Small Company Financial Reporting

Small Company Financial Reporting

Steve Collings FMAAT FCCA

Bloomsbury Professional

Published by
Bloomsbury Professional Ltd, Maxwelton House, 41–43 Boltro Road, Haywards Heath, West Sussex, RH16 1BJ

Bloomsbury Professional is an imprint of Bloomsbury Publishing Plc

British Library Cataloguing-in-Publication Data.
A catalogue record for this book is available from the British Library.

ISBN 978 1 78043 874 0

Typeset by Phoenix Photosetting, Chatham, Kent
Printed and bound in Great Britain by CPI Group (UK) Ltd, Croydon, CR0 4YY

Foreword

Small companies have benefitted from a period of stability in financial reporting for a number of years. Apart from the advent of the Companies Act 2006 which increased the small company thresholds and extended the entitlement to audit exemption, the basic principles have been established for ten years or more. As a result, accounts preparers and auditors alike have built up a strong body of knowledge and practical experience which they can apply in preparing and reporting on small company accounts. A large part of that stability has derived from the Financial Reporting Standard for Smaller Entities (FRSSE). The FRSSE has been the big success story of small company financial reporting over nearly 20 years, enabling developments in financial reporting at a large company level to be adapted for the small company environment. In particular, it has had a key role to play in ensuring that accounting disclosure for small companies remained proportionate.

Now, partly as a result of the implementation of a new UK GAAP regime and partly as a consequence of changes in accounting law at a European level all that is about to change. From 2016, FRS 102 will become the primary arbiter of recognition and measurement for many more UK companies, bringing derivative instruments on balance sheets, introducing fair values and obliging many companies to restate their balance sheets and profit and loss accounts. New small company regulations will restrict the mandatory disclosure burden, while still maintaining the overriding obligation for accounts to give a true and fair view. At the same time, a new standard, FRS 105, will provide a much simpler alternative regime for the smallest companies.

All this presents a significant challenge for accountants, auditors and their clients, a challenge that can't be overcome simply by relying on accounting software. In this book, Steve Collings takes us through the ramifications of the new financial reporting landscape, giving illustrations of the impact of new choices and worked examples of how the new rules will apply 'in real life'. I am sure that his clear and practical approach will be invaluable to anyone wanting to get to grips with small company reporting in a post-FRSSE world.

Stephanie Henshaw

Technical Partner
Francis Clark LLP

October 2015

Preface

This is the first edition of *Small Company Financial Reporting* reflecting the significant changes that have taken place with UK GAAP. This book has been designed to give a clear, concise and comprehensive reference to the new financial reporting framework for small and micro-entities.

Accountants will be aware of the move across to a financial reporting regime which is based on International Financial Reporting Standards. The UK and Republic of Ireland have undergone one of the most significant changes in a generation, with small and micro-entities following suit in 2016. The abolition of FRSs/SSAPs/UITFs marked the end of UK GAAP as we have known it in the UK and Republic of Ireland. The FRSSE has also seen its demise with the final version of the FRSSE being the FRSSE (effective January 2015).

The introduction of the EU Accounting Directive meant that the Financial Reporting Council could not maintain the FRSSE because the disclosure requirements, and some accounting methodologies, were significantly different following the transposition of the EU Accounting Directive into company law and hence some of the disclosure requirements of the FRSSE would have been prohibited by the Companies Act 2006.

The government was given until July 2015 in which to transpose the EU Accounting Directive into company law and this was completed and became effective on 6 April 2015. The revised Companies Act 2006 is effective for accounting periods commencing on or after 1 January 2016 and for accounting periods commencing on or after 1 January 2015 but before 1 January 2016, should the directors so choose. This early-adoption clause was incorporated into the Companies Act 2006 as the government estimated some 11,000 medium-sized companies could be reclassified as small under the revised Act and hence take advantage of a less burdensome financial reporting regime.

Micro-entities can report under a separate regime, being that of FRS 105 *The Financial Reporting Standard applicable to the Micro-entities Regime*. This new framework was introduced because the disclosure requirements and accounting methodologies are markedly different for micro-entities than they are for small companies and hence it was sensible to have a separate standard for micro-entities.

Small companies are brought under the scope of FRS 102 *The Financial Reporting Standard applicable in the UK and Republic of Ireland*. FRS 102 has been amended so that the presentation and disclosure requirements pertinent to a small company are contained in a separate section (Section 1A *Small Entities*). Useful appendices have been included in Section 1A by the FRC as follows:

- Appendix A *Guidance on adapting the balance sheet formats*
- Appendix B *Guidance on adapting the profit and loss account formats*
- Appendix C *Disclosure requirements for small entities*
- Appendix D *Additional disclosures encouraged for small entities*

Key features of this new publication include 'Signposts' at the start of each chapter which are designed to highlight, at a glance, the contents of the chapter. 'Focus' boxes have been included in each chapter with the objective of flagging up important concepts and points which small company directors and their accountants should take on board. This title also includes 'Pitfalls to avoid' boxes at the end of each chapter to help reduce the scope for error. Each chapter also contains a 'Chapter summary' box at the end which summarises the main content of each chapter as an aide-memoire for readers.

In addition, each chapter contains several real-life worked examples to help bring the theory within the chapter to life and to aid understanding of the new accounting methodologies and disclosures contained in the new UK GAAP.

I hope that you find this book useful and we would welcome comments or suggestions via the publisher for future editions.

I would like to take this opportunity to thank a few individuals who have been critical in bringing this book to publication.

I would like to sincerely thank my technical editor, Caroline Fox BA, FCA who has, once again, done a remarkable job on ensuring the technical accuracy of this book. I would also like to extend special thanks to Mark McLaughlin CTA (Fellow), ATT (Fellow), TEP and Pete Miller for their input into the taxation aspects of Chapter 14. I would also like to thank Stephanie Henshaw BA (Hons) FCA for writing the Foreword to this book.

Finally I would like to say thank you to the editors, Dave Wright, Claire McDermott, Claire Banyard and Jane Bradford and the rest of the team at Bloomsbury Professional for their input and support during the production of this book.

Steve Collings FMAAT FCCA

August 2015

Contents

Table of Statutes

[All references are to paragraph numbers]

Table of Statutory Instruments and Other Guidance

[*All references are to paragraph numbers*]

INTERNATIONAL ACCOUNTING STANDARDS

Table of Examples

[*All references are to paragraph numbers*]

Chapter 1

Introduction

SIGNPOSTS

- Financial reporting has seen considerable changes over the recent months due to the introduction of the new UK GAAP (see **1.1**).
- The UK now reports under a four-tier financial reporting framework due to small companies being moved under the scope of FRS 102 and micro-entities having a standalone accounting standard (see **1.2**).
- The Financial Reporting Standard for Smaller Entities (the FRSSE) has been withdrawn with effect for accounting periods commencing on or after 1 January 2016 (see **1.2**).
- The requirement to prepare financial statements for small companies which give a true and fair view under the Companies Act 2006 is still a crucial concept (see **1.4**).
- The Financial Reporting Council issued a document in June 2014 titled *True and Fair* which confirms that the true and fair requirements remain of fundamental importance in both IFRS and UK GAAP (see **1.5**).
- The proper application of accounting standards enables the financial statements to give a true and fair view and merely disagreeing with the content of an accounting standard does not give a valid reason to depart from the requirements of the standard (see **1.6**).
- Auditors of small entities corroborate the truth and fairness of the financial statements by gathering sufficient and appropriate audit evidence to support the amounts and disclosures in the financial statements (see **1.7**).
- The document *True and Fair* issued by the Financial Reporting Council outlines four points which preparers should take into account when considering whether the financial statements continue to be of a high standard (see **1.8**).
- The Financial Reporting Council is responsible for issuing accounting standards in the UK and Republic of Ireland and it is supported by three committees (see **1.9**).
- UK GAAP now consists of six FRSs (see **1.10**).

- The *Foreword to Accounting Standards* acknowledges that accounting standards need not be applied to immaterial items (see **1.11**).
- The issue about applying accounting standards to transactions which took place prior to the issuance of a standard has been addressed by the Financial Reporting Council (see **1.12**).
- Where the introduction of a standard, or an amendment to an existing standard, may have unforeseen consequences, the parties to any financing arrangement or loan agreement may wish to insulate the agreement from the effect of a future accounting standard, or a future amendment (see **1.13**).
- It is possible to early-adopt the provisions of an Exposure Draft, but care must be taken when doing so (see **1.14**).
- Financial statements are prepared to UK GAAP and the Companies Act 2006 requirements and changes in legislation often have an impact on the accounting requirements (see **1.15**).
- There may be occasions when the provisions of an accounting standard require departure from legislative requirements in order to give a true and fair view. Particulars of such departures must be disclosed in the financial statements (see **1.16**).
- The filing obligations to Companies House have changed as a result of the transposition of the EU Accounting Directive into the Companies Act 2006 (see **1.17**).
- Micro-entities no longer have to prepare a directors' report but there are also filing requirements for entities which do not prepare such a report (see **1.18**).
- Audit reports must also contain the name of the auditor and (where the auditor is a firm), the name of the person who signed the auditor's report in the capacity of senior statutory auditor (subject to some specific exceptions) (see **1.19**).
- UK tax legislation requires that financial statements are prepared to UK GAAP and the definition of UK GAAP is found in section 1127 of the Corporation Tax Act 2010 (see **1.20**).
- Transitional adjustments will often have some tax consequences and HM Revenue and Customs have issued an Overview Paper clarifying the tax treatment of such adjustments (see **1.21**).

OVERALL AIMS AND OBJECTIVES OF THE BOOK

1.1 Financial reporting has seen considerable changes over recent months with the introduction of new UK GAAP (FRS 102 *The Financial Reporting Standard applicable in the UK and Republic of Ireland*) and the introduction of the micro-entities legislation together with a brand new small companies' financial reporting framework. It is inherently difficult to keep up with the sheer volume of changes that these new regimes have introduced, from new ways of accounting for certain transactions and events to the difficulties in ensuring that financial statement disclosures achieve a true and fair view.

Small companies make up the vast majority of companies existing in the United Kingdom and Republic of Ireland and the majority of small to medium-sized accounting firms will have an extensive portfolio of clients which fall into the small and medium-sized entity (SME) sector. Advances in technology have resulted in some powerful accounts production software being available on the market and whilst such software is often the 'backbone' of an accountancy practice, invariably the software will not be able to produce certain types of information on its own without some user input. Over-reliance on accounts production software is one of the main culprits of firms receiving criticism from file reviewers or professional body regulators because often over-reliance results in 'boiler plating' or 'gold plating' policies and disclosures being made in the financial statements (ie generic wording without any sort of tailoring to be client-specific). Such criticisms have been on the increase over recent years and hence professional bodies actively encourage member firms to ensure that boiler plating is discouraged in all financial statements, regardless of the client's size.

The overall aim of this book is to offer practical help and guidance to preparers of financial statements for small companies. Its focus is on both technical theory and practical examples as the two go hand-in-hand. Accountants traditionally tend to favour worked examples when it comes to publications such as this book; however it is important to understand *why* something is done in a certain way or disclosed in a certain way rather than to accept the accounting treatment or disclosure simply because '... it has always been done that way.'

Therefore this book outlines the theory where considered necessary so that readers have an in-depth understanding of why something is done in a different way than it was previously and also why transactions and events affecting the financial statements are disclosed in a certain way to enable preparers of small company financial statements to tailor certain disclosures to their client or company. This theory is then brought to life through the use of practical examples which are based on real-life experiences in professional practice. Different clients and companies will have their own challenges and this book tries, wherever possible, to cater for most real-life scenarios presented to preparers of small company financial statements.

1.2 When the (now defunct) Accounting Standards Board initially embarked on their proposals for a new UK GAAP, they did so with the intention of reducing the number of financial reporting tiers that were in existence in the UK and Republic of Ireland. What has actually occurred, some years later, is a four-tier financial reporting framework which is structured as follows:

- Micro-entities can apply FRS 105 *The Financial Reporting Standard applicable to the Micro-entities Regime*. This framework is optional for companies that qualify as a micro-entity (see **Chapter 2** for further details on the qualifying criteria).

- Small entities which are not micro-entities (or those which could otherwise qualify as a micro-entity but choose not to adopt the regime) can apply FRS 102 *The Financial Reporting Standard applicable in the UK and Republic of Ireland* with reduced disclosure requirements through the application of Section 1A *Small Entities*. The disclosure requirements are contained in Appendix C to Section 1A *Disclosure requirements for small entities* and Appendix D *Additional disclosures encouraged for small entities*.
- Entities which apply EU-adopted IFRS in the preparation of their financial statements will continue to do so (please note this book does not consider any provisions in EU-endorsed IFRS as most companies that prepare financial statements under such GAAP are listed companies which are beyond the scope of this book).
- Qualifying entities can prepare financial statements in accordance with FRS 101 *Reduced Disclosure Framework*.

The number of financial reporting tiers has increased from three to four which is due to the introduction of the EU Accounting Directive which has been transposed into companies' legislation and takes effect from 6 April 2015. It applies to accounting periods commencing on or after 1 January 2016 and can be early-adopted for accounting periods commencing on or after 1 January 2015 but before 1 January 2016, if the directors so wish. As a direct consequence, the FRSSE (effective January 2015) is withdrawn with effect for accounting periods commencing on or after 1 January 2016 which brings its 18-year life to an end. A point worthy of note is that a micro-entity or a small company can still choose to apply a more comprehensive financial reporting framework in the preparation of their financial statements. For example, a micro-entity could choose not to apply FRS 105, but instead choose FRS 102 with reduced disclosure requirements; or full FRS 102; or EU-adopted IFRS. It is likely that the latter two frameworks will be very rarely used by such entities as the disclosure requirements in both full FRS 102 and EU-adopted IFRS would not be proportionate to the size and nature of a micro-entity.

1.3 This book is only concerned with small companies (including micro-entities) and whilst it does consider the recognition and measurement requirements in full FRS 102 (as these will still apply to small companies), it does not consider the full disclosure requirements that a company that is not classed as small would apply in their financial statements. This book also does not deal with topics which are likely to be of concern to Public Limited Companies whose shares are publicly traded on a stock market (such as the London Stock Exchange).

TRUE AND FAIR VIEW

1.4 It has been a long-established and overarching concept in the United Kingdom and Republic of Ireland that financial statements have to give a true and fair view under the provisions in section 393 of the Companies Act 2006.

The requirement to prepare financial statements which give a true and fair view is also carried over where new UK GAAP is concerned.

Section 393 of the Companies Act 2006 says that the directors of a company must not approve financial statements unless they are satisfied that they give a true and fair view of the state of the company's affairs. Many have debated the meaning of 'true and fair' in the context of legal opinion, but the courts have never attempted to define the concept.

1.5 In June 2014, the Financial Reporting Council (FRC) published a document, *True and Fair*. The purpose of the document was to confirm that the true and fair requirement remains of fundamental importance in both IFRS and UK GAAP. The document acknowledges that concerns have been raised on the operation of the true and fair override in IFRS and acknowledges that the absence of the concept of 'prudence' also raises these concerns (at the time of writing, the International Accounting Standards Board are considering re-instating the concept of 'prudence' in the Conceptual Framework). The FRC have confirmed in the *True and Fair* document that the true and fair concept remains of fundamental importance when it comes to preparing the financial statements of an entity under UK GAAP, whether those statements are prepared to IFRS or FRS 100 to 105. To achieve a true and fair view, the FRC also acknowledge that professional judgement must be applied and that professional judgement is needed, for example:

- where a choice in accounting policy exists: in such situations the accounting policy adopted must be appropriate and take into consideration the circumstances of the reporting entity;
- in developing accounting policies for items which are not specifically dealt with by accounting standards, or where the transaction(s) or event(s) are unclear;
- in making judgements, for example, concerning valuations which are aimed at giving a true and fair view;
- to avoid not applying detailed accounting rules as an excuse for poor accounting;
- in considering what is and what is not material;
- in making appropriate disclosures within the financial statements even where such disclosures may not be legally required or required by the applicable financial reporting framework;
- in ensuring that significant information is not obscured by immaterial or irrelevant disclosures (clutter); and
- in looking at the financial statements at the end of the preparation process and ensuring that they do give a true and fair view.

The above list is certainly not exhaustive and directors will have to make additional judgements, where necessary, to ensure that the reporting entity's financial statements do give a true and fair view. This requirement has, to a large extent, been accentuated by the fact that the Companies Act 2006 now incorporates the EU Accounting Directive (the Directive) issued in June 2013 and the Directive restricts Member States' ability to mandate additional disclosures in their small entities' financial statements. Indeed, the reduction from some 17 mandatory disclosures to 13 will require more judgement calls on the parts of directors (and their advisors) as to whether the inclusion of additional disclosures are needed in the small entity's financial statements so that they do give a true and fair view.

Focus

- While the mandatory disclosure requirements in law have reduced for small companies, directors of small companies must make sure the financial statements they prepare give a true and fair view in order to comply with their legal obligations. In addition to the encouraged disclosures in Appendix D to Section 1A, the directors must make further disclosures where such disclosures will enable a true and fair view to be achieved.

True and fair and the application of accounting standards

1.6 The overarching objective of accounting standards is to prescribe the recognition, measurement and disclosure requirements for specific aspects of transactions and events that are needed in the financial statements to give a true and fair view. The exercise itself in achieving a true and fair view is not a separate exercise.

Applying the provisions in accounting standards will enable financial statements to give a true and fair view and only in rare situations are departures from the standards necessary in order to give a true and fair view (with appropriate disclosures concerning the departure given in the notes to the financial statements). Merely disagreeing with an accounting standard does not mean the directors have a valid reason to depart from the requirements of the standard. In addition, where an accounting standard addresses a particular issue, but the overall requirements of the standard are insufficient so as to fully explain the issue, the entity will normally make additional disclosure (often in the notes to the accounts). Notwithstanding the revised Companies Act 2006 relating to the minimum disclosures for small companies, company directors must continue to make additional disclosures where considered necessary for a true and fair view of the financial statements to be achieved.

In cases where the directors of an entity consider it appropriate to depart from the requirements of an accounting standard because complying with the requirements of the standard will not result in a true and fair view being given by the financial statements, it is crucial that an informed and unbiased judgement is employed to devise an appropriate alternative treatment. The alternative treatment must be consistent with the economic and commercial characteristics of the circumstances concerned. The importance of this cannot be over-emphasised because the FRC, through its Conduct Committee, and the Department for Business, Innovation and Skills have set procedures in place to investigate complaints about financial statements which depart from the requirements of accounting standards and the Companies Act, including the requirement to give a true and fair view.

1.7 Auditors are particularly interested in whether the financial statements give a true and fair view because this is the overall objective of their audit. The obligations of an auditor when giving an opinion on the financial statements are set out in the Companies Act in sections 393(2), 495 and 497 and those obligations include stating whether, in the auditor's opinion, the financial statements give a true and fair view. Small company audits are considered further in **Chapter 13**.

Auditors in the UK and Republic of Ireland are required to conduct their audit in accordance with ISAs (UK and Ireland) issued by the FRC. In reality, the majority of small companies tend not to have their financial statements externally audited; however this does not preclude the directors from ensuring the financial statements give a true and fair view and in many cases the financial statements are prepared by external accountancy firms who should undertake rigorous procedures to ensure compliance with the true and fair concept.

Where small entities do have an audit of their financial statements, the auditors will apply the provisions in ISAs (UK and Ireland) and gather sufficient and appropriate audit evidence to give reasonable (but not absolute) assurance that the financial statements are free from material misstatement, whether caused by fraud or error. Where auditors are to discharge their legal and professional responsibilities properly, they should also stand back and undertake an objective view of the financial statements and consider whether the financial statements, as a whole, give a true and fair view; this is normally undertaken during the completion phase of an audit.

1.8 The FRC's *True and Fair* document concludes by outlining four points that preparers of financial statements must take on board to ensure that accounts prepared in the UK and Republic of Ireland continue to be of a high standard:

- always stand back and ensure that the accounts as a whole do give a true and fair view;
- provide additional disclosures when compliance with an accounting standard is insufficient to present a true and fair view;
- use the true and fair override where compliance with the standards does not result in the presentation of a true and fair view; and
- ensure that the consideration they give to these matters is evident in their deliberations and documentation.

DEVELOPMENT OF ACCOUNTING STANDARDS

1.9 Accounting standards in the UK and Republic of Ireland are issued by the FRC. The FRC are responsible for promoting high quality corporate governance and reporting so as to encourage investment.

Prior to the FRC taking over the responsibility for standard-setting in the UK in July 2012, the (now defunct) Accounting Standards Board had responsibility for issuing standards.

The board of the FRC is supported by three committees:

- the Codes and Standards Committee;
- the Executive Committee; and
- the Conduct Committee.

1.10 The Codes and Standards Committee advise the board of the FRC on matters concerning codes, standard-setting and policy questions and on areas relating to its Accounting, Actuarial and Audit and Assurance Councils. The Executive Committee supports the board of the FRC by advising them on strategic issues as well as providing day-to-day oversight of the FRC's work. The Conduct Committee have responsibility in advising the board of the FRC on matters relating to conduct activities to promote high-quality corporate reporting, which includes monitoring, oversight, investigative and disciplinary functions.

UK GAAP has seen significant change recently with the introduction of an IFRS-based accounting framework in the forms of:

- FRS 100 *Application of Financial Reporting Requirements* (issued November 2012).
- FRS 101 *Reduced Disclosure Framework* (September 2015).
- FRS 102 *The Financial Reporting Standard applicable in the UK and Republic of Ireland* (September 2015).
- FRS 103 *Insurance Contracts* (issued March 2014).
- FRS 104 *Interim Financial Reporting* (issued March 2015).[1]
- FRS 105 *The Financial Reporting Standard applicable to the Micro-entities Regime* (issued July 2015).

Accounting standards which are developed by the FRC are designated *Financial Reporting Standards* (FRSs) and the overall objective of the accounting standards developed by the FRC are to enable users of accounts to receive high-quality, understandable financial reporting proportionate to the size and complexity of the entity and users' information needs.

1 FRS 104 is not an accounting standard and hence there is not a new requirement to prepare interim financial statements.

1.11 New accounting standards, or amendments to existing standards, are consulted on through an Exposure Draft. An Exposure Draft is published by the FRC so as to outline their intentions and receive comments which are then reviewed by the FRC and incorporated where considered appropriate. Generally comment periods are open for around three months, but this period can be shorter if the need for a standard or an amended standard is considered urgent.

Once feedback has been incorporated where necessary into the Exposure Draft, it is then developed into a final standard for implementation. All new and amended standards have an 'effective from' date incorporated and more often than not, a new or amended standard can be adopted early – although in some cases standards might not be available for earlier-adoption, particularly if the change is due to changes in legislation which might not be available for earlier-adoption.

Accounting standards are applicable to financial statements of a reporting entity which are intended to give a true and fair view (statutory accounts). The *Foreword to Accounting Standards* acknowledges that accounting standards need not be applied to immaterial items and the determination of what is and what is not immaterial is a judgement call. To that end, accounting standards should be applied to UK and Republic of Ireland group financial statements, which also includes any amounts that relate to overseas entities included in those group financial statements. However, accounting standards are not intended to apply to financial statements of overseas entities which are prepared for local purposes.

1.12 Accounting standards issued by the FRC are authoritative and they prescribe the required treatment for particular types of transactions and other events and this is how the financial statements will give a true and fair view. As well as early adoption of standards, the question also arises as to how to deal with transactions which the entity may have entered into prior to the standard being issued.

The general policy of the FRC is that the provisions of accounting standards should be applied to all *material* transactions, regardless of the date on which the transaction was entered into. The reasoning behind this concept is that exempting certain transactions from the provisions of accounting standards and applying a certain standard from, say, the 'effective from' date would lead to transactions being accounted for differently within the same set of accounts. This will affect the comparability of the financial statements from one period to the next or affect the comparison of financial information from one entity with another.

There may be occasions when, for example, applying the provisions of accounting standards to past transactions will result in considerable work on the part of the entity. The FRC have acknowledged that this would also possibly result in information which is difficult for the user of the financial statements to interpret. As a 'workaround', when the FRC draft a standard, they will also consider including transitional provisions which provide exclusions for transactions which took place prior to the promulgation of the standard.

1.13 When a new, or amended, standard is issued, there may be unforeseen consequences when the application of the standard or amendment is included in the financial statements. This is particularly the case where the entity may have, for example, loan covenants in existence by its financiers which may impose limits on measures such as net assets or gearing levels.

The FRC have acknowledged that the developing nature of accounting is a long-established fact which would be known to the parties at the time the agreement was entered into. As a result, the FRC's view is that it is up to the parties concerned to determine whether any agreements should be protected from the effects of a future accounting standard. If the parties choose not to insulate the agreement from the effects of future accounting standards, then the agreement may be renegotiated to reflect the changes in financial reporting as opposed to changes in the underlying financial position. In light of this, the FRC does not have a policy of exempting transactions which occur prior to a specific date from the requirements of new accounting standards.

Early-adoption of Exposure Drafts

1.14 Exposure Drafts are issued by the FRC to outline their intentions in either introducing new accounting requirements in the form of a standard, or by amending existing standards. Exposure Drafts are issued for comment and are subject to revision and before any Exposure Draft is converted into an accounting standard, the requirements of existing accounting standards remain in force.

Some entities may wish to include additional information in their financial statements which reflect the FRC's proposals in an Exposure Draft. If this is the case, there are two ways in which this can be achieved:

- To the extent that the information does not conflict with existing accounting standards, it could be incorporated into the financial statements. Care must be exercised, however, because the proposals contained in the Exposure Draft could change before it either forms part of, or becomes, an accounting standard and hence entities would be well-advised to consider the consequential changes to the Exposure Draft.
- The information could be provided in supplementary form.

INTERACTION OF ACCOUNTING STANDARDS WITH LEGISLATION

1.15 As mentioned earlier in this chapter, company directors have a legal responsibility to ensure that the financial statements prepared for the entity give a true and fair view. The Companies Act 2006 forms the primary source of UK company law and supersedes the Companies Act 1985. The Companies Act 2006 starts by setting out the requirements for small private companies, it then goes on to give the further requirements for larger companies.

Part 15 of the Companies Act 2006 deals with the accounts and reports of an entity and the latest version (effective 6 April 2015) of the Companies Act 2006 also incorporates the requirements of the EU Accounting Directive which deals with the financial reporting aspects of small and micro-entities. The 2015 version of the Companies Act 2006 applies for accounting periods commencing on or after 1 January 2016 and for accounting periods commencing on or after 1 January 2015, but before 1 January 2016, if the directors so wish.

Changes to legislation are made for varying reasons. However, when they are made there may well be a consequential impact on related accounting standards. The introduction of the EU Accounting Directive was a typical example of how changes in legislation affect financial reporting. As the EU Accounting Directive essentially restricts the number of legally required disclosures in the financial statements of a small entity (not a micro-entity), the FRC had to make changes to UK GAAP as a result. This had the effect of the Financial Reporting Standard for Smaller Entities (the FRSSE) being withdrawn and replaced with Section 1A *Small Entities* in FRS 102.

Focus

- When FRS 102 was first introduced, a notable change related to the amortisation period for goodwill and intangible assets. FRS 102 said that where management are unable to assign a reliable estimate of goodwill or intangible assets' useful lives, they are to be written off over a five-year period.
- In the revisions to the Companies Act 2006, the Department for Business, Innovation and Skills changed the legislation so that if the directors could not assign a reliable estimate of the useful life of goodwill it should be written off over no shorter than five years and no longer than ten years. This then resulted in a consequential change to FRS 102 which now caps goodwill amortisation to ten years where management are unable to reliably estimate the useful life of goodwill. This issue is considered further in **Chapter 12**. It is worth noting that the FRC would only expect accelerated amortisation charges on transition to FRS 102 in exceptional circumstances.

1.16 While accounting standards do not prevail over legislation, it is the application of accounting standards issued by the FRC which result in a true and fair view being achieved.

As mentioned earlier in this chapter, there may be occasions (albeit rare occasions) where the directors deem it necessary to depart from the requirements of an accounting standard to give a true and fair view. Accounting standards might require departure from certain provisions of the Companies Act 2006 so that the financial statements give a true and fair view. This was the case with investment property that was carried under the Alternative Accounting Rules under old UK GAAP. Revaluations of investment property via the Alternative Accounting Rules meant that the true and fair override was invoked. This is not the case under the new regime as can be seen in the following example.

Example 1.1 – Revaluation of investment property under the new UK GAAP

Lunar Limited (Lunar) has an investment property on its statement of financial position (balance sheet) which it is carrying at fair value in accordance with Section 16 *Investment Property* in FRS 102 with changes in fair value going through profit or loss at each reporting date. As the property is being carried at fair value at each reporting date, Lunar does not provide for depreciation on the property. The investment property is material to the financial statements.

The Companies Act 2006 requires a company to depreciate all its fixed assets. However, in this example Lunar is not depreciating its investment property because it is applying the fair value accounting rules to the property (ie fair value through profit and loss). Investment properties carried at fair value through profit or loss (as required under Section 16) fall under the Fair Value Rules in the Companies Act 2006 and hence there is no longer any true and fair override.

It therefore follows that while accounting standards and legislation are closely interrelated, there is often a need to depart from one or the other to enable the financial statements to give a true and fair view. Care, however, must be taken to ensure that the departure is justified and adequately disclosed in the financial statements so as not to impede on the true and fair requirements and, where audited, to put an unqualified audit opinion in jeopardy.

COMPANIES HOUSE REQUIREMENTS

1.17 Small companies have traditionally filed 'abbreviated' financial statements with the Registrar of Companies (Companies House). The filing obligations of companies which are subject to the small companies' regime are contained in section 444 of the Companies Act 2006. Section 444(1) requires the directors of a company subject to the small companies' regime to deliver, for each financial year, a copy of the balance sheet drawn up as at the last day of the year. The directors may also deliver a copy of the company's profit and loss account and directors' report for that year.

> **Focus**
>
> - Where only the balance sheet is filed with the Registrar of Companies, the small company is also required to file the notes.

Where the directors deliver a copy of the company's profit and loss account under section 444(1)(b)(i) of the Companies Act 2006, the directors must also deliver a copy of the auditor's report on the accounts (and any directors report). This requirement will not apply to companies that are exempt from the statutory audit requirement and the directors have taken advantage of that exemption.

> **Focus**
>
> - The concept of 'abbreviated' financial statements, as accountants were traditionally familiar with, has been repealed in the revised Companies Act 2006 for accounting periods commencing on or after 1 January 2016 and care must be taken with the terminology used in referring to 'abbreviated' financial statements. There is some crossover in the terminology between the traditional abbreviated financial statements that were filed at Companies House and the concept of 'abridged' financial statements which have also been referred to as 'abbreviated' financial statements. Small companies (other than charities) are able to choose to prepare abridged financial statements.

Micro-entities' filing obligations

1.18 Micro-entities are not required to prepare a directors' report for inclusion in their financial statements under the micro-entities legislation. The filing obligations of companies which are entitled to small companies' exemption in relation to the directors' report are set out in section 444A of the Companies Act 2006.

Section 444A(1) requires companies which are entitled to small companies' exemption in relation to the directors report to deliver a copy of the annual accounts for that year and may deliver any directors' report which the entity voluntarily chooses to include. In addition, if the entity has been subject to external audit, a copy of the auditor's report on the accounts (and any directors' report) should also be delivered to Companies House. This requirement will not apply to companies that are exempt from the statutory audit requirement and the directors have taken advantage of that exemption.

1.19 The balance sheet and any directors' report delivered to Companies House must include the name of the person who signed it on behalf of the board. Companies House have been known to reject accounts in the past where they do not include the name of the person(s) signing on behalf of the board, or date of approval of the financial statements.

Where an auditor's report is delivered to Companies House, section 444A(4) of the Companies Act 2006 requires the name of the auditor and (where the auditor is a firm), the name of the person who signed the auditor's report in the capacity of senior statutory auditor. If the conditions in section 506 (circumstances in which names may be omitted) are met, a statement should be made that a resolution has been passed and notified to the Secretary of State in accordance with that section.

INTERACTION OF TAX LEGISLATION WITH FINANCIAL STATEMENTS

1.20 The financial statements of a small company will heavily influence the amount of tax that is paid to HM Revenue and Customs (HMRC) or repaid back to the company in the event of losses carried back and offset against previous liabilities.

Accounts prepared for tax purposes must be prepared under GAAP. Section 1127 of the Corporation Tax Act 2010 (CTA 2010) says that GAAP for corporation tax purposes is UK GAAP and in relation to the affairs of a company or other entity that prepares IAS accounts, in the Corporation Tax Acts 'generally accepted accounting practice' means generally accepted accounting practice in relation to IAS accounts (s 1127(4) of the CTA 2010). Consolidated financial statements have no influence on the tax position of entities.

Focus

- The term 'IAS' accounts also includes 'IFRS'. International Accounting Standards (IAS) were issued by the International Accounting Standards Committee (IASC) which was taken over by the International Accounting Standards Board in April 2001 who took on all of the IASC's standards but then began to issue its own standards; International Financial Reporting Standards (IFRSs).

In a large number of cases the tax treatment of transactions within the financial statements will follow the accounting treatment. However, tax legislation is such that HMRC may not recognise certain transactions for tax purposes and will disallow them in the computation of taxable profit. The main expense where this is the case is in relation to depreciation.

1.21 When an entity is transitioning onto a new financial reporting framework (for example from the previous FRSSE to FRS 102 with reduced disclosures), transitional provisions will be applied to apply the new framework as far back as the date of transition. The date of transition is the start date of the earliest period reported in the financial statements and the requirement to apply a new financial reporting framework as far back as this date is so that the financial statements are prepared as if the new framework had always been applied.

Because adjustments will inevitably arise when applying a new financial reporting framework (such as FRS 102 with reduced disclosures), HMRC have issued an Overview Paper which outlines their interpretation as to an entity's tax position. This is to give preparers an idea as to what is, and what is not, deductible/taxable when it comes to transitional adjustments and errors.

In all cases, appropriate tax legislation should be consulted to ensure the correct treatment of items within the financial statements. HMRC can, and often do, issue penalties and charge interest for erroneous tax computations and returns.

PITFALLS TO AVOID

- While the revised Companies Act 2006 only requires a minimum number of legally required disclosures, it must not be forgotten that the directors have a legal obligation to prepare financial statements which give a true and fair view, and hence additional disclosure requirements should be made, where appropriate.
- Do not forget that abbreviated financial statements are no longer in existence for accounting periods commencing on or after 1 January 2016.
- Always try to keep up with the changes in legislation and accounting standards because these can have a particular impact on companies' financial statements.

CHAPTER SUMMARY

- This book aims to provide a comprehensive insight into the new regime for small and micro-entities.
- The Companies Act 2006 has been revised for accounting periods commencing on or after 1 January 2016, and for accounting periods commencing on or after 1 January 2015, but before 1 January 2016, where the directors so wish.
- Small companies must continue to prepare financial statements which give a true and fair view and to that end the application of accounting standards and including the required disclosures should allow for this concept to be achieved.
- The concept of abbreviated financial statements has been abolished in the revised Companies Act 2006 and the filing requirements are contained in section 444 of the revised Companies Act 2006.
- HM Revenue and Customs also require financial statements to be prepared which conform to Generally Accepted Accounting Principles.

Chapter 2

The New Small Companies Regime

SIGNPOSTS

- The EU Accounting Directive which was transposed into the Companies Act 2006 in 2015 aims to allow more companies to have access to a less burdensome financial reporting regime (see **2.1**).
- The EU Accounting Directive achieves its overall objective by applying a 'think small first' approach (see **2.2**).
- The most notable change in the revised Companies Act 2006 is an increase in size thresholds for micro-entities, small companies and groups, medium-sized companies and groups and large companies and groups (see **2.3**).
- For short accounting periods the turnover limit is pro-rated (see **2.4**).
- UK GAAP will comprise FRS 100 to 105 together with EU-adopted IFRS (see **2.6**).
- Reporting entities can choose a more comprehensive reporting framework if they so wish (see **2.7**).
- Micro-entities can report under FRS 105 *The Financial Reporting Standard applicable to the Micro-entities Regime* but strict eligibility criteria are contained within the FRS and only incorporated companies can use the standard despite the term 'micro-entities' and hence LLPs and Charities are exclude from its scope (see **2.8**).
- The disclosure requirements in FRS 105 are very minimal and careful consideration needs to be made as to the appropriateness of applying FRS 105 (see **2.9**).
- FRS 105 has been developed from the requirements of FRS 102 *The Financial Reporting Standard applicable in the UK and Republic of Ireland* (see **2.10**).
- Financial statements prepared under the micro-entities legislation are 'presumed' to give a true and fair view (see **2.11**).
- There are a lot of differences between FRS 105 and the previous FRSSE (effective January 2015) which preparers of financial statements need a sound understanding of (see **2.12**).

- Whilst certain transactions are infrequent, the Financial Reporting Council have included cross-references for particular transactions to reduce divergent practices emerging (see **2.13**).
- There are only four disclosure requirements contained in FRS 105 (see **2.14**).
- This chapter contains illustrative disclosure notes which comply with FRS 105 principles (see **2.15**).
- The FRSSE (effective January 2015) is withdrawn for accounting periods commencing on or after 1 January 2016 (see **2.16**).
- It is crucial that company directors reporting under FRS 102 with reduced disclosures consider whether the disclosure requirements in the financial statements achieve a true and fair view and where this is not the case, the directors must make additional disclosures over and above the legal minimum to achieve a true and fair view (see **2.17**).
- The presentation and disclosure requirements for small entities are contained in Section 1A *Small Entities* of FRS 102 (disclosure requirements are in Appendix C *Disclosure requirements for small entities* and Appendix D *Additional disclosures encouraged for small entities*). The full recognition and measurement principles within FRS 102 are applied for small entities (see **2.18**).
- FRS 102 is a whole new financial reporting framework which is based on *IFRS for SMEs* (see **2.19**).
- There are some considerable changes to accounting methodologies and principles brought in by FRS 102 (see **2.20–2.52**).
- The content of the financial statements will depend on whether the company reports under FRS 102 for small entities or the micro-entities legislation (see **2.53–2.55**).

INTRODUCTION

2.1 The EU Directive was implemented in the UK by The Companies, Partnerships and Groups (Accounts and Reports) Regulations 2015. The Regulations came into force on 6 April 2015 (SI 2015/980) and will be effective for accounting periods commencing on or after 1 January 2016, with early adoption permitted for periods beginning on or after 1 January 2015. (The effective date relating to disclosures about related undertakings in group accounts is effective for accounts approved on or after 1 July 2015.)

The way in which small companies prepare their financial statements was subject to significant change in 2015 by virtue of Directive 2013/34/EU of the European Parliament and of the Council (the EU Accounting Directive). It replaced the 4th and 7th Accounting Directives and established minimum legal requirements for financial statements in the EU as well as providing 100 Member States with options. The options contained in the Accounting Directive (the Directive) set out to allow more companies to have access to a less burdensome financial reporting regime and the Directive set out three core objectives which are to:

- simplify accounting requirements so as to reduce the administrative burden on companies with particular emphasis focused on smaller companies;
- increase the clarity and comparability of financial statements of companies so as to reduce the cost of capital and increase the level of cross-border trade and merger and acquisition activity; and
- protect essential user needs by retaining necessary accounting information for users.

The EU introduced the Directive in order to simplify accounting requirements for small entities and at the same time reduce the levels of disclosure that were contained in the previous Companies Act 2006. This was introduced because the EU felt that the cost to small companies in disclosing information previously required by national jurisdictions was too excessive and hence the Directive brings in a mandatory minimum number of disclosures. Notwithstanding the simplicity brought about by the Directive, paragraph 9 of the Directive says:

> 'Annual financial statements should be prepared on a prudent basis and should give a true and fair view of an undertaking's assets and liabilities, financial position and profit and loss. It is possible that, in exceptional cases, a financial statement does not give such a true and fair view where provisions of this Directive are applied. In such cases, the undertaking should depart from such provisions in order that they give a true and fair view. The Member States should be allowed to define such exceptional cases and to lay down the relevant special rules which are to apply in those cases. Those exceptional cases should be understood to be only very unusual transactions and should, for instance, not be related to entire specific sectors.'

2.2 The requirement to prepare financial statements which give a true and fair view is a concept that has been enshrined in companies' legislation for many years. In light of paragraph 9 of the Directive, and the fact that the true and fair concept in the Companies Act 2006 has not been repealed or changed because of the provisions of the Directive, it is likely that company directors (and their advisors) will have to use professional judgement in ensuring that the overall content of the financial statements give a true and fair view. The Financial Reporting Council acknowledged in its consultation on the new financial reporting framework that this is likely to be burdensome for small company directors because even though the Directive imposes a mandatory 13 disclosure notes (some of which may not be applicable to some companies), some additional disclosures will need to be made so that the financial statements give a true and fair view.

The Directive seeks to simplify accounting requirements for small entities within its scope and hence reduce the levels of disclosure contained in a small entity's financial statements. The Directive achieves this objective by applying a 'think small first' approach and this approach:

- introduces a 'building block' approach to the statutory financial statements whereby disclosure levels are increased depending on the size of the undertaking;
- reduces the number of options available to preparers in respect of recognition, measurement and presentation; and
- creates a largely harmonised small company regime and, for the first time, limits the amount of information which Member States are permitted to require small undertakings to place in their annual financial statements.

Focus

- The EU Accounting Directive was transposed into the Companies Act 2006 and this was laid before Parliament on 26 March 2015 to come into effect on 6 April 2015 by virtue of SI 2015/980.

CLASSIFICATION OF SMALL, MEDIUM AND LARGE COMPANIES

2.3 The Directive says that small, medium-sized and large undertakings should be defined and distinguished by reference to balance sheet total, net turnover and the average number of employees during the financial year because this criteria generally provides objective evidence as to the size of the undertaking. The Directive also allowed Member States the option of using maximum mandatory thresholds to determine the size of a company or minimum mandatory thresholds. In January 2015, BIS issued their response to its consultation in which it confirmed its decision to take advantage of the maximum thresholds and according to BIS, this will allow 11,000 medium-sized companies to be re-categorised to small, thus allowing them to make less disclosures in their financial statements than would otherwise have been the case under the previous Companies Act 2006. In their response to its consultation, BIS also confirmed that they will also apply mandatory increases in the thresholds for medium-sized and large companies.

With effect for accounting periods commencing **on or after 1 January 2016**, the following regime will apply:

	Turnover	**Balance sheet total**	**Average no. of employees**
Micro-entity	Not more than £632,000	Not more than £316,000	Not more than 10
Small company	Not more than £10.2 million	Not more than £5.1 million	Not more than 50

	Turnover	Balance sheet total	Average no. of employees
Small group	Not more than £10.2 million net OR Not more than £12.2 million gross	Not more than £5.1 million net OR Not more than £6.1 million gross	Not more than 50
Medium-sized company	Not more than £36 million	Not more than £18 million	Not more than 250
Medium-sized group	Not more than £36 million net OR Not more than £43.2 million gross	Not more than £18 million net OR Not more than £21.6 million gross	Not more than 250
Large company	£36 million or more	£18 million or more	250 or more
Large group	£36 million net or more OR £43.2 million gross or more	£18 million net or more OR £21.6 million gross or more	250 or more

The above regime can be applied to accounting periods commencing on or after 1 January 2015, but before 1 January 2016, if the directors so wish.

Focus

- Where the table above refers to 'gross' this means before set-offs and other group transactions (ie prior to elimination of intra-group trading and the effects thereof). 'Net' means after set-offs and other group transactions have been eliminated.

2.4 The qualifying conditions above are met by a company, or a group, in a year in which it satisfies two, or more, of the turnover, balance sheet total and employee head count criteria. Section 382(4) of the Companies Act 2006 says that if a company has a short accounting period the turnover figure should be proportionately adjusted.

Example 2.1 – Short accounting period

A company has recently started up in business and has an accounting reference date of 31 December. It commenced trading on 1 April 2016 and the directors are considering which financial reporting framework to adopt. Ideally the directors would like to use the micro-entities regime in FRS 105 *The Financial*

Reporting Standard applicable to the Micro-entities Regime and for the year-ended 31 December 2016 the company's reported turnover is £520,000 and it has a balance sheet total of £410,000.

The turnover threshold for a micro-entity is £632,000 and this is based on annual turnover. However, the business has only been trading for 9/12 of the year and hence the turnover thresholds needs to be pro-rated accordingly. For the purposes of determining its size and eligibility to use the micro-entities regime, the directors should use £474,000 for the turnover threshold (£632,000 × 9/12).

As the company has turnover in excess of the £474,000 pro-rated threshold and a balance sheet total of £410,000, it fails to qualify as a micro-entity and hence must use FRS 102 with reduced disclosures as a minimum.

Focus

- The term 'balance sheet total' is defined in paragraph 3 of Article 11 of the Directive which says:

  > 'The balance sheet total referred to in paragraph 1 to 7 of this Article shall consist of the total value of the assets in A to E under "Assets" in the layout set out in Annex III or of the assets in A to E in the layout set out in Annex IV.'

- Therefore, where reference is made to 'balance sheet total', it is taken to mean fixed assets **plus** current assets. Some confusion often arises as to this term and net assets have been used in error which is net of liabilities and hence is not gross.

Average number of employees

2.5 Section 382(6) of the Companies Act 206 says that the number of employees means the average number of employees employed by the company in a year. This figure is determined as follows:

- find for each month in the financial year the number of persons employed under contracts of service by the company in that month (whether throughout the month or not);
- add together the monthly totals; and
- divide by the number of months in the financial year.

Example 2.2 – Calculating the average number of employees

A company has a 31 December 2016 accounting reference date and has a relatively high turnover of staff due to the nature of its production. The human resources department has extracted the following information from the payroll files in respect of the employee numbers during the year:

January	56
February	52
March	58
April	49
May	52
June	52
July	58
August	57
September	56
October	56
November	55
December	53

The average number of persons employed by the company during the accounting period is 55 which is calculated as the sum of the monthly numbers of staff divided by 12 months (rounded up).

Focus

- The requirement to disclose the average number of employees during the year is a new requirement for small companies.

APPLICABLE FINANCIAL REPORTING FRAMEWORKS

2.6 The transposition of the EU Accounting Directive has resulted in UK GAAP becoming consistent with an IFRS-based regime as follows:

- FRS 100 *Application of Financial Reporting Requirements*.
- FRS 101 *Reduced Disclosure Framework*.
- FRS 102 *The Financial Reporting Standard applicable in the UK and Republic of Ireland*.
- FRS 103 *Insurance Contracts*.
- FRS 104 *Interim Financial Reporting*.
- FRS 105 *The Financial Reporting Standard applicable to the Micro-entities Regime*.

Listed companies (including those on the Alternative Investment Market) will continue to report under EU-adopted IFRS.

In general, UK GAAP starts off with the micro-entities regime, flows through to the small companies' regime, through to full FRS 102 and then ends up with EU-adopted IFRS. The financial reporting requirements of each regime gets progressively more complex and comprehensive the further up the suite of standards you go. This increase in complexity represents the increasing size and complexity of the entities which are most likely to apply a given standard.

2.7 The regime is not rigid; in other words, an entity does have the option to choose to adopt a more comprehensive financial reporting framework if it wishes. The FRC acknowledged that some entities may decide, for example, not to choose to report under the micro-entities regime but instead choose to report under FRS 102 with reduced disclosures or full FRS 102 (although the latter is not expected to be a common option). Factors which the FRC have suggested should be considered are:

- Whether an entity is eligible to apply that particular regime. Eligibility criteria may include the type of financial statements (ie an individual or a group) being prepared, company size thresholds and entity type.
- Where a choice of regime exists, entities should consider which of the regimes is the most appropriate to the individual circumstances of the entity. Factors to consider will differ from company to company and may relate to certain characteristics or restrictions of a particular regime, the resources available and the information needs of users of the accounts, amongst many others.

In terms of eligibility criteria, these are summarised in the following table:

Eligibility criteria		
Regime	**Micro-entities regime**	**Small entities regime**
Source of eligibility criteria	Sections 384A to 384B of the Companies Act 2006	Sections 382 to 384 of the Companies Act 2006
Eligible entities	Companies only (Note: whilst the legislation and consequently FRS 105 uses the term micro-entities regime, it is only currently available under law to companies)	Companies Limited liability partnerships Any other type of entity that would have met the criteria of the small companies regime had it been a company incorporated under company law (for example charities)
Size thresholds	A company qualifies if it does not exceed two or more of the following criteria: Turnover £632,000 Balance sheet total £316,000 No. of employees 10	A company qualifies if it does not exceed two or more of the following criteria: Turnover £10.2m Balance sheet total £5.1m No. of employees 50

Eligibility criteria		
Regime	**Micro-entities regime**	**Small entities regime**
Ineligible entities	Any companies excluded from the small companies regime Financial institutions including credit and insurance institutions Charities Small parent companies that choose to prepare group accounts Companies that are not parent companies but their accounts are included in consolidated accounts	Public companies Financial institutions including insurance companies and banking companies

Some entities which currently use EU-adopted IFRS on a voluntary basis may now wish to switch back to UK GAAP as this was made easier to do from 1 October 2012.

MICRO-ENTITIES FRAMEWORK

2.8 The micro-entities legislation was issued by the EU in June 2013 and in the UK it applied for years-ending on or after 30 September 2013 for financial statements that are filed with the Registrar of Companies (Companies House) on or after 1 December 2013. In response to the requirement to incorporate this regime into UK GAAP, the Financial Reporting Council (FRC) incorporated the micro-entities legislation into the FRSSE (effective April 2008) and (effective January 2015). This was never intended to be a long-term solution, but merely a temporary measure so that companies qualifying as a micro-entity and preparing their financial statements under the micro-entities regime could do so having regard to the FRSSE.

The FRC decided to 'carve out' the micro-entities regime into its own standard in the form of FRS 105 *The Financial Reporting Standard applicable to the Micro-entities Regime*. A point worth noting is that at the time of writing, there was no equivalent legislation for micro-entities in the Republic of Ireland although the Irish Department of Jobs, Enterprise and Innovation had consulted on the possible enactment of the micro-entities legislation in its *Consultation on the transposition of the EU Accounting Directive 2013/34/E.* Should the Republic of Ireland introduce this legislation, FRS 105 will become available to companies in the Republic of Ireland which qualify as micro-entities.

2.9 FRS 105 is optional and a company which would qualify as a micro-entity could choose to adopt a more comprehensive framework if it so wishes, such as FRS 102 with reduced disclosures. Directors should carefully consider the most appropriate framework and not simply be guided by the complexities of alternative frameworks – the regime which meets the individual company's needs and circumstances should be carefully considered in choosing the applicable financial reporting framework.

The disclosure requirements in FRS 105 are very minimal and consideration should be given as to the view adopted by banks, creditors and other interested parties which may require additional non-statutory information so as to corroborate the financial stability of the entity.

2.10 FRS 105 has been developed from the requirements in FRS 102 *The Financial Reporting Standard applicable in the UK and Republic of Ireland.* This was a sensible approach because all UK GAAP will then be based on a consistent framework. However, in drafting FRS 105, the FRC have made further simplifications to the regime (which are examined later in this section). In addition, FRS 105 has also been developed around the legal framework from the requirements of FRS 102. The content of FRS 105 does not follow the same structure as that of FRS 102 because certain sections have been removed as they do not apply to micro-entities. Chapter 11 *Financial Reporting for Micro-Entities* examines this in more detail.

Key features of FRS 105

2.11 Notable features of FRS 105 can be summarised as follows:[1]

Primary financial statements	There are only two primary financial statements which are prepared under FRS 105, being a statement of financial position and an income statement.[1]
Condensed information	The information presented in the statement of financial position and income statement is condensed; for example fixed assets are not split between intangible, tangible and investment properties.
Fair value and revaluation amounts	No assets are allowed to be measured at fair value or at revaluation. The consequence of this is that on transition any previous revaluations will have to be removed.
Disclosure requirements	There are considerable disclosure reductions under FRS 105 which follows the minimum legal disclosure requirements in the legislation.

1 The terminology from the FRS is used. Readers may be more familiar with the statement of financial position being referred to as a balance sheet and the income statement as a profit and loss account.

Deeming provisions	There are deeming provisions within the legislation which say that financial statements prepared under the minimum legislative requirements for micro-entities are *presumed* to give a true and fair view and hence there is no requirement for directors to consider what additional information may be needed in order for the accounts to give a true and fair view.
Deferred tax	Deferred tax is not accounted for under FRS 105.
Directors' report	There is no requirement to include a directors' report in the financial statements of a micro-entity.
Equity-settled share-based payment transactions	There is no requirement to account for equity-settled share-based payment transactions.
Defined benefit pension plans	Defined benefit pension plans of a micro-entity can be accounted for as a defined contribution pension plan.
No accounting policy choices	All accounting policy choices have been removed in FRS 105.

Focus

- The micro-entities legislation says that accounts prepared in accordance with the minimum legal requirements are presumed to give a true and fair view. There is, however, no restriction on a micro-entity including more voluntary disclosure information if it so chooses.

FRS 105 compared to old UK GAAP (the FRSSE)

2.12 As with any new financial reporting regime, differences between what small entities have done in the past and what they will do under the new requirements are bound to arise and FRS 105 is no different.

Preparers of small company financial statements are advised to gain an understanding of the differences inherent with the new regime because they are based on principles found in FRS 102 which, in itself, is based on the provisions in *IFRS for SMEs*. As a consequence, some accounting methodologies are very different under the new framework than was previously the case.

Focus

- The importance of carefully considering whether FRS 105 is appropriate to the individual entity's circumstances cannot be overemphasised. The disclosure reductions are considerable under FRS 105 and some entities which may qualify to apply FRS 105 might do so at their detriment if the entity-specific factors are not carefully considered. An impact assessment is worthwhile undertaking when considering which framework to adopt.

The table below gives a general overview of the differences between FRS 105 and the old UK GAAP (the FRSSE (effective January 2015)).

Comparison of FRS 105 to FRSSE (effective January 2015)	
True and fair view	Financial statements which are prepared in accordance with the legal requirements of the micro-entities regime are *presumed* to give a true and fair view. As a result, directors are not required to consider any additional information which may be needed within the financial statements to give a true and fair view. The FRSSE placed a legal obligation on directors to ensure that the financial statements gave a true and fair view.
Number of primary financial statements	Under FRS 105, micro-entities are only required to prepare a balance sheet (statement of financial position) and a profit and loss account (income statement). There is no requirement to prepare a statement of total recognised gains and losses nor a cash flow statement.
Format of the profit and loss account (income statement)	Under FRS 105 the profit and loss account (income statement) can only be prepared under Format 2. Under the FRSSE an entity could choose between Formats 1, 2, 3 and 4 depending on the company's circumstances. Under the new Companies Act 2006, Formats 3 and 4 have been abolished.
Condensed formats of the financial statements	The statutory formats for the profit and loss account (income statement) and balance sheet (statement of financial position) are condensed when compared to the FRSSE. For example, fixed assets are not disaggregated into 'intangible', 'tangible' and 'investment properties' and current assets are not disaggregated into 'stock and work-in-progress', 'trade debtors', 'cash at bank' and 'cash in hand'.
Reduced number of disclosure requirements	Micro-entities are only legally required to provide two disclosures under the balance sheet (statement of financial position). There is no requirement to provide any additional disclosures. Micro-entities can, however, provide more voluntary disclosure if they so choose, but in contrast the FRSSE required significantly more disclosures to be made in the financial statements.
Simplified accounting treatments	FRS 105 has incorporated further simplifications to the regime such that micro-entities will not be required to account for deferred tax and equity-settled share-based payment transactions. Where micro-entities also have defined benefit pension plans, these can be accounted for as a defined contribution pension plan.
Fair value and revaluation models prohibited	Micro-entities are not permitted to fair value or subject any assets (fixed or current) to the revaluation model. Hence, all assets and liabilities (such as land and buildings and investment properties) must be held at cost. In contrast, the FRSSE permitted certain assets to be revalued. On transition to FRS 105, all revalued amounts must be removed and this could cause considerable changes to a micro-entity's balance sheet (statement of financial position).

Comparison of FRS 105 to FRSSE (effective January 2015)	
No accounting policy choices	All accounting policy options have been removed in FRS 105. The mandatory treatments essentially result in earlier recognition of income/expenses in the profit and loss account (income statement) as opposed to being deferred in the balance sheet (statement of financial position).
Inclusion of more guidance	In many instances, the requirements of FRS 105 do not differ from those which were included in the FRSSE; however, FRS 105 contains more guidance to help preparers to apply and interpret the requirements correctly.
Reproduction of company law requirements	Not all of the reporting requirements from company law applicable to micro-entities have been reproduced in FRS 105 which was the case in the previous FRSSE. However, company law requirements which apply to the financial statements are reproduced. As a result, micro-entities will need to ensure that they have met all their legal requirements.
Terminology	The terminology used in FRS 105 is consistent with FRS 102 and hence preparers will note the 'balance sheet' is referred to as the 'statement of financial position' and such like (see Focus box below). A Table of Equivalence is included in Appendix II to FRS 105 for convenience.

Focus

- While FRS 105 (and FRS 102) refer to international terminology within the body of the standards, the names of the primary financial statements are derived from the Companies Act 2006 and hence it is likely that 'balance sheets' and 'profit and loss accounts' will still be referred to as such within the new regime. Indeed paragraph 3.22 of FRS 102 allows alternative titles to be used for the financial statements (provided they are not misleading).

Infrequent transactions associated with a micro-entity

2.13 FRS 105 is based on the principles contained in FRS 102. However, there are a number of areas which have been removed due to the fact that the Accounting Council do not consider them to be appropriate to micro-entities; this was done intentionally in order to reduce the complexity of the standard. However, as all entities (including micro-entities) are different, the Accounting Council took the decision to include certain types of transactions, even though such transactions are considered to be infrequent, so as to reduce divergent practice emerging. These transactions are as follows:

- intermediate payment arrangements (Section 7: Subsidiaries, Associates, Jointly Controlled Entities and Intermediate Payment Arrangements);
- trade and asset acquisitions (Section 14: Business Combinations and Goodwill);

- compound financial instruments (Section 17: Liabilities and Equity);
- cash-generating units (Section 22: Impairment of Assets); and
- foreign branches (Section 25: Foreign Currency Translation).

Disclosure requirements under FRS 105

2.14 The most notable aspect of FRS 105 and the micro-entities' regime is the fact that the disclosure requirements are significantly reduced. The following disclosures should be made in the micro-entities' accounts, where applicable:

- the total amount of any financial commitments, guarantees or contingencies that are not included in the balance sheet;
- an indication of the nature and form of any valuable security which has been provided;
- the amounts of advances and credits granted to members of the administrative, managerial and supervisory bodies with indications of interest rates, main conditions and any amounts repaid or written off or waived; and
- any commitments entered into on their behalf by way of guarantees of any kind, with an indication of the total for each category.

Focus

- As mentioned earlier in this chapter, there is no restriction on a micro-entity including more voluntary disclosure information if it so chooses.

2.15 The EU Accounting Directive at Article 36(1)(b) requires that the disclosure requirements of Article 16 points (d) and (e) must be disclosed at the foot of the balance sheet (statement of financial position). These are as follows:

- the total amount of any financial commitments, guarantees or contingencies that are not included in the balance sheet, and an indication of the nature and form of any valuable security which has been provided; any commitments concerning pensions and affiliated or associated undertakings shall be disclosed separately;
- the amount of advances and credits granted to members of the administrative, managerial and supervisory bodies, with indications of the interest rates, main conditions and any amounts repaid or written off or waived, as well as commitments entered into on their behalf by way of guarantees of any kind, with an indication of the total for each category.[2]

In drafting FRS 105, the FRC acknowledge that – legally – only two disclosure requirements are made and, on the face of it, FRS 105 may require four

2 EU Accounting Directive, Article 16(d) and (e).

disclosures (ie more than the legal minimum). This is not the case and the FRC have split out the two disclosure requirements to be more succinct and help preparers to understand exactly what needs to be disclosed; in addition other areas of the Companies Act 2006 require disclosures to be made in connection with the legally required minimum. Therefore, while there does appear to be four disclosure requirements, the micro-entity will be complying with its legal obligations in making the disclosures mandated by FRS 105. Section 6 in FRS 105 contains an appendix outlining the required disclosures in detail.

Example 2.3 – Illustrative disclosure notes

1. Directors' benefits: advances, credits and guarantees

During the year the company made an advance of £500 to a director of the company as an advance towards the cost of a personal item of expenditure. The balance was fully repaid by the year-end.

2. Guarantees and other financial commitments

The company is currently involved in a legal claim with one of its customers who has lodged a claim in the court for damage to property. The company's legal advisers have advised that the maximum potential liability amounts to £10,000. The legal advisers have informed the directors that the claim is likely to be unsuccessful and hence no provision has been made in the financial statements.

The company had capital commitments contracted, but not provided for, in the financial statements amounting to £5,000.

FRS 102 AND SMALL COMPANY REPORTING REQUIREMENTS

2.16 The inclusion of the EU Accounting Directive within the Companies Act 2006 has had a significant impact on the way that financial statements for small companies will report their financial information. The impact has been in the form of legislative changes and changes to financial reporting requirements.

The original intention by the (now defunct) Accounting Standards Board was to have all medium-sized and large companies that do not report under EU-adopted IFRS to report under full FRS 102 *The Financial Reporting Standard applicable in the UK and Republic of Ireland* principles. Once those companies were on the new regime, the intention was to align the Financial Reporting Standard for Smaller Entities (the FRSSE) with FRS 102 requirements. This was necessary because there were disparities between the FRSSE and FRS 102 which needed to be addressed so that all companies were reporting in a broadly consistent way.

The introduction of the EU Accounting Directive (the Directive) in 2013 meant that the FRC had concluded that it was no longer possible to sustain the FRSSE in its current format due to the significant changes in disclosure requirements which the Directive brought about. As a result, a consultation was opened in September 2014 by the FRC (at the same time that the Department for Business, Innovation and Skills opened their consultation into the Directive). On 19 February 2015, three Exposure Drafts were published by the FRC:

- FRED 58 *Draft FRS 105 'The Financial Reporting Standard applicable to the Micro-entities Regime'*;
- FRED 59 *Draft Amendments to FRS 102 – Small entities and other minor amendments*; and
- FRED 60 *Draft Amendments to FRS 100 'Application of Financial Reporting Requirements'* and *FRS 101 'Reduced Disclosure Framework'*.

The comment period for these FREDs closed on 30 April 2015 and the new standards for small and micro-entities were issued on 16 July 2015 and are mandatory for accounting periods commencing on or after 1 January 2016, although earlier adoption is possible.

The overall effect of the above is twofold:

- small companies reporting under FRS 102 with reduced disclosures will apply the full recognition and measurement principles contained in FRS 102 but retain the presentation and disclosure requirements that are applicable to a small company; and
- there will be a reduction in the need for significant changes in accounting for certain transactions as the entity grows.

2.17 The new financial reporting framework for small companies is based on the full recognition and measurement requirements of FRS 102. It is only the disclosure requirements that differ because these are based on the legal minimum, although FRS 102 with reduced disclosures does encourage additional disclosure requirements in order that the financial statements give a true and fair view in Appendix D to Section 1A *Additional disclosures encouraged for small entities*.

Focus

- It is crucial that directors appreciate that the true and fair view concept enshrined within the Companies Act 2006 has not changed for small companies. Company directors have a legal obligation to ensure that the financial statements of a reporting entity give a true and fair view and it follows that the application of the legal minimum disclosures may not, necessarily, enable the financial statements to give a true and fair view and hence the directors must make additional disclosures to ensure the true and fair view concept is achieved. This may involve liaising with professional advisers so that company directors discharge their legal obligations properly.

2.18 The presentation and disclosure requirements of FRS 102 are outlined in Section 1A *Small Entities* of FRS 102 and are proportionate to small entities. They are split into two component parts: Appendix C *Disclosure requirements for small entities* outlines the disclosure requirements in the Companies Act 2006; Appendix D *Additional disclosures encouraged for small entities* deals with those disclosures which the FRC encourage to enable the financial statements to give a true and fair view.

The decision to apply the full recognition and measurement requirements of FRS 102 was made to improve financial reporting by small entities to ensure there are no differences between FRS 102 for medium and large entities and FRS 102 for small entities. In addition, those micro-entities following the principles in FRS 105 *The Financial Reporting Standard applicable to the Micro-entities Regime* will also find that the recognition and measurement principles are largely based on FRS 102 (albeit with no fair value or revaluation models included).

Focus

- Small entities which fall under the scope of FRS 102 with reduced disclosure will not be required to produce a cash flow statement, nor will a small entity reporting under FRS 102 for small entities be required to produce a statement of total comprehensive income or a statement of changes in equity (although the statement of changes in equity is encouraged if necessary). Small entities reporting under FRS 102 principles will also be exempt from the requirement to prepare group accounts.

Recognition and measurement differences under FRS 102

2.19 The move across to FRS 102 for small entities may cause concern to some preparers who may be unfamiliar with the detailed contents of FRS 102, or who may not have any experience of undertaking a transition to a new financial reporting regime. To all intents and purposes, it is not expected that the size of the financial statements under FRS 102 for small entities will significantly increase (nor significantly decrease) in size because small entities will still be able to benefit from the reduced presentation and disclosure requirements in Section 1A.

FRS 102 is a whole new financial reporting framework which brings about changes to the way that certain transactions and events are accounted for and disclosed in the financial statements. It is based on the *IFRS for SMEs* which, in turn, is based on full IFRS which is essentially where the regulators wanted the UK and Republic of Ireland to be in terms of financial reporting as most countries are now adopting an IFRS-based framework to report their financial information and hence it followed that the UK and Republic of Ireland should follow this trait to ensure comparability across borders as well as achieving consistency.

2.20 There are some considerable changes to the way in which certain transactions are accounted for under the provisions in FRS 102 from what practitioners and company accountants may be used to.

> **Focus**
>
> - This book is only concerned with small company aspects and there are notable differences in the way that consolidated financial statements are concerned. As small companies are generally exempt from the requirement to prepare consolidated financial statements this chapter does not cover the issue, but readers are advised to familiarise themselves with the differences in consolidated financial statements under FRS 102 principles where these are prepared.

The most notable differences between the FRSSE and FRS 102 for small entities are within the following areas:

- Accounting policies.
- Cash flow statement.[3]
- Deferred tax.
- Defined benefit pension schemes.
- Employee benefits.
- Fair value accounting.
- Financial instruments.
- Fixed assets.
- Goodwill and intangible assets.
- Intra-group loans.
- Investment property.
- Leases.
- Prior period adjustments.
- Revenue recognition.
- Stock valuations.

> **Focus**
>
> - Whilst this section of the book primarily concerns small companies, at the end of each of the following differences will be points that are applicable to micro-entities also to help contextualise the differences between the new small companies' regime and the micro-entities regime insofar as FRS 102 recognition and measurement principles are concerned.

3 Many small entities do not prepare a cash flow statement but due to the significant presentational differences, this book has covered the differences for clarity.

Accounting policies

2.21 Accounting policies are the 'backbone' in the way that financial statements are prepared. Other than for micro-entities, there are no changes to the requirement to disclose critical accounting policies for small entities under the scope of FRS 102. In addition, there are no changes to the way in which a change in accounting policy is applied and Section 10 *Accounting Policies, Estimates and Errors* deals with such transactions. A notable difference, however, where accounting policies are concerned relates to the rare situation where FRS 102 does not cover a transaction or event. Paragraph 10.4 says that if FRS 102 does not specifically address a transaction, or other event or condition, an entity's management must develop an accounting policy which is:

- **Relevant** – information is relevant to aid the decision-making process of the users.
- **Reliable** – this will result in financial statements faithfully representing the financial position, performance and cash flows. In addition, the policy must also reflect the economic substance of the transaction(s)/event(s)/condition(s) rather than merely reflecting the legal form. To achieve reliability the policy adopted must also be neutral, prudent and complete in all material respects.

The FRSSE was very similar and where an entity applying the FRSSE (effective January 2015) undertook a new transaction which was not dealt with under the FRSSE, management were required to develop an accounting policy, having regard to FRS 102 but not as a mandatory document, but rather as a means of establishing current practice.

Micro-entities

2.22 Micro-entities have no accounting policy options within FRS 105 and hence are not required to disclose nor develop any accounting policies.

Cash flow statement

2.23 Small companies are generally exempt from the requirement to produce a cash flow statement (statement of cash flows) in the general purpose financial statements. However, it is worth pointing out the difference in the event that a small company grows and reports under full FRS 102 and hence would be required to prepare a cash flow statement (unless it applies the provisions in FRS 101 *Reduced Disclosure Framework* and takes advantage of the exemption from preparing a cash flow statement).

Previous UK GAAP required the cash flow statement to be prepared under several standard headings as follows:

- Operating activities.
- Dividends from joint ventures and associates.

- Returns on investments and servicing of finance.
- Taxation.
- Capital expenditure and financial investments.
- Acquisitions and disposals.
- Equity dividends paid.
- Management of liquid resources.
- Financing.

Section 7 *Statement of Cash Flows* requires the cash flow statement to be prepared using only three types of cash flow classification:

- Operating activities.
- Investing activities.
- Financing activities.

Operating activities are the day-to-day revenue-producing activities of the business which are not investing or financing activities. The operating activities category is essentially a default category, encompassing all cash flows which do not fall within investing or financing activities.

Investing activities are activities which are the acquisition and disposal of long-term assets and other investments which are not included in cash equivalents. These can include the purchase and sale of fixed assets (including intangible fixed assets), payments to acquire equity or debt instruments or cash receipts from the repayment of advances and loans that have been made to other parties.

Financing activities are those activities which change the borrowing and equity structure of the business. These can include the proceeds from a share issue, repayments of loans and other amounts borrowed and payments in respect of the outstanding liability for a finance lease.

Example 2.4 – Classification of corporation tax payment

Westhead Ltd has a year-end of 31 December 2016 and has always produced a cash flow statement as part of its complete set of financial statements on the basis that the directors wish to have an understanding of how the company has generated and spent cash during the accounting year.

The finance director has prepared a cash flow statement under FRS 102 principles but the accountant is unsure where to classify the corporation tax payment in the cash flow statement as previously it would have been included under the 'Taxation' cash flow classification of which there is not such a classification under FRS 102.

Under FRS 102, Section 7 at paragraph 7.4(e), payments or refunds of income tax would fall to be classed as operating activities unless they can be specifically identified with financing and investing activities.

Micro-entities

2.24 A micro-entity is not required to produce a cash flow statement.

Deferred tax

2.25 Deferred tax under FRS 102 is inherently more complex because there are additional circumstances which require deferred tax considerations. However, comfort should be taken in the fact that deferred tax considerations could have been a lot worse under the previous Exposure Drafts of the new UK GAAP.

FRS 102 is based on the principles in IFRS. Under IAS 12 *Income Taxes*, deferred tax is calculated using the 'temporary difference' approach. In the UK and Republic of Ireland, preparers of financial statements have always been used to calculating deferred tax under the 'timing difference' approach and there is a considerable difference between the two methods. Under the first round of Exposure Drafts published by the (now defunct) Accounting Standards Board (ASB), the calculation of deferred tax was based on the temporary difference approach. The temporary difference method calculates the tax that would be paid if the net assets of the reporting entity were sold at book value. A temporary difference is the difference between the carrying amount of an asset or a liability and its tax base. The 'tax base' is the amount at which the item is recognised for the purposes of tax.

The timing difference approach, on the other hand, is based on the difference between an entity's accounting profit and taxable profit. Therefore, the temporary difference method focuses on the balance sheet (statement of financial position), whereas the timing difference approach focuses on the profit and loss account (income statement). Under the temporary difference method, the calculation of deferred tax is inherently more complex than under the timing difference method and hence would have caused accountants more difficulties.

At the time the ASB took on board feedback from critics of this method and staff were instructed to redraft the contents of Section 29 of FRS 102 under the premise that deferred tax in the UK and Republic of Ireland should not be too different than the calculation of deferred under the IAS 12 approach. This instruction was to ensure that no significant disparities existed between the deferred tax principles in FRS 102 and IAS 12.

The ASB completed its work on Section 29 and came up with the timing difference 'plus' approach which has now been incorporated within Section 29 (a Section which is notably very different than Section 29 in *IFRS for SMEs*). The timing difference plus approach builds on the old timing difference approach, but essentially eradicates some of the exemptions from deferred tax contained in previous UK GAAP. As a consequence, there are three additional situations when deferred tax must be calculated and are in respect of:

- revaluations of non-monetary asses (including investment property);
- fair values in business combinations; and
- unremitted earnings in overseas subsidiaries and associates.

Example 2.5 – Deferred tax on investment property

A company has an investment property on its balance sheet (statement of financial position) as at 31 December 2015 with a carrying value of £100,000. It has completed its transition to FRS 102 with reduced disclosures and as at 31 December 2016 the fair value of the investment property has increased to £130,000. The company pays tax at a rate of 20%. The entries in the books for this entire transaction are:

DR investment property	£30,000
CR fair value adjustments (profit or loss)	(£30,000)

Being increase in fair value of investment property at 31 December 2016

DR Deferred tax expense (profit or loss)	£6,000
CR Deferred tax provision	(£6,000)

Being deferred tax on fair value gain

Under previous UK GAAP and the FRSSE (effective January 2015), there would not have been any deferred tax recognised on the above transaction, unless:

- there was a binding agreement to sell the revalued asset; and
- the entity had recognised the gains and losses expected to arise on the sale.

Another difference between previous UK GAAP and FRS 102 (which is largely going to go unnoticed) is the fact that under FRS 102 principles, an entity is prohibited from discounting deferred tax balances to present day values.

Micro-entities

2.26 Micro-entities are exempt from the requirements of accounting for deferred tax.

Defined benefit pension schemes

2.27 Very few small companies have defined benefit pension schemes in operation; although there are some small companies which do have them. FRS 102 deals with such schemes (and defined contribution pension schemes) at Section 28 *Employee Benefits*. Paragraph 28.18 provides a number of simplifications where the valuation basis (the Projected Unit Credit Method) would require undue cost or effort. FRS 102 also does not require the use of an independent actuary to perform the valuation as previous UK GAAP did. Comprehensive annual valuations are also not required under FRS 102, provided that there has not been any significant change in the assumptions used since the last valuation was completed.

The reality is that where small companies do have a defined benefit pension scheme in operation, the majority are going to have to engage the services of a professionally-qualified independent actuary to perform the valuations because such calculations are very complex.

Micro-entities

2.28 Where a micro-entity has a defined benefit pension scheme in operation, FRS 105 allows the micro-entity to account for the scheme as a defined contribution scheme (although liabilities should be recognised for amounts in relation to a schedule of contributions to the extent that it relates to a deficit).

Employee benefits

2.29 Employee benefits are dealt with in Section 28 *Employee Benefits*. Section 28 requires an entity to make accruals for short-term employee benefits which have been accrued by the employee by the reporting date, but which are paid in the subsequent accounting period. The most notable effect this is going to have is on those entities that have not previously accounted for unpaid holiday entitlement at the year-end. The difficulty here is potentially in the calculation of holiday pay that is to be carried forward for future use and pulling this information together, especially for the transition to FRS 102.

Example 2.6 – Holiday pay accrual: holiday year is coterminous with the financial year

A company has an accounting reference date and holiday year-end of 30 June 2016. An employee has 30 days' holiday per year and is allowed to carry forward up to five days into the next holiday year. At the year-end 30 June 2015, the employee has taken 26 days' holiday.

The accountant should make an accrual for four days' holiday entitlement which will be taken in the next accounting period.

Example 2.7 – Holiday pay accrual: holiday year is not coterminous with the financial year

A company has an accounting reference date of 30 June 2016 and a holiday year of 31 December 2016. An employee has 30 days' holiday per year and at the year-end had taken 20 days' holiday in 2016.

In this case there will be a prepayment of five days' holiday ((30 days × 6/12) – 20 days).

Micro-entities

2.30 A micro-entity will be expected to account for short-term employee benefits accrued at the year-end and paid in the subsequent accounting period.

Fair value accounting

2.31 FRS 102 places more emphasis on fair value accounting and there are a number of areas within the financial statements which are likely to be affected by the increased use in fair value accounting as follows:

- *Biological assets* (living animals and plants) can be measured using fair values where such values can be obtained reliably. Fluctuations in fair value are taken through profit or loss. Such polices must be applied consistently to each class of biological asset and its related agricultural produce. The use of the fair value model is not mandatory – the cost model may also be used instead.
- *Business combinations* where intangible assets are acquired and whose values can be reliably measured, they should be separated from goodwill at acquisition (such as intellectual property, in-process research and development and customer lists). The objective of doing this is to reduce the number of assets acquired which are subsumed within goodwill.
- *Financial instruments* including derivatives and investments in equity shares must be carried at fair value with changes in fair value going through profit or loss. Examples of derivative instruments include forward foreign currency contracts, interest rate swaps and options and commodity contracts.
- *Investments* in subsidiaries, associates and jointly controlled entities can be held in the separate financial statements of the parent company at either cost less impairment or at fair value with changes in fair value going through either profit or loss or other comprehensive income.
- *Investment property* whose fair value can be measured reliably should be carried at each reporting date at fair value with fluctuations in fair value passing through profit or loss.

- *Property, plant and equipment* can be measured using the revaluation model or the depreciated historic cost model. On transition to FRS 102, a reporting entity could use fair value as deemed cost on transition and then choose to carry those assets under the cost model going forward.

Micro-entities

2.32 Fair value accounting is not permitted for micro-entities. In addition, any previous revaluations will have to be removed on transition to FRS 105 *The Financial Reporting Standard applicable to the Micro-entities Regime*.

Financial instruments

2.33 FRS 102 splits financial instruments into two classifications: 'basic' and 'other'. *Basic* financial instruments include items such as:

- trade debtors;
- trade creditors;
- straightforward bank loans; and
- cash.

When a financial instrument falls to be classed as basic, it is generally measured at amortised cost. Most trade debtors and trade creditors which are classified as current assets or current liabilities will be measured at the undiscounted amount of cash expected to be received or paid. Basic financial instruments are accounted for under the provisions of Section 11 *Basic Financial Instruments*.

Focus

- Where payment terms are deferred beyond normal terms of credit, this will become a financing transactions and will have to be discounted on initial recognition at a market rate of interest for a similar debt instrument.

Other financial instruments are accounted for under the provisions in Section 12 *Other Financial Instruments Issues*. Section 12 will include instruments such as foreign currency exchange contracts and loans with complex features. Section 12 requires all financial instruments which are not basic to be measured at fair value at each reporting date with movements in fair value passing through profit or loss. The main difference here between FRS 102 and previous UK GAAP is that under previous UK GAAP many of these instruments would not have been recognised on the balance sheet (statement of financial position), but merely disclosed – for example derivative instruments.

The requirement to include instruments such as foreign exchange forward contracts and loans with complex terms attached is going to affect reporting entities' balance sheets (statements of financial position).

In terms of the accounting for basic loans under Section 11, the accounting treatment is again different than would have been the case under previous UK GAAP and is unfortunately more arduous. This is because Section 11 requires the use of the *amortised cost method* which uses the *effective interest rate method* for interest recognition. This can be a fairly complex method and involves the use of discounting to arrive at an effective interest rate.

Example 2.8 – Calculating amortised cost using the effective interest method

A company borrows £1m on 1 January 2015 for a 10-year period by issuing loan notes with a coupon rate of 7% and the lender charges an arrangement fee of £12,500. Interest is payable at a rate of 7% and this is payable annually starting at the inception of the loan. The redemption amount of the loan is at par at the end of year 10. The company has chosen not to prepay any of the loan amounts and the discount rate which would be necessary so as to be equivalent to 10 annual payments of £70,000 (£1m × 7%) plus the redemption amount at maturity of £1m to the initial carrying value of £987,500 (£1m less the arrangement fee of £12,500) is 7.179%.

Using the amortised cost and effective interest method, the loan interest is allocated to the profit and loss account over the life of the loan as follows:

Date	Opening balance	Interest charge at 7.179%	Cash outflow	Closing balance
1.1.15	£987,500	£70,893	(£70,000)	£988,393
31.12.15	£988,393	£70,957	(£70,000)	£989,350
31.12.16	£989,350	£71,025	(£70,000)	£990,375
31.12.17	£990,375	£71,099	(£70,000)	£991,474
31.12.18	£991,474	£71,178	(£70,000)	£992,652
31.12.19	£992,652	£71,262	(£70,000)	£993,914
31.12.20	£993,914	£71,353	(£70,000)	£995,267
31.12.21	£995,267	£71,450	(£70,000)	£996,717
31.12.22	£996,717	£71,554	(£70,000)	£998,271
31.12.23	£998,271	£71,729*	(£70,000)	£1,000,000
		£712,500	(£700,000)	
31.12.24	Repayment of principal			(£1,000,000)

*adjusted for rounding difference

Focus

- Before transition to FRS 102, it is advisable to scrutinise loan agreements and finance agreements for derivative financial instruments to ensure they are accounted for properly because under previous UK GAAP they would only have been recognised on settlement and hence merely disclosed (unless FRS 26 *Financial instruments: recognition and measurement* was adopted which is unlikely for a small company).

FRS 102 does incorporate an alternative method of accounting which is to opt for the recognition and measurement requirements of IAS 39 *Financial Instruments: Recognition and Measurement* or IFRS 9 *Financial Instruments*. The take-up of this option is not likely to be common where small companies are concerned.

Micro-entities

2.34 Micro-entities are unable to carry financial instruments at fair value. On initial recognition, a micro-entity must measure the instrument at transaction price, plus or minus any transaction costs that have not been recognised in profit or loss immediately. Transaction costs can be recognised immediately in profit or loss if they are considered to be immaterial. After initial recognition, a micro-entity measures financial instruments as follows:

- Investments in preference shares or ordinary shares shall be measured at cost less impairment.
- Investments in subsidiaries, associates and jointly controlled entities shall be measured at cost less impairment.
- Financial instruments other than those covered above are measured in accordance with paragraph 9.12 of FRS 105 (which is at amortised cost).

Fixed assets

2.35 Extensive guidance was included in FRS 15 *Tangible fixed assets* relating to subsequent expenditure on an existing asset. Subsequent expenditure was capitalised in the balance sheet (statement of financial position) when the expenditure:

- provided an enhancement of the economic benefits of the asset in excess of the previously assessed standard of performance;
- related to a component of a tangible asset that had been treated separately for depreciation purposes which was replaced or restored; or
- related to a major inspection or overhaul of the tangible fixed asset that restored the economic benefits of the asset(s) that had been used up by the entity and that had already been reflected in the depreciation charge.

Paragraph 6.22 of the FRSSE (effective January 2015) said that subsequent expenditure should be capitalised only if:

- it enhances the economic benefits of a **tangible fixed asset** in excess of the previously assessed standard of performance (ie if it is an improvement); or
- it replaces or restores a component that has been separately depreciated over its **useful economic life**.

Otherwise it shall be **recognised** in the profit and loss account as incurred.

Section 17 *Property, Plant and Equipment* does deal with the issue of subsequent expenditure but does not go into anywhere near the same amount of detail that FRS 15/the FRSSE did. Paragraph 17.15 states that day-to-day servicing of property, plant and equipment must be recognised in the profit and loss account (income statement) in the periods in which the costs are incurred. Those preparing financial statements to FRS 102 principles would therefore be directed to Section 2 *Concepts and Pervasive Principles* to determine whether, or not, subsequent expenditure should be capitalised and hence professional judgement will be needed.

Paragraph 17.5 deals with 'spare parts' and 'standby equipment'. FRS 15 and the FRSSE (effective January 2015) did not deal with such equipment and hence many reporting entities carried this type of expenditure in the financial statements as inventory, with recognition in profit or loss when the entity used the spare parts/standby equipment. Section 17 at paragraph 17.5 requires 'major' spare parts and standby equipment to be included in the cost of the entity's fixed assets to which the equipment relates when the business is expected to use the equipment for more than one accounting period. The treatment under FRS 102 would essentially mean that the cost of major spare parts/standby equipment would be recognised within the depreciation charge rather than through cost of sales as consumption of stock.

Where fixed assets are acquired under a deferred payment arrangement, the cost of the asset must be the present value of all the future payments so as to comply with paragraph 17.13. Such issues were not specifically covered in either FRS 15 or the FRSSE (effective January 2015) and would have resulted in the assets capitalised being understated, giving rise to a lower depreciation charge. FRS 102 addresses this issue so the net book value of fixed assets accounted for in accordance with paragraph 17.13 will be higher and hence have consequential increase in the depreciation charge.

Micro-entities

2.36 There are no differences in the way that a micro-entity will account for its fixed assets under FRS 105 (except that no fixed assets can be subjected to revaluation under FRS 105).

Goodwill and intangible assets

2.37 Intangible assets (other than goodwill) are dealt with in Section 18 *Intangible Assets Other than Goodwill.* The key difference between FRS 102 and the FRSSE (effective January 2015) is in relation to the presumed maximum life. The FRSSE (effective January 2015) followed FRS 102 principles which stated that where management were unable to arrive at a reliable estimate for the goodwill/intangible asset useful economic life, the maximum life was five years. In contrast, previous FRSSE (effective April 2008) presumed a maximum useful life of 20 years, with an option to rebut this period if a longer (or indefinite) life can be justified.

Under FRS 102 with reduced disclosures, the maximum useful life has been increased to ten years following the Department for Business, Innovation and Skills amending the period in the revised Companies Act 2006. In addition, all goodwill and intangible assets will have finite useful lives and therefore this will affect small companies which have previously not amortised goodwill or other intangible assets on the basis that the director(s) consider such lives to be indefinite as the accounting practice will have to change to comply with FRS 102 principles.

Focus

- Accelerated write-downs of goodwill and intangible assets on transition and in the comparative year in the year FRS 102 is adopted are only likely in exceptional circumstances. Under previous UK GAAP, a company would have considered the carrying amount of goodwill and intangible assets at each reporting date as part of assessing the assets for impairment. It is, therefore, not expected that many entities will be writing down goodwill or intangible assets excessively on transition to FRS 102 for small entities.

Micro-entities

2.38 There are no differences in how a micro-entity will account for its goodwill and intangible assets under FRS 105 principles (although fair value accounting is not permissible for micro-entities).

Intra-group loans

2.39 In a group situation, it is not uncommon for one member of the group to make a loan to another member of the group; for example the parent of the group may make a loan to a subsidiary. Various reasons exist as to why an intra-group loan might take place; the most common one being simplicity (as often it can be time-consuming for a company to raise finance through a third party).

FRS 102 requires a different method of accounting for intra-group loans than previous UK GAAP did and is inherently more complex. For short-term intra-group loans there is often not a problem, provided that repayment is not deferred beyond normal commercial terms. However, the situation is different for long-term business loans because measurement issues will arise if the rate of interest charged on the loan is not a market rate of interest (which is often the case where intra-group loans are concerned).

When a group member makes a loan to another group member, the loan is often a long-term loan. It is generally more common (although not always the case) for a parent company to make a loan to the subsidiary group member and the parent may decide to charge an interest rate which is lower than market rate or even charge interest at 0%. In addition, there may also be situations where intra-group balances may be due from the subsidiary which are unlikely to be recovered in a short timescale and under normal commercial terms.

Issues can be compounded in respect of intra-group loans where there are no formal loan terms attached to the finance (which is often the case). Where there are formal loan terms in existence, it is often difficult to retrospectively change these terms and so it is advisable to change these terms (or introduce terms) before the date of transition to FRS 102 (and FRS 102 with reduced disclosures) as this will avoid any measurement issues. There are also two potential ways around encountering measurement issues:

- the lender charges the borrower a market rate of interest; or
- the terms of the loan make provision for the loan to be repaid back to the lender at a very short notice period.

In the latter, consideration will have to be given to reallocating long-term loans to current.

The difficulty is often arriving at a market rate of interest and in this respect it is often simpler to charge the rate of interest which the borrower might incur from a bank. Other methods can be used to arrive at a market rate of interest which are based on the following factors:

- cash flow pattern;
- the company's credit rating;
- currency;
- maturity; and
- any collateral which has been pledged by the borrower.

In arriving at a market rate of interest, lenders should keep in mind that if the borrower already has a substantial number of other borrowings (ie it is already highly geared), then a lender would demand a higher rate of interest to reflect the increased risk. However, where the borrower has no existing borrowings and a high level of assets, the interest rate would inherently be less because the risk is lower.

When an intra-group loan attracts interest at a market rate, no accounting issues arise and the loan is recognised at fair value at the outset which is equivalent to the loan proceeds. This is because the transaction price reflects fair value.

When an intra-group loan does not attract interest at a market rate, measurement differences arise. Under the FRSSE (effective January 2015) the issue was fairly straightforward; the company receiving the loan would recognise a creditor at the amount payable and the company making the loan would recognise a debtor at the amount receivable. The group member carrying the debtor in the balance sheet would also make provision for any amounts which may not be recoverable through an impairment test.

Example 2.9 – Loan not charged at a market rate

A parent company owns 100% of a subsidiary. The parent has agreed to make a working capital loan to its subsidiary and charge a rate of interest of 5%. Market rates of interest from its bank would be 10%. The loan terms state that the loan is repayable immediately on demand.

Where interest rates on intra-group loans are at a below market rate of interest, then the loan should be initially measured at fair value. This will be the proceeds of the transaction. In the subsidiary's books the loan should be recorded at not less than the amount repayable. As the loan is below market rate, the subsidiary will record the loan at the amount immediately payable to comply with paragraph 12.11 of FRS 102.

Where a parent company agrees to make a fixed-term loan to a subsidiary which does not contain any demand features, or the subsidiary has the option to repay the loan early, the parent recognises the loan at fair value and so will the subsidiary. An accounting issue arises as to how to deal with the difference between fair value and present value.

If a fixed-term loan is charged at a rate of interest which is below market rate, and the borrower (in this case the subsidiary) has the option to repay the loan early, the accounting treatment for this loan would normally be the same as that of a fixed-rate loan without the option of early repayment. This is because the company receiving the loan and being charged a rate of interest below market rate would not normally exercise the option to repay the loan early.

In the parent's books, the difference between the fair value and the present value of the loan will be recognised as an investment in the subsidiary. In the subsidiary's accounts, the difference between the fair value and the present value will be recognised as a capital contribution.

Example 2.10 – Fixed-term loan

A parent (P) agrees to lend its subsidiary (S) an amount of £10,000 on 1 January 2015 with repayment taking place on 31 December 2016. S's bank provided a quotation and would have charged 10% on the same loan and P has agreed to charge an interest rate of 5%. The loan is fixed-term and the terms do not have any demand features.

Workings – present value

Year	Cash flow	Discount factor	Present value
	£		£
2015	500	0.9091	455
2016	10,500	0.8264	8,677
			9,132

Workings – interest charge

Year	Opening balance	Interest (10%)	Payments	Closing balance
	£	£	£	£
2015	9,132	913	(500)	9,545
2016	9,545	955	(10,500)	–

In the parent's books the journals are:

	DR	CR
Loan receivable	9,132	
Investment in subsidiary	868	
Cash at bank		10,000
Initial recognition of loan		
Cash at bank	500	
Loan receivable	413	
Interest income (profit or loss)		913
Interest charge to 31 December 2015		
Cash at bank	500	
Loan receivable	455	
Interest income (profit or loss)		955
Interest to 31 December 2016		
Cash at bank	10,000	
Loan receivable		10,000
Redemption of capital		

In the subsidiary's books the journals are:

	DR	CR
Cash at bank	10,000	
Loan payable		9,132
Capital contribution (equity)		868
Initial recognition of loan		
Interest expense (profit or loss)	913	
Cash at bank		500
Loan payable		413
Interest to 31 December 2015		
Interest expense (profit or loss)	955	
Cash at bank		500
Loan payable		455
Interest to 31 December 2016		
Loan payable	10,000	
Cash at bank		10,000
Redemption of loan		

Focus

- Taking the difference between the fair value of the loan and the present value to the investment in subsidiary in the parent's books (and hence recognising a corresponding capital contribution in the subsidiary's books) reflects the fact that the parent has contributed to the subsidiary by lending funds at a below market rate of interest.

Loan from subsidiary to parent

2.40 In a reversed role, where the subsidiary lends funds to its parent, it is often the case that these loans are at a below market rate of interest. Two situations can be considered:

Scenario 1

The subsidiary lends funds to its parent. The loan is a fixed-term loan with no demand features and the parent has the option to repay the loan early. Interest is charged by the subsidiary at a rate of 5% with market rates being 10%.

The subsidiary recognises the loan at fair value and the initial measurement difference is recognised as a distribution to the parent.

The parent recognises the loan at fair value and the initial measurement difference is recognised as income from the subsidiary.

Scenario 2

The subsidiary lends funds to its parent. The loan is repayable on demand at the option of the subsidiary. Interest is charged by the subsidiary at a rate of 5% with market rates being 10%.

The subsidiary recognises the loan at fair value and the initial measurement difference is recognised as a distribution to the parent.

The parent recognises the loan at the amount payable. This amount is discounted from the demand date, where material.

In both cases the accounting treatment adopted reflects the fact that the subsidiary has essentially made a distribution to the parent by making a loan at a below market rate of interest.

Example 2.11 – Loan from subsidiary to parent

A subsidiary (S) agrees to lend its parent (P) an amount of £10,000 on 1 January 2015 with repayment taking place on 31 December 2016. The loan attracts interest at a rate of 5% and market rates are 10%.

Workings – present value

Year	Cash flow	Discount factor	Present value
	£		£
2015	500	0.9091	455
2016	10,500	0.8264	8,677
			9,132

Workings – interest charge

Year	Opening balance	Interest (10%)	Payments	Closing balance
	£	£	£	£
2015	9,132	913	(500)	9,545
2016	9,545	955	(10,500)	–

In the parent's books the journals are:

	DR	CR
Cash at bank	10,000	
Loan payable		9,132
Income from subsidiary (profit or loss)		868
Initial recognition of loan		
Interest expense (profit or loss)	913	
Cash at bank		500
Loan payable		413
Interest to 31 December 2015		
Interest expense (profit or loss)	955	
Cash at bank		500
Loan payable		455
Interest to 31 December 2016		
Loan payable	10,000	
Cash at bank		10,000
Redemption of loan		

In the subsidiary's books the journals are:

	DR	CR
Loan receivable	9,132	
Distribution to parent (equity)	868	
Cash at bank		10,000
Initial recognition of loan		
Cash at bank	500	
Loan receivable	413	
Interest income (profit or loss)		913
Interest charge to 31 December 2015		

Cash at bank	500	
Loan receivable	455	
Interest income (profit or loss)		955
Interest to 31 December 2016		
Cash at bank	10,000	
Loan receivable		10,000
Redemption of loan		

Focus

- There is little in the way of guidance as to whether either treatment (loan from parent to subsidiary and vice versa) gets caught by the rules on distributions. Despite the accounting treatment above accounting for the difference as a distribution, it is not necessarily a distribution for legal purposes. It has been a long established practice for group members to make interest-free loans to each other and in the past this has not been regarded as giving rise to distributions for legal purposes. Because of the revised accounting treatment under FRS 102, attention will be drawn to the issue and hence companies should exercise caution when they enter into such transactions in the absence of distributable reserves. Alternatively it might be appropriate in the circumstances to seek legal advice.

As the discount on the loan unwinds, it will be debited or credited to profit or loss. FRS 102 is silent on the adjustment to the cost of the investment and associated capital contribution and hence it could be left as they are (or they could be adjusted if management so wish). An adjustment is achieved by writing down the cost of the investment to match the unwinding discount passing through the profit and loss account and then adjusting the capital contribution via a movement on reserves. Alternatively (in the absence of guidance), it could also be appropriate to leave the cost of the investment and the capital contribution as they are and deal with them as part of any impairment adjustment.

Loan from subsidiary to subsidiary

2.41 It is not always the case that a parent company is involved in an intra-group loan (either making or receiving the loan). Intra-group loans can arise between subsidiary companies which could also be set at below market rates of interest.

Scenario 1

Subsidiary B lends funds to Subsidiary C. The loan is a fixed-term loan and contains no demand features with C having the option to repay the loan early. Interest is being charged by B at a rate of 5% with market rates being at 10%.

B recognises the loan at fair value with the initial measurement difference being recognised as a distribution as, in substance, the loan will have been authorised through the parent.

C recognises the loan at fair value and the initial measurement difference is recognised as a capital contribution – again reflecting the fact that the loan has been authorised through the parent.

Scenario 2

Subsidiary B lends funds to Subsidiary C. The loan is repayable on demand at the option of B. Interest is being charged by B at a rate of 5% with market rates of interest being 10%.

B recognises the loan at fair value and the initial measurement difference is recognised as a distribution, as the loan will have been authorised through the parent.

C recognises the amount payable. This amount is then discounted from the date, where material.

Example 2.12 – Loans between subsidiaries

Subsidiary B agrees to lend Subsidiary C an amount of £10,000 on 1 January 2015 with payment taking place on 31 December 2016. B charges C a below market rate of interest of 5% with market rates being 10%.

Workings – present value

Year	Cash flow	Discount factor	Present value
	£		£
2015	500	0.9091	455
2016	10,500	0.8264	8,677
			9,132

Workings – interest charge

Year	**Opening balance**	**Interest (10%)**	**Payments**	**Closing balance**
	£	**£**	**£**	**£**
2015	9,132	913	(500)	9,545
2016	9,545	955	(10,500)	–

In Subsidiary B's books the journals are:

	DR	**CR**
Loan receivable	9,132	
Distribution (equity)	868	
Cash at bank		10,000
Initial recognition of loan		
Cash at bank	500	
Loan receivable	413	
Interest income		913
Interest charge to 31 December 2015		
Cash at bank	500	
Loan receivable	455	
Interest income		955
Interest to 31 December 2016		
Cash at bank	10,000	
Loan receivable		10,000
Redemption of loan		

In Subsidiary C's books the journals are:

	DR	CR
Cash at bank	10,000	
Loan payable		9,132
Capital contribution (equity)		868
Initial recognition of loan		
Interest expense	913	
Cash at bank		500
Loan payable		413
Interest to 31 December 2015		
Interest expense	955	
Cash at bank		500
Loan payable		455
Interest to 31 December 2016		
Loan payable	10,000	
Cash at bank		10,000
Redemption of loan		

Micro-entities

2.42 Where micro-entities are involved in group transactions such as intra-group loans, these are recognised at transaction price.

Investment property

2.43 Under the provisions in Section 16 *Investment Property*, an investment property is defined as follows:

> 'Investment property is property (land or a building, or part of a building, or both) held by the owner or by the lessee under a **finance lease** to earn rentals or for capital appreciation or both, rather than for:

(a) use in the production or supply of goods or services or for administrative purposes; or

(b) sale in the ordinary course of business.'

The FRSSE (effective January 2015) required such properties to be classified in the balance sheet (statement of financial position) at their open market value with changes in the market value being recognised through a revaluation reserve account within equity and reported via the statement of total recognised gains and losses.

Where investment property is carried at fair value, paragraph 16.7 extinguishes the use of the revaluation reserve and requires all changes in the fair value of investment property to be recognised in profit or loss. The effect of this accounting treatment is that reported profit or loss would be different than what would have been the case under previous UK GAAP. The gain or loss taken to the profit and loss account (income statement) is ignored for the purposes of tax.

Focus

- Under the provisions of FRS 102, if fair value cannot be reliably measured with relative ease, then the cost less depreciation is used. However, this was not permitted under the FRSSE (effective January 2015), nor in previous UK GAAP.

A key point to emphasise where FRS 102 is concerned is that any gains that are taken to the profit and loss account (income statement) in respect of investment properties are not distributable as a dividend to shareholders. This is because the gain is unrealised for the purposes of dividend distribution.

In addition to the dividend point, it is also worth noting that the requirement to account for deferred tax on the fair value gain is also a requirement of Section 29 *Income Tax*. Paragraph 29.16 says:

> 'Deferred tax relating to **investment property** that is measured at **fair value** in accordance with Section 16 Investment Property shall be measured using the tax rates and allowances that apply to the sale of the asset, except for investment property that has a limited **useful life** and is held within a business model whose objective is to consume substantially all of the economic benefits embodied in the property over time.'[4]

Under the previous UK GAAP, deferred tax would have been ignored unless there was a binding agreement to sell the asset at the reporting date and the disposal had been accounted for.

4 FRS 102, Section 29, para 29.16.

Example 2.13 – Investment property on transition to FRS 102 with reduced disclosures

A company with a 31 December 2016 year-end has run an opening trial balance as at 1 January 2015 (based on the 31 December 2014 closing trial balance). The opening trial balance shows a revaluation surplus in respect of investment property of £120,000. The tax rate is 20%.

On transition to FRS 102, the company should make the following transitional adjustments to its opening balances in order to arrive at an FRS 102-compliant opening balance sheet (statement of financial position):

DR revaluation reserve	£120,000
CR accumulated profit and loss	(£120,000)

Being reclassification of investment property revaluation surplus on transition to FRS 102.

Under FRS 102, the company will also have to account for deferred tax in respect of the investment property's fair value as follows:

DR accumulated profit and loss	£24,000
CR deferred tax provision	(£24,000)

Being deferred tax on investment property revaluation surplus.

If it is assumed that in 2015 (the comparative year) the value of the investment property had increased by £5,000 the entries (under the FRSSE (effective January 2015)) would have been:

DR investment property	£5,000
CR revaluation reserve	(£5,000)

Being uplift in the market value of investment property under the FRSSE (effective January 2015).

The concept of the revaluation reserve does not apply to investment property accounted for under FRS 102 and so a transitional adjustment will also have to be made to the 2015 financial statements as follows:

DR revaluation reserve	£5,000
CR profit and loss account	(£5,000)

Being reclassification of investment property fair value gain.

DR profit and loss account tax charge £1,000

CR deferred tax provision (£1,000)

Being deferred tax on the investment property revaluation.

From the above worked example, it can be noted that there will be an overall increase in previously reported profit of £4,000 (£5,000 gain on revaluation less the deferred tax charge of £1,000). This overall gain cannot be distributed as a dividend.

Focus

- Many commentators are suggesting the use of a separate reserve account within equity to record reserves which cannot be distributed. While there is nothing in company law that requires this, it would be permissible so as to keep a record of the levels of distributable and undistributable reserves which the company has.

Micro-entities

2.44 Where a micro-entity has an investment property, it must be carried under normal fixed asset rules (ie at cost less depreciation and less impairment losses). All previous revalued amounts must be removed on transition to FRS 105.

Leases

2.45 The Glossary to the FRSSE (effective January 2015) and SSAP 21 *Accounting for leases and hire purchase contracts* set out a specific numeric benchmark when determining whether a lease was a finance or an operating lease. This 'bright line test' was where the minimum lease payments equated to 90% or more of the fair value of the asset subject to the lease and if they did, the lease was treated as a finance lease.

The classification under FRS 102 does not refer to a 90% benchmark, but instead offers examples of the various situations which, individually or collectively, would give rise to a lease being classified as a finance lease as follows:

- The lease transfers ownership of the asset to the lessee by the end of the lease term.
- The lessee has the option to purchase the asset at a price that is expected to be sufficiently lower than the fair value at the date the option becomes exercisable for it to be reasonably certain, at the inception of the lease, that the option will be exercised.
- The lease term is for the major part of the economic life of the asset even if title is not transferred.

- At the inception of the lease the present value of the minimum lease payments amounts to at least substantially all of the fair value of the leased asset.
- The leased assets are of such a specialised nature that only the lessee can use them without major modifications.

Three other indicators that a lease is a finance lease are:

- If the lessee can cancel the lease, the lessor's losses associated with the cancellation are borne by the lessee.
- Gains or losses from the fluctuations in the residual value of the leased asset accrue to the lessee (eg in the form of a rent rebate equalling most of the sales proceeds at the end of the lease).
- The lessee has the ability to continue the lease for a secondary period at a rent that is substantially lower than market rent.

The classification criterion are based on the risks and rewards of ownership of the associated asset and which party retains those risks and rewards. There are a number of factors that can determine whether risks and rewards have, or have not, been transferred from the lessor to the lessee and therefore paragraph 20.7 of FRS 102 acknowledges that the examples of the above indicators are not conclusive in every respect and consideration must therefore be given to other indicators that risks and rewards may (or may not) have transferred from lessor to lessee.

In some cases, lessees may receive an incentive payment to take up a lease. Paragraph 20.15A does make reference to the effect of incentive payments relating to operating leases. It says that the lessee must recognise the aggregate benefit of lease incentives as a reduction to the expense over the lease term on a straight-line basis unless another systematic basis is representative of the time pattern of the lessee's benefit from the use of the leased asset.

Example 2.14 – Lease incentive

Alex Ltd enters into a ten-year lease with the landlord of a commercial property. The terms of the lease allow for a break-clause to be exercised after a five-year period has elapsed, after which the lease rentals will revert to market rate. The lease incentive is equal to a one-year rental of £10,000.

Under previous UK GAAP, the £10,000 lease incentive would be recognised up to the point of the break clause (ie amortised over a five-year life). Under FRS 102, the lease incentive would be recognised over the lease term of ten years. Transitional provisions exist in paragraph 35.10(p) for leases which commenced before the date of transition to FRS 102 and a first-time adopter has the option of recognising any residual benefit or cost associated with a lease incentive on the same basis that applied under previous UK GAAP.

Micro-entities

2.46 Micro-entities will still account for leases as either a finance or operating lease depending on whether risks and rewards of ownership of the asset remain with the lessor or are transferred to the lessee.

Prior period adjustments

2.47 The difference in this area relates to error correction. Error correction is dealt with in Section 10 *Accounting Policies, Estimates and Errors*. Paragraph 10.21 of FRS 102 requires an entity to correct a *material* error through prior period adjustment in the first set of financial statements which are authorised for issue after discovery of the error.

This is different than what was the case under previous UK GAAP. FRS 3 *Reporting financial performance* required an error to be corrected where that error was a 'fundamental error'. The standard defined *fundamental errors* as those which destroy the true and fair view of the financial statements as well as the validity of those financial statements. The FRSSE (effective January 2015) referred to fundamental errors in its definition of a prior period adjustment in the Glossary.

The terms 'material' and 'fundamental' could be interpreted differently among accountants, but it is expected that more errors are going to be corrected by way of a prior period adjustment than was the case under previous UK GAAP.

Micro-entities

2.48 Micro-entities will follow the same principles under FRS 105 in that material errors are corrected through a prior period adjustment.

Revenue recognition

2.49 There are slight variations to the wording relating to the measurement of revenue. For example, paragraph 23.3 refers to revenue being the fair value of the consideration 'received' or 'receivable'. The FRSSE (effective January 2015) said that a seller recognises revenue under an exchange transaction with a customer when, and to the extent that, it obtained the 'right to consideration' in exchange for its performance. This wording was quite specific when compared to FRS 102's 'received or receivable' approach.

> **Focus**
>
> - There was no intention of allowing entities to potentially delay revenue recognition under FRS 102 by virtue of the different wording contained in the standard and it is still intended that reporting entities will continue recognising revenue when they receive a right to consideration. The Financial Reporting Council has said that if entities abuse the wording in the standard they will issue an Abstract to clarify the intentions.

Paragraph 23.15 of FRS 102 refers to a 'specific act' and a 'significant act'. The paragraph says that when a specific act is much more significant than any other act, the entity postpones revenue recognition until the significant act is executed. The FRSSE (effective January 2015) was more prohibitive in that it required revenue to be recognised in line with performance (ie passing a 'milestone' or the occurrence of a 'critical event') and hence earning the right to consideration. Again, this different wording is not intended to have any consequential effect to the timing of revenue recognition and entities must still continue recognising revenue when they receive a right to consideration.

Paragraph 23.16 of FRS 102 says that where an entity cannot estimate the outcome of a service contract (which is more likely to apply to construction contracts), then the entity should only recognise revenue to the extent of costs incurred. In contrast, paragraph 10 of SSAP 9 *Stocks and long-term contracts* said that where the outcome of a long-term contract could not be assessed with reasonable certainty, no profit should be reflected in the profit and loss account and suggested showing as turnover a proportion of total contract value using a zero estimate of profit.

Micro-entities

2.50 Micro-entities will continue recognising revenue when they receive a right to consideration.

Inventories (stock)

2.51 The FRSSE (effective January 2015) did permit, but did not favour, stock being valued using the last-in first-out (LIFO) method of valuation. Indeed, SSAP 9 *Stocks and long-term contracts* specifically required directors of companies using the LIFO method to have justifiable reasons for its use. The FRSSE in Appendix III confirmed that the use of LIFO would often result in stocks being stated in the balance sheet (statement of financial position) at amounts that bear little relationship to recent cost levels.

Paragraph 13.18 follows the same stance as its international counterpart, IAS 2 *Inventories* which outlaws the use of the LIFO method as a basis for inventory valuation.

Micro-entities

2.52 Micro-entities will also be prohibited from valuing stock using the LIFO method.

CONTENT OF THE FINANCIAL STATEMENTS

2.53 The content of the financial statements will depend on whether the entity is:

- a small entity reporting under FRS 102 with reduced disclosures; or
- a micro-entity.

FRS 102 with reduced disclosures

2.54 Under FRS 102 with reduced disclosures, reporting entities are required to prepare (for each financial year):

- A directors' report.
- An income statement (profit and loss account).
- A statement of financial position (balance sheet).
- Notes to comply with Section 1A *Small Entities* (see Appendices C and D in Section 1A of FRS 102) and the Companies Act 2006.

Entities reporting under FRS 102 with reduced disclosures are encouraged to provide a statement of changes in equity and the following disclosure notes:

- A statement of compliance with FRS 102.
- A statement that the entity is a public benefit entity (if relevant).
- If relevant, the disclosures relating to going concern.
- Dividends declared and paid or payable during the period.
- On first-time adoption of FRS 102, an explanation of how the transition has affected its financial position and financial performance.

Micro-entities

2.55 For micro-entities reporting under FRS 105 *The Financial Reporting Standard applicable to the Micro-entities Regime* a micro-entity is required to prepare:

- A Format 2 income statement (profit and loss account) for the year.
- A Format 1 or Format 2 statement of financial position (balance sheet).
- Notes as follows:

- the total amount of any financial commitments, guarantees or contingencies that are not included in the balance sheet;
- an indication of the nature and form of any valuable security which has been provided;
- the amounts of advances and credits granted to members of the administrative, managerial and supervisory bodies with indications of interest rates, main conditions and any amounts repaid or written off or waived; and
- any commitments entered into on their behalf by way of guarantees of any kind, with an indication of the total for each category.

PITFALLS TO AVOID

- Incorrect classification of a company as small by using net assets instead of gross assets and actual rather than average employee numbers.
- Reporting under FRS 105 when this framework is not appropriate in the company's circumstances or the entity is not eligible (eg a charity).
- Accounting for certain transactions in accordance with the FRSSE which may have been different than the treatment required under FRS 102 or FRS 105 principles.
- Failing to make additional disclosures in small company financial statements where such disclosures would give a true and fair view.

CHAPTER SUMMARY

- The Companies Act 2006 has been revised for accounting periods commencing on or after 1 January 2016 and earlier adoption for accounting periods commencing on or after 1 January 2015, but before 1 January 2016, is allowed if the directors so wish.
- The small companies' regime has effectively been split into two components: small companies and micro-entities.
- Micro-entities can report under FRS 105 *The Financial Reporting Standard applicable to the Micro-entities Regime* and this standard is optional; a micro-entity could report under FRS 102 with reduced disclosures if it so chooses.
- The FRSSE (effective January 2015) is withdrawn for accounting periods commencing on or after 1 January 2016 and small companies will report under FRS 102 with reduced disclosures.
- There are some accounting and disclosure differences that companies will have to understand on transition to FRS 102 or FRS 105.

- Small companies can prepare 'abridged' financial statements and 'adapted' financial statements. The concept of abbreviated financial statements is withdrawn for accounting periods commencing on or after 1 January 2016.

Chapter 3

The Financial Statements

SIGNPOSTS

- Section 1A *Small Entities* of FRS 102 *The Financial Reporting Standard applicable in the UK and Republic of Ireland* outlines the presentation and disclosure requirements for a small company but the full recognition and measurement principles of full FRS 102 apply (see **3.1**).
- A reduced number of legally required disclosures are needed in small company financial statements as a result of the transposition of the EU Accounting Directive into company law (see **3.2**).
- Micro-entities do not have to prepare a directors' report, but small companies are still required to prepare such a report (see **3.3**).
- The small companies' exemption relating to the directors' report can be claimed where two conditions are met (see **3.4**).
- The directors' report for a small company is fairly brief (see **3.5**).
- More disclosure is required in the directors' report for a small company which has an external audit (see **3.6**).
- An auditor must obtain 'relevant audit information' in order to prepare their report on the small company's financial statements (see **3.7**).
- It is a criminal offence to deliberately mislead the auditors of a company and the directors can be heavily punished under the Companies Act 2006 (see **3.8**).
- There are only two formats for the income statement (profit and loss account) under the revised Companies Act 2006 (see **3.9**).
- Some notable differences are in relation to exceptional items, fair value adjustments, operating profit and discontinued operations (see **3.13–3.17**).
- A dual statement approach can be used where the small company will prepare a 'statement of comprehensive income' (see **3.18**).
- Under the revised Companies Act 2006, a small company may adapt the statutory formats of the financial statements (see **3.19**).
- Format 1 and Format 2 remain for the statement of financial position (balance sheet) (see **3.20**).

- Micro-entities can also prepare a statement of financial position (balance sheet) under either Format 1 or Format 2 (see **3.24**).
- Where an adapted balance sheet has been prepared, there are certain items which must be distinguished between current and non-current (see **3.25**).
- A statement of changes in equity is encouraged, but not mandated (see **3.26**).
- Paragraph 6.3 of FRS 102 requires certain transactions to be disclosed separately in the statement of changes in equity (see **3.27**).
- A statement of cash flows (cash flow statement), by definition, is prepared on a cash basis using three cash flow classifications (see **3.28** and **3.29**).
- There are two permissible methods for the statement of cash flows (cash flow statement) being either the 'indirect' or 'direct' method (see **3.33–3.34**).
- Small companies would be encouraged to disclose 'non-cash transactions' relating to the statement of cash flows (cash flow statement) elsewhere in the financial statements where such transactions are material (see **3.36**).
- A reconciliation of the amounts presented in the statement of cash flows (cash flow statement) need not be presented if they are the same as the amounts in the balance sheet (statement of financial position) (see **3.37**).
- For small entities holding significant cash and cash equivalents which are not available for use by the entity, disclosure of such may need to be made to give a true and fair view (see **3.38**).
- Section 1A of FRS 102 contains the required disclosures that are needed to be made in the notes to the financial statements in Appendix C *Disclosure requirements for small entities* and Appendix D *Additional disclosures encouraged for small entities* (see **3.39–3.59**).
- There are four disclosure requirements contained in FRS 105 for micro-entities (see **3.60**).
- Abridged financial statements only show those line items which are preceded by letters and Roman numerals in the statutory formats (see **3.61–3.64**).
- A charity cannot prepare abridged financial statements and for other small companies all the members must unanimously agree to abridged financial statements being prepared (see **3.65–3.66**).
- The application of accounting standards enable the financial statements to give a true and fair view and accounting standards are only applied to material items (see **3.67–3.69**).

- A small company can claim audit exemption if certain criteria are met and where audit exemption is taken a statement that such exemption has been claimed must be made on the balance sheet (statement of financial position) (see **3.70** and **3.71**).
- Not all small companies choose audit exemption and there are benefits for a small company choosing to have an external audit (see **3.72**).

INTRODUCTION

3.1 This chapter will outline the overall content of a set of general purpose financial statements (the term 'general purpose financial statements' refers to the annual financial statements prepared by a small company).

Many small companies will use FRS 102 *The Financial Reporting Standard applicable in the UK and Republic of Ireland* and Section 1A *Small Entities* when preparing their financial statements. While Section 1A outlines the **presentation** and **disclosure** requirements needed for small companies' financial statements, it is important to emphasise that the **full** recognition and measurement requirements of FRS 102 are applied in the preparation of the amounts in the financial statements. For example, where a small company has tangible fixed assets (excluding investment property carried at fair value), it will apply the full recognition and measurement requirements of Section 17 *Property, Plant and Equipment*.

3.2 The incorporation of the EU Accounting Directive (the Directive) by the Department for Business, Innovation and Skills in 2015 has meant that there are fewer disclosure notes required by law and while the Directive essentially limits the amount of information which Member States are permitted to require small undertakings to place in their annual financial statements, it must be borne in mind that small company financial statements must still give a true and fair view in order to comply with the Companies Act 2006.

Focus

- The importance of ensuring the financial statements give a true and fair view cannot be over-emphasised. Directors of small companies will be committing a criminal offence if they recklessly prepare financial statements which fail to give a true and fair view.

For micro-entities applying the provisions of FRS 105, the legislation governing the preparation of financial statements for micro-entities contains 'deeming provisions' which state that financial statements prepared under the micro-entities' legislation are *presumed* to give a true and fair view. As a consequence of these deeming provisions, directors of micro-entities are not required to consider what additional information is required for the financial statements to give a true and fair view.

THE DIRECTORS' REPORT

3.3 At the outset it is important to point out that a micro-entity does not have to prepare a directors' report for inclusion in the annual financial statements as per section 415(1) of the Companies Act 2006 and hence this section of the chapter will only be concerned with the directors' report pertinent to small companies reporting under the provisions of FRS 102.

The requirements to prepare a directors' report are contained in the Companies Act 2006 in Part 15, Chapter 5 *Directors' Report* at sections 415 to 419A. Whilst not applicable to small companies, for the sake of completeness, section 417 *Contents of directors' report: business review* was repealed by The Companies Act 2006 (Strategic Report and Directors' Report) Regulations 2013, SI 2013/1970, regulations 2 and 5, with effect from 1 October 2013 for financial years ending on or after 30 September 2013 (although hardly any small companies prepared a business review as this requirement was confined to medium-sized and large entities).

3.4 Section 415(1) requires that the directors of a company must prepare a directors' report for each financial year for the company. This requirement extends to small companies, although section 415A outlines the small companies' exemption relating to the directors' report.

Focus

- The directors' report for a small company is very brief insofar as the contents are concerned, but must still be prepared and form part of the annual financial statements so as to comply with the Companies Act 2006.

Section 415A(1) of the Companies Act 2006 says that a company is entitled to the small companies exemption relating to the directors' report for a financial year where two conditions are met:

- it is entitled to prepare accounts for the year in accordance with the small companies regime; or[1]
- it would be so entitled but for being or having been a member of an ineligible group.[2]

Contents of the directors' report for small companies

3.5 As mentioned above, the contents of the directors' report for a small company are brief and this is because section 416(1) only requires the names of the persons who, at any time during the financial year, were directors of the company.

1 Companies Act 2006, s 415A(1)(a).
2 Companies Act 2006, s 415A(1)(b).

> **Focus**
>
> - Section 416(1) requires the names of the persons to be disclosed in the directors' report who **at any time during the financial year** were directors of the company. This means that if a director resigned part-way through the financial year, they should still be disclosed as a director during the year, together with the dates on which they resigned.

It is to be noted that section 416 does not require disclosure of the amount (if any) which the directors recommend should be paid by way of dividend for small companies. Companies not taking advantage of the small companies' regime must comply with the provisions in section 416(3) and make this disclosure.

Statement as to disclosure to auditors

3.6 Relatively few small companies have their financial statements audited; however the fact that a company is a small company does not preclude it from having an independent audit as audit exemption is optional and some small companies do have their financial statements audited. Audit exemption is examined at the end of this chapter and where a company does choose to have an external audit, **Chapter 13** examines the auditing issues for a small company in more detail.

Where a small company has an independent audit, the directors' report will contain more detail than a company that has not had an independent audit. This is because additional disclosures have to be made by the directors relating to the audit.

Section 418 outlines the contents of the directors' report where the company is subject to external audit. In particular, section 418(2) says that where the company is subjected to audit, there must be a statement to the effect that, in the case of each persons that were directors at the time the directors' report is approved:

- so far as the director is aware, there is no relevant audit information of which the company's auditor is unaware; and[3]
- he has taken all the steps that he ought to have taken as a director in order to make himself aware of any relevant audit information and to establish that the company's auditor is aware of that information.[4]

Example 3.1 – Illustrative disclosure

So far as the directors are aware, there is no relevant audit information (as defined by section 418 of the Companies Act 2006) of which the company's

3 Companies Act 2006, s 418(2)(a).
4 Companies Act 2006, s 418(2)(b).

auditors are unaware, and each director has taken all the steps that he ought to have taken as a director in order to make himself aware of any relevant audit information and to establish that the company's auditors are aware of that information.

Section 418(2)(b) refers to '... the steps that he ought to have taken as a director to make himself aware of any relevant audit information ...'. Section 418(4) says that a director will have taken all those steps where he has:

- made such enquiries of his fellow directors and of the company's auditors for that purpose; and[5]
- taken such other steps (if any) for that purpose, as are required by his duty as a director of the company to exercise reasonable care, skill and diligence.[6]

Relevant audit information

3.7 When the financial statements of a small entity are subject to external audit, section 418(a) and (b) refers to the term 'relevant audit information'. Relevant audit information is information which the auditor requires so that they can prepare their audit report. For example, a company's auditor will want to obtain sufficient and appropriate audit evidence that transactions with related parties have been adequately disclosed within the financial statements. Part of this process will be to establish those related parties and the directors of the company should inform the auditors as to who those related parties are.

Falsifying the statement of disclosure to auditors

3.8 Every director of a company must ensure that the statement as to disclosure to auditors made under section 418 of the Companies Act 2006 is accurate. It is a criminal offence to deliberately mislead the auditors of a company and where a directors' report contains the statement required by section 418 and is subsequently approved, but the statement is, in fact, false, then section 418(5) of the Companies Act 2006 says that every director of the company who:

- knew that the statement was false, or was reckless as to whether it was false; and[7]
- failed to take reasonable steps to prevent the report from being approved, commits an offence.[8]

5 Companies Act 2006, s 418(4)(a).
6 Companies Act 2006, s 418(4)(b).
7 Companies Act 2006, s 418(5)(a).
8 Companies Act 2006, s 418(5)(b).

The punishment for making a false statement of disclosure to the auditor can result in the director(s) being liable:

- on conviction on indictment, to imprisonment for a term not exceeding two years or a fine (or both);[9]
- on summary conviction:
  - — in England and Wales, to imprisonment for a term not exceeding twelve months or to a fine not exceeding the statutory maximum (or both);
  - — in Scotland or Northern Ireland, to imprisonment for a term not exceeding six months, or to a fine not exceeding the statutory maximum (or both).[10]

THE PROFIT AND LOSS ACCOUNT (INCOME STATEMENT)

3.9 The statutory formats for the profit and loss account (income statement) are prescribed in the Companies Act 2006. The inclusion of the EU Accounting Directive into the legislation saw the repealing of Format 3 and Format 4 of the profit and loss account (income statement) and hence there are now only two permissible formats, being Format 1 and Format 2.

This book deliberately starts with the profit and loss account (income statement) first, then takes a look at the balance sheet (statement of financial position) formats rather than following the order of the Companies Act 2006 and starting with the balance sheet first, then the profit and loss account. This is because in a real-life set of financial statements the profit and loss account would come first followed by the balance sheet.

> **Focus**
>
> - Micro-entities preparing their financial statements under the provisions of FRS 105 *The Financial Reporting Standard applicable to the Micro-entities Regime* can only prepare a profit and loss account (income statement) under Format 2 principles. There is no option to prepare a Format 1 profit and loss account (income statement).

The profit and loss account (income statement) is a performance statement in that it shows the small entity's trading performance throughout the year. The two formats for the profit and loss account (income statement) which were revised following the inclusion of the EU Accounting Directive into the Companies Act 2006 are as follows:

9 Companies Act 2006, s 418(6)(a).
10 Companies Act 2006, s 418(60)(b)(i) and (ii).

Profit and loss account – Format 1

3.10

(1) Turnover.

(2) Cost of sales. *(11)*

(3) Gross profit or loss.

(4) Distribution costs. *(11)*

(5) Administrative expenses. *(11)*

(6) Other operating income.

(7) Income from shares in group undertakings.

(8) Income from participating interests.

(9) Income from other fixed asset investments. *(12)*

(10) Other interest receivable and similar income. *(12)*

(11) Amounts written off investments.

(12) Interest payable and similar expenses. *(13)*

(13) Tax on profit or loss.

(14) Profit or loss after taxation.

(15) Deleted.

(16) Deleted.

(17) Deleted.

(18) Deleted.

(19) Other taxes not shown under the above items.

(20) Profit or loss for the financial year.

Profit and loss account – Format 2

3.11

(1) Turnover.

(2) Change in stocks of finished goods and in work in progress.

(3) Own work capitalised.

(4) Other operating income.

(5) (a) Raw materials and consumables.

(b) Other external charges.

(6) Staff costs:

(a) Wages and salaries.

(b) Social security costs.

(c) Other pension costs.

(7) (a) Depreciation and other amounts written off tangible and intangible fixed assets.

(b) Amounts written off current assets, to the extent that they exceed write-offs which are normal in the undertaking concerned.

(8) Other operating expenses.

(9) Income from shares in group undertakings.

(10) Income from participating interests.

(11) Income from other fixed asset investments. *(12)*

(12) Other interest receivable and similar income. *(12)*

(13) Amounts written off investments.

(14) Interest payable and similar expenses. *(13)*

(15) Tax on profit or loss.

(16) Profit or loss after taxation.

(17) Deleted.

(18) Deleted.

(19) Deleted.

(20) Deleted.

(21) Other taxes not shown under the above items.

(22) Profit or loss for the financial year.

Notes on the profit and loss account formats

3.12

(11) Cost of sales: distribution costs: administrative expenses

Format 1: items 2, 4 and 5 must be stated after taking into account any necessary provisions for depreciation or diminution in value of assets.

(12) Income from other fixed asset investments: other interest receivable and similar income

Format 1: items 9 and 10 and Format 2: items 11 and 12 – income and interest derived from group undertakings must be shown separately from income and interest derived from other sources.

(13) Interest payable and similar expenses

Format 1: item 12 and Format 2: item 14 – the amount payable to group undertakings must be shown separately.

3.13 With regards to the profit and loss account (income statement) and FRS 102, it is worthwhile pointing out some differences inherent within FRS 102:

Exceptional items

3.14 The term 'exceptional items' is not used in FRS 102 (although it does use the term 'extraordinary items'). The standard does permit the use of additional line items to be included to aid an understanding and so, for example, if a small company has a large one-off bad debt during the year, it may wish to include this on the face of the profit and loss account (income statement). This flexibility would not apply to a micro-entity as the financial statement formats cannot be adapted in any way for a micro-entity.

Fair value adjustments on investment properties and financial instruments

3.15 Under the provisions of FRS 102, fair value gains and losses on investment properties and some financial instruments are recognised in profit or loss (as opposed to a revaluation reserve account). Such transactions could be included in a separate line item (within 'operating profit' if used) as 'Fair value adjustments'.

Operating profit

3.16 FRS 102 does not require the use of 'operating profit' as a separate line item on the face of the profit and loss account (income statement). Where a small entity uses this line item, it must be used appropriately.

Discontinued operations

3.17 Discontinued operations must be presented line-by-line on the face of the income statement (profit and loss account). This means more detail on discontinued operations is given under FRS 102 than was the case under the FRSSE (effective January 2015). An Appendix to Section 5 in FRS 102 outlines the format, and broadly follows this approach:

	2016			2015		
	Continuing operations	**Discontinued operations**	**Total**	**Continuing operations (as restated)**	**Discontinued operations (as restated)**	**Total**
Turnover	X	X	X	X	X	X
Cost of sales	(X)	(X)	(X)	(X)	(X)	(X)
Gross profit	X	X	X	X	X	X
Administrative expenses	(X)	(X)	(X)	(X)	(X)	(X)
Other operating income	X	–	X	X	–	X
Profit on disposal of operations	=	X	X	=	=	=
Operating profit	X	X	X	X	(X)	X
Interest receivable and similar income	X	–	X	X	-	X
Interest payable and similar charges	(X)	=	(X)	(X)	=	(X)
Profit on ordinary activities before tax	X	X	X	X	(X)	X
Taxation	(X)	(X)	(X)	(X)	X	(X)
Profit on ordinary activities after taxation and profit for the financial year	X	X	X	X	(X)	X
Other comprehensive income						
Actuarial losses on defined benefit pension plans			(X)			(X)
Deferred tax movement relating to actuarial losses			X			X
Total comprehensive income for the year			X			X

Statement of comprehensive income

3.18 Small companies may choose to prepare a statement of comprehensive income where items of income and expense which have been taken to other comprehensive income are shown underneath the main income statement.

Example 3.2 – Illustrative statement of comprehensive income

	31.12.2016	**31.12.2015**
	£	£
Profit for the year	X	X
Other comprehensive income		
Revaluation of property	X	X
Actuarial gains and losses	X	X
Total comprehensive income for the year	X	X

The above example illustrates the use of the dual statement approach; however it is expected that most small companies will just prepare a profit and loss account (income statement) which is known as the 'single statement approach'.

Adapted profit and loss account

3.19 Part 1 (general rules and formats) of Schedule 1 (Companies Act individual accounts) to the Small Companies Accounts Regulations was amended following the transposition of the EU Accounting Directive which now allows small companies to adapt the statutory formats of the financial statements. Paragraph 1B(2) says that the company's directors may adapt one of the profit and loss account formats in Section B, provided that—

- the information given is at least equivalent to that which would have been required by the use of such format had it not been thus adapted; and
- the presentation is in accordance with generally accepted accounting principles or practice.[11]

Where a small business chooses to adapt one of the profit and loss account formats, paragraph 1AB.3 of FRS 102 says that, as a minimum, the following line items must be included in the adapted profit and loss account (income statement) which present the following amounts for the period:

- **revenue**;
- finance costs;

11 Companies Act 2006, Sch 1, para 1B(2).

- share of the profit or loss of investments in associates (see Section 14 *Investments in Associates*) and jointly controlled entities (see Section 15 *Investments in Joint Ventures*) accounted for using the equity method;
- profit or loss before taxation;
- **tax expense** excluding tax allocated to other comprehensive income or equity; and
- profit or loss.[12]

Focus

- In addition to 'adapted' financial statements, the revised Companies Act 2006 also allows 'abridged' financial statements to be prepared and these are considered later in the chapter.

BALANCE SHEET (STATEMENT OF FINANCIAL POSITION)

3.20 The balance sheet (statement of financial position) is a snapshot of the financial position of the small company as at the reporting date (the year-end). It shows what the business owns, or more precisely, controls (assets) and what the business owes (liabilities) as well as the equity interests of the business (shareholders' funds).

In transposing the EU Accounting Directive into the Companies Act 2006, there have been no changes to the number of formats. For both micro-entities and small companies, there is a choice in preparing either a Format 1 or a Format 2 balance sheet (statement of financial position).

The statutory formats for the balance sheet (statement of financial position) are outlined below:

Balance sheet – Format 1

3.21

A. Called up share capital not paid *(1)*

B. Fixed assets

  I. Intangible assets

    1. Goodwill *(2)*

    2. Other intangible assets *(3)*

  II. Tangible assets

    1. Land and buildings

    2. Plant and machinery etc.

12 FRS 102, Appendix B, para 1AB.3.

III. Investments

1. Shares in group undertakings and participating interests
2. Loans to group undertakings and undertakings in which the company has a participating interest
3. Other investments other than loans
4. Other investments *(4)*

C. Current assets

I. Stocks

1. Stocks
2. Payments on account

II. Debtors *(5)*

1. Trade debtors
2. Amounts owed by group undertakings and undertakings in which the company has a participating interest
3. Other debtors *(1)*

III. Investments

1. Shares in group undertakings
2. Other investments *(4)*

IV. Cash at bank and in hand

D. Prepayments and accrued income *(6)*

E. Creditors: amounts falling due within one year

1. Bank loans and overdrafts
2. Trade creditors
3. Amounts owed to group undertakings and undertakings in which the company has a participating interest
4. Other creditors *(7)*

F. Net current assets (liabilities) *(8)*

G. Total assets less current liabilities

H. Creditors: amounts falling due after more than one year

1. Bank loans and overdrafts
2. Trade creditors
3. Amounts owed to group undertakings and undertakings in which the company has a participating interest
4. Other creditors *(7)*

I. Provisions for liabilities

J. Accruals and deferred income *(7)*

K. Capital and reserves

- I. Called up share capital *(9)*
- II. Share premium account
- III. Revaluation reserve
- IV. Other reserves
- V. Profit and loss account

Balance sheet – Format 2

3.22 ASSETS

A. Called up share capital not paid *(1)*

B. Fixed assets

- I. Intangible assets
  - 1. Goodwill *(2)*
  - 2. Other intangible assets *(3)*
- II. Tangible assets
  - 1. Land and buildings
  - 2. Plant and machinery etc.
- III. Investments
  - 1. Shares in group undertakings and participating interests
  - 2. Loans to group undertakings and undertakings in which the company has a participating interest
  - 3. Other investments other than loans
  - 4. Other investments *(4)*

C. Current assets

- I. Stocks
  - 1. Stocks
  - 2. Payments on account
- II. Debtors *(5)*
  - 1. Trade debtors
  - 2. Amounts owed by group undertakings and undertakings in which the company has a participating interest

3. Other debtors *(1)*

III. Investments

1. Shares in group undertakings

2. Other investments *(4)*

IV. Cash at bank and in hand

D. Prepayments and accrued income *(6)*

CAPITAL, RESERVES AND LIABILITIES

A. Capital and reserves

I. Called up share capital *(9)*

II. Share premium account

III. Revaluation reserve

IV. Other reserves

V. Profit and loss account

B. Provisions for liabilities

C. Creditors *(10)*

1. Bank loans and overdrafts

2. Trade creditors

3. Amounts owed to group undertakings and undertakings in which the company has a participating interest

4. Other creditors *(7)*

D. Accruals and deferred income *(7)*

Notes to the balance sheet formats

3.23

(1) Called up share capital not paid

Formats 1 and 2, items A and C.II.3:

This item may either be shown at item A or included under item C.II.3 in Format 1 or 2.

(2) Goodwill

Formats 1 and 2, item B.I.1:

Amounts representing goodwill must only be included to the extent that the goodwill was acquired for valuable consideration.

(3) Other intangible assets

Formats 1 and 2, item B.I.2:

Amounts in respect of concessions, patents, licences, trademarks and similar rights and assets must only be included in a company's balance sheet under this item if either—

(a) the assets were acquired for valuable consideration and are not required to be shown under goodwill, or

(b) the assets in question were created by the company itself.

(4) Others: Other investments

Formats 1 and 2, items B.III.4 and C.III.2:

Where amounts in respect of own shares held are included under either of these items, the nominal value of such shares must be shown separately.

(5) Debtors

Formats 1 and 2, items C.II.1 to 3:

The amount falling due after more than one year must be shown separately for each item included under debtors and in the case of Format 2, the aggregate amount falling due after more than one year must also be shown.

(6) Prepayments and accrued income

Formats 1 and 2, item D:

This item may alternatively be included under item C.II.3 in Format 1 or 2.

(7) Other creditors

Format 1, items E.4, H.4 and J and Format 2, items C.4 and D:

There must be shown separately:

(a) the amount of any convertible loans, and

(b) the amount for creditors in respect of taxation and social security.

Payments received on account of orders must be included in so far as they are not shown as deductions from stocks.

In Format 1, accruals and deferred income may be shown under item J or included under item E.4 or H.4, or both (as the case may require). In Format 2, accruals and deferred income may be shown under item D or within item C.4 under liabilities.

(8) Net current assets (liabilities)

Format 1, item F:

In determining the amount to be shown under this item any prepayments and accrued income must be taken into account wherever shown.

(9) Called up share capital

Format 1, item K.I and Format 2, Liabilities item A.I:

The amount of allotted share capital and the amount of called up share capital which has been paid up must be shown separately.

(10) Creditors

Format 2 Liabilities items C.1 to 4:

Amounts falling due within one year and after one year must be shown separately for each of these items and for the aggregate of all of these items.

3.24 The balance sheet (statement of financial position) consists of two formats, Format 1 and Format 2. Both formats are permissible for small entities as long as a consistent format is adopted. Micro-entities preparing financial statements to FRS 105 principles are also permitted to use Format 1 or Format 2 for their balance sheet (statement of financial position) and consistency must be adopted for those also.

Adapted balance sheet (statement of financial position)

3.25 As is the case for the profit and loss account (income statement), the revised Companies Act 2006 also allows a small company to prepare an adapted balance sheet (statement of financial position) so as to distinguish between current and non-current items in a different way (this will aid consolidation of the financial statements where the parent's consolidated financial statements are prepared to EU-adopted IFRS). However, there are conditions where current and non-current items are distinguished in a different way which are:

- the information given is at least equivalent to that which would have been required by the use of such format had it not thus been adapted; and
- the presentation of those items is in accordance with generally accepted accounting principles or practice.[13]

Where the company prepares an adapted balance sheet (statement of financial position), paragraph 1AA.3 of FRS 102 says that, as a minimum, the statement of financial position must contain line items that present the following and distinguish these between items which are current and items which are non-current:

(a) **property, plant and equipment**;

(b) **investment property** carried at **fair value** through profit or loss;

(c) **intangible assets**;

(d) **financial assets** (excluding amounts shown under (e), (f), (j) and (k));

13 Companies Act 2006, Sch 1, para 1B(1)(a) and (b).

(e) investments in **associates**;

(f) investments in **jointly controlled entities**;

(g) **biological assets** carried at cost less accumulated **depreciation** and impairment;

(h) biological assets carried at fair value through profit or loss;

(i) **inventories**;

(j) trade and other receivables;

(k) **cash** and **cash equivalents**;

(l) trade and other payables;

(m) **provisions**;

(n) financial liabilities (excluding amounts shown under (l) and (m));

(o) liabilities and assets for **current tax**;

(p) **deferred tax liabilities** and **deferred tax assets** (classified as non-current);

(q) **non-controlling interest**, presented within equity separately from the equity attributable to the owners of the parent; and

(r) equity attributable to the owners of the parent.

In addition to the above items, paragraph 1AA.4 of FRS 102 also requires further sub-classifications of the line items presented in the small entity's balance sheet (statement of financial position) and the following can either be shown on the face of the balance sheet (statement of financial position) or within the notes:

(a) property, plant and equipment in classifications appropriate to the small entity;

(b) **goodwill** and other intangible assets;

(c) investments, showing separately shares and loans;

(d) trade and other receivables, showing separately amounts due from **related parties** and amounts due from other parties;

(e) trade and other payables, showing separately amounts payable to trade suppliers and amounts payable to related parties; and

(f) classes of equity, such as called up share capital, share premium, retained earnings, revaluation reserve, fair value reserve and other reserves.

STATEMENT OF CHANGES IN EQUITY

3.26 The statement of changes in equity is not a mandatory primary financial statement under the new small companies' regime. However, Section 1A of FRS 102 encourages small companies to present a statement of changes in equity (or a statement of income and retained earnings) as part of their complete set of financial statements and this is advisable where there have been movements on items within equity (such as a material revaluation gain on property, plant and equipment).

> **Focus**
>
> - Paragraph 1A.9 says that where a small entity has taken gains or losses to other comprehensive income, it is encouraged to present a statement of total comprehensive income.

Section 1A cross-references users to Section 5 *Statement of Comprehensive Income and Income Statement* and Section 6 *Statement of Changes in Equity and Statement of Income and Retained Earnings*.

3.27 The aim of the statement of changes in equity is to present movements in equity during the current and previous periods relating to the following:

- profit or loss for the period;
- other comprehensive income for the period;
- the effects of changes in accounting policies and corrections of errors recognised in the period;
- investments by equity investors; and
- dividends and other distributions to equity investors during the period.

Paragraph 6.3 of FRS 102 requires certain transactions to be separately disclosed as follows:

- total comprehensive income for the period, showing separately the total amounts attributable to owners of the parent and to non-controlling interests;
- for each component of equity:
  - — the effects of changes in accounting policies;
  - — the effects of correction of material errors;
  - — a reconciliation between the carrying amount at the beginning and end of the period, separately disclosing the changes resulting from:
    - (i) profit or loss;
    - (ii) other comprehensive income;
    - (iii) issue of shares;
    - (iv) purchase of own shares;
    - (v) dividends and other distributions to owners; and

(vi) changes in ownership interests in subsidiaries that do not result in a loss of control.

An illustration of the statement of changes in equity where there are no items of other comprehensive income is shown below:

	Note	**Share capital**	**Share premium**	**Profit and loss reserves**	**Total equity**
		£	£	£	£
Balance at 1 January 2015		X	X	X	X
Profit for the year				X	X
Total comprehensive income for the year				X	X
Dividends paid	(iv)			(X)	(X)
Issue of share capital	(xiii)	X	X		X
Balance at 31 December 2015		X	X	X	X
Profit for the year				X	X
Total comprehensive income for the year				X	X
Dividends paid	(iv)			(X)	(X)
Issue of share capital	(xiii)	X	X		X
Balance at 31 December 2016		X	X	X	X

Focus

- Where the small entity chooses to include a statement of changes in equity, the statement must be presented as a primary statement. It cannot be presented as a note to the financial statements.

THE STATEMENT OF CASH FLOWS (CASH FLOW STATEMENT)

3.28 The statement of cash flows (cash flow statement) is, by definition, prepared on the cash basis (not the accruals) basis of accounting. The aim of the statement is to show how the small entity has generated and spent cash during the reporting period. The cash flow statement is not a mandatory statement, although some small companies do prepare a cash flow statement as part of their complete set of financial statements.

Where the small entity chooses to include a cash flow statement as part of the complete set of general purpose financial statements then it must be prepared under the principles contained in Section 7 *Statement of Cash Flows* of FRS 102.

Focus

- There are considerable presentational differences between a cash flow statement prepared under Section 7 and a cash flow statement which was prepared under the FRSSE (effective January 2015). These differences are examined in **Chapter 2**.

3.29 Section 7 requires a small company that is preparing a statement of cash flows to categorise the cash flows under three separate headings:

- operating activities;
- investing activities; and
- financing activities.

Operating activities

3.30 Operating activities are the cash flows which arise from entity's day-to-day revenue-producing activities, such as:

- cash receipts from the sale of goods and rendering of services;
- cash receipts from royalties, fees, commissions and other revenue;
- cash payments to suppliers for goods and services;
- cash payments to, and on behalf of, employees;
- cash payments or refunds of income tax, unless they can be specifically identified with financing and investing activities;
- cash receipts and payments from investments, loans and other contracts held for dealing or trading purposes, which are similar to inventory acquired specifically for resale; and
- cash advances and loans made to other parties by financial institutions.

Example 3.3 – Operating activities

During the year, Emery Ltd paid corporation tax of £15,000 to HM Revenue and Customs. The company prepares a cash flow statement as part of its complete set of financial statements and under the FRSSE (effective January 2015) the company would have classified this under the 'taxation' cash flow heading.

Section 7 does not have a 'taxation' classification and would, instead, classify the corporation tax payment as an operating cash flow classification unless the tax can be specifically identified with financing and investing activities.

Investing activities

3.31 Cash flows from investing activities arise from the acquisition and disposal of an entity's long-term assets and other investments which are not included in cash equivalents. Examples include:

- Cash payments to acquire property, plant and equipment (including self-constructed property, plant and equipment), intangible assets and other long-term assets. These payments include those relating to capitalised development costs and self-constructed property, plant and equipment.
- Cash receipts from sales of property, plant and equipment, intangible and other long-term assets.
- Cash payments to acquire equity or debt instruments of other entities and interests in joint ventures (other than payments for those instruments classified as cash equivalents or held for dealing or trading).
- Cash receipts from sales of equity or debt instruments of other entities and interests in joint ventures (other than receipts for those instruments classified as cash equivalents or held for dealing or trading).
- Cash advances and loans made to other parties.
- Cash receipts from the repayment of advances and loans made to other parties.
- Cash payments for futures contracts, forward contracts, option contracts and swap contracts, except when contracts are held for dealing or trading, or the payments are classified as financing activities.
- Cash receipts from futures contracts, option contracts and swap contracts, except when the contracts are held for dealing or trading, or the receipts are classified as financing activities.

Example 3.4 – Investing activities

Weaver Ltd manufactures chemicals for use in domestic detergent products. It has four branches throughout the UK and has a year-end of 30 September 2016. Demand for the company's products has seen a sharp rise in the last two years and, on 1 July 2016, the company opened another branch in the south of the UK and purchased a building outright to house their operations which resulted in an outflow of cash amounting to £100,000.

Only expenditure that results in a recognised asset in the balance sheet (statement of financial position) is eligible to be classified as an investing activity and therefore the cash payment of £100,000 will be treated as a cash flow from investing activities.

Financing activities

3.32 Financing activities are those activities which result in a change in the size and composition of the contributed borrowings and equity structure of the business. Examples include:

- cash proceeds from a share issue or issue of other equity instruments;
- cash payments to owners to acquire or redeem the entity's shares;
- cash proceeds from issuing debentures, loans, notes, bonds, mortgages and other short-term or long-term borrowings;
- cash repayments of amounts borrowed; and
- cash payments by a lessee for the reduction of outstanding liabilities relating to a finance lease.

Example 3.5 – Financing activities

Finch Ltd has a year-end of 30 June 2016. On 20 June 2016, the company declared a dividend to its ordinary shareholders which gave rise to a cash outflow of £50,000 which occurred on 23 June 2016.

Dividends are permitted to be treated as a financing cash flow because they are a cost of obtaining financial resources.

Indirect and direct method

3.33 Section 7 of FRS 102 allows two possible methods for reporting cash flows from operating activities:

- the indirect method; or
- the direct method.

Indirect method

3.34 Under the indirect method, the net cash flows from operating activities is arrived at by adjusting profit or loss for the effects of non-cash items reported in profit or loss and fluctuations during the accounting period in stock, debtors and creditors as well as all other items for which the cash effects relate to investing or financing activities of the entity.

Example 3.6 – Indirect method

	2016	2015
	£	£
Operating profit	6,261	6,063
Depreciation charges	539	475
Loss on disposal of fixed assets	–	62
Gain on disposal of fixed assets	(125)	–
Equity-settled share-based payment expense	156	208
Decrease (increase) in trade and other receivables	(140)	139
Decrease (increase) in inventories	27	(14)
(Decrease) increase in trade and other payables	222	149
Cash generated from operations	**6,940**	**7,082**
Interest paid	(1,650)	(1,110)
Interest received	12	14
Corporation tax paid	(1,254)	(1,657)
Cash flow from operating activities	**4,048**	**4.329**

Direct method

3.35 UK GAAP does prefer the use of the direct method of preparing the cash flow statement. However, the reality is that, in practice, where small companies do prepare a cash flow statement, the indirect method is the method which is most common (and is equally acceptable).

Under the direct method, information is disclosed about the major classes of gross receipts and gross cash payments. An example of this method is as follows:

Example 3.7 – Direct method

	2016	2015
	£	£
Collections from trade receivables	4,217	4,420
Payments to suppliers	(2,142)	(2,162)
Payments to employees	(657)	(569)

	2016	**2015**
	£	£
Payments of corporation tax	(64)	(138)
Payments relating to retirement benefits	(235)	(252)
Cash flows from operating activities	**1,119**	**1,299**

Non-cash transactions

3.36 The cash flow statement is prepared, by its very nature, using a cash-based, rather than an accruals-based method to show the user of the financial statements how the entity has generated and spent cash during the accounting period.

On this basis, Section 7 requires small entities that choose to prepare a cash flow statement to exclude investing and financing transactions that do not require the use of cash or cash equivalents. For such transactions, the standard requires disclosure of these transactions elsewhere within the financial statements in a way that provides all the relevant information.

Focus

- Whilst a small company would not be legally required to make disclosure of non-cash transactions, directors of small companies would be advised to make such disclosures if so doing would enable the financial statements to give a true and fair view.

Example 3.8 – Disclosure of non-cash transactions

Jones Ltd has a year-end of 30 September 2016. On 17 December 2015 it issued 100 new shares to convertible loan note holders in settlement of £50,000 of capital and interest outstanding on the loan notes. The remaining capital and interest liabilities were satisfied through a rights issue: £5,000 was raised in cash with the remainder being an exchange of shares.

Such transactions would be disclosed as a footnote to the cash flow statement. Other examples of non-cash transactions, in addition to the conversion of debt to equity, are the acquisition of assets by assuming directly related liabilities or by means of a finance lease and issuing equity as consideration during a business combination.

Components of cash and cash equivalents

3.37 Paragraph 7.20 of Section 7 requires reporting entities that produce a cash flow statement to present the components of cash and cash equivalents as well as presenting a reconciliation of the amounts presented in the cash flow statement to the equivalent items presented in the balance sheet (statement of financial position). Paragraph 7.20 does not require reporting entities to present this reconciliation if the amount of cash and cash equivalents presented in the cash flow statement is the same as the amount shown in the balance sheet (statement of financial position).

Cash and cash equivalents not available for use by the entity

3.38 Where the small entity holds significant cash and cash equivalents, but those cash and cash equivalents are not available for use by the entity, paragraph 7.21 of FRS 102 would require disclosure of such balances. Small companies would not legally be required to make such disclosure, but where they are considered material, the directors would be advised to make such disclosures.

NOTES TO THE FINANCIAL STATEMENTS

3.39 The transposition of the EU Accounting Directive into companies' legislation has resulted in the legal minimum number of disclosure notes being reduced from 17 to 13. In addition, EU Member States are restricted as to the amount of information which they require small undertakings to place in their financial statements. The objective of this restriction is to reduce the burden on small companies as well as creating a largely harmonised small companies regime.

Focus

- A point worth emphasising at the outset is that the financial statements of a small company must always give a true and fair view. For this reason, paragraphs 1A.5 and 1A.6 requires an entity to present sufficient information in the notes to meet this requirement. Paragraphs 8.3 and 8.4 of FRS 102 are applicable to small companies in the way that the notes are structured.

3.40 Because of the EU Accounting Directive, a small entity need not comply with the disclosure requirements of paragraph 8.7 and Sections 9 to 35 of FRS 102. However, a reporting entity must consider and provide any of those disclosures which are relevant to its transactions, other events or conditions in order to meet the requirement to give a true and fair view; hence the general principal is that if the mandatory minimum disclosures do not allow the financial statements to give a true and fair view, the directors must make additional disclosures to enable a true and fair view to be given.

Appendix C to Section 1A of FRS 102 *Disclosure requirements for small entities* sets out the disclosure requirements in company law. The notes are to be presented in the order in which (where relevant) the items to which they relate are presented in the statement of financial position (balance sheet) and income statement (profit and loss account).

MANDATORY DISCLOSURES

Accounting policies

3.41 A small company must disclose the policies which it has adopted in establishing the amounts which are included in the balance sheet (statement of financial position) and arriving at profit or loss. Policies in respect of depreciation and impairment of assets are also required. Paragraph 1AC.3 also cross-references to paragraph 8.5 and 8.6 of FRS 102.

Development costs

3.42 Where the small entity has capitalised development costs, the accounting policies notes must disclose:

- the period over which the amount of those costs are being written off; and
- the reasons for capitalising the development costs.

A cross-reference to paragraph 18.27(a) of FRS 102 is included.

Where the entity has development costs on its balance sheet, and the amount is not treated as a realised loss as there are special reasons for this, the reasons why development costs have been capitalised and not treated as a realised loss should be disclosed to comply with section 844 of the Companies Act 2006.

Intangible assets and goodwill

3.43 In the rare situation that management cannot arrive at a reliable estimate for the useful life of intangible assets, including goodwill, the notes to the financial statements must disclose the period over which those intangible assets including goodwill are being written off, together with the reasons why that period has been chosen.

A cross-reference to paragraphs 18.27(a) and 19.25(g) of FRS 102 is included.

Changes in presentation, accounting policies and correction of errors

3.44 Where a small company changes its presentation of items in the balance sheet or profit and loss account, such changes are to be given in a note to the financial statements in the period in which the new presentation is used, together with supporting reasons for the change.

A cross-reference to paragraphs 3.12 and 3.13 of FRS 102 is included.

If the corresponding amount for the immediately preceding financial year is not comparable with the amount to be shown for the item in question, and the entity changes the corresponding amount, the particulars of the non-comparability together with any adjustment should be disclosed in a note to the financial statements. This situation will more than likely arise where there has been an accounting policy change or a prior period error has been corrected.

For any amounts relating to a preceding reporting period that are included in an item in the profit and loss account, the effect must be disclosed.

True and fair override

3.45 When special reasons mean that the small company must depart from any requirements of company law in preparing its financial statements, it is permitted to do so. However, the company must disclose details of the departure, the reasons for the departure and any of the departure's effects in the notes to the financial statements.

The FRC have acknowledged that it is expected that the true and fair override will be invoked only in special circumstances.

Notes to the statement of financial position (balance sheet)

Fixed assets

3.46 In respect of items included within a company's fixed assets, the company must disclose the components of cost for each class of asset:

- cost or valuation at the start of the period;
- revisions to cost or valuation during the period;
- additions during the period;
- disposals during the report; and
- transfers made during the period.

In respect of depreciation and provisions, disclose:

- depreciation at the start of the period;
- impairments at the start of the period;
- provisions for depreciation or impairment during the period;
- adjustments to depreciation or impairment due to disposals during the period; and
- other adjustments made in respect of provisions for depreciation or impairment during the period.

The term 'fixed assets' includes all fixed assets including investment property, property, plant and equipment, intangible fixed assets and goodwill, fixed asset investments, biological assets and heritage assets.

Prior period comparatives are not required in respect of this note.

Fixed assets at revaluation

3.47 Where a small company carries fixed assets under the revaluation model, it must disclose the items affected and the basis of valuation adopted by the company within the accounting policies section of the notes. This will apply if the small company:

- carries investments in subsidiaries, associates and/or joint ventures at fair value through other comprehensive income;
- carries items of property, plant and equipment under the revaluation model; and
- intangible assets (other than goodwill) are revalued under the revaluation model in Section 18 *Intangible Assets other than Goodwill.*

The above does not apply to investment properties and biological assets carried at fair value through profit or loss.

The disclosure requirements in respect of fixed assets carried at revaluation are:

- the years (if known to the directors) which the assets were severally valued and the several values; and
- where assets have been valued in the reporting period, the names of the persons who valued them, or particulars of their qualifications for doing so and the basis of the valuation.

Cross-references are made to paragraphs 17.32A(a) and (c), 18.29A(a) and (c) and 34.55(e)(ii) of FRS 102.

Additional notes must be disclosed which show the comparable amounts of fixed assets subjected to revaluation at the amounts that would have been determined under the historical cost model. The comparable amounts refer to the aggregate cost, accumulated depreciation and impairment losses. Cross-references have been made to paragraphs 17.32A(d) and 18.29(A)(d) of FRS 102.

Tabular form information is also required in respect of the following relating to fixed assets at revaluation:

- movements in the revaluation reserve during the reporting period and an explanation of the tax treatment of the items therein; and
- the carrying amount that would have been shown in the balance sheet had the historical cost model been followed.

Cross-references are made to paragraphs 6.4A, 17.32A(d), 18.29A(d) and 29.27(a) of FRS 102.

A note should also be disclosed relating to the tax treatment of amounts credited or debited to the revaluation reserve and a cross-reference is made to paragraph 29.27(a) of FRS 102.

Capitalisation of borrowing costs

3.48 Where the small company has adopted a policy of capitalising borrowing costs, the inclusion of interest in determining the cost of the asset and the amount of interest included is to be disclosed.

A cross-reference to paragraph 25.3A(a) to FRS 102 is made.

Impairment of assets

3.49 A small company should disclose impairments separately in a note to the financial statements where they are not shown separately in the profit and loss account (income statement) and a cross-reference to paragraph 27.32(a) of FRS 102 is made in paragraph 1AC.20.

Where previously recognised impairment losses have been reversed, the company should disclose the reasons why the issues giving rise to the original impairment have ceased to apply together with the amounts involved in the notes to the financial statements if they are not separately shown in the profit and loss account (income statement). A cross-reference is made to paragraph 27.32(b) of FRS 102.

Fair value measurement

3.50 If the small entity has measured financial instruments or other assets at fair value through profit or loss the following disclosures must be made:

- the significant assumptions which underlie the valuation models and techniques used in determining fair values;
- for each category of financial instrument or other asset, the fair value of the asset in that category and the change in value which has been included within profit or loss or credited to or debited from the fair value reserve.

> **Focus**
>
> - The above does not apply in respect of financial instruments or other assets measured at fair value only on initial recognition.

Where financial instruments or other assets are measured at fair value through profit or loss, there must be disclosed for each class of derivative instrument, the extent and nature of the instruments which should also include the significant terms and conditions which may affect the amount, timing and certainty of cash flows.

Tabular-form disclosures must be included in the financial statements which relate to amounts transferred to, or from, the fair value reserve during the reporting period including:

- the opening balance on the fair value reserve at the start of the reporting period and as at the reporting date; and
- the amount transferred to, or from, that reserve during the year.

In respect of amounts credited or debit to or from the fair value reserve, the tax treatment of such amounts should be disclosed in the notes.

Paragraphs 1AC.22 to 1AC.25 make cross-references to various other paragraphs in FRS 102 which will help to ensure the disclosures made in respect of fair value measurement are correct.

Financial instruments measured at fair value

3.51 Where the small company accounts for financial instruments under IFRS some instruments may be included in the financial statements at fair value. Where this is the case the disclosure requirements in the relevant IFRSs need to be made.

Indebtedness, guarantees and financial commitments

3.52 In respect of all items shown under 'creditors' in the financial statements, the total of the following amounts should be disclosed:

- the amount of any debts included under 'creditors' which are payable or repayable otherwise than by instalments which fall due for payment (or repayment) after the end of the period of five years starting with the first day after the end of the reporting period (ie 1 January for a 31 December year-end); and
- in respect of any debts so included which are payable (or repayable) by instalments, the amount of any instalments which will fall due for payment after the end of that period.

If the small company has provided any security in respect of amounts included under 'creditors', the aggregate amount of such debts should be disclosed together with an indication of the nature and form of any such security pledged by the company.

A cross-reference is made to paragraphs 11.146, 13.22(e), 16.10(c), 17.32(a) and 18.28(c) of FRS 102 to aid application of the disclosures.

Financial commitments, guarantees and contingencies not on the balance sheet

3.53 In respect of financial commitments, guarantees and contingencies which are not on the small company's balance sheet (statement of financial position), the total amount of such items is to be disclosed in the notes.

In respect of pension commitments, these are to be disclosed separately.

Separate disclosure is also required of any commitments which are undertaken on behalf of, or for the benefit, of:

(a) any parent, fellow subsidiary or any subsidiary of the small company; or

(b) any undertaking in which the small company has a participating interest.

> **Focus**
>
> - Those commitments in (a) must be separately disclosed from those within (b).

Cross-references are made to various paragraphs in FRS 102 in paragraph 1AC.29 which will aid application of these disclosures.

Disclosure must also be made of the nature and form of any valuable security pledged by the small company in respect of its commitments, guarantees and contingencies.

Where a small company has been a party to arrangements which are not reflected on the balance sheet (statement of financial position) and the risks or benefits arising from those arrangements are material at the reporting date, the company must disclose the nature and business purpose of these arrangements.

Notes to the income statement (profit and loss account)

3.54 Where any individual items of income or expense are of an exceptional size or incidence (for example a large bad-debt) then the amount and nature of the income or expense should be disclosed. A cross-reference is made to paragraph 5.9A of FRS 102.

> **Focus**
>
> - A new requirement under the revised Companies Act 2006 is in respect of the average number of employees which requires disclosure. This was not previously required under the FRSSE but disclosure of such must be made in the small entity's financial statements.

Related party disclosures

3.55 If the small company is a subsidiary, the following must be disclosed in respect of the parent of the smallest group for which consolidated financial statements are drawn up of which the small company is a member:

- the name of the parent drawing up the consolidated financial statements;
- the address of the parent's registered office (whether inside or outside of the UK); and
- where the parent is incorporated, the address of its principal place of business.

If transactions have not been undertaken under normal commercial terms (ie not on an arm's length basis), with:

- owners which have a participating interest in the company;
- companies in which the small entity has a participating interest; and
- the directors of the small company (or members of its governing body),

then disclosures need to be made which include:

- the amount of the transactions concerned;
- the nature of the related party relationship; and
- any other information which is considered appropriate for an understanding of the financial position of the small company.

Transactions can be aggregated according to their nature, but separate disclosure should be made where it is necessary for an understanding of the effects of the related party transactions on the financial position of the entity.

Focus

- Transactions between wholly-owned group members need not be disclosed in the financial statements, but the group members concerned MUST be wholly-owned within the group.

Paragraph 1AC.35 confirms that transactions with directors, or members of the company's governing body, include directors' remuneration and dividends paid to directors.

Advances, credit and guarantees to directors

3.56 Details of any advances, credit granted to the small company's directors and guarantees of any kind entered into by the small company on behalf of its directors must be disclosed in the notes to the financial statements.

For *advances* and *credits*, disclosure is required of:

(a) its amount;

(b) an indication of the interest rate;

(c) its main conditions;

(d) any amounts repaid;

(e) any amounts written off; and

(f) any amounts waived.

Monetary amounts must be disclosed in respect of (a), (d), (e) and (f).

For *guarantees*, disclosure is required of:

(a) its main terms;

(b) the amount of the maximum liability that may be incurred by the small entity; and

(c) any amounts paid and any liability incurred by the small entity for the purpose of fulfilling the guarantee (the disclosure should also include any loss incurred due to the enforcement of the guarantee).

Monetary amounts must be disclosed in respect of (b) and (c) above.

Other disclosures

3.57 Paragraphs 1AC.37 to 1AC.39 require certain other disclosures to be made including:

- the part of the UK in which the small company is registered;
- the registered number of the small company;
- whether the small company is a public or a private company and whether it is limited by shares or limited by guarantee;
- the registered office address; and
- in the circumstances of a winding-up, the fact that the small company is being wound up.

Where the statutory formats assign Arabic numbers and these have been combined, the individual amounts of any items which have been combined should be disclosed in the notes (unless these amounts are immaterial).

Events after the reporting date

3.58 Where material, non-adjusting events that arise after the reporting date must be disclosed to comply with Schedule 1, paragraph 64 of the Companies Act 2006.

ENCOURAGED DISCLOSURES

3.59 The FRC are keen to ensure that directors of small companies understand the importance of ensuring that the financial statements give a true and fair view. In light of this, the FRC encourage the following disclosures to be made in the small entity's financial statements in Appendix D to Section 1A *Additional disclosures encouraged for small entities:*

- a statement of compliance with this FRS as set out in paragraph 3.3 (adapted to refer to Section 1A);
- if relevant, a statement that it is a public benefit entity as set out in paragraph PBE3.3A;
- if relevant, the disclosures relating to going concern set out in paragraph 3.9;
- dividends declared and paid or payable during the period (for example, as set out in paragraph 6.5(b)); and
- on first-time adoption of this FRS an explanation of how the transition has affected its financial position and financial performance as set out in paragraph 35.13.

Micro-entities' disclosure requirements

3.60 FRS 105 *The Financial Reporting Standard applicable to the Micro-entities Regime* sets out the disclosure requirements in Section 6 *Notes to the Financial Statements* (Section 6 also has a useful Appendix *Company law disclosure requirements* to help correct disclosures to be made). There are considerably fewer disclosure requirements due to the micro-entities' legislation. However, there is no restriction on a micro-entity including more voluntary disclosure information if it so chooses, but if it does choose to make additional disclosures, it needs to follow the requirements of the relevant section which the disclosures relate to.

The disclosure requirements applicable to a micro-entity are:

- the total amount of any financial commitments, guarantees or contingencies that are not included in the balance sheet;
- an indication of the nature and form of any valuable security which has been provided;
- the amounts of advances and credits granted to members of the administrative, managerial and supervisory bodies with indications of interest rates, main conditions and any amounts repaid or written off or waived; and
- any commitments entered into on their behalf by way of guarantees of any kind, with an indication of the total for each category.

Focus

- In respect of the filing requirements for a micro-entity, the micro-entity will lodge the balance sheet, including the disclosures at the foot of the balance sheet, with Companies House. No notes to the accounts are required. The balance sheet filed will be exactly as prepared because the information is considered concise enough.

ABRIDGED FINANCIAL STATEMENTS

3.61 Schedule 1 to the Small Companies Regulations (specifically paragraph 1(A)) allows a small company to prepare 'abridged' financial statements. Abridged financial statements are where certain line items in the statutory formats are combined and this reduces the amount of information shown in the financial statements.

Focus

- Schedule 1 to the Regulations requires that **all** members (shareholders) of the company must agree to the company preparing abridged financial statements. The agreement **must** be unanimous and can only be made in respect of the financial statements for the **preceding** financial year. As a result, the agreement is an annual process (ie one agreement will not cover all subsequent financial years).

Abridged balance sheet

3.62 If it is appropriate in the company's circumstances, the company's directors may (having regard to one of the formats in Section B of the Regulations) draw up an abridged balance sheet. The abridged balance sheet will only show those line items which are preceded by letters and Roman numerals in the statutory formats.

Focus

- Typically in practice the alphabetic and Roman numeral items appear on the face of the small company's balance sheet. The Arabic numerals are usually disclosed in the notes to the financial statements. Therefore in almost all circumstances, the face of the balance sheet will remain unaltered from traditional practice; it will only be the notes to the balance sheet which will reduce.

3.63 There are certain restrictions that apply to an abridged balance sheet which are as follows:

- Where the small company prepares a Format 1 balance sheet, note (5) to the notes to the formats must be complied with.
- In the case of a Format 2 balance sheet, notes (5) and (10) of those formats have to be complied with.

Notes 5 and 10 refer to the disclosure of debtors and creditors which fall due after more than one year.

Abridged profit and loss account

3.64 In addition to the abridged balance sheet, the revised Companies Act 2006 allows a small company to prepare an abridged profit and loss account. Again, all the members must agree **unanimously** to the company preparing an abridged profit and loss account and the agreement is only in respect of the **preceding** financial year. One agreement will not cover all subsequent years and hence the agreement is an annual process.

When an abridged profit and loss account is prepared, the most notable difference will be the fact that both turnover and cost of sales will be combined and hence the abridged profit and loss account will start at 'Gross profit or loss'.

Where a Format 1 profit and loss account is prepared, the following can be combined:

- Turnover.
- Cost of sales.
- Gross profit or loss.
- Other operating income.

Where a Format 2 profit and loss account is prepared, the following can be combined:

- Turnover.
- Change in stocks of finished goods and in work in progress.
- Own work capitalised.
- Other operating income.
- Raw materials and consumables.
- Other external charges.

Focus

- Under Formats 1 and 2, gross profit includes other operating income. Under Format 2 it excludes staff costs and hence excludes direct staff costs which would otherwise have been included within cost of sales and hence within gross profit.

3.65 It is important to emphasise that the Regulations do not allow a company to prepare an abridged set of financial statements if, at any time during the year, the company was a charity.

3.66 Where the directors of a small company have prepared abridged financial statements, section 444(2A) says that the directors must deliver to the registrar a statement that all the members have consented to the abridgement. Reputable accounts production software systems should produce this statement as a matter of course, but it is worthwhile making sure that the statement is included where the small company has produced abridged financial statements to ensure compliance with the Companies Act.

Focus

- Where the company prepares abridged financial statements, the directors must have regard to paragraph 1AA.2 and 1AB.2 in Appendix A and B to Section 1A which requires directors to consider the requirements of paragraph 1A.16 in relation to disaggregation of the balance sheet and presentation of turnover.

APPLICATION OF ACCOUNTING STANDARDS

3.67 Financial statements for a small company must give a true and fair view. For micro-entities which are prepared under the provisions in FRS 105 *The Financial Reporting Standard applicable to the Micro-entities Regime*, the financial statements will be *presumed* to give a true and fair view.

The Companies Act 2006 governs the legalities relating to the financial statements including the form and content, certain recognition and measurement principles and the duty of directors where the financial statements are concerned. It is the application of accounting standards that enable the financial statements to give a true and fair view.

Materiality

3.68 Materiality has to be of relevance where financial statements are concerned – even for small companies. This is because in many cases financial statements will contain some degree of estimation and uncertainty where the figures in the primary financial statements are concerned (for example work in progress, accruals and provisions). The Glossary to FRS 102 defines the term 'material' as:

> 'Omissions or misstatements of items are material if they could, individually or collectively, influence the economic decisions of users taken on the basis of the **financial statements**. Materiality depends on the size and nature of the omission or misstatement judged in the surrounding

circumstances. The size or nature of the item, or a combination of both, could be the determining factor.'[14]

Accounting standards only deal with material items. It follows, therefore, that where an item is judged to be immaterial then there will be no requirement to apply accounting standards in dealing with the item.

Focus

- It is important to consider the materiality of an item both individually and in combination with other items which are considered to be immaterial on their own. Several individual immaterial items may become material when aggregated and this should be borne in mind when dealing with issues such as deferred tax, unpaid holiday pay accruals and other such items.

3.69 The issue of materiality is not simply confined to small companies that have an external audit. Materiality considerations apply to all companies. However, what may be material in one small company may not be material in another company.

Materiality is judged in both *qualitative* and *quantitative* terms. It follows, therefore, that materiality is not just concerned about the numerical aspects of the financial statements; narrative disclosures may also be material (particularly in relation to going concern, which is an encouraged disclosure in Section 1A of FRS 102 Appendix D where there are material uncertainties about the small entity's ability to continue as a going concern for the foreseeable future).

AUDIT EXEMPTION

3.70 The vast majority of small companies do not have their financial statements audited because the directors claim audit exemption.

For financial years ending on or after 1 October 2012, a company can claim audit exemption if it can meet at least two of the following criteria (see **Focus** box below):

- Annual turnover of not more than £6.5 million.
- Balance sheet total (fixed assets *plus* current assets) of not more than £3.26 million.
- 50 or fewer employees (on average).

14 FRS 102 Glossary.

Focus

At the time of writing, the Department for Business, Innovation and Skills were considering having a separate audit threshold for smaller companies because many commentators suggest that a £10.2 million turnover company should still be required to have an audit and not be able to claim audit exemption on the grounds that it is now a small business as the revised turnover threshold is considered by many to be too excessive for audit exemption.

Statement on the balance sheet

3.71 Where the company is eligible to, and does claim, audit exemption, then the following statement should be made at the foot of the balance sheet:

> 'For the year-ended [date], the company was entitled to exemption from audit under section 477 of the Companies Act 2006 relating to small companies.
>
> The members have not required the company to obtain an audit of its accounts for the year in question in accordance with section 476.
>
> The directors acknowledge their responsibilities for complying with the requirements of the Act with respect to accounting records and preparation of accounts.
>
> These accounts have been prepared in accordance with the provisions applicable to companies subject to the small companies' regime.'

3.72 Some small companies that may qualify for audit exemption do, in fact, subject their financial statements to external audit. This has the advantage that the directors and shareholders can gain reasonable assurance that the financial statements are free from material misstatement whether caused by fraud or error.

In addition, certain stakeholders (such as HM Revenue and Customs and banks) gain additional comfort from the fact that the financial statements have been subjected to an independent external audit.

Where small company audits are concerned, these are often much less complicated than the audit of a large company and this book examines the audit requirements of a small company in **Chapter 13**.

PITFALLS TO AVOID

- Reporting as a micro-entity and ignoring wider and longer-term implications.
- Reporting as a micro-entity when it is actually illegal due to being an ineligible type of company.
- Using an out-of-date format for the profit and loss account (income statement).
- Using other than the two prescribed profit and loss account formats for a small company.
- Using other than the one prescribed profit and loss account format for a micro-entity (Format 2).
- Ignoring additional disclosures just because they do not form part of the legal minimum.
- Not considering the appropriateness of the encouraged disclosures (see **3.59** above).
- Omitting the statement of unanimous agreement to preparing abridged statements.
- Omitting additional disclosures necessary with abridged statements (see **3.66** above).

CHAPTER SUMMARY

- The Companies Act 2006 was revised as a result of the EU Accounting Directive and was made a Statutory Instrument on 26 March 2015 and came into effect on 6 April 2015.
- The directors' report is still required for small company financial statements, but is not required in a set of financial statements for a micro-entity.
- The balance sheet (statement of financial position) is a primary statement which is a 'snapshot' of the financial position of the business at the end of the reporting period, showing all the assets the company owns, the liabilities it owes and the equity construction of the business.
- The profit and loss account (income statement) is a performance statement and can be prepared under a single statement approach, or a dual statement approach which will include items of income and expense taken to other comprehensive income.

- A statement of changes in equity is encouraged, but is not mandated. A small company's directors would, however, be advised to include the statement of changes in equity as a primary statement in its complete set of financial statements where there have been material changes within the composition of equity.
- The statement of cash flows (cash flow statement) is not required for a small company, but for those small companies that choose to include a cash flow statement as part of the complete set of financial statements they should follow the principles in Section 7 *Statement of Cash Flows*.
- There are 13 legally required disclosures for a small company (some of which may not be applicable in every case). Notwithstanding this minimum, small company directors must make additional disclosures where necessary to enable the financial statements to give a true and fair view.
- Micro-entities' financial statements prepared under the principles of FRS 105 *The Financial Reporting Standard applicable to the Micro-entities Regime* are *presumed* to give a true and fair view.
- Where abridged financial statements are prepared, all the members must have unanimously agreed to the small company preparing abridged accounts.
- A true and fair view is achieved by the correct application of accounting standards. However, accounting standards are only applied to material items. Care must be taken to ensure that immaterial items in isolation do not become material when combined with other isolated immaterial items.
- Many small companies claim audit exemption and a statement to this effect is required at the foot of the balance sheet. For companies which choose to have an audit, directors, shareholders and other stakeholders can take comfort in the fact that they have reasonable assurance that the financial statements are not materially misstated.

Chapter 4

The Elements of Financial Statements

SIGNPOSTS

- There are five elements of the financial statements which relate to both the balance sheet (statement of financial position) and the profit and loss account (income statement) (see **4.1**).
- The definition of an asset is based on 'control' rather than ownership (see **4.2**).
- Financial statements must report the 'substance' of transactions (ie the commercial reality) rather than the legal form (see **4.3**).
- Liabilities can arise when a small company has either a legal or a constructive obligation (see **4.4**).
- Equity can involve multiple components rather than just merely share capital and retained earnings (see **4.5**).
- Some items taken to equity cannot be distributed to shareholders as a dividend (see **4.6**).
- The term 'income' relates to income from the principal activity of the business and income from gains and a distinction must be made between the two (see **4.7**).
- Reperforming the profit and loss on disposal calculation and agreeing this to the trial balance can indicate whether disposal proceeds from the sale of fixed assets have been correctly accounted for (see **4.8**).
- Expenses can relate to those incurred in the ordinary course of business and those incurred from losses (see **4.9**).
- Correct distinction between business expenses and losses needs to be made to ensure correct accounting treatment (see **4.10**).
- Financial statements must be prepared using the accruals basis of accounting (see **4.11–4.13**).
- Going concern is a fundamental characteristic and it is important that company directors make an assessment using the correct time period (see **4.14**).

- Guidance has been issued by the Financial Reporting Council on the assessment of going concern (see **4.15**).
- The EU Accounting Directive has restricted the legally required disclosure levels and the Financial Reporting Council *encourage* disclosures to be made where going concern appears to be an issue (see **4.16**).
- The guidance issued by the Financial Reporting Council is based on three principles (see **4.17**).
- There is no 'one-size-fits-all' where the assessment of going concern is concerned (see **4.18**).
- Assessing going concern for smaller companies is inherently less complex than for a medium-sized or large entity (see **4.20**).
- There are procedures which are relevant to all companies to assess going concern and procedures which are relevant to medium and large businesses (see **4.21–4.23** and **4.24**).
- Auditors are required to evaluate the directors' assessment of going concern – they are not responsible for concluding on whether the entity is a going concern (see **4.25**).
- The review period should be for at least 12 months from the date of approval of the financial statements – not 12 months from the reporting date (see **4.26**).
- Auditors must report where the review period is less than 12 months from the date of approval and this fact has not been disclosed in the financial statements (see **4.27**).
- Principle 3 in the guidance outlines the disclosure requirements for going concern (see **4.28–4.32**).
- There are ten key characteristics which must be present in all general purpose financial statements prepared under FRS 102 (see **4.32–4.42**).

INTRODUCTION

4.1 Section 2 *Concepts and Pervasive Principles* of FRS 102 *The Financial Reporting Standard applicable in the UK and Republic of Ireland* and FRS 105 *The Financial Reporting Standard applicable to the Micro-entities Regime* outlines certain elements that are contained within the financial statements. Financial statements are focussed on the financial position and financial performance of the business. Whilst the cash flow statement (statement of cash flows) is also required for a business reporting under full FRS 102, this chapter does not consider the cash flow statement any further as there are relatively few small companies which produce a cash flow statement as part of their annual financial statements (**Chapter 3** looks at the cash flow statement in more detail). Paragraph 1.12 allows a qualifying entity (ie a small company) to take advantage of the disclosure exemption from preparing a cash flow statement in accordance with Section 7 *Statement of Cash Flows* principles.

There are five elements of the financial statements which relate to the both the balance sheet (statement of financial position) and the profit and loss account (income statement) and include:

- Assets.
- Liabilities.
- Equity.
- Income.
- Expenses.

In terms of the recognition and measurement issues in FRS 102, **Chapter 5** examines these concepts in more detail. This chapter will focus on the classification of the elements within the financial statements.

ASSETS

4.2 The definition of an asset is no longer simply something which the reporting entity owns. Its definition has become wider and potentially quite complex because emphasis is placed on the concept of 'control'. In order to recognise an asset on its balance sheet (statement of financial position), the reporting entity must control that asset.

The Glossary to FRS 102 defines an asset as 'A resource controlled by the entity as a result of past events and from which future economic benefits are expected to flow to the entity.' From this definition, it is clear that nowhere in the definition is the word 'own' or 'owns'. The key point to note in the definition is that the resource must be *controlled* by the entity.

Example 4.1 – Staff employed by a reporting entity

An accounts junior has questioned why a client's staff are not on the company's balance sheet (statement of financial position). The accounts junior said that without the staff the company would not be able to generate sales and it does not seem right (having regard to the definition of an asset) that the staff costs are charged immediately to profit and loss.

The point with regards to staff illustrates the control concept within the definition of an asset. The entity cannot control its staff – they could leave at any time and hence they are not capitalised in the balance sheet (statement of financial position).

An asset is recognised in the balance sheet (statement of financial position) when it contributes to the economic-benefit generating activities of the business. For example, a manufacturing company will be plant-intensive due to the nature of its business and the plant will manufacture the goods which are then sold and result in economic benefits flowing to the business in the form of sales. In addition, economic benefits can be derived from the sale of such assets.

4.3 The concept of 'substance over form' has been enshrined within financial reporting for decades and **Chapter 5** considers this concept in more detail. The financial statements of a reporting entity must report the substance of transactions and not merely their legal form. A transaction which illustrates this concept perfectly is a leasing transaction. FRS 102 outlines the accounting for a leasing transaction depending on which party bears the risks and rewards associated with the asset being subjected to the lease. If the risks and rewards transfer to the lessee on inception of the lease, the lease is accounted for as a finance lease and hence an asset is recognised together with an associated finance lease liability. This is because, in substance, the entity has acquired an asset which has been financed through a leasing arrangement.

Where the risks and rewards of ownership of the asset remain with the lessor, this will be indicative of an operating lease and therefore lease rentals are charged to the profit and loss account (income statement) as and when they fall due. The accounting for leases is dealt with in **Chapter 12** of this book.

When substance over form is applied to a finance lease, the entity recognises an asset as the asset will serve towards the economic-benefit generating activities of the business. It will also recognise a finance lease creditor which represents the value of the leasing payments which will be paid to the lessor.

Focus

- The issue of leasing transactions has become a controversial topic for some entities whereby the leasing arrangements have been deliberately engineered to achieve a desired outcome (usually to achieve operating lease status and hence no recognition of an asset or corresponding liability). Care should be taken by preparers to adequately scrutinise the terms of the lease to ensure correct accounting treatment is applied.

LIABILITIES

4.4 As with an asset, the definition of a liability has become more complicated over the years and is not simply something that the entity owes – although to all intents and purposes this is what a liability represents. However, the recognition of a liability will depend on whether the reporting entity has a present obligation as a result of a past event. The Glossary defines a liability as 'A present obligation of the entity arising from past events, the settlement of which is expected to result in an outflow from the entity of resources embodying economic benefits.'

What this definition is essentially saying is that the entity must recognise a liability when it has a present obligation to act or perform in a particular way. In many instances it is clear cut when a liability has arisen – for example the entity may purchase goods from a supplier which has agreed payment terms of 30 days from the date of invoice. This will give rise to a liability in the financial statements until the liability has been discharged – which will normally occur when the reporting entity pays its invoices. Liabilities usually arise in two situations and are when the reporting entity has either:

- a legal obligation; or
- a constructive obligation.

A legal obligation is legally enforceable as part of a binding contract or statutory obligation and in many cases it is clear when the entity has a legal obligation as a result of past events. Issues can arise when a *constructive* obligation might have been created.

The Glossary to FRS 102 defines a 'constructive obligation' as follows:

> 'An obligation that derives from an entity's actions where:
>
> (a) by an established pattern of past practice, published policies or a sufficiently specific current statement, the entity has indicated to other parties that it will accept certain responsibilities; and
>
> (b) as a result, the entity has created a valid expectation on the part of those other parties that it will discharge those responsibilities.'[1]

Example 4.2 – Closure of a division

Finch Industries (Finch) is a manufacturing company that manufactures three types of washing powder: EcoWash, GreenWash and BriteWash. The BriteWash brand has seen a decline in sales over the last couple of years and on 31 October 2015 the directors unanimously agreed to close the division that makes the BriteWash brand. Finch has a year-end of 31 December 2015 and on 1 November 2015 made an announcement to those staff affected by the closure of the division that they will be made redundant as they cannot be deployed elsewhere within the company. The manufacturing division will close on 31 January 2016.

The announcement to the staff on 1 November 2015 gave rise to a constructive obligation that the directors will close the BriteWash manufacturing division and that they will make the staff redundant. This constructive obligation has

1 FRS 102 Glossary **Constructive obligation**.

given rise to a liability which will be recognised in the financial statements to 31 December 2015 and the amount of the liability will be the best estimate for the cost of the redundancies together with any other incremental costs associated with the closure.

EQUITY

4.5 Equity is defined in the Glossary to FRS 102 as 'The residual interest in the **assets** of the entity after deducting all its **liabilities**.'[2]

A typical example of equity would be the leftover profit for the year-end after an entity has provided for corporation tax and has paid out dividends to shareholders. Anything left would be classed as equity and reinvested back into the entity.

The components of equity within the balance sheet (statement of financial position) may also include:

- share capital which the investors have subscribed to;
- equity component of preference shares;
- equity component of convertible debt;
- revaluation surpluses on property, plant and equipment accounted for under Section 17 *Property, Plant and equipment*;
- other items of other comprehensive income (such as accumulated actuarial gains and losses on defined benefit pension plans).

4.6 Care must be taken when dealing with items within equity because some items taken to equity may not be distributable to shareholders in the form of a dividend. This is particularly the case where fair value gains and losses have arisen on investment properties. Such fair value gains and losses are taken directly to profit or loss (as opposed to a revaluation reserve under previous UK GAAP). These are then transferred into profit and loss account reserves on the first day of the new accounting period but care must be taken not to pay out these 'undistributable' reserves as a dividend because such fair value adjustments are not realised gains for dividend purposes. **Chapter 12** takes a look in more detail at the accounting treatment for investment properties under the new small companies' regime.

INCOME

4.7 Some small entities receive income in various guises; such as income from turnover, bank interest, rental income, management recharges and such

2 FRS 102 Glossary **Equity**.

like. Not all transactions which result in economic benefits flowing to the business will be regarded as income and therefore it is important to distinguish between:

- income from the business's principal activity; and
- income from gains.

The Glossary to FRS 102 defines 'income' as 'Increases in economic benefits during the **reporting period** in the form of inflows or enhancements of **assets** or decreases of **liabilities** that result in increases in **equity**, other than those relating to contributions from equity investors.'[3]

For the purposes of FRS 102, income from 'revenue' is essentially income generated through the day-to-day sales of the business. For example, a supermarket will generate revenue from the sales of goods whereas an accountancy firm will generate revenue from the rendering of accountancy and tax services. Revenue from such sources will increase the value of the entity's assets through the recognition of a trade debtor who will eventually pay (if the sale has been made on credit terms), the balance will then turn into cash and hence whilst trade debtors will decrease, the value of the company's cash at bank balance will increase.

4.8 Revenue from gains is where the company may, for example, sell a fixed asset. When a company disposes of a fixed asset, income may be received from the sales proceeds. These proceeds are not recognised as turnover because the income will form part of the disposal of the fixed asset; instead the income will contribute to a profit or loss on disposal.

Example 4.3 – Disposal proceeds

The principal activity of Breary Enterprises Ltd is the manufacture of roller shutter doors which are fitted to the exterior of commercial premises for security purposes. It has a machine that manufactures the curtains used for the shutters and during the year disposed of its existing machine and purchased a newer model.

The machine which has been disposed of had a net book value at the year-end 30 September 2015 of £20,000 and the company's policy is to charge a full year's depreciation charge in the year an asset is acquired, but not to charge any depreciation in the year of disposal. The machine was sold for £22,000.

The net book value of the machine that has been sold is £20,000 and the company has received £22,000 for it and hence there is a profit on the disposal of this machine amounting to £2,000. The disposal proceeds will not be included

3 FRS 102 Glossary **Income**.

within turnover, but instead the entries in the books of Breary Enterprises Ltd on receipt of the proceeds will be:

DR cash at bank	£22,000
CR profit and loss on disposal of fixed assets	(£22,000)

Being disposal proceeds for old machine

If we assume that the cost of the machine was £30,000 and accumulated depreciation was £10,000 (hence giving a net book value of £20,000) the journals are:

DR profit and loss on disposal of fixed assets	£20,000
DR accumulated depreciation	£10,000
CR plant and machinery disposal	(£30,000)

Being removal of machine from balance sheet

Once the balance sheet disposal has been accounted for (ie the cost and accumulated depreciation is removed and taken to the disposal account) the profit and loss account (income statement) will show a profit on disposal of fixed assets amounting to £2,000.

Focus

- It is often beneficial to carry out a reperformance of the profit and loss on disposal of fixed assets to agree the figure in the trial balance – particularly for smaller entities that may have taken up audit exemption. This is because occasionally the bookkeeper may not fully understand how to account for a fixed asset disposal and may inadvertently include the sales proceeds within turnover or 'other income'. Reperforming the profit and loss on disposal will help to identify such transactions and therefore correctly reallocate any misposted items of income from fixed asset disposals.

EXPENSES

4.9 As with income, expenses are split into two component parts:

- expenses incurred in the ordinary course of business; and
- losses.

The distinction between the two is important and the Glossary to FRS 102 defines 'expenses' as 'Decreases in economic benefits during the **reporting period** in the form of outflows or depletions of **assets** or incurrences of **liabilities** that result in decreases in **equity**, other than those relating to distributions to equity investors.'[4]

Expenses which the business incurs in the ordinary course of business would be items such as depreciation, payroll costs, cost of sales, light and heat and motor expenses and would all be classified in their individual line items within the financial statements. The definition above refers to '... form of outflows' or '... depletions of assets ...'. A 'form of outflow' would be the cash used to settle the liability and a 'depletion of assets' would be charges such as depreciation or amortisation for a fixed asset.

4.10 Losses, on the other hand, are losses which are incurred by the business but which do not arise from the principal activities of the business. The most common type of loss would be the loss incurred when a company disposes of a fixed asset and can be illustrated using the following example:

Example 4.4 – Disposal proceeds

The principal activity of Haslam Enterprises Ltd is the manufacture of roller shutter doors which are fitted to the exterior of commercial premises for security purposes. It has a machine that manufactures the curtains used for the shutters and during the year disposed of its existing machine and purchased a newer model.

The machine which has been disposed of had a net book value at the year-end 30 September 2015 of £20,000 and the company's policy is to charge a full year's depreciation charge in the year an asset is acquired, but not to charge any depreciation in the year of disposal. The machine was sold for £18,000.

The net book value of the machine that has been sold is £20,000 and the company has received £18,000 for it and hence there is a loss on the disposal of this machine amounting to £2,000. The entries in the books of Haslam Enterprises Ltd on receipt of the proceeds will be:

DR cash at bank	£18,000
CR profit and loss on disposal of fixed assets	(£18,000)

Being disposal proceeds for old machine

If we assume that the machine cost £30,000 and had accumulated depreciation of £10,000 (hence a net book value of £20,000), the journals will be:

4 FRS 102 Glossary **Expenses**.

DR profit and loss on disposal of fixed assets	£20,000
DR accumulated depreciation	£10,000
CR plant and machinery disposal	(£30,000)

Being removal of machine from balance sheet

Once the balance sheet disposal has been accounted for (ie the cost and accumulated depreciation is removed and taken to the disposal account) the profit and loss account (income statement) will show a loss on disposal of fixed assets amounting to £2,000.

The example above illustrates the need to correctly distinguish expenses from losses incurred by the business. Of course, there are other transactions which will give rise to losses being incurred (such as impairment losses) and such transactions must be shown in the most appropriate line items within the financial statements.

ACCRUALS BASIS OF ACCOUNTING

4.11 Under UK GAAP, a small entity is required to use the *accruals* basis of accounting to prepare the financial statements. This method recognises transactions on an arising basis rather than a cash paid or received basis. For unincorporated entities which may only prepare accounts for tax purposes, HM Revenue and Customs would require the accruals basis of accounting to be applied to arrive at profits for the purposes of tax.

Under the accruals basis of accounting, income is recognised when it is earned. This is an important concept that small entities must interpret correctly. Section 23 *Revenue* in FRS 102 is notably different in terms of wording of the timing of revenue recognition than previous UK GAAP was. Under previous UK GAAP, terms such as the 'right to consideration' and the occurrence of a 'critical event' or the 'passing of a milestone' were frequently cited as the point in time when revenue should be recognised. Indeed, the introduction of Application Note G (or UITF 40 *Revenue recognition and service contracts*) caused a considerable outcry within the profession because this required reporting entities (more commonly professional firms) to recognise revenue earlier than they would have done prior to the issuance of UITF 40 and to recognise revenue when they received the right to consideration which, in some circumstances, would have been much earlier than the entity would have invoiced their customer/client.

The concepts within previous UK GAAP should still be followed under FRS 102 for small entities and small entities will still be required to recognise revenue when they receive the right to consideration (although the term 'right to consideration' is not explicitly referred to in FRS 102).

4.12 In a similar manner to income, expenditures are recognised in the financial statements to match the income to which they relate. Care must be taken where such expenses are included in the financial statements (for example by way of an accrual) so as to reliably estimate the value of the accrual within the financial statements. When considering provisions for liabilities, for example, care should also be taken to reliably estimate the value of the provision because there will often be associated tax consequences.

4.13 The recognition of transactions within the financial statements using the accruals basis of accounting will give rise to the recognition of an asset (normally a debtor) and the recognition of a liability (normally a creditor or an accrual). Other liabilities can be recognised within the financial statements to bring in the value of other liabilities at the reporting date, such as amounts owed to HM Revenue and Customs for the monthly PAYE/NIC liabilities at the year-end, or VAT liabilities.

GOING CONCERN

4.14 Going concern is one of the most important characteristics of financial statements and is an issue which is material for all businesses, large and small. The concept of going concern has been under increasing scrutiny in recent years, due in large part to the global economic crisis.

The Glossary to FRS 102 defines 'going concern' as follows:

> 'An entity is a going concern unless management either intends to liquidate the entity or to cease trading, or has no realistic alternative but to do so.'[5]

When the directors of a small company are preparing their financial statements, they must carefully consider whether the going concern basis of accounting is appropriate. In assessing the company's going concern status, the directors must take account of all information and facts that they have at their disposal and the going concern basis should be for a period of 12 months from the date of approval of the financial statements.

Focus

- The going concern assessment period should be done for a period of 12 months from the date of approval of the financial statements and not 12 months from the reporting date. Clearly the majority of small companies have their annual financial statements drawn up some months after the year-end and therefore it would be inappropriate to base a going concern assessment on a period of 12 months from the reporting date.
- Particular care should be taken by small companies that have their financial statements independently audited because failing to carry out a going concern assessment using the appropriate period could affect the audit report.

5 FRS 102 Glossary **Going concern**.

Guidance issued by the Financial Reporting Council on going concern

4.15 The Financial Reporting Council (FRC) have issued guidance to directors of companies in relation to going concern. This guidance was issued in 2009 and applies to all companies, including small companies. It is expected that this guidance will be updated soon given the time which has elapsed since it was originally issued by the FRC.

Going concern has moved up the ranks in the focus of the profession over recent years, due in large part to the economic crisis – indeed even the most profitable companies can see themselves in financial difficulty due to cash flow constraints or in the worst cases the reporting of profits which are not cash-backed to mislead users into thinking the entity's financial position and performance is better than it actually is.

While the concept of going concern is a fundamental concept, it is still one that often causes a certain element of confusion among practitioners – particularly when it comes to the disclosure requirements. In the past companies have been severely criticised for inadequate disclosures (as have audit firms who have audited such companies) and as a consequence, professional regulators have issued various amounts of guidance regarding the issue of going concern.

4.16 It is the responsibility of the directors of companies to satisfy themselves that the use of the going concern basis of accounting is reasonable so as to conclude that the financial statements give a true and fair view. The EU Accounting Directive has restricted the number of disclosure requirements which member states can impose on small companies and the Companies Act 2006 restricts these disclosure requirements to a minimum of 13 disclosures (**Chapters 2** and **3** both examine these issues in more detail).

In light of the fact that the Companies Act 2006 requires directors of small companies to ensure that the financial statements give a true and fair view, the FRC have included five *encouraged* disclosures in paragraph 1AD.1. One of these encouraged disclosures are disclosures relating to going concern set out in paragraph 3.9 of FRS 102. Therefore, where the directors have identified issues relating to going concern, directors of small companies must ensure that they make adequate disclosures.

Focus

- The point about financial statements giving a true and fair view cannot be over-emphasised. Directors of small companies cannot under-estimate the level of professional judgement which will be needed to ensure that the financial statements achieve a true and fair view and advice should always be sought from professional advisers in the event of ambiguity or misunderstanding of the requirements. More responsibility is therefore passed on to directors under the new small companies' regime to determine what additional disclosure requirements may be needed in the financial statements to achieve a true and fair view.

Guidance on going concern assessments and disclosures

4.17 In October 2009, the Financial Reporting Council (FRC) issued a document titled *Going Concern and Liquidity Risk: Guidance for Directors of UK Companies 2009*. Whilst this document was issued some five years ago, it still has particular relevance today.

The guidance itself brings together the requirements of the Companies Act 2006, accounting standards and the Listing Rules on going concern and liquidity risk for small, medium and large companies as well as providing guidance on their application.

The document itself is fairly brief, spanning just 26 pages, and deals with three principles in dealing with going concern:

(1) Assessing going concern.

(2) The review period.

(3) Disclosures.

The Appendices then offer examples of going concern disclosures in certain situations as well as key questions for boards.

The guidance applies to accounting periods ending on or after 31 December 2009 and superseded the guidance which was issued in 1994 for directors of listed companies. The 2009 version of the guidance extends to all sizes of companies for both annual and half-yearly financial statements. It is expected that the guidance will be updated in the foreseeable future to bring it up to date.

Assessing going concern

4.18 The first principle in the guidance deals with the assessment of going concern. Principle 1 says:

> 'Directors should make and document a rigorous assessment of whether the company is a going concern when preparing annual and half-yearly financial statements. The process carried out by directors should be proportionate in nature and depth depending upon the size, level of financial risk and complexity of the company and its operations.'

There is no 'one-size-fits-all' where the assessment of going concern is concerned and directors of all companies are required to make a going concern assessment. The directors of a company cannot use the going concern basis of accounting if they intend to cease trading, or go into liquidation or they have no realistic alternative but to do so.

Change in basis of preparing the financial statements

4.19 Where the directors of a company cannot use the going concern basis of accounting, this will mean a change of basis in preparing the financial statements, which will have an impact on the carrying amounts of assets and liabilities recognised in the financial statements.

Where the going concern basis is considered not appropriate, the directors must use an alternative basis, which will usually be the 'break-up' basis. The break-up basis, whilst being the most appropriate basis when the going concern basis is not appropriate, is not specifically referred to; nor is the method of how a company should reclassify items in the financial statements under the break-up basis referred to. Usually, applying the break-up basis will mean fixed assets are reclassified to current assets at their expected realisable value. Long-term liabilities will be reclassified to current and additional disclosures will be made within the financial statements to explain that the company is not regarded as a going concern and to explain the basis on which the financial statements have been prepared.

Example 4.5 – Going concern basis not appropriate

A company has lost a large contract in the year to 30 November 2016. In addition, the company's bankers have also expressed their unwillingness to continue to support the company and have 'called in' both the bank loan and overdraft. The loan and overdraft in combination are significant and the directors have been unsuccessful in negotiating refinancing with other banks and finance houses. The directors have concluded that they have no realistic alternative but to place the company into liquidation and cease trading.

Clearly in this scenario the going concern basis of preparing the financial statements as at 30 November 2016 will not be appropriate and in such cases the 'break-up' basis of accounting is used. Fixed assets will be reclassified to current assets at their realisable value and long-term liabilities will be reclassified to current liabilities. Additional disclosures should also be made to explain why the company is not a going concern together with an explanation of the basis applied in preparing the financial statements.

4.20 The guidance issued by the FRC acknowledges that small companies must still have regard to the going concern status of the entity. However, the extent of the directors' review process will depend on both the nature and size of the company as well as the complexity of the business. In reality, assessing going concern in a smaller enterprise is likely to be much simpler than that for medium-sized and large companies as small companies tend only to have one business activity and a limited number of creditors and providers of finance. Notwithstanding this simplicity, the directors' must still document and address, to the extent necessary, their plans to manage the company's borrowing requirements, cash flow timings and the company's exposure to contingent liabilities.

Example 4.6 – Going concern assessment in a subsidiary

Company B is a subsidiary company and has a year-end of 30 November each year. The directors of Company B are not planning on making any going concern assessments in the belief that this is the responsibility of the parent company.

The directors of Company B are incorrect in their belief that the going concern assessment of a subsidiary is the responsibility of the parent company. The guidance confirms that directors of subsidiary companies need to make their going concern assessment taking into account:

- the need for support[6] from the parent company or fellow subsidiaries;
- the ability and willingness of the parent company or fellow subsidiaries to provide such support; and
- the risks to the company's going concern status arising from support that it has undertaken to provide to other members of the group.

In assessing the going concern status of the subsidiary, the subsidiary's directors should also consider the degree of autonomy the subsidiary company has and how the subsidiary fits into the group's activities and future plans. The directors should also consider the particular business risks which might arise that could threaten the appropriateness of the going concern basis when preparing the individual subsidiary financial statements.

The amount of evidence which the directors of a subsidiary company collates and retains to support their assessment of going concern is a matter of judgement – again there is no 'one-size-fits-all' where this is concerned. The directors' judgement will also usually involve their experience of dealing with the parent company over a period of time as well as taking into current facts, events and circumstances pertinent to the subsidiary.

Procedures relevant to all companies

4.21 *Going Concern and Liquidity Risk: Guidance for Directors of UK Companies* 2009 offers procedures which all companies should generally adopt when assessing going concern, including:

Budgets and forecasts

4.22 The guidance recognises that budgets and forecasts prepared by an entity are long-established techniques in business management. Assumptions used in the preparation of such budgets and forecasts can be subjected to sensitivity analysis or 'stress-tested' which tends to offer a more likely outcome.

6 'Support' for this purpose means both financial and non-financial support.

The guidance suggests that directors should prepare a budget, trading estimate, cash flow forecast or other equivalent analysis covering such a period as they consider appropriate.

Borrowing facilities

4.23 Directors should carefully consider the terms of borrowing arrangements (especially where covenants have been incorporated by the financiers). This is primarily to ensure that the terms and conditions are not breached which might result in the lender 'calling in' the loan which would then potentially bring into question the entity's ability to continue as a going concern.

It is the responsibility of the directors to be satisfied that there are adequate financing arrangements in place for the entity. Where there are any potential deficits, arrears or breaches which may arise then directors should enter into discussions with the lender sooner rather than later to avoid potential problems crystallising.

Procedures relevant to medium and large businesses

4.24 The guidance issued by the FRC includes some areas which are specific to medium and large businesses. As this book is only concerned with small company reporting, the procedures relevant to medium and large businesses are beyond the book's scope.

Auditor's responsibilities over the going concern assessment

4.25 Where the small entity is independently audited, it is not the responsibility of the auditor to conclude whether the entity is a going concern – this responsibility rests with the directors. The auditor's responsibility is to evaluate the directors' assessment of the company's ability to continue as a going concern.

The review period

4.26 The second principle in the guidance deals with the review period for going concern. Principle 2 says:

> 'Directors should consider all available information about the future when concluding whether the company is a going concern at the date they approve the financial statements. Their review should usually cover a period of at least twelve months from the date of approval of financial and half-yearly financial statements.'

The important aspect concerning principle 2 is the period of review. This should be for at least 12 months from the date of approval of the financial or half-yearly financial statements – not 12 months from the reporting date which is where some companies have gone wrong with this guidance.

In undertaking their review, directors should consider all available information about the future including information which they have obtained from budgets and forecasts. FRS 102 and EU-adopted IFRS all provide for a minimum period that should be reviewed by the directors when assessing going concern (although the extent of the review period is a matter of judgement and in some situations it might be appropriate to obtain information for longer periods).

Auditor's report

4.27 If the review period of the directors' assessment of going concern is less than 12 months from the date of approval of the financial statements and this fact has not been disclosed within the financial statements, the auditor is required to make reference to the review period being less than 12 months from the date of approval of the financial statements in their report.

Where the auditor determines that a material uncertainty exists which may cast significant doubt over the entity's ability to continue as a going concern, then the auditor will modify the report (but not the opinion) by the inclusion of an 'emphasis of matter' paragraph in the audit report (directly underneath the opinion paragraph). This is, of course, subject to the disclosures in the financial statements concerning the material uncertainty being adequate.

Disclosures

4.28 After the directors have undertaken an assessment of going concern using the appropriate review period and have assessed the going concern basis having regard to all the available information at their disposal, the directors are then required to make appropriate disclosures within the financial statements relating to the entity's going concern ability.

Principle 3 in the guidance says:

> 'Directors should make balanced, proportionate and clear disclosures about going concern for the financial statements to give a true and fair view. Directors should disclose if the period that they have reviewed is less than twelve months from the date of approval of annual and half-yearly financial statements and explain their justification for limiting their review period.'

Once the going concern review is done, there are three conclusions which can be drawn:

(1) the going concern basis of accounting is appropriate because there are no material uncertainties related to events or conditions that may cast

significant doubt about the ability of the company to continue as a going concern; or

(2) the use of the going concern basis is appropriate but there are material uncertainties related to events or conditions that may cast significant doubt about the ability of the company to continue as a going concern; or

(3) the going concern basis is not appropriate.

Going concern basis is appropriate

4.29 If the directors conclude that the going concern basis is appropriate and there are no material uncertainties relating to the company's going concern status, in practice no additional disclosure note is included in the financial statements. The FRC's 2009 guidance does include an example where a company concludes that the going concern basis is appropriate and there are no material uncertainties relating to going concern and does suggest the inclusion of a disclosure note to that effect; however many companies simply do not make any disclosures where there are no material uncertainties to going concern. Under the new small companies' financial reporting regime, this would not be an issue because disclosures relating to going concern are an encouraged disclosure and if the company does not have any issues relating to going concern then non-disclosure would comply with the small companies' regime.

Going concern basis is appropriate but material uncertainties exist

4.30 It may be the case that in carrying out their assessment of going concern, directors come across material uncertainties which may cast significant doubt about the ability of the small company to remain a going concern for the foreseeable future. Notwithstanding these uncertainties, the directors may still prepare the financial statements under the going concern basis.

Appendix D to Section 1A of FRS 102 at paragraph 1AD.1(c) encourages a small entity to make disclosures relating to going concern in accordance with paragraph 3.9 of FRS 102. Paragraph 3.9 of FRS 102 says:

> 'When management is aware, in making its assessment, of **material** uncertainties related to events or conditions that cast significant doubt upon the entity's ability to continue as a going concern, the entity shall disclose those uncertainties. When an entity does not prepare financial statements on a going concern basis, it shall disclose that fact, together with the basis on which it prepared the financial statements and the reason why the entity is not regarded as a going concern.'[7]

7 FRS 102, para 3.9.

Example disclosure 4.7 – Material uncertainty exists but the going concern basis is deemed appropriate

The company has orders for work for the next two months. However, despite significant efforts, it has so far proved impossible to obtain additional sales orders. If new orders are not forthcoming, the directors will need to close the factory and make the employees redundant.

The directors have concluded that a material uncertainty exists that casts significant doubt upon the company's ability to continue as a going concern and that, therefore, the company may be unable to realise its assets and discharge its liabilities in the normal course of business. However, given the continuing efforts to secure new orders, the directors continue to adopt the going concern basis of accounting.

Going concern basis is not appropriate

4.31 In the unfortunate instance that the directors deem the company not to be a going concern, then the financial statements cannot be prepared using the going concern presumption. Whilst FRS 102 does not specifically refer to the 'break-up basis' of accounting, this would be the most appropriate basis on which to prepare the financial statements. Fixed assets are restated to current assets at their net realisable value and long-term liabilities are reclassified as current.

Example disclosure 4.8 – Going concern basis not appropriate

The company's borrowing facilities are scheduled for renewal at the end of November 2016 and the bank have expressed their unwillingness to continue to support the company. The directors have not been able to refinance the business and have concluded that they have no alternative but to liquidate the entity. The financial statements have not been prepared on the going concern basis, but have been prepared under the 'break-up' basis of accounting. Fixed assets have been restated to current assets at their fire sale value and long-term loans have been reclassified to current liabilities.

Focus

- This chapter has covered issues relating to going concern in some depth. Directors of small businesses must take care when dealing with going concern assessments because they are crucially important. In addition, where the directors have identified material uncertainties relating to going concern, they are encouraged to make the disclosures required in paragraph 3.9 of FRS 102 to enable the financial statements to give a true and fair view.

QUALITATIVE CHARACTERISTICS

4.32 The *Concepts and Pervasive Principles* in Section 2 of FRS 102 contain ten key characteristics which must be present in all general purpose financial statements that are prepared under FRS 102 principles as follows:

- Understandability.
- Relevance.
- Materiality.
- Reliability.
- Substance over form.
- Prudence.
- Completeness.
- Comparability.
- Timeliness.
- Balance between benefit and cost.

Understandability

4.33 Clearly financial statements must be presented in an understandable manner for the user of them. The *Concepts and Pervasive Principles* acknowledges that information should be presented in such a way so as to make it comprehensible by users who have an adequate degree of knowledge about the entity and economic activities as well as accounting and who are prepared to study the information presented with reasonable diligence. An important point within this particular concept is that information should not be omitted on the grounds that it may be too complicated for some users to understand.

Relevance

4.34 Information presented in general purpose financial statements must be relevant in order to aid the decision-making of users. The *Concepts and Pervasive Principles* acknowledges that information is relevant when it is capable of influencing the economic decisions of users by helping them evaluate past, present or future events or confirming, or correcting, their past evaluations.

Materiality

4.35 The concept of materiality has been an important principle for many years and is as important today as it was many years ago. The *Concepts and Pervasive Principles* confirms that information is material – and therefore has relevance – if its omission or misstatement, individually or collectively, could influence the economic decisions of users taken on the basis of the financial statements.

Materiality is not something that can be pre-determined or quantified as a whole – it is purely entity-specific and how material an item is will depend on the size and nature of the entity, the size and nature of the omission or misstatement. The *Concepts and Pervasive Principles* says that it is inappropriate to make, or leave uncorrected, immaterial departures from FRS 102 to achieve a particular presentation of an entity's financial position, financial performance or cash flows.

Reliability

4.36 Reliability is influenced by materiality in that the *Concepts and Pervasive Principles* consider information to be reliable when it is free from material error and bias and represents faithfully that which it either purports to represent or could reasonably be expected to represent. In order to achieve reliability, financial statements must not be manipulated in such a way as to achieve a desired outcome (for example by employing methods to achieve off-balance sheet finance).

Substance over form

4.37 This concept was looked at earlier in the chapter and is one of the key qualitative characteristics of financial statements. In essence, financial statements must report the commercial reality (ie the substance) of transactions and not their legal form and the *Concepts and Pervasive Principles* acknowledges that such a characteristic will enhance the reliability of financial statements. **Chapter 5** considers the reporting of the substance of transactions in more detail.

Prudence

4.38 Prudence is a long-established principle in financial reporting and is the inclusion of a degree of caution in the preparation of financial statements. It works on the basis that assets and income are not overstated whilst liabilities and expenses should not be understated (one could argue that it works on the 'worst case scenario' approach). A key example of this is in relation to construction contracts. If losses are foreseen on a construction contract, such losses are recognised within the financial statements as soon as they are foreseen, and not when they are actually incurred.

Completeness

4.39 Information presented within the financial statements must be complete within the boundaries of materiality and cost. The *Concepts and Pervasive Principles* acknowledges that financial information will be misleading and unreliable in terms of its relevance if the information presented in the financial statements is not complete.

Comparability

4.40 In order to make rational, economic decisions, users of the financial statements must be able to compare the results from one period to another or with different entities in the same sector in order to evaluate the financial position, performance and cash flows of the entity. It is for this reason that financial statements must also disclose the reporting entity's critical accounting policies as well as disclosing details of any changes in those accounting policies together with the effects of such changes.

Timeliness

4.41 The *Concepts and Pervasive Principles* acknowledges that *timeliness* involves providing the information within the decision time frame. It works on the basis that information is more relevant the more timely it is presented – for example, financial information may well lose its relevance the more time that elapses. However, in contrast, some financial information may well become more relevant with the passage of time, for example to assess trends.

Balance between benefit and cost

4.42 The costs of providing information to users should not exceed the benefits of such provision and the *Concepts and Pervasive Principles* acknowledges that such evaluations of costs and benefits is substantially a judgemental process. It also acknowledges that financial reporting information assists capital providers in making better decisions, which in turn results in more efficient functioning of capital markets and a lower cost of capital for the economy as a whole. From an individual-entity level, such entities will enjoy improved access to capital markets and perhaps also lower costs of capital. Benefits may also include better management decisions on the grounds that financial information prepared for internal use is essentially based on (at least partly) information that is prepared for general purpose financial reporting purposes.

PITFALLS TO AVOID

- Forgetting that 'gains' and 'losses' are distinguished differently than 'income' and 'expenses'.
- Using the going concern basis if the directors intend to cease to trade or liquidate (or have no realistic alternative but to cease to trade or liquidate) the business.
- Ignoring going concern disclosures because they are not legally required; the FRC have included them as an encouraged disclosure in Appendix D to Section 1A of FRS 102.
- Forgetting about the qualitative characteristics which all financial statements must contain.

CHAPTER SUMMARY

- The 'elements' of the financial statements include assets, liabilities, income, expenses and equity.
- Financial statements in the UK and Republic of Ireland must be prepared using the accruals basis of accounting (ie transactions are recognised on arising basis rather than a paid or received basis).
- The Financial Reporting Council have issued guidance to directors of UK companies on going concern to help them to apply the requirements correctly.
- Where the directors intend to liquidate the business, or cease trading, or have no realistic alternative to do so, the going concern basis cannot be used and an alternative basis is used instead (ie the 'break-up' basis).
- Financial statements must contain certain qualitative characteristics.

Chapter 5

Reporting the Substance of Transactions

SIGNPOSTS

- The financial statements of a company must report the substance of transactions rather than their legal form (see **5.1**).
- Recognition of the assets and liabilities of a small company is achieved by having regard to the *Concepts and Pervasive Principles* which are contained in Section 2 of FRS 102. Financial statements must also give a true and fair view and more responsibility will be placed on the directors of small companies to ensure their legal obligations have been adequately discharged (see **5.2**).
- There are two criterion which have to be met before an asset can be recognised on the balance sheet (statement of financial position) (see **5.3**).
- A liability is an obligation as a result of a past event and there are three criterion which have to be met before a liability is recognised on the balance sheet (statement of financial position) (see **5.4**).
- Subsequent measurement of assets and liabilities can be at historical cost or at fair value (see **5.5** and **5.6**).
- Where the substance of transactions are concerned, leasing transactions lend themselves to a significant amount of subjectivity which can result in 'off balance sheet' finance becoming a problem (see **5.7**).
- The concept of finance leases is carried over into FRS 102 but the legal title cannot be considered in isolation as this will not report the substance of a leasing transaction (see **5.8**).
- Derecognition of assets and liabilities should be carried out with care in some instances, but in the case of derecognising a financial asset, more analysis work may be needed to ensure derecognition is appropriate (see **5.9** and **5.10**).
- Derecognition of a fixed asset will often result in a profit or loss on disposal which needs to be reported correctly within the profit and loss account (income statement) (see **5.11**).

- There are certain criterion which have to be met before a financial asset can be derecognised (see **5.12**).
- An investment property can be derecognised or recategorised to property, plant and equipment in certain situations (see **5.13**).
- Inventory (stock) can be subjected to write-down to estimated selling price less costs to complete and sell if this value is lower than cost and in some cases can result in inventory being derecognised from the balance sheet (statement of financial position) completely (see **5.14**).
- Amounts owed to the entity in respect of receivables (trade or other) are essentially derecognised when the contractual rights to the cash flows from the financial asset expire or are settled (see **5.15**).
- The derecognition of a financial liability is less complex than the derecognition of a financial asset and a financial liability is derecognised when the obligation is extinguished (see **5.16**).
- Trade creditors are derecognised when the entity pays those creditors or where the obligation is cancelled (see **5.17**).
- The derecognition of financial liabilities in respect of loans or other financing agreements takes place when they are settled or when they are cancelled or discharged (see **5.18**).
- Recognising revenue can be complex in some situations and care needs to be taken when exercising professional judgement in the context of Section 23 *Revenue* (see **5.19**).
- Revenue should be recognised having regard to the economic substance of a sale agreement and in some cases an 'apparent' sale might not be a sale (see **5.20** and **5.21**).
- Linked presentation for certain non-recourse finance arrangements are no longer permitted under FRS 102 principles (see **5.22** and **5.23**).

INTRODUCTION

5.1 One of the most crucial aspects of financial statements is that they must report the substance of the arrangement which the entity has entered into. When we refer to the 'substance' of transactions, what we are referring to is the commercial reality.

Over the years accounting standards and financial reporting have had to evolve to deal with the increasing complexity attached to business. Businesses now enter into varying types of financial arrangements, including derivative contracts, complex leasing arrangements and loans with complex terms. While many accountants view such arrangements as only being confined to the large multi-nationals, this is not always the case and even smaller entities will enter into some arrangements which need to be dealt with properly in the financial statements to ensure the financial statements give a true and fair view.

This chapter focuses on the commercial reality of the transactions and takes a look at the recognition and measurement requirements when it comes to assets and liabilities (the concepts of which are discussed in **Chapter 4**).

RECOGNITION OF ASSETS AND LIABILITIES

5.2 The *Concepts and Pervasive Principles* contained in Section 2 of FRS 102 outlines the overall objective of financial statements and this objective underpins the remainder of FRS 102 (including FRS 102 applicable to small entities). The overall objective of financial statements according to the *Concepts and Pervasive Principles* is to provide information about the financial position, performance and cash flows of the reporting entity which is useful to enable third parties to make rational decisions about the entity where those users are not in a position to demand reports that are tailored to meet particular information needs.

The provisions of the EU Accounting Directive which were transposed into companies' legislation in January 2015 reduces the levels of disclosure requirements for small companies. However, a pivotal concept that has been enshrined within the Companies Act 2006 for several years is the fact that financial statements prepared by reporting entities must give a true and fair view. Correct application of financial reporting standards (such as FRS 102) will enable the financial statements to give a true and fair view. It is vital that directors of small companies discharge their obligations correctly under the Act because failure to do so will result in the financial statements failing to give a true and fair view and hence the committing of a criminal offence.

5.3 A small business will recognise an asset when the transaction satisfies the following criteria:

- it is probable that any future economic benefit associated with the item will flow to or from the entity; and
- the item has a cost or value that can be measured reliably.

Focus

- An important point to emphasise where financial statements for small businesses are concerned is that a failure to recognise transactions in the financial statements is not corrected by way of a disclosure note or a disclosure of an accounting policy.

Where an item fails to qualify for recognition at a specific point in time, it may qualify for recognition later and in order to achieve a true and fair view, the directors may well consider that additional disclosures within the notes to the financial statements are warranted. In order to make this determination, the directors of small companies should 'stand back' and take an objective look at the financial statements, having regard to the facts and knowledge at their disposal, and consider whether additional disclosures may be needed to give a true and fair view.

5.4 Once transactions meet the recognition criteria they are included within the financial statements – usually at cost and the components of cost might include purchase or production price plus other incremental costs in getting the asset to its present location and condition (for example import duties which are irrecoverable).

An *asset* must be recognised in an entity's balance sheet (statement of financial position) when it is probable that the future economic benefits associated with the asset will flow to the entity and the entity can place a reliable value on the asset. *Contingent assets* are never recognised in an entity's balance sheet, but where these are material the directors should consider making appropriate disclosures in the notes to the financial statements.

A *liability* is recognised when three criteria have been met:

- the entity has an obligation at the end of the reporting period as a result of a past event;
- it is probable that the entity will be required to transfer resources embodying economic benefits in settlement; and
- the settlement amount can be measured reliably.

Like with *contingent assets*, a *contingent liability* is never recognised in the financial statements because such liabilities fail to meet the recognition criteria. Instead, such contingent liabilities may need to be disclosed in the notes to the financial statements where the directors consider these to be material.

Income is recognised in the statement of comprehensive income (or income statement, if presented) when an increase in future economic benefits related to an increase in an asset, or the decrease of a liability has arisen and the amount of the income can be measured reliably.

Expenses are recognised in the entity's income statement when a decrease in future economic benefits related to a decrease in an asset or the increase in a liability has arisen and the amount of the expense can be measured reliably.

After initial recognition, the entity needs to consider how the transaction is subsequently measured in the financial statements and there are generally two measurement principles:

- historical cost; and
- fair value.

Historical cost

5.5 Historical cost is the amount of cash or cash equivalents that an entity pays, or the fair value of the consideration given, to acquire assets at the time of acquisition. For liabilities, historical cost is the amount of proceeds or cash or cash equivalents received or the fair value of non-cash assets received in exchange for the obligation at the time the obligation is incurred. The phrase *amortised historical cost* refers to the historical cost of an asset or liability plus or minus that portion of its historical cost previously recognised as an expense or income.

Fair value

5.6 *Fair value* is the amount for which an asset could be exchanged, a liability settled or an equity instrument granted between knowledgeable and willing parties in an arm's length transaction.

FRS 102 places more emphasis on fair value accounting as this method of accounting has risen up the ranks over the years. Fair value is potentially more accurate than historical cost because obtaining fair values at specific intervals, or with sufficient regularity, will ensure that the carrying amounts of assets in the financial statements more truly reflect their current value.

Care must be taken when choosing an accounting policy of historical cost or fair value accounting. This is because if the fair value option is chosen, it is inherently very difficult to go back to historical cost. Reverting back to historical cost would be considered a change in accounting policy (and hence would be applied retrospectively in accordance with Section 10 *Accounting Policies, Estimates and Errors*) and a small company would only change an accounting policy if the revised policy resulted in more relevant and reliable information being produced in the general purpose financial statements. It is very difficult to justify that historical cost would result in the financial statements offering more relevant and reliable information than fair value and hence the switch to fair value accounting needs to be considered carefully as generally it is a one-way switch only and obtaining fair values for certain assets (eg buildings) can prove to be a costly exercise for some small entities.

Leasing transactions

5.7 Care must be taken where leasing transactions are concerned because the concept of substance over form is particularly relevant where these transactions are concerned. The complexities inherent in leasing transactions are looked at in more detail in **Chapter 6** and the accounting for such is considered in **Chapter 12**.

Focus

- Standard-setters around the world acknowledge that some leasing contracts are deliberately engineered so as to achieve a specific outcome and the issue of 'off-balance sheet finance' is a prevalent problem around the world. The problem with off-balance sheet finance is that it results in an inaccurate and incomparable picture of certain measures (such as 'return on assets'). Standard-setters try to combat the issue of off-balance sheet finance by trying to change accounting standards so as to reduce the scope for leases to be classed as an operating lease and hence force companies to recognise finance leases on the balance sheet. This is the case at the present time in IFRS whereby, at the time of writing, a new leasing standard is scheduled for issuance during the second half of 2015 which specifically targets off-balance sheet finance. While the UK's Financial Reporting Council has not intimated that the UK and Republic of Ireland equivalent Section 20 *Leases* will change, it is an issue that small companies need to be aware of and ensure that the substance of the lease is reported and not the legal form.

In a leasing transaction a lessee will enter into an agreement with a lessor to lease an asset for a specified period of time. Section 20 of FRS 102 works on the 'risks and rewards' basis which says that if the risks and rewards associated with the ownership of the asset pass from the lessor to the lessee then this indicates the lease is a finance lease. In a finance lease the leased asset is brought onto the balance sheet as an asset and a corresponding lease creditor is also recognised. This treatment recognises the 'substance' of the arrangement which is the lessee has acquired an asset for use in the business which will generate economic benefits and has acquired this asset through lease finance.

Where the risks and rewards of ownership of the asset remain with the lessor, then this arrangement will be indicative that the lease falls to be classed as an operating lease. Operating leases are inherently easier to account for because the lease payments are simply charged to profit or loss on an arising basis.

5.8 The example of a lease illustrates the concept of substance over form perfectly. In a finance lease, while legal title does not pass to the lessee at the inception of the lease, the substance of the arrangement is that an asset has essentially been acquired through a financing transaction (the lease). If small companies were to default to the legal title treatment, no finance lease would be recognised on the balance sheet and this is where some leasing arrangements have been deliberately engineered to achieve a desired outcome.

Focus

- Hire purchase agreements are often finance leases, whereas some contract hire arrangements will fall to be classed as operating leases. The key to achieving the correct outcome for companies is to carefully scrutinise the terms of the lease and assess whether the risks and rewards of ownership have passed from lessor to lessee or remained with the lessor. The accounting issues relating to leasing transactions are examined in more detail in **Chapter 12**.

DERECOGNISING ASSETS AND LIABILITIES

5.9 It is important that assets and liabilities are recorded in the financial statements when transactions meet the definitions of such assets and liabilities (as per the *Concepts and Pervasive Principles* in Section 2) and also that they are derecognised when it is no longer appropriate to recognise such assets and liabilities.

Derecognising an asset

5.10 In the broadest sense of the concept, an entity will derecognise an asset when it is no longer probable that economic benefits will flow to the entity, or it has sold the asset and all the risks and rewards of ownership have been passed to the new owner, or the contractual rights to the cash flows associated with a financial asset have been expired, discharged or cancelled.

Focus

- Where financial assets are concerned, it is important that the derecognition criteria in paragraph 11.33 of FRS 102 are complied with.

Assets can involve (among others):

- non-current (fixed) assets;
- financial assets;
- investment property;
- inventory (stock); and
- amounts owed to the entity.

In some cases it is fairly clear when the asset should be removed from an entity's balance sheet. In other cases (as with financial assets), more analysis work will be needed to ensure appropriate derecognition takes place.

Non-current (fixed assets)

5.11 A reporting entity will remove a non-current (fixed) asset from its balance sheet when it is no longer probable that economic benefits will flow to the entity from that fixed asset. Examples of circumstances where this could be the case are:

- the asset is no longer in working order and has been scrapped;
- the asset has been sold to a third party; and
- the asset has been exchanged for another asset in a transaction that possesses commercial substance.

When a fixed asset is removed from the books of a reporting entity, the net book value is compared to any sales proceeds received and the resulting surplus or deficit will be reported as a profit or loss on disposal of the fixed asset(s). As discussed in **Chapter 4**, it is important to make a distinction between gains and losses on disposal of such assets and revenue and expenses from the ordinary course of business. Ordinarily, a reporting entity would report any profit or loss on disposal of a fixed asset in profit or loss as a profit or loss on disposal as opposed to revenue or expense.

Example 5.1 – Disposal of a machine

Pilau Co Ltd has disposed of a machine in its manufacturing division during the year to 31 December 2016. On 31 December 2015 the machine had a carrying value in the financial statements of £36,000, made up of £60,000 cost £24,000 accumulated depreciation. The company's declared accounting policy in respect of depreciation is to charge a full year's depreciation in the year a fixed asset is acquired, with no depreciation being charged in the year of disposal. The machine was sold on 31 March 2016 for £40,000 to an unconnected third party.

As the company's depreciation policy is to charge a full year's depreciation charge in the year of acquisition and no depreciation in the year of disposal, the carrying value of £36,000 will be compared to the sales proceeds (£40,000) and this will result in a profit on disposal of the machine of £4,000. The journals to remove the machine from the books of Pilau Co Ltd will be as follows:

To remove the net book value at the date of disposal

DR plant and machinery disposal account (P&L)	£60,000
CR plant and machinery disposal cost (balance sheet)	(£60,000)

Being removal of original cost

DR plant and machinery eliminated depreciation (balance sheet)	£24,000
CR plant and machinery disposal account (P&L)	(£24,000)

Being removal of accumulated depreciation on the machine

DR bank	£40,000
CR plant and machinery disposal account (P&L)	(£40,000)

Being sales proceeds on machine disposal

The disposal account will show a £4,000 credit balance on the trial balance after these entries representing the cost credited (£60,000), the eliminated depreciation charge debited (£24,000) and the sales proceeds credited (£40,000). This profit may be reported in cost of sales as disposal of manufacturing plant, or the company may choose to show it within administrative expenses. In any case the profit on disposal (and the disposal proceeds) must not be categorised as turnover.

Financial assets

5.12 Financial assets can encompass a number of things including long-term investments in equity shares and long-term loans. Extensive guidance is included in Section 11 *Basic Financial Instruments* which also outlines some examples of financial assets.

A reporting entity can only derecognise a financial asset when the following criteria are met:

- the contractual rights to the cash flows from the financial asset expire or are settled; or
- the entity transfers to another party substantially all of the risks and rewards of ownership of the financial asset; or
- the entity, despite having retained some significant risks and rewards of ownership, has transferred control of the asset to another party and the other party has the practical ability to sell the asset in its entirety to an unrelated third party and is able to exercise that ability unilaterally and without needing to impose additional restrictions on the transfer. In this case, the entity shall:
  - — derecognise the asset; and
  - — recognise separately any rights and obligations retained or created in the transfer.

Example 5.2 – Sales ledger sold to a finance house

Bury Enterprises Ltd (Bury) has recently seen a decline in activity during the last couple of years which has been largely due to a downturn in the market. Despite the company's sales volumes and related profits experiencing a decline, the company's sales ledger has increased in size as its customers are demanding longer terms of credit as they, themselves, are waiting on payment from their customers.

On 2 January 2016 Bury completed the sale of its sales ledger to the bank. The proceeds received from the bank were less than the fair value of the debtors, but gave Bury access to immediate working capital to help it continue in the difficult period. Whilst Bury has sold the ledger onto the bank it still continues to collect monies in from the customers and send out monthly statements. To recompense Bury for this service, the bank pays them a monthly service charge which is at market rate. Bury must remit all monies received from customers to the bank immediately and there is no recourse on Bury if any of the customers are late in paying their debts or if they are unable to pay due to cash flow difficulties or liquidation.

In this example Bury has transferred all the risks and rewards associated with the sales ledger to the bank. The terms of the agreement make no recourse to Bury in the event a customer is slow in making paying or fails to make payment and the debt is subsequently written off.

As the risks and rewards have been transferred, Bury must remove all the debtors from its balance sheet and recognise a loss on derecognition of these balances which is calculated as the fair value of the proceeds received by the bank less the carrying value of the debtors at the time of the sale (2 January 2016).

The proceeds received from the bank are not recognised as a liability in the balance sheet. Bury will only recognise a liability to the extent that it has received monies in from the customers but which have not yet been remitted to the bank.

In the above example, the risks and rewards had been transferred from Bury to the bank and hence the financial asset (the receivables ledger) qualified for derecognition. In some cases it may not be as clear cut that the risks and rewards of ownership have been transferred.

Example 5.3 – Sales ledger sold to a finance house

The facts are the same as in the example above. However, this time Bury has agreed to buy back any customer debts which are in arrears for more than 90 days.

In this example, Bury has retained a significant risk which is the risk that customers may be slow in making payment or may not pay at all.

Bury will not derecognise the trade receivables in this respect and they will continue to be reported on the balance sheet. The proceeds from the bank will be recognised as a loan which is secured by the receivables. Receivables will continue to be recognised as assets until they are collected or they have been written off due to uncollectibility.

Investment property

5.13 Investment property is dealt with in Section 16 *Investment Property* in FRS 102. An entity will derecognise investment property when the property itself has been sold or transferred (with the risks and rewards of ownership also being transferred). In addition, investment property may need to be derecognised as such and **reclassified** as owner-occupied property in the following situations:

- when a reliable measure of fair value is no longer available without undue cost or effort on the part of the reporting entity; or
- when the investment property no longer meets the definition of an investment property.

Where a reliable measure of fair value is no longer available, investment property is derecognised and recognised as owner-occupied property, plant and equipment and hence accounted for in accordance with Section 17 *Property, Plant and Equipment* until a reliable measure of fair value becomes available. On the date that it is reclassified, the carrying value is treated as deemed cost going forward.

Focus

- When investment property is reclassified as property, plant and equipment, it is not a change in accounting policy, but instead is a change in circumstances. Paragraph 16.10(e)(iii) requires disclosure of transfers to property, plant and equipment when a reliable measure of fair value is no longer available without undue cost or effort. For small companies reporting under FRS 102, this is not a mandatory disclosure, but the directors would need to consider making this disclosure in order that the financial statements give a true and fair view (**Chapter 6** examines the application of disclosure requirements to achieve a true and fair view in more detail).

Inventory (stock)

5.14 Essentially this links into the revenue recognition section (see next section). The risks and rewards concept which was illustrated above in the sales ledger examples also applies to items of inventory (hereon in referred to as 'stock'). In the order of current assets in the balance sheet, stock is the least liquid asset because the theory is that the stock will be sold, it will then turn into a debtor (a receivable) which will then eventually be paid and turn into cash in the bank.

Assets such as stock are derecognised when the risks and rewards of ownership of the stock have passed to the buying customer. This is also covered by the revenue recognition section in Section 23 *Revenue* which outlines the procedures for recognising revenue within the financial statements.

Stock can also be derecognised (or partly derecognised) through an allowance account (ie a provision). Section 13 *Inventories* requires stock to be valued at the lower of cost and estimated selling price less costs to complete and sell (the new term in FRS 102 for 'net realisable value').

Where the estimated selling price less costs to complete and sell is lower than cost, a write-down will be required. In some cases the write-down of the stock will be its entire cost because the estimated selling price less costs to complete and sell will be nil. However, this is only done where there is evidence that such stock has an estimated selling price less costs to complete and sell of nil.

Example 5.4 – Stock write-down

Cory Computers Ltd manufactures laptop computers. During the year to 31 December 2016, the company manufactured a batch of computers which cost £8,000 to make, but on final testing before being available for sale it was discovered that the computers did not work. Upon investigation it was found that this batch of computer equipment was faulty due to a faulty mechanism within the machines themselves and this particular type of computer has been withdrawn from the market by the directors and further stock will not be sold. The computer equipment was scrapped on 16 January 2017 and did not have any scrap value.

In this case the assets costing £8,000 will be derecognised from the inventory and recognised at estimated selling price less costs to complete and sell of £nil to comply with the principles in Section 13.

Amounts owed to the entity

5.15 Amounts owed to the entity can be in respect of trade debtors (trade receivables) or other debtors, such as loans to employees or recoverable taxes.

Debtors (whether trade or other) essentially constitute a financial instrument and the same provisions for derecognising a financial asset will equally apply.

Amounts owed to an entity in respect of receivables are derecognised when the contractual rights to the cash flows from the financial asset expire or are settled. It follows, therefore, that a trade debtor is derecognised when the customer pays or when the amounts are written off.

Derecognising a liability

5.16 The general rule in FRS 102 is that a reporting entity will derecognise a financial liability (or part thereof) only when it is extinguished. The term 'extinguished' means when the obligation giving rise to the liability is discharged, cancelled or expires.

Liabilities generally include (among other things):

- amounts owed to suppliers and other creditors;
- amounts owed in respect of loans and other financing agreements.

Amounts owed to suppliers and other creditors

5.17 In practice, a financial liability in respect of suppliers and other creditors is derecognised when the entity pays that (other) creditor. This usually happens as a matter of course, but there may be other situations which give rise to a financial liability being derecognised, such as where the obligation is cancelled or expires.

Example 5.5 – Entity wins a legal dispute

In the year to 31 December 2016, Heyes Haulage Co Ltd (Heyes) was taken to court by a member of the public claiming personal injury and loss of earnings in respect of one of Heyes' drivers who was alleged to have caused damage to the person's motor vehicle on a busy motorway. The vehicle that was damaged was written off by the insurers and the injured person is also claiming damages for injuries sustained by Heyes' lorry. The driver of the lorry has always maintained that the damage and the injuries were caused by the driver himself.

At 31 December 2016 Heyes' lawyers advised that it was probable that the company would be found guilty and hence the accountant made a provision for costs and damages in the sum of £35,000. However, CCTV footage has emerged showing that the claimant was driving dangerously and erratically and it was subsequently found that the claimant caused the crash in which his vehicle was written off. The judge found in favour of Heyes.

The financial liability that has been recognised in the accounts (the provision for costs and damages) should be removed from the books because it has now been cancelled.

Amounts owed in respect of loan and other financing agreements

5.18 Generally, liabilities in respect of loans and other financing agreements are derecognised from the financial statements when they are settled. This can occur over time (eg when the company is making instalments) or it can happen at a specific point in time (eg a creditor may agree to write off any remaining loan balance).

Example 5.6 – Company completes a company voluntary arrangement

Five years ago, a company entered into a voluntary arrangement with its creditors because it had run into cash flow difficulties due to the recession. It had lost a number of contracts and the majority of creditors agreed to the arrangement.

The company has now successfully completed the arrangement and has paid all the creditors in accordance with the formal company voluntary arrangement (CVA). The accountant is unsure what accounting entries to make in respect of the balance which has been agreed to be waived by the creditors.

Amounts should only be written off in a CVA when the CVA itself has been successfully completed (not before). Therefore in a successful CVA, the company's obligations in relation to the remaining balance which has been waived by the creditors has been cancelled and hence the entries would be:

DR creditors

CR profit or loss (usually as an exceptional item)

Other loans and financing arrangements can be discharged by the holder of the financial instrument if provisions exist in the loan agreements, such as where 'convertible debt' is concerned.

Example 5.7 – Convertible debt

On 1 January 2012 a company borrowed £20,000 from a third party. The terms of the loan agreement said that a market rate of interest is payable annually and that on maturity, the loan note holder has the option to convert the remaining principal amount into shares, rather than demand repayment, at the discretion of the loan note holder. The loan matures on 31 December 2016.

On 31 December 2016, the company's cash balance was fairly restricted due to money being tied up in inventory and in debtors. In addition, the company was also undergoing an asset replacement cycle by replacing all plant used in the manufacturing process so as to increase market share.

The loan note holder has exercised the option to convert the principal amount of £20,000 into shares of the company as she has recognised that the company's long-term plans are looking very healthy.

On 31 December 2016, the financial liability (the loan note) will be derecognised and will be reallocated to equity to recognise the additional shares which are now owned by the loan note holder. This is an example of a financial liability being discharged in forms other than cash.

REVENUE RECOGNITION

5.19 At the time of writing, revenue recognition had been in the headlines a lot over in 2014/15 and readers might be aware of the puzzlement that the supermarket chain, Tesco, could, at one stage, have revenues sailing comfortably into profit and loss and then it seems there has been a re-think as to how revenue has been booked. Revenue recognition has always been a contentious issue within the accountancy profession because previously in UK GAAP there has not been any specific standards on the subject (despite revenue often being the headline figure in financial statements – particularly small company financial statements). The FRSSE (effective January 2015) dealt with revenue recognition in Section 4 *Revenue recognition* and gave guidance on the basic principles of revenue recognition as well as the principles involved in recognising revenue from the sale of goods and revenue from the rendering of services and construction contracts.

Previous UK GAAP used terminology such as a *'right to consideration'* through its *'performance'*. The overarching objective of the FRSSE (effective January 2015) was to specify that a small entity is to recognise revenue at the point it receives the right to consideration because contractual obligations (or some of the contractual obligations) have been fulfilled. Revenue was therefore recognised in cases where invoices had not yet been raised and this principle is carried over into FRS 102 for small entities. Revenue recognition issues are examined further in **Chapter 12**.

5.20 While FRS 102 does not use the terminology 'right to consideration' anywhere within Section 23, the concept itself is still relevant because the financial statements of a small company must still report the substance of transactions and revenue recognition always lends itself to subjectivity where this issue is concerned.

FRS 102 is, itself, based on IFRS and it requires preparers of general purpose financial statements to consider the economic substance of a sale agreement in determining whether, or not, a sale has occurred. In many cases this is fairly clear cut, but in other cases it might not be so apparent (especially in complex construction contracts). The term 'economic substance' refers to the commercial reality of a transaction and this can be illustrated as follows:

Example 5.8 – Commercial substance

Victor's Vehicles (Victor) has a fleet of prestigious vehicles which can be sold to members of the public and are held in the stock of Victor. Due to cash flow difficulties, it has approached a third party who has agreed to buy these prestigious vehicles for cash and Victor will repurchase this inventory back from the third party in six months' time at a premium which will compensate the third party for the time value of money.

On the face of it, the sale of the vehicles to the third party and the purchase of these vehicles from Victor may be deemed to be two separate transactions where Victor will recognise the sale of the inventory as such and the subsequent repurchase in six months' time. However, the financial statements have to reflect the commercial substance of the arrangement and the economic reality in this transaction is that no sale has, in fact, occurred but instead a financing arrangement has been entered into by Victor with the third party. Victor has obtained a loan from the third party and the security of this loan is the fleet of prestigious vehicles.

Therefore, no sale is recognised, but Victor will recognise a creditor (a payable) for the loan obtained which will be derecognised when repayment is made to the third party. The excess over the loan amount received and the amount repaid back to the third party which represents the compensation for the time value of money will be recognised in Victor's profit and loss account (income statement) as an interest expense.

The example above highlighted a key issue where the substance of transactions is concerned and any such contract between a small company and a third party should be carefully scrutinised so as to ensure that the financial statements report the economic substance of the transaction. Clearly, if the loan proceeds were inadvertently recognised as turnover there would be a whole host of complications, notwithstanding the excessive corporation tax which would essentially be payable by recognising the loan proceeds incorrectly as turnover.

5.21 Revenue recognition has inherently involved a lot of professional judgement and the more complex and diverse an entity's operations, the more judgement is required. UK GAAP has always adopted a principles-based approach and small companies reporting under FRS 102 will welcome the additional guidance which Section 23 in FRS 102 brings. However, there is still an element of professional judgement required by preparers who must consider whether the risks and rewards inherent in the good(s) or service(s) have been transferred from the reporting entity to its customer. Where this has taken place then a sale can be recognised.

LINKED PRESENTATION FOR CERTAIN NON-RECOURSE FINANCE ARRANGEMENTS

5.22 Under previous GAAP, where a small company had, for example, entered into a debt factoring arrangement with a bank or a finance house, FRS 5 *Reporting the substance of transactions* permitted a linked presentation which effectively showed the finance on the face of the balance sheet (statement of financial position) as a deduction from the gross amount of the item which it financed.

5.23 Linked presentation is not permitted under FRS 102 principles and therefore small companies will have to recognise the assets in their entirety, together with the associated liabilities on a gross basis.

PITFALLS TO AVOID

- Inappropriate recognition of assets on the balance sheet, without having regard to the definition of an asset and the recognition criteria outlined in Section 2 *Concepts and Pervasive Principles* of FRS 102 and FRS 105 *The Financial Reporting Standard applicable to the Micro-entities Regime*.
- Inappropriately derecognising assets and liabilities (particularly financial assets and financial liabilities).
- Disproportionately delaying or accelerating revenue to achieve a desired outcome.
- Including linked-presentation for certain non-recourse finance arrangements despite FRS 102 not recognising such a concept.

CHAPTER SUMMARY

- An asset can only be recognised on the balance sheet when it is probable that future economic benefits will flow to the entity and a reliable measure of the asset's price can be obtained.
- Liabilities can arise through a legal or a constructive obligation. A constructive obligation arises through an entity's past practices or published policies.
- After initial recognition a transaction can be measured under historical cost or fair value models.
- Leasing transactions pose particular problems for reporting entities as they need to be correctly classified between a finance or an operating lease depending on which party bears the risks and rewards of ownership. The accounting treatment for both of these types of leases is considerably different and the accounting for such leases is considered in more detail in **Chapter 12**.

- A financial asset can only be derecognised when certain criterion have been met; whereas a financial liability is derecognised when the obligation has been discharged, cancelled or expired.
- Revenue should be recognised when the small entity has fulfilled its obligations within a contract and this can occur prior to an invoice being raised so care needs to be taken to correctly recognise revenue at the time that a right to consideration arises.
- Linked presentation for certain non-recourse transactions is not permitted in FRS 102 and small companies will have to recognise the assets in their entirety together with the associated liabilities on a gross basis.

Chapter 6

Contentious Areas of the Financial Statements

SIGNPOSTS

- There are key areas of the financial statements which can lend themselves to contention or involve a large degree of professional judgement (see **6.1**).
- Small companies (not micro-entities) must apply the full recognition and measurement principles of FRS 102 *The Financial Reporting Standard applicable in the UK and Republic of Ireland* (see **6.2**).
- Leasing transactions are the most problematic transaction which cause 'off balance sheet finance' (see **6.3**).
- A finance lease must be recognised on the balance sheet (statement of financial position) to recognise the substance of the transaction, not the legal form of the leasing agreement (see **6.4**).
- There is no 90% benchmark prescribed in Section 20 *Leases* of FRS 102, but eight indicators that a lease is a finance lease (see **6.5**).
- Where the present value of the minimum lease payments are *lower* than the fair value of the leased asset under Section 20, the lease is recognised at the present value of the minimum lease payments determined at the start of the lease (see **6.6**).
- Leases which are not finance leases are accounted for as operating leases (see **6.7**).
- Where financial instruments are concerned, FRS 102 splits these into 'basic' instruments and 'complex' instruments (see **6.8**).
- A basic financial instrument is generally accounted for using the 'amortised cost' method and the 'effective interest' method (see **6.9**).
- Section 12 *Other Financial Instruments Issues* deals with instruments such as options, swaps, forward contracts, financial instruments that qualify, and are designated, as hedging instruments and loans with complex features (see **6.10**).
- Financial instruments accounted for in accordance with Section 12 will (with limited exceptions) be carried at fair value with changes in fair value going through profit or loss (see **6.11**).

- Most transactions which are recorded in small company financial statements will have a tax consequence. The timing of these taxation impacts needs to be considered and the accounting entries necessary in terms of deferred tax (see **6.12**).
- There are three additional situations under FRS 102 principles which now require deferred tax to be calculated (see **6.13**).
- While accounting standards only deal with material items, care must be taken when considering whether an item is immaterial when combined with other items considered to be immaterial (see **6.14**).
- Deferred tax assets are commonly recognised when the company has unutilised tax losses but care must be taken to ensure sufficient taxable profit can be generated in the future to offset the deferred tax asset (see **6.15**).
- Micro-entities do not have to account for deferred tax (see **6.16**).
- Section 28 *Employee Benefits* deals with two types of post-employment benefit plan (see **6.17**).
- Defined contribution pension plans are not recognised on the balance sheet (statement of financial position) of a small company (see **6.18**).
- Defined benefit pension plans are recognised on the balance sheet (statement of financial position) (see **6.19**).
- Where actuarial information is concerned, Section 28 is less onerous than previous UK GAAP (see **6.20**).
- Revenue recognition policies have been the subject of extreme controversy over recent years by introducing a 'right of consideration' model which remains under new UK GAAP (see **6.21**).
- The wording in Section 23 *Revenue* is not as explicit as was the case under previous UK GAAP and preparers must ensure appropriate recognition of revenue to avoid further contentious issues (see **6.22**).
- Disclosure levels are significantly reduced under the new Companies Act 2006 due to the introduction of the EU Accounting Directive (see **6.23**).
- There are only 13 legally required disclosures but directors of small companies have a legal duty to ensure the financial statements give a true and fair view (see **6.24** and **6.25**).
- Preparers of small company financial statements should take an objective look at the financial statements to ensure they do, in fact, achieve a true and fair view (see **6.26**).

INTRODUCTION

6.1 Certain areas in the financial statements lend themselves to a degree of subjectivity and hence professional judgement will need to be applied in arriving at amounts (and, where applicable, related disclosures) to include within the financial statements.

Some of the amounts contained in the financial statements are not an exact science; in other words they are not stated 'to the penny'. This is because of the need to estimate certain figures (for example work in progress balances at the year-end) and even where 'best estimates' are concerned, these will always be a 'ballpark' amount. Accounting issues for micro-entities are examined in detail in **Chapter 11**.

> **Focus**
>
> - It is not absolutely categorical where contentious issues in the financial statements lie; and this chapter covers some which are likely to prove difficult in real-life for small companies. Different entities will encounter various types of difficulty depending on the industry it operates in. For example, a further education provider may encounter complexities in ensuring holiday pay accruals are picked up correctly. The way to avoid 'issues' where difficult or problematic areas are concerned is to pay particular attention to documentation because relatively subtle changes in contracts or commitments could make the accounting more straightforward.

Difficulties arise where accounting estimates are concerned and in the interpretation of the substance of transactions. This chapter looks at some of the most common contentious areas of the financial statements and how professional accountants should deal with such issues. The accounting aspects relating to the areas covered below are also found in **Chapter 12**. Areas which invariably involve professional judgement include:

- classification of leasing transactions;
- financial instruments;
- deferred taxation;
- post-employment benefit plans; and
- revenue recognition.

Focus

- The concept of materiality has to be of relevance in financial reporting. Accounting standards only deal with material issues. However, an important point to emphasise is that while a monetary amount may, on the face of it, be immaterial in isolation, the amount may become material when aggregated with other amounts that are considered to be immaterial in isolation. In addition, it is important to emphasise that FRS 102 does not permit immaterial items to be ignored so as to achieve a desired outcome. Items can be material in monetary terms as well as being material in nature.

6.2 For small (not micro) entities, the full recognition and measurement principles of FRS 102 will apply. Micro-entities will follow the provisions in FRS 105 *The Financial Reporting Standard applicable to the Micro-entities Regime* and this is examined in detail in **Chapter 11**. FRS 102 is a principles-based financial reporting framework which involves a lot more professional judgement than previous UK GAAP. Practical problems inherent with subjective areas are accentuated by the fact that more judgement is required by the directors in preparing the financial statements under FRS 102 principles. In the event of any confusion it is always advisable to seek advice because matters concerning the treatments prescribed in FRS 102 can be interpreted differently among preparers.

Leasing transactions

6.3 Although there are many commercial reasons why it makes sense for a company to lease assets (and for smaller company it may be particularly suitable to lease rather than buy to delay cash outflows), leasing transactions have long since been problematic within the profession; not only for practitioners themselves, but also for regulators. The main problem is the classification between a finance lease which is recognised on the balance sheet (statement of financial position) and an operating lease (which is not recognised on the balance sheet, lease rentals are simply charged to profit or loss).

The Glossary to FRS 102 defines a *finance lease* as:

> 'A **lease** that transfers substantially all the risks and rewards incidental to ownership of an **asset**. Title may or may not eventually be transferred. A lease that is not a finance lease is an operating lease.'[1]

It also defines an *operating lease* as:

> 'A **lease** that does not transfer substantially all the risks and rewards incidental to ownership. A lease that is not an operating lease is a **finance lease**.'

1 Glossary to FRS 102.

Focus

- Standard-setters around the world have always looked unfavourably at the concept of 'off-balance sheet finance' which is where assets and liabilities are purposefully kept off the balance sheet. In some cases assets remain off the balance sheet for genuine reasons (ie because the lease is a genuine operating lease). However, in some cases, lease agreements have been deliberately engineered to achieve a desired outcome.
- This has been tackled by the International Accounting Standards Board who plan to issue a revised lease accounting standard during the second half of 2015. In the broadest terms, companies reporting under IFRS will report all leases on the balance sheet, unless the lease is a short-term lease (ie one with less than 12 months to run) or is a lease for small types of assets (eg computers). In the future, UK GAAP might also follow the same stance as the international standard-setters, although at the time of writing, the Financial Reporting Council has not intimated that it intends to follow such a course.

6.4 It is more complex to account for a finance lease than it is accounting for an operating lease. However, in recognition of the fact that a set of general purpose financial statements prepared under FRS 102 principles must report the **substance** of an arrangement rather than a transaction's **legal form**, it follows that where the *risks* and *rewards* associated with the ownership of the asset pass from the lessor to the lessee then, in substance, the lessee has acquired an asset which it has acquired through a financing transaction (ie the lease contract). It is for this reason that a finance lease is reported on a small company's balance sheet. If legal form were to be followed, finance leases would not appear on a company's balance sheet.

6.5 The Glossary to the previous FRSSE (effective January 2015) contained a 90% 'bright line test'. This bright line test was where the minimum lease payments (ie the unavoidable payments inherent in the lease) equated to 90% or more of the fair value of the asset subjected to the lease and where this was the case, the lease was accordingly treated as a finance lease. Mainstream UK GAAP that time at SSAP 21 *Accounting for hire purchase and lease contracts* did accept that there may be situations where, although the 90% test applied, the lease should not be treated as a finance lease; although it also indicated that this was only likely to arise 'in exceptional circumstances'.

Section 20 *Leases* of FRS 102 does not contain a 90% threshold. Instead, the section offers eight situations that a lease is, in fact a finance lease which are as follows:

- The lease transfers ownership of the asset to the lessee at the end of the lease term.
- The lessee has the option to purchase the asset at a price that is expected to be sufficiently lower than fair value at the date the option becomes

exercisable for it to be reasonably certain, at the inception of the lease, that the option will be exercised.

- The lease term is for the major part of the economic life of the asset, even if title is not transferred.
- At the inception of the lease the present value of the minimum lease payments amounts to at least substantially all of the fair value of the leased asset.
- The leased assets are of such a specialised nature that only the lessee can use them without major modifications.
- If the lessee can cancel the lease, the lessor's losses associated with the cancellations are borne by the lessee.
- Gains or losses from the fluctuations in the residual value of the leased asset accrue to the lessee (eg in the form of a rent rebate equalling most of the sales proceeds at the end of the lease).
- The lessee has the ability to continue the lease for a secondary period at a rent that is substantially lower than market rent (sometimes referred to as a 'peppercorn rent').

Finance leases: accounting treatment

6.6 Where any of the above indicators in **6.5** are met, Section 20 would require the lease to be classified as a finance lease. Lessees will recognise an asset and a corresponding lease creditor in the balance sheet (statement of financial position) at amounts which are equal to the fair value of the leased asset. However, where the present value of the minimum lease payments are *lower* than the fair value of the leased asset, the lease shall be recognised at the present value of the minimum lease payments determined at the start of the lease.

A lessor recognises assets held under a finance lease as a receivable (a debtor) at an amount that is equal to the 'net investment in the lease'. The 'net investment in the lease' is the *gross* investment which is then discounted at the interest rate implicit in the lease. **Chapter 12** examines the accounting treatments in more detail.

Focus

- Hire purchase contracts of a financing nature should be accounted for in the same way as a finance lease.

Operating leases: accounting treatment

6.7 Leases which are not finance leases are accounted for as operating leases. The lessee will recognise the operating lease rentals in profit or loss on an arising basis. Lease incentives will be recognised as a reduction to the expense charged to profit or loss over the term of the lease on a straight-line basis, unless another systematic basis is representative of the time pattern of the lessee's benefit from the use of the leased asset (**Chapter 12** looks at lease incentives in more detail).

Lessors recognise assets subjected to operating leases as non-current assets (fixed assets) depending on the nature of the asset. Income from the asset is recognised in the lessor's profit and loss account on a straight-line basis over the lease term, unless another systematic basis is appropriate, or the payments to the lessor are structured so that they increase in line with expected general inflation.

Financial instruments

6.8 Accounting for financial instruments under FRS 102 is unfortunately more complex because of the methods involved. All companies will have some form of financial instrument in existence; for example:

- share capital;
- trade debtors and trade creditors;
- directors' loans; and
- bank/cash balances.

Such 'basic' financial instruments are dealt with in Section 11 *Basic Financial Instruments*. More complicated financial instruments (such as derivative instruments and loans with complex features) are dealt with in Section 12 *Other Financial Instruments Issues*.

6.9 When a financial instrument falls to be classed as 'basic', it is generally measured at amortised cost (the amortised cost method and the effective interest method are considered in more detail in **Chapter 12**). Most trade debtors and creditors which are classed as current assets or current liabilities will be measured at the undiscounted amount of cash expected to be received or paid (as was the case under the previous small companies' regime).

Focus

- Basic trade debtors are accounted for in the same way that they were accounted for under previous UK GAAP – ie at undiscounted invoice price. However, care must be taken because if the transaction becomes a **financing transaction** (ie the entity agrees to defer payment which is beyond normal business terms, or it is financed at a rate of interest which is not a market rate) then it must be measured at the present value of the future payments which are discounted at a market rate of interest for a similar loan.

It is to be noted that micro-entities do not use the amortised cost method in FRS 105 as this is considered to be too onerous for such entities. Chapter 11 examines the accounting for financial instruments for micro-entities

6.10 'Other' financial instruments are essentially those financial instruments which are not basic and are accounted for under Section 12. Section 12 financial instruments include instruments such as:

- options;
- swaps;
- forward contracts;
- financial instruments that qualify, and are designated, as hedging instruments;
- loans with complex features.

Section 11.6(a) also refers to 'asset-backed securities' such as collateralised mortgage obligations, repurchase agreements and securitised packages of receivables. Whilst they are contained in the basic financial instruments chapter, they are not considered further in this book due to their specialised nature and application.

6.11 Section 12 requires virtually all financial instruments which are not basic financial instruments to be measured at fair value at each reporting date and movements in fair value are taken to the entity's profit or loss. This would apply, for example, where the small company has investments in shares in a listed company. At each reporting date the investment will be carried at fair value and any gains or losses on fair value are taken to profit or loss as value adjustments. However, any fair value gains taken to profit or loss would not be distributable as a dividend to shareholders because the gain would not be a realised gain for the purposes of distributions.

In addition, Section 12 requires certain financial instruments to be recognised on a small company's balance sheet which previous UK GAAP (the FRSSE) did not, such as derivative instruments.

Focus

- A derivative financial instrument is an instrument which 'derives' its value from an underlying asset. A common derivative instrument entered into by a small company would be a forward foreign currency exchange contract. The derivative financial instrument within the foreign exchange contract will 'derive' its value from changes in the foreign exchange rate. On initial recognition the derivative is recognised at its fair value which is usually zero. Changes in this fair value (which are driven by changes in foreign exchange rates) are taken to profit or loss. A detailed example is contained in **Chapter 12.**

The challenges faced by small companies is accounting for a derivative instrument. This is because under previous UK GAAP they were not accounted for on the balance sheet of a small company until settlement.

Example 6.1 – Foreign exchange derivative

A company operates in the disposable clothing industry. In December 2015 the company ordered a new machine from a US supplier to manufacture certain types of disposable clothing for $750,000. Delivery was made at the beginning of March 2016 and settlement will take place in June 2017. It has entered into a forward foreign currency contract to purchase $1.5:£1 (ie $750,000 for £500,000 in June 2017). The company has a financial year-end of 31 March and on 31 March 2016 the rate had moved to $1:£1.

Under FRS 102 principles, the forward contract is recorded at fair value. On initial recognition the fair value is nil (which is usually the case with derivative instruments) but at 31 March 2016 it will have to be recorded on the balance sheet at fair value.

The derivative instrument 'derives' its value from the changes in foreign exchange rates and the fair value of the derivative instrument at the year-end is calculated as follows:

	£
Forward contract value	£500,000 ($750,000 @ $1.5:£1)
Closing rate of exchange	£750,000 ($750,000 @ $1:£1)
Fair value	£250,000 asset
The entries at 31 March 2016 will be:	
DR forward currency contract (asset)	£250,000
CR profit or loss	£250,000

Because of the forward contract, the company has the benefit of purchasing $750,000 for £500,000 due to the 'locked in' exchange rate. As exchange rates have moved to $1:£1 if it had not entered into the forward foreign currency it would have cost more to purchase the dollars at the year-end hence the derivative instrument is valued at an asset of £250,000 and this is reported as a gain in the profit and loss account.

Deferred tax

6.12 Small companies reporting under the scope of FRS 102 will have to account for deferred tax and this concept is examined in more detail in **Chapter 12**.

Most transactions and events which are recorded in small company financial statements have a tax consequence. The future tax consequences of transactions and events which have occurred by the reporting date cannot be avoided because whatever happens in the future, the small entity will have to pay less or more tax than it would have done if those transactions and events had not taken place. It is therefore necessary to recognise the tax effects of all income, expenditure, gains and losses, assets and liabilities in the same period which they are recognised in the financial statements themselves and not at the point in time that they form part of taxable profit. The method by which this is done is by way of deferred tax.

Timing difference 'plus' approach

6.13 Over the years, many in the profession have argued against the concept of deferred tax; but inherently the concept is a 'matching' concept to match the tax effects with the transactions that have given rise to those tax effects.

The contentious issue which arises in deferred tax is that it becomes more onerous under the provisions of FRS 102 and **Chapter 12** examines the concept of current and deferred tax in more detail. FRS 102 is based on IFRS principles and under IAS 12 *Income Taxes*, deferred tax is calculated using the 'temporary difference' approach which focuses on the value at which assets and liabilities are received and paid in comparison to their tax written down values (tax base); whereas the timing difference approach focuses on the inherent differences between accounting profit/loss and taxable profit/loss, hence focuses on profit and loss.

The 'plus' part essentially removes some of the exemptions from deferred tax which were found in previous UK GAAP, notably:

- Revaluations of non-monetary assets subjected to the revaluation model.
- Fair values in business combinations.
- Unremitted earnings in overseas subsidiaries and associates.

As a consequence, more transactions and events will give rise to deferred tax considerations under FRS 102. However, the calculations of deferred tax balances under the timing difference plus approach will not be too dissimilar than what would have been calculated under the temporary difference approach.

> **Focus**
>
> - Deferred tax under FRS 102 must always be recognised gross; it is prohibited to discount deferred tax balances to present day values under FRS 102 (discounting was allowed under previous UK GAAP). In reality, few small companies discounted deferred tax balances to present day values and hence this prohibition is going to go largely unnoticed, but some entities do have a policy of discounting deferred tax balances and hence on transition, they will need to gross them back up with the discounting portion taken to profit and loss reserves as a transitional adjustment at the date of transition and then do a comparative year adjustment also.

6.14 Accounting standards only deal with material items and hence it follows that if deferred tax is immaterial, then the entity does not need to account for it in the financial statements. Care must be taken, however, where materiality issues are concerned because something that is immaterial in isolation may not be material when aggregated with other items that are also considered immaterial in isolation.

> **Focus**
>
> - Professional bodies have been known to criticise financial statements for appearing to ignore the concept of deferred tax. As mentioned in **6.14** above, while immaterial amounts of deferred tax do not need to be accounted for within the financial statements, it is the fact that some practitioners and company accountants fail to consider deferred tax requirements that regulators are concerned with. Having a working paper on file to demonstrate that deferred tax has been considered would suffice and this would also help the practitioner in forming a conclusion as to whether the deferred tax balance is immaterial (and hence does not need to be accounted for) which will need professional judgement exercising in the light of other misstatements/balances which are also considered immaterial.

Deferred tax assets

6.15 Deferred tax assets have always been a contentious issue, mainly because of the restrictive approach accounting standards take when it comes to recognising deferred tax assets and (in some instances) the directors' desire to reduce the impact of losses on the year-end financial statements to appease shareholders or creditors.

As discussed in further detail in **Chapter 12**, there are various situations which can give rise to (potential) deferred tax assets being recognised and over recent years the most familiar situation has been unutilised tax losses which are carried forward to future accounting periods and offset against taxable profit. This is effectively a 'tax reducer' as it reduces the amount of corporation tax that an entity would otherwise pay had the tax losses not existed.

Accounting standards are restrictive when it comes to recognising such deferred tax assets because assets cannot be carried in the financial statements at any more than recoverable amount. This is why care must be taken prior to recognising any deferred tax assets in the financial statements because Section 29 says that the very existence of unrelieved tax losses is strong evidence that there may not be other future taxable profits against which the losses will be relieved.

Focus

- Where potential deferred tax assets are concerned, the entity must have convincing evidence that future taxable profits will be yielded against which unrelieved tax losses can be offset. This can, for example, be evidence that the company has been awarded a lucrative contract in the succeeding financial year which will generate profit or a healthy order book. In any case, the company should not simply recognise a deferred tax asset because it has got unutilised tax losses without evidence that such an asset will be utilised. This is to ensure that assets are not carried in the balance sheet (statement of financial position) at any more than recoverable amount.

6.16 It is worth pointing out that micro-entities reporting under FRS 105 *The Financial Reporting Standard applicable to the Micro-entities Regime* are exempt from the requirement to account for deferred taxes of any kind in the financial statements.

Post-employment benefit plans

6.17 The Glossary to FRS 102 defines a *post-employment benefit plan* as:

> '**Employee benefits** (other than **termination benefits** and short-term employee benefits) that are payable after the completion of employment.'[2]

Section 28 *Employee Benefits* deals with the issue concerning post-employment benefit plans and these are examined in more detail in **Chapter 12**. There are two types of post-employment benefit plans which are dealt with in Section 28:

- defined contribution plans; and
- defined benefit plans.

6.18 A defined contribution plan is a plan where post-employment benefits are defined by the value of contributions paid into the plan. The company

2 FRS 102 Glossary **Post-employment benefit plans**.

does not have any legal obligation to pay additional contributions into the plan if the plan does not have sufficient assets available to meet post-employment obligations to its members. This is because, in substance, actuarial risk and investment risk is not borne by the company and as a result, the value of any surplus or deficit in the plan itself is not recognised on the company's balance sheet (statement of financial position). The only effect that the plan has on the company's financial statements is the value of the pension charge for the year in the profit and loss account.

6.19 Defined benefit plans, on the other hand, are a contentious issue among companies – especially over the last couple of decades because in many cases defined benefit plans are in deficit; in other words the value of the plan's obligations exceeds the value of the assets in the plan.

The contention is accentuated by the fact that in a defined benefit plan, actuarial risk and investment risk do, in substance, fall on the part of the reporting entity. As a result, not only does the company have a legal obligation to make additional contributions in situations where the assets of a plan are insufficient to meet the plan's obligations to its members, but it also has to report the value of the pension plan on the balance sheet. In some cases the value of a defined benefit plan can run into millions of pounds of deficits and this is clearly a situation which concerns directors of small companies that operate such plans. It is for this reason that many defined benefit pension plans are closed to new members, but they were (and still are) an attractive benefit to employees that are covered by them because the value of post-employment benefits are based on the employees' salary at the retirement date (hence they are frequently referred to as 'final salary schemes').

6.20 Actuarial information is needed so that the entity can properly account for the movements in the defined benefit plan's assets and liabilities as well as make the relevant disclosures. Section 28 is less onerous than previous FRS 17 *Retirement Benefits* and the FRSSE and does not require an entity to engage an independent actuary to perform the comprehensive actuarial valuation. Nor does Section 28 require annual comprehensive valuations to be done. In instances where a small company does not get an annual valuation (as the principal actuarial assumptions have not significantly changed), the defined benefit obligation can be calculated by adjusting the prior period measurement for changes in employee demographics, for example the number of employees and salary levels.

Focus

- While Section 28 does not mandate the entity to engage the services of an independent actuary, actuarial information would be needed to ensure correct figures are included in the financial statements and to ensure that the net pension asset/liability is also carried at an appropriate value in the balance sheet (statement of financial position).

Revenue recognition

6.21 Revenue recognition is examined in **Chapter 5** and **Chapter 12**.

Revenue recognition policies have always had an element of controversy surrounding them, and this has become increasingly the case as the whole notion of revenue has become more complex in the current commercial environment where, even for small companies, packages and deals often obscure clear determination of what, and when, revenue can be accounted for. Under previous UK GAAP, revenue recognition did not have a specific standard and on 10 March 2005, the controversial UITF 40 *Revenue Recognition and Service Contracts* was issued. There was an element of outcry in the profession when this Abstract was issued by the (now defunct) Accounting Standards Board because it required certain entities, notably (but not exclusively) professional service organisations, to recognise revenue earlier than they would have done prior to the issuance of the Abstract. This, in turn, meant an increase in profit and hence a corresponding increase in tax (although HM Revenue and Customs did introduce 'spreading provisions' in the earlier years that UITF 40 was introduced so as to 'spread' the amount of tax payable on the accelerated revenue).

6.22 Revenue recognition policies have also come under the spotlight of late due to the Tesco scandal in which the supermarket chain allegedly accelerated revenue from suppliers. This is not a confined case and there have been instances where smaller companies have had revenue recognition policies challenged by authorities such HM Revenue and Customs which have resulted in additional amounts of tax being paid (usually because revenue has been disproportionately delayed).

The introduction of UITF 40 meant that some companies had to recognise revenue when they received a 'right to consideration' or when they had performed certain obligations for their customer, regardless of the fact that the work had not yet been invoiced. Phrases such as a 'right to consideration' and the occurrence of a 'critical event' were used to indicate the point at which an entity would be required to recognise revenue.

Section 23 *Revenue* does not contain such explicit terminology and the issue here relates to the potential manipulation of the wording in Section 23 because it says that an entity shall measure revenue at the fair value of the consideration 'received' or 'receivable'. This terminology appears to be more relaxed than the previous UK GAAP, but it was not the intention by the FRC to allow companies to disproportionately delay, or accelerate, revenue recognition through the relaxed wording (indeed the term 'receivable' may be interpreted differently among companies).

Focus

- Companies are advised to continue recognising revenue when the company receives the right to consideration. This will usually occur when a performance obligation(s) has been met. The FRC have also intimated that if there is any abuse of the relaxed wording in Section 23, they will issue an Abstract to clarify the position. Because of the complexities over revenue, it is more important than ever that practitioners dealing with small companies understand the whole business and sales models of their clients.

Applying disclosures to achieve a true and fair view

6.23 On 6 April 2015, The Companies, Partnerships and Groups (Accounts and Reports) Regulations 2015, SI 2015/980 came into effect and they apply to:

- financial years beginning on or after 1 January 2016; and
- a financial year of a company beginning on or after 1 January 2015, but before 1 January 2016, if the directors so decide.

These new Regulations came into effect because of the transposition of the EU Accounting Directive into company law. The EU Accounting Directive (the Directive) replaced the 4th and 7th Accounting Directive and one of the most notable features of the Directive is that it establishes minimum legal requirements for financial statements in the EU and also reduces the burden placed on companies insofar as disclosures were concerned in the previous version of the Companies Act 2006.

The overall aim of the Directive is to simplify accounting requirements for small entities within its scope and the way it does this is through reduced disclosure requirements. It applies a 'think small first' approach by:

- introducing a 'building block' approach to the statutory accounts whereby disclosure levels are increased depending on the size of the undertaking;
- reducing the number of options available to preparers in respect of recognition, measurement and presentation; and
- creating a largely harmonised small company regime and, for the first time, limiting the amount of information which Member States are permitted to require small undertakings to place in their annual financial statements.

Focus

- Micro-entities are subjected to their own disclosure regime which is contained in FRS 105 *The Financial Reporting Standard applicable to the Micro-entities Regime* which only legally requires two disclosures to be made (see **Chapter 2** and **Chapter 11** for further details).

6.24 The disclosure requirements that are contained in the revised Companies Act 2006 have been reduced from some 17 mandatory disclosures to 13 and are:

(1) Accounting policies adopted.

(2) Fixed assets revaluation table.

(3) Fair valuation note.

(4) Financial commitments, guarantees or contingencies not included in the balance sheet.

(5) The amount of advances and credit granted to members of the administrative, managerial and supervisory bodies (along with supporting information).

(6) Exceptional items.

(7) Amounts due or payable after more than five years and entire debts covered by valuable security.

(8) Average number of employees during the financial year.

(9) Fixed asset note (in addition to the mandatory revaluation table).

(10) Name and registered office of the undertaking drawing up the consolidated financial statements of the smallest body of undertakings of which the undertaking forms part.

(11) Nature and business purpose of arrangements not included in the balance sheet.

(12) Nature and effect of post balance sheet events.

(13) (Limited) related party transactions.

6.25 Notwithstanding the fact that the revised Companies Act 2006 only mandates 13 legally required disclosures, there is still a legal requirement for small company directors to ensure the financial statements give a true and fair view. Simply applying the minimum legally required number of disclosures (some of which will not be applicable to every small company) may result in the financial statements not giving a true and fair view. Where directors knowingly approve financial statements that do not give a true and fair view, a criminal offence will be committed, which can result in a fine, imprisonment (or both).

Focus

- The disclosures required by the Companies Act 2006 are fully outlined in **Chapter 3** and in Section 1A of FRS 102 in Appendix C *Disclosure requirements for small entities*. There are also encouraged disclosures covered in **Chapter 3** and in Appendix D of Section 1A *Additional disclosures encouraged for small entities*.

6.26 The Financial Reporting Council are keen to make sure that directors:

- understand their responsibilities to ensure that the financial statements give a true and fair view; and
- discharge their legal responsibilities properly.

As a result, it is important that once the financial statements of a small company are prepared, the preparer 'stands back' and takes an objective look at them to see if they do, in fact, give a true and fair view, having regard to all the facts and circumstances concerning the company at their disposal. This may mean making disclosures over and above the legally required minimum so as to enable the financial statements to give a true and fair view.

Example 6.2 – Additional disclosures over and above the legal minimum

Palbarro Enterprises Ltd is a building contractor. Over the last couple of years the company has experienced an increased demand for its services, due in large part to the improved economy. It has taken on more staff and is in the process of constructing a new building which will be used as storage facilities. The company obtained a loan exclusively for the new building and writes off the interest charges on this loan to profit or loss each year.

During the year to 31 December 2016, it has been awarded a lucrative contract to build 50 new houses for a social housing provider. This contract is due to start in June 2017 and the directors have taken the decision to build a further storage facility for the additional equipment that will be needed to service this new contract. The bank have agreed to a further loan for this new storage facility as the contract is lucrative and forecasts suggest that the company will be more than able to meet its commitments under the loan facilities.

The finance director has decided to change the company's accounting policy for the loan interest and rather than write these amounts off to profit and loss, it has been agreed that they should be capitalised as part of the cost of the new storage facilities. The finance director has correctly accounted for the change in accounting policy, which has been deemed as material to the accounts and the director suggests making additional disclosures relating to the change in accounting policy so that they give a true and fair view.

The finance director is correct in suggesting additional disclosure for the accounting policy change as the change is considered to be material. As a result, the company should apply the provisions in paragraph 10.14 of Section 10 *Accounting Policies, Estimates and Errors* of FRS 102 and disclose:

(a) the nature of the change in accounting policy;

(b) the reasons why applying the new accounting policy provides reliable and more relevant information;

(c) to the extent practicable, the amount of the adjustment for each financial statement line item affected, shown separately:

    (i) for the current period;

    (ii) for each period presented; and

    (iii) in the aggregate for periods before those presented; and

(d) an explanation if it is impracticable to determine the amounts to be shown in (c) above.

Focus

- Where a small company deems it appropriate to make additional disclosures over and above those required by law, it should make the disclosures in line with the disclosure requirements of the relevant section of FRS 102. In the example above, the disclosures made comply with the requirements of Section 10 in respect of a voluntary change in accounting policy.

PITFALLS TO AVOID

- Incorrectly classifying a lease as an operating lease when it should be a finance lease (or vice versa).
- Ignoring the amortised cost method for accounting for basic loans and using 'traditional' methods in previous UK GAAP.
- Not recognising derivative financial instruments on the balance sheet at fair value with changes in fair value going through profit or loss.
- Ignoring deferred tax for revaluations of non-monetary assets subject to the revaluation model, fair values in business combinations and unremitted earnings in overseas subsidiaries and associates.
- Accounting for deferred tax in a micro-entity's financial statements.
- Disproportionately delaying or accelerating revenue due to the different wording in Section 23.
- Not making additional disclosures because they are not legally required; there are no 'deeming provisions' in the Companies Act 2006 and small company directors still have a legal obligation to ensure the financial statements give a true and fair view.

CHAPTER SUMMARY

- Certain areas of the financial statements lend themselves to areas of contention; notably leases, financial instruments, deferred taxation, post-employment benefits and revenue recognition. However, different companies operating in different industries will also encounter other areas of contention as 'contentious areas' are not formally categorised.
- Some companies have deliberately engineered leasing contracts to achieve a desired outcome or in some cases not reported leases, which may fall to be classed as a finance lease, on the balance sheet (off-balance sheet finance).
- Financial instruments are split into two components under FRS 102 for small entities: basic and other. Trade debtors, trade creditors, share capital and bank balances are some examples of basic instruments; whereas options, swaps, forward contracts and loans with complex features are examples of other instruments.
- Derivative instruments must now be recognised on the balance sheet of small companies reporting under the provisions of FRS 102.
- There are three additional situations giving rise to deferred tax: revaluations of non-monetary assets, fair values in business combinations and unremitted earnings in overseas entities.
- Care must be taken to ensure the recognition of deferred tax assets is appropriate.
- Revenue recognition policies are vital for small companies (revenue often being the highest number in the financial statements) and the principle of recognising revenue when the entity has received a right to consideration is still carried over into FRS 102.
- While there are only 13 disclosures required under the revised Companies Act 2006, company directors still have a legal duty to ensure the financial statements give a true and fair view and this may mean making additional disclosures, over and above those legally required.

Chapter 7

Small Company Legal Requirements

SIGNPOSTS

- Provided there have been no acts of wrongdoing, company directors are not personally responsible for the debts a business cannot pay if it runs into financial difficulties (see **7.1**).
- Various information must be submitted to Companies House prior to a company being incorporated and the company has legal obligations once it has been created (see **7.2** and **7.3**).
- Abbreviated accounts are abolished in the revised Companies Act 2006 but companies must still deliver accounts and reports to the Registrar which will be made available on the public record (see **7.4–7.9**).
- Penalties can be imposed in law if a company fails to file information by due dates, which can become excessive if filing deadlines are repeatedly missed (see **7.10–7.12**).
- It is possible to change a company's year-end date and have a short or a long accounting period (see **7.13**).
- Annual returns are to be sent to Companies House until 2016 when they will be abolished (see **7.14–7.15**).
- The Small Business, Enterprise and Employment Act received Royal Assent on 26 March 2015 and has a staging timetable (see **7.16–7.30**).

INTRODUCTION

7.1 This chapter takes a look at some of the more common legal issues (such as filing requirements) which a small company must comply with. The chapter is not a comprehensive overview of all statutory requirements which companies and directors must comply with; instead it looks at some of the statutory obligations in the context of small company financial statements and other accounting related issues which company directors must ensure they comply with. Directors can be fined, prosecuted or disqualified for ignoring legal responsibilities and should continue to keep abreast of responsibilities in this area.

Focus

- There are other legal requirements relating to small companies beyond those covered in this chapter and hence readers may wish to visit www.gov.uk for more information which does not strictly relate to accounting and hence not covered in this chapter. For example, a change of director(s) or registered office. Limited liability partnership issues are contained in a separate publication *Audit and Accounts of Limited Liability Partnerships* which is available from www.bloomsburyprofessional.co.uk.

A limited company will always have shareholders and directors. In a small company, the shareholders and the directors are often the same people; although it is also common for some small companies to have directors who do not own shares in the company. For most limited companies, the term 'limited' means that the shareholders' responsibilities are limited to the value of shares that they own. Provided there have been no acts of wrongdoing on the part of the directors of a limited company, they are not personally responsible for the debts which the business cannot pay if it runs into financial difficulty. However, directors will be held responsible if acts of wrongdoing can be proved (such as wrongful or unlawful trading) and the powers given to the Secretary of State have been increased following the introduction of The Small Business, Enterprise and Employment Act 2015 which is covered in the final section of this chapter.

Example 7.1 – A company in financial difficulty

Sarah and Neil both own 50 shares each in S & N Developments Ltd. One share was worth £1 when it was originally incorporated ('incorporated' means set up). However, Sarah and Neil have only paid £25 each for these shares (hence they have only both paid half of the par value for their shares).

During the year to 31 December 2016, S & N Developments Ltd ran into financial difficulty and ceased trading.

The maximum which Sarah and Neil have to pay as shareholders towards the debts the company owes to its creditors is £50 which represents the 25 shares each which they have not paid for.

7.2 In order to set up a limited company it must be registered at Companies House. In order to do this, the person setting up the limited company will need:

- the company name (there are certain names which cannot be used, such those similar to a name of an existing company);
- an address for the company;

- at least one director;
- at least one shareholder (as limited companies are limited by shares);
- a memorandum of association;
- details of the share capital of the company together with the rights attached to those shares; and
- the articles of association.

Once all this information has been received by Companies House, the Registrar of Companies will issue a certificate of incorporation which confirms the company legally exists and the certificate of incorporation will contain the company number and the date on which the company was legally formed.

7.3 As the shareholders of a limited company are limited to the value of their shares, the price to pay for this limitation is filing certain information with Companies House which is then available on the public record (such as annual returns/annual confirmation statements and the company's accounts). There are penalties which Companies House will levy in the event that statutory documentation is filed late and in some cases these penalties can be very expensive (see the later section *Late filing penalties*).

Focus

- In addition to the statutory filing obligations which Companies House require, HM Revenue and Customs (HMRC) also require copies of the company's annual accounts and corporation tax return. Penalties and interest will also be levied by HMRC if the company's tax documentation is not filed with them on time. Companies must ensure that they allow sufficient time for the accounts to be prepared and approved and then submitted to HMRC and Companies House.

FILING OBLIGATIONS FOR SMALL COMPANIES

7.4 On 6 April 2015 the revised Companies Act 2006 came into force in the UK following the transposition of the EU Accounting Directive. This brought about certain changes to the filing requirements for small companies and micro-entities. Prior to the changes to the Companies Act 2006, small companies could opt to file 'abbreviated' financial statements (which most small companies chose to do). Abbreviated financial statements were previously dealt with in Schedule 4 of The Small Companies and Groups (Accounts and Directors' Report) Regulations 2008.[1]

Regulation 8(3) made amendments to section 444 of the Companies Act 2006 regarding Companies House filing obligations for small companies. The

1 SI 2008/409.

revised Companies Act 2006 now reflects the fact that small companies are no longer entitled to file abbreviated accounts.

7.5 Section 444(1) of the Companies Act 2006 says that the directors of a company which is subject to the small companies' regime:

- must deliver to the registrar for each financial year a copy of the balance sheet drawn up as at the last day of that year, and[2]
- may also deliver to the registrar—
  - — a copy of the company's profit and loss account for that year, and
  - — a copy of the directors' report for that year.[3]

Focus

- Companies may choose whether or not to file the profit and loss account and directors' report but, as a minimum, they must file the balance sheet prepared as at the last day of the financial year. The balance sheet will not be 'abbreviated' as was done in the majority of cases for small companies prior to the revisions to section 444, but may be abridged if the members (shareholders) unanimously agree (see **7.8**).

7.6 Where directors of small companies choose to deliver a copy of the company's profit and loss account to Companies House, section 444(2) requires a copy of the auditor's report to be filed together with any directors' report. However, where the small company takes advantage of audit exemption, section 444(2) will not apply.

Focus

- Where the directors of a small company choose **not** to file a profit and loss account or a copy of the directors' report, the balance sheet which is delivered to Companies House must contain (in a prominent position) a statement that the annual accounts and reports have been delivered in accordance with the provisions applicable to companies which are subject to the small companies' regime.

7.7 With the exception of micro-entities (as defined in sections 384(A) and 384(B)), where the directors have not chosen to file a copy of the company's profit and loss account, section 444(5A)(a) requires the balance sheet which is filed to state that fact.

If a small company has not taken advantage of audit exemption and has had its financial statements subjected to statutory audit, but has chosen not to file a

2 Companies Act 2006, s 444(1)(a).
3 Companies Act 2006, s 444(1)(b).

profit and loss account, section 444(5B) requires that the notes to the balance sheet:

- state whether the auditor's report was qualified or unqualified;
- where the report was qualified, disclose the basis of the qualification (reproducing any statement under section 498(2)(a) or (b), if applicable);
- where the report was unqualified, include a reference to any matters to which the auditor drew attention by way of emphasis; and
- state:
  - the name of the auditor and (where the auditor is a firm) the name of the person who signed the auditor's report as senior statutory auditor; or
  - if the conditions in section 506 (circumstances in which names are omitted) are met, that a resolution has been passed and notified to the Secretary of State in accordance with that section.[4]

Focus

- The copy of the balance sheet and any directors' report which has been delivered to Companies House under section 444 must state the name of the person who signed it on behalf of the board as per section 444(6). In addition, section 444(7) requires that any auditor's report must state the name of the auditor and (where the auditor is a firm) the name of the person signing in the capacity of senior statutory auditor. However, in circumstances where names are omitted and the conditions under section 506 are met, the report must state that a resolution has been passed and notified to the Secretary of State in accordance with that section.

7.8 Where a small company prepares an abridged balance sheet or an abridged profit and loss account pursuant to paragraph 1A of Schedule 1 to The Small Companies and Groups (Accounts and Directors' Report) Regulations 2008, the directors must deliver a statement to the Registrar that all members have consented to the abridgement.

Focus

- The members (shareholders) of a company can only prepare an abridged balance sheet or an abridged profit and loss account where **all** the members agree (ie the agreement has to be unanimous). In addition, the members can only agree to prepare an abridged balance sheet and an abridged profit and loss account in respect of the preceding year (hence the agreement is an annual process).

4 Companies Act 2006, s 444(5B).

Filing requirements for the directors' report

7.9 Directors of small companies which are entitled to small companies' exemption in relation to the directors' report must file a copy of the company's annual accounts for that year in accordance with section 444A(1)(a). However, section 444A(1)(b) allows the company directors to choose whether, or not, to submit the directors' report on those annual accounts.

Where the small company is subject to audit, the directors must file a copy of the auditor's report together with the directors' report (but this will not apply to small companies which have taken up audit exemption).

Late filing penalties

7.10 Accounts and reports have to be filed to Companies House in recognition of the limited liability afforded to companies. Companies House introduced late filing penalties in 1992 as a means of encouraging company directors to submit their accounts and reports on time. Strict filing deadlines are applied to all companies whether they are large or small and the law will impose penalties if these accounts and reports are late.

7.11 Where a company's first accounts are a long accounting period (a 'long' accounting period is more than 12 months), then Companies House will require these to be submitted within 21 months from the date of incorporation for private companies (this period is reduced to 18 months for public companies), or three months from the accounting reference date, whichever is the longer.

For subsequent financial years, private companies have nine months from the end of the accounting period in which to file its accounts and reports with Companies House (a public company has six months).

Example 7.2 – Filing deadline

Pete's Pottery Co Ltd has an accounting reference date of 31 August each year. Companies House must receive their accounts and reports no later than 31 May each year to avoid the law imposing penalties for late filing.

Focus

- The term 'delivery to Companies House' means the date on which Companies House actually receive the accounts and reports in the correct format. Sufficient time should be set aside to prepare the accounts and file them (electronically or by post) to ensure receipt in good time to avoid penalties. Even if the accounts and reports are one day late, the law will impose a penalty on the business.

7.12 The level of filing penalties will depend on how late Companies House receive the accounts. The table below outlines the penalties that are currently in force at the time of writing. The penalties are measured from the date on which the accounts are due at Companies House:

Length of delay	**Private company**
Not more than one month	£150
More than one month but not more than three months	£375
More than three months but not more than six months	£750
More than six months	£1,500

Penalties are higher in respect of a public company that files its financial statements late, although these penalties are beyond the scope of this book.

Penalties will be doubled where a company files accounts late in two successive financial years, hence if a company has filed three weeks' late in year 1 it will receive a £150 fine. If it files three weeks' late again in year 2 the fine will be £300.

Change of an accounting reference date

7.13 Where an accounting period is shortened (ie it is less than 12 months), section 442(4) says that the period allowed for filing accounts for a small company will be nine months from the end of the accounting reference date or three months from the date of a notice given by the company under section 392 of the Companies Act 2006 *Alteration of accounting reference date*, whichever expires last.

Companies can also extend their accounting reference date and various reasons exist as to why this may be the case. However, section 442 (5A) says that any such extension must not have the effect of extending the period for filing to more than 12 months after the end of the relevant accounting reference period.

Annual returns (until April 2016)

7.14 Until April 2016, all companies must submit an annual return once a year. Annual returns are usually submitted one year after either:

- the date of incorporation; or
- the date the company last filed an annual return.

The majority of companies will file an annual return at a different time than when they file their accounts at Companies House.

> **Focus**
>
> - Annual returns are being abolished from April 2016 and will be replaced with annual 'confirmation statements'. See **7.25** below.

7.15 The annual return includes the following information:

- details of the directors and, where applicable, the company secretary;
- the company's activities including standard industrial classifications (SIC codes);
- the type of company (eg private or public);
- the company's registered office;
- the 'single alternative inspection location' (SAIL) which is the address where records are kept if not at the registered office address;
- a statement of capital where the company has shares; and
- shareholder details (where required) and depending on how long since the company last reported them.

Nowadays annual returns are completed online and incur a £13 filing fee. However, in circumstance when an annual return cannot be filed online then it can be submitted by post but costs £40 and the company must send a cheque with the company number written on the back of the cheque.

> **Focus**
>
> - Annual returns can be filed up to 28 days after the due date. Where a company fails to send in annual return a fine of up to £5,000 can be imposed by Companies House and the company can be struck off. In addition, it is the directors who could find themselves criminally liable and facing a fine.

THE SMALL BUSINESS, ENTERPRISE AND EMPLOYMENT ACT 2015

7.16 In an attempt to deter illegal activity in business, such as money-laundering and tax evasion, there has been a change to UK company law in the form of The Small Business, Enterprise and Employment Act 2015 which received Royal Assent on 26 March 2015 and forms part of the Government's 'Transparency and Trust' proposals. The Act itself hit the statute books on 26 March 2015 but in recognition of the fact that companies will need time to prepare, a staged timetable has been introduced for implementation of the Act.

Unfortunately the new legislation is going to cause an element of upheaval among private companies and the following table highlights the main changes to company law, together with the implementation dates:

Change in the law	**Implementation date**
The prohibition of bearer shares	26 May 2015, with a nine months' transitional period for existing bearer shares.
Prohibition of corporate directors, with exceptions	October 2015, with a 12 months' transitional period for existing corporate directors
Maintenance of a public register of people with significant control for unquoted companies	January 2016 and details of these people to be provided annually to Companies House from April 2016
Replacement of annual returns	From April 2016 the annual return will be replaced with annual 'confirmation statements'
Ability to keep statutory registers at Companies House instead of having to keep own registers	April 2016

Register of persons with significant control

7.17 One of the most controversial aspects of this new piece of legislation is that individuals who have 'significant control' over a private company are to be named on a public register. In broad terms, a person will have significant control where he or she holds or controls more than 25% of the company's shares or voting rights. In addition, a person will have significant control where they have the power to appoint, or remove, a majority of the board (this can be directly, or indirectly, through a majority stake in another company).

While the above test may seem fairly simple to apply, at the time of writing there were already emerging problems that had presented themselves, such as where an individual may have significant influence or control over an unquoted company or exercises control through a partnership or trust. In this respect, the government is expected to issue additional guidance on the definition of 'significant influence or control' by October 2015.

In general, the five specified conditions which constitute 'significant control' are:

- direct/indirect ownership of 25% or more of a company's shares;
- direct/indirect control of 25% or more of a company's voting rights;
- direct/indirect right to appoint/remove a majority of the board's directors;
- exercise/right to exercise significant influence or control over a company; and/or

- exercise/right to exercise significant influence or control over activities of a trust or firm which itself meets one, or more, of the first four conditions.

7.18 There will be a legal obligation for an unquoted company to identify and keep up-to-date a register of persons with significant control. Those persons with significant control over the company will be obliged to disclose their identities to the company. Anyone will be able to inspect the register of persons with significant control if they have a 'proper purpose'.

Companies will be required to provide information concerning persons with significant control to Companies House and this information will be available on the public record. To start with, this will be on an annual basis, but from 2017 the government is planning to increase the frequency for Companies House filings to bring the new rules in line with the EU Fourth Money Laundering Directive.

The register of persons with significant control must include similar details to those which are currently on the register of directors along with the nature of the control that the person has over the company. The residential address of a person with significant control will be protected (as is the case now for directors); however other information relating to the person with significant control may only be withheld in very limited circumstances, for example where the person with significant control is at a risk of serious violence or intimidation due to the company's activities.

Failure to comply

7.19 The new rules only apply to unquoted companies (ie private companies). Listed companies (including AIM-listed companies) are exempt from the requirements on the grounds that the disclosure requirements in DTR 5 already apply to shareholders of listed companies.

Problems are likely to emerge for private companies in identifying their significant controllers by serving information requests. In addition, the new regime is likely to be extended to LLPs (although formal proposals for this had not been published at the time of writing).

Where persons with significant control do not comply with their disclosure obligations, the company can impose sanctions such as loss of voting rights and transfer restrictions. A similar regime exists with listed companies, but PLCs have to go to court to impose such sanctions, whereas private companies will not have to go to court.

Where a company fails to comply with its obligations under the new law, criminal penalties can also be imposed and such penalties will also extend to the company's directors and, where applicable, company secretary.

Implementation of the register of persons with significant control

7.20 The government has confirmed that it plans to issue further guidance on implementing the register of persons with significant control; however, based on the current timetable, companies must start to maintain a register from January 2016. Companies will also be required to file information concerning persons with significant control annually from April 2016.

Bearer shares

7.21 Bearer shares are fairly uncommon nowadays and so this issue is unlikely to affect very many small companies. However, from 26 May 2015 companies will no longer be able to create bearer shares. Over the years such shares have been criticised because they allow the shareholders to remain anonymous. From 26 May 2015, existing holders of bearer shares will have nine months to swap their shares and be listed on the register of shareholders, after which time the shares will be cancelled. It is important, therefore, that companies which have holders of bearer shares, notify such holders as quickly as possible as to the consequences of not surrendering their shares.

Corporate directors

7.22 The new Act prohibits companies and other corporate entities from being appointed as directors. The reason for this prohibition is to restrict the use of corporate structures to hide illegal activity. The ban on corporate directors is expected to commence from October 2015 and for companies which currently have a corporate director, they will have a one-year transitional period in which to appoint replacement directors.

Despite the ban being primarily to restrict illegal activity, the government have acknowledged that in some instances corporate directors are appointed for genuine reasons and hence the government have said that they may introduce some exemptions from the prohibition of a corporate director. At the time of writing, the government were currently consulting on whether a corporate director should be permitted if all of its directors (or equivalent officers) are natural persons and their details are held on a public register, such as that held at Companies House.

Shadow directors

7.23 The general duties of directors under sections 170–177 of the Companies Act 2006 will apply to shadow directors, to the extent that they are capable of applying. Shadow directors are not formally appointed as directors but the board follows the orders of such shadow directors. This change applies from 26 May 2015 but at the time of writing, it was currently unclear how this will operate in practice. Current advice to investors is to avoid 'crossing the line' between board engagement and board control and while the Act does empower the government to introduce further rules in this area, no such proposals had been published when this book went to print.

Insolvency and disqualification of directors

7.24 The Act provides for a number of measures which have the objective of making it easier to pursue directors that do not comply with their obligations. The Act will allow liquidators and administrators to bring law suits against directors for acts such as wrongful or unlawful trading as well as applying for creditor compensation orders against directors which have been disqualified.

In addition, the disqualified directors regime has also been updated and improved and will allow the Secretary of State to disqualify directors for misconduct in connection with companies that are located overseas. The courts will also be able to take account of a wider range of factors in arriving at a decision whether, or not, to ban a director.

The length of time that the Secretary of State will have in bringing disqualification action against a director following formal insolvency of a company has also been extended from two years to three years.

Annual returns and confirmation statements

7.25 The annual return which is lodged at Companies House (see earlier section in this chapter at **7.14** and **7.15**) is being replaced with an annual 'check-and-confirm confirmation statement'. This form will also make the statements of capital easier to complete because the statement of capital is to be amended to remove the requirement for companies to include the amount paid up and unpaid on each share. Instead, companies will be required to specify the aggregate amount unpaid on the total number of issued shares.

The changes relating to the annual return are scheduled to come into force in April 2016 and companies will have to adjust to the new annual reporting regime. However, a benefit of the new regime is that it should be easier to align the timing of the preparation of the company's confirmation statement with its annual accounts as the annual return is filed at a different time than the company's annual accounts.

Company registers

7.26 Private companies will have the option to maintain certain information on the public register rather than on statutory registers. This will include information concerning shareholders, directors, secretaries and persons with significant control being maintained on a register at Companies House rather than maintaining their own registers.

Focus

- While this may sound helpful due to the reduced administration, it may be worthwhile for a private company to maintain their own register where such information changes infrequently, or where there are reduced confidentiality concerns.

Directors' dates of birth

7.27 In an attempt to reduce fraudulent activity, the day that a director was born will not be made public at Companies House – only the month and year will be visible on the public register and this is expected to come into force from October 2015. The issue with this is that the new rules do not appear to remove historic data and hence for existing directors, the new rule on dates of birth will probably be of little benefit. In addition, protection will also not be available where a private company opts to keep its register of directors at Companies House. The rules on dates of birth will also extend to persons with significant control.

Director and registered office disputes

7.28 When a director is appointed, they will not have to countersign a Companies House form to indicate their consent. Instead, Companies House will notify directors that they have been appointed as a company director. This will give the director chance to object and have their names removed if an erroneous appointment has been lodged at Companies House, or if the registration is bogus. These new rules are expected to come into force in October 2015 with additional provisions which will allow Companies House to alter the registered office of a company where the use of the address is disputed.

Striking off companies

7.29 The amount of time it takes for a company to be dissolved (whether voluntary or not) has been reduced from three months to two months following publication of notice in the *Gazette*. This accelerated timescale is expected to come into force in October 2015.

Companies House changes

7.30 In light of the above changes brought about by The Small Business, Enterprise and Employment Act 2015, improvements will be made to the services offered by Companies House. At the time of writing there were three services offered by Companies House:

- Webfiling;
- Webcheck; and
- Companies House Direct.

The above will all be replaced by one unified online service – *The Companies House Service*. Webfiling, Webcheck and Companies House Direct will all run in parallel during the implementation of the new unified online service. There are some notable changes to the existing offering which include:

- the removal of the subscription-based *Companies House Direct* to a free of charge service;
- access to all document images on a free of charge basis, which will also include mortgage charges;
- removal of the form-based filing to a 'click and confirm' process which will make it easier to maintain company information; and
- an updated and user-friendly interface which will make searching for information easier and quicker.

PITFALLS TO AVOID

- Leaving the preparation of the company's accounts too late forgetting that they have to be filed at Companies House within nine months from the year end (assuming it is not a company's first year).
- Preparing accounts using incorrect formats resulting in rejection by Companies House (Companies House recently announced statistics showing that over 10% of company accounts are rejected).
- Forgetting to include the name of the person signing the accounts on behalf of the board.
- Filing annual returns/annual confirmation statements late resulting in striking-off proposals being issued.
- Omission of, or incorrect wording, of the statement relating to the financial statements being prepared under the small companies' regime.
- Forgetting to deliver the statement to the Registrar of Companies that all members have consented to abridged financial statements where these are prepared.

CHAPTER SUMMARY

- All limited companies have to be registered at Companies House.
- Various information is needed to set up a limited company at Companies House including the company name, address and details of directors and shareholders.
- Because of the protection afforded to directors and shareholders of a limited company, Companies House require various documentation to be filed on a public register (including the company's accounts).
- The revised Companies Act 2006 which came into effect on 6 April 2015 abolishes abbreviated accounts.

- Companies must file a balance sheet and may also deliver the company's profit and loss account and directors' report together with an audit report (if applicable).
- Penalties are levied by the law if a company files their accounts and reports late.
- The penalties levied for late filing are doubled when the company files their accounts and reports late for two successive years.
- Annual returns must be sent to Companies House (although these are being abolished from April 2016 and replaced with an annual confirmation statement).
- The Small Business, Enterprise and Employment Act 2015 places additional responsibilities on private companies and the timetable to implement this legislation is staged.

Chapter 8

Consolidated Financial Statements

SIGNPOSTS

- Small groups are not required to prepare consolidated financial statements, but may choose to do so and more medium-sized groups will fall to be classed as small due to rises in the small groups thresholds as a result of the EU Accounting Directive (see **8.1** and **8.2**).
- A parent-subsidiary relationship can exist even where the parent owns less than 51% of the voting rights in the subsidiary (see **8.3**).
- Group structures can become complex and careful thought needs to be given to direct and indirect ownerships (see **8.4** and **8.5**).
- Control passes from the date of acquisition which may not necessarily be the same date on which the acquisition legally completes (see **8.6**).
- Where a relationship is not that of a parent-subsidiary, it will usually be one of an associate, joint venture or simple investment (see **8.7**).
- There are various steps involved in preparing consolidated financial statements including eliminating intra-group trading and dealing with pre- and post-acquisition reserves (see **8.11–8.17**).
- The process of consolidation involves identifying an acquirer and measuring and allocating the cost of the combination (see **8.18–8.24**).
- Estimates and adjustments may have to be made for business combinations which are still ongoing at the reporting date (see **8.25**).
- Subsidiaries should use the same year-end and accounting policies as that of the parent (see **8.26** and **8.27**).
- Whilst the consolidated profit and loss account is relatively straightforward, the consolidated balance sheet is inherently more complex (see **8.28** and **8.29**).

INTRODUCTION

8.1 Small groups are not legally required to prepare consolidated financial statements, but section 398 of the Companies Act 2006 says that at the end of a financial year, where a company is subject to the small companies' regime and is also a parent company, the directors may prepare group accounts for the year as well as their own individual accounts.

Focus

- Where a company may qualify as a micro-entity and is the parent of a group which prepares group accounts, or the micro-entity has its individual financial statements consolidated in group accounts, it cannot adopt FRS 105 *The Financial Reporting Standard applicable to the Micro-entities Regime*.

While the Companies Act 2006 allows a small group to take advantage of the exemption from preparing consolidated financial statements, medium-sized groups must prepare group accounts. The Companies Act 2006 has not been redrafted in this area as a result of the transposition of the EU Accounting Directive into company law.

8.2 The table below outlines the size thresholds for a group qualifying as a small or medium-sized group:

	Turnover	**Balance sheet total**	**No. of employees**
Small group	Not more than £10.2 million net or Not more than £12.2 million gross	Not more than £5.1 million net or Not more than £6.1 million gross	Not more than 50
Medium-sized group	Not more than £36 million net or Not more than £43.2 million gross	Not more than £18 million net or Not more than £21.6 million gross	Not more than 250

The requirements above are met by a group in a year in which the group satisfies two, or more, of the turnover, balance sheet total and employee head count criteria.

Section 399 of the Companies Act 2006 (which does not apply to small groups) says that where an undertaking is a parent company, then it must prepare group accounts unless the company is exempt from the requirement to do so (ie it is a small group choosing not to prepare group accounts).

Focus

- In the revised Companies Act 2006, section 399(2A) says that a company is exempt from the requirement to prepare group accounts if:
  - it would be subject to the small companies regime but for being a public company; and
  - it is not a traded company.[1]

1 Companies Act 2006, s 399(2A)(a)(b).

8.3 *Consolidated Financial Statements*

Paragraph 1A.22 of FRS 102 says that where a small entity which is a parent chooses to prepare consolidated financial statements, it:

- shall apply the consolidation procedures set out in Section 9 *Consolidated and Separate Financial Statements*;
- is encouraged to provide the disclosures set out in paragraph 9.23;
- shall comply so far as practicable with the requirements of Section 1A as if it were a single entity (Schedule 6 of the Small Companies Regulations, paragraph 1(1)), subject to any restrictions or exemptions set out in legislation; and
- shall provide any disclosures required by Schedule 6 of the Small Companies Regulations.

The remainder of this chapter will be concerned with a small group choosing to prepare group accounts.

IDENTIFYING A SUBSIDIARY

8.3 FRS 102 *The Financial Reporting Standard applicable in the UK and Republic of Ireland* defines a 'subsidiary' as:

> 'An entity, including an unincorporated entity such as a partnership that is **controlled** by another entity (known as the **parent**).'[2]

'Control' of an entity on the part of the parent is the power to govern the entity's financial and operating policies to allow the parent to benefit from the entity's activities. This is a crucial term for the purposes of deciphering whether, or not, a parent-subsidiary relationship exists. Where control does not exist, there cannot be a parent-subsidiary relationship.

In a majority of cases, control is obtained by the parent entity over the subsidiary where the parent owns more than 50% of the voting rights in the subsidiary. This is not absolute, and a parent company may still obtain control with a holding of less than 51% of the voting rights; this is because control may still be evidenced by power:

- over more than half of the voting rights by virtue of an agreement with other investors;
- to govern the financial and operating policies of the entity under statute or an agreement;
- to appoint or remove the majority of the board of directors; or
- to cast the majority of votes at meetings of the board of directors.

2 FRS 102 (August 2014), Glossary.

Focus

- The above points illustrate that control can be obtained by a parent over a subsidiary where the holding of the voting rights is less than 51%. For small groups, it is more likely that control will be obtained through a holding of more than 50% of the voting rights in a subsidiary, but it is important to clarify than a numeric benchmark is not always an indicator that control exists. Where control exists, a parent-subsidiary relationship is established and hence group accounts can be prepared where the small group so chooses.

Example 8.1 – Control via ownership interest

On 1 January 2016, Bart Ltd acquired 80% of the net assets in Molly Ltd.

As Bart Ltd has acquired more than 50% of the net assets in Molly Ltd, a parent-subsidiary relationship has been established. The directors of Bart Ltd may decide to prepare group accounts on the basis of the parent-subsidiary relationship.

Example 8.2 – Control obtained through other means

On 1 January 2016, Bart Ltd acquired a 40% stake in Molly Ltd.

From a numerical perspective it would appear that Bart Ltd does not have control over Molly Ltd as it has only acquired 40% of the net assets and, therefore, it might seem more appropriate for Bart to account for its investment in Molly as an investment in associate (as 40% would indicate Bart has significant influence over Molly rather than control).

However, if Bart had the power to appoint, or remove, a majority of Molly's board of directors, despite only having an ownership interest of 40%, this would give rise to control regardless of the ownership interest of 40% and in these circumstances a parent-subsidiary relationship would exist.

8.4 Generally small groups are relatively simple to account for and the identification of a subsidiary may well be straightforward (as it would often be by virtue of ownership interest). However, there are situations where complexities arise in the overall structure of the group and the scope for such situations presenting themselves is increased because of the increased size thresholds in small and medium-sized groups (where more medium-sized groups will fall to be classed as small in the revised Companies Act 2006).

Example 8.3 – Vertical group structure

The following group structure relates to the Heaton Group:

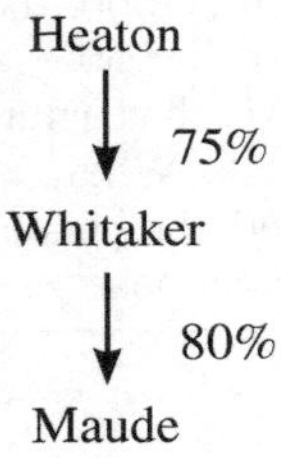

In this group structure, Heaton owns 75% of Whitaker; and Whitaker owns 80% of Maude. It follows, therefore, that Whitaker is a subsidiary of Heaton and Maude is a subsidiary of Whitaker. The question arises as to whether Maude is a subsidiary of Heaton.

Where such structures are concerned, Maude will be a subsidiary of Heaton on the grounds that Heaton controls Maude through its control of Whitaker and hence Maude is a subsidiary of Heaton. Heaton's effective ownership interest in Maude is calculated as 75% × 80% = 60% of Maude. This calculation is a useful tool to bring into the consolidation exercise, but is irrelevant when it comes to determining the status of the investment because the status is always based on control.

8.5 Whilst 'D-shaped' groups are fairly uncommon among small groups, they can exist and the scope of their existence under the small groups' regime is also increased because of the increased size thresholds.

Example 8.4 – 'D-shaped' group

The following group structure relates to the Heaton Group:

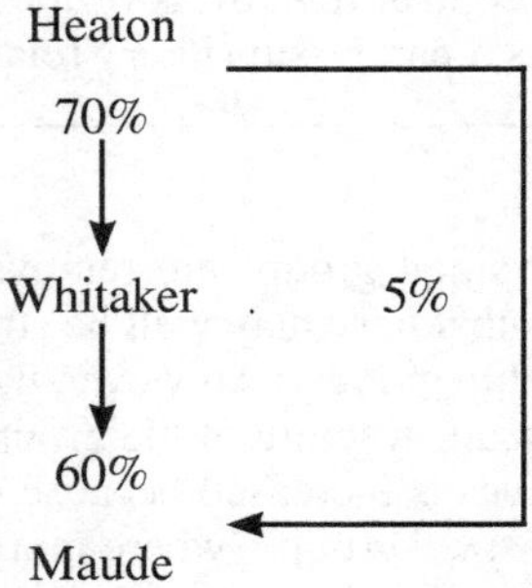

As an overview, Heaton owns 70% of Whitaker; Whitaker owns 60% of Maude and Heaton owns 5% of Maude. Where this structure (referred to as a 'D-shaped group') exists, Heaton's indirect and direct ownership interest must be established. Clearly, Whitaker is a subsidiary of Heaton and Maude is a subsidiary of Whitaker. Heaton's indirect and direct ownership is calculated as follows:

Indirect ownership:	
70% × 60%	42%
Direct ownership:	
Per group structure	5%
Heaton's Ownership interest	47%
Non-controlling interest	53%

8.6 In **8.3** above, the concept of 'control' was examined. In addition to establishing whether control exists or not, for group members acquired during the period ('in-year acquisitions') it will also be necessary to identify the *date of acquisition*. The date of acquisition may not necessarily be the date that the sale completed; it could be at a later date, but in any event a parent obtains control over a subsidiary at the *later* of:

- the date the parent acquired the subsidiary; and
- the date the subsidiary acquired the sub-subsidiary.

Example 8.5 – Establishing the date of acquisition

Company A acquires 60% of Company B on 30 June 2017. Company B acquires 70% of Company C on 31 July 2018.

In this example the date of acquisition of Company C is 31 July 2018.

If, for example, Company A acquires 60% of Company B on 30 June 2017 and Company B already owned Company C, then the date of acquisition of Company C is 30 June 2017.

Classifications of other investments

8.7 So far this chapter has looked at the situations giving rise to a parent-subsidiary relationship. However, where control does not exist the investor will either have an associate, joint venture or a simple investment.

Associate

8.8 An investor will have an investment in an associate where it has 'significant influence' over that investment and such investments are dealt with in FRS 102 at Section 14 *Investments in Associates*. Ordinarily significant influence can be achieved with an ownership interest of between 20% and 50%. However, as is the case with control, significant influence can be demonstrated by characteristics other than ownership interest, such as:

- interchange in managerial personnel;
- material transactions between the investor and the investee;
- participation in the policy-making process;
- provision of essential technical information; or
- representation on the board of directors or equivalent governing body.

Focus

- Where an investor holds between 20% and 50% of the voting rights in an investee then, unless it can be clearly demonstrated that significant influence does not exist, it is presumed that significant influence is obtained. This can also be a reverse scenario where the investor may hold less than 20% and hence the presumption is that significant influence does not exist, unless it can be clearly demonstrated otherwise. Therefore, the substance of the arrangement must be carefully considered in all cases.

The accounting requirements for an associate are examined in more detail in **Chapter 12**. However, it is worth noting that the revised Companies Act 2006 allows the use of the 'equity method' to account for such interests in the **individual** financial statements, which is also examined in **Chapter 12**.

Joint ventures

8.9 Joint ventures are dealt with in FRS 102 at Section 15 *Investments in Joint Ventures* and the accounting issues for such ventures is examined in more detail in **Chapter 12**. However, Section 15 recognises three categories of joint venture:

- jointly controlled operations;
- jointly controlled assets; and
- jointly controlled entities.

In a jointly controlled operation, each venturer:

- uses their own resources (eg their own assets);

- carries out their own part of the joint operation separately from the activities of the other venturer(s);
- owns and controls their own resources;
- incurs their own expenses and liabilities; and
- raises their own finance.

Where a jointly controlled asset is concerned, each venturer must recognise:

- their share of the jointly controlled asset(s);
- any liabilities which the venturer has incurred on behalf of the joint venture;
- their share of any joint liabilities incurred by the joint venture;
- their share of income and expense incurred by the joint venture; and
- any expenses which the venturer has incurred in respect of its interest in the joint venture in the venturer's own financial statements.

Jointly controlled entities are more complex because this involves the creation of a company or an unincorporated entity (such as a partnership) which is jointly controlled by the venturers. Such concepts are examined in further detail in **Chapter 12**.

Focus

- Where joint ventures are concerned, it is important to emphasise that a joint venture is a *contractually agreed* sharing of control. There cannot be a controlling party because that would fail to meet the definition of a joint venture. Joint control can only exist where there is a contract in place in which the strategic financial and operating decisions of the activity require the *unanimous* consent of all parties in the venture. Decisions cannot be made unilaterally, or without the consent of **all** parties within the venture as this will also give rise to the joint venture failing to meet the definition of such.

Simple investments

8.10 Where neither control nor significant influence is achieved, then such investments are accounted for in accordance with Section 11 *Basic Financial Instruments* or Section 12 *Other Financial Instruments Issues*. For small companies, it is likely that such investments will be investments in non-convertible preference shares or non-puttable ordinary and preference shares which are accounted for under the provisions of Section 11.

OVERVIEW OF THE BASIC CONSOLIDATION REQUIREMENTS

8.11 The overarching objective of consolidated financial statements is to show the performance and financial position of the group in line with its economic substance, which is that of a single trading entity – in other words as if the group structure does not exist. The following steps are necessary to produce consolidated financial statements:

- eliminate intra-group trading;
- eliminate any intra-group profits resulting from intra-group trading;
- for new subsidiaries, goodwill is recognised (for existing subsidiaries, goodwill is amortised);
- pre- and post-acquisition reserves are calculated for mid-year acquisitions; and
- account for non-controlling interests (minority interests).

Elimination of intra-group trading

8.12 It is commonplace for group members to trade with each other. At individual company level such sales and purchases among group members will be recognised as such in the financial statements. However, as mentioned above, the consolidated financial statements must show the results of the group as if the group structure did not exist and for this reason all intra-group trading, together with any balances outstanding among group members at the reporting date, must be eliminated on consolidation.

Example 8.6 – Intra-group trading

Breary Ltd owns 100% of the net assets of Byrne Ltd and the group qualifies as a small group under the Companies Act 2006, but the directors wish to prepare group financial statements. During the year Breary Ltd sold goods to Byrne Ltd for £32,500 and at the year-end a balance of £8,200 was owed by Byrne Ltd to Breary Ltd.

On consolidation, all intra-group trading and balances must be removed so that the financial statements show the trading results as if the group structure did not exist (ie show the results of trading with the outside world only). Hence, the following consolidation adjustments must be made:

DR sales	£32,500
CR cost of sales	(£32,500)

Being removal in the consolidated figures of the sale that is accounted for by Breary and the purchase that is accounted for by Byrne

DR intra-group creditor	£8,200
CR intra-group debtor	(£8,200)

Being removal of the intra-group balances at the year-end

In the above example, the sale of goods by Breary Ltd to Byrne Ltd is merely a transfer of goods for group accounts purposes; a sale will be recognised in the consolidated accounts once the goods have been sold to Byrne Ltd's customer. For this reason all intra-group transactions are eliminated because if they were not eliminated sales, cost of sales, debtors and creditors would all be overstated, which would mislead the user of the consolidated financial statements. In the individual financial statements, the sale and corresponding cost of sale and intra-group debtor and creditor will still be recognised; the transactions are only eliminated on consolidation (see **8.28** and **8.29** below for the general principles of the mechanics of how consolidated financial statements are prepared).

Focus

- In addition to normal day-to-day sales and purchases among group members, there may also be other transactions which need elimination, such as intra-group loans, intra-group loan interest and dividends paid from the subsidiary to the parent company.

Intra-group profits

8.13 When intra-group trading has taken place during the year (especially towards the year-end), some goods (or other assets) transferred within the group are still held as assets by the receiving group member at the year-end – the most common type of transaction that would give rise to intra-group profits remaining at the year-end are sales of goods from one group member to another.

Example 8.7 – Intra-group profit in stock at the year-end

Breary Ltd has a 100% investment in Byrne Ltd with a year-end of 31 December 2016. On 1 November 2016, Breary Ltd sold goods which cost £5,000 to Byrne Ltd for £8,000*. At the year-end, Byrne Ltd had only sold half of these goods to customers outside of the group.

Section 13 *Inventories* requires inventory to be measured at the lower of cost and estimated selling price less costs to complete and sell. Byrne Ltd still has goods which it bought from Breary Ltd in its own stock valuation at the year-end. These goods were sold to Byrne at a profit of £3,000 and Byrne Ltd still has half of this stock leftover at the year-end. To comply with the principles in Section 13, for group accounts purposes, the stock in Byrne Ltd needs to be reduced by £1,500 (£3,000 profit × 50%) to bring the stock valuation back down to cost to the group at the year-end, hence the journal adjustments will be:

DR closing stock (consolidated profit and loss)	£1,500
CR stock (consolidated balance sheet)	(£1,500)

Being elimination of intra-group profit held in stock at the year-end

*The intra-group sale and purchase (and any associated intra-group debtor and creditor) will also have to be eliminated on consolidation.

The effect of removing intra-group profits means that the group financial statements show a stock valuation at cost (as per Section 13 requirements). If intra-group profits were not eliminated at the year-end, the stock valuation would be overstated and hence misleading.

Goodwill

8.14 In the consolidated financial statements, goodwill arises when the amount paid by the parent for the net assets acquired in the subsidiary is more than the net assets which they have purchased in the business combination. This is known as 'positive' goodwill.

Example 8.8 – Positive goodwill

Breary Ltd acquires 80% of the net assets of Grainger Ltd on 1 January 2017 (the date of acquisition) for a purchase price of £80,000. On this date the net assets of Grainger Ltd are as follows:

	£	£
Ordinary share capital		10,000
Revaluation reserve		8,000
Profit and loss reserves		75,000
		93,000
Goodwill is calculated as follows:		
Cost of investment		80,000
Less net assets acquired (80%):		
Share capital	8,000	
Revaluation reserve	6,400	
Profit and loss reserve	60,000	(74,400)
Goodwill on acquisition		5,600

In the consolidated financial statements, the cost of investment in Grainger Ltd (£80,000) will be replaced by the goodwill figure of £5,600. This goodwill then has to be amortised over its estimated useful life (it cannot have an indefinite useful life under Section 19 of FRS 102 *Business Combinations and Goodwill*).

> **Focus**
>
> - Where management are unable to reliably estimate the useful economic life of the goodwill, then it is amortised over a period not exceeding ten years. The period was increased from five years in the revised Companies Act 2006.

8.15 This section has focused on where there is an excess of consideration over net assets acquired and hence positive goodwill arises. This is not always the case and goodwill can, in fact, be negative. Examples of where such a case may arise is in a distressed sale where the purchase consideration paid is less than the fair value of the net assets acquired.

Where negative goodwill on an acquisition arises, Section 19 provides three steps which must be carried out by the acquirer:

(1) The acquirer must first reassess the identification and measurement of the acquiree's assets, liabilities and contingent liabilities. In addition, the acquirer must also reassess the measurement of the cost of the combination.

(2) Where the acquirer is satisfied that the assets, liabilities, contingent liabilities and cost have been identified and measured correctly, the negative goodwill arising must be recognised and presented separately on the face of the consolidated balance sheet (statement of financial position) at the date of acquisition and will be shown separately immediately below goodwill and followed by a subtotal of the net amount of goodwill and the excess.

(3) The excess up to the fair value of non-monetary assets acquired is recognised subsequently in profit or loss in the periods that the entity consumes the non-monetary assets. Where there is an excess which exceeds the fair value of the non-monetary assets acquired, this is recognised in profit or loss in the periods which are expected to benefit.

Pre- and post-acquisition reserves

8.16 A parent can only recognise post-acquisition profits of a subsidiary in the consolidated reserves of the group. All pre-acquisition reserves are included in the goodwill calculation (see Example **8.8** above).

Where a subsidiary pays a dividend out of pre-acquisition profits, the parent must deduct this dividend received from the cost of the investment in the subsidiary. This means that the dividend which has been received by the parent is not distributable to its shareholders. However, if the subsidiary pays a dividend out of post-acquisition profits, it is treated as investment income by the parent and will be added to distributable reserves (hence can be distributed as a dividend to the parent's shareholders).

Example 8.9 – Mid-year acquisition

Breary Ltd acquires 100% of the net assets of Byrne Ltd on 1 July 2016 when the reserves of Byrne Ltd stood at £120,000. Both companies have a 31 December accounting reference date and the directors of Breary Ltd have elected to prepare group accounts. At 31 December 2016 the reserves of Byrne Ltd were £180,000.

The pre-acquisition reserves of £120,000 will form part of the goodwill calculation because they will be included in the net assets which Breary Ltd is acquiring. The resulting £60,000 profit (£180,000 reserves at the year-end *less* £120,000 reserves at acquisition) will form part of the consolidated retained earnings, hence consolidated retained earnings will be:

Parent company retained earnings	£X
Share of post-acquisition profit of Byrne Ltd	£60,000
Dividends to shareholders	(£X)
Consolidated retained earnings for the group	£X

Non-controlling interests

8.17 Non-controlling interests are traditionally known in UK GAAP as 'minority interests' and represent the ownership interest of shareholders who are external to the group.

When a parent company does not own 100% of a subsidiary, adjustments occur to account for non-controlling interests. In the consolidated profit and loss account (income statement), the non-controlling interest is the share of profit which is attributable to them and is disclosed on the face of the consolidated profit and loss account under 'Profit on ordinary activities after taxation'.

In the consolidated balance sheet (statement of financial position), the parent will still account for 100% of the subsidiary's assets and liabilities after eliminating intra-group trading and balances. In other words, the parent does not merely account for its share of the subsidiary's assets and liabilities as the parent accounts for the net assets of the subsidiary which it **controls**. A liability is brought into the consolidated balance sheet which represents that part of the net assets which are controlled, but not owned, by the parent.

Example 8.10 – Non-controlling interests

Breary Ltd acquires 75% of the net assets of Byrne Ltd on 1 January 2016.

A parent-subsidiary relationship has arisen because Breary Ltd has acquired more than 50% of the voting rights in Byrne Ltd. The non-controlling interests are 25% which represent the other shareholders of Byrne Ltd who are external to the group.

The Breary Group's consolidated profit and loss account will show the amount of profit attributable to both the parent and the non-controlling interests at the foot of the consolidated profit and loss account. The consolidated balance sheet will still bring in 100% of the assets and liabilities but will include the non-controlling interest share within the equity section of the consolidated balance sheet.

PROCESS OF CONSOLIDATION

8.18 Section 19 *Business Combinations and Goodwill* outlines the method of preparing consolidated financial statements. It gives guidance on identifying an acquirer as well as measuring the cost of the business combination and allocating that cost to the assets, liabilities and provisions for contingent liabilities. Section 19 also outlines the accounting requirements for goodwill arising at the date of acquisition (both positive and negative goodwill) as well as in subsequent accounting periods.

Section 19 does not, however, deal with:

- formation of a joint venture (this is dealt with in Section 15 *Investments in Joint Ventures*); or
- acquisition of group assets which do not constitute a business.

> **Focus**
>
> - Section 19 refers to 'business combinations', hence the title *Business Combinations and Goodwill.* It is important to emphasise that when a parent company acquires a subsidiary, it is **not** a merger (Section 19 also deals with merger accounting). A merger is the combining of two businesses into one where there is no controlling party and for which strict criteria must be met. The fact that there is no controlling party in a merger distinguishes this type of business combination from a combination where a parent acquires a subsidiary. In addition, merger accounting uses book values to combine the financial statements, whereas fair values are used to consolidate the subsidiary's financial statements in with the parent's.

8.19 Section 19 uses the term the 'purchase method' in accounting for a business combination. In previous UK GAAP, this was referred to as the 'acquisition method' of accounting and the purchase method is, more or less, the same thing.

The purchase method requires the following steps to be completed:

- identify an acquirer;
- measure the cost of the business combination; and
- allocate that cost to the assets acquired and the liabilities and provisions for contingent liabilities assumed at the date of acquisition.

Identify the acquirer

8.20 The purchase method of accounting requires an acquirer to be identified. The acquirer is the party involved in the business combination which is the controlling party (ie the parent). As mentioned earlier in this chapter, a parent-subsidiary relationship exists where the parent *controls* the acquired entity and control is the power to govern the financial and operating policies of that entity so that the parent benefits from the subsidiary's activities.

Paragraph 19.10 gives some examples of situations where an acquirer exists as follows:

- Where the fair value of one of the combining entities is significantly higher than that of the other combining entity. The entity with the higher fair value is likely to be the acquirer.
- Where a business combination takes place through an exchange of ordinary equity instruments for cash or other assets. In this example the entity which gives up the cash or other assets is likely to be the acquirer.
- Where the business combination results in the management of one of the combining entities having the ability to dominate the selection of the

management team of the combined entity, the entity whose management is able to dominate such a selection is likely to be the acquirer.

Focus

- The above examples are not exhaustive and there could well be other indicators of an acquirer.

Measure the cost of the business combination

8.21 For the purposes of a business combination, the cost is the total of:

- the fair values at the date of acquisition of assets given, liabilities incurred or assumed and equity instruments which are issued by the acquirer, in exchange for control of the acquiree; plus
- costs which are directly attributable to the acquisition.

There may be occasions where an acquisition is undertaken in stages (often referred to as 'step acquisitions' or 'piecemeal acquisitions'). Where control is achieved following a series of transactions, the cost of the business combination is the total of the fair values of assets given, liabilities assumed and equity instruments issued by the acquirer at the date of each transaction in the series.

Often in a business combination, the agreement will make provision for an amount to be paid to the seller or repaid to the purchaser depending on future events occurring (or not occurring as the case may be). Where contingencies are in place, the acquirer must include the estimated amount of any adjustment in the cost of the combination at the date of acquisition where this adjustment is probable (ie more likely than not). In addition, the adjustment itself must also be able to be reliably estimated.

However, where any adjustment to the cost of the business combination is not recognised at the date of acquisition, but becomes probable after the combination has taken place and can be reliably measured, then the additional consideration is treated as an adjustment to the cost of the combination.

Example 8.11 – Cost of combination

Breary Ltd acquires 80% of the net assets of Byrne Ltd for a purchase consideration of £100,000 on 1 January 2016. Legal fees have been incurred for the combination amounting to £9,000. In addition, the directors of Breary Ltd have agreed to pay a further £10,000 to the outgoing shareholders of Byrne Ltd if the entity makes profits above £65,000 for the year-ended 31 December 2016, failing which the £10,000 additional consideration will be waived. Historically, the company has always made profits well over this benchmark, but there are concerns that some customers may leave because of the combination, although current forecasts show that this profit target will be achieved.

The cost of the combination will include the £100,000 purchase price plus the legal fees of £9,000 as these are incremental to the business combination. The additional £10,000 contingent consideration will also be included in the cost of the combination because it is expected that Byrne Ltd will hit the profit target of £65,000 and the amount has already been estimated. The total cost of the combination will therefore be £119,000.

Allocate the cost of the combination

8.22 On the date of acquisition, an acquirer should allocate the total cost of the business combination by recognising the identifiable assets and liabilities (as well as making a provision for contingent liabilities) at fair value at the date of acquisition. Any difference arising once the cost of the combination has been allocated is recognised as goodwill.

> **Focus**
>
> - Provisions are not generally made for contingent liabilities under Section 21 *Provisions and Contingencies*. However, in a business combination provisions are made for such liabilities only if the fair value can be measured reliably. Where such a fair value cannot be measured reliably then there will be a resulting effect on the amount of goodwill that is recognised and disclosure of the contingent liability should be made as per Section 21.

For contingent liabilities which are recognised separately in a business combination, after initial recognition they must be subsequently measured at the *higher* of:

- the amount which would be recognised in accordance with Section 21; and
- the amount initially recognised deducting amounts previously recognised as revenue in accordance with Section 23 *Revenue*.

8.23 When allocating the costs of the business combination, the acquirer allocates the cost to the identifiable assets and liabilities and provisions for contingent liabilities as necessary. Such assets, liabilities and contingent liabilities can only be recognised if they satisfy the following criteria at the date of acquisition:

- For assets other than intangible assets, it is probable that any associated economic benefits associated with the asset will flow to the acquirer and the asset's fair value can be reliably measured.

- For liabilities other than contingent liabilities, it is probable that an outflow of resources will be required to settle the obligation and the liability's fair value can be reliably measured.
- For intangible assets or contingent liabilities, fair values can be reliably measured.

In respect of the above, there are three exceptions relating to assets and liabilities:

- Deferred tax assets or liabilities in a business combinations are accounted for in accordance with Section 29 *Income Tax* (see **Chapter 12**).
- Assets or liabilities in respect of the acquiree's employee benefit arrangements are recognised and measured in accordance with Section 28 *Employee Benefits* (see **Chapter 12**).
- Share-based payment arrangements are recognised and measured in accordance with Section 26 *Share-based Payment* (see **Chapter 12**).

Focus

- An acquirer can recognise liabilities for terminating or reducing the activities of the acquiree as a result of the business combination to the extent that the acquirer has an existing liability for restructuring in accordance with Section 21 at the date of acquisition. The acquirer cannot, however, recognise liabilities for future losses or other costs to be incurred as a result of the business combination at the date of acquisition.

Consolidated profit and loss account (income statement)

8.24 In the consolidated profit and loss account (income statement), the acquiree's profits or losses after the date of acquisition are included at an amount which is based on the cost of the business combination to the acquirer. Therefore, in respect of fixed assets owned by the acquiree, these will be valued at fair value from the date of acquisition (which may be different from book values). The associated depreciation charge in the consolidated financial statements will be calculated based on fair values of these fixed assets because the depreciable amount of such assets will also be based on the cost to the acquirer.

Ongoing combinations at the reporting date

8.25 Some business combinations may take a long time to complete and it may be the case that a business combination which has commenced prior to the reporting date is still ongoing at the end of the reporting period (ie at the year-end). Where this situation occurs, the acquirer recognises provisional amounts for the items for which the accounting is incomplete. These will, of course, be based on best estimates.

Within 12 months of the acquisition date, the acquirer must make a retrospective adjustment to the provisional amounts it has recognised in respect of assets and liabilities at the date of acquisition to reflect the new information obtained. Once this 12-month period has elapsed following the date of acquisition, the acquirer should only make adjustments to the initial accounting for the business combination to correct a material error in accordance with Section 10 *Accounting Policies, Estimates and Errors*.

Coterminous year-ends and accounting policies

8.26 Paragraph 9.16 of Section 9 *Consolidated and Separate Financial Statements* in FRS 102 requires the financial statements of a parent and its subsidiaries to be prepared to the same reporting date (ie they should have coterminous year-ends), unless it is impracticable to do so (for example because of legal reasons).

Where the parent and a subsidiary do not have coterminous year-ends the consolidated financial statements must be made up:

- from the financial statements of the subsidiary as at the last reporting date prior to the parent's reporting date and adjusted for the effects of significant transactions or events which take place between the date of those financial statements and the date of the consolidated financial statements, provided that the reporting date is no longer than three months before that of the parent's reporting date; or
- from interim financial statements prepared by the subsidiary as at the parent's reporting date.

Focus

- For the vast majority of small groups it is unlikely that a subsidiary's year-end date will be different from the parent's and for a new subsidiary it is quite easy to change a year-end so that it is coterminous with the parent's. For the purposes of Companies House, where a subsidiary's accounting reference date is changed to be coterminous with the parent's, the accounting period cannot be any longer than 18 months.

8.27 Paragraph 9.17 also requires consolidated financial statements to be prepared using uniform accounting policies for similar transactions and events and conditions encountered in similar circumstances. Where this is not possible, or impracticable, appropriate adjustments must be made to the subsidiary's financial statements so as to prepare consolidated financial statements for the group.

Method of preparing the consolidated profit and loss account

8.28 Each member of the group will prepare their own individual financial statements which are often referred to as the entity's 'separate' financial statements. Each separate set of financial statements are combined and are then subjected to consolidation adjustments to arrive at a set of consolidated financial statements which show the results of the group as a single trading entity.

Preparing the consolidated profit and loss account (income statement) is relatively straightforward as it involves consolidating, line-by-line, up to the levels of profit after tax. After profit after tax, the amounts attributable to the parent and the non-controlling interests are shown, therefore:

Up to profit after taxation:	amalgamate on a line-by-line basis
Non-controlling interests:	represents the non-controlling interest(s) share of the subsidiary's after-tax profit.

The elimination of intra-group trading has been examined above (see Example **8.6** above). Where intra-group dividends and interest are concerned, dividends from the subsidiary to the parent are eliminated from the group's investment income and the full amount of interest is eliminated from investment income and interest payable.

Method of preparing the consolidated balance sheet

8.29 It is more complex preparing the consolidated balance sheet (statement of financial position) than it is preparing the consolidated profit and loss account. The assets and liabilities of the consolidated balance sheet show the net assets which are controlled by the parent, whereas the equity section of the consolidated balance sheet reflects the ownership split between the parent and the non-controlling interests.

The method of preparing the consolidated balance sheet is shown in the following table:

Area	**Method**
Assets	Amalgamate on a line by line basis
Liabilities	Amalgamate on a line by line basis
Share capital	Parent company only
Reserves	Reserves comprise: parent's reserves; and share of subsidiary post-acquisition profit/loss
Goodwill	Capitalise and amortise over useful economic life (where this cannot be reliably estimated it is deemed to be no longer than ten years)
Non-controlling interests	Non-controlling interest's share of net assets at the reporting date

All intra-group balances should cancel each other out. Where they do not cancel each other out it is likely to be due to cash or stock in transit. In-transit items are adjusted for by adding them back into stock/bank and amending the intra-group balance in the accounts of the receiving company prior to the consolidation exercise taking place.

Intra-group dividends should also cancel each other out. Only dividends payable to non-controlling interests should be reflected in the consolidated balance sheet as a liability.

DISCLOSURES

8.30 Paragraph 1A.22(d) requires any disclosures to be made in the consolidated financial statements which are required by Schedule 6 of the Small Companies Regulations.

Reduced disclosures are available for qualifying subsidiaries in FRS 101 *Reduced Disclosure Framework.*

Where advantage is taken of disclosure exemptions, the subsidiary must disclose:

- a brief summary of the disclosure exemptions adopted; and
- the name of the parent of the group in whose consolidated financial statements the subsidiary's financial statements are consolidated, and from where those financial statements may be obtained.

PITFALLS TO AVOID

- Forgetting to eliminate intra-group trading and balances on consolidation. Assuming control is only obtained if the parent owns more than 50% of the voting rights.
- Forgetting to apportion pre- and post-acquisition reserves for 'in-year' acquisitions.
- Omitting to show the split of profit attributable to owners of the parent and non-controlling interests on the face of the consolidated profit and loss account.
- Time-apportioning assets and liabilities for an 'in-year' acquisition.

CHAPTER SUMMARY

- Small groups are not legally required to prepare consolidated financial statements, but may do so where the directors feel this is of benefit.
- The size thresholds for a small and medium-sized group have been increased in the revised Companies Act 2006 with effect for accounting periods commencing on or after 1 January 2016.

- A parent-subsidiary relationship will arise when the parent has the ability to control the financial and operating policies of the subsidiary and benefit from the subsidiary's activities.
- Control can be obtained by the parent even with a shareholding of less than 51% and hence the substance of the arrangement takes precedence over the legal form.
- Whilst not particularly common for small groups, a complex group structure needs to be looked at carefully to identify the indirect interest a parent may have in another subsidiary. More complex group structures will fall to be classed as small due to the raising of the small groups threshold.
- Other forms of investment which do not constitute a parent-subsidiary relationship include investments in associates, joint ventures and simple investments. Different sections of FRS 102 deal with these transactions.
- The consolidated financial statements of a group must show the financial results of the group in line with its economic substance, which is that of a single trading entity.
- All intra-group trading (including intra-group profits, dividends and interest) must be eliminated on consolidation.
- Goodwill arising in a business combination can be both positive and negative.
- Positive goodwill is amortised over its estimated useful life and where this useful life cannot be reliably estimated it is amortised over a period not exceeding ten years.
- Negative goodwill requires more analysis to ensure it is, in fact, negative.
- Pre-acquisition reserves are included in the goodwill calculation whilst post-acquisition reserves form part of the consolidated reserves.
- The process of a business combination involves identifying an acquirer, measuring the cost of the combination and then allocating that cost.
- Subsidiaries should use the same accounting reference date and accounting policies as that of the parent, unless it is impracticable to do so.
- Whilst the consolidated profit and loss account is relatively straightforward to prepare, the consolidated balance sheet is a little more complex.

Chapter 9

Related Parties

SIGNPOSTS

- While related party disclosure requirements have become increasingly complex over the years, the revised Companies Act 2006 only requires limited related party disclosures to be made for a small business. The directors of a small company do, however, have a legal duty to ensure the financial statements give a true and fair view which may mean making additional disclosures over and above the legally required minimum (see **9.1**).
- The objective of related party disclosures is to draw attention to the fact that reported financial information may have been influenced by the existence of transactions with related parties (see **9.2**).
- Section 33 *Related Party Disclosures* in FRS 102 outlines the circumstances when a person is a related party of an entity and also when another entity is a related party (see **9.3** and **9.4**).
- Two entities are not related to each other simply because they have a director in common but they can become related in more complex situations (see **9.5**).
- Transactions among group members need not be disclosed, provided the group members are wholly-owned members of the group (see **9.6**).
- Companies under common control are deemed to be related parties (see **9.7**).
- Section 33 outlines certain parties which it does not consider to be related to each other and where parties are related, the section gives a useful overview of examples of related party transactions (see **9.8** and **9.9**).
- The Companies Act 2006 outlines the legally required minimum disclosures but additional disclosure information may be needed to give a true and fair view (see **9.10** to **9.16**).

INTRODUCTION

9.1 Related party issues have proven to be problematic over the years for companies because of their subjective nature as well as the reluctance by some directors to make related party disclosures in an attempt to conceal certain transactions (either due to fraud or an unwillingness to make disclosure). Over the years the standards which have dealt with related party issues have become more complex because the way in which businesses have developed have also become complex. In addition, while many small companies or small groups tend not to have an audit, where these are subjected to external audit, related parties have proved to be somewhat of a challenge to auditors simply because of the reliance on the part of the directors to disclose related party relationships (although auditing standards at ISA (UK and Ireland) 550 *Related parties* does outline the procedures to obtain sufficient and appropriate audit evidence over related party relationships and transactions).

The transposition of the EU Accounting Directive into company law has resulted in related party issues for small companies being less arduous than was the case in previous UK GAAP. While Section 33 *Related Party Disclosures* in FRS 102 tries to deal with related party issues in a comprehensive manner, small companies need only make limited related party disclosures to comply with the revised Companies Act 2006.

Focus

- Notwithstanding the fact that the revised Companies Act 2006 only requires limited related party disclosures to be made, the directors of a small company still have a legal duty to ensure the financial statements give a true and fair view. This legal responsibility will mean that the directors must also consider additional disclosure requirements that may be needed in order that the financial statements do give a true and fair view. Application of the legally required minimum disclosures may not be enough to give a true and fair view, so whilst the legal requirements are less arduous for small companies, the additional duty to consider whether the true and fair requirements in company law are achieved will mean more responsibility for directors of small companies and groups. Paragraph 1AC.35 of FRS 102 also says that where a small entity discloses all transactions with related parties, it would still be complying with company law.

9.2 Related party transactions can take many forms, but for small companies they are generally confined to transactions which are undertaken in the normal course of business. The overall objective of the related party disclosures standards are to draw attention to the fact that reported financial information may have been influenced by the existence of related parties and material transactions between those related parties which may undermine the financial statements if disclosure of such transactions is not made.

Focus

- The revised Companies Act 2006 at paragraph 66 of Schedule 1 to the Regulations says that disclosure of transactions which the company has entered into with related parties **must** be given where such transactions are material and have not been concluded under normal market conditions. This is also reflected in paragraph 1AC.35 of FRS 102.

IDENTIFYING RELATED PARTIES

9.3 A related party can be an individual or a business entity, whether incorporated or a sole trader, a partnership or a Limited Liability Partnership (LLP). Related parties can also consist of a group of individuals who may act 'in concert' in respect of the financial and operating policies of the business.

The definition of a related party in Section 33 of FRS 102 is comprehensive and splits related parties into two distinct components: *persons* who may be related parties (paragraph 33.2(a)) and *entities* who may be related parties (paragraph 33.2(b)).

Focus

- It is important that where a small business is considering possible related party relationships, it does so in the context of the substance of the relationship and not merely the legal form as this is a requirement of paragraph 33.3 of FRS 102.

Persons who may be related parties

9.4 While only limited related party disclosures are needed for small companies, it is important at the outset to understand when a related party relationship exists because that relationship may then trigger the related party disclosure requirements laid down in the Regulations to the Companies Act 2006.

Paragraph 33.2(a) of FRS 102 says that a person, or a close member of that person's family, becomes a related party if that person:

- has control, or joint control, over the reporting entity;
- has significant influence over the reporting entity; or
- is a member of the key management personnel of the reporting entity or of a parent of the reporting entity.

Focus

- 'Control' can be obtained with a shareholding of more than 50% of the voting rights of the small business (although there can be other characteristics which may indicate that an individual may exert control over the business, even where the person has a holding of less than 51%). Also, 'significant influence' would be obtained with a holding of between 20 and 50% of the voting rights in the small business (although, as with control, there may be other characteristics which could indicate an individual may have the ability to exert significant influence over the small business despite a holding in the voting rights of the entity of less than 20%).

Paragraph 33.2(b) of FRS 102 then looks at how an entity may become a related party of the reporting entity and in this respect, there are seven conditions which may give rise to a related party relationship existing between two, or more, entities and these conditions are where:

- the entity and the reporting entity are both members of the same group;
- one entity is an associate or joint venture of the other entity;
- both entities are joint ventures of the same third party;
- one entity is a joint venture of a third party, whilst the other entity is an associate of the third entity;
- the entity is a post-employment benefit plan (a retirement benefit plan) for the benefit of the employees of either the reporting entity or an entity which is related to the reporting entity; where the post-employment benefit plan is itself a plan, then the sponsoring employees will become related parties of the reporting entity;
- the entity is controlled or jointly controlled by a person in paragraph 33.2(a) (see above); or
- the individual identified in paragraph 33.2(a)(i) has significant influence over the reporting entity or is a member of the key management personnel (which would include a parent of the entity).

Directors in common

9.5 Section 33 does not consider two entities to be related parties simply because they have one director (or other key management personnel) in common or because a member of the key management personnel has significant influence over the other entity.

Example 9.1 – One director in common

Miss Emery is the sole director of Alpha Ltd and Beta Ltd. During the year to 31 December 2016, Alpha Ltd sells goods to Beta Ltd for £10,000 plus value added tax.

Under the provisions in Section 33, two companies are not related parties just because they have a director in common. More often than not, a director can have influence over the running of the company, but this does not necessarily give rise to Alpha and Beta becoming related parties as both companies would be expected to go about their own business for the benefit of their respective shareholders.

Example 9.2 – Security pledged for borrowings

The facts are the same as the above, but now consider a situation where Alpha Ltd had pledged security for Beta's borrowings. This would mean that Alpha Ltd has put Beta's interests before its own and in this case Alpha and Beta would become related parties for the entire accounting period.

Example 9.3 – Controlling nucleus of directors

Alpha Ltd and Beta Ltd both have a controlling nucleus of six directors each, five of whom were directors of both companies. In this case, Alpha Ltd and Beta Ltd would be related parties because they would be under common control.

TRANSACTIONS AMONG MEMBERS OF A GROUP

9.6 It is commonplace when a group structure exists (particularly among small groups) for intra-group trading to take place.

There is a specific exemption in paragraph 33.1A (and paragraph 1AC.35) of FRS 102 which says that related party disclosures need not be made in the financial statements relating to transactions which have been entered into between two, or more, members of a group. Care, however, needs to be taken because there is a condition attached to this disclosure exemption which says that any subsidiary which is a party to the transaction must be wholly-owned by such a member before the exemption from disclosing transactions among group members can be taken.

Example 9.4 – Intra-group trading

The following is the group structure of the Heyes Group:

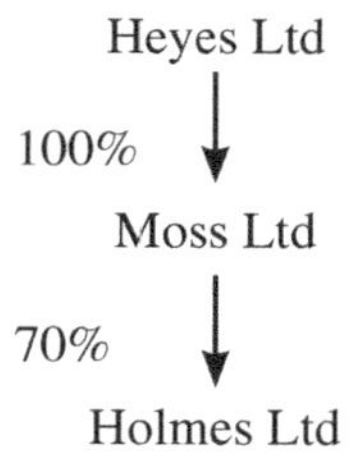

All three companies trade with each other during the year to 31 December 2016 and the 30% non-controlling interests (minority interests) in Holmes Ltd are external to the group.

In this example, Moss Ltd is a wholly-owned subsidiary of Heyes Ltd. Moss Ltd also has control over Holmes Ltd because it owns more than 50% of the voting rights in Holmes Ltd. However, Holmes Ltd is not a wholly-owned group member and hence transactions with Holmes Ltd would be disclosed in Heyes Ltd and Moss Ltd financial statements.

If, however, Heyes Ltd owned the remaining 30% of the voting rights in Holmes Ltd, then Holmes Ltd would become a wholly-owned subsidiary within the group and hence the group could take advantage of the exemption from disclosing related party transactions.

Companies under common control

9.7 Common control can arise, for example, where two companies are subject to common control by the same party.

Example 9.5 – Common control

Westhead Ltd owns 100% of the voting rights of Heaton Ltd and Whitaker Ltd. Heaton Ltd and Whitaker Ltd have both entered into transactions with each other during the accounting period.

Westhead Ltd is a related party of both Heaton Ltd and Whitaker Ltd. Both Heaton Ltd and Whitaker Ltd are also related parties because they are subject to common control.

PARTIES WHO ARE NOT RELATED PARTIES

9.8 In addition to two entities not being related parties because they have a director or other key management personnel in common, paragraph 33.4 of FRS 102 identifies other parties that Section 33 does not consider to be related parties which include:

- two venturers which share control over a joint venture;
- any of the following parties by virtue of their normal dealings with the small company regardless of the fact that they may affect the freedom of action of an entity or participate in the decision-making process:
  - providers of finance (eg a bank);
  - trade unions;
  - public utilities; and
  - government departments and agencies.

Customers, suppliers, franchisors, distributors or general agents are also not considered to be related parties in Section 33 by virtue of the resulting economic dependence.

Focus

- Section 33 defines a related party at paragraph 33.2 and an associate would also include subsidiaries of that associate and a joint venture includes subsidiaries of that joint venture. Hence, it follows that an associate's subsidiary and the investor which has significant influence over the associate are related to each other.

EXAMPLES OF RELATED PARTY TRANSACTIONS

9.9 As discussed earlier in this chapter, over the years the standard-setters have broadened the boundaries for related party transactions in an attempt that the accounting standards become a 'catch all' for related party transactions. This was done so that users of financial statements can have a clear understanding of the impact that such related party transactions have had on the financial performance and position of the business.

Paragraph 33.12 of FRS 102 gives a useful list of examples of transactions that would fall to be classed as related party transactions as follows:

- purchases or sales of goods (whether finished or unfinished);
- purchases or sales of property and other assets;
- the rendering or receiving of services;
- leasing transactions (eg a subsidiary renting an asset from a parent or vice versa);

- transfers of research and development;
- financing arrangements (eg loans and equity contributions);
- provisions of guarantees and collateral;
- the settling of liabilities on behalf of the entity or by the entity on behalf of another party; and
- participation by a parent or a subsidiary in a defined benefit pension plan which shares risks among group members.

Example 9.6 – Arm's-length transaction

Alpha Ltd and Beta Ltd are subsidiaries of the Alpha Group of Companies but are not wholly-owned subsidiaries. During the year to 31 December 2016, Alpha sold goods to Beta Ltd at a heavily discounted price, which would not have otherwise been given had Beta Ltd not been a group member. Disclosure of this transaction has been made in the financial statements of both companies and reference has also been made to the transaction being on an arm's-length basis.

In this example, clearly the transaction has not been undertaken on an arm's-length basis because the discount that has been given to Beta Ltd would not have been granted to it had the company not been a group member. Paragraph 33.13 of FRS 102 does not allow related party transactions to be disclosed as being on terms equivalent to those which prevail in an arm's-length transaction where this is not the case. Related parties can only make disclosure of transactions being on an arm's-length basis when that basis can be substantiated.

Key management compensation

9.10 The term 'key management personnel' include those individuals that have authority and responsibility for planning, directing and controlling the activities of the company (either directly, or indirectly). The scope of key management personnel extends to both executive and non-executive directors.

'Compensation' paid to key management personnel includes all types of employee benefit (eg wages and salaries, medical benefits, provisions of company cars etc). Employee benefits also include all forms of consideration paid, payable or provided by the company (or on behalf of the company) in exchange for services rendered.

Focus

- The definition of 'key management personnel' is therefore wider than just the statutory directors and compensation paid to these personnel requires disclosure.

DISCLOSURE REQUIREMENTS

9.11 Section 33 of FRS 102 and paragraph 1AC.35 does not require the names of the transacting related parties to be disclosed; only the nature of the related party relationship.

For a small reporting entity, Regulation 66(1) says that an entity **may** disclose details of transactions which the company has entered into with related parties. However, Regulation 66(1) does specifically require disclosure of material transactions which have not been undertaken under normal market conditions with:

- owners holding a participating interest in the company;
- companies in which the company has a participating interest; and
- the company's directors.

> **Focus**
>
> - The disclosure requirements for related parties are also outlined in **Chapter 3** and in FRS 102 Section 1A Appendix C at paragraphs 1AC.34–1AC.36.

9.12 Where disclosure of the above transactions are made, Regulation 66(2) requires the following to be disclosed:

- the amount of such transactions;
- the nature of the related party relationship; and
- other information about the transaction necessary for an understanding of the effects of the related party transactions on the financial position of the company.[1]

9.13 Where transactions have been entered into between related parties that are similar in nature, then these may be aggregated for the purposes of disclosure. However, Regulation 66(3) would require separate disclosure where this would be necessary for an understanding of the effects of the related party transactions on the financial position of the company.

> **Focus**
>
> - The above disclosure requirements are the legally required minimum as per the Regulations. However, it must be borne in mind that directors of small companies have a legal duty to ensure the financial statements give a true and fair view and hence directors should consider whether additional related party disclosures need to be made in order to achieve this.

1 Companies Act 2006, reg 66(2)(a)–(c).

Key management personnel compensation

9.14 The total of key management personnel must be disclosed.

Ultimate controlling party

9.15 A small company (or group) may choose to disclose the ultimate controlling party. Control is the ability to influence the financial and operating policies of a small company. The controlling party will have a view to gaining economic benefit from such control and more often than not for small companies, control is obtained when more than 50% of the voting rights in the company are obtained.

Example 9.7 – Controlling party

Mr and Mrs Smyth both run a small consultancy business. Mr Smyth owns 75% of the voting rights, with the remaining 25% being owned by Mrs Smyth.

In this example, Mr Smyth would be the ultimate controlling party by virtue of his controlling shareholding in the business and disclosure may be made of this in the financial statements. Reference does not have to be made to Mr Smyth's actual holding in the shares of the company.

9.16 It may be the case that a small business has more than two director-shareholders who all actively co-operate to exercise control or influence over the business. Where this occurs, control is obtained and may be disclosed in the financial statements. This is because the directors actively co-operate in respect of the financial and operating policies of the entity (although this is not explicitly spelt out in FRS 102 with reduced disclosures, but companies may choose to make disclosure of such control).

Example 9.8 – Directors actively co-operating in the business

Gabriella Enterprises Ltd has four directors who all own 25% of the voting rights of the entity. All the directors are actively involved in the financial and operating policies of the entity.

In this example, no one director has overall control. However, as all four directors are actively involved in the financial and operating policies of the business, they are deemed to be acting in concert and hence will be the controlling parties. A typical disclosure in this situation may be as follows:

> 'The directors are regarded as controlling parties by virtue of their ability to act in concert in respect of the operations of the company.'

PITFALLS TO AVOID

- Failing to correctly disclose transactions with related parties which have not been concluded under market conditions.
- Making additional disclosures to enable a true and fair view to be given.
- Taking advantage of the disclosure exemptions related to wholly-owned group members when some (or all) members of the group are not wholly-owned.
- Failing to consider the substance of related party relationships and merely considering the legal form of such relationships.
- Failing to disclose the ultimate controlling party (particularly where individuals may act in concert).

CHAPTER SUMMARY

- Small companies are only legally required to make limited related party disclosures according to Regulation 66(1) in the Companies Act 2006. However, directors of small companies must also consider the need to make additional related party disclosures where this would be necessary for the financial statements to give a true and fair view.
- Related party transactions can take many forms but generally for a small business, they are confined to transactions which are undertaken in the normal course of business.
- Section 33 defines a related party in the context of both persons and entities.
- Control of a business can be obtained with a holding of more than 50% of the voting rights in the reporting entity; however other characteristics may be present where control is obtained even with a holding of less than 51%. A similar principle exists for significant influence and hence in considering each possible related party relationship, an entity must assess the substance of the relationship and not merely its legal form.
- Two entities are not related to each other simply because they have one director (or other key management personnel) in common. This could, however, change if, for example, one of the entities pledges security over another entity's borrowings or there is a controlling nucleus of directors.
- Transactions among group members which are wholly-owned need not be disclosed.

- Companies under common control are not necessarily related to each other.
- Paragraph 33.4 confirms those parties which Section 33 does not consider as being related to each other.
- Paragraph 33.12 gives a useful list of transactions which should be considered when disclosing related party transactions as such transactions are not confined to intra-group sales and purchases.
- The revised Companies Act 2006 is less arduous in its requirements than was previously the case insofar as related party disclosures for a small business are concerned. A small business *may* choose to disclose details of the transactions which the company has entered into with related parties, but is not mandated to in law (although a small company should make such disclosures where so doing enables a true and fair view to be given).
- Similar transactions can be aggregated when disclosures are being made, but separate disclosures should be made where so doing enables an understanding of the effects of the related party transactions on the financial position of the company.
- A company can choose to disclose its ultimate controlling party which may be one individual (by virtue of their controlling shareholding in the company) or by virtue of acting in concert in respect of the financial and operating policies of the business.

Chapter 10

Transactions with Directors

SIGNPOSTS

- Transactions with directors are very common in a small company and there are certain provisions of the Companies Act 2006 which deal with these transactions (see **10.1**).
- Dividends paid to directors in their capacity as shareholders should be disclosed in the financial statements (see **10.2**).
- The term 'directors' remuneration' comprises a number of transactions and is not confined to just wages and salaries (see **10.3**).
- Advances, credit and guarantees should be disclosed appropriately in the financial statements to comply with the Companies Act 2006 and FRS 102 (see **10.8**).
- Drawings against directors' current accounts in credit might also give rise to the need to disclose related party transactions (see **10.14**).

INTRODUCTION

10.1 Transactions with directors are very common in small companies and the following provisions of the Companies Act 2006 are those most relevant where transactions with directors are concerned:

- Small Companies and Groups (Accounts and Directors' Report) Regulations 2008: Schedule 3, Information about directors' benefits: Remuneration (Companies Act or IAS accounts).
- Section 190: Substantial property transactions: requirement of members' approval.
- Section 197: Loans to directors: requirement of members' approval.
- Sections 252–254: Persons connected with a director etc.
- Section 413: Information about directors' benefits: advances, credit and guarantees.

10.2 The directors' report which accompanies small company financial statements has seen reductions over the years in the content which is legally required. Indeed, in 2013 the Companies Act 2006 was revised in respect of the directors' report in various areas and these changes related to all companies, large and small. All companies, including those which qualify to use the small companies' regime to prepare their financial statements must still include a directors' report (a directors' report is not required for a micro-entity). However, certain disclosure requirements were repealed, including:

- disclosure of charitable donations;
- the acquisition of own shares (by private companies);
- asset values; and
- the policy and practice on payment of creditors (which was not usually disclosed in a small company's directors' report).

In addition, the requirement to disclose the principal activity of the business was also repealed.

> **Focus**
>
> - The rules regarding approval have remained unchanged. The directors' report must be approved by the board and signed on its behalf by a director (or company secretary where appropriate). The directors' report does not have to be approved by the same individual.

In 2007 disclosure about the directors' shareholding was repealed and this opened up a controversial issue concerning the disclosure of dividends. In a small company it is often the director(s) who own the shares of the company and the question arose as to how the related party requirements were satisfied in terms of identifying the amount of dividends paid to directors in their capacity as shareholders.

The professional bodies acknowledged that dividends to directors in their capacity as shareholder were disclosable as a related party transaction (ie in the full financial statements given to the shareholders). Prior to the repealing of the requirement to disclose directors' shareholdings in the directors report, it was generally accepted that the related party issues were satisfied because it was quite easy to calculate the amount of dividend paid to directors' in their capacity as shareholders from the information in the directors' report.

10.3 The transposition of the EU Accounting Directive into company law means that certain transactions with directors' are to be disclosed in the financial statements to comply with company law, whereas insofar as related party transactions are concerned, only transactions which are not concluded under market conditions (ie on an arm's length basis) require disclosure.

DIRECTORS' REMUNERATION

10.4 Directors' remuneration is not necessarily confined to a director's monthly salary. The term 'remuneration' is fairly wide-ranging and includes items such as:

- salaries;
- fees;
- bonuses;
- expense allowances which are chargeable to tax; and
- benefits in kind.

'Golden hellos' can also form part of a director's remuneration package.

There are certain transactions which are not considered to form part of directors' remuneration, including:

- the value of share options granted, or the amount of any gains made when a director exercises such options;
- pension contributions which are paid by the company;
- any money or assets paid to, or receivable by, the director under long-term incentive plans; and
- employers' national insurance contributions.

Focus

- The final bullet point relating to employers' national insurance contributions has often resulted in companies' making erroneous disclosures in their financial statements by including such national insurance contributions in the 'directors' remuneration and other benefits' disclosure note. The director derives no benefit from employers' national insurance contributions and hence they are specifically excluded from the definition of directors' remuneration.

Example 10.1 – Payment to a director

Osbourne Ltd has asked the sales director of one of its competitors to join them and has agreed to pay him an up-front fee to join their company.

This fee is viewed as being part of the director's remuneration and should be included as such in the financial statements.

In the above example the company agreed to pay a fee for a director to join them. Conversely, where the company would, for example, pay compensation for loss of office, this would also form part of the director's remuneration package.

DIRECTORS' BENEFITS IN KIND

10.5 Where the company provides benefits in kind to a director these will form part of the director's remuneration package. Benefits in kind are wide in their scope, but for a small company would typically include:

- company cars;
- medical benefits;
- accountancy fees paid by the company for the preparation of the director's self-assessment income tax return; and
- loans to the director.

> **Focus**
>
> - Reimbursed expenses paid to directors incurred when undertaking their role are not part of their remuneration package.

10.6 When a company provides a director(s) with benefits in kind there is an additional charge to employer's national insurance (class 1A national insurance). This is currently payable at a rate of 13.8% on the cash equivalent of the benefit.

Example 10.2 – Class 1A national insurance

Cahill Ltd provides its sales director with a company car which has a list price of £50,000 and CO_2 emissions of 205. The car is 3 litre diesel and the tax year to which this car has been supplied is 2015/16. The value of the benefit in kind for tax purposes has been assessed at £18,500.

A class 1A national insurance charge will be payable by the company of £2,553 (£18,500 × 13.8%). The value of the benefit for the purposes of the director's remuneration disclosure is £18,500.

10.7 In some accounts production software programs, the value of the benefits provided by the company to a director are incorporated into the accounts by a single-sided journal entry because there is no actual cash flow associated with the benefit provided. This one-sided journal entry increases the value of directors' remuneration for disclosure purposes, but does not affect the directors' remuneration per the trial balance. Therefore the remuneration charge per the trial balance reflects what has been paid (and payable) to the director, but any disclosures included in the notes to the financial statements will also include benefits in kind.

Focus

- The provision of benefits in kind can often be missed when preparing the financial statements of a small company. The information can be found on the directors' P11D forms and such benefits should be included in the directors' remuneration disclosure note as benefits in kind form part of the overall directors' remuneration.

Advances, credit and guarantees

10.8 Many small companies provide loans to directors and these are covered by the Companies Act 2006 at section 197 *Loans to directors: requirement of members' approval* and section 413 *Information about directors' benefits: advances, credit and guarantees.*

Companies Act 2006 at section 197 allows certain transactions to be approved by shareholders (sometimes referred to as 'members'), provided disclosure is made in advance of:

- the nature of the transaction;
- the amount of the loan (or quasi-loan or credit transaction, where appropriate) and the purpose for which it is required; and
- the extent of the company's liability under any transaction connected with the loan (or quasi-loan or credit transaction, where appropriate).

Focus

- Section 197(1) says that:
- A company may not—
  - — make a loan to a director of the company or of its holding company, or
  - — give a guarantee or provide security in connection with a loan made by any person to such a director,
- unless the transaction has been approved by a resolution of the members of the company.[1]

There is an exception to the above rule regarding loans to directors. Section 204: *Exception for expenditure on company business* in the Companies Act

1 Companies Act 2006, s 197(1)(a)(b).

2006 does not require shareholder approval for any expenses which are to be incurred by a director for the purpose of the company or for the purpose of enabling the director to properly carry out his/her duties as officer of the company. Authorisation is also not required in such instances to enable the director to avoid incurring such expenditure.

> **Focus**
>
> - While section 204 provides an exemption from shareholder approval in respect of expenditure on company business, the value of such expenses must not exceed £5,000. If they do exceed £5,000 shareholder approval needs to be obtained.

10.9 Section 413 of the Companies Act 2006 has not been without controversy since the Act came into force – largely because of how the disclosure requirements are worded. Section 197(1) of the Companies Act 2006 does make a general prohibition on loans to directors and also related guarantees or provisions of security where the approval of shareholders' is not obtained. Such approval, however, is not required for 'minor' transactions (ie where the aggregate value of the loan(s) does not exceed £10,000) and therefore companies are not prohibited under company law to make such loans.

Shareholder approval must be obtained where loans to directors exceed £10,000 and this is usually by way of a board resolution, regardless of the fact that the shareholder and the director may be the same person(s) in a small company.

When a small company makes an advance to a director personally and the aggregate exceeds £10,000 at any time, the legal requirement for shareholder approval must be obtained. Many small companies might not be aware of this legal requirement until someone (ie an accountant) tells them, but failure to follow correct protocol might cause problems further down the line if there is a fall out between shareholders (for example a husband and wife who divorce) or the company goes into liquidation or administration. It is always advisable, therefore, to ensure that a copy of a resolution is on the company's files to demonstrate that protocol has been followed.

Advances to directors

10.10 There was quite a lot of confusion in the accountancy profession when the Companies Act 2006 came into effect as it became apparent that the disclosure requirements in section 413 may result in excessive amounts of disclosures where directors' loans were concerned. Under section 413 the following details have to be disclosed in respect of an advance to a director:

(1) its amount;

(2) an indication of the interest rate;

(3) its main conditions; and

(4) any amounts repaid.

The notes to the financial statements also require disclosure of the amounts in (1) and (4) above.

The disclosure of advances to a director is the most controversial area in section 413 of the Companies Act 2006 and a lot of confusion arose as to how to make this disclosure because all transactions which result in an overdrawn director's current account need disclosure. For companies where directors' current accounts are overdrawn, making disclosure of each individual entry was considered impracticable by the profession as a whole. Those in support of the specific disclosure requirements cite the fact that a company and its directors are two distinct bodies and the directors should not be using the company bank account as their own personal bank account.

10.11 Financial statements for a small company must give a true and fair view. The directors are under a legal obligation to ensure the financial statements give a true and fair view and essentially more responsibility has been placed on the part of the directors to do this given the fact that the revised Companies Act 2006 will require more judgement in making additional disclosures, where necessary, to achieve a true and fair view.

In a lot of cases, advances to directors will consist of several items which make up an overdrawn balance as at the end of the reporting period. However, consider a company which makes a £50,000 advance to a director towards the purchase of a house – this is likely to be a highly material transaction for a small company and will require disclosure in the financial statements. Disclosure of such a transaction could be as follows:

> 'During the year, the company made a short-term loan to Mr X amounting to £50,000 for the purposes of a house purchase. Interest at a rate of 4.75% per annum is payable half-yearly and the loan is repayable on 31 December 2018.'

For many small companies, the issue is not as clear-cut as in the example above and the director's current account could consist of several transactions. This common scenario gave rise to a number of commentators criticising section 413 of the Companies Act 2006 because to disclose such transactions would be impracticable.

The professional bodies in the UK offered guidance in disclosing such transactions and in cases where directors' current accounts consist of several transactions, a potential solution could be to determine the materiality of advances and repayments; aggregate the immaterial transactions and separately disclose the material items, using the following template:

	£
Opening balance	X
Plus:	
Loans made in the period (advances)	X
Private expenditure in the period	X
	X
Less:	
Undrawn remuneration	(X)
Loan repayments in the period	(X)
Dividends declared in the period	(X)
Closing balance	X

10.12 Where items of expenditure or repayment are considered to be material to the financial statements, or are dissimilar in terms of those expenses which have been aggregated, then these should be disclosed separately.

Focus

- Where the small company has its financial statements audited and the directors' current accounts are overdrawn, the auditors must be satisfied that the disclosures enable the financial statements to give a true and fair view and hence the template disclosure shown in **10.11** above is persuasive rather than prescriptive. In addition it can also be tricky to 'template' such disclosures because client circumstances vary so much so care needs to be taken in this respect.

10.13 It is worthwhile noting that where an overdrawn director's current account is cleared immediately prior to the year-/period-end, this does not preclude the disclosures from being made in the financial statements. The existence of an advance or overdrawn current account balance **at any time during the year** triggers the disclosure requirements. Professional regulators frequently cite examples of accounts where this simple rule has been overlooked so care must be taken to ensure compliance with company law requirements.

Drawing against a credit balance

10.14 When a director makes a drawing against a director's current account which is in credit balance, the transactions are not advances to directors. However, they might be related party transactions and hence the related party disclosure issues should be considered.

Guarantees

10.15 Section 413 of the Companies Act 2006 requires details of guarantees of any kind entered into by the company on behalf of its directors to be disclosed in the financial statements. Specifically, disclosure should be made of:

(1) the guarantee's main terms;

(2) the amount of the maximum liability that may be incurred by the company (or its subsidiary); and

(3) any amount paid and any liability incurred by the company (or its subsidiary) for the purpose of fulfilling the guarantee (including any loss incurred by reason of enforcement of the guarantee).

In respect of (2) and (3) above, the total amounts should be disclosed in the financial statements.

DISCLOSURE REQUIREMENTS: DIRECTORS' ADVANCES AND CREDITS

10.16 **10.15** above outlines the disclosure requirements in respect of guarantees of any kind entered into by the company on behalf of its directors.

Paragraph 1AC.35 of FRS 102 confirms that transactions with directors, or members of an entity's governing body, include directors' remuneration as well as dividends paid to directors in their capacity as shareholders.

In respect of an advance or credit, paragraph 1AC.36 requires disclosure of:

(1) its amount;

(2) an indication of the interest rate;

(3) its main conditions;

(4) any amounts repaid;

(5) any amounts written off; and

(6) any amounts waived.

In respect of (1), (4), (5) and (6), the notes to the financial statement should also include the totals.

Dividends declared and paid or payable to directors in their capacity as shareholders are encouraged to be disclosed in the financial statements by paragraph 1AD.1(d).

PITFALLS TO AVOID

- Not obtaining shareholder approval for loans to directors exceeding £10,000 in aggregate.
- Disclosing ownership interest which the director(s) have in the shares of the company within the directors' report.
- Treating 'template' disclosures in respect of directors' advances and credits as prescriptive disclosures (template disclosures are not contained in the Companies Act 2006).
- Forgetting related party issues where transactions with directors have occurred which are not under normal market conditions (although the name of the director does not need disclosure).

CHAPTER SUMMARY

- Transactions with directors' are dealt with in the Companies Act 2006 and therefore must be disclosed within the financial statements to comply with company law.
- Certain transactions may also give rise to related party issues – for example the withdrawal of amounts against a credit balance in a director's current account.
- Directors' remuneration includes salaries, fees, bonuses, expense allowances which are chargeable to tax and benefits in kind.
- Benefits in kind should also be included in the total directors' remuneration disclosure in the financial statements.
- Loans to directors need shareholder approval if they exceed £10,000 in aggregate.
- A 'template' disclosure in relation to advances and credits can be used but material amounts should be shown separately – care needs to be taken when using template disclosures to ensure they are appropriate to the company's circumstances.
- Where the company is subject to audit, the auditors need to be satisfied that the disclosures enable the financial statements to give a true and fair view.
- Any guarantees entered into by the company on behalf of its directors must also be disclosed in the financial statements.

Chapter 11

Financial Reporting for Micro-entities

Table of Contents

SIGNPOSTS

- The micro-entities regime was borne out of the EU Accounting Directive in the form of Statutory Instrument 2013/3008 but the eligibility criteria is very restrictive (see **11.1** and **11.2**).
- Care must be taken in ensuring FRS 105 is appropriate for the micro-entity as it might be beneficial for the entity to report under a more comprehensive framework (see **11.3**).
- The structure of FRS 105 is different than the structure of FRS 102 because certain types of transactions and events do not apply to micro-entities (see **11.4**).
- 'Deeming provisions' are incorporated into the micro-entities' legislation which state that accounts prepared for micro-entities to the legally required minimum are *presumed* to give a true and fair view (see **11.5**).
- There are key accounting differences between FRS 105 and the FRSSE (effective January 2015) and additional simplifications were made by the Financial Reporting Council (see **11.6** and **11.7**).
- Accounting requirements for micro-entities are outlined in this chapter (see **11.8–11.29**).

INTRODUCTION

History

11.1 On 1 December 2013, legislation was introduced in the form of Statutory Instrument (SI) 2013/3008 The Small Companies (Micro-Entities' Accounts) Regulations 2013 which was introduced by the EU with the objective of reducing costs for small businesses.

The legislation is effective for financial years ending on or after 30 September 2013 for financial statements filed with the Registrar of Companies on or after 1 December 2013. Under the SI, a company qualifies as a micro-entity if it meets at least two of the following three conditions:

- Turnover not more than £632,000
- Balance sheet total (gross assets) not more than £316,000
- Not more than ten employees.

Focus

- At the time of writing the micro-entities' legislation had not been enacted in the Republic of Ireland and hence cannot be applied in the Republic of Ireland until such time that the Irish Department for Jobs, Enterprise and Innovation enact the legislation.

11.2 The micro-entities' legislation allows qualifying companies to take advantage of significantly reduced disclosure levels. The definition of a micro-entity is contained in sections 384A and 384B of the Companies Act 2006, and despite the term 'micro-entity' the eligibility criteria is extremely restrictive and the micro-entities' regime is not applicable to:

- any companies excluded from the small companies' regime;
- financial institutions including credit and insurance institutions;
- charities;
- small parent companies that choose to prepare group accounts;
- companies that are not parent companies but their accounts are included in consolidated accounts; and
- limited liability partnerships.

FRS 105 THE FINANCIAL REPORTING STANDARD APPLICABLE TO THE MICRO-ENTITIES REGIME

11.3 The micro-entities' regime has been in place since 2013 and the Financial Reporting Council (FRC) incorporated the provisions of the regime into the FRSSE and subsequently re-issued both the FRSSE (effective April 2008) and (effective January 2015) on 29 April 2014 as these two versions were in operation at the time. This was never intended to be a long-term solution, but the FRC had to amend the FRSSEs to reflect the legislation.

On 16 July 2015, the FRC issued FRS 105 *The Financial Reporting Standard applicable to the Micro-entities Regime* which applies to micro-entities' financial statements for accounting periods commencing on or after 1 January 2016 (earlier adoption is permitted). FRS 105 has been developed around the legal framework (reflecting the EU Accounting Directive) and simplified requirements from FRS 102 *The Financial Reporting Standard applicable in the UK and Republic of Ireland*.

The FRC felt it appropriate to have a separate standard for micro-entities because of the lack of accounting policy choices and the significantly reduced disclosure levels. It is the least complex financial reporting framework in the new suite of FRSs which form UK GAAP, but it is important that companies carefully consider whether FRS 105 is appropriate for them.

Focus

- FRS 105 is optional and just because a micro-entity may meet the eligibility criteria, it might not necessarily be the most appropriate standard to report under and hence a more comprehensive framework might be more suited to the entity's circumstances (such as FRS 102 with reduced disclosure or full FRS 102). An impact assessment is advisable to ensure FRS 105 is appropriate in the micro-entity's circumstances.

Structure of FRS 105

11.4 When FRS 105 was first issued as an Exposure Draft, the FRC used the same section numbers as FRS 102. The problem with this approach was that many sections of FRS 102 were not applicable to micro-entities and this also resulted in some sections having no content. The FRC took on board feedback during the comment period and the final version of FRS 105 removes all sections of FRS 102 which do not apply to micro-entities. The consequence of this is that the section numbers in FRS 105 are not the same as the section numbers in FRS 102 which can be seen from the comparison in the table below of the content of both FRSs:

Section number	**FRS 102**	**FRS 105**
1	Scope	Scope
2	Concepts and Pervasive Principles	Concepts and Pervasive Principles
3	Financial Statement Presentation	Financial Statement Presentation
4	Statement of Financial Position	Statement of Financial Position
5	Statement of Comprehensive Income and Income Statement	Income Statement
6	Statement of Changes in Equity and Statement of Income and Retained Earnings	Notes to the Financial Statements
7	Statement of Cash Flows	Subsidiaries, Associates, Jointly Controlled Entities and Intermediate Payment Arrangements
8	Notes to the Financial Statements	Accounting Policies, Estimates and Errors
9	Consolidated and Separate Financial Statements	Financial Instruments
10	Accounting Policies, Estimates and Errors	Inventories
11	Basic Financial Instruments	Investments in Joint Ventures
12	Other Financial Instruments Issues	Property, Plant and Equipment and Investment Property
13	Inventories	Intangible Assets other than Goodwill
14	Investments in Associates	Business Combinations and Goodwill
15	Investments in Joint Ventures	Leases
16	Investment Property	Provisions and Contingencies
17	Property, Plant and Equipment	Liabilities and Equity

Section number	FRS 102	FRS 105
18	Intangible Assets other than Goodwill	Revenue
19	Business Combinations and Goodwill	Government Grants
20	Leases	Borrowing Costs
21	Provisions and Contingencies	Share-based Payment
22	Liabilities and Equity	Impairment of Assets
23	Revenue	Employee Benefits
24	Government Grants	Income Tax
25	Borrowing Costs	Foreign Currency Translation
26	Share-based Payment	Events after the End of the Reporting Period
27	Impairment of Assets	Specialised Activities
28	Employee Benefits	Transition to this FRS
29	Income Tax	
30	Foreign Currency Translation	
31	Hyperinflation	
32	Events after the End of the Reporting Period	
33	Related Party Disclosures	
34	Specialised Activities	
35	Transition to this FRS	

The removal of sections which do not apply to micro-entities (such as related party disclosures) means that the standard is less cumbersome than it was at the Exposure Draft stage. In terms of the accounting methodologies contained in FRS 105, these are simpler in FRS 105 than the FRSSE or remain unchanged from the FRSSE.

True and fair view

11.5 The micro-entities' regime has proved to be somewhat a controversial framework. Some accountants support the standard because of the reduced disclosures regime; others question how such financial statements give a true and fair view.

Section 396 of *The Small Companies (Micro-Entities' Accounts) Regulations 2013* at sub-section 2A says that in the case of the individual accounts of a micro-entity which contain the minimum accounting items included, such accounts are 'presumed' to give a true and fair view.

The fact that the accounts of a micro-entity which are prepared in accordance with the legally required minimum information are presumed to give a true and fair view has proved to be the most controversial aspect of the legislation. This is because under the FRSSE (effective January 2015), prior to the introduction of the micro-entities' legislation, and indeed under FRS 102 with reduced disclosures for small companies, directors of a micro-entity would have had to make additional disclosures within the financial statements so that they give a true and fair view. Under FRS 105, the presumption that preparing the financial statements to the legally required minimum will achieve a true and fair view means that the directors of a micro-entity will not have to consider making any additional disclosures if they choose not to.

Focus

- The FRC have highlighted that the directors of a micro-entity may voluntarily choose to disclose more information and this should be carefully considered by a micro-entity in certain situations (for example where there are material uncertainties relating to the micro-entity's ability to continue as a going concern).

Accounting differences: FRS 105 versus the FRSSE

11.6 While many of the accounting treatments in FRS 105 are the same as the FRSSE (effective January 2015) or simpler, there are some notable differences between FRS 105 and the FRSSE (effective January 2015) which are outlined in the following table:

Area	FRS 105	FRSSE
True and fair view	Financial statements prepared to the legally required minimum are presumed to give a true and fair view and hence the directors do not need to consider any additional disclosures to achieve a true and fair view.	Directors have a legal obligation to ensure that the financial statements give a true and fair view and hence must make appropriate disclosures where necessary.
Profit and loss account	Only a Format 2 profit and loss account is permitted under FRS 102.	A Format 1 or Format 2 profit and loss account is permitted.
Primary financial statements	A Format 2 profit and loss account and a Format 1 or Format 2 balance sheet is required. A statement of total recognised gains and losses and a cash flow statement is not required.	A cash flow statement is encouraged but not mandated and a statement of total recognised gains and losses is required where items have been taken directly to equity.

Area	FRS 105	FRSSE
Disaggregation of the balance sheet	No disaggregation of the balance sheet is permitted and therefore fixed assets will not be split between intangible, tangible and investment property. Similarly current assets are not disaggregated into the order of liquidity (stocks, debtors, bank and cash).	The balance sheet is disaggregated into various component parts.
Disclosure requirements	Only disclosures in respect of advances, credit and guarantees in respect of directors and financial commitments, guarantees and contingencies need to be shown at the foot of the balance sheet. No other disclosures are needed as the accounts are presumed to give a true and fair view.	More disclosure requirements are needed under the FRSSE as the financial statements must show a true and fair view.
Fair values and revaluation amounts	No fair values or revaluations can be used and hence all previous fair value or revaluations must be removed on transition and in the comparative year.	The FRSSE allows the revaluation or fair value model of accounting to be applied (eg in respect of investment property).
Accounting policy choices	No accounting policy choices exist in FRS 105 and hence most transactions will be recognised in profit or loss rather than deferred in the balance sheet.	The FRSSE allows more options in respect of accounting policies such as capitalisation of development and borrowing costs or writing such expenses off to profit or loss.
Deferred tax	Micro-entities are prohibited from accounting for deferred tax under FRS 105.	Deferred tax is recognised using the timing difference approach.
Equity-settled share-based payment transactions	There is no requirement to account for equity-settled share-based payment transactions (or to disclose such transactions).	Equity-settled share-based payment transactions are disclosed in the notes to the financial statements.

More guidance has been included in FRS 105 to aid users given in the correct preparation of micro-entity financial statements. FRS 105 does not, however, contain all of the company law reporting provisions which the FRSSE did; although it does include the company law provisions which relate to the financial statements themselves.

Simplifications to FRS 102 to arrive at FRS 105

11.7 FRS 105 has been developed from the requirements in FRS 102 which have been adapted, where necessary, to reflect the legal requirements of the micro-entities' regime as well as making further simplifications. The Accounting Council have acknowledged that they would not have recommended some of the simplifications reflected in FRS 105 (including the omissions of some of the disclosure requirements of FRS 102) if it had not been necessary so as to be compatible with company law. Indeed, the Accounting Council states that it believes investment property should always, where practicable, be measured at fair value as this provides more relevant information to users of the financial statements on an investment property company's financial position and performance. The legislation does not make any provision for revaluations or fair values and hence such assets must be measured at cost less depreciation and impairment.

In light of the fact that the micro-entities' regime is intended to be deregulatory, the Accounting Council have made further simplifications to the principles in FRS 102 to arrive at FRS 105. There are no accounting policy choices in FRS 105 and this is intentional so as to reduce complexity for preparers of micro-entity financial statements. This decision was based on the lack of detail in the formats of the financial statements and the lack of supporting disclosures which would have explained the policy choice adopted.

Key areas where simplifications have been made are as follows:

Deferred tax

Micro-entities are prohibited from accounting for deferred tax under FRS 105 as the Accounting Council view this as a complex area and the lack of supporting disclosures means that it would not be possible to make a distinction between current or deferred tax.

Equity-settled share-based payment transactions

Equity-settled share-based payment transactions do not require accounting for in the financial statements under FRS 105 which is due to the prohibition of the use of fair values and the lack of supporting disclosures.

Pension contributions

Contributions paid into a post-employment benefit plan are treated as an expense (subject to a liability being recognised in respect of a schedule of contributions to the extent that it relates to the deficit). This simplification was made on the grounds that few micro-entities have defined benefit pension plans in place.

Functional and presentation currency

There is no distinction between an entity's functional and presentation currency on the basis that it would be extremely rare for a micro-entity to have a different functional and presentational currency.

Contracted rate for foreign currency

When a micro-entity enters into a forward foreign currency contract it can use the contracted rates to translate assets and liabilities denoted in a foreign currency rather than spot rates. This is to allow for simplification.

Borrowing and development expenditure

All borrowing costs in respect of the construction of a fixed asset and development expenditure are expensed to profit or loss – there is no option to capitalise such costs as this is the simplest option of accounting for such costs.

Government grants

Government grants are accounted for using the accrual model as this is considered to be the easiest option to account for grants.

Financial instruments

The effective interest rate method in FRS 102 is considered to be too onerous for micro-entities and hence these requirements have been simplified. The requirement to impute a market-rate of interest where lending arrangements are undertaken at non-market rates has been removed on the basis that the costs would outweigh the benefits.

Equity instruments

There are simplified requirements in respect of the classification of financial instruments as debt or equity transactions as most micro-entities will issue simple equity instruments.

Intangible assets

There is a prohibition on recognising separately identifiable intangible assets in a trade and asset acquisition. This is due to the fact that these are not required items in the financial statement formats.

Hyperinflation

There is no requirement for a micro-entity to account for hyperinflation as this is not likely to be an issue for micro-entities.

Specialised activities

There are no accounting requirements in respect of specialised activities (eg extractive activities and service concession arrangements) because micro-entities will not typically enter into such transactions.

ACCOUNTING FOR SPECIFIC TRANSACTIONS AND EVENTS

11.8 While most transactions will be similar to the FRSSE (effective January 2015), there are also simplified accounting methodologies contained in FRS 105 in light of the standard's target audience. This section of the chapter will outline a basic overview of how the accounting for specific transactions and events works in FRS 105. The requirements of FRS 105 must be consulted in the event of any ambiguous or complex transactions.

Accounting policies, estimates and errors

11.9 Accounting policies, estimates and errors are dealt with in Section 8 of FRS 105 *Accounting Policies, Estimates and Errors*.

Where FRS 105 does not specifically address a transaction or event, paragraph 8.4 of FRS 105 requires the micro-entity's management to develop an accounting policy which:

- faithfully represents the transactions, other events or conditions;
- reflects the economic substance of the transactions, other events and conditions rather than its legal form;
- is neutral; and
- is prudent.

Focus
• The term 'neutral' means free from bias.

Accounting policies must be applied consistently for all similar transactions, other events and conditions.

Changes in accounting policy

11.10 A change in accounting policy must be applied by a micro-entity if it is required by FRS 105 or if the change results in the financial statements providing reliable and more relevant information about the effects of transactions, other events or conditions which affect the micro-entity's financial position and financial performance.

A change in an accounting policy is applied retrospectively by applying the revised policy to comparative information. This will mean the financial statements reflect the revised policy as if that policy had always been in place and hence will result in financial information which is both consistent and comparable. An example of a change in accounting policy is shown in **Chapter 12** at **12.10**.

Changes in accounting estimates

11.11 A change in an accounting estimate is not applied retrospectively; instead it is applied prospectively (ie going forward). A typical change in an accounting estimate will be a change in depreciation method.

A micro-entity will usually change an accounting policy when new information or new developments emerge and they are not a correction of errors.

Correction of errors

11.12 Prior period errors arise because of a failure by the micro entity to use, or misuse, information that is reliable and:

- was available when the financial statements for the accounting period were authorised for issue; and
- could have been expected to have been obtained and taken into account in the preparation and presentation of those financial statements.

Errors can arise due to:

- mathematical error;
- human error;
- oversights;
- misinterpretation of facts; and
- fraud.

An error is to be corrected by way of a prior period adjustment when it is material.

A prior period adjustment is done by restating the comparative amounts in respect of the prior period(s) presented in which the error occurred. If the error occurred prior to the earliest period reported in the financial statements, then the opening balances of assets, liabilities and equity are restated for the earliest period presented.

> **Focus**
>
> - Where it is impracticable to establish the period-specific effects of the error on the comparative financial statements, the opening balances of assets, liabilities and equity for the earliest period for which retrospective restatement is practicable are restated. The earliest period might be the current accounting period.

Financial instruments

11.13 Financial instruments are dealt with in Section 9 *Financial Instruments* of FRS 105. Section 9 provides a list of examples of financial instruments within its scope and includes:

- cash;
- trade debtors and trade creditors;
- commercial paper and commercial bills held;
- demand and fixed-term deposits with banks or similar institutions;
- bonds, loans and similar instruments;
- investments; and
- options, warrants, futures contracts, forward contracts and interest rate swaps.

There are certain types of financial instruments which are not covered by Section 9 which are shown in the following table:

Financial instrument	**Relevant section of FRS 105**
A micro-entity's own equity and the equity component of compound financial instruments	Section 17 *Liabilities and Equity*
Leases	Section 15 *Leases*
Employers' rights and obligations under employee benefit plans	Section 23 *Employee Benefits*
Share-based payment transactions	Section 21 *Share-based Payment*
Reimbursement assets and financial guarantee contracts	Section 16 *Provisions and Contingencies*
Contracts for contingent consideration in a business combination	Section 14 *Business Combinations and Goodwill*

Initial recognition of financial assets and financial liabilities

11.14 Only when a micro-entity becomes a party to a financial instrument can it recognise a financial asset or financial liability.

On initial recognition, a financial asset or financial liability is recognised at cost (also referred as the 'transaction price').

Example 11.1 – Loan from a bank

Microco Ltd obtains a four-year bank loan from its bank.

A loan is recognised at the amount borrowed. Where the micro-entity provides a loan, it would recognise the debtor at the amount loaned.

Trade debtors and trade creditors are recognised at the invoice price, unless the transaction is a financing transaction (ie payment is deferred beyond normal commercial terms).

Example 11.2 – Deferred payment

Microco Ltd sells goods to one of its customers for £5,000. Customers are usually given credit terms of 30 days from the date of invoice, but Microco agrees to defer payment for one year. If payment was not deferred for one year the cash sale price of the goods on normal credit terms would be £4,000.

This transaction becomes a financing transaction because of the one-year deferred payment terms. The sale is recognised at the cash sale price of the goods supplied on normal credit terms of £4,000. The difference is recognised as interest income over the term of the deferred payment arrangement.

Transaction costs which are associated with financial instruments are added to the cost of a financial asset or deducted from the cost of a financial liability.

Focus

- Paragraph 9.7 of FRS 105 allows transaction costs to be recognised immediately as an expense in profit or loss provided they are not material.

Example 11.3 – Purchase of shares in an entity

Microco Ltd purchases shares in another entity for £2,000. Lawyers fees to complete the transaction amount to £500 and the financial director regards the legal fees as being material.

As the legal fees are deemed to be a material transaction, they are added to the cost of the investment and hence the investment is recognised at £2,500.

Subsequent measurement

11.15 The following table outlines how financial instruments should be subsequently measured after initial recognition:

Instrument	**Subsequent measurement**
Investments in preference shares or ordinary shares and investments in subsidiaries, associates and jointly controlled entities	Cost less impairment
Derivative instruments	Transaction price plus transaction costs not recognised in profit or loss less impairment losses recognised to date allocated to profit or loss over the term of the contract on a straight-line basis unless another systematic basis of allocation is more appropriate
Other financial instruments	Transaction price; *plus* (for financial assets) or *minus* (for financial liabilities) transaction costs not yet recognised in profit or loss; *plus* Cumulative interest income or expense recognised in profit or loss to date; *minus* Repayments of the capital amount and all interest payments or receipts to date; *minus* For a financial asset any reduction for impairment or uncollectability.

Interest income or expense

11.16 Total interest income or expense is the difference between the transaction price of the financial asset or financial liability and the total amount of receipts or payments in respect of the financial asset or financial liability.

The total interest income or expense is allocated to profit or loss over the term of the instrument as follows:

(1) for transactions with deferred settlement terms, the interest income or expense is allocated on a straight-line basis over the term of the contract; and

(2) for all other types of instrument, interest income or expense is allocated to profit or loss at a constant rate on the carrying amount of the financial asset or financial liability excluding transaction costs not yet recognised in profit or loss.

Focus

- In (2) above, the rate will normally be the rate specified in the contract and this could be a fixed rate or variable rate.

Example 11.4 – Two-year loan

Microco Ltd receives a loan of £2,000 on 1 January 2017 and pays an arrangement fee of £100. Interest is payable on the loan at a rate of 5% annually in arrears and the loan is repayable on 31 December 2018. The financial controller has confirmed that the arrangement fees are material and hence recognises the loan at transaction price which is the value of the loan less the arrangement fee and the arrangement fee is recognised in profit and loss on a straight-line basis over the life of the loan (ie over two years). The loan is allocated as follows:

Year	Opening balance	Interest @ 5%	Transaction costs (P&L)	Cash flow	Closing balance
	£	£	£	£	£
31.12.17	(1,900)	(100)	(50)	100	1,950
31.12.18	(1,950)	(100)	(50)	2,100	–

Impairment of financial assets

11.17 In respect of financial assets, at the end of each reporting period the micro-entity must assess any financial assets for indicators of impairment. Examples of such indicators could be a breach in the terms of the loan, the debtor has entered into (or is about to enter to) bankruptcy or an arrangement to pay with its creditors, the contract has become onerous or concessions have been granted by the micro-entity which would not otherwise have been granted (eg extended arrangements to pay).

Impairment losses in respect of financial assets are recognised as follows:

Type of financial asset	Measurement of impairment loss
Preference or ordinary shares; and investments in subsidiaries, associates and jointly controlled entities	Recognised if the asset's carrying amount exceeds the best estimate of the asset's selling price at the reporting date
Derivative instrument	Recognised if the derivative's carrying value exceeds its fair value less costs to sell
Other financial assets	Recognised if the asset's carrying amount exceeds the total of estimated net cash flows which could be generated from the asset. Where the time value of money is material, the amount of the cash flows is the present value of the estimated net cash flows and the micro-entity uses the current contractual rate to discount the cash flows

Reversing an impairment loss

11.18 A micro-entity can reverse a previously recognised impairment loss in a subsequent accounting period when the amount of the impairment loss previously recognised decreases and this decrease can be attributed to an event occurring after the impairment was recognised. An example of such a case could be where a debtor's credit-rating subsequently improves. Any reversals of previously recognised impairment losses are recognised in profit or loss immediately.

Onerous contracts

11.19 A contract becomes an 'onerous contract' when the expected unavoidable payments relating to the contract outweigh any benefit to be received. Paragraph 9.20 of FRS 105 refers specifically to derivative financial instruments (such as a forward foreign currency contract) and a derivative will become onerous when the expected payments exceed the expected receipts. An example of where a derivative becomes onerous would be where the micro-entity enters into an interest-rate swap, repays a loan earlier than the contracted maturity date but the interest rate swap cannot be terminated hence the payments due under the interest rate swap exceed the receipts. In this case the interest rate swap becomes an onerous contract because the micro-entity will not derive any benefit from it.

The present obligation within an onerous contract is measured in accordance with Section 16 *Provisions and Contingencies.*

Derecognising a financial asset

11.20 A micro-entity can derecognise a financial asset when:

- all the contractual rights to the cash flows have expired or have been settled;
- substantially all the risks and rewards of ownership have been passed to another party; or
- no future economic benefits are expected to be received from the financial asset.

Example 11.5 – Sales ledger sold to a factoring company

On 20 July 2017, Microco Ltd (Microco) sold its sales ledger to a factoring company. The sale completed at less than the sales ledger's carrying amount and the terms of the contract state that Microco will not have any obligation to the factoring company in respect of slow or non-payment. Microco will continue to administer the sales ledger (ie send out monthly statements and collect cash from the debtors). On receipt of monies from the trade debtors, Microco is required to immediately remit those to the factoring company.

In this scenario, Microco has transferred substantially all of the risks and rewards of ownership of the debtors. As a result it must remove the debtor balances from its balance sheet and as they have been sold at less than fair value, a loss is recognised in profit or loss. The loss is calculated as the difference between the proceeds received from the bank less the carrying value of the debtors at the date of the disposal. A liability is recognised at each reporting date reflecting any amounts collected from trade debtors which have yet to be remitted to the factoring company.

Derecognising a financial liability

11.21 A micro-entity can derecognise a financial liability when the financial liability is extinguished (ie when the contractual obligations are discharged, cancelled or expire).

Presentation of financial assets and financial liabilities

11.22 A micro-entity should present financial assets and financial liabilities separately. A micro-entity can offset a financial asset against a financial liability, but only in two situations:

- the micro-entity has a legally enforceable right of set-off of the recognised amounts; and
- the micro-entity intends to settle on a net basis or to realise the asset and then settle the liability at the same time.

Disclosure requirements

11.23 The disclosure requirements in respect of financial instruments are as follows:

- the amount of financial commitments, guarantees and contingencies which are not recognised on the balance sheet (statement of financial position) should be disclosed within the total amount of financial commitments, guarantees and contingencies; and
- an indication of the nature and form of any financial asset which has been pledged as security in respect of the micro-entity's commitments, guarantees and contingencies should be disclosed.

Inventories

11.24 Section 10 *Inventories* of FRS 105 deals with the recognition and measurement of a micro-entity's stock (inventory) and work in progress. It does not, however, deal with:

- work in progress in relation to construction contracts – Section 18 *Revenue* deals with this; and

- biological assets which relate to agricultural activity and agricultural produce at the point of harvest – Section 27 *Specialised Activities* deals with these.

A micro-entity measures its inventories at the lower of cost and estimated selling price less costs to complete and sell. This is a similar principle to what was involved in the FRSSE (effective January 2015) which required an entity to measure its inventories at the lower of cost and net realisable value.

Components of cost

11.25 The cost of inventories is not necessarily confined to purchase price, but it can also include costs of conversion (of raw materials into goods) and the costs incurred in bringing the inventories to their present location and condition (eg freight and shipping costs). Where the micro-entity incurs import duties or other taxes which are irrecoverable from the tax authorities, these are also included in the cost of inventories.

Total cost is reduced for the effects of trade discounts, rebates and other similar items (such as volume discounts).

If deferred payment arrangements have been entered into between the micro-entity and its supplier, the purchase price is the cash price at the date of purchase. Any excess between the deferred settlement amount and the cash price at the date of purchase is recognised as interest in the profit and loss account.

Excluded costs

11.26 The following types of cost are not included in the cost of inventories and are written off to profit or loss immediately in the period in which they are incurred:

- abnormal amounts of wasted material, labour and other production-related costs;
- storage costs where these are not necessary during the production process;
- administrative overheads incurred by the micro-entity which are not attributable to bringing the inventories to their present location and condition; and
- selling costs.

Costs of conversion

11.27 Manufacturing companies often convert raw materials into finished goods and the cost of converting these goods include costs which are directly related to the units of production (ie direct labour). Fixed and variable overheads are also included on a systematic basis which relate to the conversion process. The term 'fixed production overheads' relates to those overheads which remain static regardless of the levels of production (such as the cost of factory management or plant depreciation). 'Variable overheads' are indirect costs which vary according the levels of production.

> **Focus**
>
> - Production overheads can also include the costs for obligations which are accounted for under Section 16 *Provisions and Contingencies*. Such costs could be incurred for the dismantling and restoration of a site on which an item of property, plant and equipment is located which are incurred during the reporting period as a result of having used that item of property, plant and equipment to produce inventories during the reporting period.

Allocating production overheads

11.28 Production overheads are allocated to the costs of conversion on a normal capacity basis. The term 'normal capacity' means the production levels expected to be achieved on average over a number of periods or seasons under normal circumstances. Losses due to planned maintenance are also taken into consideration.

> **Focus**
>
> - In periods of abnormally high production levels, the amount of fixed overhead which is allocated to each unit is decreased because if they are not it will result in a valuation of inventory which is above cost. Variable production overheads are allocated to each unit of production based on actual use of the production facilities.

Service providers

11.29 Where a service provider has inventories, they are measured at cost which would normally include the costs of labour and other costs associated with the personnel involved in the provision of the service (including supervisory personnel). As with the production of goods, costs in relation to sales and general administrative personnel must not be included in the measurement of cost and these costs are written off to profit or loss as they are incurred. In addition, the cost of inventories must not include profit margins or overheads which are included in the prices charged by the service provider.

Measurement of cost and cost formulas

11.30 It is permissible for a micro-entity to use methods such as:

- the standard cost method;

- the retail method; or
- most recent purchase price,

to value inventories.

In addition, a micro-entity can use the first-in first-out (FIFO) method or the weighted average cost formula to measure its inventories. It cannot, however, use the last-in first-out (LIFO) method as this method is specifically prohibited in FRS 105 as it results in a valuation of inventories which bears little relationship to actual costs.

Focus

- An example of how the FIFO and average cost method works is shown in **Chapter 12** at **12.77** and **12.78**.

Impairment

11.31 There is an implicit requirement in the concept of 'lower of cost and estimated selling price less costs to complete' which means that a micro-entity must consider whether any of its inventories is showing signs of impairment. Impairment may arise due to obsolescence or damage (or both) or because selling prices have reduced. Where inventory (or a group of inventories) is showing signs of impairment the micro-entity must write these down to recoverable amount by way of an impairment loss which is recognised in profit or loss.

A micro-entity can reverse a previously recognised impairment loss in respect of its inventory where it is clear that the circumstances giving rise to the previously recognised impairment loss no longer apply and selling price less costs to complete and sell have increased.

Focus

- The reversal of a previously recognised impairment loss is restricted to the amount of the original impairment loss.

Disclosure requirements

11.32 FRS 105 requires details of any inventory that the micro-entity may have pledged in respect of its commitments, guarantees and contingencies to be disclosed.

Investments in joint ventures

11.33 Joint ventures are dealt with in Section 11 *Investments in Joint Ventures* in FRS 105. A joint venture is an agreed sharing of control over an activity. An important point to emphasise where joint ventures are concerned is that there must be unanimous consent required by all parties insofar as the financial and operating policies of the venture are concerned. To that end there must be a contractual agreement in place which confirms that there is joint control (in other words one party in the venture cannot have control because this would not give rise to a joint venture).

FRS 105 recognises two types of joint venture:

- jointly controlled operations; and
- jointly controlled assets.

Jointly controlled operations

11.34 In a jointly controlled operation, each venturer will use its own fixed assets (property, plant and equipment) and carry its own inventories. It will incur its own expenses and liabilities and raise its own finance.

In the individual financial statements, a venturer will recognise:

- the assets which it controls and the liabilities which it incurs; and
- the expenses which it has incurred together with its share of the revenue from the joint venture.

Jointly controlled assets

11.35 In some joint ventures, each venturer will jointly control an asset or a group of assets (for example two venturers may have joint control over an investment property).

In the individual financial statements, each venturer will recognise:

- its own share of the jointly controlled assets which are to be classified according to Section 4 of FRS 105 *Statement of Financial Position*;
- any liabilities which it has incurred;
- its own share of any liabilities which it has incurred jointly with the other venturer(s) in relation to the joint venture;
- its share of revenue and expenses; and
- any expenses which it has incurred in respect of its own interest in the joint venture.

Disclosure requirements

11.36 In respect of joint ventures, a micro-entity is only required to disclose the amount of any financial commitments, guarantees and contingencies which are not recognised in the balance sheet which have arisen as a result of its jointly controlled operations and jointly controlled assets and are required to be disclosed within the total amount of financial commitments, guarantees and contingencies.

Property, plant and equipment and investment property

11.37 Section 12 *Property, Plant and Equipment and Investment Property* deals with tangible fixed assets of a micro-entity (ie those fixed assets which possess a physical form and which are intended for use on a continuing basis). The scope of Section 12 does not include biological assets which are related to agricultural activity.

Initial recognition

11.38 There are two criterion which have to be met **before** an asset can be recognised in the statement of financial position (balance sheet):

(1) it is **probable** (ie more likely than not) that the micro-entity will receive future economic benefit associated with the asset; and

(2) the cost of the asset can be measured reliably.

Section 12 also deals with the issue relating to major spare parts and standby equipment. The standard recognises that in some cases spare parts and servicing equipment are consumed through inventory and recognised in profit or loss through cost of sales. FRS 105 takes a different view to previous UK GAAP and says that where major spare parts and standby equipment (including spare parts and servicing equipment) can be used for more than one accounting period, or if the spare parts and servicing equipment can be used only in connection with an item of property, plant and equipment, then they are to be capitalised in the balance sheet as part of property, plant and equipment.

There are some items of property, plant and equipment which may need major components replacing at regular intervals, or may need major inspections performing at regular intervals. Where parts of an item of property, plant and equipment need regular replacement then the replacement parts can be capitalised as property, plant and equipment, provided that the replacement part will provide future economic benefit to the entity. In such cases component accounting is used where the parts are recognised separately from the asset to which they relate and are derecognised once they are replaced.

In respect of major inspections, the cost of each major inspection is included in the carrying amount of an item of property, plant and equipment. Any remaining amount of the previous inspection is derecognised.

Where the micro-entity acquires land and buildings, these are to be accounted for as separate assets, regardless of the fact that the company might have acquired them together.

Subsequent measurement

11.39 All tangible fixed assets are measured at cost less accumulated depreciation and any accumulated impairment losses under FRS 105. There is no option to carry such assets using the revaluation model.

> **Focus**
>
> - This may present problems for some micro-entities on transition where they may have an investment property in the balance sheet which was carried at open market value under the previous FRSSE. On transition such revaluations will have to be removed and the property will have to be carried under normal fixed asset rules, ie at cost less accumulated depreciation and accumulated impairment. In some cases this is likely to have a detrimental impact on the company's balance sheet and hence should be part of the impact assessment when considering the most appropriate framework.

If the micro-entity wishes to carry investment property, or other types of fixed asset, using the revaluation model then it must adopt FRS 102 with reduced disclosures as a minimum. It cannot use the provisions of FRS 105 because the micro-entities' legislation does not recognise any revaluation or fair value amounts.

Depreciation

11.40 Component depreciation should be used where the major components of an item of property, plant and equipment have significantly different patterns of consumption of economic benefit.

Example 11.6 – Component accounting

Microco Ltd has a blast furnace which is being depreciated over its estimated useful life of 20 years. The lining in the blast furnace has to be replaced every five years.

The lining will be accounted for using component accounting and will be depreciated separately from the main asset to which it relates. At the end of five years, the old lining will be derecognised and the new lining will be capitalised and also depreciated over five years.

All amounts in respect of depreciation are to be recognised in profit or loss, unless another part of FRS 105 requires it to be taken to assets; such as Section 10 *Inventories* which would require the depreciation of manufacturing property, plant and equipment to be included in the cost of inventories.

Depreciable amount and period of depreciation

11.41 The depreciable amount of an asset is calculated as the cost of the asset less the expected residual value the company could receive at the end of the asset's useful economic life. This depreciable amount is then depreciated on a systematic basis over its useful life.

Once the directors have arrived at a residual value for the asset, it must be reviewed at each reporting date because factors may indicate that the residual value has, in fact, changed. Where circumstances indicate that the residual value has changed, a micro-entity reviews its previous estimates and, where expectations differ, it will amend the residual value, depreciation method or useful life (note residual values can go in an upward direction under FRS 105 as well as reduce). Any changes to such residual values, depreciation methods or useful lives are applied prospectively (ie going forward) as they are a change in estimation technique rather than a change in accounting policy.

Depreciation must commence as soon as the asset is available for use. The term 'available for use' means that the asset is in the location and condition necessary for it to be capable of operating in a manner intended by management. All depreciation must cease when the asset is derecognised (ie when it is sold or scrapped).

Example 11.7 – Asset becomes idle

Microco Ltd has an asset which it uses to produce one flavour of bottled water. Due to customer complaints, this particular flavour has been withdrawn from the market and the asset which was used to produce the bottled water has not been used for four months. The financial controller has not recognised any depreciation in respect of this asset.

Paragraph 12.19 of FRS 105 states that depreciation does not cease when an asset becomes idle or is retired from active use (unless the asset is fully depreciated). However, in some instances the depreciation charge might well be zero if the company uses the 'usage method' of depreciation and hence the depreciation for the four months in which the asset was out of use might well be zero while there is no production.

When determining the useful life of an asset, there are certain factors which should be taken into consideration:

- The expected use of the asset.
- Expected levels of wear and tear.
- Technical or commercial obsolescence.
- Legal or similar limits on the use of the asset.

Depreciation method

11.42 FRS 105 does not specify which depreciation method to use for certain types of asset and Section 12 requires management to select a depreciation method which reflects the pattern in which the company will consume the benefits associated with the asset. Ordinarily a micro-entity will use the straight-line method of depreciation or the reducing balance method (sometimes referred to as the 'diminishing balance' method). A manufacturing company might also opt for the usage method, particularly if the goods they produce are seasonal and hence machinery is only active at certain times of the year.

Impairment of assets

11.43 Assets should not be carried in the balance sheet (statement of financial position) at any more than recoverable amount. Where an asset is showing signs of impairment then it must be written down to recoverable amount through an impairment loss which is recognised immediately in the profit and loss account. Paragraphs **11.98–11.106** of this chapter examine impairment of assets in more detail.

If the micro-entity is to receive some form of compensation from a third party in respect of an impairment loss, it can only recognise that compensation when its receipt is virtually certain.

Derecognition of a fixed asset

11.44 There are two instances where a micro-entity will derecognise an item of property, plant and equipment and investment property:

(1) when the micro-entity disposes of the asset; or

(2) when no future economic benefits are expected to be received from owning the asset or disposing of the asset.

Any gain or loss on disposal is recognised in profit or loss. If a gain on disposal occurs, this is not recognised as turnover in the profit and loss account (income statement).

Example 11.8 – Disposal of an item of property, plant and equipment

Microco Ltd has a machine which cost £10,000 and has accumulated depreciation of £4,000 at the date of disposal. The company sold this machine to an unconnected third party for £3,500. The loss on disposal can be calculated as follows:

	£
Cost price	10,000
Accumulated depreciation	(4,000)
Net book value	6,000
Disposal proceeds	(3,500)
Loss on disposal	2,500

The journals to remove this asset from the books are as follows:

DR cash at bank	3,500
DR accumulated depreciation	4,000
DR profit and loss on disposal	2,500
CR plant disposal	(10,000)

Being disposal of machine in the year

Disclosure requirements

11.45 If the micro-entity has any financial commitments which are not recognised in the balance sheet (statement of financial position) in respect of acquiring property, plant and equipment or investment property, it must disclose the amount within the total amount of financial commitments, guarantees and contingencies.

Where the micro-entity has pledged any security it must disclose an indication of the nature and form of any items of property, plant and equipment and investment property which have been pledged in respect of its commitments, guarantees and contingencies.

Intangible assets other than goodwill

11.46 Intangible assets are those fixed assets which do not possess a physical form. Section 13 *Intangible Assets other than Goodwill* deals with all such assets (with the exception of goodwill). It also deals with internally generated intangible assets, other than intangible assets which are held for sale in the ordinary course of business as these are dealt with in Section 10 *Inventories* and Section 18 *Revenue*.

Initial recognition

11.47 Separately acquired intangible assets are recognised as intangible assets.

Any internally generated intangible assets must not be recognised as an asset, but must instead be written off to profit or loss as an expense in the period in which the expenditure took place.

In addition, all research **and development** expenditure must also be written off to profit or loss.

> **Focus**
>
> - The capitalisation of development expenditure used to be an accounting policy option in the FRSSE (effective January 2015). FRS 105 does not contain such options and hence the micro-entity has no choice but to write off such costs to profit or loss. This is one of the areas that must be carefully considered when establishing whether FRS 105 is the most appropriate framework to use because if the micro-entity is involved in research and development activities, and has previously capitalised development costs, then it may wish to continue capitalising development expenditure in which case it must use FRS 102 with reduced disclosures as a minimum.

Other types of costs which cannot be recognised as intangible assets include:

- internally generated brands, logos, publishing titles, customer lists and items similar in substance;
- start-up costs including legal and secretarial costs or expenditure incurred in opening up a new facility of business and expenditure for launching new products or processes;
- training activities;
- advertising and promotion costs;
- relocation or reorganisation costs; and
- internally generated goodwill.

Where an intangible asset qualifies for recognition in the balance sheet it must be recognised at cost. Cost can comprise of several components including:

- purchase price;
- irrecoverable taxes (eg import duties); and
- costs which are directly attributable to preparing the asset for its intended use.

If the micro-entity receives any discounts or rebates, these are deducted from the cost price.

Exchange transactions

11.48 If a micro-entity receives an intangible asset in exchange for a non-monetary asset(s) or a combination of non-monetary assets and monetary assets, then the cost of the intangible asset is its fair value. This will not be the case where the exchange transaction lacks commercial substance or fair value for the asset received or the asset given up is not reliably measurable. In such cases the asset's cost is measured at the carrying value of the asset which has been given up.

Subsequent measurement

11.49 After initial recognition at cost, an intangible asset must be carried at cost less accumulated amortisation and any accumulated impairment losses. There is no option to revalue intangible assets under FRS 105.

Amortisation

11.50 All intangible assets will have a finite useful life. For those intangible assets which have been acquired through contractual or other legal rights, the useful life must not exceed the period of the contractual or legal right. The useful life can, however, be shorter depending on how long the micro-entity might use the intangible asset for. If the contractual or legal rights can be renewed at a subsequent date, the useful life can include the renewal period provided there is evidence to support renewal by the micro-entity without incurring significant costs.

> **Focus**
>
> - Where the micro-entity is unable to reliably estimate the useful economic life of intangible assets, the life must not exceed ten years.

Residual value

11.51 It is often difficult to assign a residual value to an intangible asset and in recognition of this, paragraph 13.13 of FRS 105 has a default presumption that the residual value of an intangible asset is zero.

There may, however, be instances where a residual value can be ascertained for the intangible asset, for example:

- where there is a commitment by a third party to purchase the asset at the end of its useful life; or
- there is an active market for the asset where residual values can be determined and it is probable that such a market will exist at the end of the asset's useful life.

An 'active market' is one where the intangible asset is frequently traded and in which market prices are therefore available.

Amortisation period and method

11.52 The 'depreciable amount' of an intangible asset is calculated in the same way as the depreciable amount for a tangible fixed asset, ie at cost less residual value. This depreciable amount is then written off on a systematic basis over the useful life of the intangible asset. Amortisation charges are recognised immediately in profit or loss, unless another part of FRS 105 requires the charge to be recognised elsewhere (eg in inventories or cost of property, plant and equipment).

Ordinarily a micro-entity will use the straight-line method as a basis for amortisation, but may also choose an alternative method if the alternative reflects the pattern in which it expects to consume the asset's future economic benefits.

Amortisation must begin when the intangible asset is available for use. The term 'available for use' means when the intangible asset is in the location and condition necessary for it to be usable in the manner intended by management.

Focus

- Amortisation periods and methods must be reviewed to check if the residual value or useful life of an intangible asset has changed since the most recent annual reporting date. Where such indicators exist, the micro-entity must review its previous estimates and if current expectations differ, they must change the residual value, amortisation method or useful life accordingly. This change is accounted for prospectively as it represents a change in accounting estimate rather than a change in accounting policy.

Impairment of intangible assets

11.53 As with tangible fixed assets, management must determine whether a separately acquired intangible asset is impaired by applying the principles in Section 22 *Impairment of Assets* (see **11.98–11.106** below).

Derecognising an intangible asset

11.54 An intangible asset is derecognised from the micro-entity's balance sheet and a corresponding gain or loss recognised in profit or loss:

- when the micro-entity disposes of the intangible asset; or
- when no future economic benefits are expected to be received from the intangible asset (either through use or disposal).

Disclosure requirements

11.55 The micro-entity must determine the amount of any financial commitments, guarantees and contingencies which are not recognised in the balance sheet for the acquisition of separate intangible assets and disclose that amount within the total amount of financial commitments, guarantees and contingencies.

The micro-entity must also disclose the nature and form of any intangible assets which it has pledged as security in respect of commitments, guarantees and contingencies.

Business combinations and goodwill

11.56 If the micro-entity is involved in a business combination in which the trade and assets of another business are acquired, it must apply the provisions in FRS 102 at Section 19 *Business Combinations and Goodwill* (see **Chapter 12** at **12.176**). There are some exceptions which specifically apply to micro-entities where business combinations and goodwill are concerned:

- the micro-entity must not separately identify and recognise **intangible assets**;
- no **deferred tax assets** or **liabilities** are recognised;
- the micro-entity does not apply paragraph 19.23 which relates to subsequent measurement of goodwill; instead it follows the requirements in paragraph 14.2 (see below);
- **share-based payment transactions** are not measured in accordance with Section 28 *Employee Benefits* in FRS 102, but are accounted for in accordance with Section 23 *Employee Benefits* in FRS 105 (see **11.94–11.97** below); and
- none of the disclosure requirements in Section 19 of FRS 102 are required to be made.

Goodwill in a business combination

11.57 Goodwill arising in a trade and asset acquisition is measured at cost less amortisation and accumulated impairment. Goodwill will always have a finite useful life and is amortised on a systematic basis over that useful life (usually, but not always, on a straight-line basis). Where a reliable estimate of the useful life is unable to be made, the life must not exceed ten years.

Any impairment of goodwill is recognised in accordance with Section 22 *Impairment of Assets* (see **11.98–11.106** below).

Disclosure requirements

11.58 The micro-entity must disclose the amount of any financial commitments, guarantees and contingencies not recognised in the balance sheet for trade and asset acquisitions. This is disclosed within the total amount of financial commitments, guarantees and contingencies.

Leases

11.59 Section 15 *Leases* in FRS 105 applies to all leases other than licensing agreements in relation to:

- motion picture films;
- video recordings;
- plays;
- manuscripts;
- patents; and
- copyrights.

> **Focus**
>
> - Management must have regard to the substance of the leasing arrangement when considering whether an arrangement is, or contains, a lease.

Finance versus operating lease

11.60 The Glossary to FRS 105 defines a 'finance lease' as:

> 'A **lease** that transfers substantially all the risks and rewards incidental to ownership of an **asset**. Title may or may not eventually be transferred. A lease that is not a finance lease is an **operating lease**.'[1]

The Glossary defines an 'operating lease' as:

> 'A **lease** that does not transfer substantially all the risks and rewards incidental to ownership. A lease that is not an operating lease is a **finance lease**.'[2]

Where the lease substantially transfers all the risks and rewards of ownership from the lessor to the lessee, the lease falls to be classed as a finance lease. A lease is an operating lease where the risks and rewards incidental to ownership do not substantially transfer to the lessee (ie they remain with the lessor).

1 FRS 105 Glossary **Finance lease**.
2 FRS 105 Glossary **Operating lease**.

There are eight indicators of situations which may indicate a lease is a finance lease contained within FRS 105 as follows:

(a) the lease transfers ownership of the asset to the lessee by the end of the **lease term**;

(b) the lessee has the option to purchase the asset at a price that is expected to be sufficiently lower than the **fair value** at the date the option becomes exercisable for it to be reasonably certain, at the **inception of the lease**, that the option will be exercised;

(c) the lease term is for the major part of the economic life of the asset even if title is not transferred;

(d) at the inception of the lease the **present value** of the **minimum lease payments** amount to at least substantially all of the fair value of the leased asset;

(e) the leased assets are of such a specialised nature that only the lessee can use them without major modifications;

(f) if the lessee can cancel the lease, the lessor's losses associated with the cancellation are borne by the lessee;

(g) **gains** or losses from the fluctuation in the **residual value** of the leased asset accrue to the lessee (eg in the form of a rent rebate equalling most of the sales proceeds at the end of the lease); and

(h) the lessee has the ability to continue the lease for a secondary period at a rent that is substantially lower than market rent.[3]

> **Focus**
>
> - The examples above are indicators of a finance lease, but they are not conclusive in every respect and where it is clear that the lease does not transfer substantially all the risks and rewards incidental to ownership to the lessee then the lease is an operating lease.

The classification of a lease is made at the start of the lease and is not changed during the term of the lease (ie it cannot go from a finance lease to an operating lease part-way through the accounting period). The only exception to this would be where the lessee and the lessor agree to change the provisions of the lease (other than simply renewing the lease) in which case the lease classification is then re-assessed.

Finance lease recognition: lessees

11.61 When a lease falls to be classed as a finance lease, the lessee recognises an asset in the balance sheet together with a corresponding finance lease creditor. The asset is recognised at the fair value of the leased asset (or

3 FRS 105, paras 15.6 and 15.7.

the present value of the minimum lease payments determined at the inception of the lease if lower). A corresponding finance lease obligation is also recognised.

Where the lessee incurs incremental costs associated with the lease (such as legal fees) these can be included in the cost of the asset. The term 'incremental costs' in this context means those costs which could have been avoided had the lessee not entered into the finance lease.

Example 11.9 – Fair value of a leased asset

Microco Ltd enters into a three-year lease for an item of machinery with a fair value of £15,000. The finance lease has been drawn up by the solicitor who has levied a fee of £1,500 plus VAT in respect of the lease.

Microco should recognise the asset in the balance sheet at a cost of £16,500 (fair value of the asset of £15,000 plus the legal fees of £1,500). The finance lease creditor will be the fair value of the leased asset of £15,000. The double-entry is as follows:

DR property, plant and equipment	£16,500
DR VAT control	£300
CR finance lease creditor	(£15,000)
CR trade creditors	(£1,800)

Interest payments in respect of finance leases are allocated to each period over the life of the lease so as to produce a constant periodic rate of interest on the remaining balance of the liability. Examples of how to allocate interest payments in a finance lease are shown in **Chapter 12** (at **12.209**).

Focus

- Contingent rents are recognised as expenses in the period in which they are incurred.

Finance lease recognition: lessors

11.62 A lessor recognises a finance lease as a debtor in the balance sheet at an amount which is equal to the net investment in the lease. The net investment in the lease is the lessor's gross investment in the lease which is discounted at the rate implicit in the lease. The gross investment in the lease is the total of:

- the minimum lease payments which are to be received by the lessor under a finance lease; and
- any unguaranteed residual value accruing to the lessor.

12.212 in **Chapter 12** illustrates how this works in practice.

Any costs which are incurred in arranging the lease (eg legal fees) are included in the initial measurement of the finance lease debtor and will reduce the amount of income recognised over the term of the lease.

Finance income is recognised in profit or loss on a basis which reflects a constant periodic rate of return on the lessor's net investment in the finance lease. Where there is evidence that the estimated unguaranteed residual value that has been used in calculating the lessor's gross investment in the lease has significantly changed, the income allocation over the term of the lease is revised and any reduction in respect of accrued amounts is recognised in profit or loss.

Operating lease recognition: lessees

11.63 Operating lease rentals are simply charged to profit and loss as they are incurred on a straight-line basis over the lease term unless another basis is reflective of the time pattern of the entity's benefit (this can be the case even if the payments are not made on that basis).

Lease incentives are recognised as a reduction to operating lease expense over the lease term on a straight-line basis (unless another basis is reflective of the time pattern of the lessee's benefit from the use of the leased asset).

If an operating lease becomes onerous, the micro-entity applies Section 16 *Provisions and Contingencies* (see **11.68–11.74** below).

Operating lease recognition: lessors

11.64 Income from operating leases in the lessor's books is recognised in profit or loss on a straight-line basis over the lease. An alternative method of income recognition can be used if this method is representative of the time pattern over which the lessor's benefit from the leased asset is diminished.

As the asset subject to the lease is recognised in the lessor's balance sheet, costs such as depreciation are recognised as an expense. The depreciation policy for such assets must be consistent with the lessor's policy for similar assets.

Where the lessor incurs costs in arranging and negotiating an operating lease (eg legal fees), it should recognise such costs within the cost of the asset and recognise these incremental costs as an expense over the term of the lease on the same basis as the lease income (ie match the expense with the income it has generated).

> **Focus**
>
> - Lessors must review the assets subject to operating leases for impairment in the same way as normal fixed assets and hence apply the provisions in Section 22 *Impairment of Assets* in FRS 105.

Manufacturer and dealer lessors

11.65 Manufacturer or dealer lessors can offer customers two options: lease the asset or buy the asset outright (this usually happens with motor vehicles). It follows, therefore, that a finance lease of an asset by a manufacturer or dealer lessors gives rise to two forms of income:

- profit or loss arising from an outright sale (net of any volume or trade discounts); and
- finance income over the lease term.

Where a lease is taken out, the sales revenue is the fair value of the asset or, where lower, the present value of the minimum lease payments which accrue to the lessor (which are calculated at a market rate of interest). Cost of sales at the commencement of the lease is the cost, or carrying amount if different, of the leased asset *less* the present value of the unguaranteed residual value. Any remaining difference is the selling profit which is recognised in accordance with the micro-entity's policy in respect of outright sales.

> **Focus**
>
> - If an artificially low rate of interest has been quoted, selling profit must be restricted to that which would apply if a market rate had been used. All costs incurred by a manufacturer or dealer lessor in negotiating and arranging a lease are recognised as an expense at the point that selling profit is recognised.

Sale and leaseback arrangements

11.66 There are two possible outcomes in a sale and leaseback arrangement:

- the sale and leaseback arrangement results in a finance lease; or
- the sale and leaseback arrangement results in an operating lease.

If the sale and leaseback arrangement results in a **finance lease**, the seller-lessee does not recognise any proceeds received immediately as income. Such income is deferred in the balance sheet and amortised over the term of the lease.

If the sale and leaseback arrangement results in an **operating lease** at fair value, the seller-lessee recognises any profit or loss immediately. Where the sales price is below fair value, the seller-lessee recognises any profit or loss immediately unless the seller-lessee is going to be compensated for such losses by way of payments which are at below market rates. If this is the case, the seller-lessee defers and amortises such a loss in proportion to the lease payments over the period for which the asset is expected to be used by the micro-entity.

Where the sales price is above fair value, the seller-lessee defers the excess and amortises it over the period for which the lease is expected to be used. It should not recognise any excess immediately in profit or loss.

Disclosure requirements

11.67 The amount of any financial commitments, guarantees and contingencies which are not recognised in the balance sheet arising from a sale and leaseback transaction should be disclosed within the total amount of financial commitments, guarantees and contingencies.

Provisions and contingencies

11.68 Section 16 *Provisions and Contingencies* of FRS 105 covers all provisions, contingent liabilities and contingent assets with the exception of those covered in other sections of FRS 105. Section 16 also does not cover:

- Financial instruments which are under the scope of Section 9 *Financial Instruments*. The exception to this is if the contract becomes onerous or it is a financial guarantee contract.
- Executory contracts unless they are onerous contracts.

Focus

- The term 'provision' is interchangeable. The term can also relate to a 'provision for bad debts' or a 'provision for depreciation'. Such provisions are reductions of the carrying amount of assets rather than under the scope of a provision under Section 16.

Initial recognition

11.69 The following three criterion must be fulfilled before a provision can be recognised:

- There must be a legal or constructive obligation as a result of a past event.
- It is probable (ie more likely than not) that the micro-entity will have an outflow of economic benefit to settle the obligation.
- The amount of the obligation can be reliably measured.

Where such criteria are met, the micro-entity can recognise the provision as a liability in the balance sheet (statement of financial position) with a corresponding expense (unless another section of FRS 105 requires the debit to go elsewhere, eg into property, plant and equipment).

Focus

- A 'legal' obligation is one which is enforceable by law, such as a contract. A 'constructive' obligation is one which has arisen because of the past practices of the micro-entity. A typical example would be where the management of a micro-entity have notified certain staff that they are being made redundant before the reporting date. In such cases, management have created a valid expectation in the mind-sets of those affected that they will discharge their obligation (ie pay them redundancy amounts). Section 16 contains a useful appendix *Examples of recognising and measuring provisions.*

When an amount meets the recognition criteria for a provision, the micro-entity must recognise the provision at the best estimate of the amount required to settle the obligation at the reporting date. The best estimate is the amount which is likely to be paid by the micro-entity in order to settle the obligation.

Example 11.10 – Provision for returns

Microco Ltd sells electrical goods to the general public with a warranty which covers customers for the costs of repairs which occur during the first six months from the date of purchase. The company is preparing its financial statements for the year ended 31 March 2017 and has calculated that if all the products sold contained minor defects the cost of the repairs would be £50,000. If major defects occurred in all the products the cost of the repairs would be £150,000.

Management have concluded that past experience, and future expectations, suggest that for the coming year 75% of the goods sold will contain no defects; 20% will contain minor defects and 5% will have major defects.

The provision for the year-ended 31 March 2017 is calculated as follows:

	£
75% × £nil	–
20% × £50,000	10,000
5% × £150,000	7,500
Total provision	17,500

If the micro-entity is expected to be reimbursed for any provision by a third party – such as an insurance company, then the reimbursement can be recognised as a separate asset only when the receipt is virtually certain (ie there is evidence that the third party will reimburse the micro-entity). The amount of the reimbursement asset cannot exceed the amount of the provision and the asset must **not** be offset against the liability in the balance sheet (statement of financial position). However, the income and the expense in the profit and loss account (income statement) can be offset.

The time value of money should be taken into consideration (where material) for provisions which are expected to be long-term. However, the vast majority of micro-entities will only have short-term provisions and hence the time value of money becomes immaterial.

Subsequent measurement

11.70 Expenses can only be charged against provisions which directly relate to the provision originally recognised.

At each reporting date the micro-entity must assess the provisions and make adjustments where necessary to reflect the current best estimate of the amount which would be required to settle the obligation. Such adjustments are recognised in profit or loss unless the provision was originally recognised as part of an asset.

Contingent liabilities and contingent assets

11.71 Contingent liabilities are not recognised in the financial statements because they fail to meet the recognition criteria. The only exception to this is where a micro-entity undertakes a trade and asset acquisition and will recognise a provision for contingent liabilities of an acquiree. In cases where a micro-entity is jointly and severally liable for an obligation, the part of the obligation which is expected to be met by the other parties is treated as a contingent liability.

Contingent assets are also not recognised in the financial statements of a micro-entity. The exception to this is where it becomes virtually certain that the micro-entity will receive economic benefit (ie cash) and hence recognition is then appropriate.

Onerous contracts

11.72 Where a contract becomes onerous (the term 'onerous' means the unavoidable costs of meeting the obligations exceed the benefits to be received under the contract) then the present obligation is recognised and measured as a provision.

Future operating losses and restructuring provisions

11.73 A micro-entity cannot make any provision for future operating losses. Such losses must be recognised in the period in which they are incurred.

Insofar as restructuring provisions are concerned, a micro-entity can only recognise a provision for restructuring if there is a constructive obligation. A constructive obligation will arise when the micro-entity:

- has a detailed formal plan for the restructuring identifying at least:
  - — the business or part of a business concerned;
  - — the principal locations affected;
  - — the location, function and approximate number of employees who will be compensated for terminating their services;
  - — the expenditures that will be undertaken; and
  - — when the plan will be implemented; and
- has raised a valid expectation in those affected that it will carry out the restructuring by starting to implement that plan or announcing its main features to those affected by it.[4]

Example 11.11 – Restructuring provision

Microco Ltd has an accounting reference date of 31 October. It has five depots spread across the country.

Over the last two years the depots in Yorkshire and Newcastle have been sustaining heavy losses due to a downturn in business. On 30 September 2016 the board of directors decided to close those depots and transfer the business to its head office located in Bolton. This intention was communicated to all staff in the Yorkshire and Newcastle depots on 4 October 2016 and the staff concerned were given their redundancy notices. Both depots will close on 1 December 2016. Redundancy calculations have been undertaken by the human resources department and these have been agreed by the board of directors.

In this example the company is going through a restructuring exercise in which it has identified the business which has been affected by the downturn, it has identified the locations affected, the number of employees which will be compensated for the termination of their services and the plan has already been started. In addition, the company has also communicated its intentions to the staff concerned and hence has created a valid expectation in their minds that the company will discharge its obligations. In this respect the company can make a restructuring provision in its financial statements to 31 October 2016.

---

4 FRS 105, para 16.15.

Disclosure requirements

11.74 The micro-entity must determine the amount of any financial commitments, guarantees and contingencies which have not been recognised in the balance sheet and disclose this amount within the total amount of financial commitments, guarantees and contingencies. There is no requirement to disclose the amount of a contingent liability where the possibility of an outflow of resources is remote.

Liabilities and equity

11.75 Section 17 *Liabilities and Equity* in FRS 105 gives guidance on the principles involved in classifying financial instruments as either debt (ie a liability) or equity. It also examines the concept of 'convertible debt' which is debt that contains a mixture of both debt and equity and outlines the accounting treatment involved for such instruments. In addition, Section 17 also deals with the issue of issuing shares and making distributions to shareholders as well as the situation when a micro-entity may repurchase its own equity.

Focus

- This particular section does not deal with share buybacks, bonus issues or rights issues. Readers are directed to **Chapter 12** at **12.245** which deals with such issues.

There are some types of financial instrument which are not dealt within Section 17 which are outlined in the following table:

Instrument	**Relevant section of FRS 105**
Investments in subsidiaries and associates and interests in jointly controlled entities	Section 9 *Financial Instruments*
Employer's rights and obligations under employee benefit plans	Section 23 *Employee Benefits*
Financial instruments, contracts and obligations under share-based payment transactions	Section 21 *Share-based Payment*
Financial guarantee contracts	Section 16 *Provisions and Contingencies*

Classifying an instrument as liability or equity

11.76 A financial instrument becomes a financial liability where there is an obligation to pay cash, or transfer other assets, to the holder of the instrument. This can include the periodic payment of interest or where the financial instrument has a redemption feature.

Example 11.12 – Preference shares

Microco Ltd issues 5% preference shares to a shareholder. The company is required to pay the shareholder a fixed rate of dividend each year.

Despite the name 'preference shares', Microco has an obligation to deliver cash to the shareholder each year (the 5% dividend). As a result these preference shares will be recognised as a financial liability in the financial statements.

A financial instrument becomes equity where the issuer can be required to settle the obligation in cash or by way of another financial asset if the micro-entity liquidates.

Paragraph 17.6 of FRS 105 outlines some examples of instruments and their classification as equity or liabilities as below:

(a) An instrument is classified as equity if the only payment holders of the instruments are entitled to receive is a pro rata share of the net assets of the micro-entity on liquidation.

(b) An instrument is classified as a liability if it obliges the micro-entity to make payments to the holder before liquidation, such as a mandatory dividend.

(c) A preference share that provides for mandatory redemption by the issuer for a fixed or determinable amount at a fixed or determinable future date, or gives the holder the right to require the issuer to redeem the instrument at or after a particular date for a fixed or determinable amount, is a financial liability.[5]

Ordinary shares

11.77 Ordinary shares are equity instruments because the micro-entity does not have an obligation to pay the holder of those shares cash or other assets. Dividends on ordinary shares are generally discretionary hence ordinary shares are classed as equity.

If the micro-entity receives payment before the shares are issued, and the micro-entity is not required to repay the cash (or other resources received), then it recognises the corresponding increase in equity to the extent of the cash (or other resources) received.

If the ordinary shares have been subscribed to but not issued (or called up) and the micro-entity has not received cash (or other resources) in exchange, no increase in equity is recognised.

5 FRS 105, para 17.6.

> **Focus**
>
> - Any transaction costs of an equity transaction are recognised as a deduction from equity, net of any related income tax benefit.

Convertible debt

11.78 Convertible debt is debt which contains a mixture of liability and equity. The most common form of convertible debt is a convertible loan where the loan note holder has the option to convert the capital amount into shares at a later date, if it so wishes.

When a micro-entity issues convertible debt, it must first determine the liability component as the fair value of a similar liability which does not have a conversion feature or similar associated equity component. Once this has been established, the residual left is the equity component. Any transaction costs incurred are split between the debt component and the equity component on the basis of their relative fair values.

After initial recognition, the liability component is accounted for in accordance with Section 9 of FRS 105.

> **Focus**
>
> - In **Chapter 12, 12.253** contains an example of how to account for convertible debt.

Treasury shares

11.79 Treasury shares are shares which have been previously issued by the micro-entity and then re-acquired by the micro-entity.

Where treasury shares are concerned, the micro-entity must deduct the fair value of the consideration given for the treasury shares from equity. No gain or loss on the purchase, sale, transfer or cancellation of the treasury shares is recognised in profit or loss.

Distributions to shareholders

11.80 Distributions to shareholders (usually dividends) are shown as a reduction of equity reserves. They are not charged as an expense in the profit or loss account.

Revenue

11.81 Section 18 *Revenue* deals with four types of revenue stream:

- revenue from the sale of goods;
- revenue from the rendering of services;
- construction contract revenue where the micro-entity is the contractor; and
- use by others of the micro-entity's assets yielding interest, royalties or dividends.

Revenue arising from a leasing contract is dealt with in Section 15 *Leases* (see **11.59–11.67** above).

Measurement of revenue

11.82 Revenue is to be measured at the amount receivable which should take into account any discounts (trade, settlement or volume). It must not include any revenue which it collects on behalf of a third party (such as in an agent/principal arrangement).

Deferred payment arrangements

11.83 Where a micro-entity agrees to deferred payment arrangements (ie arrangements which are beyond normal commercial terms), this effectively becomes a financing arrangement. The amount of revenue recognised is equal to the cash price of the sale on the date the sale is made. Any excess between the deferred payment amount and the sales price is recognised as interest.

Exchange of goods or services

11.84 If a micro-entity exchanges goods or services which are of a similar nature or value; or are of a dissimilar nature of value but lack commercial substance, then no revenue is recognised.

A micro-entity can recognise revenue for the exchange of dissimilar goods or services in a transaction which has commercial substance. A transaction is said to have commercial substance when it is expected that the future cash flows of a business will change as a result of the transaction. In such cases, the micro-entity will measure the transaction:

(a) at the fair value of the goods or services received – this amount will be adjusted for any cash transferred;

(b) where the amount under (a) cannot be reliably measured, then at the fair value of the goods or services given up – this amount is also adjusted by the amount of any cash transferred; or

(c) where the fair value of neither the goods or services received, nor the goods or services given up can be reliably measured, then at the carrying amount of the goods or services given up which is also adjusted by the amount of any cash transferred.

Identifying the revenue transaction

11.85 A micro-entity must apply the recognition criteria of revenue separately to each identifiable component of a single transaction when necessary so as to reflect the substance of the transaction. This might usually be the case where the micro-entity sells a product but then includes an amount for subsequent servicing of that product.

Sale of goods

11.86 A micro-entity can recognise a sale of goods when all five of the following conditions are met:

- the micro-entity has transferred to the buyer the significant risks and rewards of ownership of the goods;
- the micro-entity retains neither continuing managerial involvement to the degree usually associated with ownership nor effective control over the goods sold;
- the amount of revenue can be measured reliably;
- it is **probable** that the economic benefits associated with the transaction will flow to the micro-entity; and
- the costs incurred or to be incurred in respect of the transaction can be measured reliably.[6]

It is often the case that when a micro-entity completes a sale, legal title also passes. In some cases, however, this might not arise and where the micro-entity retains significant risks and rewards of ownership, a sale cannot be recognised even if the goods have been despatched.

Example 11.13 – Ongoing obligation

Microco Ltd supplies five machines to a supplier based 250 miles away on 25 October 2017. The terms of the contract are that Microco will supply and fit the machines and ensure that the machines are working to full capacity before the customer signs the order off to say they are happy that the contract has been fulfilled adequately. Microco's year-end is 31 October 2017.

The fitters are scheduled to go to the customer on 6 November 2017 to install the machinery. The financial controller is proposing to recognise the revenue associated with the sale in the 31 October 2017 financial statements on the grounds that it is only a week that has passed since the year-end and he is also keen to report increased profitability.

6 FRS 105, para 18.9.

The financial controller cannot recognise this sale in the financial statements to 31 October 2017 as the company still has an ongoing obligation at the year-end to install the machines and to ensure that they are working to full capacity. Revenue can only be recognised once the customer has signed to say they are satisfied that all the contractual obligations have been fulfilled and hence the sale should not be recognised until the next financial year.

Paragraph 18.11 offers four examples of situations in which the micro-entity may retain the significant risks and rewards and hence would be unable to recognise revenue:

- when the micro-entity retains an obligation for unsatisfactory performance not covered by normal warranties;
- when the receipt of the revenue from a particular sale is contingent on the buyer selling the goods;
- when the goods are shipped subject to installation and the installation is a significant part of the contract that has not yet been completed; and
- when the buyer has the right to rescind the purchase for a reason specified in the sales contract, or at the buyer's sole discretion without any reason, and the micro-entity is uncertain about the possibility of return.

Focus

- Where a micro-entity only retains an insignificant risk of ownership, then a sale can be recognised. An insignificant risk of ownership might be where the seller retains legal title until payment is received.

Rendering of services

11.87 Service revenue can be more complicated than when a micro-entity sells goods in terms of the timing of revenue recognition. Paragraph 18.13 offers four conditions, all of which must be met, to ensure that the outcome of a transaction can be estimated reliably:

- the amount of revenue can be measured reliably;
- it is probable that the economic benefits associated with the transaction will flow to the micro-entity;
- the stage of completion of the transaction at the end of the reporting period can be measured reliably; and
- the costs incurred for the transaction and the costs to complete the transaction can be measured reliably.

A micro-entity recognises revenue in a service transaction by reference to the stage of completion at the end of the reporting period.

If services are performed over an indeterminate number of acts over a period of time, revenue is recognised on a straight-line basis over the specified period. A micro-entity can adopt an alternative method if this alternative method represents the stage of completion.

> **Focus**
>
> - Paragraph 18.14 refers to a 'specific act' and 'any other act'. Where a specific act is much more significant than any other act, the micro-entity delays recognising revenue until the significant act is completed.

Construction contract accounting

11.88 In a construction contract, where the micro-entity is the contractor, contract revenue and expenses are recognised by reference to the stage of completion at the end of the reporting period. Normally the stage of completion is assessed through surveys of the work performed, but the stage of completion can also be assessed through:

- assessing the proportion that costs incurred for work performed to date (excluding costs relating to future activity, such as for materials or prepayments) bear to the estimated total costs; and
- completion of a physical proportion of the contract work or the completion of a proportion of the contract.

> **Focus**
>
> - If the micro-entity receives any progress payments or advances from its customer, they are not recognised in turnover because they do not reflect the work performed – they should be credited to the contract account instead and will form part of the 'Gross amount due to/from the customer'.

There are generally three initial outcomes for a construction contract from an accounting perspective:

- the contract will make a profit;
- the contract will make a loss;
- it is uncertain whether the contract will make a profit or a loss.

If the contract is assessed to make a profit, revenue and costs are recognised depending on the stage of completion (ie if 40% of the contract is complete, 40% of the contract price is recognised as revenue and 40% of the contract costs are recognised as costs).

If the contract is assessed to make a loss, revenue is recognised depending on the stage of completion and costs are a balancing figure to generate the required loss. Therefore, if the contract price is £5,000, the contract is expected to make a loss of £2,000 and it is 40% complete at the reporting date, revenue of £2,000 is recognised (£5,000 × 40%) and cost of sales is a balancing figure to generate the required loss, hence cost of sales is £4,000. This is because losses are recognised as soon as they are foreseen.

If the contract is uncertain, then no profit is recognised. Revenue is recognised depending on the stage of completion and cost of sales is the same figure so if revenue is £2,000 then cost of sales will be £2,000.

> **Focus**
>
> - Detailed worked examples of construction contract accounting are shown in **12.266–12.268** in **Chapter 12** of this book.

Interest, royalties and dividends

11.89 A micro-entity might make available its own assets for others to use which generate a revenue stream for the micro-entity in the form of interest, royalties or dividends. Such income streams can be recognised as revenue when:

- it is probable that the economic benefits associated with the transaction will flow to the micro-entity; and
- the amount of the revenue can be measured reliably.[7]

Interest income is recognised in accordance with paragraph 9.14 of FRS 105 (see also **11.16** *Interest income or expense* in this chapter).

Royalties are recognised on an accruals basis in accordance with the substance of the relevant agreement.

Dividends are recognised when the shareholder's right to receive the dividend is established (which may be a different date than the date on which the shareholder actually receives the dividend).

> **Focus**
>
> - Section 18 contains a useful appendix *Examples of revenue recognition under the principles in Section 18* which will aid an understanding of revenue recognition issues.

Government grants

11.90 Section 19 *Government Grants* is a short section in FRS 105 and deals with the accounting treatment for all government grants. The Glossary to FRS 105 defines a 'government grant' as:

7 FRS 105, paras 18.25(a) and (b).

> 'Assistance by government in the form of a transfer of resources to an entity in return for past or future compliance with specified conditions relating to the **operating activities** of the entity. Government refers to government, government bodies and similar bodies whether local, national or international.'[8]

Recognition and measurement

11.91 A government grant should not be recognised in the financial statements until there is reasonable assurance that:

- the micro-entity will comply with the conditions that are attached to the grant; and
- the grants will be received.

Once these conditions have been met, the grant is recognised at the fair value of the asset received (or receivable).

There are generally two types of grant:

(1) revenue-based; and

(2) capital-based.

Revenue-based grants are recognised in income on a systematic basis over the periods in which the related expenses are included in profit or loss.

Capital-based grants are recognised in the profit and loss account to match the related expenditure associated with the asset (eg depreciation) and hence are written off over the expected useful life of the asset to which the grant relates.

Focus

- The performance method of recognising grants is not permitted for micro-entities. Only the accrual method is permissible.

If any part of a government grant is repayable then the amount repayable is recognised in liabilities.

Unamortised grants relating to fixed assets must be shown as deferred income and must not be deducted from the cost price of the asset.

Borrowing costs

11.92 Section 20 *Borrowing Costs* acknowledges that borrowing costs includes:

8 FRS 105 Glossary **Government grants**.

- interest expense recognised in accordance with Section 9 *Financial Instruments*;
- finance charges in respect of finance leases recognised in accordance with Section 15 *Leases*; and
- exchange differences arising as a result of foreign currency borrowings to the extent that they are regarded as an adjustment to interest costs.

Recognition

11.93 Where a micro-entity incurs borrowing costs, they are always written off to profit or loss. There is no option to capitalise them, even if the micro-entity is constructing its own asset and has taken out borrowings to fund the construction.

Share-based payment

11.94 There are three types of share-based payment arrangement:

- equity-settled share-based payment arrangements;
- cash-settled share-based payment arrangements; and
- transactions in which the micro-entity receives, or acquires, goods or services and the terms of the arrangement provide either the micro-entity, or the supplier of those goods or services, with a choice of whether the micro-entity can settle in cash (or other assets) or equity.

Equity-settled share-based payment arrangements

11.95 Until the shares are issued, a micro-entity does not account for equity-settled share-based payment arrangements. Once the shares are issued they are accounted for in accordance with Section 17 *Liabilities and Equity* (see **11.75–11.80** above).

Cash-settled share-based payment arrangements

11.96 Once the micro-entity receives the goods or services, it recognises them in the financial statements together with a corresponding liability. Goods or services may be received over time and hence in these situations they are recognised as they are received.

Services in respect of employees are more complex. If the cash-settled share-based payments vest immediately and the employee does not have to complete any further specified period of service, the micro-entity recognises the services received in full at the date of the grant together with a corresponding liability.

If the share-based payments do not vest immediately because the employees have to complete a specified period of service, then the micro-entity recognises those services as they are rendered by the employee during the vesting period with a corresponding increase in the liability.

> **Focus**
>
> - Unless goods received or services rendered in a cash-settled share-based payment arrangement qualify for recognition as an asset, the micro-entity must recognise them as expenses.

Share-based payment arrangements with cash alternatives

11.97 A micro-entity might have the choice of settling the share-based payment arrangement with cash, other assets or equity instruments (equity instruments generally mean shares).

Where a choice of settlement exists, the micro-entity accounts for the transaction as if it was equity-settled and hence no accounting input is made until the shares are issued, at which point the micro-entity applies the requirements in Section 17 of FRS 105 (see **11.75–11.80** above).

Where a choice of settlement exists, the transaction is accounted for as a wholly cash-settled transaction if any of the following apply:

- the choice of settlement in equity instrument has no commercial substance (for example where the micro-entity cannot issue shares); or
- the micro-entity has a past practice or a stated policy of settling in cash or generally settles in cash when the counterparty asks for such settlement.

If the counterparty has a choice of receiving settlement in cash, other assets or equity shares, the transaction is accounted for by the micro-entity as cash-settled unless the choice of settlement in cash or other assets has no commercial substance. This can be because the cash settlement amount (or value of the other assets) bears no relationship to the fair value of the equity instrument, or is lower in value than the fair value of the equity instruments. In this case the micro-entity accounts for the transaction as equity-settled.

Impairment of assets

11.98 Section 22 *Impairment of Assets* in FRS 105 outlines the principles involved when an asset is showing signs of impairment. There are three types of asset which are not covered under Section 22:

- assets arising from construction contracts (see Section 18 *Revenue* and **11.81–11.89** above);
- financial assets within the scope of Section 9 *Financial Instruments* (see **11.13–11.23** above); and
- inventories (see Section 10 *Inventories* and **11.24–11.32** above).

Impairment

11.99 An asset is said to be impaired when its recoverable amount is less than its carrying amount in the financial statements. Where it is not possible to estimate the recoverable amount of an individual asset, the micro-entity must base recoverable amount on the cash-generating unit to which it belongs. This could, for example, be a group of machinery and one item in itself may not generate cash flows.

An impairment loss is immediately recognised as an expense in profit or loss and is calculated as the difference between recoverable amount and carrying amount.

Indicators of impairment

11.100 It can sometimes be clear when an asset is impaired. For example if a machine is broken beyond repair and it has a carrying amount in the fixed assets register then this carrying amount will need to be reduced to estimated selling price less costs to complete the sale (which might be £nil for a machine beyond repair). In addition, it may become apparent that a trade debtor is not going to pay all, or part, of its debt to the micro-entity and in this case a write-down to recoverable amount will be done (through either a specific or general bad debt provision).

While it may be readily apparent to those within the entity when an asset is showing indicators of impairment, paragraph 22.7 requires certain sources of information to be formally considered in terms of evidence which may indicate an asset is impaired as follows:

External sources of information

11.101

- Market values of assets have declined significantly more than would be expected through the normal passage of time or use.
- Adverse changes have taken place in the market to which the asset belongs which will affect the micro-entity.
- Market interest rates or returns on investments have increased during the period and these increases are likely to materially affect the discount rate which the micro-entity has used in calculating the asset's value in use and hence decrease the asset's fair value less costs to sell.
- The carrying amount of the asset is more than the estimated fair value of the micro-entity as a whole when, for example, valuing the business for potential sale.

Internal sources of information

11.102

- The asset is damaged or is obsolete.
- The asset is likely to become idle because of adverse changes within the micro-entity which have taken, or are likely to take, place in the future.
- The micro-entity is planning to discontinue an area of operations.
- The micro-entity is planning to dispose of the asset before the previously expected disposal date.
- Evidence has become available suggesting the economic performance of the asset is worse than previously expected.

Where indicators of impairment are present, the micro-entity should also review the remaining useful life, depreciation (amortisation) method or the residual value of the asset(s) concerned and make appropriate adjustments even if no impairment loss is recognised for such asset(s).

Recoverable amount

11.103 As mentioned earlier in this section, an asset is impaired when its carrying amount in the financial statements exceeds its recoverable amount. Recoverable amount is the *higher* of an asset's fair value less costs to sell and its value in use.

Focus

- It is not always necessary to determine both fair value less costs to sell and value in use. This is because if *either* of these amounts are higher than the carrying amount, the asset in question is not impaired.

Fair value less costs to sell

11.104 In reality, this is likely to be the most commonly used amount when determining recoverable amount because fair value less costs to sell is the amount which an independent third party would be willing to buy the asset for in an arm's length transaction less the costs, associated with the disposal. Usually fair value less costs to sell can be obtained from a binding sales agreement, or an active market.

Where there is no binding agreement or active market, fair value less costs to sell is based on the best information available to the micro-entity to reflect the amount which it could obtain at the reporting date by way of disposal in an arm's length transaction.

> **Focus**
>
> - When considering fair value less costs to sell, the micro-entity must also take into account any restrictions imposed on that asset. Costs to sell should also take into account the cost of the relaxation of the restriction so that the asset can be sold.

Value in use

11.105 Value in use calculations can be complicated for a micro-entity and in real-life are not common because fair value less costs to sell is easier to ascertain for the purpose of impairment.

Value in use calculations involve discounting the present value of the future cash flows expected to be received from the asset. For the majority of micro-entities it is going to be quite difficult in ascertaining future cash flows from a specific asset and hence where the micro-entity is undertaking value in use calculations, it might want to use recent financial budgets or forecasts to estimate such cash flows (if these are available). If they are available, the micro-entity could then extrapolate the projections using a steady or declining growth rate for subsequent years. A rising growth rate could be used, but only where this is justifiable.

When estimating future cash flows, the micro-entity must not include cash inflows or outflows from financing activities or income tax receipts or payments.

> **Focus**
>
> - When estimating future cash flows, the micro-entity must do so in respect of the asset in its current condition. Therefore if the asset is (say) a division of the business then no cash flows in respect of restructuring which the entity is not yet committed to should be included. If the asset is (say) an asset in its own right, no future cash flows in respect of improving or enhancing the asset's performance should be included.

Discount rates used in measuring an asset's value in use should not reflect risks for which the future cash flow estimates have been adjusted, so as to avoid double-counting.

Reversing an impairment loss

11.106 Any impairment loss in respect of goodwill must not be reversed in a subsequent period.

> **Focus**
>
> - The prohibition of reversing goodwill impairment losses was brought in by the EU Accounting Directive, but has yet to be brought into the Companies Act 2006 and so FRS 105 reflects the requirements of the EU Accounting Directive. Prior to the introduction of this prohibition, it was possible to reverse impairment losses against goodwill. It is likely that this prohibition will be reflected in the Companies Act 2006 to remedy the inconsistency with the EU Accounting Directive.

In respect of all other assets (excluding goodwill), if the reasons for the previously recognised impairment loss have ceased to apply then they can be reversed in a subsequent period. Where the reasons for the previously recognised impairment loss have ceased to apply, the micro-entity can reverse all, or part, of the prior impairment loss.

Where a micro-entity has previously recognised an impairment loss which was based on the recoverable amount of an individually-impaired asset, the following must be applied:

(a) The micro-entity shall estimate the recoverable amount of the asset as at the current reporting date.

(b) If the estimated recoverable amount of the asset exceeds its carrying amount, the micro-entity should increase the carrying amount to recoverable amount (subject to (c) below). This increase then represents the reversal of an impairment loss which is recognised immediately in profit or loss.

(c) An impairment loss cannot be reversed to the extent that it increases the asset above the carrying amount which would have been recognised (net of depreciation and amortisation) had no impairment been recognised previously.

(d) Once the impairment loss has been recognised, the micro-entity then adjusts the depreciation/amortisation charge for the asset in future periods so as to allocate the revised carrying amount, less residual value (if any), on a systematic basis over the remaining useful life.

Employee benefits

11.107 The term 'employee benefits' is wide-ranging but broadly means all forms of consideration given by a micro-entity to its employees in exchange for services they have rendered. 'Employees' for the purpose of Section 23 *Employee Benefits* in FRS 105 includes directors and management.

Whilst employee benefits are wide in their scope, Section 23 does not apply to share-based payment transactions which are dealt with in Section 21 *Share-based Payment* (see **11.94–11.97** above).

Section 23 deals with four types of benefits:

- short-term employee benefits (other than termination benefits) which are expected to be settled within 12 months after the reporting date after the employee renders the service;
- post-employment benefits;
- long-term employment benefits (ie those which are not short-term); and
- termination benefits.

Recognition principle for all employee benefits

11.108 Where a micro-entity has accrued short-term employee benefits, it will recognise a liability which will be after the deduction of amounts paid directly to employees, or amounts contributed to a pension fund. A prepayment will be recognised where the value of any payments made exceeds the liability at the end of the reporting date.

A corresponding expense is recognised in profit or loss, unless another part of FRS 105 requires the debit to be taken elsewhere, for example as part of the cost of inventories or property, plant and equipment.

Recognition principle for short-term employee benefits

11.109 Short-term employee benefits are those benefits paid to employees within 12 months of the reporting date. Examples of such benefits include:

- wages and salaries;
- social security contributions;
- holiday pay;
- sick pay; and
- other non-monetary benefits such as the provision of medical care, cars and housing.

For short-term employee benefits which have been accrued by the employee, but not paid by the micro-entity until the subsequent accounting period, the micro-entity recognises a liability together with a corresponding expense (unless another part of FRS 105 requires the debit to be taken elsewhere, for example to inventories or property, plant and equipment).

Focus

- Under previous UK GAAP, few entities tended to make accruals for accrued short-term employee benefits which were not paid until the next accounting period and the most commonly cited example is unpaid holiday pay. As the standard has to be applied retrospectively this might be an issue for micro-entities at the date of transition, particularly where a central record of such information has not been maintained.

Example 11.14 – Accrued holiday pay

Microco Ltd has a year-end of 30 June 3017 and gives its employees 30 days holiday entitlement per year. Employees are also allowed to carry forward up to five days holiday into the next holiday year. At the year-end an employee had taken 26 days.

An accrual should be made for four days holiday entitlement which will be taken in the subsequent accounting period.

There may be occasions when the holiday year and the financial year-end are not sequential and in such cases either an accrual or a prepayment will be needed.

Example 11.15 – Holiday year not coterminous with the financial year

Microco Ltd has a financial year which ends on 30 June 2017 and a holiday year of 31 December 2016. An employee has 30 days holiday per year and at the accounting year-end she had taken 20 days of her entitlement.

In this case there will be a prepayment of five days holiday ((30 days × 6/12) less 20 days).

Profit-sharing and bonus arrangements

11.110 Only when two criterion are met can a micro-entity recognise the expected cost of profit-sharing or bonus arrangements:

- the micro-entity has a present legal or **constructive obligation** to make such payments as a result of past events (this means that the micro-entity has no realistic alternative but to make the payments); and
- a reliable estimate of the obligation can be made.[9]

Post-employment benefits

11.111 The term 'post-employment benefits' refers to retirement benefits (pension plans) and other post-employment benefits such as post-employment life insurance and medical care.

In respect of pension plans, there are two types of plan:

- defined contribution plans; and
- defined benefit pension plans.

9 FRS 105, para 23.7(a) and (b).

Under a *defined contribution plan*, the employer has no obligation (legal or constructive) to pay additional contributions into the plan if the plan does not have sufficient assets available in which to pay all employee benefits. The term 'defined contribution' means that the amount of post-employment benefits which the employee receives is determined by the amount of contributions paid into the plan by a micro-entity (plus the employee, where the employee pays into the plan). Investment risk and actuarial risk do not, in substance, fall on the part of the micro-entity.

Under a *defined benefit pension plan*, the micro-entity does have an obligation to make additional contributions in to the plan if there are insufficient assets available in which to pay employee benefits. As a result, investment risk and actuarial risk do, in substance, fall on the part of the micro-entity.

Recognition and measurement of post-employment benefits

11.112 Contributions into a defined contribution or defined benefit pension plan which are not expected to be settled within 12 months after the end of the reporting period are discounted to present day values and the micro-entity then recognises this discounted amount as an expense together with a corresponding liability. The difference between the settlement amount and the discounted amount is recognised as interest expense in profit or loss in the period in which it arises.

To discount contributions to present day values, the micro-entity must use a rate by reference to market yields at the reporting date on high quality corporate bonds.

In respect of defined benefit pension plans, the accounting for these types of plans is generally more complex. However, simplifications have been made to FRS 105 which mean that the defined benefit pension plan is accounted for as a defined contribution plan (ie the contributions are recognised in profit or loss).

However, if the micro-entity has entered into an agreement with the plan which determines how the micro-entity will fund a deficit in the plan (for example a schedule of contributions), then the micro-entity must recognise a liability in the balance sheet (statement of financial position) which reflects the contributions payable as per the agreement, to the extent that the contributions relate to the deficit. A corresponding expense is recognised in profit or loss.

Focus

- If the micro-entity participates in a defined benefit pension plan which shares risks between entities that are under common control, the micro-entity recognises a cost which is equal to its contributions payable for the period.

Other long-term employee benefits

11.113 Paragraph 23.14 of FRS 105 offers five examples of long-term employee benefits as follows:

- long-term paid absences such as long-service or sabbatical leave;
- other long-service benefits;
- long-term disability benefits;
- profit-sharing and bonuses; and
- deferred remuneration.

When the micro-entity enters into such transactions, it must recognise a liability which is measured at the present value of the benefit obligation at the reporting date. To discount the benefits to present day values, the micro-entity will use a discount rate by reference to market yields on high quality corporate bonds. The difference between the settlement amount and the discounted amount is recognised as interest expense in profit or loss in the period in which it arises.

Termination benefits

11.114 Termination benefits will always be recognised as an expense in profit or loss because such benefits will not provide the micro-entity with future economic benefits.

To recognise a liability for the payment of termination benefits, the micro-entity must be demonstrably committed either:

- to terminate the employment of an employee (or a number of employees) before their normal retirement date; or
- be committed to providing termination benefits as a means of encouraging voluntary redundancy.

Focus

- The micro-entity is 'demonstrably committed' to a termination only when the micro-entity has drawn up a detailed plan for the termination and is without realistic possibility of withdrawing from the plan.

Once the recognition criteria has been met for termination benefits, the micro-entity recognises a liability which is calculated using the best estimate of the expenditure which would be required to be paid in order to discharge the liability and will be based on the number of staff who are expected to accept the offer of redundancy.

It is fairly uncommon for redundancy benefits to be paid longer than 12 months after the end of the reporting period, but if they are due more than 12 months from the reporting date they must be discounted to present day values. The difference between the settlement amount and the discounted amount is interest and the micro-entity uses a discount rate having regard to market yields at the reporting date on high quality corporate bonds.

Disclosure requirements

11.115 Disclosure should be made of any commitment which is not recognised in the balance sheet relating to pensions. This disclosure should be made separately from other financial commitments, guarantees and contingencies.

Income tax

11.116 Section 24 *Income Tax* of FRS 105 deals with income tax, including all domestic and foreign taxes which are based on the micro-entity's taxable profit. In addition, issues relating to value added tax (VAT) are also covered in Section 24.

The section itself is relatively short and requires a micro-entity to recognise the **current** tax implications of transactions and other events in the financial statements.

Focus

- Micro-entities are prohibited from recognising deferred tax in their financial statements. This is on the grounds that the disclosure restrictions would mean it would be impossible to distinguish between current and deferred taxes and so this section of the book only considers the current tax implications.

Recognition of current tax

11.117 Current tax due to HM Revenue and Customs (HMRC) is recognised as a liability in the balance sheet with a corresponding debit to tax expense in the profit and loss account. Where the amount of tax paid for both the current and prior periods exceeds the amount payable a current tax asset is recognised in the balance sheet to represent the amount refundable from HMRC or the amount for which future tax liabilities can be reduced.

Where a micro-entity suffers a tax loss which can be carried back to previous periods triggering a refund from HMRC, a current tax asset is also recognised.

Current tax assets and liabilities are measured using the tax rates and laws which have been enacted or substantively enacted by the reporting date and are not discounted to present day values.

Withholding tax on dividends

11.118 Where a micro-entity may pay dividends to shareholders and pay a portion of the dividend to the tax authorities on behalf of the shareholders, the amount of any dividends recognised shall include the amount of withholding tax, but any other taxes (such as attributable tax credits) are excluded.

Where the micro-entity may receive dividends and similar income, these shall also be recognised at amounts which include withholding taxes and exclude other taxes (such as attributable tax credits). Withholding tax suffered is shown as part of the tax expense in profit or loss.

Value added tax (VAT)

11.119 Where the micro-entity is VAT-registered it must exclude VAT from the turnover reported in the profit and loss account (including VAT calculated under the flat rate VAT scheme). Expenses must also exclude any irrecoverable amounts of VAT. Where VAT is irrecoverable it is usually included in expenses and in the cost of fixed assets where practicable and material.

Presentation

11.120 Changes in current tax assets and tax liabilities are presented as tax expense or (income).

Where the micro-entity has both a tax asset and a tax liability, offsetting can only take place if, and only if, it has a legally enforceable right to set off the amounts and the micro-entity intends to either settle on a net basis or recover the asset and settle the liability simultaneously.

Foreign currency

11.121 Foreign currency issues are dealt with in Section 25 *Foreign Currency Translation* and this particular section is not as detailed as the foreign currency section in FRS 102. Where a micro-entity has a foreign branch it should refer to the requirements of Section 30 *Foreign Currency Translation* in FRS 102 (see **Chapter 12** at **12.356**) to determine if the foreign branch has a different functional currency and where this is the case it should apply the requirements in FRS 102.

Accounting for foreign currency transactions

11.122 A micro-entity will enter into foreign currency transactions by:

- buying or selling goods or services in a foreign currency;

- borrowing or lending funds when the amounts payable or receivable are denoted in a foreign currency; or
- acquiring or disposing of assets, or incurring and settling liabilities, which are denoted in a foreign currency.

Example 11.15 – Purchases of goods from a foreign supplier

Microco Ltd purchases some goods from a supplier based in Spain. The invoice received from the supplier is in Euros.

Microco will translate the invoice into sterling using the exchange rate at the date of the transaction. It can also use the contracted rate where the transaction is to be settled using a contracted rate.

Where the micro-entity has entered into a forward foreign currency contract, the rate of exchange specified in that contract should be used for the transaction.

Focus

- The use of contracted rates is a simplification in FRS 105 which is not found in FRS 102.

Translating amounts at the reporting date

11.123 Unless the micro-entity is applying a contract rate, at the end of the reporting period, the micro-entity must:

- translate foreign currency monetary items at the closing rate; and
- translate non-monetary items which are measured at historical cost and denoted in a foreign currency using the exchange rate at the date of the transaction.

Exchange differences are recognised in profit or loss in the period in which they arise.

Example 11.16 – Goods purchased from an overseas supplier

Microco Ltd purchases goods from its supplier based in Farland whose currency is the Dinar (D) on 1 December 2016 for D5,000. On this date the rate of exchange was £1:D1.20. Payment is due to the supplier on 31 January 2017 and on this date the rate of exchange was £1:D1.30 and there is no contracted rate. The transaction is recorded as follows:

Record the purchase at the rate of exchange on the date of the transaction

The purchase will be recorded in the purchase ledger at £4,167 (D5,000/1.20).

Settlement of the invoice on 31 January 2017

On settlement the rate of exchange has moved from 1.20 to 1.30. Microco will pay the supplier £3,846 (D5,000 / 1.30). This will result in an exchange gain of £321 (£4,167 less £3,846) because the rate of exchange has moved since the invoice was originally recognised and hence Microco will pay less at the settlement date than when the transaction was originally recorded. This exchange gain is recorded in profit or loss on 31 January 2017.

If the year-end had been 31 December 2016, the creditor would be translated at the closing rate on 31 December 2016. Assuming this was 1.25 the closing creditor would be £4,000 (D5,000 / 1.25) which would give rise to an exchange gain of £167 (£4,167 less £4,000). This exchange difference is recorded in profit or loss at the year-end.

Events after the end of the reporting period

11.124 Section 26 *Events after the End of the Reporting Period* in FRS 105 deals with favourable and unfavourable events which take place between the reporting date and the date on which the micro-entity's financial statements are authorised for issue. There are two types of event which Section 26 deals with:

- adjusting events; and
- non-adjusting events

Adjusting events

11.125 Adjusting events are those events which provide evidence of conditions which existed at the reporting date and hence are reflected in the financial statements (ie the financial statements are adjusted to reflect the transactions or events). Examples of adjusting events include:

- bankruptcy of a customer soon after the reporting date and who owes the micro-entity money at the reporting date;

- sale of stock after the reporting date which suggests that selling price less costs to complete and sell is lower than cost and hence providing evidence of impairment at the reporting date;
- determination of amounts in profit-sharing or bonus arrangements paid after the reporting date and where the micro-entity had a legal or constructive obligation at the reporting date and hence made provision for profit-sharing or bonus arrangements; and
- discovery of fraud or error which show the financial statements are incorrect.

Non-adjusting events

11.126 Non-adjusting events are those events whose conditions did not exist at the reporting date but have occurred between the reporting date and the date on which the financial statements are authorised for issue. Because the conditions relating to non-adjusting events did not exist at the reporting date, they are not adjusted in the financial statements. Examples of non-adjusting events include:

- a decline in market investments between the reporting date and the date when the financial statements are authorised for issue. Such a decline would reflect circumstances which have occurred subsequent to the year-end and hence are not adjusting events;
- a favourable judgement being awarded in respect of a court case after the reporting date but before the financial statements are authorised for issue. At the reporting date the micro-entity would have a contingent asset in such circumstances. However, if the micro-entity and the third party agreed on an amount in settlement before the reporting date which was not previously recognised because the amount of the settlement could not be reliably measured, this may be indicative of an adjusting event.

Going concern

11.127 The going concern basis of accounting must not be used by the micro-entity if management concludes after the end of the reporting period that it intends to liquidate the micro-entity or to cease trading, or has no realistic alternative but to do so. Where the going concern basis is not appropriate the effect is usually so pervasive that it requires a fundamental change in the basis of accounting.

Where this is the case, the financial statements must be prepared on an alternative basis (usually the break-up basis).

Dividends

11.128 Dividends declared after the end of a reporting period are not recognised as a liability. This is because the micro-entity has no obligation at the reporting date.

Specialised activities

11.129 Section 27 *Specialised Activities* only deals with agriculture. Other specialised activities (such as extractive industries and service concession arrangements) are not dealt with in FRS 105.

Recognition of a biological asset or agricultural produce

11.130 A 'biological asset' is a living animal or plant from which agricultural produce is harvested. For example milk would be harvested from a cow and wool would be harvested from sheep. There are three criterion which have to be met before a micro-entity can recognise a biological asset or an item of agricultural produce:

- the micro-entity controls the **asset** as a result of past events;
- it is **probable** that future economic benefits associated with the asset will flow to the micro-entity; and
- the cost of the **asset** can be measured reliably.[10]

Measurement

11.131 In line with other assets, a micro-entity can only measure biological assets at cost less accumulated depreciation and any accumulated impairment losses. Agricultural produce is measured at the point of harvest at the lower of cost and estimated selling price less costs to complete and sell. This will also be the cost price when applying Section 10 *Inventories* or another applicable section of FRS 105.

Disclosure requirements

11.132 The amount of any financial commitments, guarantees and contingencies which are not recognised in the balance sheet for the acquisition of a biological asset is to be disclosed within the total amount of financial commitments, guarantees and contingencies.

In addition, if the micro-entity has pledged any biological asset or agricultural produce as security in respect of its commitments, guarantees and contingencies, it must disclose an indication of the nature and form of such.

Transition to FRS 105

11.133 Section 28 *Transition to this FRS* requires a micro-entity to retrospectively apply FRS 105 as far back as the date of transition. The 'date of transition' is the start date of the earliest period reported in the financial statements.

10 FRS 105, para 27.2 (a), (b) and (c).

Example 11.17 – Date of transition

Microco Ltd has a year-end of 31 December 2016 and has chosen FRS 105 as its financial reporting framework. The comparative year is 31 December 2015 and the start date of this comparative year is 1 January 2015.

The date of transition is 1 January 2015.

The objective of applying FRS 105 as far back as the date of transition is so that the financial statements reflect FRS 105 as if the standard had always been the framework applied by the micro-entity.

Process at the date of transition

11.134 The micro-entity must prepare an opening FRS 105-compliant balance sheet in which it:

- recognises all assets and liabilities which are required to be recognised by FRS 105;
- derecognise items as assets or liabilities if FRS 105 does not permit such recognition;
- reclassify items which were recognised as one type of asset, liability or component of equity under the previous framework (eg the FRSSE), but are a different type of asset, liability or component of equity under FRS 105; and
- apply FRS 105 going forward in measuring all recognised assets and liabilities.

Focus

- There is no requirement to disclose the opening FRS 105-compliant balance sheet at the date of transition.

Where it is impracticable for a micro-entity to restate the opening balance sheet at the date of transition to FRS 105 for one, or more, of the adjustments required above, it must apply this section and the next three sections 'Accounting policies', 'Mandatory exemptions from retrospective application' and 'Optional exemptions from retrospective application' (ie paragraphs 28.7 to 28.10 of FRS 105) for such adjustments in the earliest period for which it is practicable to do so.

Accounting policies

11.135 One of the main problems which micro-entities are going to face on first-time adoption of FRS 105 is the fact that if they reported under the FRSSE (effective January 2015) there are a number of accounting options which have been removed in FRS 105, notably:

- prohibition of fair value accounting or amounts in respect of revaluations (eg investment property revaluations);
- prohibition of deferred tax;
- no option to capitalise borrowing or development costs; and
- a requirement to account for accrued short-term employee benefits.

When preparing the opening FRS 105-compliant balance sheet, the directors must consider the micro-entity's accounting policies under its previous financial reporting framework (eg the FRSSE) and assess whether they are compliant with FRS 105. Where they are not, they must be changed to reflect the rules in FRS 105 and this may give rise to transitional adjustments which are recognised directly in equity reserves at the date of transition.

In addition, the comparative year financial statements must also be adjusted to reflect the provisions in FRS 105.

Focus

- Transitional and prior-period adjustments may have consequential tax effects and the tax consequences must be considered.

Mandatory exemptions from retrospective application

11.136 There are two mandatory exemptions from retrospective application which a micro-entity is required to apply on transition to FRS 105 in respect of:

- derecognition of financial assets and financial liabilities; and
- accounting estimates.

Financial assets and financial liabilities which were derecognised under the previous financial reporting framework (eg the FRSSE (effective January 2015)) cannot be recognised upon transition to FRS 105.

For financial assets and financial liabilities which were recognised under previous UK GAAP, but which would have been derecognised under FRS 105, there are two choices available to a micro-entity:

- derecognise them on adoption of FRS 105; or
- continue recognising them until they are disposed of or settled.

Accounting estimates must not be changed on adoption of FRS 105 for the benefits of hindsight.

Optional exemptions from retrospective application

11.137 There are eight optional exemptions from retrospective application which relate to:

- business combinations and goodwill;
- share-based payment transactions;
- investment properties;
- compound financial instruments;
- arrangements containing a lease;
- decommissioning liabilities included in the cost of property, plant and equipment or investment property;
- dormant companies; and
- lease incentives.

Business combinations and goodwill

Where a business combination has taken place before the date of transition to FRS 105, a micro-entity is not required to apply Section 14 *Business Combinations and Goodwill*. However, if the micro-entity opts to apply Section 14 on first-time adoption of FRS 105, it must restate any later business combinations.

Where a first-time adopter does not apply Section 14 retrospectively, it must recognise and measure all the assets and liabilities acquired or assumed in a previous business combination at the date of transition in accordance with paragraph 28.7 (see the section above 'Process at the date of transition') to 28.9 (see the section above 'Accounting policies' and 'Mandatory exemptions from retrospective application); or with the following paragraphs of this section, except that no adjustment must be made to the carrying amount of goodwill.

Share-based payment transactions

For share-based payment transactions which were settled prior to the date of transition to FRS 105, a first-time adopter is not required to apply the provisions in Section 21 *Share-based Payment*.

Investment properties

This is probably the area where some micro-entities will be affected the most. A first-time adopter does not have to apply paragraph 12.15 of FRS 105 to determine the depreciated cost of each of the major components of an investment property at the date of transition. Where advantage is taken of this exemption, a first-time adopter must:

(1) Determine the total cost of the investment property (including all its components). Where the investment property was carried at open market value under the FRSSE (effective January 2015), this is calculated by reversing any revaluation gains or losses previously recorded in equity reserves.

(2) Separate the cost of the land from the buildings, where the land has a value. This is because land and buildings are accounted for separately under FRS 105.

(3) Estimate the total depreciated cost of the investment property (excluding land) at the date of transition to FRS 105 by recognising accumulated depreciation since the date of initial acquisition. This is calculated on the basis of the useful life of the most significant component of the item of investment property (eg the main structure of the investment property).

(4) Some of the total depreciated cost calculated in (3) above is then allocated to each of the other major components of the investment property to determine their depreciated cost. This allocation is made on a basis which is reasonable and consistent.

(5) Any amount of the total depreciated cost which is not allocated under (4) above is then allocated to the most significant component of the investment property (eg the main structure).

Example 11.18 – Investment property on transition

Microco Ltd has an investment property in its balance sheet as at 1 January 2015 (the date of transition) with a carrying amount of £150,000 and an associated revaluation surplus of £25,000. Microco previously applied the provisions in the FRSSE (effective January 2015) at paragraph 6.51 and carried the investment property at open market value (ie no depreciation had been charged). The investment property was purchased on 1 January 2011 and the financial controller is unsure as to how to get the investment property back to historical cost for the purposes of transitioning to FRS 105. The value of the land is £30,000.

For the purpose of FRS 105, the financial controller can apply the transitional provision in paragraph 28.10(c)(i) to arrive at a cost for FRS 105 at the date of transition. The revaluation surplus of £25,000 can be reversed against the cost of the investment property and hence at the date of transition the investment property will have a cost of £125,000 (£150,000 less £25,000).

Once a cost has been established for the purpose of FRS 105, the value of any land is taken into consideration and accounted for separately (as land does not generally depreciate).

Example 11.19 – Calculating depreciation at transition

The financial controller has removed the previous revaluation amounts in respect of investment property to arrive at a cost price of £125,000. The financial controller has confirmed that the depreciation policy in respect of investment property will be the same as for its owned building (ie 2% on a straight-line basis calculated on the basis of the useful life of the most significant component of the item of investment property (eg the main structural elements of the building)). The depreciation charge at the date of transition is calculated as follows:

Date of purchase: 1 January 2011

Depreciable amount: Total land and buildings	£125,000
Less land element	(£30,000)
Depreciable amount	£95,000

Depreciation to the date of transition = £95,000 × 2% × 4 years = £7,600

A transitional adjustment will be made as at 1 January 2015 as follows:

DR accumulated profit and loss	£7,600
CR accumulated depreciation (investment property)	(£7,600)

Being 4 years depreciation from 1 January 2011 to 1 January 2015

On transition, the investment property has a total depreciated cost of £87,400 (£95,000 less £7,600). This depreciated cost then needs to be allocated to each of the other major components (ie excluding the most significant component) to determine their depreciated cost.

Example 11.20 – Component accounting

Continuing with the above example the financial controller has been informed that the central heating system in the investment property will need replacing in three years' time from the date of transition to FRS 105. The current cost to replace the central heating system is £12,000.

The central heating system has a considerably shorter life than the main structure of the investment property and hence it is considered that it is reasonable that it should be depreciated over a three-year period from 1 January 2015 (ie separately from the rest of the property). Therefore the depreciation charge in the 2015 comparative year will be calculated as follows:

	Residual investment property***	Central heating	Total investment property
	£	£	£
Depreciable amount	75,400	12,000	87,400
Depreciable charge	1,508*	4,000*	5,508

*£75,400 × 2% = £1,508
**£12,000 / 3 years = £4,000
*** being treated as the most significant component

Compound financial instruments

A first-time adopter does not need to separate the compound financial instrument into its debt component and equity component if the liability component is not outstanding at the date of transition to FRS 105.

Arrangements containing a lease

A first-time adopter can assess whether an arrangement contains a lease, based on facts and circumstances which exist at the date of transition to FRS 105 rather than when the arrangement was entered into.

Decommissioning liabilities included in the cost of property, plant and equipment or investment property

Where the cost of an item of property, plant and equipment or investment property includes the initial estimate of costs of dismantling and removing the item and restoring the site on which the asset is located, a first-time adopter can measure this component of cost at the date of transition to FRS 105 as opposed to the date(s) when the obligation arose.

Dormant companies

A dormant company can elect to retain its accounting policies for reported assets, liabilities and equity at the date of transition to FRS 105 until there is a change to those balances, or the company undertakes new transactions.

Lease incentives

A first-time adopter can continue applying the accounting treatment it previously used in respect of lease incentives for leases entered into before the date of transition to FRS 105.

Focus

- Paragraph 28.12 of FRS 105 says that where applicable to the transactions, events or arrangements affected by applying these exemptions, the micro-entity can continue to use the exemptions which it has applied at the transition date when preparing subsequent financial statements until such time that the assets and liabilities which are associated with those transactions, events or arrangements are derecognised.

PITFALLS TO AVOID

- Failing to consider the 'bigger picture' when considering the appropriateness of FRS 105 for an entity ie would it be preferable for the entity to select a more comprehensive accounting framework?
- Using FRS 105 for an ineligible entity (eg a charity or an LLP).
- Not removing fair values and revaluation amounts on transition to FRS 105 and in the comparative year.
- Not understanding the key differences between FRS 105 and the previous FRSSE (effective January 2015).
- Accounting for deferred tax for a micro-entity.
- Using Format 1 for the profit and loss account.

CHAPTER SUMMARY

- Micro-entities are a new concept borne out of the EU Accounting Directive issued in June 2013.
- The eligibility criteria is very restrictive and care must be taken to ensure FRS 105 is appropriate for an entity.
- Micro-entities will report under FRS 105, which is a separate accounting standard specific to such entities on the basis of the significantly reduced disclosures and lack of accounting options available.
- While FRS 105 has been developed from the requirements in FRS 102, it has been simplified further by the FRC to avoid complex accounting issues being faced by preparers of micro-entity financial statements.
- The section and paragraph numbering in FRS 105 is different than in FRS 102 as fewer sections in FRS 102 will apply to a micro-entity applying FRS 105.
- There are two mandatory exemptions from retrospective application of FRS 105 and eight optional exemptions.

Chapter 12

Financial Reporting of Key Areas of the Accounts

Table of Contents

SIGNPOSTS

- While the disclosure requirements for a small company are contained in Section 1A of FRS 102, the full recognition and measurement principles apply to reduce divergent practices among companies (see **12.1**).

- This chapter considers the accounting and disclosure issues for small companies reporting under FRS 102 with reduced disclosure. The micro-entity standards are contained in **Chapter 11** (see **12.2**).
- The recognition, measurement and disclosure issues for transactions and events covered by FRS 102 are in paragraphs **12.3–12.407**.
- An Appendix is included to this chapter outlining the differences between FRS 102 applicable to small companies and the FRSSE (effective January 2015).

INTRODUCTION

12.1 This chapter looks in detail at the accounting requirements of FRS 102 *The Financial Reporting Standard applicable in the UK and Republic of Ireland*. While Section 1A of FRS 102 *Small Entities* deals with the presentation and disclosure requirements for a set of financial statements for a small company, the full recognition and measurement principles in full FRS 102 apply. This is to reduce divergent practices among small, medium-sized and large companies and hence as a small company grows, the accounting treatment for certain transactions and events will remain the same as it moves up the suite of standards.

12.2 The accounting requirements for micro-entities are looked at in **Chapter 11** and are dealt with in a separate chapter in light of the fact that there are no accounting policy choices and no recognition of items at fair value or revalued amounts.

Chapter 2 examines the new financial reporting frameworks in terms of classification of a company and/or a group and the contents of the annual accounts (including abridged and adapted financial statements). **Chapter 3** examines the contents of the financial statements including how the application of accounting standards will achieve a true and fair view.

Focus

- Many small companies choose not to prepare a cash flow statement as part of the primary financial statements and hence this chapter does not consider the requirements in Section 7 *Statement of Cash Flows*. However, the cash flow statement is examined in **Chapter 3**.

ACCOUNTING POLICIES, ESTIMATES AND ERRORS

12.3 Accounting policies, estimates and errors are dealt with in Section 10 *Accounting Policies, Estimates and Errors* of FRS 102. Accounting policies are the 'backbone' of a small entity's financial statements because they are the specific principles, bases, conventions, rules and practices which a small company applies in preparing their financial statements. It follows, therefore, that the directors must carefully select accounting policies that are appropriate to the size, nature and complexity of the business and apply these policies consistently from one period to the next.

> **Focus**
>
> - It is possible to change an accounting policy where management deem this appropriate. However, a change to an accounting policy is not left to management's discretion as other commercial decisions might be. The 'change' in itself is governed by accounting rules which must be followed. Ordinarily a change in accounting policy will occur when FRS 102 requires such a change to be made (ie where a change to a relevant section has taken place which mandates a company to change its policy) or where management deem the accounting policy change will result in more relevant and reliable information being contained in the financial statements.

12.4 Section 10 also covers the issue relating to errors and takes a slightly different approach than the previous Financial Reporting Standard for Smaller Entities (the FRSSE) (effective January 2015). The FRSSE required the correction of errors by way of a prior year adjustment where an error(s) was *fundamental*. The term 'fundamental' was taken to mean that the error(s) destroyed the true and fair view and the validity of the financial statements and hence the correction was applied retrospectively. Section 10 says that an error is corrected when the error is *material* to the financial statements.

> **Focus**
>
> - Paragraph 2.6 of FRS 102 says that information is **material** – and therefore has relevance – if its omission or misstatement, individually or collectively, could influence the economic decisions of users taken on the basis of the financial statements. Materiality depends on the size and nature of the omission or misstatement judged in the surrounding circumstances. The size or nature of the item, or a combination of both, could be the determining factor. However, it is inappropriate to make, or leave uncorrected, immaterial departures from this FRS to achieve a particular presentation of an entity's financial position, financial performance or cash flows.[1]

It is likely that more errors will be corrected via a prior year adjustment under FRS 102 than was the case under the FRSSE (effective January 2015). Whether something is material will all depend on professional judgement and FRS 102 does not provide benchmarks for materiality; hence something which may be

1 FRS 102, para 2.6.

material in one company's financial statements may not be material in another company's financial statements.

It is generally accepted within the accountancy profession that over- or under-estimations of figures such as accruals, prepayments, tax provisions and stock provisions will often occur. Generally these estimations are going to be immaterial to the financial statements and will simply be adjusted for in the current financial year without the need for a prior year adjustment.

Selecting accounting policies

12.5 A small company is required to select accounting policies which are appropriate in the entity's individual circumstances. An example of a typical accounting policy choice would be carrying a class of fixed assets under the cost model or revaluation model as permitted in Section 17 *Property, Plant and Equipment* (see **12.134** and **12.136**). In addition, some entities that self-construct an asset may choose to capitalise borrowing costs which they incur on loans taken out specifically for the construction to take place; whereas other entities may write off such charges to profit or loss.

12.6 Small companies are also required to select measurement bases on which to subsequently measure items in the financial statements, for example:

- fixed assets can be subsequently measured using the cost model or revaluation model; and
- inventory (stock) can be subsequently measured using first-in first-out, weighted average cost or another acceptable method (but not the last-in first-out method).

Different companies will also present items in different areas of the financial statements. For example, a labour-intensive company manufacturing goods will more than likely present depreciation charges for factory equipment in cost of sales; whereas a service company might present depreciation charges relating to its computer equipment in administrative expenses. Changes in presentation would fall to be classed as an accounting policy change and hence would only be made when management deem the revised policy to present more relevant and reliable financial information.

12.7 It is important that accounting policies are applied consistently from one period to the next and it is for this reason that an accounting policy change is applied retrospectively so as to enable comparability and consistency to be achieved in the financial statements.

Transactions and events not covered by FRS 102

12.8 In instances where FRS 102 does not cover a particular transaction or event (which is likely to be rare), management must develop its own accounting policy. This is not quite as straightforward as it initially sounds, because the accounting policy developed by management must be done with reference to Section 2 of FRS 102 *Concepts and Pervasive Principles* and must be:

- **Relevant** – it must be relevant to the economic decision-making needs of users; and
- **Reliable** – so that the financial statements:
  - faithfully represent the financial position, financial performance and cash flows of the entity;
  - reflect the substance of transactions, events and conditions rather than legal form;
  - are neutral (in other words free from bias);
  - are prudent; and
  - are complete in all material respects.

When management are developing an accounting policy to deal with a transaction or event which is not covered by FRS 102, paragraph 10.5 requires management to refer to, and consider the applicability of, certain sources as follows in descending order:

- the requirements and guidance in an FRS or FRC Abstract dealing with similar and related issues;
- where an entity's financial statements are within the scope of a **Statement of Recommended Practice (SORP)** the requirements and guidance in that SORP dealing with similar and related issues; and
- the definitions, **recognition** criteria and measurement concepts for **assets**, **liabilities**, **income** and **expenses** and the pervasive principles in Section 2 *Concepts and Pervasive Principles*.[2]

Changing an accounting policy

12.9 As discussed in **12.3** above, it is possible for a small company to change an accounting policy. Where a change in accounting policy takes place, the directors must apply that change **retrospectively** to comparative information for prior periods to the earliest date for which it is practicable. This is to enable the financial statements to reflect the revised accounting policy as if it had always been applied by the entity and to allow the financial statements to be comparable and consistent.

Section 10 recognises certain transactions and events which are NOT considered to be accounting policy changes:

- applying an accounting policy for certain transactions, events or conditions which differ in substance from those which have previously occurred;

2 FRS 102, para 10.5(a), (b), (c).

- applying an accounting policy for transactions, events and conditions which had not occurred previously or which were immaterial in previous periods; and
- changes to the cost model when fair value can no longer be reliably measured (or vice versa) for assets which could be measured at fair value under FRS 102 for small companies.

Example 12.1 – Change in accounting policy

Whatmough Enterprises Ltd is a manufacturer of fine chemicals and has always been involved in a small amount of research and development. The directors decided several years ago that the company's accounting policy for development expenditure is to write it off to profit or loss as opposed to capitalising such expenditure.

However, over the last two years the company's activities in research and development have increased significantly and the directors have now decided that it would be more appropriate to capitalise development expenditure where the expenditure meets the recognition criteria in paragraph 18.8H of FRS 102.

Paragraph 10.10 of FRS 102 says that where an FRS or FRC Abstract permits a choice of accounting treatment (including the measurement basis) for a certain transaction, event or other condition, and the entity subsequently changes its previous choice, then that will give rise to a change in accounting policy. Therefore, Whatmough Enterprises Ltd must apply the decision to change writing off development costs to capitalising them retrospectively.

12.10 Paragraph 10.11 of FRS 102 requires certain accounting to be undertaken for changes in accounting policy as follows:

- Change is required by an FRS or FRC Abstract.

  Where a change in accounting policy is required by an FRS or an FRC Abstract, then the change is applied according to any transitional provisions contained in the amendment (where applicable).

- Financial instruments.

  In the rare instance that a small entity has decided to follow IAS 39 *Financial Instruments: Recognition and Measurement* and/or IFRS 9 *Financial Instruments* as opposed to Section 11 *Basic Financial Instruments* or Section 12 *Other Financial Instruments Issues* in FRS 102 and changes are made to IAS 39/IFRS 9 then the small entity must account for the change in accounting policy in accordance with any transitional provisions contained in the revised IAS 39/IFRS 9.

  It is not anticipated that the application of IAS 39/IFRS 9 will be common where small companies are concerned.

- Earnings per share, operating segments and mineral resources.

  Again, these situations are likely to be rare for small companies, but where the small business applies the provisions in IAS 33 *Earnings per Share*, IFRS 8 *Operating Segments* or IFRS 6 *Exploration for and Evaluation of Mineral Resources*, and the requirements of those standards change, then the entity must account for that change in accounting policy in accordance with any transitional provisions contained in the revised standards.

Focus

To assist small company directors in establishing whether, or not, there has been a change to an accounting policy, financial statement preparers should ask three questions:

(1) Has there been a change in the way the entity recognises amounts in the financial statements?

(2) Has there been a change in the way the entity measures amounts in the financial statements?

(3) Has there been a change in the way the entity presents amounts in the financial statements?

If the answer to any of the above questions is 'yes' then there has been a change in an accounting policy and the change is applied retrospectively.

Example 12.2 – Change in the valuation of inventory

Jones Ltd has a year-end of 31 December 2016 and manufactures outdoor garden furniture. The company has always valued its closing stock on an individual basis, however due to rapid expansion the directors have undertaken an impact assessment and have decided that the first-in first-out method (FIFO) of stock valuation would result in more relevant and reliable information being provided in the financial statements as well as being more appropriate in the company's individual circumstances.

The impact assessment shows that if the stock valuation in the prior year (2015) had been undertaken using FIFO then this would have produced a stock valuation £10,000 higher than was originally calculated. Profit and loss account reserves immediately prior to the accounting policy change amount to £90,000.

The impact of the adjustment is as follows:

The opening balance on profit on loss reserves will increase from £90,000 to £100,000 as a result of the accounting policy change.

	Year-ended 31 December 2015		
	Pre-adjustment	Adjustment	As restated
	£	£	£
Turnover	750,000	–	750,000
Cost of sales	420,000	10,000	410,000
Administrative expenses	190,000	–	190,000
Net profit (ignoring tax implications)	140,000	10,000	150,000

Information about judgements

12.11 Section 1A *Small Entities* in FRS 102 in Appendix C requires a small entity to disclose the accounting policies adopted (see **12.12** below). In addition to the summary of significant accounting policies, Section 1A Appendix C also requires information concerning the judgements made by management in the process of applying the entity's accounting policies which have the most significant effect on the amounts that have been recognised in the financial statements.

Focus

- In disclosing information about judgement within the summary of significant accounting policies, information about key sources of estimation uncertainty are not included.

Typical examples around judgements which may be applicable to small companies include:

- information concerning impairment of assets;
- bad debt provisions;
- provisions for slow-moving or obsolete items of inventory; and
- warranty provisions.

Note: the above list is not exhaustive, but is an indicator of items within the financial statements which may involve judgement on the part of management and which may require disclosure to comply with Section 1A of FRS 102.

Example 12.3 – Illustrative disclosures about judgements

Impairment of assets

Fixed assets include goodwill and items of property, plant and equipment and such assets are reviewed annually for impairment where events or changes in circumstances indicate that the carrying amount of the asset may not be recoverable.

When a review for impairment is conducted, the recoverable amount of an asset or cash-generating unit is determined based on value-in-use calculations prepared on the basis of management's assumptions and estimates.

Bad debt provisions

The company maintains a general bad debt provision which accounts for management's best estimate of losses resulting from customers' inability to make required payments. Additional provisions are made for specific customers if the financial conditions of a customer indicate a deterioration in their ability to make payment.

Provisions for slow-moving inventory

Where the company has excess amounts of inventory or inventory is showing signs of obsolescence which may indicate that estimated selling price less costs to complete and sell is below cost, then a provision is made against inventory to reduce the value of the inventory to the lower of cost and estimated selling price less costs to complete and sell to comply with the requirements of paragraph 13.4 of FRS 102.

Warranty provisions

Warranty provisions are calculated using management's best estimate of the value of warranty claims by customers for defective goods. The calculation is based on past experiences of the company.

Disclosures relating to accounting policies

12.12 The disclosure requirements for a small company in relation to its accounting policies are contained in Section 1A of FRS 102. This section requires a small company to disclose its accounting policies adopted in accordance with paragraphs 8.5 and 8.6 of FRS 102. Paragraph 8.5 requires the following to be disclosed in the summary of accounting policies:

(a) the measurement basis (or bases) used in preparing the entity's financial statements; and

(b) other accounting policies adopted by the entity which are relevant to an understanding of the financial statements.

12.13 Paragraphs 1AC.3 to 1AC.10 outline the legally required disclosures concerning a company's accounting policies. In particular, disclosure must be made of the accounting policies adopted by the company in determining amounts included in the balance sheet (statement of financial position) and profit and loss account (income statement) which should also include policies regarding depreciation and asset impairment.

Development costs

12.14 Where development costs are capitalised and management have determined the carrying amount of those intangible assets is not a realised loss, disclosure should be made of the reasons for showing development costs as an asset and that the carrying amount is not to be treated as a realised loss.

Disclosure should also be made of the period over which the amount of the development costs originally capitalised are being written off together with the reasons for capitalising those costs.

Where, in exceptional circumstances, the useful life of intangible assets cannot be reliably assessed, the company must disclose the period over which those intangible assets are being written off, together with the reasons for that period.

Changes in presentation, accounting policies and corrections of errors

12.15 The entity should disclose:

- Particulars of changes in presentation in either the profit and loss account (income statement) or balance sheet (statement of financial position) in the period in which the new presentation is used together with reasons for the change.
- Where the corresponding amount for the preceding financial year is not comparable with the current year and the corresponding amount is adjusted, the particulars of the non-comparability should be disclosed together with the adjustment (this will usually arise because of a change in accounting policy or the correction of an error).
- Where any amount which relates to a preceding reporting period is included in any item in the income statement, disclosure of the effect should be made.

True and fair override

12.16 It is permissible for a small company to depart from the requirements of company law in special circumstances in order that the financial statements give a true and fair view. Where the company does depart from a requirement in company law, it must disclose:

- the particulars of the departure;
- the reasons for the departure; and
- the effects of the departure.

Focus

- It is not expected that many companies will apply the true and fair override as it should only be undertaken in special circumstances.

Accounting estimates

12.17 A change in an accounting estimate is not the same as a change in an accounting policy. A change in an accounting estimate is an adjustment to the carrying amount of an asset or liability, or the amount of the periodic consumption of an asset. The Glossary to FRS 102 defines a change in accounting estimate as:

> 'An adjustment of the **carrying amount** of an **asset** or a **liability**, or the amount of the periodic consumption of an asset, that results from the assessment of the present status of, and expected future benefits and obligations associated with, assets and liabilities. Changes in accounting estimates result from new information or new developments and, accordingly, are not corrections of **errors**.'

Example 12.4 – Change in an accounting estimate

Hussain & Co Ltd are management consultants who have a customer base spread across the UK and Republic of Ireland. The company has a policy of depreciating their motor vehicles on a four-year straight-line basis. The financial statements for the year-ended 31 March 2017 are in the process of being completed and the board of directors have announced a change to the method of depreciating the company's motor vehicles to a 25% reducing-balance (diminishing balance) basis. This is to reflect the higher maintenance charges incurred in the later years of ownership of the vehicles and hence is the reason why management believe the revised depreciation policy is appropriate given the company's replacement cycle of motor vehicles (which is usually every five years).

A change in depreciation method is a change in estimation technique because there is no change to recognition criteria, measurement bases or presentation methods on the basis that:

- the motor vehicles are still being carried at cost less accumulated depreciation;

- the depreciation charge is still allocated to the individual accounting periods which reflect the consumption of the economic benefits of the motor vehicles; and
- the motor vehicles and depreciation are still presented in the same way in Hussain & Co's balance sheet (statement of financial position) and profit and loss account (income statement).

12.18 Accounting for a change in estimation is straightforward because it is simply applied prospectively (going forward). A change in estimation technique is not applied retrospectively and hence there will be no consequential effect on the comparative period's financial statements nor the opening balance of profit and loss reserves (retained earnings).

Disclosures relating to changes in accounting estimate

12.19 There are no legally required disclosures in respect of changes to an accounting estimate. However, where disclosure of such would enable a true and fair view to be given, the small entity should consider disclosing the nature of the change in accounting estimate as well as:

- the consequential change on assets, liabilities, income and expense for the current period; and
- where practicable, estimates of the effect of the change in one, or more, future periods.

Errors

12.20 Section 10 also deals with the issue concerning errors. As discussed earlier in the chapter, Section 10 requires the correction of an error by way of a prior period adjustment when that error is material. In contrast, the FRSSE (effective January 2015) only required the correction of errors through a prior period adjustment when the error was fundamental. It is expected that more errors will be corrected by way of a prior period adjustment under FRS 102 principles.

Paragraph 10.19 of FRS 102 says that prior period errors are omissions from, and misstatements in, an entity's financial statements for one or more prior periods arising from a failure to use, or misuse of, reliable information that:

- was available when the financial statements for those periods were authorised for issue; and
- could reasonably be expected to have been obtained and taken into account in the preparation and presentation of those financial statements.[3]

3 FRS 102, para 10.19(a) and (b).

Example 12.5 – Error discovered after the financial statements were authorised for issue

During the preparation of the financial statements for the year-ended 31 December 2017, the accountant discovered two months' worth of sales had been omitted from the prior year financial statements of Colin's Cycle Repairs Ltd. This had arisen because the bookkeeping had been done incorrectly for the last two months' of the previous year as the bookkeeper had fallen ill. The value of the omitted sales was £35,000 (net of value added tax) and this figure is considered to be material to the financial statements.

As the amount of the error is material, it must be corrected through a prior period adjustment. If, on the other hand, the error was not deemed to be material then it could be adjusted for in the current financial year.

12.21 The method of correcting an error through a prior period adjustment is similar to the principles involved in retrospectively changing an accounting policy. To correct an error through a prior period adjustment the accountant must:

- restate the comparative amount for the prior period(s) in which the error occurred; and
- where the error occurred before the earlier prior period presented, the accountant must restate the opening balances of assets, liabilities and equity for the earlier prior period presented.

Example 12.6 – Correction of a material error

The financial statements of Westhead Ltd for the year ended 31 December 2016 are in the process of being completed. These financial statements are shown below:

Westhead Ltd
Profit and Loss Account
For the year ended 31 December 2016

	2016	2015
	£'000	£'000
Turnover	4,000	3,500
Cost of sales	950	820
Gross profit	3,050	2,680
Administrative expenses	1,200	800
Profit on ordinary activities before taxation	1,850	1,880
Tax on profit on ordinary activities	700	600
Profit for the financial year	1,150	1,280

Westhead Ltd
Balance Sheet
As at 31 December 2016

	31.12.16		31.12.15	
	£'000	£'000	£'000	£'000
Tangible fixed assets		5,325		4,000
Current assets				
Stocks	400		300	
Trade debtors	175		100	
Cash at bank	250		200	
	825		600	
Creditors: amounts falling due within one year	750		350	
NET CURRENT ASSETS		75		250
TOTAL ASSETS LESS CURRENT LIABILITIES		**5,400**		**4,250**
Capital and reserves				
Called up share capital		100		100
Profit and loss account		5,300		4,150
		5,400		**4,250**

During the preparation of the financial statements for the year ended 31 December 2016, it was noticed that a large item of plant and machinery that had been purchased on 20 December 2015 had been allocated to repairs and renewals within the profit and loss account (shown within administrative expenses) amounting to £325,000. The financial statements above do not contain any amendments to the financial statements in respect of this error, which the partner in charge has deemed to be material. This error will need to be corrected by way of a prior period adjustment.

The administrative expenses in the 2015 financial statements will need to be reduced by £325,000 and the tangible fixed assets will also increase by this amount. However, the depreciation element will also have to be considered, so for the purposes of this illustration assume that the company writes off the value of all its plant and machinery over five years on a straight-line basis (hence £325,000 ÷ 5 years) = £65,000 worth of depreciation (note – the tax implications have been ignored for the purposes of this illustration).

Westhead Ltd
Profit and Loss Account
For the year ended 31 December 2016

	2016	**2015 (as restated)**
	£'000	£'000
Turnover	4,000	3,500
Cost of sales	950	820
Gross profit	3,050	2,680
Administrative expenses	1,265	540
Profit on ordinary activities before taxation	1,785	2,140
Tax on profit on ordinary activities	700	600
Profit for the financial year	1,085	1,540

Westhead Ltd
Balance Sheet
As at 31 December 2016

	31.12.16		**31.12.15**	
	£'000	£'000	£'000	£'000
Tangible fixed assets		5,520		4,260
Current assets				
Stocks	400		300	
Trade debtors	175		100	
Cash at bank	250		200	
	825		600	
Creditors: amounts falling due within one year	750		350	
NET CURRENT ASSETS		75		250
TOTAL ASSETS LESS CURRENT LIABILITIES		**5,595**		**4,510**
Capital and reserves				
Called up share capital		100		100
Profit and loss account		5,495		4,410
		5,595		**4,510**

The statement of changes in equity is an encouraged statement and given that the prior period adjustment has been deemed as material, then it should be included in the financial statements as follows:

Westhead Ltd
Statement of Changes in Equity
For the year ended 31 December 2016

	Note	Share capital	Profit and loss	Total
		£'000	£'000	£'000
Balance at 1 January 2015	14	100	2,870	2,970
Profit for the year			1,280	1,280
Balance at 31 December 2015		100	4,150	4,250
Prior period adjustment			260	260
Profit for the year			1,085	1,085
Balance at 31 December 2016		100	5,495	5,595

The prior period adjustment has been calculated as:

Cost of asset capital	£325,000
Less depreciation (five years' straight line)	(£65,000)
Prior period adjustment	£260,000

Disclosures relating to error correction

12.22 Paragraph 1AC.8 makes reference to paragraph 10.23 of FRS 102 which requires disclosure of:

(a) the nature of the prior period error;

(b) to the extent practicable, for each prior period presented in the financial statements, the amount of the correction for each line item in the financial statements affected;

(c) to the extent practicable, the amount of the correction at the beginning of the earlier prior period presented in the financial statements; and

(d) where it is not practicable to determine the amounts to be disclosed in (b) or (c) above, an explanation of the adjustments.

Focus

- There is no need to repeat these disclosures for subsequent accounting periods.

FINANCIAL INSTRUMENTS: BASIC AND OTHER INSTRUMENTS

Basic financial instruments

12.23 FRS 102 splits financial instruments into two classifications: 'basic' and 'other'. *Basic* financial instruments include items such as:

- trade debtors;
- trade creditors;
- straightforward loans;
- bonds and similar debt instruments; and
- investments in non-convertible preference shares and non-puttable ordinary and preference shares.

When a financial instrument falls to be classed as a basic instrument they are accounted for under the provisions in Section 11 and are then generally accounted for at amortised cost. Most trade debtors and trade creditors will continue to be measured at the undiscounted amount of cash expected to be received or paid.

> **Focus**
>
> - Care must be taken with trade debtors where these are granted payment terms which are beyond normal commercial terms because where this happens, the transaction will become a financing transaction and hence the asset must be measured at the present value of the future payments which are then discounted at a market rate of interest for a similar debt instrument.

12.24 Paragraph 11.6 of FRS 102 gives examples of financial instruments which would not normally satisfy the criteria to be classed as a basic financial instrument and these relate to:

- asset-backed securities such as collateralised mortgage obligations, repurchase agreements and securitised packages of receivables;
- options, futures contracts, rights, forward contracts, warrants and interest rate swaps which may be settled by cash or through an exchange of other assets;
- financial instruments which qualify and have been designated as hedging instruments under the provisions in Section 12 *Other Financial Instruments Issues*; and
- commitments to make a loan and commitments to receive a loan whereby the commitment can be settled net in cash.

The following are also not dealt with under Section 11 principles:

Type of financial instrument	Applicable section or standard
Investments in subsidiaries.	Section 9 *Consolidated and Separate Financial Statements.*
Investments in associates.	Section 14 *Investments in Associates.*
Investments in joint ventures.	Section 15 *Investments in Joint Ventures.*
Financial instruments meeting the definition of an entity's own equity and the equity component of a compound financial instrument which contains both equity and liability.	Section 22 *Liabilities and Equity.*
Leasing transactions (except in relation to the derecognition requirements in paragraphs 11.33–11.35 and impairment requirements in paragraphs 11.21–11.26 which apply to the derecognition and impairment of debtors recognised by a lessor and the derecognition principles in paragraphs 11.36–11.38 which apply to creditors recognised by a lessee under a finance lease). Section 12 *Other Financial Instruments Issues* apply to leases with characteristics specified in paragraph 12.3(f).	Section 20 *Leases.*
Employers' rights and obligations in an employee benefit plan (note paragraphs 11.27–11.32 do apply in determining the fair value of plan assets).	Section 28 *Employee Benefits.*
Share-based payment arrangements.	Section 26 *Share-based Payment.*
Insurance contracts (including reinsurance contracts).	FRS 103 *Insurance Contracts.*
Financial instruments containing a discretionary participation feature.	FRS 103 *Insurance Contracts.*
Reimbursement assets accounted for under Section 21 *Provisions and Contingencies.*	Section 21 *Provisions and Contingencies.*
Financial guarantee contracts.	Section 21 *Provisions and Contingencies.*

Classifying a financial instrument as a basic instrument

12.25 For the majority of small companies, most financial instruments will meet the criteria to be accounted for under Section 11 principles, especially where the instruments are:

- cash;
- debt instruments which meet the conditions in paragraph 11.9 of FRS 102;

- commitments to make or receive a loan to another entity which cannot be settled net in cash and where the conditions in paragraph 11.9 can be met; and
- investments in non-convertible preference shares and non-puttable ordinary shares or preference shares.

12.26 For a debt instrument to be classified as basic, the criteria is outlined in paragraph 11.9 of FRS 102 which says the conditions to be met are:

(a) The contractual return to the holder (the lender), assessed in the currency in which the debt instrument is denominated, is:

(i) a fixed amount;

(ii) a positive fixed rate or a positive variable rate; or

(iii) not used;

(iv) a combination of a positive or a negative fixed rate and a positive variable rate (eg LIBOR plus 200 basis points or LIBOR less 50 basis points, but not 500 basis points less LIBOR).

(aA) The contract may provide for repayments of the principal or the return to the holder (but not both) to be linked to a single relevant observable index of general price inflation of the currency in which the debt instrument is denominated, provided such links are not leveraged.

(aB) The contract may provide for a determinable variation of the return to the holder during the life of the instrument, provided that:

(i) the new rate satisfies condition (a) and the variation is not contingent on future events other than:

(1) a change of a contractual variable rate;

(2) to protect the holder against credit deterioration of the issuer;

(3) changes in levies applied by a central bank or arising from changes in relevant taxation or law; or

(ii) the new rate is a market rate of interest and satisfies conditions (a).

Contractual terms that give the lender the unilateral option to change the terms of the contract are not determinable for this purpose.

(b) There is no contractual provision that could, by its terms, result in the holder losing the principal amount or any interest attributable to the current period or prior periods. The fact that a debt instrument is subordinated to other debt instruments is not an example of such a contractual provision.

(c) Contractual provisions that permit the issuer (the borrower) to repay a debt instrument or permit the holder (the lender) to put it back to the issuer before maturity are not contingent on future events other than to protect:

(i) the holder against the credit deterioration of the issuer (eg defaults, credit downgrades or loan covenant violations), or a change in control of the issuer; or

(ii) the holder or issuer against changes in levies applied by a central bank or arising from changes in relevant taxation or law.

The inclusion of contractual terms that, as a result of the early termination, require the issuer to compensate the holder for the early termination does not, in itself, constitute a breach of this condition.

(d) [not used]

(e) Contractual provisions may permit the extension of the term of the debt instrument, provided that the return to the holder and any other contractual provisions applicable during the extended term satisfy the conditions of paragraph (a) to (c).[4]

> **Focus**
>
> - Section 11 contains some useful examples of debt instruments which are accounted for under Section 11 or Section 12 depending on whether they are basic or otherwise.

Initial recognition of a basic debt instrument

12.27 A company can only recognise a financial asset or a financial liability when it becomes a party to the contractual terms of the instrument. When it is evident that the small business has become a party to the debt instrument, the financial asset or financial liability is initially recognised at its transaction price, which will include transaction costs.

> **Focus**
>
> - Transaction costs are not included in the transaction price of a financial asset or financial liability which has been designated as being measured at fair value through profit or loss on initial recognition.

Example 12.7 – Investments in another entity

Fallon Ltd invests in two companies: Heysham PLC (a company listed on the London Stock Market) and Antley Ltd.

4 FRS 102, para 11.9(a)–(e).

The investment in Heysham PLC should be initially recorded at the cost of the investment which **excludes** transaction costs. Transaction costs are expensed to profit or loss when they are incurred because the investment will subsequently be measured at fair value through profit or loss as the fair value of the investment can be measured reliably at each reporting date due to the listed status of the investee.

The investment in Antley Ltd should be initially recorded at the cost of the investment which **includes** transaction costs. This is because it will not be possible to obtain a reliable fair value of the investment at each reporting date.

12.28 Section 11 also deals with the issue of financing transactions. A financing transaction will take place where payment for sales of goods or rendering of services is deferred beyond normal commercial terms. A financing transaction can also arise where the transaction is financed at a rate of interest which is not at market rate. In such instances, the company must measure the financial asset or financial liability at the present value of the future payments which are then discounted at a market rate of interest for a similar debt instrument.

Example 12.8 – Sale of goods on deferred payment terms

Appliances R Us sell domestic appliances to members of the public. During the year to 31 July 2017 it sells a 65-inch wide-screen TV to a member of the public on two-years' interest-free credit for £3,500. The current cash sales price of the TV is £2,950.

In this example, the provisions of paragraph 23.5 of FRS 102 would apply and Appliances R Us would recognise a debtor of £2,950 (being the current cash sales price of the TV). After initial recognition, the company would account for the debtor using the amortised cost method and hence the difference between the present value of the debtor (£2,950) and the expected consideration amount of £3,500 (£550) is treated as interest revenue over the two-year period.

Other types of instruments which are pertinent to a small business, together with how they are initially recognised in the financial statements are as follows:

Transaction	**Initial recognition**
Long-term loan made to another entity	A debtor is recognised representing the present value of the cash receivable which will include interest and capital
Goods sold to a customer on short-term credit	Invoice price

Transaction	Initial recognition
Goods sold to a customer on three-years' interest free credit	A debtor is recognised at the current cash sale price for that item (as the cash sales price would normally approximate present value) – if the current cash sales price is unknown it is estimated using the present value of the cash receivable which is then discounted using prevailing market rates for a similar transaction
Purchase of an entity's ordinary shares	Cash paid to acquire the shares
Bank loan from a bank	A creditor is recognised representing the present value of the cash payable to the bank which will include interest and capital
Goods purchased from a supplier on short-term credit	Invoice price

Subsequent measurement of a basic financial instrument

12.29 Generally a debt instrument accounted for under Section 11 will be subsequently measured using the amortised cost method, which in turn uses the effective interest method.

> **Focus**
>
> - Debt instruments which are payable or receivable within one year (ie current assets or current liabilities) are measured at the undiscounted amount of the cash or other consideration expected to be received.

Debt instruments can be designated at fair value through profit or loss on initial recognition and subsequently measured at fair value through profit or loss after initial recognition. However, this treatment is expected to be quite rare for small businesses. Debt instruments accounted for under Section 11 can only be designated at fair value through profit or loss where so doing provides more relevant information because:

- an accounting mismatch (a measurement or recognition inconsistency) is eliminated or significantly reduced by recognising and measuring at fair value; or
- a group of debt instruments or financial assets and debt instruments are managed, and their performance evaluated, on a fair value basis.

> **Focus**
>
> - For the second bullet point above, there has to be a documented risk management or investment strategy in place. In addition, information about the instruments within the group have to be provided to the entity's key management personnel. This is likely to be rare for small companies.

Shares (either investments in non-convertible preference shares and/or non-puttable ordinary shares or preference shares) which are publicly traded (or where fair value can be reliably measured) should be measured at fair value with fluctuations in fair value going through profit or loss.

Amortised cost method

12.30 The vast majority of financial instruments accounted for under Section 11 principles for a small entity are likely to be accounted for using the amortised cost method. Paragraph 11.15 of FRS 102 says that the amortised cost of a financial asset or financial liability at each reporting date is the **net** of the following four amounts:

(1) the value at which the financial instrument is measured at initial recognition;

(2) *minus* repayments of capital;

(3) *plus* or *minus* the cumulative amortisation of the instrument using the effective interest rate method (see next section) of any difference in the amount at initial recognition and the amount at maturity; or

(4) *minus* – in the case of a financial asset – any reduction for impairment or uncollectibility.

Focus

- Financial assets and financial liabilities which:
  - have no stated interest rate;
  - do not give rise to a financing agreement; and
  - are classified as payable or receivable within one year

  are initially measured at an undiscounted amount and hence (3) above will not apply.

Effective interest method

12.31 The effective interest method is a method of calculating the amortised cost of a financial asset or financial liability (ie the carrying value of the instrument in the balance sheet (statement of financial position)) and then allocating the interest income/expense over the relevant period on an actuarial basis using the effective interest rate.

The *amortised cost* of a financial asset or financial liability is the present value of future cash receipts/payments which are then discounted at the *effective interest rate*.

The effective interest rate is the rate which exactly discounts estimated future cash payments or receipts through the expected life of the financial instrument (or, where appropriate, a shorter period) to the carrying value of the financial asset or financial liability.

Example 12.9 – Application of the effective interest method

A company borrows £200,000 for a five-year period and the loan attracts fixed interest payments amounting to £11,800 per annum over the life of the loan. The terms of the loan state that it is to be repaid at a premium of £25,000 (ie the total to be repaid is £225,000).

Total finance costs amount to £84,000 which are made up as follows:

	£
Interest payments (5 × £11,800)	59,000
Debt premium	25,000
	84,000

Using the internal rate of return in *Excel*, we can calculate the effective interest rate to be 8.029%. This is the rate which exactly discounts the future cash payments through the expected life of the loan to the carrying amount of the financial liability. In an *Excel* spreadsheet this is worked out as follows:

Cell number	**Value**
A1	(£200,000)
A2	£11,800
A3	£11,800
A4	£11,800
A5	£11,800
A6	£236,800 (made up of £11,800 interest + £25,000 premium + £200,000 capital)

The formula to use will be =IRR(A1:A6) and this will calculate the effective interest rate to be 8.029%. Please note the internal rate of return function will not work if there is not at least one negative number.

The finance charges on the loan can be allocated as follows:

Year	**Opening balance**	**Interest (8.029%)**	**Cash flow**	**Closing balance**
	£	£	£	£
1	200,000	16,058	(11,800)	204,258
2	204,258	16,400	(11,800)	208,858
3	208,858	16,769	(11,800)	213,827
4	213,827	17,168	(11,800)	219,195
5	219,195	17,605*	(11,800)	225,000
		84,000		

*adjusted for rounding throughout the period of the loan.

12.32 Some finance houses may charge fees for arranging loans or transactions costs and other premiums or discounts. These are to be amortised over the expected life of the financial instrument. However, care must be taken for instruments where fees, finance charges/income, transactions costs, premiums or discounts are repriced to market rates prior to the maturity of the financial instrument. This is usually the case for loans where a fixed rate is given for a specified period of time which is then increased to market rates after that specific period of time has elapsed. In these instances, the appropriate amortisation period will be the period to the next repricing date.

Where loans attract variable interest rates, regular re-estimation of the cash flows to take account of the change in interest rates will alter the effective interest rate. Therefore, if the entity recognises a variable rate financial instrument at an amount equivalent to the capital element receivable or payable when the instrument matures, re-estimating the future interest payments would not normally have a significant effect on the carrying amount of the asset or liability.

Example 12.10 – Payment profile is revised

During the year to 30 April 2017, Irene's Interiors Ltd renegotiated its interest payments to one of its loan note holders who provided a working capital loan.

Where revisions to an entity's payments or receipts takes place in respect of financial instruments, the entity must make an adjustment to the carrying value of the financial asset or financial liability to reflect actual and revised cash flows attached to the instrument.

Irene's Interiors Ltd must recalculate the carrying value by calculating the present value of the estimated future cash flows using the instrument's original effective interest rate. The adjustment will then be recognised as income or expense in profit or loss at the date the revision took place.

Impairment of financial instruments

12.33 As is the case for other types of assets, a financial asset cannot be carried in the balance sheet (statement of financial position) in excess of its recoverable amount. As a result, where the small entity has financial assets, management must assess whether there is objective evidence that such assets are impaired. Where there are indicators of impairment, the financial asset must be written down to recoverable amount via an impairment loss which is recognised in profit or loss immediately.

There are various indicators that a financial asset has become impaired, some of which are outlined as follows:

- the borrower has got significant cash flow difficulties;

- the borrower has breached the terms of the loan agreement by defaulting on payments;
- revised conditions have been agreed between the borrower and the lender which would not normally be agreed to otherwise;
- the borrower is likely to enter into bankruptcy or other financial arrangements with creditors; and
- a change in industry conditions means that cash flows associated with a group of financial assets are likely to be lower than originally anticipated.

When assessing financial assets for impairment, management must:

- undertake an assessment of all equity instruments regardless of how significant they are; and
- assess other financial assets which are deemed to be individually significant for impairment.

Example 12.11 – Impaired financial asset

Cory Construction Ltd agrees to provide a loan to Breary Bricks Ltd amounting to £20,000. The term of the loan is five years and will be redeemed on maturity at a premium of £25,000. The coupon rate of the loan is 3% and £750 worth of interest is payable at the end of each year. The effective interest rate on this loan has been calculated at 8%. The loan profile is as follows:

Year	Opening balance	Interest (8%)	Cash flow	Closing balance
	£	£	£	£
1	20,000	1,600	(750)	20,850
2	20,850	1,668	(750)	21,768
3	21,768	1,741	(750)	22,759
4	22,759	1,821	(750)	23,830
5	23,830	1,920*	(25,750)	–

*adjusted for rounding throughout the period of the loan.

At the end of year 2 the amortised cost of the debt instrument is £21,768. One of Breary Ltd's customers has gone into liquidation and the company has suffered a significant bad debt. As a result, Cory Construction Ltd agrees to waive the remaining amount of interest but the capital element of the loan will be repaid.

The present value of the principal repayment in three years' time is £19,846 (£25,000/1.08^3). As a result, Cory Construction Ltd will recognise an impairment loss in profit or loss amounting to £1,922 (£21,768 less £19,846).

12.34 When an instrument is carried at amortised cost, any impairment loss is calculated as the difference between the carrying value in the financial statements and the present value of the estimated cash flows which are discounted using the instrument's original effective interest rate.

Focus

- Where a financial instrument has a variable interest rate, the discount rate for measuring an impairment loss is the current effective interest rate which has been established under the contract.

12.35 Where an instrument is measured at cost less impairment, any impairment loss is calculated as the difference between the carrying value of the instrument and a best estimate of the amount which the entity would receive for the financial asset if it were to be sold at the reporting date (this amount could be zero).

Reversal of an impairment loss

12.36 In practice circumstances change and it may be the case that the conditions which gave rise to an impairment loss being recognised on a financial asset may no longer apply.

Example 12.12 – Improvement in a customer's credit-rating

During the year to 30 June 2017 a major customer of McSharry Ltd announced that it was encountering serious cash flow difficulties due to the loss of one of its customers. A provision was made against this debt to write it down to recoverable amount as the customer's credit-rating had also significantly deteriorated. Payments were, however, continuing to be made in equal instalments against the debt.

During the year to 30 June 2018, the customer had announced that it had overcome the cash flow difficulties and had secured several lucrative contracts and that the debts owed to its suppliers would be paid in full over the next two months' and the credit-rating duly improved.

In this example, the conditions which gave rise to the initial impairment loss have now ceased to apply and McSharry can reverse the previously recognised impairment loss.

Where reversals of impairment losses take place, it is important to emphasise that the amount of the reversal cannot be such that the carrying amount of the financial asset (net of any allowance account) exceeds the value at which the financial asset would have been carried had no impairment loss been recognised.

Investments whose fair value can be measured reliably

12.37 While many financial assets and financial liabilities will be carried in a small company's financial statements at amortised cost, the fact that the business is small does not preclude it from carrying financial instruments at fair value through profit or loss where the investment's fair value can be measured reliably (eg by reference to the stock exchange).

Where, for example, non-convertible preference shares and non-puttable ordinary shares or preference shares are publicly traded, or if their fair value can be measured reliably, then paragraph 11.14(d)(i) would require these to be carried at fair value through profit or loss.

Example 12.13 – Fair value of shares available

Slevin Ltd invested in some shares several years ago for £50,000 (the investment did not give rise to the creation of a subsidiary, associate or joint venture). Slevin previously reported under the FRSSE (effective January 2015) and carried the shares at cost in its financial statements. The notes to the financial statements confirmed the following fair values:

31 December 2014	£120,000
31 December 2015	£135,000

The company does not qualify to prepare financial statements under FRS 105 *The Financial Reporting Standard applicable to the Micro-entities Regime* and hence is reporting under FRS 102. As the fair value of the shares can be measured reliably, then they should be carried in the financial statements at fair value to comply with paragraph 11.14(d)(i) of FRS 102.

On transition to FRS 102, Slevin will include the following journals:

<u>31 December 2014 (date of transition)</u>

DR investment	£70,000
CR profit and loss reserves*	(£70,000)

Being increase in fair value of shares at 31 December 2014

<u>31 December 2015 (comparative year)</u>

DR asset	£15,000
CR profit and loss*	£15,000

Increase in fair value of shares at 31 December 2015

*the increase in the fair value of the shares will not be distributable as a dividend.

In addition, as the shares are non-monetary assets which are carried at fair value (ie at revaluation), there will be associated deferred tax implications. Assuming Slevin pays corporation tax at 20%, the journals will be:

<u>31 December 2014 (date of transition)</u>

DR profit and loss reserves	£14,000 (£70,000 × 20%)
CR deferred tax provision	(£14,000)

Being deferred tax on fair value gain at date of transition

<u>31 December 2015 (comparative year)</u>

DR tax expense	£3,000
CR deferred tax provision	(£3,000)

Being deferred tax on fair value gain in comparative year

12.38 Comprehensive guidance is given in Section 11 at paragraphs 11.27–11.32 of FRS 102 on how to obtain fair values which is known as the 'fair value hierarchy' which should be followed in order as follows:

<u>Level 1</u>

The best evidence of fair value is a quoted price obtained from an active market. This means that prices are available for similar transactions because they are frequently traded in that market and the quoted price is usually the current bid price.

<u>Level 2</u>

Where quoted prices are unavailable, fair value can be obtained from the price of a recent transaction for a similar asset, provided there has been no significant changes in economic circumstances, or a significant amount of time has elapsed since the last transaction. Where it can be substantiated that the price obtained in such situations is not a fair price (for example where the price has been reduced for liquidation purposes or a distressed sale) then that price is adjusted to reflect fair value.

<u>Level 3</u>

Valuation techniques are the final port of call where a market for the asset is not active and recent transactions are not a good indicator of fair value. The overarching objective of a valuation technique is to estimate what the fair value would have been in an arm's-length transaction undertaken in a normal business environment.

> **Focus**
>
> - For small companies the most common transaction that will be carried out at fair value is likely to be an investment in shares where the shares are publicly traded. Detailed guidance on determining fair values is set out in paragraphs 11.27–11.32 of FRS 102.

Loans among related parties

12.39 The issue concerning loans with related parties (for example intra-group loans) has become more complex under the provisions in FRS 102. This is because Section 11 uses the amortised cost method to account for such loans and difficulties present themselves when related parties enter into loans which are below market rates of interest. The difficulties are in the form of 'measurement differences' which arise that reflect the fact that the lender has made a loan to the borrower at a rate of interest which is below market rate and hence has provided an additional benefit to the borrower and this additional benefit has to be reflected in the financial statements. The most common type of loan at below market rate is an intra-group loan.

Intra-group loans

12.40 Many groups enter into intra-group loans for a variety of reasons; some usually because of convenience (ie the group member may require finance at a relatively short notice period and the parent, or another group member, may provide that finance quicker than, say, a bank). In addition, the borrower may be unable to secure finance from its bank (or other finance houses) because of a poor credit-rating or a lack of assets available to pledge as security. A borrower may also have existing borrowings and the bank may want to charge a higher rate of interest to the borrower to reflect the increased risk which the group may not be willing to accept and hence another group member may provide the loan.

Whatever the reasons for group members entering into intra-group loans, the accounting for such loans will need to be made correctly in the individual financial statements of both the lender and the borrower. Where a small group prepares consolidated financial statements, the intra-group loan and interest charges/income will be eliminated on consolidation.

12.41 Under previous UK GAAP in the FRSSE (effective January 2015), the issue of intra-group loans was fairly straightforward. The borrower would recognise a creditor at the amount payable and the lender would recognise a corresponding debtor. The only complex issue concerning this arrangement would have been that the lender would consider the amount recognised as a debtor at each reporting date for any evidence of impairment and where evidence of such impairment existed, the lender would write-down the debtor to recoverable amount (in much the same way as the impairment loss example worked in Example **12.11** above).

12.42 It is important to emphasise that there will not normally be an issue with short-term intra-group trade debtors and short-term intra-group trade creditors because these are normally recognised in the individual financial statements at their undiscounted invoice amount. However, where payment is deferred beyond normal trading terms this will constitute a financing arrangement and paragraph 11.13 of FRS 102 would require such arrangements to be recognised at the present value of the future payments which are discounted to a market rate.

12.43 For long-term intra-group loans there are two issues to consider:

- Is there a rate of interest being charged on the loan?
- If there is, is the rate of interest a market rate?

Problems begin to emerge where loans are charged at zero rates of interest or interest rates which are below market rate because measurement differences arise. To avoid measurement differences the lending group company should be advised to charge a market rate of interest. Alternatively, they can also be advised to include provisions in the loan terms which enable the lender to demand repayment at a very short notice period. Including repayment terms at very short notice periods could (potentially) get around the issue of measurement differences because the loan which is repayable on demand will then be recorded in the borrower's books at not less than the amount repayable so as to recognise the demand feature of the loan.

Focus

- Including repayment demand features on a loan may not necessarily get around **all** measurement differences (particularly for the lender) because even where the loan is repayable on demand, immediate repayment may not be possible as the funds could be tied up in projects and hence take time to release.

Example 12.14 – Intra-group loan at market rate

A parent company agrees to a five-year working capital loan for its wholly-owned subsidiary. The terms of the loan say that a market rate of interest is to be charged on the intra-group loan.

Where a market rate of interest is charged by the lending company, there will not be any complex accounting issues to consider because the transaction price (ie the loan proceeds) will reflect fair value. The parent would, however, need to test the intra-group debtor annually at each reporting date for any indicators of impairment.

12.44 Obtaining a market rate of interest for a company will depend on various factors such as:

- the duration of the loan;
- the type of security pledged (if any);
- the company's gearing levels;
- the company's credit-rating; and
- the basis of interest.

A market rate of interest for a company may well be the rate of interest which the company's bank would charge on an equivalent loan and for small companies this is probably the best indicator of a market rate of interest.

Focus

- Where the borrowing entity is already highly geared and has relatively few (or no assets) available which it could pledge as security, market rates of interest will be higher to reflect the increased risk faced by the lender. Conversely, a company which has lower levels of gearing and assets available which can be pledged as security would attract a lower rate of interest as the risk to the lender is reduced.

Loan from parent to subsidiary at below market rate

12.45 It is not uncommon for a parent company to provide finance to a subsidiary and in many cases these loans will be at below market rates of interest or even at zero percent. Because of the way that the amortised cost method works, measurement differences will arise which can be illustrated as follows:

Example 12.15 – Measurement difference arising

A parent company agrees to provide a loan to its subsidiary for £20,000 on 1 January 2015. The loan is repayable on 31 December 2016. Market rates of interest are at 5%, but the parent agrees to charge an interest rate of 2% on the loan.

Under FRS 102 principles, the first step is to discount the cash flows to present day values as follows:

Year	Cash flow	Discount factor (5%)	Present value
	£		£
2015	400*	0.952	381
2016	20,400	0.907	18,503
			18,884

*The £400 is calculated as the interest rate charged by the parent on the loan of £20,000 (ie £20,000 × 2% = £400). In 2016 another year's worth of interest will be charged plus the redemption amount of £20,000. A measurement difference has arisen on the fair value of the loan proceeds (£20,000) and the present value of the future cash flows (£18,884).

The measurement difference in this scenario amounts to £1,116 (£20,000 less £18,884). The question arises as to how to account for this measurement difference in the individual financial statements of both the parent and the subsidiary. The key to this issue is to look at the substance of the transaction.

In the parent's books, the measurement difference is taken to the cost of the investment in the subsidiary (as a debit). This reflects the fact that the parent has contributed to the subsidiary by giving it a loan at a rate of interest which is below market rate and hence the journals will be:

	£
Debit intra-group debtor	18,884
Debit investment in subsidiary	1,116
Credit cash at bank	(20,000)

Being initial recognition of intra-group loan to subsidiary

In the subsidiary's books, the measurement difference is credited to equity as a capital contribution to reflect the fact that the parent has contributed to the subsidiary by providing a loan at below market rates interest, hence the journals are:

	£
Debit cash at bank	20,000
Credit intra-group creditor	(18,884)
Credit capital contribution (equity)	(1,116)

Being initial recognition of intra-group loan from parent

Once initial recognition of the loan and measurement difference has taken place, the next step will be to allocate the interest income/charge to the profit and loss account (income statement). The interest charge in profit or loss reflects the **market** rate of interest charged on the loan rather than the actual interest payments made/received.

Example 12.16 – Allocation of the interest

Continuing with the example above, the present value of the loan is £18,884 after initial recognition and market rates of interest are at 5%. The loan can be profiled as follows:

Year	Opening balance	Interest (5%)	Cash flow	Closing balance
	£	£	£	£
2015	18,884	944	(400)	19,428
2016	19,428	972	(20,400)	–

Journals in the books of the parent

<u>2015</u>	£
Debit cash at bank	400
Debit intra-group loan	544
Credit interest income	(944)

Being interest income on loan to subsidiary in 2015

<u>2016</u>	
Debit cash at bank	400
Debit intra-group loan	572
Credit interest income	(972)

Being interest income on loan to subsidiary in 2016

Debit cash at bank	20,000
Credit intra-group loan	(20,000)

Being redemption of loan

Journals in the books of the subsidiary

<u>2015</u>	£
Debit interest expense	944
Credit cash at bank	(400)
Credit intra-group loan	(544)

Being interest charge on loan from parent in 2015

<u>2016</u>	
Debit interest expense	972
Credit cash at bank	(400)
Credit intra-group loan	(572)

Being interest charge on loan from parent in 2016

Debit intra-group loan	20,000
Credit cash at bank	(20,000)

Being redemption of loan

As can be seen from the above worked example, measurement differences can cause additional complexities and these should be factored into any impact assessment during a transition so that small groups can be advised appropriately.

Focus

- With regard to any subsequent adjustment to the cost of the investment in the parent and corresponding capital contribution in the subsidiary arising from the measurement difference, FRS 102 is silent on this treatment. The group could choose to write off the additional cost of the investment so as to match the unwinding of the discount passing through profit or loss and then adjust the capital contribution in the subsidiary via a movement on reserves. Alternatively, the group may choose to leave the measurement difference within the cost of the investment and corresponding capital contribution and deal with any adjustment (ie write-down) as part of an impairment review.

Loan from subsidiary to parent

12.46 It is not always the case that a parent company will lend funds to a subsidiary and indeed the reverse scenario is not uncommon (ie where the subsidiary lends funds to the parent). Where a subsidiary makes an intra-group loan to its parent which is below market rate the measurement difference is treated as a distribution to the parent.

Example 12.17 – Loan from subsidiary to parent

A subsidiary lends £20,000 to its parent on 1 January 2015 and charges an interest rate of 2% on the loan. Market rates are set at 5%. The present value of the loan at initial recognition is £18,884 and a measurement difference has arisen amounting to £1,116 (£20,000 fair value less £18,884 present value).

The journals to record this loan are as follows:

In the books of the subsidiary

	£
DR intra-group loan	18,884
DR distribution (equity)	1,116
CR cash at bank	(20,000)

Being initial recognition of loan to parent

In the books of the parent

	£
DR cash at bank	20,000
CR intra-group loan	(18,884)
CR income from subsidiary	(1,116)

Being loan from subsidiary

This accounting treatment recognises that the subsidiary has contributed to the parent by way of providing a loan at below market rates of interest and hence the measurement difference is treated as a distribution to the parent. Interest charges/income will be calculated in the same way as the example in paragraph **12.42** where the parent makes a loan to the subsidiary.

Focus

- Care must be taken where a measurement difference is treated as a distribution to the parent by the subsidiary where the subsidiary has little (or no) distributable reserves because the distribution above is not necessarily a distribution for legal purposes. The way that the accounting treatment works in Section 11 for intra-group loans at below market rates means that more attention will be drawn to the transaction and hence in some situations it may be advisable to seek legal advice.

Loans between subsidiaries

12.47 Loans can take place among subsidiaries and where these do arise, it is generally the case that the parent has authorised the loan to take place. The substance of this arrangement, therefore, is that the subsidiaries have entered into the loan through the parent (because of the parent's authority) and hence the lending subsidiary records the loan as if it was made to the parent and the borrowing subsidiary records the loan as if it had been received from the parent. This is regardless of the fact that the transaction will not affect the parent's own financial statements.

Example 12.18 – Loans between subsidiaries

Subsidiary A lends £20,000 to Subsidiary B on 1 January 2015. The loan is repayable on 31 December 2016 and the parent has instructed Subsidiary A to charge Subsidiary B a rate of interest of 2%. Market rates are at 5%. The present value of the loan is £18,884 and a measurement difference has arisen amounting to £1,116 (£20,000 fair value less £18,884 present value).

The journals to record this loan are as follows:

Subsidiary A	£
DR intra-group loan	18,884
DR distribution (equity)	1,116
CR cash at bank	(20,000)

Being initial recognition of loan to Subsidiary B

Subsidiary B	£
DR cash at bank	20,000
CR intra-group loan	(18,884)
CR capital contribution (equity)	(1,116)

Being initial recognition of loan from Subsidiary A

Interest income and expense will be recognised in the same way as in Example **12.16** above.

Loans between companies under common control

12.48 An individual may own several companies and those companies may not be members of the same group but are related parties because they are owned and controlled by the same person. Companies in this situation may enter into loans with each other at below market rates and where this does arise measurement differences will still arise and need accounting for.

Example 12.19 – Loan made by a company under common control

Cecilia owns several companies but there is no formal group structure in place. On 1 January 2015 Company A lends £20,000 to Company B (both companies are owned by Cecilia). Company A is charging a 2% interest rate on the loan and market rates are at 5%. The present value of the loan is £18,884 and a measurement difference has arisen of £1,116 (£20,000 fair value less £18,884 present value).

In this example there is no group structure so the loan has not been made among subsidiaries; however the accounting treatment of the loan would be similar to that of a loan among subsidiaries. The measurement difference in Company A (the lender) would be recorded as a distribution within equity to Cecilia and Company B (the borrower) would record the measurement difference as a capital contribution in equity from Cecilia.

Directors' loans

12.49 It is extremely common for small companies to have directors' current accounts (often referred to as 'directors' loan accounts') in operation. Loans to, or from, a director have to be looked at carefully and assessed as to whether the loan has been made to, or received from, the director in his/her capacity as a director or as an employee of the company.

Example 12.20 – Director introduces funds

Cecilia owns the entire share capital of Westhead Ltd. On 1 January 2015 Cecilia introduces funds into the business amounting to £20,000. The present value of the loan discounted at a market rate of 5% is £18,884 resulting in a measurement difference of £1,116 (£20,000 fair value less £18,884 present value).

The measurement difference represents the additional investment by Cecilia which the entity records as a capital contribution. The journals for the loan are as follows:

	£
DR cash at bank	20,000
CR director's current account	(18,884)
CR capital contribution (equity)	(1,116)

Being introduction of funds by the director

12.50 It is also commonplace for directors' of small companies to withdraw funds as loans from the company. There are additional legal considerations where this takes place (such as shareholder approval for loans over £10,000).

Example 12.21 – Loan provided to a director

Cecilia owns 100% of Westhead Ltd. On 1 January 2015 the company lends Cecilia £20,000 and the present value of this loan discounted at a market rate of 5% is £18,884 resulting in a measurement difference of £1,116 (£20,000 fair value less £18,884 present value).

The measurement difference represents a distribution from Westhead Ltd to Cecilia Ltd and hence the journals to record this loan are as follows:

	£
DR director's current account	18,884
DR distribution to owner (equity)	1,116
CR cash at bank	(20,000)

Being loan made to the director

Focus

- The above two examples focussed on a scenario where the director had ownership interest in the company. This is not always the case and a director may not necessarily own any of the business. The reality is that it is unlikely that a director with no ownership interest in an entity will provide an interest-free loan to the company because they will not derive any benefit from doing this. However, the company may provide an interest-free loan to a director who is not a shareholder and in both cases the entity would account for the transaction in the same way that it would do if the transaction had taken place with another unrelated party.

Loans from or to a director where a small entity is concerned can often have no loan terms attached to them and in such cases they are regarded as being on-demand loans. As such they will always be regarded as current and usually stated at the amount of the loan so as to recognise the on-demand feature.

Derecognising a financial asset

12.51 Financial assets can be quite complex when it comes to derecognising them from the balance sheet (statement of financial position) and careful analysis might need to be undertaken to ensure that the conditions for derecognition have, in fact, been met.

There are three situations which allow a small company to derecognise a financial asset:

- the contractual cash flows attached to the financial asset are settled (or have expired);
- the company transfers all of the risks and rewards of the ownership of the financial asset to a third party; or
- where the entity has retained some of the significant risks and rewards of the asset, but has transferred control of the financial asset to a third party, that third party then has the power to sell the financial asset in its entirety to an unrelated third party and this decision can be made unilaterally on the part of the third party; in such cases the entity:
  - derecognises the financial asset; and
  - recognises separately any rights and obligations which have been retained or created as a result of the transfer.

12.52 For many small companies it is usually fairly clear cut when a financial asset can be derecognised, for example where the small company has a trade debtor and that trade debtor settles its invoices, this will mean that the contractual cash flows have been settled and hence derecognition can take place.

However, some transactions or arrangements may not be as clear cut and a typical example will involve debt factoring.

Example 12.22 – Sales ledger sold to a factoring organisation with recourse

Cahill Ltd (Cahill) has agreed to sell a group of trade debtors to an invoice factoring company at less than fair value so as to release cash tied up within its debtors as it is going through a rapid expansion programme. The sale of the trade debtors completes and the terms of the arrangement are that Cahill will still continue to collect monies from the debtors on the invoice factoring company's behalf, send out monthly statements of account and generally administer the sales ledger for which the invoice factoring company pays a market rate for administration services. The agreement stipulates that Cahill must buy back any trade debtors which fall overdue for payment for more than 120 days.

In this scenario Cahill has retained the risk of slow (or non) payment for its debtors which is considered to be a significant risk where debtors are concerned. In accordance with paragraph 11.34 of FRS 102, Cahill should continue to recognise the full amount of the trade debtors in its balance sheet (statement of financial position). The consideration received from the invoice factoring company should be recognised as a financial liability (linked presentation is not considered in FRS 102 and hence the asset (the full amount of trade receivables) is shown gross and the proceeds are shown as a liability secured by the debtors).

Example 12.23 – Sales ledger sold to a factoring organisation with no recourse

The facts are similar to the above, except that Cahill does not have to buy back any debts which fall due for more than 120 days from the invoice factoring company.

In this scenario, Cahill has transferred the significant risks and rewards of the debtors to the invoice factoring company. As a result, it removes all of the trade debtors from its balance sheet (statement of financial position) and also shows no liability in respect of the funds received from the invoice factoring company on completion of the sale of the sales ledger. Because the sales ledger has been bought by the invoice factoring company at below fair value, a loss is recognised in profit or loss calculated as the difference between the carrying value of the trade debtors at the time the sale completed and the proceeds received from the invoice factoring company. The only liability that is recognised at each reporting date is in respect of cash collected from trade debtors that has not yet been remitted to the invoice factoring company.

Derecognising a financial liability

12.53 Generally, a small company will derecognise a financial liability (or part of a financial liability) when the liability is *extinguished*. The term 'extinguished' is taken to mean discharged, cancelled or expires.

Example 12.24 – Company voluntary arrangement

Scanlon Ltd has suffered from serious cash flow difficulties over the last couple of years due in large part to a downturn in demand for its goods. The directors think they have found a way to turn the business around and have entered into a 'company voluntary arrangement' (CVA) with its creditors.

In an attempt to improve the balance sheet position, the financial controller has reduced the value of creditors in the balance sheet (statement of financial position) to reflect the actual amount that will be paid to the creditors in the CVA and the corresponding credit has been taken to the profit and loss account (income statement) as an exceptional item.

It is incorrect to reduce the value of the creditors in the balance sheet before the CVA has been completed. Despite the fact that the majority of the creditors must agree to the CVA, there is still an obligation to comply with the terms of the CVA and the liabilities can only be cancelled once the creditors have formally cancelled the obligation – which is likely to be on successful completion of the CVA. As a result, the financial controller must reinstate the value of the creditors and reverse the credit to profit and loss.

12.54 Where an existing borrower and lender agree to substantially modified loan terms on an existing debt, then both parties account for the change in terms as a cancellation of the original debt and will then recognise the new debt reflecting the new terms agreed.

Where a borrower and lender exchange financial instruments which have substantially different terms, both entities account for the transaction by extinguishing the old financial liability and then recognise a new financial liability.

A profit or loss will be recognised between any financial liability extinguished or transferred and the amount paid which will also include any non-cash assets transferred or liabilities assumed.

Focus

- Offsetting financial liabilities against financial liabilities can only take place if, and only if, the entity:
  - has a legally enforceable right to set-off the recognised amounts; and
  - the entity intends to either settle on a net basis, or to realise the financial asset and settle the financial liability at the same time.

OTHER FINANCIAL INSTRUMENTS ISSUES

12.55 Section 12 *Other Financial Instruments Issues* deals with the more complex types of financial instruments. In reality the majority of small companies (and small groups) will account for financial instruments under Section 11 provisions (see above); but Section 12 instruments may also be applicable to the small company.

The scope of Section 12 applies to all financial instruments which are not considered basic, including:

- derivative instruments;
- loans with complex features;
- financial instruments which qualify and are designated as hedging instruments; and
- commitments to make a loan to another entity and commitments to receive a loan from another entity if the commitment can be settled net in cash.

The following types of transactions are beyond the scope of Section 12:

Type of transaction	**Relevant area of FRS 102**
Basic financial instruments	Section 11 *Basic Financial Instruments*
Investments in subsidiaries	Section 9 *Consolidated and Separate Financial Statements*
Investments in associates	Section 14 *Investments in Associates*
Joint ventures	Section 15 *Investments in Joint Ventures*
Employers' rights and obligations in an employee benefit plan	Section 28 *Employee Benefits*
Insurance contracts (including reinsurance contracts)	FRS 103 *Insurance Contracts*
Financial instruments meeting the definition of an entity's own equity and the equity portion of a compound financial instrument	Section 22 *Liabilities and Equity*
Leasing transactions	Section 20 *Leases*
Contracts for contingent consideration in a business combination	Section 19 *Business Combinations and Goodwill*
Forward contracts between an acquirer and a selling shareholder to buy/sell an acquiree which would result in a business combination at a future acquisition date	–
Financial instruments, contracts and obligations in share-based payment arrangements	Section 26 *Share-based Payment*
Financial instruments with a discretionary participation feature	FRS 103 *Insurance Contracts*
Reimbursement assets accounted for in accordance with Section 21 *Provisions and Contingencies*	Section 21 *Provisions and Contingencies*
Financial guarantee contracts	Section 21 *Provisions and Contingencies*

Initial recognition of a Section 12 financial instrument

12.56 As with basic financial instruments, a small entity can only recognise a financial asset or financial liability under Section 12 when the entity becomes a party to the contractual provisions of the instrument.

Once the entity becomes a party to the contractual provisions of the instrument, the financial instrument is recognised initially at fair value which includes all associated transaction costs.

Focus

- Transaction costs are not included in the initial recognition of financial instruments which are measured at fair value through profit or loss (for example the purchase of shares in a listed company). Instead such costs are expensed immediately. This is because fair values will be available for such shares (eg a quoted price on the stock market).

Subsequent measurement

12.57 After initial recognition at fair value, all financial instruments accounted for under the provisions in Section 12 are measured at fair value with changes in fair value going through profit or loss. There are three exceptions to this rule:

- where investments in equity instruments are not traded on a recognised stock market and hence fair values cannot otherwise be ascertained reliably (this also applies to contracts linked to such instruments) and such instruments will then be measured at cost less impairment;
- hedging instruments which are in a designated hedging relationship and accounted for in accordance with the hedge accounting rules in paragraph 12.23; and
- financial instruments which cannot be measured at fair value through profit or loss because Regulations (including the LLP Regulations) prohibit measurement at fair value and hence these shall be measured at amortised cost.

Paragraphs 11.27–11.32 of FRS 102 give comprehensive guidance on fair value measurements in accordance with Section 12 (as well as applying to fair value measurements for Section 11 also).

Focus

- Where an equity instrument is initially recognised and subsequently measured at fair value through profit or loss, but a reliable measure of fair value is no longer available, then the fair value at the last date the equity instrument was reliably measurable becomes the instrument's cost. The entity must then measure the instrument at this cost, less applicable impairment, until a reliable measure of fair value becomes available again.

Impairment of Section 12 financial instruments

12.58 Where financial instruments have been measured at cost less impairment, the directors must assess the financial instrument for any indicators that the instrument is impaired. Where evidence confirms that the financial instrument's carrying value is less than recoverable amount, the asset must be written down to recoverable amount immediately through an impairment loss which is taken to profit or loss (**12.33–12.36** above outline the impairment requirements associated with financial instruments). For Section 12 financial instruments, the impairment requirements only relate to financial instruments measured at cost less impairment.

Derecognising a Section 12 financial instrument

12.59 The principles addressed in **12.51–12.54** above apply to a small company derecognising a financial asset or a financial liability. In substance, for a financial asset, the risks and rewards of the contractual cash flows attached to the instrument must have been substantially transferred to a third party, discharged, cancelled or expired before a financial asset can be derecognised.

Similarly, where a financial liability is concerned, such a liability can only be derecognised when the company's obligations under the contract have been discharged, cancelled or expired.

Hedge accounting

12.60 Comprehensive guidance is included in Section 12 at paragraphs 12.15–12.25A which relate to hedge accounting.

A small company may choose to hedge its exposure to risk by either adopting the hedge accounting provisions in Section 12 or not. In some situations the company may not be allowed to adopt the hedge accounting provisions if it is unable to meet the criteria in paragraph 12.18.

Focus

- Hedge accounting is optional but in reality many small companies/ small groups choose not to apply hedge accounting because of its complexity and hence this section of the chapter will look at the main aspects of hedge accounting, but readers are encouraged to gain an understanding of the hedge accounting requirements in Section 12 where hedge accounting becomes relevant because it is a very complex topic.

12.61 In the broadest terms, hedge accounting recognises the offsetting effects within profit or loss of both changes in fair values of the hedging instrument and the hedged item. The idea behind this is that the profit and loss account recognises the effects of both the hedged item and the hedging instrument in the same accounting period (so as to reduce volatility). It follows, therefore, that if hedge accounting is not applied then gains and losses on assets and liabilities which are managed together may be recognised in profit or loss in different accounting periods.

Example 12.25 – Interest-rate swap

Williams Ltd (Williams) entered into a fixed-rate loan with its bank several years ago and this loan still has seven years until maturity. This loan falls to be classed as basic and hence has been accounted for under FRS 102 at amortised cost.

Interest rates are likely to fall shortly and so Williams enters into a fixed-to-floating interest rate swap so as to manage the interest rate risk.

Under Section 12, the interest rate swap will be a derivative instrument (see the section 'Derivative financial instruments' at **12.64**) and is measured at fair value through profit or loss.

Where hedge accounting is not applied, gains and losses on the interest rate swap would be recognised in profit or loss immediately. In contrast, gains and losses on the debt component of the loan are recognised on a different basis because the debt portion is measured at amortised cost and not fair value. Hence, if Williams chooses not to apply hedge accounting, gains and losses on the interest rate swap will be recognised in profit and loss at a different time than gains and losses on the debt.

Conditions for hedge accounting

12.62 There are five conditions which have to be met before hedge accounting can be applied:

(a) The hedging relationship consists only of a hedging instrument and a hedged item.

(b) The hedging relationship is consistent with the entity's risk management processes for undertaking hedges.

(c) An economic relationship exists between the hedged item and the hedging instrument.

(d) Documentation exists clearly identifying the hedging relationship and the hedging instrument.

(e) The entity has determined and documented the causes of hedge ineffectiveness.

Focus

- The condition in (c) above says that an economic relationship must exist between the hedged item and the hedging instrument. Such a relationship exists when the entity expects the value of the hedged item and the hedging instrument to move in opposite directions in response to movement in the same risk (which is the hedged risk).

Types of hedging relationships

12.63 There are three types of hedge:

Fair value hedge

A fair value hedge is where the risk being hedged relates to changes in the fair value of an instrument, such as the fair value risk on a fixed-rate loan which can be hedged with a fixed-for-floating interest rate swap (see Example **12.25** above).

Cash flow hedge

A cash flow hedge relates to uncertain cash flows. For example a company may have a loan with a variable rate and such risks can be hedged by using a floating-for-fixed interest rate swap.

Hedge of a net investment in a foreign operation

This is likely to be rare for small companies and hence is not covered in this publication. An example of a hedge of a net investment in a foreign operation would be where a company enters into a forward foreign exchange contract in order to hedge the risk of foreign currency exchange gains and losses on the net investment.

> **Focus**
>
> - In practice, smaller companies are more likely to enter into fair value hedges or cash flow hedges.

Example 12.26 – Hedge accounting

On 1 January 2016, Heaton Ltd received a ten-year variable-rate bank loan of £500,000. Interest is payable at a variable rate of 2% above the Bank of England base rate. To protect against interest rate increases, Heaton entered into an interest rate swap with the same bank in which it will pay 5% fixed rate and receive the same variable rate as the loan it has just taken out for a ten-year term. This has the effect that Heaton will effectively be paying a fixed rate of interest on the loan as opposed to variable rates.

For the year-ended 31 December 2016 interest rates remain at 0.5% and the settlement value of the interest rate swap is (£75,000).

Using hedge accounting the entries for this transaction for the year-ended 31 December 2016 are:

	£
DR cash at bank	500,000
CR loan payable	(500,000)

Being initial recognition of loan

DR interest payable	25,000
CR cash at bank	(25,000)

Being interest charges for the year-ended 31 December 2016 at 5%

DR fair value of interest rate swap	75,000
CR interest rate swap liability	(75,000)

Being fair value of the interest rate swap

The fair value of the interest rate swap is taken to other comprehensive income rather than charged to profit or loss because hedge accounting is being used. If Heaton had not used hedge accounting then the fair value loss would have been taken to profit or loss.

Derivative financial instruments

12.64 As can be seen from the above section relating to hedge accounting, Section 12 requires derivative instruments to be recognised on the balance sheet (statement of financial position) of a company which was not the case under the FRSSE (effective January 2015). Under the FRSSE (effective January 2015) derivative instruments were accounted for on settlement and this new requirement may cause an element of disruption among small businesses.

A derivative instrument derives its value from an underlying asset – for example a forward foreign currency contract will derive its value from changes in foreign exchange rates and this type of contract is probably one of the most common types of contract a small business will enter into (as well as an interest rate swap which derives its value from fluctuations in interest rates).

12.65 If a company enters into a forward foreign currency contract one month prior to the year-end to sell foreign currency one month after the year-end, then on the date the contract is entered into the derivative instrument will usually have a fair value of £nil. Over the next two months' foreign currency exchange rates are likely to change (either go up or go down) and it is this change which will generate a value for the contract which is then brought onto the balance sheet (statement of financial position) at the end of the reporting period.

Example 12.27 – Accounting for a forward foreign currency contract derivative

Colgan Ltd prepares financial statements to 31 March each year and is reporting under FRS 102. On 1 February 2017 Colgan sells goods to a customer based in the United States for $120,000. Payment is to be received in three months' time (ie on 30 April 2017).

Colgan enters into a forward foreign currency contract to sell $120,000 on 30 April 2017 at a contracted rate of £1:$1.65. Foreign exchange rates are as follows:

	Spot rate	**Forward rate to 30 April 2017**
Date	£1:$	£1:$
1 February 2017	1.63	1.65
31 March 2017	1.60	1.62
30 April 2017	1.58	–

Under the FRSSE (effective January 2015), Colgan would have accounted for this transaction at the contracted rate of 1.65 (although Colgan could have also chosen to account for the transaction using the spot rate).

Step 1 – Recognise the debtor at the year-end

Colgan would have accounted for this transaction using the rate in the contract (1.65) under the FRSSE (effective January 2015) and hence would have recognised a debtor of £72,727 (being $120,000 / 1.65).

Paragraph 30.7 of FRS 102 requires foreign currency transactions to be recorded at the spot rate at the date of the transaction and hence Colgan will translate the $120,000 at 1.63 and the journals will be:

DR trade debtors	£73,620
CR turnover	(£73,620)

Being translation of the sale at spot rate ($120,000 / 1.63)

The difference of £893 (£73,620 less £72,727) is equal to the difference arising on $120,000 translated at spot rate of 1.63 (£73,620) and $120,000 translated at contracted rate of 1.65 (£72,727).

Step 2 – Calculate the derivative instrument for the year-end 31 March 2017

As the contracted rate cannot be used under FRS 102 principles, a derivative financial instrument has to be recognised at fair value at Colgan's year end. This is calculated as follows:

	£
$120,000 @ contracted rate of 1.65	72,727
$120,000 @ year-end forward rate of 1.62	74,074
Loss on derivative	1,347

The loss on the derivative has arisen because of what has happened with the exchange rates. If Colgan were to sell at the year-end forward rate of 1.62, they would receive £74,074; however as they are selling at a contract rate of 1.65, they will only receive £72,727 and hence a loss has been generated on the contract at the year-end which has to be recognised in the financial statements to comply with Section 12 of FRS 102. The entries in the books of Colgan are:

	£
DR loss on derivative – profit and loss account	1,347
CR derivative liability – balance sheet	(1,347)

Being loss on derivative at fair value

Under previous UK GAAP no entries would have been needed as Colgan would have accounted for the transaction at the contracted rate which could have been used to measure the monetary asset.

Step 3 – Work out the foreign exchange gain/loss at the year-end 31 March 2017

Colgan will have to work out the foreign exchange gain or loss for the year-end as follows:

	£
$120,000 at year-end spot rate (1.60)	75,000
Less original debtor recognised	(73,620)
Foreign exchange gain at year-end	1,380

This gain is taken to profit or loss. Under previous UK GAAP, as Colgan would have used the contracted rate, there would be no gain to take to profit or loss. However, if the spot rate were to be used then a gain would arise.

Step 4 – Settlement on 30 April 2017

Once Colgan's customer has settled the invoice, the derivative needs to be dealt with and then the invoice should be cleared from the debtors' ledger.

To deal with the derivative, work out the fair value at the date of settlement as follows:

	£
$120,000 at settlement date spot rate 1.58	75,949
$120,000 at year-end forward rate 1.62	(74,074)
Loss on derivative at settlement date	1,875

The entries in the books of Colgan will be:

DR loss on derivative – profit and loss	1,875
CR derivative liability – balance sheet	(1,875)

Being loss on derivative at fair value

The next step is to clear the derivative and the invoice from the debtors' ledger. Colgan's customer will pay them £72,727 which is $120,000 at the contracted forward rate of 1.65. The derivative instrument is recognised as a liability of £3,222 (£1,347 + £1,875) and hence the journals are:

	£
DR bank	72,727
DR derivative liability	3,222
CR trade debtors control	(75,949)

Being removal of derivative instrument and debtor on settlement

The derivative instrument at the date of settlement (30 April 2017) can be reconciled as follows:

	£
$120,000 at settlement date spot rate of 1.58	75,949
$120,000 at contract rate of 1.65	(72,727)
Loss on foreign exchange contract	3,222

The £3,222 loss reflects the loss that Colgan has made by taking out the forward foreign currency contract – ie Colgan would have received £3,222 more had they undertook the transaction using spot rates.

A balance of £949 is left on the customer's sales ledger account and this is made up of £75,000 year-end debtor (step 3) less £75,949 ($120,000/spot rate at settlement of 1.58 (see step 4)). This represents the foreign exchange gain.

Disclosures relating to financial instruments

12.66 For small companies, the disclosure requirements relating to financial instruments are contained in Section 1A *Small Entities* in Appendix C *Disclosure requirements for small entities*.

The disclosures that may be required in respect of financial instruments measured at fair value through profit or loss are referred to in the following table which also cross-refers to other paragraphs in FRS 102 to aid small companies in ensuring the disclosure requirements are complete:

Disclosure requirement	Cross-reference other paragraphs in FRS 102
Significant assumptions underlying the valuation models and techniques which have been used where a quoted price in an active market is not available.	Paragraph 11.43
For each category of financial instrument, the fair value and changes in fair value included in profit or loss and changes which have been taken to equity.	Paragraphs 11.41(a), 11.41(d), 11.48(a)(i) and 11.48(a) (ii)
For each class of derivative instrument, the extent and nature of the instruments including significant terms and conditions which may affect the amount, timing and certainty of future cash flows.	–
A table setting out the movements in equity during the reporting period.	An example is provided in paragraph 6.3A and paragraphs 12.29(c) and (d) of FRS 102
If financial instruments have been measured at fair value and are within the scope of those listed in paragraph 11.48A, the disclosures set out in that paragraph should be made.	Paragraph 11.48A

Focus

- Other disclosures relating to financial instruments should be made within the financial statements where so doing enables the financial statements to give a true and fair view. Comprehensive disclosure requirements are contained in Section 11 in paragraphs 11.39 to 11.48C and these disclosure requirements also apply to financial instruments which are accounted for under Section 12 provisions.

STOCKS

12.67 Stock and work in progress (referred to as 'inventory' in FRS 102) is often a material figure in a small entity's financial statements and the valuation of stock can have a significant impact on a company's reported profit or loss and balance sheet position. In addition, valuations can also have a consequential impact on the entity's tax position so it is vital that the valuations of stock are as accurate as possible (particularly where a lot of estimation is needed).

Focus

- The way that stock/inventory is dealt with for management accounting purposes may be different to the way in which it must be included in the statutory financial statements.
- Section 13 of FRS 102 *Inventories* prescribes the accounting requirements for inventory as well as outlining the various methodologies which can be used to value stock at the reporting date.

Focus

- A notable difference between Section 13 and the FRSSE (effective January 2015) is the fact that under Section 13, the use of the last-in first-out (LIFO) method of stock valuation is specifically outlawed. The FRSSE (effective January 2015) did permit the use of LIFO but it did not favour its use because the use of LIFO would result in the reporting of current assets which bear little relationship to recent cost and hence it followed that where the directors of a small company used LIFO, they would have to be able to justify its use.

Scope

12.68 Section 13 prescribes the requirements for recognising and measuring inventories which are:

- held for sale in the ordinary course of business;
- in the process of production for such sale (ie work in progress); and
- in the form of materials or supplies which are to be consumed in the production process or in the rendering of services.

There are some types of inventories which are not specifically covered by Section 13 and these are shown in the following table:

Type of transaction	**Relevant section of FRS 102**
Work in progress in a construction contract	Section 23 *Revenue*
Financial instruments	Section 11 *Basic Financial Instruments* and Section 12 *Other Financial Instruments Issues*
Biological assets that are related to agricultural activity and agricultural produce	Section 34 *Specialised Activities*

12.69 Under the previous FRSSE (effective January 2015) the principle of 'lower of cost or net realisable value' was pivotal in measuring stock. This principle has been carried over into Section 13 but is instead referred to as the 'lower of cost and estimated selling price less costs to complete and sell' hence 'net realisable value' is referred to differently under FRS 102 but it amounts to the same thing.

Cost

12.70 The cost of stock is a broad definition and can include:

- the original purchase price of the stock;
- import duties (and other irrecoverable taxes);
- transport costs;
- handling costs; and
- other costs which are directly attributable to bringing the inventory to its present location and condition.

Example 12.28 – Components of cost

Alex Attires Ltd is a retailer of children's clothing with branches throughout the UK. It has a portfolio of approved suppliers who supply the company with its merchandise. The company is embarking on its ordering for the Autumn/Winter season and has placed an order with its major supplier who is located in China. The company will be charged air freight fees and transport fees from the airport to the company's head office. In addition import duties will be levied.

As Alex Attires purchases a large volume of goods through the year it is entitled to a 2% trade discount on any purchases over £10,000 and this particular order is for £20,000 worth of goods.

The cost of the goods will include:

- the overall purchase price;
- the cost of freight from China and transport costs from the airport to head office; and
- the import duties.

The discount which Alex Attires receives from its supplier will be deducted in arriving at the overall cost of purchase.

12.71 There may be occasions when a small business may purchase goods from a supplier and that supplier agrees to deferred settlement terms. Paragraph 13.7 of FRS 102 recognises that in some cases this type of arrangement effectively contains an unstated financing element which is the difference between the purchase price of the goods under normal commercial terms and the deferred settlement amount.

Where such transactions arise, the difference between the two amounts is taken to the be interest expense over the period of the financing but is NOT added to the cost of the stock unless the item of stock is a qualifying asset under the provisions in Section 25 *Borrowing Costs* (see **12.284** below) and the entity adopts a policy of capitalising borrowing costs.

Example 12.29 – Deferred settlement terms

Alicia is the purchasing director of Fraser's Furniture Store. The company has purchased some stock for resale to the general public which would have cost £75,000 under normal commercial terms. However, the supplier has agreed to defer payment for 18 months at which point the company will pay the supplier an amount of £80,000.

The difference between the purchase price under normal credit terms of £75,000 and the deferred settlement amount of £80,000 (£5,000) is the financing element and is recognised as interest expense over the 18 month deferred settlement period. It is not added to the cost of the stock which will be included at an amount of £75,000 plus any other incremental costs associated with the transaction (such as freight and handling costs).

Conversion costs

12.72 Companies may manufacture their own goods for resale or may manufacture them for resale for a retailer or other outlet. When valuing inventories, directors should take into account the costs which are directly related to the units of production (which would include direct labour). Manufacturing companies will often include a proportion of fixed and variable production overheads which are incurred in converting raw materials into finished goods.

Focus

- Fixed production overheads are those overheads which remain constant regardless of the levels of production, such as depreciation and factory maintenance. Variable overheads are indirect costs which vary with the volume of production (such as indirect materials and indirect labour).

Production overheads

12.73 Production overheads are allocated to the costs of conversion based on the normal capacity of the production facilities. The term 'normal capacity' is taken to mean the production which is expected to be achieved by the company on average over a number of periods or seasons under normal circumstances. This also takes into account any planned maintenance resulting in loss of production time (ie 'idle time').

> **Focus**
>
> - Paragraph 13.9 does allow the actual level of production to be used rather than expected levels of production where actual amounts approximate normal capacity.

Care must be taken where production is increased abnormally (for example due to a large, one-off order being received by the company). When abnormally high levels of production take place, the amount of fixed overhead which is allocated to each unit of production is reduced so that inventories are not measured above cost.

Example 12.30 – Allocation of production overheads

Zedcolour Trading Ltd manufactures outdoor garden furniture and has a year-end of 31 December 2016. Production is usually fairly static; however at the beginning of December 2016 a very large order arrived from a 'do-it-yourself' outlet which had suffered a fire at one of its premises and which had destroyed a large amount of goods. Orders like this do not occur on a regular basis and at the year-end the goods were still in production. The financial controller has increased the amount of fixed overhead allocated to each unit of production as a result of the order.

Paragraph 13.9 of FRS 102 says that where periods of abnormally high production take place, the amount of fixed overhead allocated to each unit of production should be *decreased* (the financial controller has increased the amount of fixed overhead). The finance director is incorrect to increase the amount of fixed overhead because this will result in a valuation of inventory which is in excess of cost. The principle in paragraph 13.4 should be strictly applied in the valuation of inventories and they must be valued at the lower of cost and estimated selling price less costs to complete and sell.

By-products

12.74 By-products are secondary products from a production process and are usually immaterial. When the costs of raw materials (or the conversion of each product) are not separately identifiable the business must allocate them between the products on a rational and consistent basis. Where by-products are judged as being immaterial, the entity must measure them at selling price less costs to complete and sell and this amount is then deducted from the cost of the main product. This will result in a carrying amount for the main product which is not materially different from cost.

Costs which are excluded from inventories

12.75 Generally an entity must include all costs incurred in bringing the inventories to their present location and condition in with the inventories valuation. However, Section 13 identifies certain types of costs which a company **must** exclude when valuing inventories and these relate to:

- abnormal amounts of waste materials, labour or other production costs;
- storage costs (the exception to this type of cost is where such costs are necessary during the production process – for example a whisky distillery);
- administrative overheads which are not incurred directly in bringing the inventories to their present location and condition; and
- selling costs.

When such costs are incurred, they are written off as expenditure.

Example 12.31 – Inventory relating to a service provider

A firm of accountants is valuing its work in progress at the year-end and has estimated that the labour and other costs of personnel directly engaged in providing the uncompleted services at the year-end amounts to £43,000. The senior partner has asked if this amount includes the costs relating to the marketing and administrative personnel.

Paragraph 13.14 of FRS 102 deals with the cost of inventories relating to service providers, such as firms of accountants. It specifically states that labour and other costs relating to sales and general administrative personnel are not included in the cost of inventories but are instead recognised as expenses in the periods in which the costs are incurred. In addition, the costs of inventories for a service provider will not include any profit margin or non-attributable overheads which may be included in the prices that are charged by a service provider.

Agricultural produce

12.76 Agricultural produce is harvested from a biological asset, which is a living animal or plant and these types of activities are dealt with in Section 34 *Specialised Activities* of FRS 102 (see **12.387** below). However, paragraph 13.15 says that on initial recognition, inventories which comprise of agricultural produce that have been harvested from biological assets should be measured at the point of harvest which is either:

- fair value less estimated costs to sell; or
- lower of cost and estimated selling price less costs to complete and sell.

Whichever method above is selected, this then becomes the cost of the inventories at that date for the purposes of Section 13.

Cost formulas

12.77 As mentioned earlier in this chapter, the FRSSE (effective January 2015) did not specifically prohibit the use of the last-in first-out method of stock valuation; but it did not favour its use because it recognised that the use of such a cost formula resulted in the valuation of current assets which bear little relationship to actual cost. This issue is remedied in FRS 102 because paragraph 13.18 specifically prohibits the use of the LIFO method as it follows mainstream IFRS at IAS 2 *Inventories* which also disallows the use of the LIFO method.

The only acceptable cost formulas under FRS 102 are:

- the first-in first out (FIFO) method; and
- weighted average cost (AVCO).

Paragraph 13.18 does make provision for entities that have stock of a different nature and hence different cost formulas may be used (for example a retail outlet may choose to adopt the 'retail method' of valuation).

Example 12.32 – First-in first-out

During an accounting period, Ditchfield Ltd records the following purchases and sales of its products:

Purchases

	Qty/change	**Total cost**	**Cost**
Opening stock	100	£275	£27,500
Sale 1	(70)		
Purchase 1	140	£300	£42,000
Sale 2	(110)		
Purchase 2	60	£320	£19,200
	120		

The company's cost of sales is calculated in units as follows:

Opening stock	100
Purchases	200
Closing stock	(120)
	180 units

The figure to be taken to cost of sales in the profit and loss is:

	Units	**Cost**	**Total cost**
FIFO purchase 1	100	£275	£27,500
FIFO purchase 2	80	£300	£24,000
	180		£51,500

The closing inventories figure for the balance sheet (statement of financial position) is as follows:

	Units	**Cost**	**Total cost**
FIFO purchase 1	60	£300	£18,000
FIFO purchase 2	60	£320	£19,200
	120		£37,200

Sale 1 sold 70 units which were used from the opening stock which reduced opening stock to 30 units. The company then bought an additional 140 units which totals 170 units. The company sold an additional 110 units of which 30 were still in opening stock using all of the opening stock; the remaining 80 units were sold out of purchase 1, hence 60 units of purchase 1 are still in closing stock. The company then purchased an additional 60 units resulting in 120 units being held in inventory at the year-end.

If you add the cost of sales figure of £51,500 to the closing inventories figure in the balance sheet of £37,200 this totals £88,700 which amounts to the cost of inventories in the purchasing summary.

12.78 The weighted average cost (AVCO) method of stock valuation is recommended where inventory units are similar (or nearly similar). The way AVCO works is to calculate an average unit cost by dividing the total cost of the units by the number of units. When the entity purchases a new batch of inventory, that average unit cost has to be revised which can be illustrated in the following example:

Example 12.33 – Weighted average cost method

Ditchfield's purchasing activity for the month of March 2017 is as follows:

1 March 2017	Opening stock	55 units at £16 per unit
4 March 2017	Purchase	150 units at £16.50 per unit
14 March 2017	Sale	200 units at £20 per unit
25 March 2017	Purchase	80 units at £16 per unit
30 March 2017	Sale	40 units at £19.50 per unit
Units available to sell:	55 + 150 + 80 = 285	
Units actually sold:	200 + 40 = 240	
Units in closing stock:	45	

The weighted average cost can be calculated as follows:

		Units	Cost	Total
			£	£
1 March 2017	Opening stock	55	16.00	880
4 March 2017	Purchase	150	16.50	2,475
25 March 2017	Purchase	80	16.00	1,280
		285	16.26*	4,635

*£4,635/285

	Units	Cost	Total
Cost of sales	**240**	**16.26**	**3,902**
Closing stock	**45**	**16.26**	**732**

Impairment

12.79 As with all assets, a small company must consider whether the carrying amount of inventories (including work in progress) is stated at any more than recoverable amount. While Section 13 says that inventories should be measured at the lower of cost and estimated selling price less costs to complete and sell, it must be borne in mind that estimated selling price less costs to complete and sell for certain types of inventory may be below cost and hence a write-down to estimated selling price less costs to complete and sell would be required.

Where indicators of impairment are in evidence (eg obsolete or slow-moving items of inventory) then an impairment loss is recognised in profit or loss.

Focus

- Specific requirements for inventories are outlined in Section 27 *Impairment of Assets* at paragraphs 27.2–27.4, which also includes circumstances indicating an impairment reversal. Such issues are covered in this chapter, see **12.307**).

Disclosures

12.80 Disclosures relating to inventories are fairly limited in Section 1A of FRS 102, but a small entity should disclose the accounting policies it has adopted in measuring inventories, including the cost formulas used.

In addition, FRS 102 with reduced disclosure would require the disclosure of the total carrying amount of inventories which have been pledged as security for the entity's liabilities (see paragraph 13.22(e) in FRS 102).

INVESTMENTS IN ASSOCIATES

12.81 Many small companies may invest in another company and obtain an ownership interest in the voting rights of the acquiree. FRS 102 recognises various types of investments in another entity's shares (eg a subsidiary); however, other additional types of investment include associates, joint ventures and simple investments.

Scope

12.82 This particular section examines the principles in Section 14 *Investments in Associates.* This section of FRS 102 applies to the accounting for associates in both the consolidated financial statements and the individual financial statements of an investor which is not a parent.

Focus

- Few small groups prepare consolidated financial statements as it is not a legal requirement. However, where a small group chooses to prepare consolidated financial statements, the provisions in Section 14 relating to consolidated financial statements will apply to an associate.

12.83 The Glossary to FRS 102 defines an 'associate' as:

> 'An entity, including an unincorporated entity such as a partnership, over which the investor has **significant influence** and that is neither a **subsidiary** nor an interest in a **joint venture**.'[5]

5 FRS 102 Glossary **Associate**.

The term 'significant influence' means that the investor has the power to *participate* in the financial and operating policy decisions of the associate and it follows, therefore, that this does not give rise to 'control'. 'Control' is the power to govern the financial and operating policies of another company and hence this would give rise to a parent-subsidiary relationship.

Significant influence for the purposes of FRS 102 is usually obtained by a small company when that company owns between 20% and 50% of the voting rights in the investee. As with control, this numeric benchmark is not absolute and there can be other indicators that significant influence has been achieved, even with a holding of less than 20%. Such indicators may be achieved through:

- interchange of managerial personnel;
- material transactions between the investor and the investee;
- participation in the policy-making decisions;
- provisions of essential technical information; or
- representation on the board of directors or other governing body.

Focus

- Significant influence can also be achieved 'indirectly' by the investor, for example through a subsidiary company. In addition, where another investor owns a substantial share in the investee, this does not preclude the investor from having significant influence.

Accounting policy for an associate

12.84 The accounting policy for an associate will depend on whether the investor is a parent or is not a parent.

Investor is NOT a parent

12.85 Where the investor is not a parent but has investments in entities which fall to be classed as associates and hence accounted for under the provisions in Section 14, the investments (in the individual financial statements) are accounted for using either:

- the cost model;
- the fair value model; or
- at fair value through profit or loss.

> **Focus**
>
> - Where the associate is accounted for at fair value with changes in fair value going through profit or loss, FRS 102 provides guidance on determining fair value at paragraphs 11.27–11.32. These paragraphs outline the fair value hierarchy which should be used to establish fair value.

Investor IS a parent

12.86 Where the investor is a parent and has an investment in an associate which is held as part of an investment portfolio, the associate is measured at fair value and changes in this fair value are taken through profit or loss.

> **Focus**
>
> - The term 'held as part of an investment portfolio' is defined in the Glossary to FRS 102 as follows:
>
>   'An interest is held as part of an investment portfolio if its value to the investor is through **fair value** as part of a directly or indirectly held basket of investments rather than as media through which the investor carries out **business**. A basket of investments is indirectly held if an investment fund holds a single investment in a second investment fund which, in turn, holds a basket of investments.'[6]
>
> - For the vast majority of small companies owning investments in associates, it is likely that such investments are not held as part of an investment portfolio.

Accounting for an investment in an associate

12.87 Where the investor is not a parent (which may be more common for small companies), the entity can choose to adopt the cost model for its associate. Where the cost model is chosen, the investor will measure it at cost less any accumulated impairment losses which have been recognised in accordance with Section 27 *Impairment of Assets* (see **12.307** below).

12.88 The EU Accounting Directive at Article 9.7 allows EU Member States the option to permit (or require) participating interests to be accounted for using the equity method in the investor's own financial statements. Article 2(2) says that 'participating interest':

6 FRS 102 Glossary **held as part of an investment portfolio**.

> '... means rights in the capital of other undertakings, whether or not represented by certificates, which, by creating a durable link with those undertakings, are intended to contribute to the activities of the undertaking which holds those rights. The holding of part of the capital of another undertaking is presumed to constitute a participating interest where it exceeds a percentage threshold fixed by the Member States which is lower than or equal to 20%.'[7]

In addition, the Directive also allows Member States to permit (or require) that the proportion of the profit or loss which belongs to the participating interest be recognised in the investor's profit and loss account only to the extent of the corresponding amount of dividends already received (or the payment of which can be claimed).

Prior to the transposition of the EU Accounting Directive into company law, the Companies Act 2006 did not allow the investor to use the equity method in its individual financial statements and only cost-based and fair value measurements were permitted, but investors that have associates can now use the equity method of accounting in their own (separate) financial statements.

Accounting policy options

12.89 There are three permissible methods of initially recognising an investment in an associate:

- at cost;
- at fair value through other comprehensive income; or
- at fair value with through profit or loss.

> **Focus**
>
> - For small entities, it is likely that most investments in associates will be accounted for at cost. The only exception to this rule is where an investor is a parent and has an associate which is held as part of an investment portfolio. Where this is the case, the investor must account for its associate at fair value through profit or loss (which will also apply to the consolidated financial statements where these are prepared).

Equity accounting

12.90 The equity method of accounting is a method in which the investment is initially recognised at cost (which also includes incremental costs associated

7 EU Accounting Directive, Art 2(2).

with the investment, such as legal fees). After initial recognition at cost, the value of the investment is subsequently adjusted to reflect the investor's share of the profit or loss, other comprehensive income and equity of the associate.

Focus

- Care should be taken when using the equity method to ensure that transactions are correctly recorded. Where an investor receives a dividend from the associate, the dividend is treated as a *reduction* to the carrying amount of the investment. This is because a dividend is a form of return on investment and hence is not credited to profit or loss.

The equity method works as follows:

Initial recognition at cost *plus* share of profit from associate *less* dividends received from the associate.

Example 12.34 – Carrying amount of associate

On 1 January 2016, Company A acquires a 35% interest in Company B which cost £475,000. On this date the book value of Company B's assets was £900,000. During the year to 31 December 2016 B made a profit of £80,000 and paid a dividend of £120,000.

Under the equity method, Company A would account for its investment in B as follows:

	£	£
Acquisition of investment in B		
Share of B's net assets (35% × £900,000)	315,000	
Goodwill on investment of B (£475,000 less £315,000)	160,000	
		475,000
Profit during the year		
A's share of B's profit (35% × £80,000)		28,000
Dividend received by A during the year		
£120,000 × 35%		(42,000)
		461,000

The £461,000 carrying value of A's investment in B can be reconciled as follows:

Share in book value of B's net assets:

£315,000 + 35% (£80,000 – £120,000)	301,000
Goodwill on investment of B	160,000
Carrying value of investment in A	461,000

12.91 Some general points to note where the equity method of accounting is concerned:

Distributions from the associate

12.92 Distributions received from the associate **reduce** the carrying value of the associate (they are not taken to profit or loss).

Potential voting rights

12.93 While potential voting rights are brought into consideration when establishing whether significant influence exists, the investor must measure its share of profit or loss and other comprehensive income (and its share of changes in the associate's equity) on the basis of the actual ownership interest at the reporting date and these measurements must not reflect the potential exercise or conversion of potential voting rights (eg where the investor has provided convertible debt).

Fair value adjustments

12.94 On acquisition of an associate, goodwill is the difference between the cost of the acquisition and the investor's share of the fair value of the net identifiable assets of the associate (in a similar manner to the way that goodwill in a subsidiary is calculated). The investor must adjust its share of the associate's profits or losses after acquisition so as to account for the additional depreciation or amortisation of the depreciable or amortisable assets in the associate; this is because at the date of acquisition, the associate's identifiable assets and liabilities will be fair valued and the fair values may be different than book value at the time an associate is acquired.

Impairment

12.95 Where there is evidence that an associate is impaired, the investor must test the entire carrying amount of the investment for impairment using the provisions in Section 27 *Impairment of Assets* as a single asset. Goodwill arising on the acquisition of an associate is **not** tested separately but is part of the test for impairment on the entire investment.

Investor's transactions with associates

12.96 It is not uncommon for an investor to trade with its associates (and vice versa). Where such trading takes place, the investor must eliminate all unrealised profits and losses in a two-way direction (ie 'upstream' which is trading between associate and investor and 'downstream' which is trading between investor and associate). Care must be taken here because this is not necessarily the same as eliminating intra-group trading where a subsidiary is concerned. This is because where an associate is concerned, the investor will only eliminate unrealised profits and losses to the extent of the investor's interest in the associate. In addition, it must be borne in mind that unrealised losses on such transactions may indicate that the asset transferred is impaired.

Coterminous period end

12.97 The equity method of accounting requires the associate to use the same accounting reference date as that of its investor, unless this is impracticable do so. Such impracticalities are likely to be rare for small companies, but where it does prove to be impracticable then the investor should use the most recent available financial statements of the associates and make adjustments for the effects of any significant transactions or events which take place between the two accounting period ends.

Accounting policies

12.98 Where the associate uses accounting policies which differ from those used by the investor, the investor must adjust the associate's financial statements so that they reflect the accounting policies for the purposes of applying the equity method, unless it is impracticable to do so. Again it is likely to be rare for small companies that impracticalities will occur.

Losses in excess of the investment

12.99 Where the investment makes losses to the extent that the investor's share of the associate's losses exceeds the carrying amount of the investment, the investor must discontinue recognising further losses (ie it cannot recognise a negative investment on the balance sheet). When the investor's interest is zero any additional losses are recognised as a provision but only to the extent that the investor has incurred a legal or a constructive obligation which will necessitate the recognition of a provision (Section 21 *Provisions and Contingencies* applies here see **12.223** below). In addition, the investor may also recognise a provision where it has made payments on behalf of the associate.

When the associate subsequently reports a profit, the investment can then resume recognising its share of those profits, but only where its share of the profits is equivalent to the share of losses not recognised.

Cessation of the equity method

12.100 Generally the equity method of accounting is stopped from the date that the investor no longer has significant influence over the investment. The equity method will also no longer apply where the investor becomes a subsidiary (ie the investor increases its ownership interest in the associate to the extent that the investor controls the previous associate). Where control is achieved, the investor applies the provisions in Section 19 *Business Combinations and Goodwill* (see **12.176**). Conversely if the associate becomes a joint venture, the investor also ceases to use the equity method and accounts for the joint venture in accordance with Section 15 *Investments in Joint Ventures* (see **12.104–12.115**).

Where the equity method is discontinued for whatever reason, the accounting for such is as follows:

- Where significant influence is lost as a result of a full or partial disposal, the associate is derecognised from the balance sheet (statement of financial position) and the difference between the sale proceeds and the carrying value of the investment is recognised in profit or loss. Any interest which the investor has retained following the disposal is accounted for using Section 11 *Basic Financial Instruments* or Section 12 *Other Financial Instruments Issues* as appropriate. The carrying value of the associate on the date of disposal is then regarded as cost on initial measurement of the financial asset.
- If other reasons apply for the loss of significant influence other than a partial disposal of the investment, the investor regards the carrying value of the investment as at that date as the new cost and the investment is accounted for under the provisions of Section 11 or Section 12 as appropriate.

Focus

- The gain or loss recognised on disposal should also include all amounts which have been recognised in other comprehensive income which relate to the associate subject to the disposal and where such amounts have to be reclassified to profit or loss on disposal. Where amounts cannot be recycled through profit or loss, they are transferred directly to retained earnings.

Investments in associates at fair value

12.101 It is not expected that very many investments in associates will be carried at fair value as many are likely to be carried at cost (see **12.90**). However, where an investor carries an investment in an associate at fair value it is done so at transaction price.

Focus

- Transaction price does not include incremental costs of the transaction (transaction costs). Such costs are expensed to profit or loss as and when they are incurred.

12.102 After initial recognition, an investor (which is not a parent) that has chosen to adopt the fair value model will account for any subsequent changes in the fair value of the investment in other comprehensive income. The fair value guidance in paragraph 11.27–11.32 of FRS 102 should be considered.

Because the value of the investment is at fair value any dividends or other distributions received from the associate are not recognised as a reduction to the carrying amount, as is the case for an investment in an associate carried under the cost model. Instead such dividends and other distributions are recognised as income regardless of whether such distributions are from accumulated profits of the associate arising before, or after, the date of acquisition.

Example 12.35 – Dividend from an associate carried at fair value

Company A acquired 35% of the net assets of Company B several years ago and both companies have a 31 December accounting reference date. During the year to 31 December 2016, Company B pays a dividend to Company A amounting to £50,000.

As the associate in this example is being carried under the fair value model, the entries in the books of Company A are:

DR cash at bank	£50,000
CR income from associate (profit or loss)	(£50,000)

Being dividend received from associate

In contrast, had the investment in the associate been carried at cost (see **12.90**) then the credit would have been to the cost of the investment in the associate in the balance sheet to reduce the carrying amount.

If Company A had acquired the associate during the current accounting period, it would not matter whether the dividend received from the associate was made out of accumulated profits before or after the date of acquisition.

Disclosures

12.103 The disclosures relating to investments in associates may include:

- The accounting policy for investments in associates.

- The cost or fair value at the beginning of the reporting period.
- Additions, disposals and transfers during the period.
- Accumulated impairment losses at the beginning and end of the reporting period.
- Impairment losses during the reporting period.
- Where associates are carried at revalued amounts, a table showing:
  - the movement in the revaluation reserve in the reporting period with an explanation of the tax treatment (where appropriate); and
  - the carrying amount of the investment in the balance sheet (statement of financial position) had the investment not been revalued.
- Where the investment is carried at fair value through profit or loss, disclose:
  - the significant assumptions underlying the valuation models and techniques used where a quoted price is unavailable; and
  - the fair value, changes in value included directly in profit or loss and changes in fair value in equity.

Additional disclosures should be provided relating to investments in associates where these are considered material.

INVESTMENTS IN JOINT VENTURES

12.104 Section 15 *Investments in Joint Ventures* deals with the accounting for joint ventures. The section itself applies to both the consolidated financial statements (where these are prepared) and the individual financial statements.

12.105 In order for a venture to qualify as a joint venture, there must be a contractually-agreed sharing of control in existence. This is crucial in a joint venture because joint control can only be evident where the venture requires the unanimous consent of the parties involved in the venture in respect of the venture's financial and operating decisions.

> **Focus**
>
> - In a joint venture no one party can have overall control of the venture because to do so would give rise to the controlling party becoming a parent and the venture becoming a subsidiary and hence a parent-subsidiary relationship would arise.

12.106 There are three types of joint venture dealt with under Section 15:

- jointly controlled operations

- jointly controlled assets
- jointly controlled entities

Jointly controlled operations

12.107 A joint venture may be set up which involves the use of the assets and resources of individual venturers as opposed to the creation of a separate vehicle to operate the joint venture through (ie a company, partnership or other form of entity).

In a jointly controlled operation, each venturer will use their own assets (property, plant and equipment) and carry their own inventory. The venturer will incur their own expense and liabilities and be responsible for raising their own finance.

In terms of the accounting for a jointly controlled operation in the individual financial statements, a venturer recognises:

- the assets which it controls and the liabilities which it incurs; and
- the expenses which it incurs and its share of the income which it earns from the sale of goods or services by the joint venture.

Example 12.36 – Jointly controlled operation

Mark and Neil enter into a contractual arrangement under which they will combine their operations, resources and technical expertise to manufacture, market and distribute aircraft aimed at the high-volume, low-cost carrier market.

The two individuals will carry out different parts of the manufacturing process. Both parties will bear their own costs and be entitled to a share of the revenue from the sale of the aircraft. The basis for allocating revenue is determined in accordance with the terms of the contractual arrangement.

Mark and Neil both have joint control over the manufacturing operations as described in paragraph 12.95 above and the joint venture takes the form of a jointly controlled operation. As a result, in the separate financial statements of Mark and Neil both will recognise the assets they control and the liabilities and expenses each party incurs and their share of the income which they earn from the sale of the aircraft.

Jointly controlled assets

12.108 A joint venture may be created whereby the venturers both control and own one or more assets which have been contributed to the venture. Where such jointly controlled assets exist, each venturer will recognise (in their own financial statements):

- their share of the jointly controlled assets which are to be classified according to the nature of the assets;
- any liabilities which they have incurred;
- the venturer's share of any liabilities incurred jointly with the other venturers which relate to the joint venture;
- any income from the sale or use of its share of the output of the joint venture as well as its share of any expenses incurred by the joint venture; and
- any expenses which it has incurred in respect of its interest in the joint venture.

Example 12.37 – Jointly controlled asset

Pete and Jenny both own a residential property which is let out to a third party to earn rentals.

In the individual financial statements of Pete and Jenny each venturer will recognise their share of the jointly controlled asset (being the property itself) and their own share of the income generated from the rental business. They will also recognise their own liability for mortgage payments on the property as well the interest charge on the borrowings.

Jointly controlled entities

12.109 Jointly controlled entities are complex to account for in comparison to jointly controlled operations and jointly controlled assets.

A jointly controlled entity involves the creation of a separate vehicle through which the jointly controlled entity will operate (eg an incorporated company or partnership). The joint venture itself will operate in much the same way as other entities, however a notable difference is that there will be a contractual arrangement in place between the venturers which will establish joint control over the economic activity of the company.

Focus

- The contractual arrangement is pivotal in a jointly controlled entity because it will specify that there is joint control over the financial and operating policies of the joint venture which will allow the joint venture to be classified as such.

Accounting policy choice

12.110 There are three accounting policy options in respect of a jointly controlled entity which a venturer which is not parent can choose:

- the cost model;
- the fair value model; or
- at fair value with changes in fair value going through profit or loss.

Where the venturer is a parent company and produces consolidated financial statements the venturer must use the equity method of accounting for its interest in jointly controlled entities (see **12.90** which outlines how the equity method works).

> **Focus**
>
> - The equity method referred to in FRS 102 uses the terms 'significant influence' and 'associate' in Section 14. For the purposes of joint ventures, 'significant influence' is replaced by the term 'joint control' and 'associate' is replaced by the term 'jointly controlled entity'.

Where the venturer is a parent and the jointly controlled entity is held as part of an investment portfolio such investments must be measured at fair value with changes in fair value going through profit or loss in the consolidated financial statements.

Cost model

12.111 This is likely to be the most common type of model for a small company accounting for its interest in a jointly controlled entity. Under the cost model the investment in the jointly controlled entity is measured at cost less any accumulated impairment losses. Dividends received from the jointly controlled entity are recognised as income regardless of whether the dividends have been paid out of accumulated profits of the jointly controlled entity prior to the date of acquisition or not.

Fair value model

12.112 Under the fair value model, a venturer which is not a parent, measures its investment in the jointly controlled entity at transaction price. After initial recognition at transaction price, the venturer measures its investment in a jointly controlled entity at fair value using the fair value guidance in FRS 102 at paragraphs 11.27–11.32. Changes in the fair value of a jointly controlled entity are reported through other comprehensive income. The exception to this requirement is where a fair value gain reverses a revaluation decrease of the same jointly controlled entity which was previously recognised in profit or loss.

Example 12.38 – Revaluation gain

Bury Enterprises Ltd has a jointly controlled entity which suffered a revaluation loss in 2015. In 2016 the circumstances giving rise to the loss have expired and the jointly controlled entity has seen an increase in its fair value.

The entries in the books of Bury Enterprises to recognise the increase in fair value will be:

DR investment in jointly controlled entity	X
CR profit or loss	(X)

Revaluation gains and losses are recognised in other comprehensive income to the extent that there is a credit balance on the revaluation surplus. Where a revaluation decrease exceeds the accumulated revaluation gains which have been accumulated in equity, the excess is taken to profit or loss.

12.113 If it is impracticable to measure the fair value of a jointly controlled entity reliably without incurring undue cost or effort, the venturer should use the cost model.

In terms of dividends and other distributions received from the jointly controlled entity, these are to be recognised as income in the profit and loss account (income statement) regardless of whether the distributions have been paid out of accumulated profits of the jointly controlled entity which arise prior to the date of acquisition.

Transactions between a venturer and a joint venture

12.114 It is not uncommon for transactions to take place between a venturer and a joint venture. A key point to emphasise, however, is that where a venturer contributes or sells assets to a joint venture, any gain or loss must reflect the substance of the transaction.

If the venturer has transferred the risks and rewards of ownership to the joint venture, the venturer should only recognise that gain or loss which belongs to the interests of the other venturers. Conversely, the venturer will recognise the full amount of any loss when the contribution or the sale provides evidence of an impairment loss.

Example 12.39 – Transactions between a venturer and a joint venture

Leyla is one of the venturers in Westhead Ltd which is a jointly controlled entity. On 31 December 2016 she purchased goods from the venture for onward sale in her own company.

When a venturer purchases goods or other forms of assets from a joint venture, they must not recognise any share of the profits of the joint venture from the purchase until the goods or assets are sold to an unconnected party. However, Leyla would recognise her share of the losses from any such transactions where these provide evidence of impairment.

Disclosures

12.115 Disclosures relating to joint ventures may include:

- Accounting policies adopted in respect of joint ventures.
- Where joint ventures are measured at fair value, a table showing:
  - — movements in the revaluation reserve in the reporting period; and
  - — the carrying amount in the balance sheet (statement of financial position) that would have been recognised had the joint venture not been revalued.
- Where joint ventures are measured at fair value through profit or loss, disclose:
  - — the significant assumptions underlying the valuation models and techniques used where a quoted price in an active market is not available;
  - — the changes in value included directly in profit or loss and the changes in value included in equity; and
  - — a table showing movements in equity during the reporting period.
- The aggregate amounts of the joint venture's commitments including its share in the capital commitments that have been incurred jointly with other venturers, as well as its share of the capital commitments of the joint ventures themselves.

INVESTMENT PROPERTY

12.116 Investment property is dealt with in Section 16 *Investment Property* in FRS 102 and this particular section brings about significant changes in the accounting for such properties than was the case under the FRSSE (effective January 2015).

Section 16 applies to investment property which is carried in the balance sheet (statement of financial position) at fair value. Where such properties are not carried at fair value (which is likely to be rare) then they are accounted for under the provisions in Section 17 *Property, Plant and Equipment* (see **12.127**). Section 16 also deals with property interests held by a lessee under an operating lease.

Focus

- Unlike the FRSSE (effective January 2015), Section 16 provides for circumstances where obtaining a fair value for investment property would cause undue cost or effort. In such situations the investment property is accounted for under the normal fixed asset rules in Section 17 (ie at cost less depreciation and any applicable impairment losses) until a reliable measure of fair value becomes available.
- It is unlikely that the undue cost or effort provision will be exercised by many small companies that have investment property on their balance sheet (statement of financial position) because obtaining a fair value for investment property at each reporting date is straightforward and would have been obtained in any event to comply with the requirements of the FRSSE (effective January 2015).

Investment property defined

12.117 In the vast majority of cases it is clear when a property can qualify for classification as an investment property. Paragraph 16.2 of FRS 102 says that investment property:

> '… is property (land or a building, or part of a building, or both) held by the owner or by the lessee under a **finance lease** to earn rentals or for capital appreciation or both, rather than for:
>
> (a) use in the production or supply of goods or services or for administrative purposes; or
>
> (b) sale in the ordinary course of business.'

This definition is fairly restrictive and has to be applied to properties on a case-by-case basis. Where the definition is not met then the property will be accounted for under the provisions in Section 17.

There are a couple of exceptions to the definition and the following types of property will **not** qualify to be classified as investment property:

- Property which is held primarily for the provision of social benefits (such as social housing held by a public benefit entity).
- Mixed-use property where the fair value of the investment component of the property cannot be reliably measured without the incurrence of undue cost or effort.

In both of the above cases, the properties are to be accounted for under Section 17.

Measurement at initial recognition

12.118 Where a small company acquires a property which meets the definition of investment property as per paragraph 16.2 (a) and (b) of FRS 102, it is initially recognised at cost. Cost can comprise a number of different elements including:

- initial purchase price;
- incremental costs (such as legal fees in connection with the purchase);
- property transfer taxes; and
- other transaction costs which are directly attributable to the investment property.

'Other transaction costs' will be those costs which could have been avoided by the small company had it not acquired an investment property.

Where a small company self-constructs its own investment property, the provisions in paragraphs 17.10 to 17.14 of FRS 102 are to be followed.

12.119 Where the investment property is held under a lease, the property must be treated as a finance lease in accordance with paragraphs 20.9 and 20.10 of FRS 102 and this applies even if the lease would otherwise be classed as an operating lease if the property fell under the scope of Section 20 *Leases*. This treatment requires the asset to be recognised at the *lower* of the fair value of the property and the present value of the minimum lease payments with a corresponding amount being recognised in the balance sheet (statement of financial position) as a finance lease creditor. Premiums paid in respect of such leases are treated as part of the minimum lease payments and hence included in the composition of cost, but they are excluded from the finance lease creditor in the balance sheet (statement of financial position).

Subsequent measurement of investment property

12.120 Generally, investment property will be fair valued at each reporting date provided such values can be obtained without undue cost or effort. Under the previous FRSSE (effective January 2015), fair value gains and losses were taken to a revaluation surplus and reported in equity via the statement of total recognised gains and losses. The exception to this accounting treatment was where the deficit (or its reversal) on an individual investment property was expected to be permanent, in which case it was charged (or credited) to profit or loss in the period that it arose. Hence under previous UK GAAP the accounting treatment for uplifts in the market value of an investment property were to debit the investment property in the balance sheet and credit the revaluation reserve in equity.

Section 16 of FRS 102 extinguishes the use of the revaluation reserve for investment property and all fair value changes (gains and losses) are to be taken to profit or loss. This will have a major impact in some instances for small companies; particularly those with several investment properties on their balance sheets (statements of financial position) because reported operating profit is likely to be significantly different than was the case under previous UK GAAP.

Example 12.40 – Accounting treatment under Section 16

Ditchfield Ltd has an investment property on its balance sheet and an accounting reference date of 31 December. On 31 December 2017 the valuation agent confirmed that the market value of the investment property had increased by £15,000. The entries in the books of Ditchfield will be:

DR investment property	£15,000
CR profit or loss	(£15,000)

Being increase in fair value of investment property

The effect of this revised accounting treatment is that reported profit is £15,000 (gross of deferred tax) more than would have been the case under the previous FRSSE (effective January 2015).

Focus

- An important point to emphasise where the £15,000 gain is concerned is that the gain is **not** a realised profit and hence cannot be distributed to shareholders. As a consequence, small companies will experience a higher level of undistributable profit. Some commentators are advising that small entities keep a track of unrealised gains in a separate reserve account within equity so as not to inappropriately distribute gains on investment property. Whilst there is nothing in legislation that requires this, it is important that small companies do keep a track of such undistributable reserves because the gains (and losses) must pass through profit or loss (ie they cannot simply be taken directly to reserves).

Deferred tax issues on investment property

12.121 Section 29 *Income Tax* at paragraph 29.16 requires deferred tax relating to investment property measured at fair value be brought into account at the tax rates and allowances which would apply to the sale of the asset. The exception in this case would be where the investment property has a limited useful life and is held within a business model whose objective is to consume substantially all of the economic benefits associated with the property over time. In reality, where the company is going to hold the investment property for several years, the tax rate used in the calculation of deferred tax will be the latest rate currently known by the company as announced by the Chancellor.

Under previous UK GAAP, deferred tax on fair value gains and losses for investment property would have been ignored unless there was a binding agreement to sell the asset at the reporting date and the disposal had been accounted for in the financial statements. This exception has been withdrawn in FRS 102 to arrive at the timing difference 'plus' approach.

Investment property in group situations

12.122 Under previous UK GAAP there was a scope exemption which meant that properties which were let out to group members were specifically excluded from the definition of an investment property. Under Section 16 there is no scope exemption for properties which are rented out to other group members and this is going to have an impact on the consolidated financial statements of a small group where these are prepared.

Example 12.41 – Property let out to a subsidiary company by the parent

Westhead Enterprises Ltd (Westhead) has a wholly-owned subsidiary, Heaton Enterprises Ltd (Heaton) which it acquired several years ago. Heaton rents an office building which is owned by Westhead and under the previous FRSSE (effective January 2015), both parties accounted for the arrangement as an operating lease. Westhead carried the property under previous UK GAAP at depreciated historic cost as a tangible fixed asset in its balance sheet. The group qualifies as a small group but prepares consolidated financial statements.

<u>Accounting treatment by Westhead</u>

Section 16 does not contain any scope exemption for properties which are let out to other group companies and therefore to comply with the provisions in Section 16, the property which is rented out will have to be treated as an investment property. In Westhead's individual financial statements, the property will be held at fair value with fluctuations in fair value passing through profit or loss. Westhead will have to perform a one-off valuation at the date of transition and restate the prior year's financial statements by removing the depreciation charge and replacing it with a charge or credit which represents the change in value for the prior year.

<u>Treatment by Heaton</u>

In the individual financial statements of Heaton, nothing has changed because it still has an operating lease in place with Westhead to rent the building.

Treatment in the group accounts

From a group perspective, the property is owner-occupied and hence the treatment as an investment property is only permitted in the lessor's (Westhead's) financial statements. In the group accounts the investment property will form part of property, plant and equipment.

Mixed-use property

12.123 Section 16 addresses the issue of mixed-use property and paragraph 16.4 requires such property to be separated between the investment property component and the owned property (property, plant and equipment) component. Once this split has been established, the fair value of the let-out portion of the property should be established. Sometimes this can be straightforward if there is a separate floor within the building which is rented out; however, such issues may not be so straightforward as can be illustrated in the following example:

Example 12.42 – Parent rents part of a building to its subsidiary

Westhead Enterprises Ltd (Westhead) rents out part of its manufacturing space to its wholly-owned subsidiary, Heaton Enterprises Ltd (Heaton) for which it receives rental income. In preparation for its transition to FRS 102, Westhead has been trying to establish a fair value for the part of the building which is occupied by Heaton but difficulties have arisen in arriving at fair value because it is on the same floor as Westhead.

Where the fair value of the investment property component cannot be measured reliably, then paragraph 16.4 of FRS 102 says that the entire property is to be accounted for as property, plant and equipment in accordance with Section 17. Therefore, Westhead will account for the entire building under Section 17 rather than Section 16.

Investment property on transition to FRS 102

12.124 Where a small company has an investment property on its balance sheet (statement of financial position) at the date of transition to FRS 102 it is going to have to deal with a couple of additional complexities.

To comply with the provisions in the previous FRSSE (effective January 2015), the small company would have carried the investment property at open market value with changes in this open market value passing through a revaluation reserve account. Any remaining surplus on the revaluation reserve account at the date of transition will be taken to profit and loss reserves, or an alternative component of equity (such as an 'undistributable reserve' account). Deferred tax will also have to be accounted for at the date of transition in respect of the investment property because it is a non-monetary asset which is subject to revaluation, hence Section 29 *Income Tax* requires such assets to have related deferred tax accounted for. This is because an opening FRS 102-compliant balance sheet has to be prepared at the date of transition to comply with Section 35 *Transition to this FRS* principles and so that the financial statements reflect the requirements of FRS 102 as if FRS 102 had always been the financial reporting framework that the company reports under.

Example 12.43 – Investment property on transition to FRS 102

Robyn Ltd (Robyn) has run an opening trial balance as at 1 January 2015 which is based on the closing 31 December 2014 trial balance. The opening trial balance as at 1 January 2015 shows a revaluation surplus in respect of investment property of £120,000. Robyn pays tax at 20%.

On transition to FRS 102, Robyn should make the following transitional adjustments to its opening balances in order to arrive at an FRS 102-compliant set of opening balances:

DR revaluation reserve	£120,000
CR accumulated profit and loss	(£120,000)

Being reclassification of investment property revaluation surplus on transition.

Under FRS 102, Robyn will have to account for deferred tax in respect of the investment property's fair value as follows:

DR accumulated profit and loss	£24,000
CR deferred tax provision	(£24,000)

Being deferred tax on investment property revaluation surplus

If it is assumed that in the 2015 (the comparative year) the value of the investment property had increased by £5,000 the entries under the FRSSE (effective January 2015) would have been to debit investment property with the increase and credit revaluation reserve.

The concept of the revaluation reserve does not apply to investment property accounted for under FRS 102 and so an adjustment is required to the comparative year as follows:

DR revaluation reserve	£5,000
CR profit and loss	(£5,000)

Being reclassification of investment property fair value gain

The associated deferred tax charge will also have to be included in the comparative year as follows:

DR tax expense	£1,000
CR deferred tax provision	(£1,000)

Being deferred tax on the investment property revaluation

From the above worked example, it can be seen that there will be an overall increase in previously reported profit of £4,000 (£5,000 gain on revaluation less deferred tax of £1,000). This overall gain cannot be distributed to shareholders.

> **Focus**
>
> - While the provisions in Section 16 require all fair value gains and losses on investment property to be reported in profit or loss and hence extinguishes the use of a revaluation reserve account, the concept of a revaluation reserve account does still apply to assets carried under the revaluation model in Section 17 *Property, Plant and Equipment* hence an owned building carried under the revaluation model will still have an associated revaluation reserve account for fair value gains.

Transfers of investment property

12.125 In situations where a reliable measure of fair value is no longer available for an investment property without the company incurring undue cost or effort, the company has to account for its investment property in accordance with Section 17 principles until a reliable measure of fair value becomes available. The carrying amount on the date that a fair value is no longer available becomes cost for the purposes of Section 17 and because this will give rise to a change in accounting policy, disclosure as such should be made in the financial statements if material and would achieve a true and fair view.

The only other situation where a property can be transferred to, or from, investment property is when the property first meets, or ceases to meet, the definition of investment property in paragraph 16.2 of FRS 102.

Disclosures

12.126 Disclosures relating to investment property may be as follows:

- Accounting policies adopted (and any changes in accounting policy because of a transfer to/from investment property classification).
- The methods and significant assumptions applied in determining fair value of investment property.

- A reconciliation between the carrying amounts of investment property at the beginning and end of the reporting period, showing separately:
  - — additions, showing separately those additions arising through a business combination;
  - — net gains or losses from fair value adjustments;
  - — transfers to property, plant and equipment when a reliable measure of fair value is no longer available without undue cost or effort;
  - — transfers to and from inventories and owner-occupied property; and
  - — other changes; and
- Contractual obligations to purchase, construct or develop investment property or for repairs, maintenance or enhancements.

Additional disclosures may be necessary so that the financial statements of the small company give a true and fair view (for example where no such valuations have been obtained and the extent to which fair value for investment property is based on a valuation by an independent valuer who holds a recognised and relevant professional qualification and has recent experience in the location and class of investment property being valued).

PROPERTY, PLANT AND EQUIPMENT

12.127 Section 17 *Property, Plant and Equipment* deals with tangible fixed assets (but it does not deal with investment properties which are carried at fair value and accounted for under Section 16 *Investment Property*). Section 17 only deals with *tangible* fixed assets; intangible assets other than goodwill are dealt with in Section 18 *Intangible Assets other than Goodwill* and goodwill itself is dealt with in the provisions of Section 19 *Business Combinations and Goodwill.*

While the scope of Section 17 does not include investment property carried at fair value, it does cover investment property whose fair value cannot be measured without undue cost or effort as Section 16 says that where this is the case, the investment property must be accounted for under Section 17 principles (paragraph 16.7 of FRS 102).

Property, plant and equipment defined

12.128 Section 17 says that property, plant and equipment are tangible assets which are held for use in the production or supply of goods or services, for rental to others or for administrative purposes and are expected to be held by the reporting entity for more than one accounting period (hence the term in FRS 102 as 'non-current'). There are some types of assets, which are not dealt with under the provisions in Section 17 and relate to:

- biological assets related to agricultural activity (see Section 34 *Specialised Activities*); and
- mineral rights and mineral reserves, such as oil, natural gas and similar non-regenerative resources (also dealt with in Section 34).

Recognising a tangible fixed asset

12.129 A small company reporting under FRS 102 must have regard to the *Concepts and Pervasive Principles* at Section 2 of FRS 102 in determining whether to recognise an item as property, plant and equipment (notably paragraph 2.27). Two specific criterion have to be fulfilled:

- it is probable that future economic benefits associated with the item will flow to the entity; and
- the cost of the item can be measured reliably.

The term 'probable' is defined in the Glossary to FRS 102 as *'more likely than not'*.

Focus

- The term 'economic benefits associated with the item' means that there will be a flow of another asset to the entity from the asset in question. For example, an item of plant in a manufacturing company will manufacture goods for resale which will then turn into inventory (stock), the inventory will turn into a debtor once it is sold to a customer who will then eventually settle the bill and realise the sale into cash. The company may also receive income streams from an asset (such as rentals) and these would also fall to be classed as economic benefits.

Major spare parts and standby equipment

12.130 When a small business carries items such as spare parts and servicing equipment, Section 17 acknowledges that these are usually carried as inventory and recognised in the profit and loss account (income statement) as and when the assets are consumed. Care needs to be taken with 'major' spare parts and standby equipment because these should be recognised as property, plant and equipment under Section 17 when the small company expects to use such equipment for more than one accounting period. Also, where spare parts and servicing equipment can only be used in connection with an item of property, plant and equipment, they are considered to be property, plant and equipment and hence should be recognised as such in the balance sheet (statement of financial position).

Component accounting

12.131 Section 17 acknowledges that there are some items of property, plant and equipment which may require replacement at regular intervals – in other words 'components' of a tangible fixed asset which have different useful economic lives than the main asset itself. The section cites an example of a roof on a building and the accounting for such expenditure is largely similar to that of the FRSSE (effective January 2015) and FRS 15 *Tangible fixed assets* relating to subsequent expenditure. If the replacement part is expected to provide incremental future benefits to the entity then it is capitalised as part of the cost of the asset and the carrying amount of the part(s) replaced are derecognised.

Example 12.44 – Component accounting

A frequently cited example of a scenario which gives rise to component accounting is the replacement of an aircraft's engine. While it is acknowledged that very few small companies will have aircrafts on the balance sheet (statement of financial position) the example itself is a good illustration of how component accounting works in practice. The engines of an aircraft will have to be replaced at regular intervals (such as every five years) and hence the engines will have a much shorter useful economic life than the actual aircraft itself. The engines, therefore, may be accounted for separately than the main aircraft and hence the engines will be depreciated separately over, say, a five-year period.

Section 17 also cites an example of a bus that is subjected to major inspections for faults at periodic intervals regardless of whether parts of the item are replaced. Where each major inspection is undertaken, the cost of the inspection is included in the carrying value of the asset as a replacement should the recognition criteria be satisfied. Any remaining carrying amount of the cost of the previous major inspection which has been distinguished from physical parts is therefore derecognised. The section also allows an estimated cost of a future similar inspection may be used as an indication of what the cost of the existing inspection component was when the item was acquired or constructed.

Example 12.45 – Land and buildings

Whitaker Ltd has acquired a property during the year to 31 December 2016. The value of the building is £100,000 and the value of the land on which it is built has been established by the valuation agent at £25,000. The financial controller of Whitaker Ltd has accounted for the entire cost as one complete asset.

Paragraph 17.8 of FRS 102 recognises that land and buildings are both separable assets and hence it follows that Whitaker Ltd should account for them separately regardless of the fact that they have both been acquired together.

Initial recognition of an asset

12.132 When an asset meets the recognition criteria, it is initially measured at cost on the balance sheet (statement of financial position). An asset's 'cost' can be made up of several elements and is not necessarily just the purchase price. Other elements of cost can include:

- legal and brokerage fees;
- import duties;
- non-refundable purchase taxes;
- costs directly attributable in bringing the asset to the location and condition necessary for it to be capable of operating in the manner which management intended;
- initial estimates of the costs involved in dismantling and removing the item and restoring the site on which the asset is located; and
- borrowing costs which may be capitalised in accordance with Section 25 *Borrowing Costs*.

12.133 While the cost of an asset can clearly be made up of several components, the following types of cost cannot be recognised as part of the cost of an asset:

- costs incurred in opening a new facility;
- costs incurred for introducing a new product or service (for example, advertising and promotion);
- costs which the business incurs in conducting business in a new location or with a new class of customer; and
- administration and overhead costs.

Such costs must be expensed to profit or loss as soon as they are incurred.

Example 12.46 – Exchange of assets

Cahill Ltd acquires an asset in exchange for one of its assets in an exchange transaction. The financial controller is trying to establish a cost price for the acquired asset and is proposing to recognise the addition at fair value.

The financial controller can use fair value for the acquired asset as permitted by paragraph 17.14 of FRS 102. However, there are two exceptions where fair values cannot be used:

(1) where the exchange transaction lacks commercial substance (see **Focus** box below); or

(2) the fair value of neither the asset received, nor the asset given up, is reliably measurable.

Where these exceptions apply the cost of the asset is measured at the carrying value of the asset given up.

Focus

- A transaction has 'commercial substance' when it is expected that the future cash flows of the business will change as a result of the transaction. Where the cash flows of the business will not change as a result of the transaction then the transaction will not have commercial substance.

Measurement after initial recognition

12.134 After initial recognition at cost, the small company then has two accounting policy choices to subsequently measure property, plant and equipment.

(1) at cost; or

(2) at revaluation.

Focus

- The revaluation model is not permitted for micro-entities reporting under FRS 105 *The Financial Reporting Standard applicable to the Micro-entities Regime*. See **Chapter 11** for issues regarding the micro-entity accounting standards.

Cost model

12.135 When the small company uses the cost model, it measures property, plant and equipment at cost less any accumulated depreciation and impairment losses. In practice this method is usually the most common method in measuring tangible fixed assets because of its ease of use and it is also inherently less costly than the revaluation model.

Where payment for an item of property, plant and equipment is deferred beyond normal credit terms, the cost of the item is recognised as the present value of all future payments as the deferral of payment beyond normal credit terms will give rise to the transaction being a financing transaction.

> **Focus**
>
> - Under previous UK GAAP at the FRSSE (effective January 2015) it was inherently very difficult to initially recognise an asset at cost, then choose the revaluation model and then go back to the cost model. This is because a change from cost to revaluation is a change in accounting policy and changes in accounting policy are only generally undertaken when the change results in the financial statements giving a more true and fair view and hence a switch back from revaluation to cost would be very difficult to justify.
> - The provisions in Section 35 *Transition to this FRS* at paragraph 35.10(d) permit a revaluation amount to be used as deemed cost on transition. Therefore it is possible on transition to FRS 102 to use a previous GAAP revaluation as deemed cost and then continue to measure the asset(s) under the cost model. Care must be taken however, because the previous GAAP valuation must be **at, or before, the date of transition**. It cannot be after the date of transition.

Revaluation model

12.136 Under the revaluation model, property, plant and equipment whose fair value can be reliably measured may be carried at revalued amounts in the balance sheet (statement of financial position). There is no change from previous FRSSE (effective January 2015) requirements in this respect.

Revaluation is the fair value at the date of revaluation less subsequent accumulated depreciation and subsequent impairment losses.

> **Focus**
>
> - Under the FRSSE (effective January 2015) revaluations had to be undertaken at least every five years, with valuations in the intervening years where a material change in value may have occurred. Section 17 does not specify a timeframe for revaluations other than saying that reporting entities must obtain revaluations with 'sufficient regularity' so that the entity is not carrying the asset in the balance sheet (statement of financial position) at an amount which is materially different from that which would be determined using fair value at the end of the reporting period.

12.137 The revaluation model is more commonly applied to land and buildings and fair values of such assets are usually obtained from the market in which similar properties are bought and sold and are normally arrived at by professionally-qualified valuers who have recent experience in valuing such properties.

12.138 Fair values for plant and equipment are usually arrived at by reference to market values determined by appraisal and Section 17 refers preparers to paragraphs 11.27–11.32 of FRS 102 which offers further guidance on the determination of fair value.

Where no market-based evidence exists of fair value due to the specialist nature of the item of property, plant and equipment and the item is rarely sold (such as a school building) then fair value may need to be estimated using an income or depreciated replacement cost approach.

Gains and losses on revaluation

12.139 When the carrying value of an asset which is subjected to the revaluation model increases as a result of the revaluation, the increase is recognised in other comprehensive income in equity under the heading of 'revaluation surplus'. Any increases which reverse a revaluation decrease of the same asset previously recognised in profit or loss should be taken to profit or loss.

Focus

- A revaluation reserve account within equity is permissible for items of property, plant and equipment carried at revaluation. This accounting treatment has not changed from the FRSSE (effective January 2015) and should not be confused with the notably different change in accounting methodology for investment property carried at fair value where fair value gains and losses are taken directly to profit or loss (see **12.120** above).

Example 12.47 – Downward revaluation

A company owns its own freehold property and measures this building using the revaluation model in Section 17 of FRS 102. It has an accounting reference date of 30 June each year. On 30 June 2015 the external valuation agent confirmed the building had increased in value from £110,000 to £120,000 and hence the company accountant made the following entries in the books:

DR property, plant and equipment	£10,000
CR revaluation surplus	(£10,000)

Being increase in fair value of property

The valuation of the revaluation surplus at 30 June 2015 after this entry had been made was £15,000.

On 30 June 2017 the directors decided to commission another valuation of the building because they suspected there had been a material change in carrying value. The valuation agent said that the investment property had reduced in value to £100,000.

Paragraph 17.15F says that the decrease of an asset's carrying value as a result of a valuation is to be recognised in other comprehensive income (ie via the revaluation reserve) to the extent of any previously recognised revaluation increases which have been accumulated in equity. To reflect this requirement, of the £20,000 revaluation decrease (£120,000 carrying value less £100,000 revaluation) £15,000 is debited to the revaluation reserve account to reduce this to nil. The remaining £5,000 is taken to profit or loss.

Depreciation

12.140 Items of property, plant and equipment will continue to be depreciated as this is mandatory under Section 17 and the Companies Act 2006 (unless the useful economic life is deemed to be indefinite as is the case with land).

Section 17 places emphasis on component accounting for depreciation whereby the major components of an item of property, plant and equipment have different useful economic lives than the asset itself and hence in these cases the entity must allocate the initial cost of the asset to its major components and depreciate each component separately over its useful life.

Example 12.48 – Component depreciation

Gareth's Glassware Co Ltd manufactures ornamental glass. It has a blast furnace that has a lining which needs replacing every five years for technical reasons. The blast furnace itself has a useful economic life of 15 years.

The useful economic life of the lining in the blast furnace is significantly less than the blast furnace itself. As a result, the lining will be depreciated over its estimated useful life of five years and the remaining asset will be depreciated over its estimated useful life of 15 years.

Depreciation charges continue to be recognised in profit or loss under Section 17 principles unless another section requires the depreciation expense to be recognised as part of the cost of an asset and in this respect Section 17 cites an example of the depreciation of manufacturing property, plant and equipment which is included in the cost of inventories.

Depreciable amount

12.141 The depreciable amount of an asset is the cost of the asset less the asset's estimated scrap value (residual value) at the end of its useful economic life. This depreciable amount is then depreciated on a systematic basis over the asset's useful economic life.

> **Focus**
>
> - FRS 102 uses a 'current cost' approach to residual values and acknowledges that factors such as a change in how an asset is used, significant unexpected wear and tear, technological advancement and changes in market values might indicate that the residual value of an asset (or the asset's useful life) has changed since the most recent reporting date. In such situations, the entity must review its previous estimates and where current expectations differ, amend the residual value depreciation method or useful life accordingly. This could mean that residual values see an upward direction, which is notably different than the FRSSE (effective January 2015) which did not take account of expected future price changes.

Where the entity experiences a change in residual value, depreciation method or useful life, it recognises this as a change in accounting estimate as per Section 10 *Accounting Policies, Estimates and Errors*. Such changes in estimation techniques are accounted for prospectively (ie going forward – no retrospective change is applied to the comparative period's financial statements).

12.142 Depreciation commences when the asset is available for use. An asset is said to be available for use when it is in the location and condition necessary for it to be capable of operating in the way that management intended. Conversely, depreciation of an asset will cease when the entity derecognises the asset (ie it sells the asset or it is scrapped). Depreciation does not cease when the asset becomes idle or is retired from expected use.

> **Focus**
>
> - Even though depreciation will not cease to apply when the asset is idle, there may be instances where the depreciation charge for a period is zero and this will usually apply where the entity is not producing any goods and the asset is being depreciated under the 'usage method'. Such a policy is acceptable under FRS 102.

12.143 In arriving at an estimated useful life for an asset, Section 17 requires that management take into consideration certain factors, including:

- the expected usage of the asset (by reference to the asset's expected capacity or physical output);
- expected physical wear and tear;
- technical or commercial obsolescence; and
- legal or similar limits on the use of the asset.

The above factors are not exhaustive and other company/asset-specific issues should be taken into consideration in arriving at an estimated useful life for the asset.

Depreciation method

12.144 Section 17 does not prescribe depreciation methods for certain assets; however it does require that the entity selects a depreciation method which reflects the pattern in which it expects to consume the asset's future economic benefits. Small companies commonly use the straight-line or reducing balance (diminishing balance) method of depreciation. However, these are not the only permissible methods of depreciation and an entity may choose a method based on usage (such as the 'units of production method').

Paragraph 17.23 requires an entity to consider the pattern by which the entity is consuming the asset's future economic benefits and this assessment must be done on an annual basis. If current expectations differ, then the depreciation method must reflect the revised assessment of consumption of the asset and this could result in accelerated or decelerated depreciation charges. A change in depreciation method is accounted for as a change in accounting estimate and is applied prospectively (ie no prior period adjustment is carried out).

Impairment

Recognition and measurement

12.145 The underlying principle in financial reporting is that assets should not be carried in the balance sheet (statement of financial position) at any more than their recoverable amount. It follows, therefore, that at the end of each reporting period an entity must consider whether any assets are showing indicators of impairment and where it is evident that an asset is impaired then it should be written down to its recoverable amount and the debit is taken to profit or loss.

Compensation

Sometimes an entity which has suffered impairment on an asset(s) may be entitled to compensation from a third party. Compensation receivables can only be recognised when it is 'virtually certain' that the compensation will be received.

Example 12.49 – Insurance proceeds for a destroyed asset

McSharry Haulage Ltd is a haulage company with an accounting reference date of 31 October. On 21 September 2017 one of its lorries was involved in an accident and the insurance company wrote the lorry off. The driver of the lorry was not at fault and the company has claimed on the other driver's insurance. The insurance company has agreed to the claim and on 26 October 2017 McSharry Haulage received written confirmation from the insurance company that it will pay the company compensation for the lorry.

Paragraph 17.25 of FRS 102 says that where compensation from a third party is 'virtually certain' then the company can include such compensation in profit or loss. In this example the receipt of the insurance proceeds is virtually certain because McSharry Haulage has received written confirmation from the insurance company confirming it will pay out.

Paragraph 17.25 uses the term 'virtually certain' but this term is not defined in the Glossary to FRS 102. However, an entity would be able to account for such a transaction where they receive confirmation from the third party that the third party will reimburse the reporting entity.

Plan to sell

Any plans to sell an asset before the expected date of disposal will trigger a test for impairment.

Example 12.50 – Disposal triggering an impairment test

The management of Leah Lighting Co Ltd have decided to sell a group of machines five years before their expected disposal date on the basis that the machinery currently produces goods which are being withdrawn by the entity.

When an item of property, plant and equipment is going to be disposed of before the previously expected date of disposal, this will trigger the impairment test requirements in Section 27 *Impairment of Assets* and hence the assets' recoverable amount will have to be calculated in order to determine whether the asset is impaired and hence needs writing down to recoverable amount.

Derecognition of an item of property, plant and equipment

12.146 There are two means by which a company will derecognise an item of property, plant and equipment:

(1) the entity disposes of the asset; or

(2) there are no future expected economic benefits expected to arise from the asset's use or disposal.

Gains or losses on disposal are recognised as such in the profit and loss account (income statement) and are not recognised as revenue. The gain or loss on disposal is calculated as the difference between the sale proceeds and the net book value of the asset at the date of disposal.

Example 12.51 – Disposal of a machine

Patricia's Pantry Ltd has an accounting reference date of 30 September and on 20 June 2017 the company sells an industrial fridge which had a net book value as at 30 September 2016 of £5,000 for £3,500. The company's depreciation policy is to charge a full year's depreciation in the year of acquisition and none in the year of disposal, hence in the financial statements to 30 September 2017 (prior to the disposal being accounted for) the fridge had a net book value of £5,000.

A loss on disposal has arisen on the sale of this asset amounting to £1,500 which is the difference between the net book value at the date of acquisition (£5,000) and the proceeds from the disposal (£3,500). This £1,500 loss will be reported as a loss on disposal of fixed asset in Patricia's Pantry's profit and loss account.

Disclosures

12.147 The disclosures relating to items of property, plant and equipment may be as follows:

- When fixed assets have been measured at revalued amounts, a table should be presented showing:
  - — movements in the revaluation reserve in the reporting period, with an explanation of the tax treatment of the items therein; and
  - — the carrying amount in the balance sheet (statement of financial position) that would have been recognised had the fixed assets not been revalued.
- For fixed assets which have been revalued (excluding listed investments), disclose:
  - — the years in which the assets were valued and the revalued amounts; and
  - — for fixed assets that have been revalued during the reporting period, the names of the persons who valued them or particulars of their qualifications and the basis of valuation.
- The existence and carrying value of property, plant and equipment to which the entity has restricted title or that is pledged as security for the entity's borrowings.
- The amount of contractual commitments for the acquisition of property, plant and equipment.
- For each class of fixed assets (including heritage assets), a table showing:
  - — the purchase price or production cost or, where an alternative basis of measurement has been followed, the fair value or revalued amount at the beginning and end of the reporting period;

- — additions, disposals and transfers during the reporting period;
- — the accumulated depreciation and impairment losses at the beginning and end of the reporting period;
- — separately, depreciation and impairment losses recognised during the reporting period;
- — movements in accumulated depreciation and impairment losses in respect of additions, disposals and transfers during the reporting period; and
- — when an entity adopts a policy of capitalising borrowing costs, the amount capitalised during the reporting period.

- Where impairment losses are recognised, or reversed, disclose:
  - — the amount of impairment losses recognised in profit or loss during the period and the line item(s) in the statement of comprehensive income (or income statement/profit and loss account) in which those impairment losses are included; and
  - — the amount of reversals of impairment losses recognised in profit or loss during the period and the line item(s) in the statement of comprehensive income (or income statement/profit and loss account) in which those impairment losses are reversed.

INTANGIBLE ASSETS (EXCLUDING GOODWILL)

12.148 Section 18 *Intangible Assets other than Goodwill* deals with those assets held in a small company's balance sheet (statement of financial position) which do not possess a physical form. Goodwill is specifically excluded from the scope of Section 18 as this is dealt with in Section 19 *Business Combinations and Goodwill* and generally goodwill will only arise in a business combination (internally generated goodwill is not capitalised). Section 18 also does not apply to the following types of intangible assets:

- intangible assets held by the small company in the ordinary course of business (Section 13 *Inventories* and Section 23 *Revenue* apply);
- financial assets (Section 11 *Basic Financial Instruments* and Section 12 *Other Financial Instruments Issues* apply);
- heritage assets (Section 34 *Specialised Activities* applies); or
- mineral rights and mineral reserves (Section 34 applies).

Identifying an intangible asset

12.149 One of the main problems which is inherent with an intangible asset (and which is distinguishable from a tangible asset) is the fact that in a lot of cases they are subjective. An example using goodwill will be used to demonstrate the problem faced with many intangible assets.

Over the years many companies have included goodwill on their balance sheets (statements of financial position) as the directors believe the goodwill represents the value attached to their business (ie the 'reputable value' of the business). This was particularly prevalent in the early 2000's when the Chancellor announced that corporation tax for small businesses up to taxable profits of £10,000 was to be set at zero percent. When this announcement took place lots of sole traders rushed to become incorporated entities (companies) so as to take advantage of the reduced corporation tax rates. This involved the transfer of the sole trader/partnership's assets and liabilities into a limited company and in many cases goodwill was created on the newly formed company's balance sheet which was then subsequently credited to the directors' current accounts.

The problem with this approach is that the goodwill failed to meet the recognition criteria in accounting standards because:

- the goodwill would generally fail the test as to whether it is identifiable; and
- the goodwill would have no reliable cost attached to it because there would not be an active market in which to derive such a cost.

12.150 Under Section 18, an intangible asset is said to be an 'identifiable non-monetary asset without physical substance.' The key phrase in this definition is the word 'identifiable'. In order to be identifiable, an intangible asset must:

- be separable; in other words it must be capable of being separated or divided from the business and sold, transferred, licensed, rented or exchanged (either individually or in combination with a related contract, asset or liability); or
- arise from contractual or other legal rights, regardless of whether those rights are themselves transferable or separable from the business or from other rights and obligations.

Examples of intangible assets

12.151 Intangible assets can take the form of many items and some of the more common examples of an intangible asset include:

- Intangible assets arising from contract-related activities – for example franchises, service and supply contracts and licensing agreements.
- Goodwill arising through a business combination – the goodwill element will be the excess of the consideration over the net assets acquired (see **12.176** and Section 19 *Business Combinations and Goodwill*).
- Motion pictures or works of art.
- Customer list and relationships.

Example 12.52 – Taxi licence

Graham is a taxi driver in the UK. In order to operate his cab in the UK he needs to be issued with a licence for which he pays a fee.

The taxi licence would meet the recognition criteria as an intangible asset because the asset arises from legal rights. The fact that the licence cannot be separable from the underlying taxi business is not taken into account in this example because it can only be transferred to other taxi drivers.

Recognition of an intangible asset

12.152 The recognition criteria is more or less the same as the recognition criteria for a tangible asset. A small business should only recognise an intangible asset if, and only if:

(a) it is probable that the expected future economic benefits that are attributable to the asset will flow to the entity; and

(b) the cost or value of the asset can be measured reliably.

Focus

- As mentioned earlier in this section, many companies that incorporated to take advantage of the zero percent corporation tax rate in the early 2000's would have failed the test to recognise (internally generated) goodwill on their balance sheets because of (b) above.

12.153 In order to obtain an understanding of the 'future economic benefits', paragraph 18.5 of FRS 102 requires management to assess the probability of expected future economic benefits using reasonable and supportable assumptions that represent management's best estimate of the economic conditions that will exist over the useful life of the asset. The degree of certainty attached to the flow of future economic benefits associated with the asset should be done on the basis of the evidence available to management at the time of initial recognition and greater weight must be given to external evidence.

Focus

- The probability that expected future economic benefits will flow to the entity is always fulfilled for intangible assets which are separately acquired.

12.154 When a business combination takes place and the acquiring company acquires an intangible asset, the recognition criteria is often fulfilled because: (a) future economic benefits will be expected to flow to the entity, and (b) the fair value of the intangible asset(s) can be measured with sufficient reliability. The fair value of the intangible asset will be known at the date of acquisition in a business combination because the company being acquired will fair value its assets and liabilities as at the date of acquisition.

There is an exception to this rule, however. Intangible assets in a business combination that arise from legal or other contractual rights where there is no history or evidence of other exchange transactions for the same (or similar) asset are not recognised. This is because the fair value attributed to such assets would ultimately depend on immeasurable variables.

Internally generated intangible assets

12.155 One of the most common issues facing a small business is the recognition of internally generated intangible assets on the balance sheet (statement of financial position). In many cases a small business will not be subjected to audit and the financial statements produced as part of the compilation exercise will be based on information and explanations provided to the accountant by the client. Management often want to report internally generated intangible assets on the balance sheet as they believe that the asset has a value. FRS 102 would not generally allow an internally generated intangible asset to be capitalised on the balance sheet because in the majority of cases a reliable measure of cost would not be available.

Example 12.53 – Internally generated brand

A company manufactures washing powder under the brand name of EcoWash and the business has been in operation for 25 years. The directors of the company feel that this brand is widely recognised and have approached their accountant with a view to capitalising the brand as an intangible asset.

Paragraph 18.8C would prohibit the directors from capitalising the EcoWash brand on the balance sheet on the basis that the brand is internally generated and hence has no reliable measure of cost because no active market exists for that internally generated brand.

Focus

- The term 'active market' is defined in the Glossary to FRS 102 as:

  'A market in which all the following conditions exist:

  (a) the items traded in the market are homogeneous;

  (b) willing buyers and sellers can normally be found at any time; and

  (c) prices are available to the public.'[8]

8 FRS 102 Glossary **Active market**.

12.156 Section 18 at paragraph 18.8C outlines certain types of expenditure which must **not** be recognised as an intangible asset on a company's balance sheet and which must instead be written off to the profit and loss account as an expense:

- All internally generated brands (see the example above).
- Logos, publishing titles, customer lists and items which are similar in substance.
- Expenses incurred on start-up activities and will include:
  - — legal and secretarial costs;
  - — expenditure to open a new facility (including pre-opening expenditure); and
  - — expenditure incurred in starting new operations and/or launching new products or processes;
- Training costs and costs for training activities.
- Advertising and promotional expenses (the exception here would relate to advertising and promotional activities which meet the definition of inventories held for distribution at no or nominal consideration).
- Relocation or reorganisation of part of an entity.
- Internally generated goodwill.

Example 12.54 – Prepaid expense

Sam's Supermarket Ltd (Sam) is expanding its operations and has built another supermarket in the south of the country. Sam has an accounting reference date of 31 October and on 1 October 2016 it received an invoice from its local radio station for advertising services for the period 1 November 2016 to 31 October 2017 which it paid on 30 October 2016. The financial controller has posted the entire cost of this advertising service to advertising expenditure within profit or loss as she is aware that paragraph 18.8C prohibits advertising expenditure being recognised on the balance sheet.

While paragraph 18.8C does prohibit advertising and promotional expenditure being recognised as part of the cost of an intangible asset, it does not preclude the business from recognising a prepayment as an asset when payment for goods or services has been made in advance of the delivery of goods or rendering of services. Therefore the financial controller should recognise the cost as a prepayment for the year-ended 31 October 2016 rather than a cost.

Research and development costs

12.157 Research and development expenditure is also dealt with in Section 18 and where a small business deals with research and development projects, expenditure must be split into two distinct phases:

(1) the research phase; and

(2) the development phase.

Research phase

12.158 Reporting entities must write off all research expenditure to the profit and loss account when this expenditure is incurred – it cannot be capitalised. This is because in the research phase of an internal project, the entity will be unable to demonstrate whether the intangible asset will generate probable future economic benefits. Examples of research activities per Section 18 are:

- Activities aimed at obtaining new knowledge.
- The search for, evaluation and final selection of, applications of research findings and other knowledge.
- The search for alternatives for materials, devices, products, processes, systems or services.
- The formulation, design, evaluation and final selection of possible alternatives for new or improved material, devices, projects, processes, systems or services.

Development phase

12.159 Once the research phase has been completed, the internal project may well move on to the development phase. Development expenditure can be recognised as an intangible asset on the balance sheet (statement of financial position) if the company can demonstrate **all** of the following criteria:

- The technical feasibility of the project so that the intangible asset will be ready for use or for subsequent sale.
- The company's intention to complete the intangible asset and then use it or sell it.
- The company's ability to use or sell the intangible asset.
- How the intangible asset will generate probable future economic benefits for the company. The company must also be able to demonstrate the existence of a market for the output of the intangible asset, or the intangible itself. Where the intangible asset is to be used internally, the company must be able to demonstrate the usefulness of the intangible asset.

- The availability of adequate technical, financial and other resources in order that the company can complete the development so as to use or sell the intangible asset.
- The company's ability to reliably measure the expenditure attributable to the intangible asset during the development phase.

Example 12.55 – Development of a new accounts production software system

Cory's Computer Software Ltd is in the process of rapid expansion and is considering the development of a new accounts production software system for firms of accountants based in the Far East so as to enable them to become more efficient in the way that they prepare financial statements and undertake other assignments for their clients.

The project team involved have structured the project as follows:

(1) Identify the need for a new accounts production system.

(2) Commission research for any existing equivalent accounts production systems in that part of the world.

(3) Commission research for any existing equivalent accounts production systems that may have the features which Cory's Computers believe are currently only unique to themselves.

(4) Undertake research for any other competitors that may be involved in producing equivalent accounts production systems in the timescale which the project team have devised.

(5) Commission the design of the new accounts production system.

(6) Prepare a shortlist from step 5 above.

(7) Obtain a budget from the finance department for the new system and then compare this budget to the shortlist prepared in 6.

(8) Prepare a further shortlist of two possible alternatives based on feedback from the project management.

(9) Send the final two shortlisted candidates to the board of directors for their approval.

(10) Develop the new accounts production system.

(11) Undertake testing.

(12) Roll out the new system.

The recognition criteria at each stage should be considered in order to establish when capitalisation of development costs can commence and hence when the recognition criteria has been met. At stage 5 of the project, the technical feasibility of completing the project has been confirmed. At the end of stage 7 it has been established how the project will generate future economic benefits. At stage 10 all of the recognition criteria have been met and the board of directors have approved the project which in turn provides evidence of the company's intention to complete the project. The budgeted information will also provide evidence of the entity's ability to measure the expenditure.

> **Focus**
>
> - Capitalisation of development costs is an accounting policy choice. The small business can also choose to write off development costs to profit or loss if it so wishes. However, such policies must be applied consistently from one period to the next.

Initial measurement of an intangible asset

12.160 Once expenditure on an intangible asset qualifies for recognition on the balance sheet (statement of financial position), the business must first measure it at cost. The cost is the sum of expenditure incurred from the date when the intangible asset first meets the recognition criteria. In the case of a separate acquisition, cost will comprise:

- the purchase price, including import duties and non-refundable purchase taxes, after deduction of trade discounts and rebates; and
- any directly attributable costs of preparing the asset for its intended use.

Cost of internally generated intangible assets

12.161 Paragraph 18.10B says that the cost of internally generated intangible assets which meet the recognition criteria (ie development expenditure) are those costs necessary to create, produce and prepare the asset so as to be capable of operating in the manner intended by management. Examples of costs which are suggested to be 'directly attributable costs' are:

- costs of materials and services used or consumed in creating the intangible asset;
- the cost of employee benefits (as per Section 28 *Employee Benefits*) which arise from the creation of the intangible asset;
- fees incurred by the reporting entity to register a legal right; and
- amortisation of patents and licences which are used to create the intangible asset.

In addition to the above, a small business might also be able to capitalise interest on borrowings as part of the cost of an intangible asset. **12.284** below examines borrowing costs in more detail and such costs are dealt with in Section 25 *Borrowing Costs* of FRS 102.

12.162 An intangible asset may be acquired through means other than the direct exchange of cash or other assets.

Example 12.56 – Acquisition of an intangible asset in a business combination

North Ltd has just acquired 100% of the net assets of South Ltd in a business combination. As part of the business combination, North has acquired a group of patents.

The cost of the intangible assets acquired in the business combination (ie the patents) will be the patents' fair value at the date of acquisition.

Example 12.57 – Acquisition of an intangible asset by way of government grant

East Ltd has acquired a fishing licence to obtain fish in certain waters by way of a government grant.

The fishing licence will fall to be treated as an intangible asset and accounted for under Section 18 provisions. The cost of the licence is the fair value at the date the grant is received or receivable in accordance with Section 24 *Government Grants*.

Exchanges of assets

12.163 In some cases (which are expected to be uncommon for small businesses), a company might exchange an intangible asset for another non-monetary asset(s) or a combination of monetary and non-monetary assets. Where such exchanges of assets takes place, the intangible asset is measured at fair value on the date of exchange. There are two exceptions to this rule:

(1) Where the exchange transaction lacks commercial substance (see Example **12.46** above).

(2) Where the fair value of neither the asset received, nor the asset given up can be reliably measured.

Focus

- Where exception (2) applies, the asset's cost is the carrying amount of the asset given up.

Past expenditure on an intangible asset

12.164 Where previously incurred expenditure on an intangible asset was written off to the profit and loss account, it will not be possible to reclassify that expenditure as part of the cost of the intangible asset at a later date.

Example 12.58 – Previously written off expenditure

A company has recognised costs in relation to the development of an intangible asset in its profit and loss account in the previous financial year (for which the financial statements have been approved and lodged at Companies House and HM Revenue and Customs and distributed to shareholders). The directors have decided that these costs should now be recognised as part of the cost of the intangible asset to which they relate and are proposing to reallocate these expenses to intangible assets in the current year's financial statements by way of a prior period adjustment. The financial director is particularly keen to do this as the results for the current year are not as good as previously anticipated due to the incurrence of a large bad debt in the year.

The directors cannot reclassify previously recognised expenditure on an intangible asset as part of the cost of the intangible asset as paragraph 18.7 of FRS 102 will prohibit this treatment.

Measurement after initial recognition

12.165 After initial recognition at cost, there are two permissible methods for subsequent measurement:

(1) the cost model; and

(2) the revaluation model.

Cost model

12.166 Under the cost model, the reporting entity measures intangible assets at cost less any accumulated amortisation and impairment losses. In practice this is the most commonly applied method for two reasons – first, it is a straightforward method of measuring intangible assets and second it is less onerous than the revaluation model which can be restrictive due to the nature of intangible assets.

Revaluation model

12.167 Under the revaluation model, the intangible asset is carried at a revalued amount, which is the intangible asset's fair value at the date of revaluation less any subsequent accumulated amortisation and subsequent impairment losses. A key point to emphasise is that the revaluation model can only be used where there is an **active market**. An active market is a market in which the items traded are homogeneous; willing buyers can be found at any time and prices are available to the public. The revaluation model is only used after the asset has been initially recognised at cost as it is an accounting policy choice.

Focus

- The reality is that few intangible assets will be part of an active market and hence in practice the cost model will be the most frequently used method of measurement after initial recognition.

12.168 The revaluation model is restrictive, largely due to the inherent nature of intangible assets as well as the fact that an active market is unlikely to exist for the majority of intangible assets. Where a small company does qualify to use the revaluation model as a measurement method for its intangible asset(s), it cannot use the model for the revaluation of intangible assets which have not been previously recognised as assets. In addition, the revaluation model does not allow the initial recognition of intangible assets at amounts other than cost.

12.169 Once an intangible asset is being measured under the revaluation model, the entity must obtain fair values for the intangible asset with **sufficient regularity** so as to prevent the carrying value of the intangible asset differing materially from that which would otherwise be determined using fair value at the end of the reporting period. The term 'sufficient regularity' is not defined in FRS 102 and hence it will be a case of management exercising their professional judgement at each reporting date to establish whether the fair value is materially disparate from carrying value.

Example 12.59 – Fair value no longer available

Spring Ltd has an intangible asset on its balance sheet which is being measured under the revaluation model. Its year-end is 31 January 2017 and on 31 January 2016 the fair value of this intangible asset was £8,000. However, during the year it became apparent that the fair value could no longer be determined due to factors beyond the control of the management of the entity. The financial controller is unsure how to arrive at a fair value in the absence of a reliable measure and has left the carrying value at £8,000.

The financial controller is correct to leave the carrying value at £8,000. This is because paragraph 18.18E says that where a reporting entity carries an intangible asset under the revaluation model and a reliable measure of fair value can no longer be determined by reference to an active market, the carrying amount of the intangible asset is to be the revalued amount at the date of the last revaluation by reference to the active market, less any subsequent accumulated amortisation and any subsequent impairment losses.

Gains and losses on revaluation of an intangible asset

12.170 Any revaluation gains in respect of an intangible asset will be recognised in other comprehensive and accumulated in equity (under the heading of 'revaluation surplus'). Gains can be recognised in profit or loss, but only to the extent that the gain reverses a revaluation decrease of the same asset previously recognised in profit or loss.

Revaluation losses are recognised in other comprehensive income to the extent of any previously recognised gains and accumulated in equity. Where losses exceed the accumulated revaluation gains, further losses are taken to the profit and loss account.

Amortisation

12.171 All intangible assets which fall under the scope of Section 18 are considered to have finite useful lives. This is in contrast to previous UK GAAP where an intangible asset could have had an indefinite useful life and hence the company would have tested the intangible asset annually for impairment. This is no longer the case under FRS 102 principles and therefore where a reporting entity has previously not amortised intangible assets on the grounds that management considered them to have indefinite useful lives, the accounting practice will have to be changed.

Focus

- Where management are unable to make a reliable estimate of the useful life of an intangible asset, the useful economic life will not exceed ten years. This was increased from five years in the previous version of FRS 102 and the FRSSE (effective January 2015) following the transposition of the EU Accounting Directive into company law.

12.172 The depreciable amount of the intangible asset will be allocated to the profit and loss account on a systematic basis over the intangible asset's useful life and amortisation must commence when the intangible asset is available for use (in other words, when it is in the location and condition necessary for it to be usable in the manner intended by management). Conversely, amortisation must cease when the intangible asset is derecognised. These principles are much the same as depreciation for a tangible fixed asset.

Section 18 of FRS 102 uses the straight-line method of amortisation as the benchmark amortisation method, unless the small business can demonstrate that an alternative amortisation method accurately reflects the entity's consumption of the intangible asset.

Example 12.60 – Intangible asset with a residual value

Autumn Ltd acquires an intangible asset on 1 January 2016. Management have calculated the depreciable amount by assuming a residual value of £5,000 (ie cost less £5,000 = depreciable amount). There is no commitment by a third party to acquire the intangible asset at the end of its useful economic life, nor is there an active market available for the asset.

FRS 102 at paragraph 18.23 assumes a residual value for an intangible asset as being **zero**, unless:

- there is a commitment by a third party to purchase the asset at the end of its useful life; or
- there is an active market for the asset, and:
  - residual value can be determined by reference to that market; and
  - it is probable that such a market will exist at the end of the asset's useful life.

Therefore, management should assume a residual value of zero when calculating the depreciable amount of the intangible asset for amortisation purposes.

Review of amortisation period and method

12.173 If the intangible asset is showing signs of impairment since the most recent annual reporting date, the company must review previous estimates of residual value and the asset's useful economic life. Where current expectations differ, management should amend the residual value, amortisation method or useful economic life as appropriate. Where such changes are made they are considered to be changes in accounting estimate and are hence applied prospectively (ie no prior period adjustment is made as it is not a change in accounting policy).

Impairment

12.174 As with all other types of assets, intangible assets must also be reviewed at the end of each reporting period to assess whether there are indicators that the asset(s) is/are impaired. Section 27 *Impairment of Assets* (see **12.307** below) examines when and how the business must review the carrying amount of its assets and how recoverable amount is determined. An impairment loss is recognised when recoverable amount is lower than carrying value and the impairment loss is recognised in profit or loss.

Disclosures

12.175 The disclosures relating to intangible assets may be as follows:

- An explanation of the period over which intangible assets are written off.
- When development costs are capitalised as an accounting policy choice in accordance with paragraph 18.8H and the entity has determined that the carrying amount of those intangible assets is not a realised loss, the reasons for showing development costs as an asset and that the carrying amount is not to be treated as a realised loss.
- When intangible assets are measured at revaluation, a table showing:
  - movements in the revaluation reserve in the reporting period, with an explanation of the tax treatment of the items therein;
  - the carrying amount in the balance sheet (statement of financial position) that would have been recognised if the intangible assets had not been revalued;
  - the years in which the assets were valued and the revalued amounts; and
  - the names of the persons who valued them or particulars of their qualifications and the basis of the valuation.
- The existence and carrying amounts of any intangible assets to which the entity has restricted title or that are pledged as security for liabilities.
- The amount of any contractual commitments for the acquisition of intangible assets.
- The gross carrying amount and any accumulated amortisation (aggregated with accumulated impairment losses) at the beginning and end of the reporting period.
- A reconciliation of the carrying amount at the beginning and end of the reporting period showing separately:
  - additions, indicating separately those from internal development and those acquired separately;
  - disposals;
  - acquisitions through business combinations;
  - revaluations;
  - amortisation;
  - impairment losses; and
  - other changes.

  This reconciliation does not need to be presented for prior periods.
- When the entity has a policy of capitalising borrowing costs in respect of intangible assets, the amount capitalised during the reporting period.

BUSINESS COMBINATIONS AND GOODWILL

12.176 Business combinations and goodwill are dealt with in Section 19 *Business Combinations and Goodwill* and for the purposes of Section 19, a business combination is defined in the Glossary to FRS 102 as:

> 'The bringing together of separate entities or **businesses** into one reporting entity.'[9]

Section 19 gives guidance on how to identify an acquirer in a business combination, how an entity should measure the cost of the business combination and allocate that cost to:

- the assets acquired; and
- the liabilities and provisions for contingent liabilities assumed.

Goodwill is dealt with in Section 19 (as opposed to Section 18 *Intangible Assets other than Goodwill*) as it is assumed for accounting purposes that goodwill arises in a business combination.

There are three types of business which are not dealt with in Section 19:

- joint ventures (see Section 15 *Investments in Joint Ventures* and see **12.104** above);
- acquisition of a group of assets which does not give rise to a business; and
- pubic benefit entity combinations (see Section 34 *Specialised Activities* and see **12.406** below).

Defining a business combination

12.177 A business combination occurs when two separate businesses come together to form one reporting entity. Ordinarily in a business combination one party will be the acquirer and the target will be the acquiree and the acquirer will always obtain control over the acquiree. The date of acquisition is the date on which the acquirer obtains control of the acquiree and this date may be a different date than the date on which the sale completes so care must be taken in this respect.

There are a variety of means by which a business combination is paid for – the acquirer may issue shares or pay cash or obtain control through consideration which comprises a mix of shares and cash (or other assets). In addition, a business combination may involve the creation of a new entity to control the combining entities (eg a holding company) or a restructuring exercise may take place once the business combination has completed.

9 FRS 102 Glossary **Business Combinations**.

Focus

- The majority of this section relates to consolidated financial statements and whilst it is acknowledged that few small groups prepare consolidated financial statements due to them being exempt from the requirement, some small groups do prepare such consolidated financial statements and hence issues relating to the consolidated financial statements have been included in this section for completeness. Where an acquisition takes place and the group is small and does not prepare consolidated financial statements, the entries in the acquiring company's books are straightforward:

DR cost of investment (fixed asset)	X
CR cash at bank	(X)

Example 12.61 – Purchase of shares

Company A Ltd acquires the business of Company B Ltd in a share purchase (ie it purchases 100% of B's shares for cash). This is the first time that Company A has acquired another business.

In the individual financial statements, Company A will account for its investment in B at cost. If the small group chooses to prepare group financial statements (it will not be mandated to prepare such consolidated accounts, but can if it so wishes), the excess of the price paid for the shares over the fair value of the net assets acquired is recognised as goodwill. In other words, the cost of the investment in B is removed in the consolidated financial statements and replaced by goodwill.

Example 12.62 – Purchase of assets

Company A Ltd acquires the business of Company B Ltd through the transferring of B's assets and liabilities to A. This is the first time that Company A has acquired another business.

The fair value of B's individual assets less liabilities will be combined with those of A in A's financial statements. The excess of the purchase consideration over the fair value of B's net assets will be reflected as goodwill. Because the business combination is a net asset purchase the issue of consolidated financial statements (whether required or desired) becomes irrelevant.

Purchase method of accounting

12.178 When a business combination takes place it is accounted for using the 'purchase method' of accounting. The purchase method of accounting used to be referred to as the 'acquisition method' of accounting in previous UK GAAP and works in a similar manner. There are two exceptions where the purchase method is not to be used:

- in a group reconstruction using the merger method of accounting (as the merger method will use book values rather than fair values); and
- in a public benefit entity combination which are, in substance, a gift or that are a merger (such combinations will be accounted for under the provisions in Section 34 *Specialised Activities*).

12.179 There are three steps involved in applying the purchase method:

(1) identify an acquirer;

(2) measure the cost of the business combination; and

(3) at the date of acquisition, allocate the cost of the business combination to the assets acquired and the liabilities (and provisions for contingent liabilities) assumed.

Step 1: identify an acquirer

12.180 When two companies enter into a business combination, the acquirer is the entity which obtains control of the other combining business(es). The term 'control' is pivotal in identifying an acquirer; this is because control is the power to govern the financial and operating policies of the business being acquired. For small group purposes, control is usually achieved through the acquiring company obtaining more than 50% of the voting rights in the target company and hence control will then be presumed to exist unless it can be clearly demonstrated otherwise.

The 50% numeric benchmark is not necessarily the only test for a control relationship; a holding of less than 50% can still lead to a control relationship being triggered and this may be because the acquirer (the parent) has:

- the power over more than 50% of the voting rights by virtue of agreement with the other investors;
- the power to govern the financial and operating policies of the entity under statute or agreement;
- the power to appoint or remove the majority of the members of the board of directors; or
- the power to cast the majority of the votes at the meetings of the board of directors.

Example 12.63 – Identification of the acquirer

Company A Ltd acquires 60% of the voting rights in Company B Ltd.

Company C Ltd acquires 40% of the voting rights in Company D Ltd but has the power to appoint and remove the majority of the board.

Company A Ltd has obtained control of Company B because it has obtained a majority ownership interest in the voting rights of Company B Ltd.

Company C has only obtained a 40% ownership interest in the voting rights of Company D and on the face of it, numerically, it does not have control. However, because Company C has the power to appoint or remove the majority of the board of directors it has assumed control and hence does have the power to govern the financial and operating policies of Company D.

As can be seen from the above examples, a numeric benchmark is not necessarily an indicator that control has, or has not, been obtained. For the majority of small business combinations (resulting in a small group being created) control will usually be evident through the ownership interest of the parent; but other considerations need to be brought into account where it is not immediately clear.

12.181 Where it is not immediately clear which party is the acquirer in a business combination, FRS 102 offers some helpful indicators of who the acquirer in a business combination will be as follows:

- Where the fair value of one of the combining companies is significantly higher than that of the other combining company, the one with the greater fair value is likely to be the acquirer.
- Where the business combination occurs through an exchange of voting rights (equity instruments) for cash or other assets, the party which gives up cash or other assets is likely to be the acquirer.
- When the business combination results in the management of one of the companies being able to dominate the selection of the management team of the acquiring company, the company whose management is able to dominate the other company's management is likely to be the acquirer.

Step 2: measure the cost of the business combination

12.182 Once an acquirer has been identified and it is clear that a business combination under the purchase method of accounting has taken place, the next step is to measure the cost of the business combination. The acquirer (ie the purchasing company) measures the cost of the business combination as the total of:

- the fair values at the date of acquisition of the target's assets, liabilities incurred or assumed and equity instruments issued by the acquirer in exchange for control of the target; and
- any incremental costs which are attributable to the business combination.

Focus

- Incremental costs associated with the business combination are those costs which could have been avoided by the acquiring company had the business combination not taken place – such as legal fees or due diligence fees.

Example 12.64 – Cost of a business combination

On 30 September 2018, Irene's Interiors Ltd (Irene) acquired the entire share capital of Spike's Soft Furnishings Ltd (Spike) for a consideration of 1,000 shares in Irene and £65,000 in cash. This is the first time that Irene has acquired a business and has no other investments. The following costs were incurred in respect of the business combination:

- £1,250 costs in respect of the share issue; and
- £4,500 in respect of legal fees.

The cost of the business combination will not include the £1,250 costs in respect of the share issue – these are instead accounted for as a deduction from equity to comply with paragraph 22.9 of FRS 102 (this is because transactions costs of an equity transaction is to be deducted from equity, net of any related income tax benefit).

The £4,500 costs in respect of legal fees will be included in the cost of the business combination.

12.183 For the majority of small business combinations, control is likely to be achieved in one go at the date of acquisition. However, such transactions may involve control being achieved in stages (sometimes referred to as 'step acquisitions' or 'piecemeal acquisitions'). Where such acquisitions take place the cost of the business combination is the total of the fair values of the assets given, liabilities assumed and equity instruments issued by the acquirer at the date of each transaction in the series.

12.184 A contract to acquire a business may make provision for an adjustment to be made to the cost of the business combination and this adjustment may be dependent upon future events occurring, or not occurring, as the case might be. Where such provisions are included, the acquirer must include the estimated amount of the adjustment in the cost of the combination at the date of acquisition where this adjustment is probable and can be measured reliably.

Example 12.65 – Contingent consideration

On 30 September 2018, Irene's Interiors Ltd (Irene) acquired the entire share capital of Spike's Soft Furnishings Ltd (Spike) for £65,000 in cash and incurred legal fees of £4,500 in respect of the acquisition. The terms of the sale contract make provision for additional consideration of £25,000 to be paid if the profits of Spike achieve an agreed benchmark. Budgets have been prepared which have been subjected to due diligence and these suggest that the profit targets will be met.

Provided there is reasonable evidence to support the estimated contingent consideration, this amount will be capitalised as part of the cost of the business combination with the corresponding credit entry going to provisions for liabilities.

The contingent consideration will need reviewing on an annual basis in light of the latest available information at the disposal of the management and where it is probable that the amount of contingent consideration will reduce, the cost of the business combination and associated provision for liability should be adjusted accordingly. Conversely, further consideration should be provided if the amount payable is probable and can be measured reliably.

Step 3: allocate the cost of the business combination

12.185 At the date of acquisition, the acquirer must allocate the cost of a business combination so as to recognise the acquiree's identifiable assets and liabilities (together with a provision for those contingent liabilities) at their fair values at that date. Any resulting difference between the cost of the business combination and the ownership interest in the identifiable assets, liabilities and provisions for contingent liabilities is goodwill and this can be either positive or negative (see the section *Goodwill* below).

In respect of assets and liabilities there are some additional considerations which small companies need to be aware of where Section 19 is concerned:

- Assets, other than intangible assets, can only be recognised at the date of acquisition if it is probable that any future economic benefits will flow to the acquiring company and fair value can be reliably measured.
- For a liability (not a contingent liability) to be recognised at the date of acquisition, it is probable that an outflow of resources will be required to settle the obligation and the liability's fair value can be measured reliably.
- Where an intangible asset or a contingent liability is concerned, it should only be recognised if its fair value can be measured reliably.

Focus

- For deferred tax assets or liabilities in a business combination at the date of acquisition, these should be accounted for in accordance with Section 29 *Income Tax* (see **12.346** below).

12.186 A company that has been acquired as part of a business combination may have share-based payment arrangements in place with its employees. In this respect the acquiring company will account for such share-based payment transactions in accordance with Section 26 *Share-based Payment* (see **12.290** below). Other employee benefit arrangements (excluding share-based payment arrangements) should be accounted for in accordance with Section 28 *Employee Benefits* (see **12.328** below).

Incomplete business combinations

12.187 In some business combinations the entire transaction may not be fully complete at the end of the reporting period in which the business combination takes place. In such instances the acquiring company must recognise provisional amounts for the items for which the accounting is not complete. The amounts will be a best estimate and will be retrospectively adjusted within 12 months after the acquisition date (in other words the assets and liabilities will be adjusted to reflect the values as if they took place at the date of acquisition) so as to reflect the new information which the acquiring company has obtained.

After 12 months has elapsed since the date of acquisition any adjustments to the initial accounting for the acquisition are to be recognised only to correct a material error. Corrections of such errors will be made having regard to the provisions in Section 10 *Accounting Policies, Estimates and Errors* (see **12.3** above).

Other accounting aspects of a business combination

12.188 Once the cost of the business combination has been allocated there are certain other aspects which need to be considered when it comes to accounting for the acquired business.

Fair value adjustments

12.189 The application of the purchase method of accounting requires the target company to fair value the assets and liabilities (including provisions for contingent liabilities) at the date of acquisition. These fair values will often differ from book values in the individual financial statements of the target company. The acquirer's statement of comprehensive income/income statement must include the acquiree's profits or losses subsequent to the date of acquisition by including income and expense which is based on the cost of the business combination to the acquirer.

Example 12.66 – Depreciation expense

Summer Ltd acquires 80% of the net assets of Winter Ltd. The date of acquisition was 2 January 2017 (which is the date when control passed to Summer Ltd). On that date the fair value of Winter's depreciable assets was £50,000. Book values of the same assets are £35,000.

The depreciation expense to be included in the consolidated financial statements of the group will be based on the fair values of the depreciable assets (ie £50,000) which is the cost to Summer Ltd.

Restructuring costs

12.190 When a company is bought out it is often the case that the acquiring company will restructure the business so it has strategic fit. Unfortunately this may involve the loss of jobs through redundancy or the discontinuation of certain parts of the business.

The acquirer can recognise a liability for terminating or reducing the activities of the acquiree as part of the allocating the cost of the business combination only to the extent that the acquiree has an existing liability for restructuring at the date of acquisition. Where such a liability exists then it is accounted for under the provisions in Section 21 *Provisions and Contingencies* (see **12.236** below).

Provision for future losses/costs

12.191 The acquiring company will not be able to recognise any provision for future losses or additional costs to be incurred as a result of the business combination when allocating the cost of the combination. This is because such costs must be recognised in profit or loss as and when they are incurred rather than brought forward to the date of acquisition.

Contingent liabilities

12.192 A contingent liability is a liability which is of uncertain timing or amount. Under the provisions of Section 21 *Provisions and Contingencies*, it is not possible to recognise a contingent liability because of this uncertainty; instead such liabilities are disclosed where they are considered to be material to the financial statements.

When a business combination takes place, paragraph 19.15(c) requires the acquirer to separately recognise a provision for a contingent liability of the acquiree only where a reliable measure of fair value of the contingent liability can be obtained. Where it is not possible to obtain a reliable measure of fair value then there will be a resulting effect on the amount which the acquiring company recognises as goodwill in the consolidated financial statements (where these are prepared). This will essentially increase the value of the goodwill in the consolidated accounts because the net assets acquired will be higher. Where 'negative' goodwill has arisen then the amount of negative goodwill will inherently be lower because it will be based on a reduced overall liabilities figure.

Subsequent measurement of contingent liabilities

12.193 After initial recognition of provisions for contingent liabilities, such liabilities are measured separately at the *higher* of:

- the amount which would have been recognised in accordance with Section 21; and
- the amount initially recognised *less* amounts previously recognised as revenue in accordance with Section 23 *Revenue*.

Goodwill

12.194 Goodwill has often been a subjective topic in the world of financial reporting and some companies have, over the years, recognised goodwill on their balances sheets when, in fact, it would have failed the recognition criteria laid down in accounting standards. For the purposes of FRS 102, goodwill is said to arise in a business combination when the fair value of the net assets and liabilities acquired and assumed are of a different value to the amount paid by the acquiring company.

Example 12.67 – Goodwill on acquisition

Heyes Ltd acquires 80% of the net assets of Moss Ltd on 1 January 2016 for £75,000. The group qualifies as small (even after the acquisition of Moss Ltd) but it has chosen to prepare group financial statements. At the date of acquisition, the net assets of Moss Ltd were as follows:

	£
Share capital	1,000
Share premium	1,500
Revaluation reserve	15,000
Profit and loss account	65,000
	82,500

Goodwill arising on the acquisition of Moss Ltd can be calculated as follows:

	£	£
Cost of investment in Moss		75,000
Less net assets acquired (80%)		
Share capital	800	
Share premium	1,200	
Revaluation reserve	12,000	
Profit and loss account	52,000	
		(66,000)
Goodwill on acquisition		9,000

The individual financial statements of Heyes Ltd will show the cost of the investment within fixed assets at £75,000. Where the group financial statements are concerned, the cost of the investment will be replaced by goodwill (as the cost of the investment will form part of the goodwill calculation).

Amortisation of goodwill

12.195 After initial recognition at cost, goodwill is then amortised over its estimated useful life.

> **Focus**
>
> - Where companies have previously not amortised their goodwill on the grounds that the directors consider it to have an indefinite useful life, accounting practices will need to be changed on transition to FRS 102 with reduced disclosures as it is no longer possible to regard goodwill as having an indefinite useful life.

Goodwill amortisation is usually amortised on a straight-line basis; however, the small group may choose to amortise goodwill using a different method where this is more representative of the pattern of consumption by the group.

A notable difference between the previous FRSSE (effective January 2015) and FRS 102 with reduced disclosures is the length of time over which goodwill can be amortised where management cannot place a reliable estimate on the useful economic life of the goodwill. Under the FRSSE (effective April 2008) there was a rebuttable presumption that the useful economic life of goodwill was no longer than 20 years. This useful economic life presumption was reduced to five years in the FRSSE (effective January 2015); but it has subsequently been increased to a maximum of ten years in FRS 102 for small companies following the transposition of the EU Accounting Directive into the Companies Act 2006 and hence **where management cannot establish a reliable estimate** of the useful life of goodwill it should be amortised over a period not exceeding ten years.

Focus

- The reduction in the presumed useful life of goodwill caused an element of confusion within the profession. The Financial Reporting Council are keen to emphasise that it will only be in exceptional circumstances that a small group will experience accelerated write-downs of goodwill on transition to FRS 102 with reduced disclosures. This is because the rules in previous UK GAAP would have required management to assess the carrying values of goodwill (and associated amortisation methods) to identify whether the carrying amount exceeded recoverable amount and where this was the case, the goodwill should have been written down to recoverable amount and this revised balance amortised over the useful economic life.

Negative goodwill

12.196 In the majority of cases it is likely that a small company acquiring another small company will pay more than the fair value of the net assets acquired in the combination, resulting in positive goodwill being recognised in the consolidated financial statements (where these are prepared). However, this is not always the case and in some situations, a bargain purchase might take place (ie where the acquiring company pays less than the fair value of the net assets acquired). This can often take place in, say, a distressed sale where a company is in financial distress and the shareholders agree to sell the company to an acquiring company at less than the fair value of the assets and liabilities.

Where negative goodwill arises, care must be taken because it might not always be the case that the sale is a distressed sale and Section 19.24 of FRS 102 outlines three procedures to take where negative goodwill arises:

- Where negative goodwill arises, the acquiring company must reassess the identification and measurement of the target's assets, liabilities and provisions for contingent liabilities as well as reassessing the measurement of cost of the combination.
- After such reassessment has taken place, and provided no issues have been found, any resulting negative goodwill is recognised on the face of the consolidated balance sheet (where prepared) at the date of acquisition, immediately below goodwill and then followed by a subtotal of the net amount of goodwill and the excess.
- The acquirer will then recognise the excess up to the fair value of non-monetary assets acquired in the business combination in the profit and loss account in the periods that the non-monetary assets are recovered. Any excess over and above the fair value of non-monetary assets acquired are recognised in profit or loss in the periods which are expected to benefit.

Group reconstructions and merger accounting

12.197 The use of merger accounting is rare (especially for small groups) and the eligibility criteria for merger accounting is very restrictive. Merger accounting can only be used in a group reconstruction where:

- it is not prohibited by the Companies Act 2006 or other legislation;
- the ultimate equity holders remain unchanged and the rights of those equity holders (relative to the others) remain unchanged; and
- no non-controlling (minority) interests in the net assets of the group are affected by the reconstruction.

12.198 Merger accounting is fundamentally different than the purchase method of accounting for an acquisition. This is because in merger accounting book values, rather than fair values, are used and hence no adjustment to fair value is needed (although adjustments to align accounting policies in the combining entities might be needed).

When applying merger accounting, the results and the cash flows of all the combining entities are brought into the financial statements of the newly combined entity **from the beginning of the financial year in which the merger took place**. The comparative financial statements are also restated by including the total comprehensive income for all the combining entities for the previous reported period as well as their balance sheets, making any necessary adjustments to reflect the alignment of accounting policies.

Focus

- If any difference arises between the nominal value of the shares issued plus the fair value of any additional consideration given and the nominal value of the shares received in exchange, it is shown as a movement on other reserves in the consolidated financial statements. Existing balances on the share premium account or capital redemption reserve of the new subsidiary are brought into account by being shown as a movement on reserves and reported through the statement of changes in equity. Merger expenses are not included as part of this adjustment and are expensed to profit or loss of the combined entity at the effective date of the group reconstruction.

Disclosures

12.199 The disclosures relating to business combinations and goodwill (according to Section 1A of FRS 102 relevant to Section 19) may be as follows:

- An explanation of the period over which goodwill is being written off. Where this exceeds ten years, supporting reasons for the amortisation period should be disclosed.

For consolidated financial statements, the disclosures below are the disclosures required by Section 19 and should be considered for small groups that choose to prepare consolidated financial statements:

For business combinations that have occurred during the reporting period

12.200

- The names and descriptions of the combining businesses.
- The date of acquisition.
- The value (in percentage terms) of voting rights acquired in the combination.
- The cost of the combination and information about the composition of cost (eg shares and cash).
- The amounts recognised as the date of acquisition for each class of the acquiree's assets, liabilities and contingent liabilities (including goodwill).
- The useful life of goodwill (where this exceeds ten years, supporting reasons for this).
- The periods in which any negative goodwill is to be recognised in profit or loss.

For all business combinations

12.201

- A reconciliation of the carrying amount of goodwill at the beginning and end of the reporting period, showing separately:
  - — changes arising from new business combinations;
  - — amortisation;
  - — impairment losses recognised;
  - — disposals of previously acquired businesses; and
  - — other changes.

The above reconciliation does not need to be presented for prior periods.

In respect of negative goodwill, the acquirer should disclose:

- The carrying amount of the negative goodwill at the beginning and end of the reporting period, showing separately:
  - — changes arising as a result of new business combinations;
  - — amounts recognised in profit or loss;

— disposals of previously acquired businesses; and
— other changes.

This reconciliation does not need to be presented for prior periods.

LEASES

12.202 Leases are dealt with in Section 20 *Leases* in FRS 102. In general the accounting for leases has not changed from the previous FRSSE (effective January 2015). However, leases have generally been a problem for the profession as a whole because of their subjective nature and the ability to manipulate leasing transactions so as to achieve a desired outcome (commonly referred to as 'off-balance sheet finance').

The scope of Section 20 applies to all leases (both lessee and lessor), but does not apply to:

- leases which are entered into to explore for minerals, oil, natural gas and similar non-regenerative resources (see Section 34 *Specialised Activities*);
- licensing agreements relating to items such as motion picture films, video recordings, plays, manuscripts, patents and copyrights (see Section 18 *Intangible Assets other than Goodwill*);
- measurement of investment property held by lessees and measurement of investment property provided by lessors under an operating lease (see Section 16 *Investment Property*);
- measurement of biological assets which are held by lessees under a finance lease and measurement of biological assets which are provided by lessors under an operating lease (see Section 34); and
- leases which could lead to a loss to the lessor or the lessee as a result of contractual terms which are not typical (see paragraph 12.3(f) of FRS 102).

Section 20 also applies to leasing agreements which transfer the right to use the asset which is subjected to the lease regardless of the fact that the lessor may be called upon to provide services to maintain the asset; however, the section does not apply to arrangements which are contracts for services which do not transfer the right to use assets from one contracting party to the other.

In some instances it may not be explicit that an arrangement between contracting parties does, in fact, contain a lease and hence an assessment is needed as to whether:

- fulfilment of the arrangement is dependent on the use of a specific asset(s); this will be the case where, for example, the supplier owns or leases a single asset with which to fulfil the obligation and it is not economically feasible, or practicable, for the supplier to perform its obligation through the use of alternative assets; and

- the arrangement which the parties have entered into specifies a right to use the asset; this will be the case where the arrangement coveys to the purchaser the right to control the use of the underlying asset.

Lease classification

12.203 Section 20 still determines the classification of a lease in much the same way as the previous FRSSE (effective January 2015). The overarching principle in the determination of whether a lease is a financing or operating lease is considered in light of the substance of the arrangement – in other words looking at who bears the risks and rewards of ownership of the asset which is subject to the lease.

12.204 When, substantially, all the risks and rewards incidental to ownership of the asset are transferred from the lessor to the lessee, this will give rise to a finance lease. In such cases the asset subjected to the lease will appear on the lessee's balance sheet (statement of financial position) together with a corresponding finance lease creditor. Where the risks and rewards of ownership remain with the lessor, the lease is classified as an operating lease and rentals are charged to profit or loss as incurred. There is no change from the accounting treatment in this respect which took place under previous UK GAAP under either the FRSSE (effective January 2015) or SSAP 21 *Accounting for leases and hire purchase contracts.*

Finance lease classification under Section 20

12.205 The FRSSE (effective January 2015) referred to a 90% 'bright line' test in the Glossary which said that if the present value of the minimum lease payments which the lessee is required to make equated to 90% or more of the fair value of the leased asset then the lease is to be classified as a finance lease. SSAP 21 provided this 90% test in the guidance notes.

Section 20 of FRS 102 does not contain any 90% benchmark which many accountants have relied upon over the years to decipher whether a lease is a finance lease. Instead, the section offers five examples of situations which individually, or in combination, would normally lead to a lease being classified as a finance lease. It also offers a further three indicators of situations which, individually or in combination, could also lead to a lease falling to be classified as a finance lease.

The first five indicators that a lease is a finance lease are:

- Ownership of the asset is transferred to the lessee at the end of the lease term.
- There is an option which allows the lessee to acquire the asset at a price which is expected to be sufficiently lower than the fair value of the asset

at the date on which the option becomes exercisable and it is expected to be reasonably certain, at the inception of the lease, that this option will be exercised by the lessee.

- The term of the lease is for the major part of the asset's economic life even if title is not transferred to the lessee at the end of the lease term.
- At the start of the lease the present value of the minimum lease payments amounts to substantially all of the fair value of the leased asset.
- The assets in the lease are of such a specialised nature that only the lessee can use them without major modifications having to be made.

> **Focus**
>
> - Bullet point four is broadly similar to the 90% benchmark test which was found in previous UK GAAP – except that the 90% numeric benchmark is replaced by the term 'substantially all'. This is going to require more judgement on the part of the accountant.

The three additional indicators of situations which could also lead to classification of a lease being a finance lease are as follows:

- If the lessee has the option to cancel the lease, the lessor's losses associated with the cancellation are borne by the lessee.
- Gains or losses which arise from the fluctuation in the residual value of the leased asset accrue to the lessee (for example in the form of a rent rebate which is equivalent to most of the sales proceeds at the end of the lease).
- The lessee may continue to lease the asset for a secondary period at a rent which is much lower than market rent (a 'peppercorn' rent).

12.206 It is important to emphasise that the eight indicators above are not exhaustive and this is reflected in the wording in paragraph 20.7 of FRS 102. The key to determining the correct classification will all depend on whether the risks and rewards of ownership have transferred to the lessee or remain with the lessor at the inception of the lease. Paragraph 20.8 says that lease classification is made at the start of the lease and is not changed during the lease term (ie changed from financing to operating or vice versa) unless the lessee and the lessor agree to a change in the provisions of the lease, rather than simply renewing the lease. Where such provisions are changed the lease classification is the re-evaluated.

Operating lease classification

12.207 The Glossary to FRS 102 says that an operating lease is a lease whereby the risks and rewards of ownership of the asset do not pass substantially to the lessee.

Example 12.68 – Lease where lessee does not have risks and rewards

Bentley Ltd (Bentley) enters into a lease with Jaguar Ltd to lease a machine for use in its production facilities. The terms of the lease make provision for ownership of the asset to transfer to Bentley for a variable payment which is equal to the fair value of the lease at the date the lease expires.

This is not a situation where 'gains or losses from the fluctuation of the leased asset's residual value accrue to the lessee' and hence the risks and rewards have not substantially passed to Bentley. The lease cannot, therefore, be classed as a finance lease.

Care needs to be taken when dealing with the lease classification criteria because the standards point to classification as finance leases rather than operating leases to combat the issue of off-balance sheet finance.

When a lease is genuinely an operating lease the asset is not recognised on the balance sheet (statement of financial position); instead the lease rentals are charged to the profit and loss account (income statement) as incurred.

Accounting for a finance lease: lessees

12.208 Once classification as a finance lease has been established by the lessee, the asset subjected to the lease is brought onto the balance sheet (statement of financial position) at fair value (or present value of the minimum lease payments determined at the inception of the lease, if this value is lower) with a corresponding lease creditor.

Focus

- The present value of the minimum lease payments must be calculated using the interest rate implicit in the lease and where the lessee is unable to determine this rate, the lessee's incremental borrowing rate should be used instead.

The term 'minimum lease payments' is defined in the Glossary to FRS 102 and for a lessee should include:

- the payments over the lease term which the lessee is, or can, be required to make (excluding contingent rentals);
- costs for services and taxes to be paid and reimbursed to the lessor; and
- any amounts guaranteed by the lessee or by a party related to the lessee.

> **Focus**
>
> - Any initial costs which are attributable to arranging and negotiating the lease should be included in the amount recognised as an asset (for example legal fees).

The term 'interest rate implicit in the lease' is defined in the Glossary to FRS 102 as:

> 'The discount rate that, at the inception of the lease, causes the aggregate present value of:
>
> (a) the minimum lease payments; and
>
> (b) the unguaranteed residual value, to be equal to the sum of:
>
> (i) the fair value of the leased asset; and
>
> (ii) any initial direct costs of the lessor.'[10]

12.209 In a finance lease the leased asset is shown as an item of property, plant and equipment in the lessee's balance sheet (statement of financial position) with a corresponding lease creditor. The profit and loss account is charged with the finance costs (using the interest rate implicit in the lease or the lessee's incremental borrowing rate) and the asset's depreciation over its useful life.

> **Focus**
>
> - Where there is no reasonable certainty that the lessee will obtain ownership by the end of the lease term, the asset is fully depreciated over the *shorter* of the lease term and the asset's useful life. The lessee must also test the asset annually for impairment.

Example 12.69 – Accounting for a finance lease

Sandiford Ltd (Sandiford) is looking to purchase a machine for use in its manufacturing process which has an estimated useful life of ten years. The machine can be purchased outright in cash for £42,800 or it can be obtained through a finance lease.

If Sandiford were to go through the finance lease route it would be required to make five annual payments of £11,600 payable in arrears. Once the five years have elapsed, Sandiford would be able to continue leasing the asset for an indefinite period for a peppercorn rent.

10 FRS 102 Glossary **Minimum lease payments**.

Sandiford has undertaken an opportunity cost exercise and has decided to go down the finance lease route. The fair value of £42,800 provides acceptable evidence as to the present value of the minimum lease payments determined at the inception of the lease, discounted at the interest rate implicit in the lease. Using the internal rate of return function in Excel, the interest rate implicit in the lease is 11.07%.

The following table shows the movement on the lease liability:

Year	Opening liability	Interest (11.07%)	Cash flow	Closing liability
	£	£	£	£
1	42,800	4,738	(11,600)	35,938
2	35,938	3,978	(11,600)	28,316
3	28,316	3,135	(11,600)	19,851
4	19,851	2,198	(11,600)	10,449
5	10,449	1,151	(11,600)	–
		15,200		

The entries in this example at the inception of the lease will be:

DR property, plant and equipment £42,800

CR finance lease liability (£42,800) (split between current and non-current)

Being recognition of new asset under a finance lease

The profit and loss account will be charged with the total finance costs of £15,200 over the life of the lease.

As the leased equipment has a useful life of ten years, the profit and loss account will also be charged with the depreciation of £4,280 over its useful life (£42,800/10).

Accounting for an operating lease: lessees

12.210 Accounting for an operating lease by a lessee is less complex than accounting for a finance lease. The payments under the operating lease (which must exclude costs for services such as insurance and repairs) are recognised as an expense in profit or loss over the term of the lease on a straight-line basis.

> **Focus**
>
> - Paragraph 20.15 suggests the use of the straight-line basis of recognising the payments under an operating lease and this is going to be the most commonly applied method for small businesses that enter into operating leases. However, another systematic basis can be used if that alternative basis is representative of the pattern of the company's benefit – even if the payments are not made on that basis. In addition, where payments to the lessor increase in line with expected inflation, an alternative basis of recognition in profit or loss may be used.

Lease incentives

12.211 It is often the case that a lessor will want to entice a lessee to enter into a lease by offering them an incentive. This is usually the case for the lease of property (although other assets may attract a lease incentive). Paragraph 20.15A says that where a lease incentive is agreed the total benefit of that incentive is recognised as a reduction to the expense over the lease term on a straight-line basis unless another systematic basis is representative of the time pattern of the lessee's benefit.

There is a difference in the accounting methodology for lease incentives in Section 20 because under previous UK GAAP, lease incentives were recognised in profit or loss up to the point at which the lease payments reverted to market values (which would normally occur if a break clause was not exercised). However, on transition to FRS 102 for small entities, there is an optional exemption from retrospective application at paragraph 35.10(p) which effectively allows a small company to continue with the same accounting treatment it applied under the FRSSE (effective January 2015) for its lease incentives. However, there are associated tax impacts which may need to be considered as can be seen in the following example:

Example 12.70 – Lease incentive under Section 20 versus the FRSSE (effective January 2015)

On 1 January 2012, West Ltd entered into a ten-year lease to rent a building to house its administration and office facilities. The terms of the lease make provision for a break-clause to be exercised on 31 December 2016. On signing the lease, the landlord agrees to a one-year rent-free period and rent of £230,000 per annum is payable.

Under the FRSSE (effective January 2015) the charge to the profit and loss account would be as follows:

Year-end	**Paid**	**P&L charge**	**Balance c/fwd**
	£'000	£'000	£'000
31.12.2012	–	184	184
31.12.2013	230	184	138
31.12.2014	230	184	92
31.12.2015	230	184	46

The journal entries in 2012 are:

DR rent expense (P&L)	£184,000
CR balance sheet incentive	(£184,000)

In the years to 31/12/2013, 14 and 15:

DR balance sheet incentive	£46,000
CR rent expense (P&L)	(£46,000)

On transition to FRS 102, West Ltd will have a choice. They can either restate as if FRS 102 for small companies has always been the reporting framework; or they continue with the previous UK GAAP treatment and spread the incentive up to the point at which the break-clause will be exercised.

Option 1: restate under FRS 102 for small entities

If West decides to restate as if FRS 102 for small entities has always been the financial reporting framework then a transitional adjustment at the date of transition will be made to the balance at the date of transition together with a prior year adjustment in the comparative year.

Year-end	**Paid**	**P&L charge**	**Balance c/fwd**
	£'000	£'000	£'000
31.12.2012	–	207	207
31.12.2013	230	207	184
31.12.2014 (Date of transition)	230	207	161
31.12.2015	230	207	138
31.12.2016	230	207	115
31.12.2017	230	207	92
31.12.2018	230	207	69
31.12.2019	230	207	46
31.12.2020	230	207	23
31.12.2021	230	207	–

At the date of transition an adjustment will be needed as follows:

DR accumulated profit and loss	£69,000
CR balance sheet incentive	(£69,000)

Being the difference between £161k and £92k

In the comparative year an adjustment will be needed as follows:

DR profit and loss expense	£23,000 (£207k less £184k)
CR balance sheet incentive	(£23,000)

Being the difference in P&L charge under FRS 102 for small entities v FRSSE

There will also be consequential tax adjustments to factor into account.

Option 2: continue with previous UK GAAP treatment

If West decides to continue with the FRSSE (effective January 2015) treatment then the position will be as follows:

Year-end	**Paid**	**P&L charge**	**Balance c/fwd**
	£'000	£'000	£'000
31.12.2012	–	184	184
31.12.2013	230	184	138
31.12.2014 (Date of transition)	230	184	92
31.12.2015	230	184	46
31.12.2016	230	184	–

As can be seen from the above comparisons, there are also tax implications to consider and in the above worked examples, it would be more advantageous from a tax perspective to use option 1 and restate as if FRS 102 had always been the reporting framework because the charge to profit and loss is higher (as the lease incentive is being written off over a longer period) and hence tax relief would be granted on the excess.

Focus

- On transition to FRS 102 for small companies it is advisable to do an impact assessment where lease incentives are concerned to ensure that the company is applying the most advantageous method.

Lessor accounting: finance leases

12.212 Lessors recognise assets which are subject to finance leases in their balance sheet (statement of financial position) as a debtor at an amount which is equal to the net investment in the lease. The net investment in the lease is the gross investment in the lease, discounted at the interest rate implicit in the lease. The gross investment is the total of:

- the minimum lease payments receivable by the lessor under the finance lease; and
- any unguaranteed residual value accruing to the lessor.

Finance income is recognised in the profit and loss account on a pattern which reflects a constant periodic rate of return on the lessor's net investment in the finance lease.

Example 12.71 – Change in residual value

A lessor has recognised a finance lease as a debtor, calculated using the gross investment in the lease and discounted at the interest rate implicit in the lease. A year later it is clear that the unguaranteed residual value which was used to calculate the gross investment in the lease has changed significantly due to technological advances.

Where there is an indication that the estimated unguaranteed residual value used in the calculation of the gross investment in the lease has changed significantly, paragraph 20.19 of FRS 102 says that the income allocation of the lease term is to be revised, and any reduction in respect of amounts accrued is recognised immediately in profit or loss.

Example 12.72 – Accounting for a finance lease by a lessor

Sandiford Ltd (Sandiford) has agreed to enter into a leasing transaction with its customer Colgan Ltd (Colgan). Colgan is going to lease a new machine for use in its manufacturing process from Sandiford. The fair value of the machine is £10,000 and it has an expected useful life of five years at which point its expected residual value has been assessed as £1,000. Colgan will make five annual rental payments to Sandiford in advance of £2,100 per annum. No incremental costs have been incurred by either party in negotiating this lease.

Sandiford's gross investment in the lease is calculated as the total rents receivable of £10,500 (£2,100 × 5) plus the unguaranteed residual value in the machine at the end of the lease term of £1,000. Sandiford will recognise a debtor on inception of the lease of £10,000 which is deemed to be the fair value of the machine at the inception of the lease and is also the present value of the gross investment in the lease discounted at the implicit interest rate of 6.62%. The finance income and lease receivable over the life of the lease is as follows:

Year	Opening debtor	Rent received	Finance income 6.62%	Gross investment at end of year	Gross earnings to future years	Closing debtor
	£	£	£	£	£	£
1	10,000	2,100	523	9,400	977	8,423
2	8,423	2,100	419	7,300	558	6,742
3	6,742	2,100	307	5,200	251	4,949
4	4,949	2,100	189	3,100	62	3,038
5	3,038	2,100	62	1,000	–	1,000
		10,500	1,500			

Over the life of the lease the gross investment will comprise the total of the rentals receivable in the future periods plus the unguaranteed residual of £1,000. For example at the end of year 3 the gross investment is £5,200 which is two years' rentals at £2,100 plus the £1,000 unguaranteed residual. The closing debtor in Sandiford's books at the end of year 3 will be £4,949 which is the gross investment at the end of year 3 of £5,200 less the earnings allocated to years 4 and 5.

Lessor accounting: operating leases

12.213 Assets which are leased to a third party under an operating lease are recognised as fixed assets in the books of the lessor. Such assets are presented in the lessor's financial statements according to the nature of the asset.

Income from the lease is recognised in the lessor's financial statements on a straight-line basis over the term of the lease and this will exclude amounts in respect of services such as insurance or repairs and maintenance.

Focus

- An alternative basis can be used to recognise income over the lease term if this alternative is representative of the time pattern of the lessee's benefit from the leased asset regardless of the fact that receipt of payments may not be received by the lessor on that basis. In addition, an alternative basis can be used if payments to the lessor are structured to increase in line with inflation (although if factors other than inflation are responsible for a variability in payments then the latter condition is not met).

12.214 As the lessor is recognising the asset subjected to the lease on its balance sheet (statement of financial position), it must depreciate the asset so as to be consistent with the lessor's normal depreciation policy for similar assets.

Example 12.73 – Recognition of an asset subject to an operating lease

A company acquires an item of machinery which it is planning to lease out to one of its customers on an operating lease. A solicitor has drawn up the lease agreement on behalf of the lessor for which a charge of £2,000 plus VAT has been levied.

The costs of the lease will be included in the cost of the asset on the lessor's balance sheet as the legal fees have been incurred as a result of the lease transaction. They will be recognised within profit or loss over the lease term on the same basis as the lease income.

Manufacturer or dealer lessors

Finance leases

12.215 A manufacturer or dealer lessor can offer customers the choice of buying or leasing an asset (such as a motor vehicle). A finance lease for a manufacturer or dealer lessor will give rise to two forms of income:

(1) profit or loss which is equivalent to profit or loss on an outright sale of the asset being leased; and

(2) finance income over the lease term.

At the commencement of the lease term, the sales revenue recognised by a manufacturer or dealer lessor is the fair value of the asset. Alternatively if the present value of the minimum lease payments (computed at a market rate of interest) are lower, this is recognised as a sale. Cost of sales at the commencement of the lease will be the cost (or carrying value where different) of the leased asset *less* the present value of the unguaranteed residual value. Any difference between the sales revenue and the cost of sales is the profit made in the transaction and is recognised in line with the entity's policy for outright sales.

Example 12.74 – Artificially low rate of interest

A dealer agrees to sell a commercial van using artificially low rates of interest and incurs lease transaction costs of £1,500.

Where artificially low rates of interest are quoted, the dealer's selling profit must be restricted to that profit which would be recognised if a market rate of interest were being charged. Any costs which are incurred by the dealer relating to negotiating the lease are recognised as an expense when the selling profit is recognised.

Operating leases

12.216 In respect of operating leases, a manufacturer or dealer lessor does not recognise any selling profit on entering into an operating lease because this is not the equivalent of a sale.

Sale and leaseback transactions

12.217 Sale and leaseback arrangements have commonly been entered into to release finance. Usually a company will enter into negotiations with its bank (or other financier) to sell an asset and then lease it back – usually such assets are buildings. Over the last few years such transactions have become increasingly more prevalent as companies struggle with cash flows during economic difficulties.

There are two very distinct component parts to a sale and leaseback arrangement:

(1) there is a sale of an asset by the seller-lessee; and

(2) there is a lease agreement in place between the seller-lessee and the buyer-lessor for the same asset.

When a sale and leaseback arrangement takes place, it is not uncommon for the fair value of the sales proceeds to be higher than the fair value of the asset being sold and this gives the seller-lessee an added benefit because there is an increased gain on the sale of the asset and also the buyer-lessor sees an increased benefit because they can charge higher rentals (as well as having a higher depreciable basis).

12.218 A sale and leaseback transaction will result in the creation of either a finance or an operating lease and the accounting treatment subsequently applied will all depend on the classification of the type of the lease.

If the sale and leaseback transaction results in the creation of a finance lease, any gain on disposal of the asset is not recognised immediately in profit or loss but is deferred and amortised over the life of the lease.

If the sale and leaseback transaction results in the creation of an operating lease and the transaction has taken place at fair value, the seller-lessee can recognise any profit or loss on disposal at the inception of the lease.

Example 12.75 – Gain on disposal of a finance leaseback

Parker Ltd has suffered from cash flow difficulties over the year to 31 December 2016 and the bank have agreed to purchase its freehold building which has net book value of £200,000 in the financial statements as at that date under a finance leaseback arrangement where Parker will leaseback the building over a three-year period. Disposal proceeds received amount to £275,000 and the £75,000 gain has been recognised as a profit on disposal in Parker's financial statements.

The recognition of the £75,000 gain in profit or loss on inception of the finance leaseback is not correct. Instead it should be deferred in the balance sheet and released to profit or loss over the term of the lease (ie at £25,000 per year (£75,000/3 years)).

If the bank had leased back the building to Parker under an operating leaseback arrangement, then the £75,000 would qualify to be recognised as a gain on disposal at the inception of the lease.

Sale and operating leaseback: additional considerations

12.219 Where a sale and leaseback arrangement results in the creation of an operating lease and the sale price is below fair value, the seller-lessee must recognise any profit or loss on the disposal of the asset immediately unless the loss is going to be recouped by way of future lease payments which are set at a below market rate.

Example 12.76 – Sale proceeds in an operating leaseback transaction at below fair value

Henley Ltd has sold its building to its bank in a sale and leaseback arrangement which has resulted in the creation of an operating lease. The fair value of the building is £150,000 and the sales proceeds received from the bank amount to £110,000. The terms of the lease arrangement make no provision for any of the difference to be recouped through rentals charged at below market rates.

In this example, the £40,000 (£150,000 less £110,000) loss is recognised immediately in profit or loss. However, if the agreement had made provision for the difference to be recouped through rentals charged at below market rates then the £40,000 would be deferred and released to profit or loss in proportion to the lease payments over the term for which the building is to be used.

12.220 Where the sales proceeds received are above fair value, the seller-lessee shall defer the excess amount and amortise it over the period for which the asset is expected to be used.

Example 12.77 – Sales proceeds in an operating leaseback transaction higher than fair value

Henley Ltd has sold its building to its bank in a sale and leaseback arrangement which has resulted in the creation of an operating lease. The fair value of the building is £110,000 and the sales proceeds received from the bank amount to £150,000.

In this example the fair value of the proceeds received is £40,000 higher than the fair value of the building. This amount will be deferred and released to profit or loss in the periods which the asset is being used. For example, if the term of the leaseback is four years, Henley Ltd will recognise £10,000 per annum in profit or loss.

Leases of investment property in a group context

12.221 It is often the case that a small group may rent out properties which it owns to other group members. Under previous UK GAAP there was a scope exemption which meant that any properties let to group members did not qualify to be classed as investment property in the lessee's financial statements. Unfortunately there is no scope exemption in Section 16 *Investment Property* and hence where a property is let out to another group member and the group member-owner receives rental income from the letting group member, the group member which owns the property will be have to reclassify the property to investment property in its own individual financial statements. In the consolidated financial statements (where these are prepared by a small group owning investment property) the investment property will be reclassified to property, plant and equipment because from a group perspective, the property is owner-occupied and hence the treatment as investment property will only be permitted in the individual group member's financial statements.

In the individual financial statements of the lessee, nothing has changed because there will still be an operating lease in existence between the lessee and the lessor.

Disclosures

12.222 The disclosures in respect of leases may be as follows:

- In respect of operating leases:
  - the total amount of future minimum lease payments under non-cancellable operating leases for each of the following periods:
    - (i) not later than one year;
    - (ii) later than one year and not later than five years; and
    - (iii) later than five years; and

- Any other disclosures which the directors consider necessary in order for the financial statements to give a true and fair view.

PROVISIONS AND CONTINGENCIES

12.223 Section 21 *Provisions and Contingencies* of FRS 102 deals with the accounting and disclosure issues relating to provisions and contingencies. In practice this can be a very difficult area to deal with because of its subjectivity and it is important to understand the circumstances in which a provision is appropriate because there are often associated tax implications to consider as well.

Before the introduction of accounting standards governing the accounting requirements for provisions, companies were quite able to 'massage' the profits (or losses) and report figures which were desired rather than figures which were factual; hence the focus would be on the bottom line (the profit or loss) and then companies would work upwards. This particular method of profit manipulation was coined 'big bath accounting' and was quite common prior to the introduction of SSAP 18 *Accounting for contingencies* which was superseded by FRS 12 *Provisions, contingent liabilities and contingent assets.* A typical scenario using big bath accounting would entail a company calculating 'actual' profits and then deciding that these were too high (usually because if profit was high in one year, shareholders would expect an even higher profit next year). Management would then create a provision for expenditure which had not actually been incurred or committed to at the balance sheet date and this would then have the effect of reducing profit and (on the face of it) increasing liabilities. In the subsequent financial year when profit was not quite as high as shareholders would like, some (or all) of the provision was reversed and it was for this reason that accounting standards were introduced in this area; in other words to prevent management from looking 'bottom up' in the profit and loss account and using the profit figure as a driver for figures above profit.

12.224 The requirements from the FRSSE (effective January 2015) and FRS 12 have been carried over into Section 21 and hence there is little in the way of change from the requirements where provisions and contingencies are concerned.

Section 21 also deals with financial guarantee contracts, unless:

- an entity has chosen to apply IAS 39 *Financial Instruments: Recognition and Measurement* and/or IFRS 9 *Financial Instruments* (which is likely to be rare for a small company); or
- an entity has elected under FRS 103 *Insurance Contracts* to continue the application of insurance contract accounting.

Section 21 does not apply to:

- financial instruments, including loan commitments, which are within the scope of Section 11 *Basic Financial Instruments* and Section 12 *Other Financial Instruments Issues*;
- insurance contracts and reinsurance contracts within the scope of FRS 103 (including financial instruments issued by an entity which contain a discretionary participation feature); and
- executory contracts unless these are onerous contracts (an executory contract is one under which neither party has performed any of its obligations or both parties have partially performed their obligations to an equal extent).

Focus

- An 'onerous contract' is one in which the unavoidable costs of meeting the obligations under the contract outweigh the economic benefit which is expected to be received.

Defining a provision

12.225 The Glossary to FRS 102 is fairly straightforward in its definition of a provision – it says that a provision is *'A **liability** of uncertain timing or amount.'*[11] The term 'provision' is also used in other contexts throughout FRS 102 including a *provision for bad debts* and a *provision for depreciation*. Such 'provisions' are merely adjustments to the carrying amount of assets as opposed to a recognition of liabilities and hence are not dealt with in Section 20.

Example 12.78 – Irrecoverable trade debtor and an impaired brand

A company supplies sunbeds to beauty salons throughout the country. The company's year-end is 31 October 2017 and on this date the management undertook a review of the aged debtors listing. Management determined that there were a number of overdue debts which they considered to be irrecoverable. In addition, the company has its own outlets and trades under its own brand. Recent adverse press reports in respect of the company's brand has resulted in a significant decline in demand for their brand and management have therefore estimated that the recoverable amount of the brand is below its carrying amount in the balance sheet. The question arises as to whether a provision for impairment in the financial and non-financial assets in the balance sheet fall under the scope of Section 21.

The impairment loss on the trade debtors is not actually a provision as far as Section 21 is concerned. The company would recognise a reduction in trade

11 FRS 102 Glossary **Provision**.

debtors (a financial asset) by way of a provision for bad debts (also referred to as an 'allowance for receivables').

In respect of the impairment of the brand, the brand should be presented net of the impairment in the balance sheet in accordance with Section 27 *Impairment of Assets*. An impairment charge is not a probable outflow of economic benefits, but is instead a reduction in the cash flows expected from the brand. As a result, an impairment charge does not fall under the scope of Section 21.

Recognition of a provision

12.226 As mentioned in the introduction to this section, in order to combat the act of 'big bath accounting', accounting standards were introduced with the objective that a provision can only be recognised once certain criteria have been met. To that end, Section 21 specifies three criteria which must be met before an amount qualifies as recognition as a provision as follows:

- The entity has an obligation at the reporting date which has arisen because of a past event.
- It is probable (which means more likely than not) that there will be a transfer of economic benefit required to settle the obligation.
- The amount of the obligation can be reliably measured.

Focus

- This criteria is rigid and all three of the above must be met before the recognition of a provision can take place. Where any of the above criteria cannot be met a provision cannot be recognised and a contingent asset/liability is disclosed where material.

12.227 The key driver in the recognition criteria is whether the company has an **obligation** at the reporting date. If the company has an obligation to a third party at the reporting date, it is likely that there will be a transfer of economic benefit required to settle the obligation and the company can reliably estimate the obligation then it has to recognise a provision for that liability in the financial statements. An obligation arises from an obligating event and such an obligation can be classified as either:

- a 'constructive' obligation; and
- a legal obligation.

Constructive obligation

12.228 Paragraphs 2.20(a) and (b) of Section 2 *Concepts and Pervasive Principles* says that a constructive obligation is one which derives from an entity's actions when:

- by an established pattern of practice, published policies or a sufficiently specific current statement, the entity has indicated to other parties that it will accept certain responsibilities; and
- as a result, the entity has created a valid expectation on the part of those other parties that it will discharge those responsibilities.

Example 12.79 – Bonus payment

Smyth Salons Ltd has been in existence for over 20 years and has a long-established practice of paying bonuses to its management team using a pre-determined formula on year-end profits if they exceed a certain benchmark. This benchmark has not been increased for the last ten years and the directors have intimated that they have no intention of increasing the benchmark.

Monthly management accounts are prepared with reasonable accuracy and at the year-end 31 December 2016 these showed a relatively high level of profit. The company accountant has made an accrual for a bonus, together with the associated employer's national insurance contributions.

The company has created a constructive obligation by way of an established pattern of past practice by paying bonuses. It is this past practice which gives rise to a constructive obligation because it has created an expectation in the mind-sets of management that they will receive a bonus. As the company has a constructive obligation, it would be permissible to recognise the bonus provision in the year-end 31 December 2016 financial statements.

The example above illustrates the situation whereby management have a valid expectation because of the company's past practice. Care, however, must be taken to ensure that the obligation can be demonstrable as a constructive obligation. If the company's past practice was NOT to pay a bonus year on year, then it would be difficult to make such a provision unless there was adequate documentation to support the obligation prior to the year-end (for example a board resolution).

Example 12.80 – No obligating event at the reporting date

A company operates in the brick industry and has an overseas depot which operates in a jurisdiction which has recently introduced legislation that now requires the use of air filters for all companies in this industry to be fitted to all buildings. The number of air filters to be fitted is determined by the size of each building. The company has calculated that it will need 250 air filters and as at 31 December 2016 the company had not fitted the air filters. The finance director has made a provision in the balance sheet for the cost of the air filters on the basis that it is a legal requirement and that the company will inevitably have to fit the air filters.

The provision should not be recognised because at the reporting date no obligating event (the fitting of the air filters) had taken place.

On 31 December 2017 the company had still not fitted the air filters. Again, there is still no obligation (despite a year passing) as no obligating event has taken place (the fitting of the air filters). There could well be good reason to make a provision for fines and penalties which may be levied under the legislation because an obligating event has arisen in this respect (the non-compliance with legislation).

Legal obligation

12.229 A legal obligation is an obligation which can be enforced by law. Normally it is clear when the company has a legal obligation (for example by contract or through a court order). Provisions can also be made for normal day-to-day transactions, such as provisions for goods and/or services received by the reporting date but not yet invoiced (accruals).

Provisions for future costs/operating losses

12.230 Section 21.6 is quite strict in its approach to an entity's future actions (ie the future conduct of its business). This is because such actions do not meet the definition of a provision and the entity has not got an obligation at the reporting date for its future actions, regardless of how likely (or unlikely) they are to occur.

Example 12.81 – Recognition of future costs

A company has an item of machinery which requires a major component to be overhauled every five years. The directors wish to make a provision for 1/5 of the cost of the future overhaul in the current year's financial statements.

The directors will not be able to make such a provision for the future overhaul. These costs are merely an intention at the reporting date rather than an obligation. The directors may well sell the item of machinery before the five years have elapsed.

Recognition and measurement of a provision

12.231 Section 21 says that where a provision qualifies for recognition, it should be recognised in the financial statements at the best estimate of the amount which will be required to settle the obligation. In many cases this will be clear – especially where monetary amounts are known. Estimates, however, may be required for such items such as interest charges or penalties.

When a provision involves a large population of items, paragraph 21.7(a) of FRS 102 requires the estimate to reflect the weighting of all possible outcomes by their associated probabilities. Where there is a continuous range of potential outcomes and each outcome is as likely as another outcome, the mid-point range is used.

Example 12.82 – Provision for defective goods

Andy's Appliances Ltd sells electrical goods such as dishwashers, washing machines, TVs and audio equipment. It sells goods to the general public with a warranty which covers customers for the costs of repairs which occur during the first six months from the date of purchase. The company is preparing its financial statements for the year-ended 31 December 2016 and it has calculated that if all the products sold contained minor defects the costs of the repairs would be £50,000. If major defects occurred in all the products the costs of repairs would be £150,000.

Management have concluded that past experience, and future expectations, suggest that for the coming year 75% of the goods sold will contain no defects; 20% will contain minor defects and 5% will have major defects.

The provision for the year-ended 31 December 2016 can be calculated as follows:

	£
75% × £nil	nil
20% × £50,000	10,000
5% × £150,000	7,500
Total provision	17,500

12.232 Where provisions are concerned, consideration must be given to the time value of money. This is because the time value of money may become a material issue to the company and paragraph 21.7 of FRS 102 requires the provision to be the expected value of the expenditure expected to be required in order to settle the obligation. Where the time value of money is material, the discount rate(s) used in discounting the obligation to present-day values must be the pre-tax rate(s) which reflect market assessments of the time value of money and risks which are specific to the liability.

Focus

- In practice, it is likely to be fairly uncommon for the effects of the time value of money to be material and in many cases no discounting will be required because the cash flows associated with the provision will not be sufficiently so far into the future for discounting to have a material impact (especially for small companies).

12.233 There are some instances when a provision may be settled by a third party (for example an insurance company). Before an entity can recognise a provision as an asset the company must consider whether the reimbursement is 'virtually certain'. The term 'virtually certain' is inherently more stringent than 'probable' and therefore an asset should only be recognised if the third party has confirmed that it *will* settle the provision.

Example 12.83 – Settlement of a provision by a third party

A firm of accountants has been sued by one its clients for the negligent preparation of a corporation tax return. The firm has made a provision for a liability in its year-end financial statements which is equivalent to the levels of penalties and interest due to HM Revenue and Customs. The firm's professional indemnity insurers have confirmed that they will reimburse the firm for these costs. This confirmation has been received from the professional indemnity insurers in writing and the reimbursement will take place after the year-end.

In this respect the firm will be able to recognise a provision in respect of the reimbursement asset because it is virtually certain that the obligation will be settled by the insurers. However, the firm must make sure that to comply with paragraph 21.9 of FRS 102, the amount of the reimbursement provided in the financial statements does not exceed the amount of the provision. In addition, the firm must not offset the asset against the provision; the two must be separately presented in the firm's balance sheet. However, the expense within the firm's profit and loss account can be presented net of the amount recognised for the reimbursement.

Subsequent measurement of a provision

12.234 At each reporting date management must conduct a review of the provisions in the financial statements and make adjustments which reflect the current best estimate of the amount which would be required to settle the obligation at that reporting date. This is important because if a provision is long-standing, information may come to light during the year which would result in a change to the estimate being made. When adjustments are made to provisions, they must be recognised in profit or loss. The only exception to this rule is if the provision was recognised as part of the cost of an asset and hence the adjustment would also be recognised in the cost of the asset.

When the time value of money is material, the entity recognises a provision at its present value of the amount required to settle the obligation. Any unwinding of the discount must be reflected as a finance cost in profit or loss during the period in which it arises.

Onerous contracts

12.235 The Glossary to FRS 102 defines an 'onerous contract' as:

> 'A contract in which the unavoidable costs of meeting the obligations under the contract exceed the economic benefit expected to be received under it.'[12]

Paragraph 21.11A says that where an entity has a contract that has become onerous, the present obligation under the contract is recognised and measured as a provision. A typical example of an onerous contract is when a company has an operating lease for a building which it cannot sub-let.

Example 12.84 – Onerous contract

Slevin Ltd occupies two properties. One of the properties is owned by Slevin Ltd and the other is occupied under an operating lease and is owned by an unconnected third party. The provisions in the lease state that Slevin Ltd will pay the landlord monthly rentals of £1,000 per annum from 1 April 2016 to 31 March 2020. However, due to a reduction in trade, Slevin Ltd has been forced to downsize and has abandoned the property it occupied under an operating lease from 1 April 2017.

Slevin Ltd has vacated a property which it held under an operating lease, but the contract is onerous as Slevin is still committed to pay the landlord future rentals until 31 March 2020. Therefore the present obligation under the contract is recognised and measured as a provision in Slevin's financial statements.

Example 12.85 – Termination of a contract

Robinson Renovations Ltd (Robinson) has a contract with a supplier and this contract is onerous. The provisions in the contract state that Robinson will enter into the contract on 1 January 2016 and it will run for three years until 1 January 2019. Robinson wishes to terminate the contract in 2017 because a competing supplier has offered more favourable terms; however, it will incur an early termination fee for terminating the contract early by the existing supplier.

12 FRS 102 Glossary **Onerous contract**.

Robinson wishes to make a provision in the 2016 financial statements for the costs of terminating the contract.

In this example the contract has been determined as an onerous contract. It should, therefore, make provision for the net cost of terminating this contract. This is because the contract has automatically be deemed to be onerous. However, consideration will need to be given as to whether the business in which the products are used in are profitable. If they are profitable, the contract will not be onerous and the early termination fee should be charged when such fees are incurred (ie in 2017).

Restructuring provisions

12.236 Paragraph 21.11C deals with the issue relating to the restructuring of a company. This paragraph says that a restructuring gives rise to a constructive obligation (and hence recognition of a provision) only when the entity:

- has a detailed formal plan for the restructuring which identifies at least:
  - the business or part of a business concerned;
  - the principal locations which will be affected;
  - the location, function and approximate number of employees which will be compensated for the termination of their services;
  - the expenditures which will be undertaken; and
  - when the plan will be implemented; and
- the company has raised a valid expectation in the mind-sets of those affected that it will carry out the restructuring by starting to implement that plan or announce its main features to those which are going to be affected.

Example 12.86 – Restructuring provision

Whatmough Ltd has an accounting reference date of 31 October. It supplies and hires plant and machinery to members of the public and to other companies throughout the UK and has five depots spread across the country.

Over the last two years the depots in Yorkshire and Newcastle have been sustaining heavy losses due to a downturn in business. On 30 September 2016 the board of directors decided to close those depots and transfer the business to its head office located in Bolton. This intention was communicated to all staff in the Yorkshire and Newcastle depots on 4 October 2016 and the staff concerned were given their redundancy notices. Both depots will close on 1 December 2016. Redundancy calculations have been undertaken by the human resources department and these have been agreed by the board of directors.

In this example the company is going through a restructuring exercise in which it has identified the business which has been affected by the downturn, it has identified the locations affected, the number of employees which will be compensated for the termination of their services and the plan has already been started. In addition, the company has also communicated its intentions to the staff concerned and hence has created a valid expectation in their minds that the company will discharge its obligations. In this respect the company can make a restructuring provision in its financial statements to 31 October 2016.

Contingent liabilities and assets

12.237 Paragraph 21.12 of FRS 102 says that a contingent liability is either a possible, but uncertain, obligation or a present obligation which is not recognised within the entity's financial statements as it fails to meet the recognition criteria for a provision.

Focus

- Contingent liabilities are not recognised in the company's financial statements. An exception to this rule, however, relates to contingent liabilities which have been assumed by the acquirer of a business in a business combination and for which the provisions in paragraphs 19.20 and 19.21 of FRS 102 apply.

12.238 Contingent liabilities should be disclosed in the financial statements unless the possibility of an outflow of economic benefits is considered to be remote.

Example 12.87 – Contingent liability

Hardacre Ltd has made a provision for damages amounting to £10,000 in its financial statements for the year-ended 31 December 2016 in respect of a legal claim brought against it by one of its customers. The legal advisers have advised the company that at the reporting date it was uncertain as to the potential outcome of this case.

The company should not recognise a provision for damages because it is not probable that an outflow of economic resources will be required to settle the case. The legal advisers are unsure as to the outcome of the case. In such situations, disclosure of a contingent liability in the notes to the financial statements should be made.

12.239 A contingent asset is directly the opposite of a contingent liability and, again, should not be reflected within the financial statements of an entity.

Contingent assets should only ever be recognised if it is 'virtually certain' that the entity will realise the contingent asset (for example an insurance company agreeing to pay out a claim to the company).

Summary of provisions and contingencies

12.240 The following table illustrates the required accounting treatment where provisions and contingencies are concerned:

Contingent Liabilities		
There is a present obligation that probably requires a transfer of economic benefits to settle.	**There is a possible obligation or a present obligation that may, or may not, require a transfer of economic benefits to settle.**	**There is a possible obligation or a present obligation where the likelihood of a transfer of economic benefits is remote.**
A provision is required and disclosures may be required relating to the provision.	No provision is recognised but disclosure as a contingent liability may be required.	No provision is recognised and no disclosure is required.
Contingent Assets		
Inflow of economic benefits is virtually certain.	**Inflow of economic benefits is probable but not virtually certain.**	**Inflow is not probable.**
The asset is not contingent, thus provision should be made.	No asset is recognised but disclosures may be made in the notes to the financial statements.	No asset is recognised and no disclosure is made.

Disclosures

12.241 The disclosures relating to provisions and contingencies may be as follows:

- Unless the possibility of any outflow of economic resources is remote, the small business must disclose (for each class of contingent liability) at the reporting date, a brief description of the nature of the contingent liability and (where practicable):
  - — an estimate of its financial effect (measured in accordance with paragraphs 21.7–21.11 of FRS 102);
  - — an indication of the uncertainties relating to the amount or timing of any outflow; and
  - — the possibility of any reimbursement.
- Where it is impracticable to make any of the above disclosures then that fact must be stated.

- In relation to contingent assets, if an inflow is probable (more likely than not) but not virtually certain, the company must disclose a description of the nature of the contingent assets at the end of the reporting period and, when practicable, an estimate of their financial effect measured in accordance with paragraphs 21.7–21.11 of FRS 102.
- Where it is impracticable to make the above disclosures then that fact must be stated.

The directors should also consider making any additional disclosures they feel are necessary concerning provisions and contingencies in order that the financial statements give a true and fair view.

LIABILITIES AND EQUITY

12.242 Section 22 *Liabilities and Equity* of FRS 102 is linked with financial instruments and the issue of distinguishing financial liabilities between liability and equity (referred to as a 'compound financial instrument'). In addition, the section also addresses the issue of equity instruments and distributions to owners of the business and how to account for purchases of a company's own equity.

There are, however, certain types of financial instruments which Section 22 does not deal with as follows:

- Investments in subsidiaries, associates and joint ventures which are accounted for in accordance with Section 9 *Consolidated and Separate Financial Statements*, Section 14 *Investments in Associates* and Section 15 *Investments in Joint Ventures*.
- Employers' rights and obligations under employee benefit plans as Section 28 *Employee Benefits* applies to these.
- Contingent consideration in a business combination as Section 19 *Business Combinations and Goodwill* applies.
- Financial instruments, contracts and guarantees under a share-based payment award as Section 26 *Share-based Payment* will apply (however, paragraphs 22.3–22.6 will apply to treasury shares purchased, issued, sold, transferred or cancelled which relate to employee share option plans, employee share purchase plans and all other share-based payment arrangements).
- Insurance contracts and reinsurance contracts to which FRS 103 *Insurance Contracts* applies.
- Financial instruments with a discretionary participation feature as FRS 103 will apply.
- Financial guarantee contracts as Section 21 *Provisions and Contingencies* applies to these.

Distinction between liability and equity

12.243 The definition of a financial liability is fairly complex but in the broadest sense of the phrase, a financial liability arises on the part of the business when they have an obligation to transfer cash or other assets to another entity or to exchange financial assets or financial liabilities with another entity so as to discharge any obligations. Such liabilities can also be settled in equity instruments (ie shares).

The term 'equity' is taken to mean the residual that is left in the company's assets after taking into account all the liabilities. Equity also means investments by the owners of the company (such as additional shares) and additions to those investments which have been earned through profits generated by the company. Any losses sustained by the business or distributions paid to owners are deducted.

Focus

- A financial liability is classified as such when the company does not have the unconditional right to avoid settling or delivering cash to a third party. Discretionary dividends paid on ordinary shares would not meet the definition of a liability at the reporting date because they are declared at the company's discretion – the holders of the shares do not have a right to receive the dividends.

Example 12.88 – Preference dividend

Jackson Ltd issues 6% preference shares to its shareholders and is required to pay them a fixed rate of dividend each year.

Despite the name preference 'shares', Jackson Ltd has an obligation to deliver cash to the shareholders each year (the 6% dividends). As a result these preference shares will be recognised as financial liabilities in the financial statements. The dividends paid to the preference shareholders are classed as interest charges.

12.244 In some cases it can be fairly obvious when a financial instrument requires payment to be made to the holder of the instrument. If a loan is made to the company which attracts interest, the interest payments and the redemption amount will give rise to the loan being classified as a liability. Where a shareholder subscribes to ordinary shares in a company this will represent equity ownership in the company and hence will fall to be treated as equity.

There are occasions when some instruments contain a mix of both liability (debt) and equity and the most common type of instance where this arises in a small company is in relation to 'convertible debt'.

Example 12.89 – Convertible debt

On 1 January 2016 Breary Ltd (Breary) received a 5% convertible loan with a nominal value of £200,000. The loan is redeemable on 31 December 2019 also at par, but the loan note holders may choose to convert the capital element of the loan into shares on 31 December 2019 if the company's cash flow is such that redemption may not be made. Breary has obtained a market rate from its bank on an equivalent loan which would be 8%. Interest has already been paid on the loan amounting to £10,000 (£200,000 × 5%) and has been taken to finance costs within the profit and loss account.

Present value rates are as follows:

		5%	**8%**
End of year	1	0.95	0.93
	2	0.91	0.86
	3	0.86	0.79
	4	0.82	0.74

The loan itself is a liability but also contains an equity component as the loan note holders have the option of converting the capital element into equity at maturity. This option has to be reflected in the financial statements and hence the instrument must be split between its debt component and its equity component.

Interest is being charged by the loan note holders at a rate of 5% but market rates are at 8% (hence the loan is below market rates). In order to correctly recognise the debt and equity components (and correct rate of interest) the loan itself has to be discounted at the market rate of 8% (the market rate being the rate which Breary's bank would charge on an equivalent loan). The calculation of the debt portion and the equity portion is as follows:

Year	**5% interest (£200k × 5%)**	**Discount factor (8%)**	**Present value**
	£		£
1	10,000	0.93	9,300
2	10,000	0.86	8,600
3	10,000	0.79	7,900
			25,800
4	210,000	0.74	155,400
Amount to be recognised as a financial liability			181,200
Initial proceeds received			(200,000)
Amount to be recognised in equity			(18,800)

The loan interest has been calculated as £10,000 in year 1 (£200,000 × 5%). However, market rates are at 8% and hence this needs to be reflected in the financial statements and so an additional £6,000 (£200,000 × 8% less £10,000) should be recognised as follows:

DR finance costs	£6,000
CR loan liability account	(£6,000)

This entry is done because while the loan note holders have agreed a rate of interest of 5%, the loan must be accounted for at market values and as the loan has been discounted to present day values using a market rate, the additional interest amounts will need to be accrued for at the end of each year of the loan so that the loan liability account on redemption or conversion equals nil.

The £18,800 taken to equity represents the value of the option to convert the loan on maturity.

Example 12.90 – Conversion of loan from liability to equity

Woodward Ltd (Woodward) receives a loan from Williams Ltd (Williams) of £100,000 on 1 January 2017. The loan becomes repayable on 31 December 2020. However on 1 November 2020 a large customer of Woodward went into liquidation leaving the company with financial difficulties. Williams has accepted 100,000 ordinary £1 shares in settlement of the loan on the basis that the management of the company will turn the business around successfully.

The journals to reallocate this loan on 31 December 2020 will be:

DR loan payable	£100,000
CR equity	(£100,000)

No gain or loss will be recognised because the loan has simply been recategorised. However, if a premium had been made on the transaction it would have been credited to a share premium account.

Example 12.91 – Conversion of a loan to equity resulting in a gain

Using the same facts as above in Woodward and Williams. If it is assumed that only 80,000 £1 shares are issued to Williams in settlement of the loan, this will result in a gain in Woodward's financial statements of £20,000 (£100,000 less share issue of £80,000). The journals in this case will be:

DR loan payable	£100,000
CR equity	(£80,000)
CR profit and loss	(£20,000)

Share splits

12.245 When a company does a share split it divides its existing shares into multiple shares. The effect of a share split is that the number of issued shares increases by a specific multiple, but the total value of the shares remain the same.

Example 12.92 – Share split

A company is keen to attract new investment to raise finance for a new product range. The shares of the company have been valued and they are currently worth £200 per share. The board of directors have expressed concern that this value may prove to be too costly for some investors and are exploring ways of getting around this issue. The financial controller has suggested that the company undertake a two-for-one share split.

In this example a shareholder would only need to pay £100 to own 100 shares rather than £200 for 100 shares as the shares have been split two-for-one.

Bonus issues

12.246 When a company makes a bonus issue of shares, it issues further shares to its shareholders in proportion to their existing holding (for example an additional one share for every five shares held). In small companies bonus issues are fairly uncommon but can be very advantageous for both the company and the shareholder. The company benefits because a bonus issue could be undertaken as opposed to paying a dividend to shareholders (hence preserving cash) and this is definitely an advantage where a company may be undercapitalised because the value of the dividend will be higher as it is based on a fairly low number of shares.

From a shareholders' perspective a bonus issue is advantageous because they will receive additional shares at no cost to them.

Focus

- In a bonus issue there is no impact on profit or loss. The only effect is to increase the number of shares which are outstanding after the issue. In addition there is no impact on earnings because no flow of funds has occurred.

Example 12.93 – Accounting for a bonus issue of shares

Holmes Ltd makes a bonus issue of shares to its existing shareholders in the year to 31 October 2017. The bonus issue is one share for every five shares held and all the shareholders have taken up the offer of the bonus issue resulting in additional shares being issued of £10,000.

The bonus issue treated as a transaction among the equity holders and the journals to record the transaction are:

DR accumulated profit and loss reserves	£10,000
CR issued share capital	(£10,000)

Rights issues

12.247 Rights issues are again fairly uncommon among small companies; but they do occasionally happen as they are a means of raising finance by selling additional shares to existing shareholders in proportion to their holding. To entice shareholders to agree to the rights issue the additional shares are usually offered to them at a discount (although this is not necessarily always the case and they can be offered at par value). A key point to bear in mind from a shareholder's point of view is that if they refuse to take the offer of a rights issue, their shareholding may become diluted because other shareholders may take up the rights issue instead.

Focus

- Care needs to be taken with a share issue where the company already has significant levels of borrowings because the fact that the company is attempting to raise even more finance should be taken as a warning sign. Little is to be achieved from a rights issue if the company is in financial distress unless there are signs that the company's finances will improve.

When a rights issue is made at a discount, the discount portion of the issue represents a bonus issue of shares because effectively the shareholders are receiving additional shares which are partly free.

Example 12.94 – Rights issue

The balance sheet of a company shows issued share capital of 100,000 £1 shares in issue. The company made a rights issue of shares of one share for every five shares held and all the shareholders took up the rights issue.

The additional shares in the rights issue are 20,000 shares (100,000 × 1/5).

Share premium account

12.248 A means of raising finance by a company is to issue additional shares. Generally for a small company the issuance of more shares is uncommon as small companies tend to approach their bank or shareholders for loans. However, in some cases a bank may require the shareholders commit to additional subscriptions of shares to demonstrate their confidence in the business. This has become more common over the recent years following the global financial crisis as banks have been reluctant to finance small businesses without commitments from their owners.

When a company issues shares for more than their par value, the excess is treated as a share premium. The Companies Act 2006 requires share premiums to be recognised in a separate component of equity from issued share capital so as to distinguish between share capital issued at par and the value of the premium (if any) on the issuance.

Example 12.95 – Shares issued at a premium

A company is experiencing rapid growth following the successful launch of a new product range. In order to fund this expansion the company has approached its bank for a working capital loan to avoid it over-trading. The bank have agreed in principal provided that the shareholders contribute additional capital to demonstrate their confidence in the business.

The company's balance sheet prior to the issuance of additional shares showed 100,000 £1 ordinary shares in issue which had all been issued at par value. The company wishes to issue a further 70,000 shares to its existing shareholders at £2 each. All the shareholders have agreed to the additional shares.

The journals for the above share issue are as follows:

DR cash at bank	£140,000
CR share capital	(£70,000)
CR share premium	(£70,000)

Being issue of shares at a £1 premium

Share buybacks

12.249 Small companies often enter into share buyback arrangements where a company will purchase their own shares from shareholders. A typical scenario would be where a shareholder is retiring and wishes to sell their shares in a company but the other shareholders are unwilling to buy them.

The Companies Act 2006 deals with the acquisition by a company of its own shares in Part 18 at sections 658 to 737.

When a company redeems or purchases shares wholly out of profit it is required to transfer a sum equivalent to the amount of which the company's share capital has reduced on cancellation of the shares to a 'capital redemption reserve'. The purpose of the capital redemption reserve is to protect creditors and to maintain the company's capital. A company can only use the capital redemption reserve to make a bonus issue of shares.

Example 12.96 – Redemption of capital and capital redemption reserve

The balance sheet of Weaver Ltd is as follows:

	£
Cash at bank	60,000
Share capital (£1 ordinary)	10,000
Profit and loss account	50,000
	60,000

The shareholders have passed a resolution to repurchase 3,000 shares at par value. The accounting entries are as follows:

DR ordinary share capital	£3,000
CR cash at bank	(£3,000)

Being repurchase of shares

A transfer must be made to the capital redemption reserve equivalent to the reduction in ordinary share capital so as to maintain the company's capital and protect creditors as follows:

DR profit and loss account	£3,000
CR capital redemption reserve	(£3,000)

Maintenance of share capital

The balance sheet of Weaver Ltd is now as follows:

	£
Cash at bank	57,000
Share capital	7,000
Capital redemption reserve	3,000
Profit and loss account	47,000
	57,000

In this example the company has repurchased shares of £3,000 from an outgoing shareholder but it is required to maintain its original level of capital to protect creditors and hence the additional transfer from profit and loss reserves to a capital redemption reserve is required by section 733 of the Companies Act 2006 as the shares have been purchased wholly out of profits.

Example 12.97 – Shares purchased at a premium

Using the same facts as in Weaver above, assume that the company repurchased the shares at a 50p premium. The journals will be as follows:

DR ordinary share capital	£3,000
DR profit and loss account	£1,500 (3,000 shares × 0.50p)
CR cash at bank	(£4,500)

Shares repurchased at 50p premium

The transfer to the capital redemption reserve will be:

DR profit and loss account	£3,000
CR capital redemption reserve	(£3,000)

Maintenance of share capital

Share buybacks out of a fresh issue of shares

12.250 The Companies Act 2006 says that any premium which is paid on shares which the company acquires must be made out of distributable profits. Section 687(4) of the Companies Act 2006 then goes on to say that if the redeemable shares were issued at a premium, any premium which is payable when it comes to the company repurchasing them can be funded from the proceeds of a new share issue. Care, however, must be taken because the amount of the premium which the Companies Act 2006 allows to be funded in this way is equal to the *lower* of:

- the aggregate of the premiums the company received on issuance of the shares which it is now redeeming; and
- the amount of the company's share premium account *after* crediting the premium (if any) on the new issue of shares it makes to fund the purchase or redemption.

Example 12.98 – Redemption of shares previously issued at a premium

On 1 January 2014, Weaver Ltd issued 200,000 ordinary £1 shares. On that date Lisa subscribed to 10,000 ordinary shares which were issued at a premium of 0.10p per share. The balance on the share premium account on issuance of the shares on 1 January 2014 was £7,000. The company experienced rapid growth and on 1 January 2016 it made a bonus issue of shares in which it used the entire balance on the share premium account resulting in the share premium becoming £nil on 1 January 2016.

Lisa has set up new business and has approached the company to buyback her shares in order that she can use the funds to inject capital into her new business. The company has agreed to purchase Lisa's shares for £3.00 per share (ie at a £2 premium). In order to do this, the company made a further issue of 10,000 ordinary at a 50p premium (ie at £1.50) and the balance to purchase Lisa's shares of £15,000 has been paid out of the company bank account.

The premium on the purchase of Lisa's shares is the lower of the initial premiums which the company received when it first issued the shares to Lisa and the balance on the share premium account after the issue of the new shares which is calculated as follows:

	£	£
Par value of shares purchased		10,000
Lower of:		
– initial premium on share issue	1,000	
– balance on share premium including premium on new issue of shares	5,000	
		1,000
Total (must not exceed the proceeds of the new issue)		11,000
Balance funded from distributable profit		19,000
Cost of purchase of Lisa's shares		30,000

To record the above the journals are:

DR cash at bank	£15,000
CR share capital	(£10,000)
CR share premium	(£5,000)

Issuance of additional 10,000 £1 shares at a premium of £0.50

DR share capital	£10,000
DR share premium	£1,000[13]
DR profit and loss	£19,000[14]
CR cash at bank	(£30,000)

Being purchase of 10,000 ordinary £1 shares at a premium of £3

In the above example no amount has been transferred to a capital redemption reserve. This is because the par value of the shares purchased (£10,000) is less than the total proceeds of the new issue (£10,000 × £1.50) £15,000 and hence the company's capital has been maintained so there is no need for a transfer to the capital redemption reserve.

Permissible capital payment

12.251 Permissible capital payment (PCP) is dealt with in section 710 of the Companies Act 2006. The PCP is the amount by which the cost of purchasing or redeeming shares exceeds the amount of:

- distributable profit; plus
- the proceeds of any new share issue.

The PCP ensures that a company purchasing or redeeming shares does so out of available profit and any proceeds from a fresh issue of shares before it makes any payments out of capital.

13 Section 692(4) allows the share premium account to be reduced by part of the premium payable on the purchase which is allowed to be funded out of the proceeds of the new share issue as opposed to it being made out of profit and loss reserves.

14 See balance funded from distributable profit in the table.

Focus

- Where the PCP is less than the nominal value of the shares redeemed or purchased, the difference is transferred to a capital redemption reserve. If the PCP is higher than the nominal value of the shares redeemed or purchased, section 734(3) says that the excess can be used to reduce any of the following:
  - capital redemption reserve;
  - share premium;
  - fully paid up share capital; or
  - revaluation reserve.

Example 12.99 – Insufficient reserves to make a share buyback

The balance sheet of Weaver Ltd is as follows:

	£	
Cash at bank	15,000	
Ordinary share capital	10,000	(£1 shares)
Profit and loss account	5,000	(all distributable)
	15,000	

A shareholder owning 7,000 £1 shares died and his estate requires the shares to be bought back by the company so the proceeds can go into his estate. The company has insufficient reserves available to repurchase the shares at par (it only has £5,000 worth of distributable reserves) and hence a payment out of capital will be required. The procedures in sections 709–723 of the Companies Act 2006 have been carried out and the journals are as follows:

DR ordinary share capital	£7,000
CR cash at bank	(£7,000)

Redemption of share capital

DR profit and loss account	£5,000
CR capital redemption reserve	(£5,000)

Maintenance of capital and protection of creditors

Weaver's balance sheet will then be as follows:

	£
Cash at bank	8,000
Ordinary share capital	3,000
Capital redemption reserve	5,000
	8,000

The PCP is £2,000 which is the shortfall on the profit and loss reserves immediately prior to the buyback. This is calculated as 7,000 £1 shares requiring redemption less £5,000 available profit immediately before the buyback.

REVENUE

12.252 Issues relating to revenue recognition have been in the headlines a lot recently. Indeed 2015 saw the Tesco scandal where questions were raised concerning the supermarket's revenue recognition practices. Inappropriate revenue recognition policies detract from the relevance and reliability aspects which financial statements have to contain and such characteristics are required as much in small company financial statements as they are needed in larger organisations' financial statements.

FRS 102 deals with revenue recognition in Section 23 *Revenue*. This section is a very comprehensive section with an Appendix of 26 worked examples so as to aid comprehension of the section. Section 23 itself covers revenue arising from:

- the sale of goods (whether produced by the entity or for the purpose of sale or purchased for resale);
- rendering of services;
- construction contracts in which the entity is the contractor; and
- the use by other of entity assets which yield interest, royalties or dividends.

There are certain income streams which a company might receive which are not covered by Section 23 as outlined in the following table:

Section 23 is NOT applicable to:	**Relevant applicable section:**
Lease agreements	Section 20 *Leases*
Dividends/other income from investments accounted for under the equity method	Section 14 *Investments in Associates* and Section 15 *Investments in Joint Ventures*

Section 23 is NOT applicable to:	**Relevant applicable section:**
Fair value changes of financial assets and financial liabilities or their disposal	Section 11 *Basic Financial Instruments* and Section 12 *Other Financial Instruments Issues*
Fair value changes in investment property	Section 16 *Investment Property*
Initial recognition and changes in the fair value of biological assets related to agricultural activity	Section 34 *Specialised Activities*
Initial recognition of agricultural produce	Section 34 *Specialised Activities*

Section 23 also does not apply to revenue which arises from transactions and events which fall under the scope of FRS 103 *Insurance Contracts*.

Measurement of revenue

12.253 Paragraph 23.3 requires that an entity measures revenue at the fair value of the consideration received or receivable. The term 'fair value' is defined in the Glossary to FRS 102 as:

> 'The amount for which an **asset** could be exchanged, a **liability** settled, or an equity instrument granted could be exchanged, between knowledgeable, willing parties in an arm's length transaction. In the absence of any specific guidance provided in the relevant section of this FRS, the guidance in paragraphs 11.27 to 11.32 shall be used in determining fair value.'[15]

Example 12.100 – A sale with a discount

A company manufactures and sells office furniture to retailers and most of its customer base has credit facilities. Terms of credit range from 30 days for smaller customers with larger customers (and those smaller customers with a long-standing association with the company) having credit terms between 60 and 90 days. Newer customers pay cash on delivery until they have become established. The company has an accounting reference date of 30 September.

On 30 September 2016, the company made a sale to one of its larger customers amounting to £10,000 (before discount and VAT). The company entered into an agreement with its customer some time ago which states that any sales up to £11,000 will attract a discount of 1% and sales to the value of £11,001 to £15,000 will attract a 2% discount. Sales discounts for orders above £15,000

15 FRS 102 Glossary **Fair value**.

are made at the discretion of the company and are agreed with the customer prior to the sale being made.

The sale on 30 September 2016 attracts a 1% discount, hence a discount of £100. Section 23 says that revenue is to be recognised at the fair value of the consideration receivable and must take into account the amount of any trade discounts, prompt settlement discounts and rebates allowed by the entity.

Therefore, the company will recognise revenue of £9,900 (£10,000 less £100). Assuming the sale falls within the scope of VAT at 20%, the VAT amount will be £1,980 (£9,900 × 20%) and hence a trade debtor is recognised of £11,880 (£9,900 + £1,980).

Principal and agent relationship

12.254 Section 23 deals with the principal versus agent relationship in paragraph 23.4 and states that the agent must only recognise revenue to the extent of its commission. Any amounts which are collected on behalf of the principal must not be recognised as revenue of the agent.

Example 12.101 – Principal/agent relationship

Stephanie is a solicitor who specialises in debt recovery and has agreed to take on a case where the client is owed an amount of £20,000 from one of its contractors who has refused to pay claiming defective work was carried out. This matter was taken to court and the courts found that no defective work had, in fact, occurred and ordered the contractor to make payment. Stephanie has been instructed by the client and they have agreed that she will charge a 5% commission for any monies which she recovers.

The contractor eventually paid the solicitor following a threat to issue a winding-up petition in the court.

Of the £20,000 (ignoring any VAT implications), 5% will be deducted by Stephanie for her agreed commission, hence £1,000 will be recognised as revenue. The remaining £19,000 will be recognised in Stephanie's books as a liability owed to the client until the funds are remitted.

Deferred payment

12.255 Deferred payments (ie where the inflow of cash or cash equivalents is deferred) may constitute a financing transaction. A financing transaction will arise, for example, when the entity provides interest-free credit to its customer or agrees to a loan which attracts interest at a rate which is below market rate.

In such cases the fair value of the consideration is the present value of all future receipts determined using an imputed rate of interest. For the purposes of Section 23, the imputed rate of interest is the more clearly determinable of:

- the prevailing rate for a similar instrument of an issuer with a similar credit-rating; or
- the rate of interest that discounts the nominal amount of the instrument to the current cash sales price of the goods or services.

Focus

- The entity will then recognise the difference between the present value of all future receipts and the nominal amount of the consideration as interest revenue.

Example 12.102 – Interest income calculation

A company sold goods amounting to £4,000 to a customer with three years' interest-free credit. The rate of interest which discounts the nominal value of the instrument to the current cash sales price of the goods is 8%. The company's accounting reference date is 31 December 2016.

For the year-ended 31 December 2016, revenue will be £3,175 (£4,000 × $1/1.08)^3$. Interest income will be recognised in the financial statements amounting to £254 (£3,175 × 8%).

For the year-ended 31 December 2017, interest income will be £274 ((£3,175 + £254) × 8%) and in the 2018 financial statements the remaining interest income will be £297.

This accounting treatment will allow the full £4,000 sale to be recognised as revenue in the company's profit and loss account over the three years.

Exchange of goods or services

12.256 Revenue should only be recognised in the financial statements in respect of exchanges of goods or services when the transaction possesses commercial substance. A transaction is said to have commercial substance when it is expected that the future cash flows of a business will change as a result of the transaction.

For exchanges of goods or services, paragraph 23.6 prohibits revenue being recognised:

- when goods or services are exchanged for goods or services which are of a similar nature and value; or

- when goods or services are exchanged for dissimilar goods or services but the transaction lacks commercial substance.

Example 12.103 – Transaction lacking commercial substance

A manufacturer of lorries has a three-year old vehicle in its stock. The company has agreed to swap this lorry for a similar sized lorry with one of its competitors. The value of the competitor's lorry has been valued at £300 less than the company's lorry.

In this scenario the transaction lacks commercial substance because the cash flows of both parties to the transaction are not likely to change as a result of the transaction.

12.257 When goods or services are exchanged for dissimilar goods or services in a transaction which DOES possess commercial substance, Section 23 requires revenue to be measured as follows:

(a) at the fair value of the goods or services received, adjusted by the amount of any cash or cash equivalents that have been transferred;

(b) if the amount under (a) cannot be reliably measured, then at the fair value of the goods or services given up which is to be adjusted by the amount of any cash or cash equivalents transferred; or

(c) if the fair value of neither the goods or services received, nor the goods or services given up, can be reliably measured, revenue is recognised at the carrying amount of the goods or services given up adjusted by the amount of any cash or cash equivalents transferred.

Sale of goods

12.258 There are five criteria which must be fulfilled before an entity can recognise revenue in relation to the sale of goods (note: **all** conditions must be fulfilled). These conditions are as follows:

- the significant risks and rewards of ownership of the goods have been transferred to the buyer;
- the company does not retain any continuing managerial involvement to the degree which is usually associated with ownership, nor has the company any effective control over the goods sold;
- the value of revenue can be reliably measured;
- it is probable (ie more likely than not) that the company will receive economic benefit from the transaction; and
- the costs incurred, or to be incurred, relating to the transaction can be measured reliably.

12.259 The key judgement call on the part of the company will be in establishing the point at which it has transferred all the significant risks and rewards of ownership of the goods. In many cases this might be clear; but in some cases it is often unclear and the transfer of risks and rewards may be at a later date than when legal title passes. To that end, paragraph 23.3 offers four examples of when the selling entity **retains** the significant risks and rewards of ownership of the goods and hence cannot recognise revenue as follows:

- the company retains an obligation for unsatisfactory performance which is not covered by normal warranties;
- receipt of the revenue associated with the sale depends on the buyer selling the goods;
- the goods are shipped to the customer but installation has yet to be completed and installation is a significant part of the contract; and
- the buyer has a right to rescind the purchase for a reason outlined in the sales contract, or at the buyer's sole discretion, and the company is uncertain about the probability of the return.

Example 12.104 – Recognition of revenue and ongoing obligations

Company A Ltd enters into a contract to sell 10 items of machinery to Company B which is located in Italy. The terms of the contract are that Company A will ship the machines to Company B, install the machines and ensure that the machines are working to full capacity prior to Company B signing the contract off to say that they are satisfied with the machines. Company A's year-end is 31 October 2016.

Due to an ongoing project, Company A's installation team have said that they are unable to install the machines until 1 December 2016 and Company B has agreed to this date. The financial controller of Company A is proposing to recognise the revenue associated with the sale in the 31 October 2016 financial statements as he believes the installation will go ahead and is keen to report increased profitability in 2016.

The financial controller cannot recognise the sale in the 31 October 2016 financial statements because the company still has an ongoing obligation after despatch of the machines to install them and to ensure that they are operating to full capacity. Revenue can only be recognised when Company B signs the contract to say that they are satisfied that the machinery is working to full capacity because it is at this point that all the risks and rewards pass from Company A to Company B. The sale, therefore, should be recognised in the year to 31 October 2017.

12.260 One of the conditions that has to be fulfilled when it comes to revenue recognition is that 'significant risks and rewards' have to be transferred from the seller to the buyer. Where the entity only retains an *insignificant* risk of ownership, the transaction falls to be classed as a sale and revenue can be recognised. This could be the case, for example, where the seller retains legal title to the goods in order that they can be taken back in the event of non-payment; a sale is recognised in this respect because the selling company have only retained an insignificant risk of ownership.

Rendering of services

12.261 This area of Section 23 lends itself to more subjectivity in terms of revenue recognition than with the sale of goods. This is because in order to qualify for revenue recognition, there often needs to be an estimate calculated of the amount of revenue to be recognised and this is done having regard to the 'stage of completion' (often referred to as the 'percentage of completion') and is dealt with in the construction contracts section of this chapter (see **12.263** below). In addition, the outcome of the transaction has to be reliably estimated and for the purposes of Section 23 and the rendering of services, the outcome of a transaction can be estimated reliably when **all** of the following conditions are satisfied:

- the amount of revenue can be measured reliably;
- it is probable that the company will receive economic benefit associated with the transaction;
- the stage of completion of the transaction can be measured reliably; and
- the costs incurred in respect of the transaction together with the costs to complete the transaction can be measured reliably.

12.262 Paragraph 23.15 of FRS 102 refers to a 'specific act' and a 'significant act'. The principle in this paragraph is that when a specific act is much more significant than any other act, the entity must postpone revenue recognition until the significant act is executed.

Example 12.105 – Services spanning more than one accounting period

A company operates in the document management industry and sells scanning equipment to companies who wish to become 'paperless'. In addition to the scanning equipment, the company also sells bespoke software and when the customer purchases the software it can choose to pay for a year's support services at the same time. The support service runs for a calendar year and the company has an accounting reference date of 31 March.

Where customers purchase the support service they will be invoiced from 1 January to 31 December each year. However, the company's financial year ends on 31 March and hence nine months' of the support service relates to the next financial year and so this portion of the services will be recognised as deferred income within creditors falling due within one year with the remaining three months' being recognised as revenue.

Construction contracts

12.263 Construction contract accounting under Section 23 uses the 'stage of completion' method which was referred to in the 'Rendering of services' section in **12.261** above.

When the outcome of a contract can be estimated reliably the entity recognises revenue and associated contract costs by reference to the stage of completion of the contract at the end of the reporting period. Paragraph 23.22 of FRS 102 offers possible methods to determine the stage of completion of a transaction or contract which include:

- the proportion that costs incurred for work performed to date bear on the estimated total costs. Such costs incurred for work performed to date will not include costs which relate to future activity (for example materials or prepayments);
- surveys of the work performed; and
- completion of a physical proportion of the contract work or the completion of a proportion of the service contract.

Example 12.106 – Progress payment received

During the course of a profitable contract, the company received a progress payment of £10,000 from the contractor. The financial controller has credited this progress payment to revenue in the profit and loss account.

Any progress payments (or advances) which are received from customers (in this case the contractor) do not reflect the work performed and hence should not be taken directly to revenue. Instead, they should be credited to the contract account in the nominal ledger and this amount will be taken into consideration when calculating the gross amount due from the contractor at the reporting date. The amount of revenue to be recognised at the reporting date should be recognised using the stage of completion method.

12.264 Where construction contracts are concerned, Section 23 is applied **separately** to each construction contract. On occasion, however, it may be necessary to apply Section 23 to the separately identifiable components of a single contract (or a group of contracts) so as to reflect the substance of a contract (or group of contracts).

In the event that a contract covers a number of assets, the construction of each contract is treated as a separate construction contract when:

- separate proposals for each contract have been submitted;

- each asset in the contract has been subjected to separate negotiation and the contractor and customer are able to accept, or reject, that part of the contract relating to each asset; and
- the costs and revenues of each asset can be identified.

Example 12.107 – Construction contract covering a number of assets

A company operates in the construction industry and is undertaking the construction of a retail park in the north of the UK. The contract is one contract but will comprise a number of individual retail outlets which include clothing retailers, a supermarket, a petrol station, a catalogue company and a 'do-it-yourself' outlet.

Each outlet has been subjected to separate proposals by the head office of each outlet which will be operating in the retail park. In addition, each outlet was subjected to a rigorous negotiation process and a number of offers were rejected by the contractor for each outlet until a satisfactory price was agreed and an undertaking from various construction companies that they would adhere to strict deadlines. As details have now been finalised, each outlet has been assigned costs and revenues by the contractor.

In this example, one contract is covering the construction of a number of assets for which separate proposals have been received. Negotiations have been completed for the construction of each outlet and the costs and revenues relating to the construction of each outlet have been assigned.

Despite one contract covering a number of assets, paragraph 23.19 of FRS 102 requires the construction of **each** asset to be treated as a **separate** construction contract.

The example above takes one contract and then separates that contract into each individual component asset. Paragraph 23.20, on the other hand, says that a group of contracts (whether with a single customer or with several customers) shall be treated as a single contract when:

- the group of contracts is negotiated as a single contract;
- the contracts are so closely interrelated that effectively they are part of a single contract with an overall profit margin; and
- the contracts are performed concurrently or in a continuous sequence.

Example 12.108 – Rectification costs

A construction company agrees to build eight new houses on a plot of land. The terms of the contract state that any remedial costs (often referred to as 'rectification costs') are to be borne by the construction company and will not be able to be recovered from the contractor. During the course of the building process the construction company incurred rectification costs of £10,000.

In such situations, the costs will not be recovered; the rectification costs are to be written off immediately to the profit and loss account.

Percentage of completion method

12.265 Accounting for construction contracts (and in many cases service contracts) will inherently involve a large degree of estimation on the part of the reporting entity. In terms of construction contracts, the starting point is to determine the outcome of the contract. There are three outcomes where construction contracts are concerned:

(1) the contract yields a profit;

(2) the contract makes a loss; or

(3) the outcome is uncertain.

Profit-making contracts

12.266 When it is expected that the contract will be profit-making, revenue and costs are recognised by way of the percentage of completion method.

Example 12.109 – Profit-making contract

On 1 May 2017 a construction company enters into a contract at a fixed price of £5 million. Costs have been analysed at the start of the contract as follows:

	£'000
Materials to date plus additional costs	1,000
Labour and other overheads	1,200
Depreciation	900
	3,100

The estimated profit in the contract is expected to be £1.9 million (£5m fixed price less £3.1m costs).

At the year-end 31 October 2017, the costs actually incurred were as follows:

	£'000
Purchase of materials	500
Labour and other overheads	600
Depreciation (£900 × 6/12)	450
Costs incurred at year-end	1,550

On 31 October 2017 the surveyor confirmed that the contract was 40% complete and the customer made a progress payment of £9,000 on that date.

As the surveyor has confirmed that 40% of the contract is complete as at 31 October 2017, 40% of the price can be recognised as revenue with 40% of the contract costs being recognised as cost of sales, ie:

	£'000
Turnover (40% × £5m)	2,000
Cost of sales (40% × £3.1m)	1,240
Gross profit	760

In the balance sheet, the gross amount due from the customer is calculated as follows:

	£'000
Costs to date:	
Purchase of materials	500
Labour and other overheads	600
Plant depreciation	450
Total costs to date	1,550
Contract profit recognised	760
	2,310
Less progress payment received	(9)
Gross amount due from customer	2,301

Loss-making contracts

12.267 When a contract is expected to make a loss, prudence needs to be exercised and the expected loss must be recognised immediately where cost recovery is not probable.

Example 12.110 – Loss-making contract

The outcome of a contract with a fixed price of £5 million has been assessed to make a loss of £900,000. At the year-end 31 October 2017 the surveyor confirms the project is 60% complete.

In this example, revenue will be recognised equivalent to 60% of the contract price (ie £3 million). The contract is expected to make a loss of £900,000 and hence cost of sales will be a balancing figure so as to generate the required loss, hence:

Turnover	£3,000,000	
Cost of sales	£3,900,000	(balancing figure)
Gross loss	£900,000	

Uncertain contracts

12.268 When the outcome of a contract is uncertain, no profit is recognised. The stage of completion method is still used to identify the amount of revenue that can be recognised on the contract, but cost of sales is again a balancing figure to generate a nil profit.

Example 12.111 – Uncertain contract outcome

The outcome of a project with a fixed price of £5 million is uncertain. At the year-end 31 October 2017 the surveyor confirms the contract is 60% complete.

In this scenario revenue will be recognised equivalent to 60% of the contract price (ie £3 million). It is uncertain whether the contract will make a profit or a loss and therefore cost of sales will also be £3 million, hence:

Turnover	£3,000,000
Cost of sales	£3,000,000
Gross profit	–

Interest, royalties and dividends

12.269 There are additional revenue streams which Section 23 deals with; namely revenue from income-yielding assets in the form of interest, royalties and dividends. Revenue in respect of such income streams can only be recognised when:

- it is probable (ie more likely than not) that the entity will receive economic benefit associated with the transaction; and
- the amount of revenue can be measured reliably.

Interest revenue

12.270 Interest revenue in the financial statements must be recognised by way of the effective interest method. The effective interest method uses the effective interest rate and in calculating the effective interest rate, the entity must include any related fees, finance charges paid or received, transaction costs and other premiums or discounts.

Example 12.112 – Interest calculated using the effective interest method

A finance company agrees to lend £1,000 at a discount of £900 over three years to a company. The instrument has a coupon rate of 5% which is paid to the lender at the end of each year and the principal amount at maturity is £1,000. Using the internal rate of return function in Microsoft Excel, the effective interest rate has been calculated at 8.95%. The loan profile in the lenders books can be analysed as follows:

Year	Opening amortised cost	Interest and principal payments	Interest income (A × 8.95%)	Debt discount amortisation (C–B)	Closing amortised cost (A+D)
	(A)	(B)	(C)	(D)	
1	900	50	81	31	931
2	931	50	83	33	964
3	964	1050	86*	36*	1000

*ignores the capital element

Focus

- The effective interest method discounts the expected future cash inflows and outflows which are expected over the life of the underlying asset.

Royalties

12.271 Royalty income is recognised as revenue on an accruals basis in accordance with the substance of the relevant agreement. In other words, it is recognised on a receivable rather than a received basis.

Dividends

12.272 Dividend income is to be recognised when the shareholder's right to receive payment is established. In some situations the right to receive the dividend may differ from the date on which the dividend is actually received and hence care must be taken to correctly recognise the timing of the dividend which is to be on a receivable, rather than a received, basis.

Disclosures

12.273 The disclosures relating to revenue may be as follows:

- The entity's accounting policy for revenue recognition.
- Where abridged financial statements have been prepared, the directors must consider disclosing the value of turnover in the notes to the financial statements.

In relation to construction contracts, a small company should present:

- The gross amount due from customers for contract work as an asset.
- The gross amount due to customers for contract work as a liability.

GOVERNMENT GRANTS

12.274 Section 24 *Government Grants* deals with the accounting requirements for government grants and while some of the accounting concepts have been brought in from the FRSSE (effective January 2015), there is a new model in Section 24 which was not in previous UK GAAP.

The Glossary to FRS 102 defines a government grant as:

> 'Assistance by government in the form of a transfer of resources to an entity in return for past or future compliance with specific conditions relating to the **operating activities** of the entity. Government refers to government, government agencies and similar bodies whether local, national or international.'[16]

The scope of Section 24 does not extend to government assistance which an entity receives in the form of benefits which are available in arriving at taxable profit (loss) or are determined or limited on the basis of income tax liability. Paragraph 24.3 cites examples of income tax holidays, investment tax credits, accelerated depreciation allowances and reduced income tax rates as such benefits. All aspects relating to income tax are dealt with in Section 29 *Income Tax* (see **12.343**).

16 FRS 102 Glossary **Government grant**.

Recognition and measurement of government grants

12.275 The underlying principle contained in Section 24 is that an entity must not recognise grants (including non-monetary grants) until there is reasonable certainty that the company will comply with the conditions which are attached to the grant. In addition, there must be reasonable certainty that the grant will be received by the company in order to recognise it in the financial statements. Once these conditions have been met, the entity then has two possible accounting policy choices:

(1) the performance model; or

(2) the accrual model.

Performance model

12.276 The performance model is a new concept in Section 24 which was not available under the FRSSE (effective January 2015) nor in SSAP 4 *Accounting for government grants*. The performance model works by recognising grant income when the grant's performance-related conditions are met. Certain grants are given by government without any conditions attached (for example to compensate for loss of income) and where grants are unconditional, they should be recognised within income when they are receivable. The performance model works as follows:

- A grant which does not impose specified future performance-related conditions on the recipient is recognised in income when the grant proceeds are receivable.
- A grant which does impose specified future performance-related conditions on the recipient is recognised in income only when the performance-related conditions are met.
- Grants received before the revenue recognition criteria are satisfied are recognised as a liability.

Example 12.113 – Early recognition of a grant

Alicia Enterprises Ltd has experienced a period of rapid expansion over the last couple of years and has an accounting reference date of 31 December. In October 2016 it opened up a new production plant in an area of high unemployment in an attempt to be seen to encourage individuals back into work. It has employed 100 members of staff and has entered into negotiations with the government to reclaim some of the costs incurred in training these new employees. The directors have calculated that they may be entitled to £5,000 worth of compensation for training these new employees and then offering them permanent employment.

In February 2017 the government agreed to the grant claim and gave the company the grant. The financial director has recognised the grant in the financial statements for the year-ended 31 December 2016 on the basis that the directors were confident that the claim would be successful.

The grant should not be recognised in the 31 December 2016 financial statements because the claim was not approved until the following February. Therefore, the grant should be recognised in the 31 December 2017 financial statements. Until the claim is approved by the government it is not certain whether the grant will be received and hence fails the recognition criteria in paragraph 24.3(A)(b) in FRS 102.

12.277 When conditions are attached to a grant, the grant can only be recognised in income when those conditions have been met. Therefore, it follows that until the performance-related conditions have been met, the grant is recognised as a liability and released to the profit and loss account when the performance conditions are met.

Example 12.114 – Conditions imposed on a grant

Alex Ltd has agreed to expand in a deprived area of the country in order to entice employment opportunities and has therefore agreed to construct a new production plant in the area. The company has entered into negotiations with the government for a setup grant amounting to £100,000. There are performance-related conditions attached to the grant which are as follows:

- Alex Ltd must ensure its production plant complies with all planning and environmental legislation.
- It must maintain a workforce of at least 100 individuals, all of whom must be employed on the commencement of trading.
- Production must commence on or before 31 December 2016.

The grant was received by the company on 1 February 2016.

Until the performance-related conditions have been met by Alex Ltd, the grant must be recognised as a liability in the balance sheet. If it is assumed that the performance-related conditions are met by the company by 31 December 2016, the liability can be derecognised and the grant taken to profit or loss. If, on the other hand, the grant conditions are not met by 31 December 2016, a liability representing the unfulfilled performance-related conditions is recognised until the conditions are met.

12.278 Grants which become repayable are recognised as a liability when the repayment meets the definition of a liability. In the example above (Alex Ltd), if the conditions were not met by 31 December 2016 then some (or all) of the grant may become repayable and hence in such cases all, or part, of the grant which is due for repayment must be recognised as a liability.

Example 12.115 – Potential repayment of a grant

James Joinery Co Ltd receives a government grant on 1 January 2017. The grant contains certain conditions, one of which is that the company must maintain a minimum number of permanent employees in its workforce over a three-year period. If the company fails to maintain the minimum number of employees, the grant is repayable in full.

Conditions are complied with

If the conditions are complied with and the company maintains the number of employees as stipulated in the grant conditions, the grant is recognised in income as it becomes non-repayable – for example on a straight-line basis over a three-year period.

Conditions are not complied with

If the company fails to comply with the conditions imposed in the grant conditions, then a liability is recognised for the amounts repayable. Any repayment is then applied to the unamortised balance of the grant with any excess being recognised in profit or loss.

The accrual model

12.279 The accrual model is the most familiar model in accounting for grants because this model has been carried over from the FRSSE (effective January 2015). There are four methods of accounting for grants under the accrual model:

- Grants relating to revenue are recognised in income on a systematic basis over the periods in which the entity recognises the related costs for which the grant is intended to compensate.
- A grant which becomes receivable as compensation for expenses or losses already incurred, or for the purpose of giving immediate financial support to the entity with no future related costs, is recognised in income in the period in which it becomes receivable.
- Grants relating to assets are recognised in income on a systematic basis over the expected useful life of the asset.
- Where part of a grant relating to an asset is deferred, it shall be recognised as deferred income and NOT deducted from the carrying amount of the asset.

12.280 When a grant is received, the first thing which the company must do is to establish whether the grant is a revenue-based grant or a capital-based grant. The accounting is then as follows:

- *Revenue-based* grants are recognised in income in the period the related costs are incurred by the entity for which the grant is intended to compensate. For grants which are received by the entity for compensation for expenses or losses which have already been incurred, the grant is recognised in income when it is received or receivable.
- *Capital-based* grants which relate to assets are recognised in income on a systematic basis over the useful life of the asset.

Example 12.116 – Capital-based grant

A company purchases an asset at a cost of £100,000 and pays cash for it. The expected useful life of the asset is ten years at which point the directors have assessed the residual value to be £20,000. The company's depreciation policy is to depreciate the asset on a straight-line basis over its expected useful life. The government have agreed to a grant of £35,000 and this was received on 1 December 2016. The company's year-end is 31 December 2016 and the depreciation policy is to charge a full year's depreciation in the year an asset is acquired with no depreciation charged in the year of disposal.

The accounting for this grant is as follows:

<u>On initial receipt of the grant</u>

DR cash at bank	£35,000
CR deferred income	(£35,000)

<u>On initial recognition of the asset</u>

DR property, plant and equipment	£100,000
CR cash at bank	(£100,000)

<u>Depreciation charge</u>

DR depreciation charge	£8,000 (£100,000 – £20,000/10 years)
CR accumulated depreciation	(£8,000)

<u>Grant income</u>

DR deferred income	£3,500 (£35,000 / 10 years)
CR grant income (profit and loss)	(£3,500)

Deferred income

This will be split between the portion falling due within one year and the portion falling due after more than one year as follows:

Falling due within one year	£3,500
Falling due after more than one year	£28,000

Focus

- Grants received in respect of capital expenditure cannot be offset against the cost of the asset. They must be deferred in the balance sheet and written off to profit or loss on a systematic basis over the useful life of the asset.

12.281 The accrual model is very different to the performance model in terms of accounting treatment. If the company were to use the performance model then it would recognise the grant in the profit and loss account as the performance-related conditions are met.

Non-monetary grants

12.282 Grants may not necessarily be made in cash – they can take other forms (such as land) and this is where problems can be encountered in terms of valuation. Paragraph 24.5 of FRS 102 says that the company must measure grants at the fair value of the asset received or receivable. Fair value is defined in **12.253** above.

Example 12.117 – Non-monetary grant

Fred's Fish Markets Ltd operates a chain of fish markets across the country and has an accounting reference date of 31 December. It has to apply to the government every five years to obtain a fishing licence and on 1 January 2016 the company received a non-transferable five-year licence to catch 15 tonnes of fish per annum. There are strict conditions attached to the grant relating to the fishing quota and if the company exceeds this quota there are substantial penalties which can be levied by the government.

The fishing licence is a government grant because the grant gives the company the right to remove up to 15 tonnes of fish per annum. The company has received the grant on the basis of the conditions attached to the grant (ie that the company will not exceed the quota). If the fair value of the grant is assessed to be £200,000 then this will be recognised as an intangible asset on the balance sheet of Fred's Fish Markets Ltd and will be amortised over a five-year period.

Under the performance model the grant of £200,000 will be recognised as income in the period in which it becomes receivable. The grant is non-transferable and hence will not be revoked as there are no future performance conditions.

Under the accrual model the grant is recognised as a liability and released to profit or loss over the life of the intangible asset (ie five years) in order to match the amortisation charge. The unamortised balance deferred in the balance sheet is separated between the portion falling due within one year and the portion falling due after more than one year.

Disclosures

12.283 The directors should consider making any disclosures necessary where grants are material so that the financial statements give a true and fair view. For example, accounting policies in respect of grants and any unfulfilled conditions pertaining to the grant.

BORROWING COSTS

12.284 Borrowing costs have been the subject of much debate over the years and accounting standards in the UK and Republic of Ireland have always allowed for an accounting policy choice in respect of such costs; they can either be capitalised or written off to profit or loss as incurred. Some years ago the (now defunct) Accounting Standards Board (ASB) issued a discussion paper *Measurement of Tangible Fixed Assets* and this discussion paper suggested that the capitalisation of borrowing costs should either be mandatory or prohibited so as to achieve consistency. The ASB concluded that the arguments for and against capitalisation were finely balanced and they decided that entities should have the option of capitalising or writing off such costs.

> **Focus**
>
> - There are some entities which incur a high level of borrowing costs, such as housing associations, and hence the accounting policy choice adopted must be applied consistency from one year to the next.

Borrowing costs are dealt with in FRS 102 at Section 25 *Borrowing Costs*. The section itself is a fairly short section and deals with the situation when a small company might use borrowings in order to construct a qualifying asset. Section 25 recognises that borrowing costs include:

- interest expense which is calculated using the effective interest method as per the requirements in Section 11 *Basic Financial Instruments*;
- finance costs relating to finance leases accounted for under Section 20 *Leases*; and

- exchange differences arising from borrowing denoted in a foreign currency to the extent which they are classed as an adjustment to interest charges.

> **Focus**
>
> - In broad terms, borrowing costs are essentially those costs which are directly attributable to the acquisition, construction or production of a qualifying asset and would have been avoided if the expenditure on the qualifying asset had not been made.

Recognition of borrowing costs

12.285 A small company can choose to capitalise or write off borrowing costs as appropriate and provided that the accounting policy choice the company chooses is applied consistently from one period to the next. Paragraph 25.2 says that only those borrowing costs which are *directly attributable* to the acquisition, construction or production of a 'qualifying asset' can be included as part of the cost of that asset. A 'qualifying asset' is defined in the Glossary to FRS 102 as follows (note words which are in bold type mean they are defined in the Glossary):

> 'An **asset** that necessarily takes a substantial period of time to get ready for its intended use or sale. Depending on the circumstances any of the following may be qualifying assets:
>
> (a) **inventories**;
>
> (b) manufacturing plants;
>
> (c) power generating facilities;
>
> (d) **intangible assets**; and
>
> (e) **investment properties**.
>
> **Financial assets**, and inventories that are produced over a short period of time, are not qualifying assets.
>
> Assets that are ready for their intended use or sale when acquired are not qualifying assets.'[17]

> **Focus**
>
> - The definition of borrowing costs includes the term '… a substantial period of time'. A substantial period of time is taken to mean longer than 12 months.

17 FRS 102 Glossary **Qualifying asset**.

Once borrowing costs qualify to be accounted for under the provisions in Section 25, an entity can either capitalise those costs as part of the cost of the asset or they can be recognised as an expense in profit or loss.

12.286 There can be two situations when a small company incurs borrowings to fund the cost of construction of a qualifying asset:

- funds are borrowed specifically for the purpose of constructing a qualifying asset; or
- general borrowings are used.

Funds borrowed specifically to construct a qualifying asset

12.287 When a company borrows funds specifically to construct a qualifying asset, paragraph 25.2B requires the company to determine the amount of borrowing costs which are eligible for capitalisation. This is calculated as the actual borrowing costs incurred on that borrowing during the accounting period *less* any investment income (bank interest received) earned by the company on the temporary investment of those borrowings. In other words the amount eligible for capitalisation is interest paid less interest received.

General borrowings are used

12.288 The issue becomes slightly more complex when general borrowings are used because paragraph 25.2C requires the amount of borrowing costs eligible for capitalisation to be determined by applying a *capitalisation rate* to the expenditure on that asset and for this purpose the expenditure on the asset is the average carrying amount of the asset during the period including borrowing costs which have been previously capitalised as part of the cost of the asset. The capitalisation rate to be used in an accounting period is the weighted average of the rates which apply to the entity's general borrowings which are outstanding during the accounting period. If the reporting entity is constructing a number of qualifying assets then any borrowings that have been obtained for the purpose of constructing these additional qualifying assets are *excluded* from the capitalisation rate calculation.

Focus

- Paragraph 25.2C restricts the amount of borrowing costs which a company can capitalise so they cannot exceed the amount of borrowing costs which the company incurred during the period.

Example 12.118 – Calculation of capitalisation rate

A company has three sources of borrowings during an accounting period as follows:

	Outstanding liability	Interest charge
Five-year loan	£15,000	£3,500
30-year loan	£425,000	£17,800
Bank overdraft	£8,000	£1,400

If all of the above borrowings are used to finance the production of a qualifying asset, the capitalisation rate is calculated as follows:

$$\frac{3{,}500 + 17{,}800 + 1{,}400}{15{,}000 + 425{,}000 + 8{,}000} \times 100 = 5.07\%$$

If the five-year loan is used to finance a specific qualifying asset, the capitalisation rate which should be used on the other qualifying asset is:

$$\frac{17{,}800 + 1{,}400}{425{,}000 + 8{,}000} \times 100 = 4.43\%$$

Example 12.119 – Suspension of construction

A company is in the process of constructing its new purpose-built headquarters. The company has a year-end of 31 December 2016 and because of an issue with the local council, construction was suspended on 1 March 2016 and did not resume until 31 October 2016.

Paragraph 25.2D of FRS 102 requires that where active development of the asset has paused then capitalisation of borrowing costs is also suspended.

Capitalisation of borrowing costs must also cease once substantially all of the activities necessary to prepare the qualifying asset for its intended use or sale are complete.

Disclosures

12.289 Disclosures relating to borrowing costs may be as follows:

- Where the entity adopts a policy of capitalising borrowing costs the company should disclose the amount of borrowing costs capitalised in the period.

The directors must also consider any additional disclosures which may be necessary where borrowing costs are concerned in order that the financial statements give a true and fair view.

SHARE-BASED PAYMENT

12.290 Section 26 of FRS 102 *Share-based Payment* outlines the accounting requirements where a small business might enter into share-based payment arrangements. The overarching objective of this section is to provide the necessary accounting treatment so as to reflect the effects of share-based payment arrangements in the profit and loss account as in some cases there is no associated cash flow. There are three types of share-based payment arrangement which Section 26 deals with:

- **Equity-settled share-based payment transactions**. These are where the entity receives goods or services in exchange for its own equity instruments (eg shares). For the purposes of Section 26 this includes both shares and share options. Equity-settled share-based payment transactions also include situations where the entity receives goods or services but does not have to pay for them.
- **Cash-settled share-based payment transactions**. These arrangements are where the entity receives goods or services and incurs a liability to transfer cash or other assets to the supplier. Such arrangements are based on the price (or value) of the entity's shares or other equity instruments of either the entity, or another group entity.
- **Transactions where a choice of settlement exists**. This is where an entity receives goods or services and the terms of the contract allows the transaction to be settled either in cash or in equity instruments.

Section 26 also deals with group members where a share-based payment transaction could be settled by another group entity (or shareholder of a group entity) on behalf of the group member receiving the goods or services. The exception to this would be where the transaction is for a purpose other than payment for goods or services supplied to the entity receiving them.

In addition, cash-settled share-based payment transactions extend to share appreciation rights. An example of this would be where the company might grant share appreciation rights to its employees whereby they become entitled to a future cash payment (rather than shares) based on the increase in the entity's share price over a period of time. The entity might also grant the employees a right to receive a future cash payment by granting them a right to shares which can be redeemable either at the choice of the employee or mandatorily by the entity. Such shares extend to shares that will be issued on the exercise of share options.

Vesting conditions

12.291 The term 'vesting conditions' means the conditions that are included in a share-based payment arrangement. Under a share-based payment arrangement, a third party has a right to receive cash, other assets or equity instruments of an entity when the third party's entitlement to cash, other assets or equity instruments are no longer conditional on the vesting conditions being satisfied and hence the cash, other assets or equity instruments become an entitlement to the third party.

An example of a vesting condition could be where the entity says that employees will receive shares in the entity if the net assets of the company rises to a pre-determined level.

The vesting date is the date on which the shares become exercisable. Where goods are received the vesting date is not relevant because the vesting date is simply the date on which the goods are received by the entity. The issue becomes more complicated where services are rendered and hence the vesting date does become relevant.

Where the small company issues shares that vest immediately these are regarded as a form of remuneration and therefore the company must immediately recognise the expense for the employee service which they have received in full on the date which the shares (or share options) have been granted.

Where the share-based payment does not vest until a specified period of service is completed by the employee then the accounting takes place when such services are rendered with a corresponding increase in equity or liabilities.

Example 12.120 – Establishing the grant date

On 5 July 2017 the directors of Smyth Ltd sent letters to its 20 employees offering them the option to subscribe in the shares of the entity. The board of directors agreed this offer in the Annual General Meeting on 4 July 2017 and the shareholders agreed to the awards on 29 July 2017.

The allotment of shares or rights to shares in general must be approved by the shareholders in a general meeting, or by the entity's articles of association. The award was approved by the directors on 4 July 2017 but was subject to shareholder approval which took place on 29 July 2017 and hence the grant date is 29 July 2017.

Recognition of a share-based payment transaction

12.292 Goods or services acquired by an entity under a share-based payment arrangement are recognised in the financial statements when the company obtains the goods or services with the corresponding credit entry being recognised within equity (if equity-settled) or liabilities (if cash-settled).

Example 12.121 – Accounting for a cash-settled share-based payment transaction

A company receives goods which are subject to a share-based payment arrangement as agreed with the supplier. The terms of the agreement provide for the transaction to be cash-settled. The bookkeeper has correctly debited the cost of the goods to the appropriate profit and loss expense account but is unsure as to where to post the corresponding credit entry.

As this arrangement is that of a *cash-settled* share-based payment arrangement, the credit entry will be taken to liabilities.

Recognition when vesting conditions exist

12.293 When share-based payments granted to employees vest immediately it means that the employee does not have to complete a specified period of service before they become unconditionally entitled to the share-based payments and unless there is information to the contrary, the entity assumes that the services have been received from the employee as consideration for the share-based payment. It follows, therefore, that on the grant date the entity will recognise the expense in profit or loss with a corresponding increase in equity (where the share-based payment is equity-settled) or as an increase in liabilities (where the share-based payment is cash-settled).

12.294 In situations where the share-based payments do not vest immediately, the entity will account for the services rendered by the employees as the employees complete the service during the vesting period. As employees render their services, the entity recognises the expense in profit or loss with a corresponding increase in equity or liabilities.

MEASUREMENT OF SHARE-BASED PAYMENTS

Equity-settled share-based payments

12.295 In respect of equity-settled share-based payment transactions, the reporting entity must measure these at fair value where a reliable measure of fair value can be obtained with a corresponding increase in equity. Where it is not possible to measure the equity-settled share-based payment at fair value, it must be measured by reference to the fair value of the equity instruments granted. This becomes inherently difficult where employees' services are concerned. In respect of transactions with employees and others the fair value of the services received is measured by reference to the fair value of the equity instruments granted.

Focus

- It is usually not possible to reliably estimate the fair value of the services received.

For transactions entered into with employees, the reporting entity should measure the fair value of the equity instruments at the grant date. The grant date in respect of transactions with third parties (excluding employees) is the date on which the entity obtains the goods or services.

12.296 When an entity is estimating the number of equity instruments which are expected to vest it must take into consideration all conditions which relate to employee service, or to a non-market performance condition (such as achieving a pre-determined profit level). This information is revised accordingly if new information emerges which indicates that the number of instruments which are expected to vest differs from the number previously expected.

Paragraph 26.9 of FRS 102 says that all market conditions and non-vesting conditions are taken into consideration when the entity is estimating the fair value of the shares or share options at the measurement date with no subsequent adjustment irrespective of the outcome of the market or non-vesting conditions (provided that all other vesting conditions are satisfied).

Focus

- In a small company it is likely that market prices are not going to be available for the purposes of fair valuing the company's shares (paragraph 26.10(a) of FRS 102). Paragraph 26.10(b) says that where an observable market price is unavailable then fair value can be measured using a recent transaction in the entity's shares; again this is unlikely to apply to a small company and it is more likely that paragraph 26.10(b)(ii) will apply which says that fair value can be derived using a recent independent fair valuation of the entity or its principal assets. Where none of these methods provides a reasonable measure of fair value then paragraph 26.10(c) says that the directors must indirectly measure the fair value of the shares using a valuation method which uses market data to the greatest extent practicable to estimate what the share price would be on the grant date in an arm's length transaction. In this scenario the directors must use their judgement to apply a generally accepted valuation method for placing a fair value on the company's shares which is also appropriate to the circumstances of the entity.

Share options and share appreciation rights which are equity-settled

12.297 In respect of share options and share appreciation rights, there is a hierarchy of valuation methods contained in paragraphs 26.11(a)–(c) in which to arrive at a fair value. The hierarchy works in the following order:

- an observable market price is used for the equity instruments granted; or
- where an observable market price is not available the fair value of the share options and share appreciation rights are measured using entity-specific market data (for example data available from a recent transaction in the share options); or
- where an observable market price is not available and it is not practicable to obtain a measurement of fair value under the second bullet point, management must indirectly measure the fair value of the share options or share appreciation rights using an alternative valuation technique using an option pricing model.

For a small company entering into such transactions it is likely that the third bullet point is going to be more common as observable prices would only be available if the shares were listed which is not going to apply to a small, privately-owned company and it is likely that the accountants performing the valuation will use appropriate software to value the share options or share appreciation rights.

Modifications to an equity-settled share-based payment arrangement

12.298 It might be the case that an entity makes a change to the terms and conditions on which equity instruments were originally granted. Where a change to the terms and conditions takes place and this change is in the employees' favour the modified terms and conditions must be taken into consideration when accounting for the share-based payment transaction as follows:

Modification increases the fair value of equity instruments granted

12.299 Where the revised terms and conditions has the effect of increasing the fair value of the equity instruments granted (and hence is favourable to the employees), measured immediately before and after the modification, the company includes the incremental fair value granted in the measurement of the amount recognised for services as the amount of consideration for the equity instruments granted. The incremental fair value granted is calculated as the difference between the fair value of the modified equity instrument and the fair value of the original equity instrument.

Where the change to the terms and conditions takes place during the vesting period, the incremental fair value granted to the employees is included in the measurement of the amount recognised for services received over the period from the modification date until the date on which the modified equity instruments vest (in addition to the amount based on the grant date fair value of the original equity instruments).

Modification reduces the fair value of equity instruments granted

12.300 Where the terms and conditions of a share-based payment arrangement are amended such that they become unfavourable to the employee (ie they reduce the total fair value of the share-based payment arrangement), the company should continue to account for employee services received as consideration for the equity instrument granted as if the modifications to the original terms and conditions had not taken place.

Example 12.122 – Modification to the terms and conditions of a share-based payment award

Zedcolour Trading Ltd (Zedcolour) operates a share option scheme for its employees. It has valued its shares using an option pricing model and the option exercise price is £20. At the Annual General Meeting, the directors decided to roll these options into a new award. As a result, Zedcolour cancelled the original share options and issued new options under the new award. The new options are granted at a price of £17 as the options were revalued using an option pricing model which suggested the value of the shares were now £16 since the grant of the old award.

The fact that Zedcolour has cancelled one award and replaced it with another would not constitute a cancellation of the old award and the creation of a new award. What Zedcolour has, in fact, done is modified the existing award because the directors have indicated that this new award replaces a cancelled award and so it is treated as if it has been modified. The company accounts for the incremental fair value of the new award at the date of modification and spreads this over the vesting period of the new award. In respect of the old award, Zedcolour would continue to charge for the original award over the original vesting period.

Cancellation or settlement of an award

12.301 If a company cancels or settles an award then it accounts for such a cancellation or settlement as an acceleration of vesting. This has the effect of immediate recognition of the amount that would otherwise have been recognised for services the company received over the remainder of the vesting period.

Example 12.123 – Cancellation of a share-based payment award

On 1 January 2015 Gabriella Gardening Equipment Ltd (Gabriella) made an award of 100 ordinary shares to its financial controller as an equity-settled share-based payment arrangement. The terms of the award are that the financial controller must remain in the employment of Gabriella for a three-year period. Gabriella has used a valuation technique to arrive at a fair value of the award on the grant date which was calculated as £1,200. The financial controller has been employed by Gabriella for a relatively long period of time and at the grant date it was expected that the award would vest.

On 1 January 2016 the financial controller indicated that she was going to leave the employment of Gabriella to retire because of ill health. As a gesture of goodwill, the company agreed to settle the award in cash on a pro-rata basis and the financial controller received an additional £400 in cash (£1,200 × ⅓). This value was accounted for in the financial statements as an expense by the new financial controller.

Paragraph 26.14 says that a company should account for a cancellation as an acceleration of vesting and must therefore recognise the full amount which would otherwise have been recognised for services received over the remainder of the vesting period. Therefore to comply with this requirement, Gabriella must recognise an additional £800 (ie the remainder of the award which would have otherwise been recognised in years two and three of the award had the previous financial controller not retired through ill health). The corresponding credit entry is taken to equity.

Cash-settled share-based payments

12.302 When a company enters into a cash-settled share-based payment plan it measures the goods or services acquired at the fair value of the goods or services received together with a corresponding increase in liabilities. Until such time that the liability is settled, the company must continue remeasuring the liability to fair value at each reporting date and fluctuations in the fair value of the liability are taken to the profit and loss account.

Example 12.124 – Cash-settled share-based payment with remeasurement

Williams Ltd grants 1,000 share options to 50 members of staff on 1 January 2016. The terms of the arrangement are that on the exercise date the employees will receive cash which will equate to the increase in the valuation of the company's net worth calculated by reference to a valuation technique since the date of the grant. All of the options vest on 31 December 2017 and can be exercised during 2017 and 2018. The directors of Williams Ltd estimate that at the date of the grant the fair value of each share option will be £10 and that 10% of the staff will leave evenly during the two-year period. The company accountants have valued the share options as follows:

31 December 2016	£13
31 December 2017	£9
31 December 2018	£12
31 December 2019	£11

The directors have estimated that 10% of management will leave before the end of 2017. The intrinsic value of each option as at 31 December 2018 was £10 and six employees exercised their options. The remaining 39 exercised their options at the end of 2019 when the intrinsic value was equal to the fair value of £11. The amount recognised as an expense and as a liability each year is as follows:

Year		**Expense**	**Liability**
		£	£
2016	45 × 1,000 × £13 × ½	292,500	292,500
2017	45 × 1,000 × £9	112,500	405,000
2018	39 × 1,000 × £12	123,000	468,000*
2019	39 × 1,000 × £11	(39,000)	0**

*the expense includes an additional £60,000 being the cash paid to those exercising their options (6 employees × 1,000 × £10).

**the liability is extinguished and the previous cost reversed as cash paid to those that have exercised their options (39 × 1,000 × £11) was less than the opening liability of £468,000.

Share-based payment with cash alternatives

12.303 Situations may present themselves where the entity or the counterparty has a cash-settlement option. The Financial Reporting Council issued an Exposure Draft FRED 61 *Draft Amendments to FRS 102 – Share-based payment transactions with cash alternatives* in April 2015. The proposal was to align the requirements of paragraph 26.15 with IFRS 2 *Share-based Payment* because the August 2014 version of FRS 102 said that where the entity or the counterparty has a cash-settlement option, such transactions are accounted for as cash-settled unless the entity has a past practice of settling by issuing equity instruments or there is no commercial substance in the cash-settlement option.

FRS 102 has been amended to state that cash-settlement accounting is only applied where the entity has a present obligation to settle in cash. A present obligation will exist where the entity has a past practice of settling such transactions in cash, or if the equity settlement option has no commercial substance or the entity has no unconditional right to avoid cash-settlement.

This change affects those shares where a one-off event exists because they can then be treated as equity-settled, whereas previously they would have been treated as cash-settled as the entity would not have had the evidence for settlement either way at the time the shares were granted. Under the amendment any transactions in which there is the option to settle in cash, the option is accounted for as cash-settled which is no different to how FRS 102 treated such transactions previously.

Focus

- It is important to emphasise that the amendment to FRS 102 does not amend the accounting requirements in respect of equity-settled or cash-settled share-based payment arrangements.

Group issues

12.304 For small groups some of the issues dealt with in paragraph 26.16 of FRS 102 will not necessarily apply, but it is worth examining them in this part of the section because they may present themselves and with more medium-sized groups falling to be classed as small under the new Companies Act 2006 this area of section 26 is given wider scope.

Paragraph 26.16 says that if a share-based payment is granted to employees of one or more members in group, it is permissible to recognise and measure the share-based payment expense on the basis of a reasonable allocation of the expense for the group.

In many cases this will be a fairly straightforward calculation because each member of the group will reflect its share of the share-based payment expense in its own separate financial statements. However, situations may present themselves where this calculation is not necessarily straightforward; for example where members of staff may work in different companies across the group or where a director may be a director of the parent company and also a director of the subsidiary company.

12.305 Where it is not clear which entity, or entities, within a group of companies should reflect the share-based payment charge in their individual financial statements, the following factors may assist:

- Where staff secondments take place within the group there may be intercompany recharges to the group member receiving the employee services and hence the share-based payment charge would follow the cost of the employee (ie the group member receiving the recharge).
- In addition for staff secondments, if the terms of the employee's contract stipulates that they may be temporarily seconded to another group member, the entity receiving the employee on secondment will be

deemed the employer for the period of the secondment and hence will reflect the share-based payment charge for the period of the secondment.

- Where a director is both a director of the parent and a director of a subsidiary there should be consideration as to whether the director receives the reward in respect of the group as a whole or for the individual subsidiary. If it is for the individual subsidiary then it will reflect the share-based payment charge.
- If one group member has overall responsibility for issuing an employee's contract and undertaking periodic appraisals of the employee's performance, and authorising overtime and bonuses then this group member would normally take the charge in respect of the employee's share-based payment award.

Disclosures

12.306 There are no legally required disclosures for small companies relating to share-based payment arrangements but directors should consider making any disclosures they feel are necessary to give a true and fair view having regard to the disclosure requirements in paragraphs 26.18–26.23 of FRS 102.

IMPAIRMENT OF ASSETS

12.307 The overarching principle in financial reporting is that assets should not be carried in the balance sheet (statement of financial position) at any more than recoverable amount. Section 27 *Impairment of Assets* in FRS 102 deals with the issue of asset impairment and recognises that an impairment loss arises when the carrying value of an asset exceeds its recoverable amount. There are, however, certain types of assets for which Section 27 does not deal with as follows:

- assets which arise in construction contracts (see Section 23 *Revenue* and **12.252**);
- deferred tax assets (see Section 29 *Income Tax* and **12.346**);
- financial assets which are accounted for under the provisions of Section 11 *Basic Financial Instruments* and Section 12 *Other Financial Instruments Issues* (see **12.23** and **12.55**);
- investment property which is measured using fair value (see Section 16 *Investment Property* and **12.116**); and
- biological assets related to agricultural activity which is measured at fair value less estimated costs to sell (see **12.387**).

In addition to the above, Section 27 also does not apply to impairment of deferred acquisition costs and intangible assets which arise from insurance and reinsurance contracts and which are accounted for under the provisions in FRS 103 *Insurance Contracts*.

Example 12.125 – Financial asset with an indicator of impairment

Havannah Ltd has a year-end of 31 August 2017 and on this date a debtors listing was extracted from the bookkeeping system. This showed a debtor owing an amount of £100,000. The debt has been outstanding for several months and the customer has told the credit controller that the company is experiencing cash flow difficulties.

The debt of £100,000 has an indicator of impairment because it may be the case that the customer goes into liquidation or ceases to trade and hence the debt becomes irrecoverable. As assets should not be stated in the balance sheet in excess of recoverable amount a provision for part, or all, of the debt should be made to write the debt down to recoverable amount.

Inventories

12.308 Section 27 deals with the issue of impairment of inventories in paragraphs 27.2–27.4. In a lot of cases a degree of judgement is needed when it comes to valuing inventory – particularly items such as work in progress. Paragraph 27.2 requires a company to make an assessment at each reporting date as to whether any items of inventory are impaired. The entity does this by comparing the carrying value of each item of inventory with its selling price less estimated costs to complete and sell. Where estimated selling price less costs to complete and sell is lower than the carrying amount, the inventory is impaired and the impairment loss is recognised in profit or loss immediately.

Example 12.126 – Item of inventory showing indicators of impairment

Computers R Us manufacture laptop and desktop computers. It has a batch of component parts valued at £25,000 for which it uses in its 'Fastpace' brand of laptop. The company has a year-end of 31 March 2017 and during this financial year the company has announced that the Fastpace brand is being withdrawn from the market with immediate effect as the brand is now considered to be obsolete. The components cannot be used in any other items and the directors have suggested that they be scrapped.

It would be inappropriate to recognise the component parts in inventory at £25,000 because this value will probably not be recovered; indeed the directors have suggested that the components be scrapped and hence estimated selling price less costs to complete and sell is estimated to be £nil. As a result the directors should write-down the value of the inventory to £nil by recognising an impairment loss in profit or loss of £25,000.

12.309 It is not unusual for small companies to have groups of inventory which are all similar in nature or relate to the same product line. Where this is the case, or if it is impracticable to determine selling price less costs to complete and sell for inventory on an item by item basis, then the company can group such items for the purposes of assessing impairment.

Impairment reversal for inventory

12.310 If a company has recognised an impairment loss in one accounting period because selling price less costs to complete and sell was lower than carrying amount, but the circumstances which gave rise to the impairment loss in the first place now cease to apply, or if there is clear evidence that selling price less costs to complete and sell have increased, then the entity can reverse the amount of the impairment previously recognised (or part thereof).

Focus

- Where impairment reversals are concerned, it is important that any reversal in a subsequent accounting period is restricted to the amount of the original impairment loss. This is to make sure that the new carrying amount is at the lower of cost and the revised selling price less costs to complete and sell.

Impairment of other assets

12.311 When an asset(s) has a carrying value in the financial statements in excess of its recoverable amount then the asset is said to be impaired. When such situations present themselves the asset must be written down to recoverable amount by way of an impairment write-down which is recognised immediately in profit or loss. However, if an asset is being measured using the revaluation model as permitted in Section 17 *Property, Plant and Equipment*, any write-down can be taken to the revaluation reserve to the extent of any previous gains recognised in the revaluation reserve in respect of that same asset(s). Any amounts in excess of the revaluation reserve are then recognised in profit or loss.

Indicators of impairment

12.312 Quite often in a small company it is fairly straightforward to determine if an asset is suffering from impairment. For example if an item of machinery is broke beyond repair and it has a carrying value in the fixed assets register then it is more than likely that the scrap value will be negligible (sometimes £nil) and hence the asset will need writing down in the accounts. Trade debtors who are experiencing cash flow difficulties may need general or specific provisions making against them to bring the amounts owed at the reporting date to recoverable amount. Whatever the situation might be, it is important that assets are not stated at an inflated value because this will render the accounts misleading.

12.313 When assessing indicators of impairment, an entity is required to consider two sources of information (as a minimum):

- external sources of information; and
- internal sources of information.

External sources of information might suggest an asset has become impaired due to:

- the market value of the asset declining more significantly than would otherwise have been the case due to passage of time;
- changes, of an unfavourable nature, have taken place (or are expected to take place) relating to technological advances, the market in which the asset belongs or the economic or legal environment in which the asset belongs;
- interest rates or market rates of return on investments have increased which are expected to materially affect any discount rate which is used in the calculation of an asset's value in use and decrease the fair value less costs to sell of the asset; and
- the entity's carrying value of its net assets is more than the estimated fair value of the entity as a whole which has been valued, perhaps, due to a potential sale.

Example 12.127 – Change in legislation

Pete's Pesticide Co Ltd (Pete) manufactures pesticides for use in the agricultural industry and has a year-end date of 31 December 2016. It has a machine in its production process that manufactures one type of pesticide. The machine can only be used to manufacture this type of pesticide because it is very dangerous and can cause death if it is used incorrectly.

During the year to 31 December 2016 the Government announced that it was going to introduce legislation to ban the use of this pesticide in the next two years because it is considered too dangerous for use and has been responsible for the deaths of a large number of wild animals.

A change in the law (ie the banning of the pesticide) is an external source of information which would give rise to a significant adverse change in which the machine used to manufacture the pesticide belongs. This is because the machine will no longer be in use after the ban is implemented and hence the directors must write-down the asset to its recoverable amount (which may be £nil).

Internal sources of information relating to impairment are also a useful source of determining whether an asset is showing signs of impairment. In this respect an asset may be impaired if:

- there is evidence of technological obsolescence or physical damage to the asset;
- significant changes are about to take place (or have taken place) at the entity which may affect the asset(s) concerned (such as a discontinued operation or the asset becoming redundant or idle);
- the entity is planning to dispose of the asset before the previously expected disposal date; or
- evidence is available which suggests that the economic performance of an asset is worse than previously expected.

Example 12.128 – Impairment through an idle asset

During the year to 30 June 2017, a company manufactured a new brand of soap and purchased a machine solely dedicated to this new brand. After launch of the product, adverse press reports were published which suggested that the soap was responsible for a number of skin complaints after its use. The company had the product tested and it was found that the allergy was caused by a manufacturing defect and the company made the decision to withdraw the brand from the market immediately and advised all shops which stocked the product to take it off the shelves and issue a product recall. The directors have also decided that this product will not be continued.

In the year to 30 June 2017 the economic performance of the asset which produced the bars of soap has become impaired because it has performed worse than was previously expected. The company is no longer producing the soap and hence the machine will become idle and should therefore be written down to its recoverable amount with the impairment loss being recognised in profit or loss immediately.

Recoverable amount

12.314 The 'recoverable amount' of an asset is the *higher* of:

- fair value *less* costs to sell; and
- value in use.

Fair value less costs to sell

12.315 Fair value less costs to sell is the amount which can be obtained from the sale of the asset in an arm's length transaction with unconnected, knowledgeable and willing third parties less the costs associated with the disposal.

Paragraph 27.14 of FRS 102 suggests that the best evidence of fair value less costs to sell of an asset is a price that is contained in a binding sale agreement or active market for the asset. An 'active market' is one in which the asset is regularly traded and where reliable measures of prices can be obtained.

Not all small companies will have binding sales agreements relating to assets which they are planning to dispose of and in this respect fair value less costs to sell should be based on the best available information which may indicate the value at which the entity will receive in an arm's length disposal.

> **Focus**
>
> - In estimating fair value less costs to sell, the entity must also take into consideration any restrictions which are imposed on that asset and costs to sell should factor in these restrictions. Where such restrictions are passed on to potential purchasers of the asset, the fair value of the asset may be lower than that of an asset which does not have any restrictions imposed on it.

Value in use

12.316 Value in use is the most complex value to obtain because it is the present value of the future cash flows expected to be received from an asset. The calculation itself involves estimating the future cash flows (which can be inherently difficult for a small company) to be received from an asset and then discounting these cash flows to present day values using an appropriate discount rate.

> **Focus**
>
> - It might not be necessary to determine *both* fair value less costs to sell and value in use. This will apply where the either amount is in excess of its carrying amount and hence if fair value less costs to sell exceeds the carrying amount of the asset, the asset is not impaired and hence calculating value in use becomes irrelevant.

12.317 Value in use calculations can become very complicated – particularly for a small company who may ask their professional advisers to assist them in arriving at such a valuation. Section 27 at paragraph 27.16 requires the value in use calculation to contain various elements which include:

(1) the estimated future cash flows which the entity expects to receive from the asset;

(2) the entity's expectations concerning any variability in the amount or timings of those cash flows;

(3) the time value of money which is to reflect the current market risk-free rate of interest;

(4) the cost of bearing the inherent uncertainty in the asset; and

(5) other factors such as illiquidity which third parties would bring into account in pricing the future cash flows which are expected to be generated from the asset.

In (1) above the estimated future cash flows which the entity expects to receive from the asset should also include:

- projected cash inflows from using the asset;
- projected cash outflows directly associated with the cash inflows from the asset, such as preparing the asset for use; and
- net cash flows (if any) to be received or paid when the asset is disposed of.

Focus

- A company might be able to use recent financial budgets or forecasts to estimate such cash flows but in any event the future cash flows must be estimated based on the asset in its current condition. However, the estimated future cash flows should **not** include cash flows from financing activities or income tax payments or refunds.

Discount rate

12.318 When calculating value in use, a discount rate has to be applied to discount the estimated future cash flows to present value. When arriving at a discount rate, the company must ensure that it uses a *pre-tax* rate which reflects:

- the time value of money; and
- the risks which are confined to the asset for which future cash flows have not been adjusted (this is to avoid double-counting).

Focus

- Where assets are held for their service potential (for example a school building), a cash flow driven valuation is likely to be inappropriate and this why such assets are generally valued at their depreciated replacement cost which is more appropriate as a measurement model; although other models may be equally as appropriate.

Cash-generating units

12.319 The Glossary to FRS 102 defines a 'cash-generating unit' as:

> 'The smallest identifiable group of **assets** that generates cash inflows that are largely independent of the cash inflows from other assets or groups of assets.'[18]

18 FRS 102 Glossary **Cash-generating unit**.

Where impairment losses for a cash-generating unit are concerned there is a certain order in which they must be apportioned to as follows:

- first, to reduce the carrying amount of any goodwill allocated to the cash-generating unit; and
- then, to the other assets of the unit pro-rata on the basis of the carrying amount of each asset in the cash-generating unit.

Under the FRSSE (effective January 2015) an impairment loss would have been allocated to goodwill first; then to any capitalised intangible fixed assets in the unit and finally to the tangible fixed assets in the unit on a pro-rata basis (or a more appropriate basis).

Example 12.129 – Allocating an impairment loss in a cash-generating unit

Morley Ltd has undertaken an impairment test on one of its groups of assets which is considered to be a cash-generating unit. Financial statement extracts for the year-ended 30 September 2017 are as follows:

	£
Goodwill	130,000
Plant and machinery	200,000

The cash-generating unit has suffered an impairment loss of £150,000 during the year. The financial director has calculated fair value less costs to sell relating to goodwill is £60,000 and the value in use figure is £50,000. The directors consider it impracticable to arrive at a fair value less costs to sell or value in use amount for plant and machinery.

The impairment loss of £150,000 is first allocated to goodwill with the remainder being applied to the plant and machinery. However, neither the goodwill, nor any asset in a cash-generating unit, can be reduced below the *higher* of:

(1) fair value less costs to sell (if determinable);

(2) value in use (if determinable); and

(3) zero.

As fair value less costs to sell is higher than value in use, fair value becomes the recoverable amount. Goodwill is to be carried at £60,000, so of the £150,000 impairment, £70,000 (£130,000 less £60,000) will be allocated to goodwill with the remaining £80,000 being charged against plant and machinery. Financial statement extracts will then be as follows:

	£
Goodwill	60,000
Plant and machinery	120,000

Impairment of goodwill

12.320 Goodwill has not been without controversy over the years – largely because of its subjective nature. This subjective nature was tested in the case of *Commissioners of Inland Revenue v Muller & Co Margarine* [1901] AC 217. The presiding judge, Lord MacNaghten said:

> 'What is goodwill? It is a thing very easy to describe, very difficult to define. It is the benefit and advantage of the good name, reputation and connection of the business. It is the attractive force which brings in custom. It is the one thing which distinguishes an old established business from a new business at its first start. Goodwill is composed as a variety of elements. It differs in its composition in different trades and in different businesses in the same trade. One element may preponderate here, and another there.'

12.321 The problem with goodwill is generally placing a value on it. In addition, paragraph 27.24 also acknowledges that goodwill on its own cannot be sold or generate cash flows which are independent of the cash flows of other assets. It therefore follows that the fair value of goodwill can never be measured directly and hence the fair value of goodwill must always be derived from measurement of the fair value of the cash-generating unit(s) to which it forms part.

When it comes to impairment testing, goodwill which has been derived from a business combination is allocated to each of the acquirer's cash-generating units which are expected to benefit from the synergies of the business combination regardless of whether other assets or liabilities of the acquiree are assigned to those units.

Example 12.130 – Apportioning an impairment loss

On 1 January 2015, Emery Ltd (Emery) acquired 80% of the net assets of Weaver Ltd and on this date control was obtained by Emery. The financial statements for the year-ended 31 December 2015 are being prepared and an impairment loss has arisen on the goodwill and the financial controller is unsure as to how the apportionment of the impairment loss is to be split.

Under Section 27, goodwill which has been acquired in a business combination is tested for impairment from the date of acquisition. The impairment loss is then allocated to each of the cash-generating units which are expected to benefit from the synergies of the combination. Emery does not wholly own Weaver as there is 20% non-controlling interests and hence 20% of the impairment loss will belong to those non-controlling interests.

The financial controller should notionally adjust the carrying amount of the cash-generating unit before comparing the unit to its recoverable amount. This is done by grossing up the carrying amount of goodwill so that it includes the goodwill belonging to the non-controlling interests. This 'grossed up' amount is then compared to the recoverable amount in order to determine whether the cash-generating unit is impaired.

12.322 Where goodwill cannot be allocated to specific cash-generating units on a non-arbitrary basis, paragraph 27.27 of FRS 102 says that the goodwill is tested for impairment by establishing the recoverable amount of either:

- the acquired entity in its entirety where goodwill relates to an acquired entity which has not been integrated (the term 'integrated' means the business subject to the acquisition has been restructured or dissolved into the reporting entity or other subsidiary companies); or
- the entire group of entities (excluding those which have not been integrated) if the goodwill relates to an entity which has been integrated.

Reversing an impairment loss

12.323 It is possible to reverse an impairment loss provided that the conditions which gave rise to the impairment loss in the first place no longer apply.

Focus

- Under the provisions of FRS 102, it is also necessary for an entity to not only consider whether an asset is impaired at each reporting date, but also to consider whether previous impairment losses no longer exist or have ceased (or partially ceased) to apply.

12.324 Where conditions have ceased, or partially ceased, and the entity wishes to reverse a previously recognised impairment loss, it must then consider whether the previous impairment loss was based on:

- the recoverable amount of that individual asset; or
- the recoverable amount of the cash-generating unit to which the asset belongs.

Impairment loss based on recoverable amount of the individual asset

12.325 If the previously recognised impairment loss was based on the recoverable amount of the individual asset the company must estimate the recoverable amount as at the current reporting date. Where the conclusion is drawn that recoverable amount is in excess of carrying amount, the entity can reverse the previously recognised impairment charge. Ordinarily the reversal will be recognised in profit or loss immediately; the exception to this rule is where another part of FRS 102 requires the credit entry to be recognised elsewhere, such as a revaluation reserve permitted by Section 17 *Property, Plant and Equipment*.

> **Focus**
>
> - An important point to emphasise is that any reversals of previously recognised impairment losses must not increase the carrying value of the asset to the amount which would have been determined (net of depreciation and amortisation charges) had no impairment loss been recognised (paragraph 27.30(c) of FRS 102).

Example 12.131 – Prior period impairment loss based on recoverable amount of an asset

On 31 January 2017, Gee Enterprises Ltd had an asset with a net book value of £70,000. The asset has had a few operational problems over the last financial year and the directors concluded that the asset had suffered impairment of £35,000 and hence wrote-down the asset to recoverable amount of £35,000. If no impairment loss had been required, the asset would have had a carrying value of £60,000 as depreciation is being charged on the asset on a ten years' straight-line basis.

After a significant overhaul the machine was deemed to be working correctly and it was considered that the circumstances giving rise to the original impairment loss no longer applied.

Had the asset not been written down to recoverable amount in 2017 the carrying value would have been £60,000 and in 2018 would have been £50,000. On the basis that the carrying amount of the asset is still £35,000 the maximum amount of the impairment that can be reversed in 2018 is £15,000 (£50,000 less £35,000). As a result, the company can only debit the carrying amount of the asset with £15,000 and credit the profit and loss account. This will then bring the asset up to its carrying amount of £50,000. The company must then adjust the depreciation charge for the asset in future periods so as to allocate the asset's depreciable amount over its remaining useful life.

Impairment loss based on recoverable amount of a cash-generating unit

12.326 If the impairment loss was previously based on the recoverable amount of a cash-generating unit, the entity must estimate the recoverable amount of that cash-generating unit as at the current reporting date.

Where it is concluded that the circumstances giving rise to the previously recognised impairment loss now no longer apply, the reversal is allocated to the assets of the unit on a pro-rata basis with the carrying amounts of those assets and goodwill in the following order:

- first to the other assets in the cash-generating unit (excluding goodwill); and
- secondly to any goodwill in the cash-generating unit.

Example 12.132 – Prior period impairment charge based on recoverable amount of a cash-generating unit

On 30 June 2015, Scanlon Ltd accounted for an impairment loss on a group of assets, which constitute a cash-generating unit, and the amount of this impairment loss was £360,000. Extracts of the financial statements for the year-end 30 June 2016 are as follows (after the depreciation charge has been accounted for). Depreciation is being charged at 20% on a reducing balance basis.

	30 June 2016	30 June 2015
	£'000	£'000
Goodwill	nil	nil
Manufacturing plant	384	480
Machinery	1,104	1,380
	1,488	1,860

The directors have received conclusive evidence that the original impairment charge of £360,000 has reversed in the sum of £310,000. The reversal is applied first to the assets, excluding goodwill, of the unit on a pro-rata basis on the basis of the carrying amount of each asset and then to any goodwill in the cash-generating unit.

Care must be taken because the reversal cannot increase the carrying amount of any asset above the *lower* of its recoverable amount and the carrying amount which would have been determined had no impairment loss been recognised.

Had no impairment loss been recognised, the assets would have been carried at the following amounts:

	£'000
Goodwill	220
Manufacturing plant	400
Machinery	1,200
	1,820

Manufacturing plant currently represents 26% (£384 / (£384 + £1,104) × 100) of the total assets in the cash-generating unit. Allocating 26% of £310,000 would take the net book value higher than the carrying amount of £400,000 if no impairment had originally been made, hence only £16,000 can be allocated.

The machinery currently has a carrying amount of £1,104,000 and if the remaining 74% of the impairment reversal is allocated against the machinery this, too, will increase the carrying amount above the £1,200,000. Therefore only £96,000 (£1,200,000 less £1,104,000) of the remaining £294,000 (£310,000 less £16,000) can be allocated to the machinery.

The remaining reversal is taken to goodwill. Once the reversal has been completed, the financial statements will show the following:

	30 June 2016	**30 June 2015**
	£'000	£'000
Goodwill	198	nil
Manufacturing plant	400	480
Machinery	1,200	1,380
	1,798	1,860

Disclosures

12.327 Disclosures relating to impairment losses and the reversals of previously recognised impairment losses may be as follows:

- the amount of impairment losses recognised in profit or loss during the period and the line item(s) in the profit and loss account (income statement) in which those impairment losses are included; and
- the amount of reversals of impairment losses recognised in profit or loss during the period and the line item(s) in the profit and loss account (income statement) in which those impairment losses are reversed.

EMPLOYEE BENEFITS

12.328 Section 28 *Employee Benefits* of FRS 102 deals with all forms of consideration given by a company to its employees and directors in exchange for the services which they render. The section itself does not, however, deal with share-based payment transactions as these are covered in a separate section (Section 26 *Share-based Payment* – see **12.290**).

The following types of employee benefits are dealt with under Section 28:

- short-term employee benefits (excluding termination benefits) that are expected to be settled before 12 months after the end of the reporting period in which the employee renders the service;
- post-employment benefits payable to employees after completion of employment;
- other long-term employee benefits other than short-term employee benefits, post-employment benefits and termination benefits; and

- termination benefits as a result of an entity's decision to terminate an employee's employment before the normal retirement date or an employee's decision to accept voluntary redundancy in exchange for those benefits.

Other long-term benefits could include:

- long-term paid absences such as long-service or sabbatical leave;
- other long-service benefits;
- long-term disability benefits;
- profit-sharing and bonuses; and
- deferred remuneration.

Focus

- The phrase 'short-term employee benefits' means those benefits which the entity expects to settle within 12 months after the year-/period-end.

Examples of short-term employee benefits include:

- wages, salaries and social security contributions;
- paid annual leave and sick leave;
- profit-sharing and bonuses; and
- non-monetary benefits such as medical care and cars.

12.329 A significant majority of small companies have previously not made accruals for short-term employee benefits which were accrued by employees but not paid until the subsequent accounting period – the main one being unpaid holiday pay. This is because the FRSSE (effective January 2015) did not specifically require companies to make such accruals – although FRS 12 *Provisions, contingent liabilities and contingent assets* did cite unpaid holiday as meeting the definition of a liability and so technically companies should have made accruals for such.

Providing for unpaid holiday entitlement in the financial statements of a small company may prove problematic – particularly where the company does not maintain a central record of such information. In addition, as FRS 102 is retrospective, adjustments to the date of transition and the comparative year will need to be made.

Example 12.133 – Holiday pay coterminous with the financial year

A company has an accounting reference date of 30 June, which is also the holiday year-end. An employee has 30 days holiday per year and is allowed to carry forward up to five days into the next holiday year. At the year-end 30 June 2016, the employee has taken 26 days.

An accrual should be made for four days holiday entitlement which will be taken in the subsequent financial year.

Example 12.134 – Holiday pay not coterminous with the financial year

A company has a financial year-end of 30 June 2016 and a holiday year of 31 December 2016. An employee has 30 days holiday per year and at the financial year-end had taken 20 days of their entitlement.

In this case, there will be a prepayment of five days holiday ((30 days × 6/12) – 20 days).

Recognition and measurement

12.330 Ordinarily a company will recognise a liability in respect of short-term employee benefits accrued by the employee but not paid until the subsequent accounting period together with an associated expense in profit or loss. The debit entry may also be taken to the balance sheet (statement of financial position) as an asset if another section of FRS 102 so requires (for example to inventories as per Section 13 *Inventories*). Where amounts paid exceed the obligation arising from service before the reporting date, the entity recognises a prepayment.

Focus

- In determining liabilities for short-term employee benefits, the entity must deduct any amounts which have been paid to the employees or contributed to an employee benefit fund. Such amounts are recognised at the undiscounted amount of short-term employee benefits expected to be paid in exchange for services.

Profit-sharing and bonuses

12.331 Some small companies operate profit-sharing and bonus arrangements for their employees. When such arrangements are in place, the entity must make provision for these, but only when:

- there is a present legal or constructive obligation to make such payments as a result of past events; and
- a reliable estimate of the obligation can be made.

These two conditions may seem familiar to many as they relate to provisions and contingencies in Section 21 *Provisions and Contingencies*. Essentially, such amounts should only be provided for if the entity has an obligation at the reporting date to make such payments and these payments are made in the subsequent accounting period.

The term 'constructive obligation' can prove to be very subjective and such an obligation arises on the part of the entity when its past practices or policies create an expectation in the mind-sets of those affected. An example of a constructive obligation would be where the directors inform the employees before the year-end date that the directors will pay a bonus after the year-end based on actual pre-tax profit. This will create an expectation in the mind-sets of the employees that they will receive a bonus and, in turn, create an obligation on the part of the company which must be reflected in the financial statements.

Pension plans

12.332 Section 28 includes guidance relating to *defined contribution* and *defined benefit* pension plans. These two types of pension plan are quite different and the accounting differences between the two types of plan are significant. In essence, as actuarial risk and investment risk do not, in substance, fall on the part of the entity where a defined contribution plan is concerned, companies' simply charge the contributions to profit or loss.

Defined benefit pension plans are inherently more complicated to account for. As investment risk and actuarial risk do, in substance, fall on the part of the entity, it must account for the defined benefit plan in the financial statements and hence recognise the surplus or deficit in the plan at the reporting date. There are occasions, however, where a defined benefit pension plan is accounted for as a defined contribution plan.

Example 12.135 – Defined benefit plan accounted for as a defined contribution plan

A school converted to academy status during the year to 31 August 2016 and it has two forms of pension plan: the Teachers' Pension Scheme (TPS) and the Local Government Pension Scheme (LGPS). The LGPS is a defined benefit pension plan and the academy receives actuarial valuations each year in order that the accounting input and relevant disclosures can be made in the financial statements.

The TPS is a multi-employer scheme and the academy is not able to identify its share of the underlying assets and liabilities of the scheme.

Under paragraph 28.11 of FRS 102, multi-employer plans and state plans are classified as defined contribution plans or defined benefit plans on the basis of the terms of the plan. In this case, there is insufficient information available for the academy to identify its share of assets and liabilities in the TPS and therefore the academy must account for the TPS as if it were a defined contribution plan.

12.333 Where defined benefit pension plans are concerned they could well be in a deficit position and the entity may have entered into an agreement which will determine how the entity will fund the deficit. Under Section 28, a company is required to recognise a liability in the balance sheet (statement of financial position) which represents the contributions payable that arise from an agreement determining how the entity will fund a deficit, to the extent that the liability relates to the deficit.

Accounting for a defined benefit pension plan

12.334 Accounting for a defined benefit pension plan is quite complicated. As actuarial and investment risk, in substance, fall on the part of the company, the surplus or deficit in the defined benefit pension plan must be reported on the balance sheet (statement of financial position).

> **Focus**
>
> - Where a deficit in a defined benefit pension plan is significant, The Pensions Regulator in the UK has the power to mandate a company to increase its contributions into a defined benefit pension scheme to bridge the deficit.

Actuarial information will be needed in order that the defined benefit pension plan can be accounted for correctly in the financial statements. Paragraph 28.15 of FRS 102 requires a company to measure the net defined benefit liability for its obligations (ie the plan's liabilities) at the net of the following amounts:

- the present value of the company's obligations under the defined benefit pension plan at the reporting date (paragraphs 28.16 and 28.21A of FRS 102 provide additional guidance to measuring this obligation); *minus*
- the fair value at the reporting date of the plan assets (if any) out of which the obligations are to be settled. Paragraphs 11.27–11.32 of FRS 102 establish requirements for determining the fair values of those plan assets. The exception is where the asset is an insurance policy which exactly matches the amount and timing of some, or all, of the benefits payable under the plan, the fair value of the asset is deemed to be the present value of the related obligation.

Focus

- When it comes to the accounting for a defined benefit pension plan, actuarial information is needed and the defined benefit obligation (together with the related profit and loss account charges) will be measured using the 'projected unit credit method'. The Glossary defines the 'projected unit credit method' as follows:

  > 'An actuarial valuation method that sees each period of service as giving rise to an additional unit of benefit entitlement and measures each unit separately to build up the final obligation (sometimes known as the accrued benefit method pro-rated on service or as the benefit/years of service method).'[19]

A summary of the accounting input is shown in the following table:

Profit and loss account	**Profit and loss account (finance costs)**	**Other comprehensive income**
Current service cost	Interest cost; *less*	Differences between actual and expected return on plan assets
Past service cost	Expected return on plan assets	Experience adjustments affecting the plan's liabilities
Gains and losses on curtailments and settlements		Effects of changes in actuarial assumptions

Remeasurement of the net defined benefit liability comprises of:

- actuarial gains and losses; and
- return on plan assets which exclude amounts included in net interest on the net defined benefit liability.

Example 12.136 – Accounting for a defined benefit pension plan

Lockland Ltd is a chemical processing company with a 31 December accounting reference date. The actuaries have provided the following information which relates to the company's defined benefit pension plan as at 31 December 2016 and 31 December 2015.

19 FRS 102 Glossary **Projected unit credit method**.

	31 December 2015	31 December 2014
	£'000	£'000
Plan assets		
Opening balance	4,197	4,021
Expected return on plan assets	218	216
Actuarial gain (loss)	230	(321)
Employer contributions	310	458
Employee contributions	31	33
Benefits paid	(141)	(210)
Plan assets at end of year	4,845	4,197
Plan liabilities		
Opening balance	5,208	4,597
Current service cost	69	67
Past service cost	nil	nil
Interest on scheme liabilities	248	259
Actuarial (gain) loss	318	462
Employee contributions	31	33
Benefits paid	(141)	(210)
Plan liabilities at end of period	5,733	5,208

The profit and loss account will include the following pension plan costs:

	31 December 2015	31 December 2014
	£'000	£'000
Current service cost	69	67
Past service cost	0	0
Total operating charge	69	67

Finance costs in the profit and loss account will include:

	31 December 2015	31 December 2014
	£'000	£'000
Expected return on plan assets	218	216
Interest on scheme liabilities	(248)	(259)
Net interest charge	(30)	(43)

Actuarial gains and losses in the defined benefit pension plan are taken to other comprehensive income and therefore the balance sheet position will be as follows:

	31 December 2015	31 December 2014
	£'000	£'000
Value of plan liabilities	(5,733)	(5,208)
Value of plan assets	4,845	4,197
Surplus (deficit) at end of period	(888)	(1,011)

Changes within a defined benefit pension plan

12.335 Changes within a defined benefit pension plan usually arise through the following:

- introductions;
- changes;
- curtailments; and
- settlements.

'Curtailments' and 'settlements' are not defined in the Glossary to FRS 102 but they arise when the liabilities within the scheme are significantly changed by circumstances other than actuarial assumptions. In old UK GAAP, a 'settlement' was defined as 'an irrevocable action that relieves the employer (or the defined benefit scheme) of the primary responsibility for a pension obligation and eliminates significant risks relating to the obligation and the assets used to effect the settlement.' A 'curtailment' was defined as 'an event that reduces the expected years of future service of present employees or reduces for a number of employees the actual amount of defined benefits for some or all of their future service.' Usually a curtailment would arise due to redundancy as a result of the discontinuation of part of an organisation.

Example 12.137 – Transfer of obligations

Lockland Ltd has had a defined benefit pension plan in place for its employees for several years. The latest actuarial valuation showed the defined benefit having a deficit of some £3 million. During the year to 31 December 2016 the company successfully transferred all the obligations in the defined benefit plan to an insurance company who has agreed to take over the plan in exchange for a cash sum.

This transfer would represent a settlement and the company would extinguish its defined benefit liability and recognise a gain in profit or loss during the reporting period. If, on the other hand, the defined benefit pension plan was in a surplus position, the company would recognise a loss.

Defined benefit pension plan in a surplus position

12.336 Not all defined benefit pension plans are in a deficit position; indeed some are shown as assets in the company's balance sheet (statement of financial position) because the plan's assets are in excess of the plan's obligations.

> **Focus**
>
> - As discussed elsewhere in this chapter, the underlying objective where assets are concerned in a company's balance sheet (statement of financial position) is that they should not be stated in excess of recoverable amount.

For the purposes of a defined benefit pension plan which is in surplus, the asset can only be recognised to the extent that the company is expected to be able to recover the asset – either through reduced contributions in the future or via refunds from the pension plan itself.

Reimbursements

12.337 Where a company is expecting a reimbursement from the pension scheme, it can only recognise an asset in respect of the reimbursement if it is 'virtually certain' that reimbursement will be made and where it is virtually certain that reimbursement will be made, it is treated as a separate asset. If it is not virtually certain then it is a contingent asset and should not be recognised.

Group defined benefit pension plans

12.338 It might be the case in a small group that a defined benefit pension plan is in place for the group and the risks associated with the defined benefit pension plan are shared among the group entities. Where this situation arises, it is important that the agreement relating to the group plan is carefully looked at. If there is no agreement in place then the defined benefit pension plan is recognised in the financial statements of the entity that is legally responsible for the plan. The other group members will recognise a cost which is equivalent to their contribution payable for the period.

If there is a contractual agreement in place, the individual group companies will recognise the net defined benefit cost of the defined benefit pension plan in accordance with the agreement.

Other long-term employee benefits

12.339 For the purposes of financial reporting, 'long-term' is taken to mean more than 12 months and paragraph 28.29 outlines five types of transaction which may be taken as being 'long-term':

- long-term paid absences such as long-service or sabbaticals;
- other long-service benefits;
- long-term disability benefits;
- profit-sharing and bonuses; and
- deferred remuneration.

If the company has any of these transactions, it must account for them in accordance with paragraph 28.30 which says that long-term employee benefits are measured at the **net** of the following amounts:

- the present value of the benefit obligation as at the reporting date; *less*
- the fair value of the plan assets (if any) at the reporting date out of which the obligations are to be directly settled.

Termination benefits

12.340 Where termination benefits are concerned, there has to be a legal or constructive obligation present (in much the same way that a provision for liabilities should only be recognised). In all cases, termination benefits – by their very nature – do not provide the entity with any future economic benefits and hence it follows that they will always be recognised in profit or loss immediately.

Paragraph 28.34 of FRS 102 says that a company can only recognise termination benefits as a liability (with an associated expense in profit or loss) when it is demonstrably committed to either:

- terminate the employment of an employee (or group of employees) before their normal retirement date; or
- to provide employees with additional termination benefits in order to encourage voluntary redundancy.

Focus

- A company can say it is demonstrably committed to a termination programme only when there is a detailed formal plan for the termination and there is no realistic possibility that the entity will withdraw the plan.

Recognition and measurement of termination benefits

12.341 Only when the company is demonstrably committed to a termination programme can it recognise a liability for such. This is initially recognised at the best estimate of the expenditure which the company is likely to incur in order to settle the obligation. For a voluntary redundancy programme, the best estimate will be based on the number of employees which are likely to take up the offer of voluntary redundancy.

If termination benefits are not due to be settled until 12 months after the end of the accounting period, then they are measured at the discounted present value. The discount rate which is to be used is determined by reference to market yields on high quality corporate bonds.

Example 12.138 – Recognition of termination benefits

Smyth Sunbeds Ltd (Smyth) operates a chain of sunbed salons across the country. Over the last couple of years the company has experienced a decline in the use of its salons. In addition, competitors with aggressive pricing policies have opened up in the areas where Smyth operates which has had a detrimental impact on the company over the last few months. The company has a year-end of 31 March 2017.

On 1 February 2017 the directors informed the staff members of four loss-making outlets that the salons will be closing with effect from 4 April 2017. The staff concerned cannot be deployed elsewhere in the company and hence they are being made redundant.

The payroll clerk has calculated the values of the redundancy payments including holiday entitlement as at 31 March 2017 and the financial controller is planning to recognise a provision for such costs in the financial statements as at 31 March 2017 even though the payments will not be made until the April 2017 payroll is run.

The provision for termination benefits can be made as the company has announced the detailed closure plan for the affected stores to those affected prior to the year-end and hence has created an expectation in the mind-sets of those concerned that the company will discharge its obligations under the plan (ie a constructive obligation).

Disclosures

12.342 The disclosures relating to employee benefits may be as follows:

(1) Where the entity treats a defined benefit multi-employer plan as a defined contribution plan due to the fact that sufficient information is not available to use defined benefit accounting, the company must disclose:

 (a) the fact that it is a defined benefit pension plan and the reason why it is being accounted for a defined contribution plan, along with any additional information concerning the plan's surplus or deficit and any implications for the entity; and

 (b) a description of the extent to which the entity can be liable to the plan for other entities' obligations under the terms and conditions of the multi-employer plan.

(2) If the company is involved in a defined benefit pension scheme which shares the risks between entities and accounts for the contributions payable for the period, the information about the plan as a whole required by paragraphs 28.41(a), (d), (h) and (i).

The information in (2) above can be disclosed by cross-reference to disclosures in another group entity's financial statements provided that:

- the group entity's financial statements separately identify and disclose the information required about the plan; and
- that group entity's financial statements are available to users of the financial statements on the same terms as the financial statements of the individual entity and at the same time as, or earlier than, the financial statements of the entity.

INCOME TAX

12.343 Section 29 *Income Tax* is fairly wide in its scope as the term 'income tax' also includes all domestic and foreign taxes which are based on a company's taxable profit. It also extends to taxes such as withholding taxes which are payable by a subsidiary, associate or joint venture when they pay dividends to the investor.

There are two types of taxes generally dealt with in Section 29: current tax and deferred tax. The section itself requires a company to account for the current and future tax consequences of transactions and other events. Section 29 also covers the issue of value added tax.

Current tax

12.344 Current tax is straightforward to account for under the provisions in Section 29. Current tax can either be a current asset or a current liability and the company will recognise such tax assets or liabilities in respect of the taxable profit (loss) for both the current and past periods. A current tax asset might also be recognised in respect of tax losses which have been carried back to previous periods and which give rise to a refund potentially being received from HM Revenue and Customs (HMRC).

> **Focus**
>
> - The rate of tax used in the calculation of current tax assets or liabilities is the rate of tax which has been enacted, or substantively enacted, by the reporting date.

12.345 In the vast majority of cases, a small company will recognise the amount of corporation tax which is based on taxable profit for the current year and this is usually worked out by business tax software programs. In this respect the journals to include the corporation tax liability (asset) is:

DR/CR tax expense (profit or loss)	X/(X)
DR/CR tax asset/tax liability (balance sheet)	X/(X)

Deferred tax

12.346 Deferred tax has always been a controversial aspect within the accountancy profession and it is fair to say that some commentators were hoping that the Financial Reporting Council would withdraw the concept of deferred tax. While this has been the case for micro-entities, small companies must continue to recognise deferred tax in accordance with the provisions in Section 29. Unfortunately FRS 102 makes deferred tax more onerous as its scope is wider than was the case under the FRSSE (effective January 2015).

The scope section of Section 29 takes the same stance as previous UK GAAP at the FRSSE (effective January 2015) in that it acknowledges that deferred tax represents the future tax consequences of transactions and events recognised in the entity's financial statements of both the current and previous accounting periods. Some additional points to note where deferred tax is concerned are as follows:

- Tax losses which are carried forward to the next accounting period which essentially give rise to a deferred tax asset must only be recognised to the extent that it is probable that they will be recovered against the reversal of deferred tax liabilities. Section 29 takes the same view as the FRSSE (effective January 2015) in that the default presumption is that the mere existence of tax losses is taken as strong evidence that there may not be other future taxable profits against which the unutilised tax losses can be relieved. There should be evidence to the contrary that the company will be able to utilise deferred tax assets – such as the awarding of a lucrative contract in the next financial year.

- Paragraph 29.8 says that deferred tax will be recognised in an entity's financial statements in respect of tax allowances for the cost of a fixed asset when these are received before or after the depreciation of the fixed asset is recognised in profit or loss. If, and when, the company has met all the conditions imposed by HMRC for retaining the relevant capital allowances, deferred tax is then reversed.

- Where the small company has a subsidiary, associate, branch or an interest in a joint venture, it must recognise deferred tax when income or expenses from these sources have been recognised in the financial statements but will subsequently be included in the tax computation in a future period. There are, however, two exceptions to this rule:
  - where the reporting entity has control over the reversal of the timing difference; and
  - there is probability that reversal of the timing difference will not take place in the foreseeable future.

Timing difference plus

12.347 In the UK, accountants have always calculated deferred tax using a timing difference approach. Timing differences are differences between a company's taxable profit (loss) and the profit (loss) as stated in the financial statements. They arise from the inclusion of gains and losses in tax assessments in periods different from those in which they are recognised in the financial statements. An example of a situation where a timing difference arises is where a company may claim HM Revenue and Custom's Annual Investment Allowance (AIA) in the year of acquiring a fixed asset, but then depreciate that asset over, say, three years. Assuming the entire cost of the fixed asset qualifies for AIA there will be a difference between the book value of the asset per the financial statements and the tax written down value of the asset which will give rise to a deferred tax liability.

12.348 Section 29 still uses a timing difference approach in calculating deferred tax; the difference however relates to the wider scope of deferred tax in Section 29. Section 29 uses a timing difference 'plus' approach and the plus part builds on the previous timing difference approach in an attempt to bridge the gap between the outcome of deferred tax under UK GAAP and the outcome that would have been calculated under international accounting standards (IAS 12 *Income Taxes*). Section 29 achieves this by extinguishing some of the exceptions which were contained in the FRSSE (effective January 2015). A typical example of this is in respect of fixed assets which are subjected to the revaluation model as permitted in Section 17 *Property, Plant and Equipment*. Under the FRSSE (effective January 2015) no deferred tax would have been recognised on a revaluation gain in respect of a non-monetary asset subjected to the revaluation model unless the company had:

- entered into a binding agreement to sell the asset; and
- had recognised the gains and losses expected to arise on the sale.

This exemption from calculating deferred tax has been removed in FRS 102 and hence deferred tax has to be applied in respect of non-monetary assets subject to the revaluation model.

Likewise with assets which are carried under the revaluation model, where a company has investment property on its balance sheet (statement of financial position) which is measured at fair value in accordance with Section 16 *Investment Property,* deferred tax is recognised using the tax rates and allowances which apply to the sale of the investment property. There is an exception to this rule in paragraph 29.16 which relates to investment property which has a limited useful life and where the company is going to use the economic benefits associated with the investment property over time.

Example 12.139 – Investment property measured at fair value

Smallco Ltd (Smallco) has an investment property on its balance sheet as at 31 December 2016 with a carrying amount of £85,000. A chartered surveyor has undertaken a valuation of this property and has confirmed that the value of the investment property has increased by £10,000 during the year. The entries in the financial statements to increase the carrying amount at the reporting date will be:

DR investment property	£10,000
CR profit or loss	(£10,000)

Being fair value gain on investment property

In addition to the above transaction, Smallco must also provide for deferred tax on the investment property. Paragraph 29.16 of FRS 102 says that deferred tax relating to investment property which is measured at fair value is to be measured using the tax rates and allowances that apply to the sale of the asset. Rates of tax in the UK are announced each year in the Chancellor's Budget. Assuming the rate of tax which will apply to the sale of the asset is 18% (as announced in the July 2015 Budget) then the deferred tax will be £1,800 (£10,000 × 18%). The entries in the books will be:

DR tax expense	£1,800
CR deferred tax provision	(£1,800)

Being provision for deferred tax on investment property

It is important to ensure the deferred tax component of any assets subjected to revaluation is taken to the correct account in the financial statements. The concept of 'tax treatment follows the accounting treatment' applies to the revaluation of non-monetary assets.

If the revaluation amount has been taken to other comprehensive income via a revaluation surplus account (for assets accounted for under Section 17 *Property, Plant and Equipment*) then the associated deferred tax must also be taken to the revaluation surplus. For investment property measured at fair value, fair value gains and losses are taken directly to profit or loss (there is no longer a revaluation surplus for investment property under Section 16 *Investment Property*) and hence the associated deferred tax will also be taken to profit or loss.

12.349 In addition to revaluation of non-monetary assets, a couple of other situations will give rise to deferred tax considerations.

Business combinations

12.350 Paragraph 29.11 says that when the tax base of an asset acquired in a business combination (with the exception of goodwill) is less than the value at which it is recognised in the acquirer's financial statements, a deferred tax liability is recognised to represent the additional tax that will be paid in the future. On the flip side, where the tax base of an asset is more than the amount recognised for the asset in the financial statements, a deferred tax asset is recognised to represent the additional tax that will be avoided in respect of that difference. A deferred tax asset or liability is recognised for the additional tax the company will either avoid, or pay, due to the difference in value at which a liability is recognised and the amount that is assessed to be owed to HM Revenue and Customs. Amounts attributed to goodwill will be adjusted by the amount of deferred tax recognised.

Example 12.140 – Deferred tax in a business combination

Westhead Enterprises Ltd (Westhead) acquires Heaton Enterprises Ltd (Heaton) on 1 January 2016. The company pays corporation tax at a rate of 20%. At the acquisition date, Heaton has an asset with the following values:

Carrying amount	£120,000
Tax written down value	£80,000
Fair value at acquisition	£150,000

At the date of acquisition, the asset will be recorded at fair value of £150,000 and the difference between fair value and the tax written down value of the same asset (£80,000) will give rise to a timing difference on which a deferred tax liability of £14,000 ((£150,000 – £80,000) × 20%) will arise.

Unremitted earnings

12.351 This situation is likely to be rare for small companies and small group but essentially where an overseas subsidiary or associate has unremitted earnings which it can distribute to the parent/investor then this will also attract deferred tax considerations.

Permanent differences and timing differences

12.352 In the vast majority of cases, a company's accounting profit will be different than taxable profit. This is because certain items are recognised in the financial statements which are not recognised for tax purposes; the most common transaction which is charged in the accounts but not recognised for tax is depreciation. It follows, therefore, that there are two types of 'difference', being a 'permanent' difference and a 'timing' difference.

A permanent difference means that certain types of income and expenditure are not taxable or tax deductible. A timing difference arises from items which are either taxable or tax deductible but are included in the tax computation in a different period than when they are included in the financial statements.

Example 12.141 – Timing difference

A company acquires new computer equipment during the accounting period for £12,000 which qualifies for HMRCs *Annual Investment Allowance* (AIA) in full. The company's declared accounting policy in respect of computer equipment is to depreciate it on a three-year straight-line basis with a full year's depreciation charge in the year of acquisition and no depreciation in the year of disposal. The directors have assessed that the residual value of the computer equipment at the end of three years will be £nil.

Extracts from the company's fixed asset register in respect of this computer equipment are shown below:

	£
Cost	12,000
Depreciation charge	(4,000)
Net book value	8,000

As the directors have taken advantage of HMRCs AIA the tax written down value of this computer equipment at the end of year 1 will be £nil. There is a difference, therefore, between the book value of £8,000 and the tax written down value of £nil. This difference will trigger a deferred tax liability and if it is assumed that the corporation tax rate is 20%, the deferred tax liability will be £1,600 (£8,000 × 20%).

This deferred tax liability has arisen because there will be a future tax consequence for the company. The company has made a cash flow saving in the year of acquisition by claiming HMRCs AIA. This allowance will not be available in the subsequent accounting period and hence the tax liability will be higher.

12.353 Timing differences are said to originate when a transaction is first included in the financial statements in one period but is included in the corporation tax computation in another period (or vice versa). Therefore it follows that the timing differences subsequently reverse over time when the transaction is reflected in the financial statements or in the tax computation whether this be in whole or in part. The effect of this reversal is that the tax charge in the later periods will be affected by transactions or events which have arisen in a previous accounting period.

Other examples of timing differences are:

- accrued pension liabilities in the financial statements which attract tax relief when the pension contributions have been paid; and
- intra-group profits in stock which are unrealised at group level and reversed on consolidation.

> **Focus**
>
> - The overarching objective of deferred tax is to balance out the effects of future tax consequences by recognising the tax effects of all items of income, expenditure, gains, losses, assets and liabilities in the same period as opposed to recognising the tax portion when the items are included in the tax computation as doing this would distort the true taxable position of the company in the financial statements.

Value added tax

12.354 Paragraph 29.20 explains the accounting treatment for value added tax (VAT). This paragraph confirms that turnover must be stated net of VAT (which is the case for VAT registered companies). Conversely, expenses are also stated net of VAT for a VAT registered entity.

Any irrecoverable amounts of VAT are included in expenses or the cost of assets.

Disclosures

12.355 The disclosures in respect of taxation may be as follows:

- The aggregate current and deferred tax relating to items that are recognised as items of other comprehensive income or equity.

FOREIGN CURRENCY

12.356 Section 30 *Foreign Currency Translation* recognises that a company may conduct foreign activities in three ways:

- undertaking transactions in foreign currencies;
- possess foreign operations; or
- present financial statements in a foreign currency.

Focus

- A 'foreign operation' is an entity which is a subsidiary, associate, joint venture or branch of a reporting entity, the activities of which are based or conducted in a country, or currency, other than those of the reporting entity.

For the vast majority of small companies, it is expected that foreign currency issues will arise as a result of the company undertaking transactions in a foreign currency (for example purchasing goods from an overseas supplier).

Functional currency

12.357 A small company is required to identify its 'functional currency'. This is generally going to be sterling or the Euro because these are the currencies which companies in the UK and Republic of Ireland trade in. Paragraph 30.3 says that the functional currency of an entity is the one in which the entity primarily generates and expends cash.

12.358 In addition, the currency in which funds from financing activities are generated will also have a bearing on an entity's functional currency (as well as the currency in which receipts from operating activities are usually retained). Whilst extremely rare for small companies, a change in functional currency can only take place if there is a change to the underlying transactions, events and conditions which apply to the entity. This could arise, for example, where there is a change of currency (for example if the UK were to adopt the Euro).

Functional currency in a group situation

12.359 A small group might have a foreign subsidiary (for example a UK company might own an Irish subsidiary) and where this is the case, paragraph 30.5 of FRS 102 outlines various additional factors which must be considered when it comes to determining the functional currency which will then lead to the conclusion as to whether the functional currency is the same as that of the parent:

- Whether the foreign operation is an extension of the reporting entity as opposed to being carried out with a significant degree of autonomy.
- Whether transactions with the reporting entity are a high or low proportion of the activities of the foreign operation's activities.

- Whether the cash flows which arise from the activities of the foreign operation have a direct effect on the cash flows of the reporting entity and are readily available for remittance to the reporting entity.
- Whether the cash flows of the foreign operation are of a level sufficient to service existing and normally expected debt obligations without funds being made available by the reporting entity.

Accounting for individual foreign currency transactions

12.360 For small companies the majority of transactions which will give rise to foreign currency issues is when a company enters into a foreign exchange transaction with an overseas supplier. The transaction will be denominated in a foreign currency and will be settled in a foreign currency. Examples include:

- The purchase or sale of goods or services whose price is denominated in a foreign currency.
- Borrowing or lending of funds when the amounts payable or receivable are denominated in a foreign currency.
- Acquisition or disposal of assets (or incurring or settling liabilities) which are denominated in a foreign currency.

On initial recognition, the transaction is accounted for using the rate of exchange prevailing on the date of the transaction. This applies whether or not the transaction is covered by a forward foreign currency contract.

Example 12.142 – Purchase of goods from an overseas supplier

A company based in the UK buys a batch of chemicals from its supplier based in Austria. The cost of the chemicals is €180,000 and the spot rate on the date of the transaction is £1:€1.45. The company does not have credit facilities with this supplier.

The invoice will be translated into sterling at the exchange rate prevailing at the date of the transaction, ie £124,138 (€180,000 / 1.45) and this is the amount that will be recorded in the supplier's purchase ledger.

In the above example it was assumed that the company purchasing the goods did not have credit facilities with its supplier. However, this is not always the case and it may be the case that payment is made in accordance with agreed credit terms.

Example 12.143 – Payment in a foreign currency in accordance with credit terms

The facts are as above. If it is assumed that the company has a four-week credit period and settles the invoice on time, but the exchange rate has moved to £1:€1.65 then there will be an exchange difference of £15,047 ((€180,000 / 1.65) – £124,138). This has risen because the exchange rate has moved from the date the transaction was entered into to the date the transaction was settled and the exchange difference is recognised as a gain on exchange in profit or loss.

If payment was made AFTER the year-end, the gain would be recorded in the subsequent year's financial statements. No exchange rate differences are accrued or prepaid which relate to settlement of foreign currency transactions after the reporting date.

12.361 At the end of each reporting period, a company that has entered into foreign exchange transactions must:

- translate foreign currency monetary items using the closing rate;
- translate non-monetary items at historical cost using exchange rates at the date the transaction took place; and
- translate non-monetary items which are measured at fair value using exchange rates which apply at the date that fair value was determined.

Example 12.144 – Monetary item translated at closing rate

On 19 December 2016, a company purchases raw materials from its supplier based in Spain for €250,000. Payment is subsequently made on 19 January 2017 and the company has a year-end date of 31 December 2016. Exchange rates are as follows:

19 December 2016:	£1:€1.20
31 December 2016:	£1:€1.26
19 January 2017:	£1:€1.29

The creditor at the year-end needs to be translated at the closing rate of exchange which will result in the creditor having a carrying amount of £198,413 (€250,000/1.26). An exchange gain of £9,920 will be recorded in profit or loss ((€250,000/1.20) – €250,000/1.26).

On 19 January 2017 the company will pay £193,798 (€250,000/1.29). The exchange gain of £4,615 (£198,413 less £193,798) will be included within profit or loss in the 2017 financial year.

Net investment in a foreign operation

12.362 This part of Section 30 is quite specific and deals with inter-company monetary items relating to a foreign operation.

A reporting entity may have a monetary item which is receivable from, or payable to, a foreign operation. If settlement of such amounts is not planned or likely to occur in the foreseeable future, such transactions will form part of an entity's net investment in that foreign operation. Such monetary items may include long-term debtors or loans but they will **not** include trade debtors or trade creditors.

Paragraph 30.12 and 30.13 outlines the requirements with debtors and/or creditors in a foreign operation where settlement of either is not planned or likely to occur in the foreseeable future (and could include long-term debtors or long-term loans). The substance of such arrangements is that they are part of the reporting entity's net investment in a foreign operation and there are specific ways of accounting for such items.

Focus

- The term 'foreseeable future' does not contain a specified period of time and there must be no intention or expectation by either party that the loan will be repaid.

Any exchange differences which arise on a monetary asset which forms part of a reporting entity's net investment in a foreign operation is recorded in profit or loss in the individual financial statements of the reporting entity or the individual financial statements of the foreign operation. If the small group prepares consolidated financial statements and the foreign operation is a subsidiary, such exchange differences are recognised in other comprehensive income and accumulated within equity. They are not recognised in profit or loss when the parent disposes of the net investment.

Example 12.145 – Long-term loan

Smallgroup Ltd has a foreign subsidiary located in Spain. In 2016 the company made a loan to the foreign subsidiary and a formal loan agreement was put in place. The terms of this agreement make provision for the loan to be repaid in 15 years' time. The financial controller wishes to treat the loan as part of the company's net investment in a foreign operation on the basis that the loan will not be repaid for a long period of time.

Where a long-term loan is made with a specified maturity it will not be possible to treat the loan as part of a net investment in a foreign operation simply on the grounds that the loan is not repayable for a long time. In order to qualify as part of a net investment in a foreign operation, management must have expressed an intention to renew the loan at maturity and the foreign operation would not be expected to make a repayment.

Example 12.146 – Accounting for a loan regarded as part of a long-term investment

Topco Ltd (Topco) has a functional and presentational currency of £ sterling. It has a foreign subsidiary, Forex Inc (Forex), whose functional currency is the Euro (€).

In the year to 31 December 2016, Topco made a loan to Forex in the sum of €10,000 when the exchange rate was £1:€1.28. On 31 December 2016 the exchange rate was £1:€1.25.

Management have confirmed that they do not expect repayment of this loan and have regarded the loan as part of the net investment in the foreign operation. Despite the group qualifying as a small group in the eyes of the Companies Act 2006, consolidated financial statements are prepared.

<u>Topco's financial statements</u>

In Topco's financial statements, the loan is initial recorded at the exchange rate prevailing on the date of the transaction, ie £7,813 (€10,000/1.28). At the financial year-end, the loan debtor will be translated at the closing rate and will therefore have a carrying amount in the financial statements of £8,000 (€10,000/1.25). The gain on exchange of £187 (£7,813 less £8,000) will be recognised in profit or loss.

<u>Forex's financial statements</u>

The loan creditor will be recorded at €10,000 and no further adjustments are necessary as the loan is denominated in Euros.

<u>Consolidated financial statements</u>

The consolidated financial statements will show the results of the group in line with its economic substance, which is that of a single reporting entity. As such the intra-group loan will be eliminated on consolidation. The exchange gain of £187 will be taken to other comprehensive income in the consolidated financial statements (not the consolidated profit and loss account). This will mean a consolidation adjustment is required by moving the gain in the individual profit and loss account of Topco and moving it to other comprehensive income.

Presentation currency

12.363 The term 'presentation currency' is the currency in which the financial statements are presented. FRS 102 acknowledges in paragraph 30.17 that an entity may present its financial statements in any currency (or currencies).

Example 12.147 – Presentation currency

Topco Ltd is the parent of two subsidiaries which operate in Germany and France. However, the majority of the group's turnover and profits are generated in the UK.

As most of the group's turnover and profits are generated in the UK, Topco Ltd chooses to present its consolidated financial statements in £ sterling.

In very rare situations a small entity's presentation currency may differ from the entity's functional currency. In such cases the entity must translate its items of income and expense and financial position into the presentation currency. This is achieved as follows:

- Assets and liabilities for each balance sheet presented (including comparatives) are translated at the closing rate at the reporting date.
- Income and expenses for each profit and loss account (and other comprehensive income), including comparatives, are translated at the exchange rates at the dates of the transactions.
- All resulting exchange differences are recognised in other comprehensive income.

Paragraph 30.19 does recognise that for practical reasons, an entity may use average rates of exchange, particularly to translate income and expense items. Care must be taken where average rates of exchange are used because the paragraph also recognises that where exchange rates have fluctuated significantly, the use of an average rate of exchange for a period will be inappropriate.

Consolidated goodwill

12.364 Where a small group acquires a foreign subsidiary, any goodwill which arises on the acquisition of the subsidiary is treated as an asset of the foreign operation. Any fair value adjustments to the carrying value of assets and liabilities arising on the acquisition of a foreign operation are treated as assets and liabilities of the foreign operation. Assets and liabilities for each balance sheet (statement of financial position) presented (which also includes comparative information) should be translated from the functional currency to the presentation currency using the closing rate at the reporting date.

Under previous UK GAAP, consolidated goodwill was regarded as an asset of the parent company and not the subsidiary.

Disclosures

12.365 There are no legally required disclosures in respect of foreign exchange transactions for a small company, but management should consider the need to make any relevant disclosures in order to achieve a true and fair view.

EVENTS AFTER THE REPORTING PERIOD

12.366 Events after the reporting period (or 'post balance sheet events' as many accountants are familiar with) are dealt with in Section 32 *Events after the Reporting Period*. Such events can have a significant impact on a company's financial statements because of the need to reflect certain transactions which take place after the year-end but which relate to conditions that existed at the year-end. Additional disclosures may be necessary for events which took place after the year-end (for which no conditions existed) but before the financial statements are approved. There are two types of event under the scope of Section 32:

- adjusting events; and
- non-adjusting events.

Adjusting events

12.367 An adjusting event is one which is reflected within the financial statements and is an event where the conditions giving rise to the adjustment existed at the year-end/period-end, but which crystallise after the year-/period-end. The key to identifying whether the event is adjusting is to ensure that it is clear that the conditions which give rise to the event were in existence at the reporting date.

Examples of adjusting events include:

- The settlement of a court case after the reporting date which confirms that the company had a liability at the reporting date.
- Receipt of information after the reporting date which confirms that an asset has suffered impairment.
- Bankruptcy of a customer after the reporting date which confirms the debtor is irrecoverable (ie impaired).
- Sale of stock after the reporting date which may give evidence relating to the stock's estimated selling price less costs to complete and sell.
- The cost of assets purchased after the reporting date, or proceeds received from the sale of assets sold prior to the reporting date.

- Determination of profit-sharing bonus payments made after the reporting date.
- Discovery of fraud and/or error.

If the conditions above existed at the reporting date they would be reflected within the financial statements (ie adjusted).

Example 12.148 – Bonus payments

A company has always paid bonuses to its two directors based on 5% of profit before tax. The draft management accounts as at 31 March 2017 include a gross bonus, plus employer's national insurance amounting to £11,500 each following the resolution to pay a bonus based on the draft financial statements supplied as at 20 March 2017. This bonus is not paid until such time that the financial statements are approved because of various adjustments which are often incorporated into the finalised financial statements. The financial statements are approved four months' after the year-end and because of a large stock write-down, the profits have reduced to such an extent that the gross bonus, plus the employer's national insurance should only be £4,500 each.

This is an example of an adjusting event because the decision to pay the bonuses was made prior to the year-end and therefore the bonuses should be reduced accordingly.

Non-adjusting events

12.368 By their definition, non-adjusting events are not adjusted in the financial statements. This is because their conditions did not exist at the reporting date. Instead, additional disclosures may be required if the non-adjusting event is considered to be material to the financial statements.

Focus

- While non-adjusting events are not legally required, directors of a small company have a legal obligation to make sure the financial statements they approve give a true and fair view. Therefore, where a non-adjusting event is considered to be material to the company, the directors should make appropriate disclosures in the financial statements.

Section 32 requires disclosure of a non-adjusting event if non-disclosure would otherwise influence the decisions which users (for example the bank) may make on the basis of the financial statements.

12.369 Section 32 offers some (non-exhaustive) examples of non-adjusting events at paragraph 32.7 and 32.11 as follows:

- A fall in value of market investments between the end of the reporting period and the date on which the financial statements are authorised for issue. A fall in the market value of, say, a listed investment does not normally relate to the condition of the investment at the end of the reporting period, but it does reflect circumstances which have arisen subsequently. Therefore the company does not make an adjustment in the financial statements itself, although the directors might consider additional disclosures to be appropriate.
- The company receives confirmation that it has incurred a debtor following the settlement of a court case after the year-end but before the financial statements are authorised for issue. The debtor would not be recognised in the financial statements at the year-end, but a contingent asset might need to be disclosed if required for the financial statements to give true and fair view. An exception to this, which may give rise to an adjusting event, would be where an agreement was reached **before** the reporting date as to the amount to be settled.
- A major business combination (ie acquisition of a subsidiary) or disposal of a major subsidiary.
- The announcement by management of a plan to discontinue an operation.
- Any major purchases of assets, disposals or plans to dispose of assets or expropriation of major assets by the government.
- Destruction of a production plant by fire.
- The announcement (or commencement) of a major restructuring of the organisation.
- Issues or repurchases of an entity's debt or equity instruments.
- Abnormally large changes in the price of assets, or foreign exchange rates.
- A change in tax rates or tax laws which are enacted or announced that may have a significant impact on current and deferred taxes.
- Entering into significant commitments, or contingent liabilities (for example issuing significant guarantees).
- The commencement of litigation which has arisen because of events that have taken place after the end of the reporting period.

Example 12.149 – Discontinuing a division

A small supermarket operates four different classes of business: groceries, mobile telephone provider, internet service provider and domestic appliances. Each division is considered material to the financial statements of the company.

The financial year-end is 31 August 2017 and the financial statements have not yet been approved. On 30 September 2017, the company directors decided that because of extremely difficult trading conditions, and the incurrence of a heavy loss, it would discontinue the domestic appliances division. This announcement was made on 1 October 2017.

This is a non-adjusting event because the decision to discontinue the division took place after the reporting date. However, because the division is considered to be material to the financial statements, it would be appropriate to make additional disclosure of a non-adjusting event in the financial statements concerning the closure of the appliances division.

Example 12.150 – Share issue after the year-end

A company has a year-end of 31 July 2017. It has approached its bank for an additional working capital loan and the bank have agreed in principal subject to the shareholders making further investment to demonstrate their commitment to the company before the bank will formally agree to any further lending. The shareholders agreed and further shares were issued on 31 August 2017.

Section 32.11 recognises issues or repurchases of an entity's debt or equity instruments as a non-adjusting event and therefore it will probably be necessary to make additional disclosure of this non-adjusting event to give a true and fair view.

Going concern

12.370 The issue of going concern is a material issue in all companies, both large and small. When preparing financial statements, the company usually does so on the going concern basis. However, a company will not be able to use the going concern basis of preparing the financial statements if management determines *after* the reporting date that it either intends to cease trading or liquidate the business, or has no realistic alternative but to do so.

In situations when the directors feel that the financial statements should not be prepared on the going concern basis, the effect is so pervasive that there has to be a change in the basis of preparation (ie a basis other than the going concern basis). This alternative basis should not merely be an adjustment to the amounts recognised in the financial statements, but should be a complete change to the basis of accounting. The 'break-up' basis is not explicitly mentioned in Section 32, but would be regarded as an appropriate basis when the going concern presumption is not used.

Focus

- Going concern disclosures are encouraged disclosures in Appendix D to Section 1A and cross-reference is made to paragraph 3.9 of FRS 102 where going concern disclosures are needed.

12.371 Where management consider that going concern disclosures are needed in the financial statements, paragraph 3.9 requires them to disclose the uncertainties about the entity having the ability to continue as a going concern, together with the basis on which the financial statements have been prepared and the fact that they have not been prepared on a going concern basis. The directors must also disclose why the company is not regarded as a going concern.

Example 12.151 – Going concern basis not appropriate

A company is preparing financial statements to 31 December 2016. On 4 February 2017, following negotiations, the bank have 'called in' the overdraft and loan of £500,000 immediately as the company has been having ongoing trading difficulties. This has had a catastrophic effect on the company as they have failed to secure borrowing facilities with other financiers and the directors have decided that they have no realistic alternative but to cease trading with immediate effect and liquidate the company.

The going concern basis is not appropriate in this company's circumstances, and hence the directors may make disclosures as follows **(please note the following disclosures are illustrative disclosures only and may not be appropriate in every situation).**

Basis of preparation of the financial statements

The basis of preparation paragraph should explain the reasons why the going concern basis is no longer appropriate in the circumstances and the effect of this approach. Such a disclosure could be as follows:

> The company has failed to reach agreement with its bankers concerning the renewal of the company's borrowing facilities. The company has ceased trading with immediate effect and therefore the financial statements have been prepared under the 'break-up' basis. Fixed assets have been restated to recoverable amount on the grounds that the company is no longer trading and are available for sale in their current condition and current assets have been stated at recoverable amounts. Creditors falling due after more than one year have been reclassified as current liabilities.

Events after the reporting period

This would be relevant in this scenario because the event causing the going concern presumption to be departed from occurred after the year-end. A disclosure example is as follows:

As disclosed in the accounting policies note at Note X, the company ceased to trade on 4 February 2016 on the grounds that the company has been unable to source additional finance to enable the business to continue as a going concern. The going concern basis is not appropriate and the directors have therefore not prepared the financial statements on that basis.

Dividends

12.372 Dividends which are proposed after the reporting date cannot be recognised in the financial statements at the year-/period-end. This requirement also applies where the financial statements have not yet been authorised for issue. This is because at the reporting date, no obligation existed.

> **Focus**
>
> - Dividends declared and paid or payable are an encouraged disclosure in Appendix D to Section 1A and should be disclosed where material so that the financial statements give a true and fair view.

Date of authorisation of the financial statements

12.373 Under Section 32 of FRS 102, the company must disclose the date on which the financial statements were authorised for issue and who gave that authorisation. This is also required for e-filing purposes. This disclosure is usually automatically produced by accounts production software and may look as follows:

The financial statements were approved by the Board of Directors on [insert date of approval] and were signed by:

....	....
J Smith – Director	*B Jones – Director*

> **Focus**
>
> - If the business owners have the power to amend the financial statements after they have been issued, the directors should consider making additional disclosure concerning this power.

Disclosures

12.374 The disclosures relating to events after the reporting period may be as follows:

- The nature and financial effect of material non-adjusting events after the reporting period.
- Going concern disclosures, where applicable, as set out in paragraph 3.9 of FRS 102.
- Dividends declared and paid or payable during the period (for example as set out in paragraph 6.5(b) of FRS 102).

RELATED PARTIES

12.375 Related parties are dealt with in FRS 102 at Section 33 *Related Party Disclosures*. A key point worth emphasising at the outset where related party disclosures are concerned is that the EU Accounting Directive restricts the amount of disclosures needed in a small company's financial statements.

The overarching objective of Section 33 is to draw attention to the possibility that an entity's financial position and profit or loss have been affected by the existence of related parties and transactions between those related parties.

Definition of a related party

12.376 Over the years the definition of a related party has become more complicated. This is in recognition of the fact that business has evolved and in order to try to attempt to be a 'catch all' the standard-setters have always tried to widen the scope of related parties to ensure that a true and fair view is given in the financial statements.

Section 33 splits related parties into two distinct component parts in its definition. Part (a) relates to individuals and part (b) relates to companies.

Individuals as related parties

12.377 Paragraph 33.2(a) says that a person, or a close member of that person's family, is related to an entity if that person:

(i) has control, or joint control, over the reporting entity;

(ii) has significant influence over the reporting entity; or

(iii) is a member of the key management personnel of the reporting entity or of a parent of the reporting entity (key management personnel being those persons having authority and responsibility for the planning, directing and controlling of the entity and can include any director (executive or otherwise)).

Entities as related parties

12.378 Paragraph 33.2(b) says that an entity is related to a reporting entity if any of the following apply:

(i) the entity, and the reporting entity, both belong to the same group (hence each parent, subsidiary and fellow subsidiary in the group is related to the others);

(ii) one entity is an associate or joint venture of the other entity (or an associate or joint venture of a member of a group of which the other company is a member);

(iii) both companies are joint ventures of the same third company;

(iv) one entity is a joint venture of the third entity and the other entity is an associate of the third entity;

(v) the entity is a retirement benefit plan for the benefit of the employees – this can either be of the reporting entity or an entity which is related to the reporting entity – where the entity itself is a retirement benefit plan the sponsoring employers are related to the reporting entity;

(vi) the entity is controlled or jointly controlled by anyone identified in part (a)(i);

(vii) any person having control or joint control has significant influence over the entity, or is a member of the key management personnel of the entity (including the parent company); and

(viii) the entity, or any member of a group of which the company is a part of, provides key management personnel services to the reporting entity, or to the parent company.

Focus

- When considering each possible related party relationship, it is important that the entity assesses the substance, and not merely the legal form, of the relationship.

Parties who are not related parties

12.379 There are certain parties who are excluded from the definition of a related party as follows:

- Two companies simply because they have a director in common. This also includes other members of key management personnel in common or a member of key management personnel of one entity that has significant influence over the other entity.
- Two venturers simply because they share joint control over a joint venture.
- Any of the following in their normal dealings with the company, regardless of the fact that they may affect the freedom of action of an entity, or be involved in the decision-making process of the company:
    - finance providers;

- — trade unions;
- — public utilities; and
- — government departments and agencies.

- Customers, suppliers, franchisors, distributors or general agents with whom a company might be involved in a significant volume of business, merely by virtue of the resulting economic dependence.

Example 12.152 – Intra-group trading

A parent company wholly owns a subsidiary company. During the year to 31 October 2017, the parent purchases goods from its subsidiary. In addition, the parent provides administration services for which a management charge is levied by the parent. The financial controller is unsure whether such transactions need to be disclosed in the financial statements.

Paragraph 33.1A says that disclosure of such intra-group trading need not be made provided that the subsidiary which is a party to the transaction is a wholly-owned group member. Had the subsidiary not been wholly-owned, disclosures of any transactions which have not been concluded under normal market conditions would need to be disclosed.

Related party disclosures for small companies

12.380 As mentioned in the introduction to this section, the EU Accounting Directive which has been transposed into the Companies Act 2006 significantly reduces the amount of disclosure requirements which a small company needs to make in its financial statements. The Financial Reporting Council does not have the power to mandate additional disclosures over and above those contained in the legislation, but company directors do have a legal duty to ensure that the related party disclosures that they choose to make (or may not make as the case might be) allow the financial statements to give a true and fair view.

Focus

- A key point to emphasise where related party disclosures are concerned is that while only limited related party disclosures need be made for a small company, if the company chooses to disclose all transactions with related parties, it will still be complying with the law.

The disclosure requirements are contained in paragraph 1AC.34 to 1AC.36 and are as follows:

Small entity is a subsidiary company

12.381 If the small company is a subsidiary company the following disclosures should be made in respect of the parent of the smallest group for which consolidated financial statements are prepared of which the small entity is a member:

- the name of the parent drawing up the consolidated financial statements;
- the parent company's registered office address (whether this be in the UK or outside of the UK); or
- where the parent is not an incorporated entity, the address of the principal place of business.

Transactions not undertaken under normal market conditions

12.382 If the small company has entered into transactions with:

- it owners who hold a participating interest in the small company;
- companies in which the small company has a participating interest; and
- directors of the company (or members of the governing body)

and these transactions are not concluded under market conditions (ie on an arm's length basis), disclosure is required of the following:

- the amount of the transactions involved;
- the nature of the related party relationship; and
- any other information about the transactions to enable the users to have an understanding of the financial position of the small company.

Focus

- It is possible to aggregate individual transactions depending on their nature. However, separate information should be disclosed where this is considered necessary for an understanding of the effects that such related party transactions has had on the financial position of the small company.

Example 12.153 – Dividends to directors

During the year to 31 January 2017, a dividend was paid to Les who is a director and a shareholder of a small company.

Paragraph 1AC.35 of FRS 102 says that transactions with directors (or members of an entity' governing body), include directors' remuneration as well as dividends to paid to directors.

Transactions with group members

12.383 Transactions with members of a group need not be disclosed, provided the group member which is a party to the transaction is wholly-owned within the group. It does not necessarily have to be a parent company which owns the subsidiary; it can be another subsidiary. If external shareholders own any non-controlling interest in the subsidiary, the subsidiary is not wholly-owned.

Directors' advances, credits and guarantees

12.384 If a company makes advances or credits to its director(s) or enters into guarantees on behalf of the directors, the notes to the financial statements must show the following:

Advances or credits to directors:

(1) the amount;

(2) the interest rate;

(3) main conditions;

(4) any amounts which have been repaid;

(5) any amounts which have been written off; and

(6) any amounts which have been waived.

In respect of (1), (4), (5) and (6) the totals must also be disclosed.

Guarantees:

In respect of guarantees, the following details are required:

(1) the main terms;

(2) the amount of the maximum liability which may be incurred by the small company; and

(3) any amounts paid, and any liability which has been incurred by the small company, for the purpose of fulfilling the guarantee. This includes any loss incurred because of enforcement of the guarantee.

In respect of (2) and (3), the notes to the financial statements outlining details of the guarantee(s) should include the amounts involved.

Focus

- If the small entity is not an incorporated company, the disclosure in respect of the guarantee should be made in relation to members of its governing body.

SPECIALISED ACTIVITIES

12.385 Section 34 *Specialised Activities* deals with a range of entity-specific activities, some of which may not be applicable to small companies. In recognition of this, this particular section of the chapter will not go into comprehensive detail and merely provide an overview of the requirements and to indicate where further information might be obtained.

12.386 Section 34 deals with the following types of specialised activities:

- Agriculture.
- Extractive Activities.
- Service Concession Arrangements.
- Financial Institutions.
- Retirement Benefit Plans: Financial Statements.
- Heritage Assets.
- Funding Commitments.
- Incoming Resources from Non-Exchange Transactions.
- Public Benefit Entity Combinations.
- Public Benefit Entity Concessionary Loans.

Agriculture

12.387 Where a small company is involved in agricultural activity it should choose an accounting policy for each class of biological asset and its related agricultural produce.

> **Focus**
>
> - A 'biological asset' is a living animal or plant and 'agricultural produce' is the harvested produce of that biological asset.

12.388 There are three recognition criteria which have to be fulfilled before an entity can recognise a biological asset or an item of agricultural produce on the balance sheet (statement of financial position):

(1) the entity has control over the asset as a result of past events;

(2) it is probable (ie more likely than not) that future economic benefits that are associated with the asset will flow to the entity; and

(3) the fair value, or cost, of the asset can be reliably measured.

Subsequent measurement

12.389 There are two models which can be used to measure biological assets and their related agricultural produce:

(1) the fair value model; or

(2) the cost model.

Focus

- Where the entity chooses the fair value as its accounting policy to subsequently measure the biological asset and their related agricultural produce, it cannot change its accounting policy to the cost model. Hence it is important to choose the policy which is most applicable to the entity at the outset.

Fair value model

12.390 Where the company opts to measure a biological asset under the fair value model on initial recognition it must carry the asset at fair value at each reporting date. Changes in fair value from one period to the next are taken to profit or loss.

Where the company opts to measure agricultural produce harvested from the biological asset it is measured at fair value less costs to sell at the point of harvest. This also becomes cost at the date the entity applies Section 13 *Inventories* to the agricultural produce.

Where the entity chooses to use the fair value model, there are four factors which need to be considered:

- Where an active market exists for a biological asset or agricultural produce (in its present location and condition), then the quoted price in that market is the most appropriate basis for arriving at a fair value for the asset. Where various types of market exist, the company should use the price which exists in the market which it expects to use.
- Where an active market does not exist, an entity can use one, or more, of the following to determine fair value:
  - — the most recent transaction price, provided there has been no significant change in circumstances between the date of the transaction and the reporting date;
  - — market prices for similar assets which are then adjusted to reflect differences; and
  - — sector benchmarks.
- If information sources considered in the three sub-bullets above suggest different conclusions relating to fair value of a biological asset or an item

of agricultural produce, the company must consider the reasons behind those differences in order to arrive at the most reliable estimate of fair value.

- Some situations might arise where a fair value price is available despite market-determined prices, or values, not being available for a biological asset in its present condition. Where this is the case the company must consider whether the present value of expected net cash flows from the asset (discounted at a current market rate) results in a reliable measure of fair value.

Cost model

12.391 This is probably the most common model where a small company has agricultural activity in place. Under the cost model, the company measures biological assets at cost less accumulated depreciation and accumulated impairment losses.

In respect of agricultural produce harvested from a biological asset, this is measured at the point of harvest at either:

- lower of cost and estimated selling price less costs to complete and sell; or
- fair value less costs to sell with any gain or loss arising on initial recognition of agricultural produce at fair value less costs to sell being included in profit or loss.

Extractive industries

12.392 Extractive industries are very specialist and are beyond the scope of this book. Readers are directed to paragraphs 34.11–34.11C of FRS 102 for the relevant accounting treatment.

Service concession arrangements

12.393 A service concession arrangement is an arrangement where a public sector body, or a public benefit entity contracts with a private sector entity to construct, operate and maintain infrastructure assets for a specified period of time (known as the 'concession period'). The private sector entity is paid for its services over the period of the arrangement.

FRS 102 deals with the accounting requirements for both the grantor (the public sector body or public benefit entity) and the operator (the private entity).

Detailed analysis of service concession arrangements are beyond the scope of this book and readers are advised to consult the requirements of paragraphs 34.12–34.16A of FRS 102 where they are affected by service concession arrangements.

Financial institutions

12.394 Financial institutions have been subjected to much debate over recent years because it was intimated that they could well be classified as 'publicly accountable' and hence report under EU-adopted IFRS. This would have caused significant problems for institutions such as small pension schemes because the levels of disclosure required by EU-adopted IFRS is vast.

However, due to the removal of the concept of public accountability in FRS 102, this problem was no longer apparent; although FRS 102 includes a significantly long definition of what it considers to be a 'financial institution'. Institutions which meet the definition of a financial institution per the Glossary to FRS 102 can adopt the provisions in FRS 102 and may also take advantage of the reduce disclosure concessions in either FRS 101 *Reduced Disclosure Framework* or FRS 102.

The Glossary to FRS 102 defines a financial institution as:

> 'Any of the following:
>
> (a) a bank which is:
>
> (i) a firm with a Part IV [Financial Services and Markets Act 2000, s 40(4)] permission which includes accepting deposits and:
>
> (a) which is a credit institution; or
>
> (b) whose Part IV permission includes a requirement that it complies with the rules in the General Prudential sourcebook and the Prudential Sourcebook for Banks, Building Societies and Investment Firms relating to banks, but which is not a building society, a friendly society or a credit union;
>
> (ii) an EEA bank which is a full credit institution;
>
> (b) a building society which is defined in section 119(1) of the Building Societies Act 1986 as a building society incorporated (or deemed to be incorporated) under that act;
>
> (c) a credit union, being a body corporate registered under the Industrial and Provident Societies Act 1965 as a credit union in accordance with the Credit Unions Act 1979, which is an authorised person;
>
> (d) custodian bank, broker-dealer or stockbroker;
>
> (e) an entity that undertakes the business of effecting or carrying out **insurance contracts**, including general and life assurance entities;
>
> (f) an incorporated friendly society incorporated under the Friendly Societies Act 1992 or a registered friendly society registered under

section 7(1)(a) of the Friendly Societies Act 1974 or any enactment which it replaced, including any registered branches;

(g) an investment trust, Irish Investment Company, venture capital trust, mutual fund, exchange traded fund, unit trust, open-ended investment (OEIC);

(h) a **retirement benefit plan**; or

(i) any other entity whose principal activity is to generate wealth or manage risk through financial instruments. This is intended to cover entities that have business activities similar to those listed above but are not specifically included in the list above.

A **parent** entity whose sole activity is to hold investments in other group entities is not a financial institution.'[20]

Disclosures for financial institutions other than retirement benefit plans

12.395 The provisions in Section 1A relating to small entities will apply, but directors should also consider the disclosure requirements in paragraphs 34.19–34.33 of FRS 102 where necessary in order to give a true and fair view.

Retirement benefit plans

12.396 Retirement benefit plans are outside the scope of this book. However, readers are advised to consult the provisions in the Statement of Recommended Practice (SORP) *Financial Reports of Pension Funds* which has been updated to reflect the provisions in FRS 102.

Readers are also directed to Section 34 and paragraphs 34.34–34.48 of FRS 102 outlining the accounting issues relating to retirement benefit plans.

Heritage assets

12.397 A 'heritage asset' is defined in the Glossary to FRS 102 as:

> 'Tangible and **intangible assets** with historic, artistic, scientific, technological, geophysical, or environmental qualities that are held and maintained principally for their contribution to knowledge and culture.'

Heritage assets are accounted for under paragraphs 34.50–34.54 and the relevant disclosure requirements for heritage assets are contained in Section 1A of FRS 102 (Appendix C, paragraph 1AC.12).

20 Glossary to FRS 102 **Financial institution**.

Recognition and measurement of a heritage asset

12.398 Heritage assets can be recognised and measured using either the cost model or the revaluation model as permitted in Section 17 *Property, Plant and Equipment*.

> **Focus**
>
> - Where heritage assets have been previously capitalised or recently purchased, then information relating to the cost or valuation of the asset will be available. Where this information is not available, the heritage asset is not recognised as an asset on the balance sheet (statement of financial position).

Disclosure requirements relating to heritage assets

12.399 Disclosures relating to heritage assets are as follows:

- Where heritage assets are recognised on the balance sheet (statement of financial position), disclose the carrying amount of heritage assets at the start and end of the reporting period, showing an analysis between classes or groups of heritage assets recognised at cost and those recognised at valuation.
- Where heritage assets are recognised at valuation, sufficient information should be disclosed to assist in understanding the valuation being recognised (this will include the date of valuation, method employed, whether the entity used an external valuer and where it did, details of their qualification and any limitations on the valuation).

Funding commitments

12.400 Where a company makes funding commitments (ie commitments to provide resources to other entities) it will recognise a liability and usually a corresponding expense when it has made that commitment.

> **Focus**
>
> - Funding commitments do not apply to commitments to make a loan because in this situation a company will apply the provisions in Section 11 *Basic Financial Instruments* (see **12.23**) or Section 12 *Other Financial Instruments Issues* (see **12.55**).

There are three conditions which have to be met in relation to funding commitments:

(1) the definition and recognition criteria for a liability have been met;

(2) the obligation (either legal or constructive) is such that the entity cannot legally withdraw from it; and

(3) the entitlement of the other party to the resources is not dependant on the satisfaction of performance-related conditions.

> **Focus**
>
> - Where commitments are performance-related, they are recognised when those conditions have been met.

Measurement of a funding commitment

12.401 A company which has entered into a funding commitment recognises the commitment at the present value of the resources which it has committed.

Disclosure requirements for funding commitments

12.402 The disclosure requirements for funding commitments are as follows:

- the commitment made;
- the timeframe of that commitment;
- any performance-related conditions which are attached to that commitment; and
- details of how the commitment will be funded.

Incoming resources from non-exchange transactions

12.403 A 'non-exchange transaction' is one whereby the receiving entity receives value from another entity without having to directly give anything in return in equal value. They can include (but are not limited to):

- cash;
- goods;
- services; and
- legacies.

> **Focus**
>
> - The accounting treatment for incoming resources from non-exchange transactions are similar to the accounting treatment for grants (Section 24 *Government Grants* and see **12.274**).

Recognition and measurement

12.404 Incoming resources from non-exchange transactions are recognised as follows:

- Transactions which do not impose specific performance-related conditions are recognised in income when they are received or receivable.
- Transactions which do impose specific performance-related conditions are recognised in income as the performance-related conditions are satisfied.
- Where the resources are received before the revenue recognition criteria is met, they are recognised as a liability (similar to deferred income).

> **Focus**
>
> - When considering incoming resources from non-exchange transactions, an entity is required to assess whether the resource can be reliably measured and whether the benefits of recognising the resource outweigh the costs involved.

Recognition and measurement: donations and other incoming resources

12.405 Sometimes a company will receive a donation. Donations of services which can be reasonably quantified will be recognised in the financial statements as income with a corresponding expense. The debit entry will only be taken to assets where the donated services are used in the production of an asset.

Donated services and facilities are measured at the value to the entity.

All other incoming resources from non-exchange transactions are measured at the fair value of the resources received or receivable.

Public benefit entity combinations

12.406 Public benefit entity combinations are beyond the scope of this book and readers are directed to paragraphs PBE34.75–PBE34.85 of FRS 102 for the accounting requirements and paragraph PBE34.86 of FRS 102 for the disclosure requirements.

Public benefit entity concessionary loans

12.407 Public benefit entity concessionary loans are beyond the scope of this book and readers are directed to paragraphs PBE34.87–PBE34.92 of FRS 102 for the accounting requirements and paragraph PBE34.93–PBE34.97 of FRS 102 for the presentation and disclosure requirements.

CHAPTER SUMMARY

- The specifications of FRS 102 as applicable to different areas of the financial statements are described in this chapter.
- The presentation and disclosure requirements applicable to a small company are contained in Section 1A in Appendix C and Appendix D of Section 1A of FRS 102.
- Appendix C outlines the disclosures required by company law.
- Appendix D outlines the disclosures encouraged by the Financial Reporting Council to enable the financial statements to give a true and fair view.
- The full recognition and measurement principles in FRS 102 apply to small companies – for example if a small company has investment property carried at fair value through profit or loss, it will apply the full recognition and measurement principles in Section 16 *Investment Property* but make the disclosures required by Section 1A of FRS 102.
- There are various differences in accounting methodology between what did apply under the FRSSE and what applies under FRS 102 (which are contained in the Appendix to this chapter).
- The transposition of the EU Accounting Directive into the Companies Act 2006 allows financial statements to be 'abridged' and 'adapted'.
- Companies classed as small in the Companies Act 2006 can apply the accounting requirements in this chapter (including companies operating in the financial services section (see **12.394**))

PITFALLS TO AVOID

- Do not assume that all the accounting methodologies contained in the FRSSE (effective January 2015) have been carried over into FRS 102 because there are some considerable changes. The Appendix to this chapter outlines some of the more *notable* changes (not every change is considered).
- Small companies still have a legal obligation to ensure their financial statements give a true and fair view and applying the minimum legally required disclosures may not achieve this and hence directors must ensure they make additional disclosures, where applicable, to give a true and fair view.
- Do not rely wholly on accounts production software programs to get the disclosures correct and consider the use of a disclosure checklist, where necessary, to ensure disclosures are not omitted or disclosed incorrectly (particularly in the early stages of first-time adoption of FRS 102 with reduced disclosures).

- As well as the accounting differences inherent in FRS 102, companies' should not ignore the associated taxation implications (particularly on transition).
- Make sure you are using the correct version of FRS 102 – ie the September 2015 version.

APPENDIX TO CHAPTER 12

Key differences in accounting requirements between the FRSSE and FRS 102

A12.1 The presentation and disclosure requirements for small companies are contained in Section 1A *Small Entities* in Appendix C *Disclosure requirements for small entities* which outlines the legally required disclosures and Appendix D *Additional disclosures encouraged for small entities*. Appendix C reflects the requirements in the Companies Act 2006 following transposition of the EU Accounting Directive in company law. Appendix D outlines those disclosures which a small entity should consider making in order to achieve a true and fair view.

Focus

- While the presentation and disclosure requirements pertaining to small companies are contained in a separate Section 1A, the **full** recognition and measurement principles in the rest of FRS 102 will apply to a small company.

A12.2 In recognition that FRS 102 is a new regime for many practitioners and preparers of financial statements, it is useful to show the key differences in the accounting methodologies between FRS 102 and the previous FRSSE (effective January 2015) which should aid preparers in understanding the impact that the new financial reporting framework will have on companies. The key differences are outlined in the following table (please note that this table only contains the **key** differences – not every difference in accounting methodology is covered and the differences are only confined to small companies).

Area	**FRS 102 September 2015**	**FRSSE (effective January 2015)**
Deferred tax	Deferred tax is calculated using the timing difference 'plus' approach which recognises deferred tax on: non-monetary assets subject to revaluation; fair values in business combinations; and unremitted earnings in overseas subsidiaries and associates.	Deferred tax was calculated using the timing difference approach which included more exemptions from deferred tax than FRS 102.
Defined benefit pension plans	The net liability is recognised as the difference between the present value of the plan's obligations and the fair value of the assets.	The resulting asset or liability is recognised on the balance sheet. The assets are valued at fair value; liabilities are valued at actuarial value.
Discontinued operations	Presented line-by-line on the face of the income statement (profit and loss account). See paragraph 3.10 of this book for an illustration.	Line-by-line presentation is not required under the FRSSE.
Employee benefits	Short-term accrued benefits (eg holiday pay) have to be accrued at the reporting date where these are subsequently paid in the next accounting period.	Short-term employee benefits such as holiday pay were not necessarily accounted for as there was no specific requirement in the FRSSE (although FRS 12 *Provisions, contingent assets and contingent liabilities* did cite unpaid holiday as an example meeting the definition of a liability).
Fair value accounting	More emphasis is placed on fair value accounting in FRS 102 including biological assets and agricultural activity.	Less emphasis was placed on fair value accounting (especially no requirement to account for derivative financial instruments which are carried at fair value under FRS 102).
Financial instruments	An imputed interest rate is required where a loan is made at rates other than market rates.	No requirement to impute interest where the loan is, say, at below market rates of interest.
Fixed assets	Major spare parts and standby equipment must be capitalised.	Major spare parts and standby equipment were not specifically covered in the FRSSE and hence were usually consumed through stock as cost of sales.

Area	**FRS 102 September 2015**	**FRSSE (effective January 2015)**
Foreign currency	Foreign currency transactions must be translated at spot rate and any derivative contract held at fair value through profit or loss. Hedge accounting must be applied if the entity wishes to achieve a similar outcome as that of the FRSSE (effective January 2015).	The contracted rate could be used instead of spot rate.
Goodwill and intangible assets	Maximum presumed economic life where management cannot reliably estimate such a useful life is presumed to be 10 years.	Maximum presumed economic life where management cannot reliably estimate such a useful life is presumed to be five years.
Grants	Can be accounted for using the performance model or the accrual model.	Only the accrual model was used in the FRSSE.
Investment properties	Fair value gains and losses are taken to the profit and loss account with associated deferred tax.	Fair value gains and losses are taken to a revaluation surplus with no deferred tax accounted for.
Inventory	Valued at the lower of cost and estimated selling price less costs to complete and sell.	Valued at the lower of cost and net realisable value.
Leases	More judgement is needed on classification of a lease between financing and operating and no numeric benchmark for lease classification is contained.	A 90% threshold was cited in the Glossary to the FRSSE (effective January 2015) which suggested that if the present value of the minimum lease payments equated to 90% or more of the fair value of the leased asset then the lease was a finance lease.
Prior period adjustments	Material errors must be corrected by way of a prior period adjustment.	Only fundamental errors needed correction through a period adjustment. A fundamental error was one which destroyed the true and fair view and the validity of the financial statements.
Related party disclosures	Limited related party disclosures are made including disclosure of transactions not concluded under normal market terms.	More extensive related parties were required (including the names of the transacting related parties).

Chapter 13

Small Company Audits and Ethical Standards

SIGNPOSTS

- Auditors must obtain evidence which is both sufficient and appropriate (see **13.1**).
- Where a UK and Ireland International Standard on Auditing (ISA) is applicable, then the entire contents of that UK and Ireland ISA must be applied (see **13.2**).
- As well as UK and Ireland ISAs, auditors must also comply with the requirements of the Ethical Standards (see **13.3–13.19**).
- Audit planning is a critical part of the audit because without adequate planning the auditor 'goes in blind' (see **13.20–13.21**).
- Once the audit strategy has been developed the auditor can then move on to the more detailed audit plan (see **13.22**).
- Audit planning is considered to be a continuous and iterative process and amendments to the audit plan may be required during the course of the audit (see **13.23** and **13.24**).
- Throughout the course of the audit, supervision and review procedures must be applied (see **13.25**).
- Planning documentation will vary according to the nature and complexity of the audit assignment (see **13.26** and **13.27**).
- Inquiry by the auditor to management or those charged with governance is not considered, on its own, to generate sufficient appropriate audit evidence (see **13.28**).
- There are various factors which the auditor should consider in gaining an understanding of the entity (see **13.29**).
- Auditors should also obtain an understanding of the entity's owners, other individuals and entities in which the owners are also involved with (see **13.30**).
- Internal controls are a key consideration when planning and executing an audit (see **13.31** and **13.32**).

- Analytical procedures must be used at the planning stage, fieldwork stage and immediately prior to finalising the audit (see **13.33**).
- There are specific audit objectives which need to be fulfilled and certain procedures will gather the evidence needed to fulfil these objectives and sampling can be used to avoid testing the whole population (see **13.34–13.64**).
- Audit reporting is a crucial aspect of the audit and the engagement partner must base their opinion on the audit evidence gathered (see **13.65**).
- Audit reports are governed by UK and Ireland ISAs in the 700 series (see **13.66**).
- The audit report must contain certain elements to comply with the UK and Ireland ISAs (see **13.67–13.76**).
- There are generally three types of audit qualification (see **13.77–13.83**).
- An emphasis of matter is not an audit qualification but a paragraph used to highlight an issue of importance (see **13.84** and **13.85**).
- Other matter paragraphs can be used in certain situations (see **13.86**).

INTRODUCTION

13.1 Whilst relatively few small companies have a statutory audit, there are some that do and this chapter examines the principles involved in small company audits. Some small companies still choose to have a voluntary audit to have additional comfort that the financial statements are free from material misstatement. Whilst an audit does not give absolute assurance concerning the truth and fairness of the financial statements, it does give reasonable assurance.

The objective of the auditor is to express an opinion as to whether the financial statements give a true and fair view of the state of the company's affairs at the reporting date. The auditor undertakes various procedures to gather sufficient and appropriate audit evidence relating to the amounts and disclosures in the financial statements. The pivotal term where audit evidence is concerned is the phrase 'sufficient and appropriate'. 'Sufficiency' is the measure of the quantity of audit evidence and this is affected by the auditor's risk assessment that the financial statements may be materially misstated. 'Appropriateness' is the measure of the quality of the audit evidence and how relevant and reliable that evidence is to support the conclusions on which the auditor's opinion is based.

13.2 This chapter does not go into every detail concerning a small company audit because each audit is different. Instead the chapter considers a basic overview of how a small company audit works from the planning phase, through to the detailed fieldwork and completion procedures. In all cases, auditors and accountants should ensure that they comply with the requirements applicable to a true and fair framework (for example compliance with accounting standards (FRS 102 with reduced disclosures) and ISAs (UK and Ireland)).

One of the main problems that auditors of small companies face is understanding some of the core principles in the ISAs (UK and Ireland). This is particularly the case for areas such as planning and completion which are frequently criticised by regulatory bodies when they inspect the work of audit firms. There is no pre-determined 'benchmark' when it comes to the amount of planning, fieldwork or completion work; indeed exercising professional judgement is prevalent within auditing, but auditors must ensure that they comply with all the requirements of the UK and Ireland ISAs.

When the clarified UK and Ireland ISAs were issued by the (now defunct) Auditing Practices Board, they were issued with the intention that where a UK and Ireland ISA was relevant, the entire standard applied. In other words, an auditor could not 'cherry pick' certain requirements of the UK and Ireland ISA and ignore other parts and this concept still applies today. For example, if the small company has related party transactions then the entire contents of ISA (UK and Ireland) 550 *Related parties* must be applied to that particular audit area. Some small firms of auditors have run into difficulties when it comes to regulatory inspections (either through external file reviewers or professional body reviews) in that certain parts of the UK and Ireland ISAs have not been applied, or have been applied incorrectly.

Focus

- Practice Note 26 (Revised) *Guidance on Smaller Entity Audit Documentation* provides a useful guidance to auditors on how to prepare smaller entity audit documentation in an efficient manner. The Practice Note itself is concerned with the audits of simpler entities, where typically:
  - ownership is confined to a small number of individuals (usually owner-managed companies);
  - the operations of the business are uncomplicated;
  - there are few sources of income and activities;
  - the processes and accounting systems are simple; and
  - there are relatively few internal controls and these may be informal.

ETHICAL STANDARDS FOR AUDITORS

13.3 Professional ethics are central to the audit and accountancy profession. Unfortunately many audit firms have run into problems over the years when it comes to complying with Ethical Standards – either deliberate non-compliance or unintentional and it is not appropriate for auditors to simply say that they would not succumb to a threat to independence or objectivity – they must demonstrate compliance with the Ethical Standards. In the UK and Republic of Ireland, there are five Ethical Standards (ES) which auditors must adhere to:

- ES 1: Integrity, objectivity and independence.
- ES 2: Financial, business, employment and personal relationships.
- ES 3: Long association with the audit engagement.
- ES 4: Fees, remuneration and evaluation policies, litigation, gifts and hospitality.
- ES 5: Non-audit services provided to audit clients.

Focus

- The Ethical Standards are updated on a periodic basis and copies of the ESs can be obtained free of charge from the Financial Reporting Council's website www.frc.org.uk.

ES 1: Integrity, objectivity and independence

13.4 To all intents and purposes, this ES tells auditors what they should already know. Auditors must act with integrity, which the standard recognises as not just including honesty, but other qualities. The standard refers to characteristics such as fairness, candour, courage, intellectual honesty and confidentiality.

Auditors have been criticised over the years for the ways in which they have approached their audit work. Indeed, auditors have also been blamed for their part in the financial crisis which started in 2007/08 with regards to failing to apply professional scepticism properly and failing to question managements' practices. Citations such as 'auditors need to demonstrate more scepticism' and 'the audit model needs to evolve' have been frequently voiced by critics of the audit profession and whether this criticism is fair or otherwise, it must be borne in mind that auditors should be, and be seen to be, objective and independent.

ES 1 considers objectivity to be a state of mind that excludes bias, prejudice and compromise. It goes on to say that applying objectivity will enable auditors to give fair and impartial consideration to all matters which are relevant. It also recognises that objectivity goes hand in hand with integrity.

13.5 Objectivity is a personal behavioural characteristic which concerns the auditor's state of mind. According to ES 1, independence is freedom from situations and relationships which would otherwise make others think that objectivity is (or could be) impaired.

The main thrust, therefore, is that integrity, objectivity and independence must be maintained at all times during the course of an audit. Where threats to independence and objectivity present themselves, they must either be reduced to an acceptably low level or eradicated in totality. Where threats to independence and objectivity cannot be mitigated then the auditor must consider resigning from the existing audit or declining a new audit. ES 1 recognises the following threats to an auditor's objectivity and independence:

- *Self-interest threat.* This can occur when the auditor or close family member has a financial interest in the audit client.
- *Self-review threat.* This occurs when the audit firm is also providing non-audit services, such as preparing the management or year-end accounts and then also acts in the capacity of auditor.
- *Management threat.* A management threat occurs when the audit firm performs non-audit services and management make judgements and take decisions based on that work. The standard itself cites the design, selection and implementation of an accounting IT system.
- *Advocacy threat.* This can arise when the audit firm acts as a legal advocate for the audit client because here the audit firm will have to adopt a position which is very similar to that of a management role.
- *Familiarity threat.* Familiarity threats could commonly arise. This is when the auditor develops close relationships with the audit client, usually because of long association. Regular partner rotation is encouraged to reduce this threat to an acceptable level.
- *Intimidation threat.* This can arise when the client is aggressive or pressure is put on the auditor to complete the audit in a disproportionately short timescale.

ES 2: Financial, business, employment and personal relationships

13.6 Auditors cannot have any financial interest in their audit client. To do so would give rise to a self-interest threat as described above and ES 2 acknowledges that there are no safeguards which can be applied to reduce this risk to an acceptable level. However, situations can arise when the family of the audit partner may have a financial interest in the audit client. ES 2 makes no allowances for such situations, but provides an exception where an immediate family member of an audit partner is not in a position to influence the conduct and outcome of the audit. Generally, however, where such financial interests are material and the audit partner has close contact with the audit engagement team, the Ethics Partner would consider the need to put safeguards in place and this may involve substituting the audit partner.

13.7 Business relationships can occur when the audit firm and the client have a common commercial interest and the standard itself recognises that this can create a self-interest, advocacy or intimidation threat. The audit firm must not enter into a business relationship with an audit client, its management or its affiliates. The ES does, however, provide for two exceptions to this rule and does allow the audit firm to enter into a business relationship where they:

- involve the purchase of goods and services from the audit client in the ordinary course of business and on an arm's-length basis and which are not material to either party; or
- are clearly inconsequential to either party.

13.8 Employment relationships occur when an audit firm employs someone from the audit client, or admits, for example, the financial director to the audit firm's partnership. The standard recognises instances when the audit firm may enter into an agreement with the audit client to supply staff (secondments). Such agreements are not permitted unless the arrangement is for a short period of time and would not involve the staff (or the partners) providing services to the client which would not be permitted under ES 5: *Non-audit services provided to audited entities*. In addition, the audit firm must also ensure that the client agrees that the staff member(s) concerned will not hold a management position, make management decisions or exercise discretionary authority to commit the audit client to a certain position or accounting treatment.

The standard is also quite strict on what happens when a staff loan assignment has been undertaken which is permissible under ES 2. Where an audit partner or member of staff of the audit firm returns after completion of the loan assignment, they must not be involved in any area of the audit which may involve a function or activity which the employee or audit partner performed or supervised during their engagement.

13.9 Where a former audit partner takes up employment with the audit client, the firm must ensure that it takes all relevant action to ensure that no significant connections remain between the firm and the individual who has joined the client. Also, where an audit partner who has been the partner in charge of the audit client leaves to take up employment with that same audit client in a key management position, or is appointed as a director of the audit client, the audit firm must resign and not be re-appointed until a two-year period has elapsed. The two-year clock starts when the former audit partner ceased to be able to influence the conduct and outcome of the audit, or when the former partner ceases to be employed by the audit client, whichever is the sooner.

13.10 Personal relationships can hinder objectivity and independence when a family member has a financial, business or employment relationship with the audited entity. ES 2 acknowledges that this can result in a self-interest, familiarity or intimidation threat arising.

The audit firm must have procedures in place whereby partners and audit staff must report any family, close family and other personal relationships which involve the audit client and which may give rise to a threat to independence and objectivity. The audit engagement partner will then assess these threats and apply safeguards which will normally involve removing the relevant individuals from the audit assignment.

ES 3: Long association with the audit client

13.11 Long association with the audit client is a fairly common threat and one which has been frequently criticised by professional regulators. Essentially the audit firm must have procedures and policies in place which monitor the length of time that an audit engagement partner and other key staff (including key partners) are involved in the audit. Where such individuals have had a long association with the audit client, the firm must assess the threat to the auditor's objectivity and independence and put in place safeguards to reduce any threats to objectivity and independence to an acceptable level. This can usually involve partner rotation, but in cases where such safeguards cannot be put in place, the audit firm must resign.

For small audit firms, the practicalities of rotation and ensuring true separation from previous audit team can present particular problems.

ES 4: Fees, remuneration and evaluation policies, litigation, gifts and hospitality

13.12 Where fees are concerned, the audit partner must ensure that fees for the audit are not influenced, or determined, by any non-audit services which the firm may provide to the audit client (for example payroll services, tax advisory services or accountancy services). In addition, fees can never be undertaken on a contingent fee basis; fees must always be calculated in accordance with the time spent on the audit and the level of skills and experience of the staff needed to perform the audit work effectively and in accordance with the firm's quality assurance procedures.

13.13 Where the audit firm provides non-audit services then care needs to be taken. ES 4 says that where it is expected that fees for both audit and non-audit work from unquoted companies (and subsidiary companies) which regularly exceed 15% of the annual fee income of the firm or, where profits are not shared on a firm-wide basis, of the part where the audit engagement partner's profit-share is calculated, then the firm shall either decline to act as auditor for the entity and shall either resign or not stand for reappointment, as appropriate.

Where fees for both audit and non-audit services from an unlisted entity are expected to regularly exceed 10% of the annual fee income of the firm, or the part of the firm by reference to which the audit engagement partner's profit share is calculated, but are not expected to regularly exceed 15%, then the audit partner must disclose this expectation to the firm's Ethics Partner as well as to those charged with governance of the audit client. The audit firm must then arrange to have an external and independent quality control review of the audit engagement prior to the audit report being finalised (a 'hot' file review).

> **Focus**
>
> - This book focuses on the requirements applicable to small companies. For listed entities, the thresholds in respect of fees for audit and non-audit work are reduced and hence auditors are advised to consult with the requirements in paragraphs 31 and 35 of ES 4.

13.14 Remuneration and evaluation policies occur when the audit firm sells non-audit services to an audit client and then subsequently judges the audit team on the amount of non-audit services which they sell to their audit clients. ES 4 at paragraph 44 requires the audit firm to establish policies and procedures to ensure that the objectives of the audit team do not include the selling of non-audit services to the audit client. In addition, any appraisals of the audit team (for the purposes of promotion or establish pay levels) must not include the success in selling non-audit services to the audit client. Remuneration levels of members of the audit team also cannot be based on their success in selling non-audit services to audit clients.

13.15 Unfortunately sometimes audit clients may not pay the auditor for the work which they have performed. There are two points to be aware of where overdue fees are concerned. Firstly, paragraph 26 of ES 4 says that in relation to fees for professional services that are overdue, and the amount concerned cannot be regarded as 'trivial', the audit engagement partner (in consultation with the Ethics Partner), shall consider whether the audit firm can continue to act as auditor, or whether it would be appropriate to resign. This is particularly the case where fees have been outstanding for a significantly long period of time and the auditor is about to issue the next auditor's report. A self-interest threat is created because the auditor may feel that by issuing an unqualified audit report, the fees for the previous year's audit will be paid. Professional regulators have also been known to criticise audit firms where fees are outstanding for a disproportionate length of time because this essentially has the characteristics of a loan to the audit client.

Secondly, where the audit client has not paid the auditor for work performed and the auditor has instigated legal proceedings to recover the fees, this may create a self-interest, advocacy or intimidation threat. Where litigation is significant, and in progress, or where the audit engagement partner considers such legal action to be probable, the audit firm must either not continue with, or accept, the audit engagement.

13.16 The relationship between the audit firm and the audit client may be very good and the audit client may want to offer hospitality or gifts to the audit team. The rules in ES 4 are clear where such gifts and hospitality are concerned.

ES 4 recognises that gifts from an audit client, unless their value is insignificant, create threats to objectivity and independence which no safeguards can eliminate or reduce. Therefore, where the value of a gift is judged to be significant, the audit team should decline the gift.

In terms of hospitality, the ES acknowledges that this is a component of many business relationships and recognises that such hospitality can also create an opportunity for developing a better understanding of the audited entity's business. Where hospitality is concerned, the ES acknowledges that it will not necessarily impair the independence and objectivity of the auditor where they accept hospitality, but this hospitality must be reasonable in terms of its frequency, nature and cost.

In theory, these areas can sound straightforward. In practice, deciding what is 'insignificant' and 'reasonable' and what constitutes 'hospitality' can be fraught with difficulty and therefore these problems need the auditor to exercise professional judgement including renewed consideration.

ES 5: Non-audit services provided to audited entities

13.17 Many small firms of auditors provide non-audit services to their smaller audit clients such as payroll, tax advisory and accounts preparation work. Essentially in such situations, the audit engagement partner must ensure that there are sufficient safeguards in place to eliminate any threats to independence and objectivity so as to ensure that threats are reduced to an acceptably low level. A typical safeguard which many small audit firms have in place is to have a file independently reviewed prior to the audit report being signed (a 'hot' review) or a review after the audit report has been signed (a 'cold' review). Where the audit firm is involved in preparation of the financial statements it may be the case that one team prepares the financial statements with another team undertaking the audit.

13.18 Where the audit engagement partner concludes that there are no safeguards available to eliminate, or reduce, the threat to independence and objectivity to an acceptable level, the audit firm must either refuse the non-audit work or not accept, or withdraw, from the audit engagement.

> **Focus**
>
> - Where the audit firm accepts both the audit and non-audit work, the audit engagement partner must document the reasons for undertaking the non-audit work, together with the safeguards which have been put in place to mitigate the threats to independence and objectivity.

13.19 ES 5 provides a number of general principles which are specific to non-audit services that should be applied. These are covered in paragraphs 54 to 168 of ES 5.

AUDIT PLANNING

13.20 Audit planning is one of the most crucial aspects of the audit. Without planning the audit properly, the auditor goes into the audit almost completely blind and may well miss high risk areas which in turn gives wider scope for expressing an incorrect audit opinion at the completion stage (ie increased audit risk). There are four UK and Ireland ISAs which are relevant to audit planning:

- ISA (UK and Ireland) 300 *Planning an audit of financial statements.*
- ISA (UK and Ireland) 315 *Identifying and assessing the risks of material misstatement through understanding the entity and its environment.*
- ISA (UK and Ireland) 320 *Materiality in planning and performing an audit.*
- ISA (UK and Ireland) 33 *The auditor's responses to assessed risks.*

13.21 ISA (UK and Ireland) 300 requires that the auditor plans the audit in such a way so that it will be performed in an effective manner.

Focus

- Whilst the overarching objective of ISA (UK and Ireland) 300 is probably obvious to many auditors, the area of planning has been frequently criticised by regulators in the past due to evidence of poor planning resulting in ineffective audit procedures being applied during the audit fieldwork and hence insufficient and inappropriate audit evidence being on file.

During the planning phase of the audit, the overall audit strategy is developed for the engagement. The objective of the audit strategy is to set the scope, timing and direction of the audit and guide the development of the audit plan. The audit plan is clearly more detailed than the audit strategy and is discussed in the next section. The establishment of the overall audit strategy is dealt with in some detail in the *Application and Other Explanatory Material* at paragraphs A8 to A11 in ISA (UK and Ireland) 300 and essentially the audit strategy involves:

- Determining the characteristics of the engagement that define its scope, such as the financial reporting framework used, industry-specific reporting requirements and the locations of the components of the entity.
- Ascertaining the reporting objectives of the engagement to plan the timing of the audit and the nature of the communications required, such as deadlines for final reporting, and key dates for expected communications with management and those charged with governance.
- Considering the important factors which will determine the focus of the engagement team's efforts, such as:
  - determination of appropriate materiality levels;
  - preliminary identification of areas where there may be higher risks of material misstatement;

— preliminary identification of material components and account balances;

— evaluation of whether the auditor may plan to obtain evidence regarding the effectiveness of internal control; and

— an identification of recent significant entity-specific, industry, financial reporting or other recent developments.

> **Focus**
>
> • ISA (UK and Ireland) 320 *Materiality in planning and performing an audit* requires both financial statement materiality and performance materiality to be calculated. Financial statement materiality is calculated for the financial statements as a whole and is often calculating using benchmarks (eg 1% of revenue, 5% of profit before tax and 2% of gross assets). Performance materiality is a lower level of materiality and is set to reduce, to an appropriately low level, the probability that the aggregate of uncorrected and undetected misstatements in the financial statements exceeds financial statement materiality.

In devising the audit strategy, the auditor must also take into consideration:

- the resources to deploy on the audit assignment; for example deploying more experienced audit team members for key high risk areas of the audit;
- the amount of resources to use on the audit assignment; for example assigning team members to attend the stock count and the extent that team members will review other members work during the course of the audit;
- at what stage these resources will be used; for example whether they are to undertake an interim audit or at key cut-off dates; and
- how such resources are to be managed, directed and supervised; for example when team briefing and de-briefing meetings will be held and the review of the work of team members by the audit engagement partner and manager (as well as external quality control reviews where necessary).

> **Focus**
>
> • The Appendix to ISA (UK and Ireland) 300 contains a useful list of examples that the auditor of a small business should take into consideration when they are establishing the overall audit strategy.

13.22 Once the overall audit strategy has been developed, the audit plan then follows. The audit plan itself is more detailed than the audit strategy and its overarching objective is to reduce audit risk (the risk that the auditor expresses an incorrect audit opinion) to an acceptably low level.

The plan itself will include the nature, timing and extent of audit procedures to be performed by the audit team. ISA (UK and Ireland) 300 recognises that planning for such procedures will occur over the course of the audit as the audit plan for the engagement develops. For example, the auditor will undertake risk assessment procedures at an early phase in the audit; planning the nature, timing and extent of audit procedures will depend on the outcome of those risk assessment procedures and in some cases additional procedures may be started earlier than other audit procedures.

Focus

- Audit planning is not undertaken by one team member; achieving the objective of audit planning involves the audit engagement partner and other key members of the audit team joining together to benefit from each other's experience and insight.

13.23 The importance of a proper programme of audit planning cannot be over-emphasised because it is at this stage of the audit that the plan ensures adequate attention is devoted to important areas of the audit. In addition, audit planning also helps to identify potential problems and difficulties and ensures that these are resolved in a timely manner. Sufficient planning will also enable the proper delegation of audit work to appropriate members of the audit team.

13.24 ISA (UK and Ireland) 300 recognises that planning is not an exercise which is commenced at the outset of the audit and ends immediately prior to attending the client's premises to undertake the detailed fieldwork. Instead, ISA (UK and Ireland) 300 recognises audit planning to be a 'continual and iterative process'. This is because issues could well arise during the course of the audit which may well result in the overall audit plan having to be amended and the auditor must update and change the plan, as necessary, during the course of the audit.

The reason that changing and updating the audit plan is mandatory is because during the course of the detailed fieldwork, unexpected events, changes in conditions or the audit evidence obtained, may give rise to the need to change and update the audit plan accordingly.

Example 13.1 – Amendment needed to the audit plan

During the course of the planning of the audit of Bury Enterprises Ltd, the auditor's initial analytical review suggested that gross profit margins had remained static on the previous year and hence she devised audit procedures to determine that this was the case. During the on-site fieldwork, the auditor discovered numerous purchase invoices that had not been accrued for at the year-end resulting in understated creditors. In addition, it appeared that cut-offs were incorrect on the closing stock valuation.

Clearly in a situation like this, the original planned audit procedures would have to be changed, which in turn results in a change to the audit plan, because more work will have to be undertaken to ascertain if the only reason the gross margins had remained static were as a result of the unaccrued purchase invoices and incorrect stock cut-offs. In addition, the auditor must also establish why the internal controls had also not picked up this omission as it may result in a significant deficiency which would need to be reported to management and those charged with governance.

Supervision and direction of the audit

13.25 Paragraph 11 of ISA (UK and Ireland) 300 requires the auditor to plan the nature, timing and extent of direction and supervision of engagement team members and a review of their work. This is an important aspect to the audit to ensure that the engagement team members have gathered sufficient and appropriate audit evidence on which the audit engagement partner can base their opinion.

Focus

- Where a sole practitioner is undertaking the audit, then clearly supervision and direction issues will not be relevant. However, the sole practitioner must consider the need to have the audit work externally reviewed (eg a 'hot' review) prior to signing the auditor's report. The fact that the sole practitioner may be conducting the auditor on their own does not relieve them of the need to consider whether the audit has been conducted in accordance with UK and Ireland ISAs.

In planning the nature, timing and extent of the direction and supervision of engagement team members, the auditor has regard to the assessed risk of material misstatement. For those areas of the audit which are determined as being high risk, the auditor must increase the extent and timeliness of the supervision and direction of engagement team members and perform a more detailed review of their work.

Planning documentation

13.26 It is important that the overall audit strategy and the audit plan (including any significant changes made during the audit engagement) are adequately documented. This is crucial because this documentation records the key decisions considered necessary in order to properly plan the audit and to communicate significant matters to the engagement team.

The documentation must include the audit plan as well as the planned nature, timing and extent of risk assessment procedures, and further audit procedures at the assertion level for each material class of transaction, account balance and disclosure in response to the assessed levels of risk.

13.27 The form and content of documentation will depend on the size and complexity of the entity, materiality levels and the extent of other documentation as well as the individual circumstances of the specific audit engagement.

> **Focus**
>
> - Practice Note 26 (Revised) *Guidance on Smaller Entity Documentation* offers practitioners guidance on the form and content of audit documentation which is pertinent for a smaller company audit.

Planning documentation may include the following (note: the following list is not exhaustive and may include additional planning information depending on the specifics of the audit client):

- Background and history of the client.
- Nature of products/services.
- Management structure.
- Details of locations.
- Risk assessment.
- Overall control environment.
- Systems and controls in place.
- Analytical review.
- Audit team members.
- Financial statement and performance materiality levels.
- Points brought forward from prior year.
- Laws and regulations.
- Audit strategy and audit plan.
- Audit team planning meeting.
- Budget.
- Timetable for review and audit team de-briefing and the audit clearance meeting with the client.

Understanding the audit client

13.28 Auditors of smaller companies need to ensure that they have a thorough understanding of the audit client and whilst many small company auditors do have a sound understanding, it is often the lack of documentation that results in audit work being criticised. ISA (UK and Ireland) 315 *Identifying and assessing the risks of material misstatement through understanding the entity and its environment* requires the auditor to gain an understanding of the client and the environment in which it operates. ISA (UK and Ireland) 315 is a particularly important standard and is concerned with the auditor gaining an understanding of the entity and the environment in which it operates so the auditor can assess the risk of material misstatement within the financial statements, together with assessing the entity's internal control environment.

The vast majority of information which the auditor obtains is from management. However, it may be useful for the auditor to discuss relevant and appropriate issues with other staff members (such as warehouse managers during the course of the stock count). This type of inquiry will serve as audit evidence; however, ISA (UK and Ireland) 500 *Audit evidence* recognises that while inquiry is a valid audit procedure, inquiry alone will not generate sufficient and appropriate audit evidence – in other words inquiry as an audit procedure complements other audit procedures.

13.29 In gaining an understanding of the entity and the environment in which it operates, there are some specific factors which may be considered. Not all small audits are the same and hence will not require the same procedures to be adopted and hence the list that follows is only an illustration of the types of factors that auditors should consider when gaining an understanding of the client:

- The entity's business operations, such as:
  - revenue streams;
  - products and services;
  - geographic dispersion;
  - key customers and suppliers;
  - legal and regulatory issues;
  - related party issues; and
  - research and development activities/expenditure.
- Investments and investment activities including any planned or recently executed acquisitions, investments in securities, capital investment activities and joint ventures and special-purpose entities.
- Financing and financing activities such as major subsidiaries and associated entities, including consolidated and non-consolidated structures, debt structure and related terms, beneficial owners and any use of derivative instruments (especially now derivative instruments have to be recognised on the balance sheet under FRS 102, Section 12 *Other Financial Instruments Issues*).
- Financial reporting issues such as the use of accounting policies and any industry-specific requirements; revenue recognition practices; fair value accounting; foreign currencies and consideration of complex transactions such as those which may give rise to 'substance over form' issues.

Nature of the entity

13.30 It is generally accepted that smaller entities tend to have less complex internal controls because they are perhaps operating in less complex industries and hence such businesses will normally have relatively straightforward and less complex internal control structures. However, notwithstanding the fact that smaller audits tend to have less complexities attached to them, the auditor has to have a thorough understanding of the nature of the entity, particularly where there may be complex structures attached.

In addition to obtaining an understanding of the nature of the entity, the auditor must also gain an understanding of the entity's owners, other individuals and entities in which the client is also involved with. This is particularly useful as it will help the auditor in understanding whether there have been, or if there are, potentially any related party transactions that need consideration; especially related party transactions which have not been undertaken on an arm's length basis (and hence would require disclosure under Section 1A *Small Entities* of FRS 102).

Focus

- As smaller audits are generally less complex, gaining an understanding of the entity and the environment in which it operates can be a relatively straightforward process. The key is ensuring that auditors document this understanding and the environment in which the client operates to ensure compliance with the UK and Ireland ISAs.

Internal controls

13.31 As part of gaining an understanding of the client and the environment in which it operates, the auditor must also understand the client's internal control environment. This allows the auditor to identify factors that affect the risk of material misstatement within the financial statements. An ineffective control environment is much more likely to give rise to material misstatement than an effective control environment.

Focus

- Even the most robust of internal control systems will not eliminate the risk of material misstatement; it will merely reduce the risk more than a less effective internal control environment.

In considering the internal control environment, the auditor should have regard to:

- the nature and complexity of the audit client;
- materiality levels;

- the diversity and complexity of the entity's operations;
- legal and regulatory requirements;
- whether, and how, a specific control (individually or collectively with others) prevents, detects and corrects material misstatements;
- the significance of the related risk; and
- the circumstances and the applicable component of internal control.

13.32 Internal control is the process designed and implemented by those charged with governance, management and other personnel to provide reasonable assurance about the achievement of the entity's objectives. Internal controls are primarily designed and implemented to address business risks identified by management (business risks are risks to the business which are externally generated, such as interest rate risk). A small owner-managed business will have less complex internal controls than, for example, a large blue-chip company, but this will not mean that the small business will be any less efficient than a larger business with more complex internal controls.

Analytical procedures

13.33 Analytical procedures must be applied as risk assessment procedures under ISA (UK and Ireland) 520 *Analytical procedures* in order that the auditor can obtain an understanding of the entity and the environment, as well as during the audit fieldwork and as an overall review at the end of the audit.

Analytical procedures used at the planning stage of the audit are used to indicate aspects of the client to which the auditor was previously unaware, which will then go to assist the auditor in assessing the risks of material misstatement in order to determine the nature, timing and extent of further audit procedures.

Focus

- Analytical procedures are not just applied to the numerical aspects of the financial statements. They can also be applied to non-financial information and ISA (UK and Ireland) 520 considers the use of analytical procedures in areas such as the relationship between sales and square footage of selling price, or volume of goods sold.

Analytical procedures can also be used as substantive analytical procedures. However, substantive analytical procedures are generally more suitable to large volumes of transactions which tend to be predictable over time. In determining the suitability of substantive analytical procedures, the auditor considers:

- the assessment of the risk of material misstatement; and
- any tests of details directed towards the same assertion.

> **Focus**
>
> - There can be a lot of detail undertaken at the planning phase of a small company audit in order to satisfy the UK and Ireland ISAs. The key to achieving compliance with the UK and Ireland ISAs is to ensure that the knowledge and understanding of the auditor is thoroughly documented; team meetings are properly recorded (including discussions concerning fraud and fraud in respect of related parties); risk assessments are appropriate and planned audit procedures are responsive to those risks. Automated audit programmes are generally used nowadays and these should be tailored, where necessary, to be client-specific.

AUDITING SPECIFIC AREAS OF THE FINANCIAL STATEMENTS

13.34 Many small company audits are completed predominantly through audit software programmes. These offer the auditor a framework in which to complete the audit, but do need to be tailored in some cases to be client-specific. As discussed earlier in this chapter, no two audits are the same and hence what may be specific to one audit client, might be irrelevant to another.

> **Focus**
>
> - Obtaining audit evidence can done through substantive procedures (ie tests of detail) and tests of control. Audit sampling is also undertaken by the auditor which is a key concept in ISA (UK and Ireland) 530 *Audit sampling*. Sampling is the application of audit procedures to less than 100% of the items in a population.

The sections that follow outline some of the more typical procedures which might be applied in a small company audit to certain areas of the financial statements. Each part starts with the overall audit objectives and then focuses on the typical types of test an auditor may wish to apply to gather sufficient and appropriate audit evidence.

> **Focus**
>
> - The audit procedures in the following sections are not exhaustive. In all cases it is important that the auditor devises specific procedures which are applicable to the client and also responsive to the assessed levels of risk.
> - Whilst many small audit firms rely on audit software to generate the required procedures, it is important that sufficient and appropriate audit evidence is gathered in all material areas so as to reduce audit risk (the risk that the auditor forms the incorrect opinion on the financial statements).

Intangible fixed assets

Audit objectives

13.35

- To ensure that the carrying values of intangible non-current assets remain appropriate.
- To consider any impairment of intangible assets and to ensure that intangible assets are not carried in the balance sheet at any more than recoverable amount.
- To ensure all additions and disposals have been properly authorised and accounted for in the financial statements.
- To ensure the entity has appropriate title to intangible assets.

Tests

13.36

- Confirm that the amortisation policy is appropriate and in line with Section 18 *Intangible Assets other than Goodwill* and/or Section 19 *Business Combinations and Goodwill*.
- Where there are indicators of impairment, carry out a review of the valuations placed on intangible fixed assets and the impairment review carried out by management to ensure that they are not recorded at any more than recoverable amount.
- Where additions and disposals have taken place during the year, obtain documentary evidence to support the additions and disposal proceeds.
- Recalculate the profit and loss of any disposals during the year and agree to the trial balance.
- Trace intangible fixed assets to their documents of title (such as patent and licences).
- Perform a reasonableness test (eg a proof in total test) on the amortisation charge for the year.

Tangible fixed assets

Audit objectives

13.37

- To confirm the opening values of cost and accumulated depreciation have been correctly brought forward into the current year and accounting policies have been consistently applied.
- To confirm that tangible fixed assets are included in the financial statements at a cost or valuation which is acceptable.

- To confirm that purchases of fixed assets during the year have been authorised and have been appropriately capitalised in the balance sheet.
- To confirm that depreciation rates are appropriate and have been correctly calculated.
- To confirm that tangible fixed assets are still in use and that no items of tangible fixed assets are carried in the balance sheet at any more than recoverable amount.
- To confirm rights and obligations of tangible fixed assets.
- To confirm that any future commitments in relation to capital expenditure have been sufficiently disclosed in the financial statements.
- To confirm correct treatment of items of tangible fixed assets which have been obtained through leasing arrangements (such as hire purchase contracts).
- To confirm that items of leasehold improvements are correctly valued in the financial statements.

Audit tests

13.38

- Obtain or prepare the reconciliation of tangible fixed assets and agree all opening cost and depreciation values to ensure that they have been correctly brought forward.
- Obtain details of all additions during the year and perform testing on a representative sample of additions, confirming via source records (such as purchase orders, goods received notes and purchase invoices) that:
  - — the item capitalised is of a capital nature;
  - — any input VAT has been correctly accounted for and any irrecoverable taxes have been included in the cost price; and
  - — the item of capital expenditure has been appropriately authorised.
- Review minutes of meetings and cross-reference any major items of capital expenditure to board meeting minutes.
- Ensure that all items in the year which have been capitalised have been done so in accordance with the definition of an asset in Section 2 *Concepts and Pervasive Principles* in FRS 102.
- Ensure that where any subsequent expenditure has been capitalised, the expenditure meets the definition of an asset in Section 2 of FRS 102.
- Obtain reconciliations of repairs and maintenance expense, computer costs, office stationery and other appropriate revenue expense accounts to ensure that all items within these nominal accounts are revenue expense and do not contain any items which may be of a capital nature.

- Obtain details of disposals in the year and trace sales proceeds to source documentation such as to sales invoices and the cash book, ensuring that the disposal has been correctly treated in the financial statements.
- Ensure that where an entity receives capital-based grants they have been correctly treated in accordance with Section 24 *Government Grants* (either using the accruals method or performance method).
- Where there are indicators of impairment, ensure that tangible fixed assets are not carried at any more than recoverable amount and undertake a review of management's impairment test.
- Where an entity adopts the revaluation model for its tangible fixed assets, ensure that the model is consistently applied to all assets within the same class and that the value is appropriate at the reporting date.
- Where an entity holds investment properties at fair value, ensure that these are accounted for properly in accordance with Section 16 *Investment Property* in FRS 102.
- Review depreciation rates and consider their reasonableness.
- Test check depreciation rates to ensure that they have been correctly calculated (eg through reasonableness tests).
- Obtain a sample of tangible fixed assets and physically inspect those assets to make sure they are in regular use and if there are any indicators of impairment. Where the entity maintains a fixed assets register, trace the items in the sample to the register.
- Discuss with senior officials the possibility of any assets which still have a carrying value which may have been scrapped.
- In respect of properties, check ownership of properties by reference to documents of title (eg title deeds). Check for any charges over the property by financiers and ensure adequate disclosure has been made (eg as secured debt).
- Where an entity obtains fixed assets under finance leases, ensure that the capitalisation method is appropriate (finance leases are capitalised, operating leases are not).
- In respect of leasehold improvements, obtain a copy of the lease and ensure that any improvement works are being depreciated appropriately having regard to the provisions in the lease.

Investments

Audit objectives

13.39

- To confirm that recorded investments exist and are owned by the entity.

- To confirm that investments are appropriately valued and that adequate provision has been made for diminution in values.
- To ensure that income from investments have been correctly recorded in the financial statements.

Audit tests

13.40

- Obtain or prepare a schedule of investments which show all movements in investments during the year.
- Agree details from the investments register to the financial statements.
- Agree additions during the year to source documents such as agreements, contracts and minutes of meetings.
- Agree the proceeds of any disposals to source documents and ensure the disposal has been correctly accounted for in the financial statements.
- Agree the investments to share certificates.
- Where evidence of impairment exists, ensure adequate provision has been made to write down the investment to recoverable amount.
- Test the value of listed investments to market values at the reporting date.
- For unlisted investments, review the value by reference to the latest financial statements.
- Where the entity has long-term investments, ensure sufficient appropriate evidence is available to support the long-term investments.
- Confirm income has been received on all income-yielding investments on a consistent basis and that it has been correctly accounted for in the financial statements.

Stock

Audit objectives

13.41

- To ensure any significant adverse variances between the current period and the previous year's stock balance is adequately investigated and sufficient explanations received.
- To confirm the existence of stock.
- To confirm that stock and work in progress are valued correctly.
- To confirm that long-term work in progress is valued correctly and that valuations are in accordance with FRS 102 requirements.

- To confirm that adequate provisions have been made, where applicable, to ensure that stock is valued at the lower of cost and estimated selling price less costs to complete and sell.
- To confirm correct recognition of stock.
- To confirm any stock which is held by third parties.
- To confirm the existence of inventory which is not physically verified at the year-end stock count.

Audit tests

13.42

- Perform analytical procedures on the stock valuation, investigating any reasons for unexpected fluctuations in the stock valuation between the previous and current year's results.
- Calculate the numbers of days' sales held in stock and consider its reasonableness.
- Where stock and work in progress are considered material, attend the stock count (see next section).
- Check sample quantities taken at the stock count and agree these counts to the final stock valuation.
- Agree the casts and cross casts on the stock sheets and ensure that all stock sheets are intact with no obvious omissions or errors.
- Test a sample of stock to source documents (eg purchase invoices) to confirm cost.
- Where the entity has work in progress, ensure that an appropriate test is undertaken to agree work in progress and finished goods to supplier invoices, material usage, labour rates and overhead absorption rates.
- Ensure that the valuation of stock complies with Section 13 *Inventories* criteria in FRS 102 (note the last-in first-out method is not permitted in Section 13).
- Review long-term work in progress and ensure that costs have been properly recorded and that profit is taken on the basis of work carried out, costs to date, expected costs to complete and total contract value.
- Where losses are foreseen on contracts, ensure adequate provisions are made as soon as losses are foreseen.
- Undertake a net realisable value test on a sample of stock ensuring that the entity is selling the product at more than cost.
- Review items of slow-moving or obsolete stock and ensure that valuations placed on these items are appropriate.
- Discuss the level of stock provisions with management.

- Undertake cut-off tests to ensure that stock is recognised in the correct accounting period.
- Where the entity has material amounts of stock which are held by third parties, obtain independent confirmation as to the value of this stock.

Attendance at stock count

Audit objectives

13.43

- To gain an understanding of the procedures adopted by management for the stock count and whether such procedures will reduce the risk of material misstatement in the final stock valuation.
- To confirm the existence and completeness of stock.

Audit tests

13.44

- Obtain a list of instructions given by management to individuals involved in the stock count.
- Tour the areas to be covered and establish the nature, location and size of the stock to be counted.
- During test counts ensure that no items of stock can be double-counted and establish how effective the procedures are in ensuring no items of stock are double-counted (eg whether they are marked as counted).
- Identify any stock which is held by third parties.
- Ensure that all stock sheets are controlled and signed.
- Select items of stock in a two-way direction (floor to sheet and sheet to floor) to test for completeness and existence respectively.
- Mark the items which have been sampled on the rough stock sheets to enable further audit tests to be carried out to ensure that these have been correctly carried through to the final stock valuation and that any discrepancies can be investigated.
- Record the number of rough stock sheets and ensure that only appropriate stock sheets are included.
- Note details of any obvious omissions or errors.
- Note details of any stock which is slow-moving or obsolete and establish the valuations placed on this stock.
- Ensure that cut-off procedures are adequate to ensure that only stock which has been purchased at the end of the reporting period is included in the count and exclude those items of stock which have been sold at the end of the reporting period.

- Obtain details of the last goods inwards notes to check that cut-offs are correct.
- If the stock count is not undertaken exactly at the year-end, undertake procedures (such as roll-back procedures) to verify the existence and completeness of stock at the year-end.

Debtors, sales and prepayments

Audit objectives

13.45

- To confirm that debtors are fairly stated and that any significant variances from the previous reporting period have been adequately investigated and explained.
- To confirm that debtors represent amounts which are properly due to the entity at the reporting date and that appropriate provision has been made to ensure that debtors are not overstated.
- To confirm that amounts in respect of debtors at the reporting date have been realised after the reporting date.
- To confirm that goods and/or services supplied by the entity are not understated and that they are properly accounted for.
- Where the entity has significant cash sales, to ensure that these are complete and correctly recorded in the financial statements.
- To ensure that prepayments are correctly calculated and represent the value of services received by the entity after the reporting date but paid for during the reporting period.

Audit tests

13.46

- Compare current year trade debtors with the prior year balance and obtain sufficient explanations for any significant variances.
- Calculate trade debtors' days for reasonableness.
- Obtain the list of trade debtors at the reporting date and trace a sample of balances, agreeing:
  - The ageing of the trade debtors to invoices.
  - To after-date cash receipts.
  - How any credit balances have arisen.
- Obtain material after-date credit notes and ensure they do not relate to sales made during the period. If they do, ensure that adequate provision has been made.

- Consider the need to undertake a trade debtors' circularisation. Chase up non-replies and where non-replies are still outstanding, consider alternative procedures (such as extended after-date cash testing).
- Perform cut-off testing to ensure that goods and/or services sold either side of the reporting date are correctly accounted for.
- Confirm income completeness by selecting a sample of source documents and agree:
  - Details of goods/services supplied to customer order.
  - Sales invoice agrees to the customer order.
  - Prices recorded on the sales invoice agree to price lists or the customer's order.
  - Casts on the invoice are correct.
  - Posting to relevant VAT accounts (where the entity is VAT registered).
  - Postings to the debtors control account.
  - Posting of the sales invoice to the sales nominal.
- If the entity deals with cash sales and these are considered material, agree the cash takings to source documents (such as receipt books or till rolls).
- Trace material sundry debtors and prepayments to source documents.
- Recalculate material prepayments.
- Ensure that where any debtor falls due after more than one year that it is correctly classified in accordance with paragraph 4.4A of FRS 102.

Cash and bank balances

Audit objectives

13.47

- To confirm that bank balances belong to the entity and exist at the reporting date.
- To confirm that payments are correctly recorded.
- To identify any large and unusual items.
- To confirm that petty cash is correctly accounted for.

Audit tests

13.48

- Obtain bank reconciliations for all accounts and agree to the financial statements.

- Agree the balance per the statement on the bank reconciliation to the bank statement at the end of the reporting period and the bank confirmation letter.
- Check casts on the bank reconciliation.
- Ensure that outstanding payments and lodgements properly clear after the reporting date.
- Review the bank confirmation letter for details of any securities and cross-reference to relevant disclosures in the financial statements ensuring such disclosures are adequate.
- Select a sample of payments from the cash book and check to paid cheques. Consider the need to obtain copies of paid cheques direct from the entity's bankers if considered appropriate.
- Trace a sample of receipts and payments from the cash book to the nominal ledger.
- Review the cash book for large and unusual items and agree to source documentation.
- Trace a sample of petty cash expenditure from source documentation and agree to the postings in the nominal ledger.
- Ensure that where the entity operates the 'imprest system' for petty cash that it is correctly applied throughout the year.
- Consider the need to attend cash counts at the reporting date where cash is considered material.

Creditors and accruals

Audit objectives

13.49

- To confirm that creditors represent amounts which are properly due by the entity at the reporting date, properly accounted for and appropriately disclosed.
- To confirm that appropriate costs are recorded completely and are properly disclosed.
- To confirm that liabilities incurred are completely and accurately recorded.
- To confirm that there are no incomplete recording of costs.
- To confirm the correct recording of purchases.
- To confirm that creditors and accruals are recorded at their full amounts and are recognised in the correct period and on a consistent basis.

- To confirm the correct accounting treatment for accruals and sundry creditors.
- To ensure that liabilities are properly classified and details of any security is properly disclosed.
- To ensure that loans are properly classified and adequate disclosure is made of any security pledged by the entity.

Audit tests

13.50

- Calculate trade creditor days for consistency and investigate the reasons for any large variances between the current year and prior year.
- Review current year trade creditors' balances against the prior year and investigate any large variances.
- Obtain a sample of supplier statements from the entity and reconcile these to the purchase ledger. Where there are only a few supplier statements, consider circularisation of creditor balances.
- Select a sample of purchase orders or goods received notes and agree the details of these to supplier invoices, checking for authorisation, casts, calculation of amounts on the invoice (including VAT where applicable) and postings into the purchase ledger and nominal ledger.
- Perform cut-off testing to ensure that goods and/or services received either side of the reporting date have been accounted for in the correct accounting period.
- Ensure the balance on the aged creditors list agrees to the trade creditors control account and trial balance.
- Review the aged creditors list and ascertain the reasons for any major debit balances.
- Review payments made after the reporting date for any undisclosed creditors or accruals.
- Review goods received notes pre year-end which have not been matched to supplier invoices and ensure that they have been accrued in the financial statements.
- Trace material non-trade creditors to underlying source documents.
- Ensure liabilities which fall due after more than one year are correctly disclosed as long-term liabilities.
- Where liabilities are secured, ensure adequate disclosure is made in the financial statements.

Hire purchase and leasing

Audit objectives

13.51

- To ensure correct classification of leases between operating and finance leases.
- To ensure that the financial statements reflect all finance leases entered into by the entity; that capital repayments and interest are correctly treated and that future operating lease obligations are adequately disclosed.

Audit tests

13.52

- Obtain copies of lease agreements and confirm correct classification as either operating or finance leases.
- Ensure correct capitalisation of finance leases.
- Ensure finance leases are split between amounts falling due within one year and amounts falling due after more than one year.
- Ensure accounting treatments for leases (either lessee or lessor) are in accordance with Section 20 *Leases* in FRS 102.
- Ensure interest payments have been calculated using the effective interest method.
- Ensure future operating lease obligations are adequately disclosed.

Share capital and reserves

Audit objectives

13.53

- To confirm that share capital is correctly recorded in the financial statements.
- To confirm that reserves are correctly recorded in the financial statements.
- To confirm that financial statements agree to statutory records (such as records held at Companies House).

Audit tests

13.54

- Agree details of the share capital to share certificates and/or statutory records lodged at Companies House.

- Ensure that any amendments to share capital have been properly notified to Companies House.
- Obtain or prepare a reconciliation of the movement in all types of equity balances in the balance sheet and agree that all transfers have been correctly made and agree such transfers to the financial statements.
- Ensure that any dividends paid or proposed are done so having regard to the sufficiency of reserves available. Where dividends have been declared in excess of available distributable reserves, consider the impact on the audit opinion.
- Ensure disclosure has been made concerning dividends paid/proposed at the year-end where such disclosure is needed for the financial statements to give a true and fair view (note – Section 1A of FRS 102 in Appendix D, paragraph 1AD.1(d)) encourages disclosures to be made concerning dividends).
- Ensure where dividends have been declared after the reporting date, that they are not included in the financial statements (disclosure of such dividends would be encouraged by Section 1A of FRS 102 – see bullet point above).
- Ensure all statutory records are up to date.
- Review minutes of board meetings to ascertain any matter which may affect the financial statements and agree any resolutions made that are relevant to the year under audit.

Payroll

Audit objectives

13.55

- To confirm expenditure on wages and salaries represents genuine payments to employees at authorised rates.
- To confirm there are no underpayments of taxes and national insurance contributions.
- To confirm that the average number of employees employed during the year is adequately disclosed.
- To confirm that correct and timely returns to HM Revenue and Customs have been made.

Audit tests

13.56

- Devise a sample of payroll deductions to test and confirm these have been correctly calculated.

- Check that a sample of employees physically exist by way of physical verification or reviewing correspondence from HM Revenue and Customs.
- Verify rates of pay are authorised by an appropriate individual within the entity.
- Check that contracts of employment are issued.
- Check that adequate segregation of duties exists in respect of payroll preparation (eg one person prepares the payroll and another person reviews the payroll).
- Agree a sample of net pay to the cash book.
- Review amounts in the cash book and be on alert for any amounts which have been paid to employees or contractors which have not been processed through the payroll records and consider any taxation implications.
- Where employees are provided with benefits, ensure that HM Revenue and Customs has been notified via a form P11D.
- Reconcile the payroll charge from the payroll records to the charge in the profit and loss account.
- Where there are a large number of employees and reperforming the payroll charge reconciliation would be time-consuming, check a sample of employees' postings from the payroll records to the payroll nominals in the accounting system.
- Vouch the year-end PAYE/NIC liability to payroll reports and confirm properly cleared after the year-end.
- Review a copy of the year-end returns submitted to HM Revenue and Customs and check a sample of these for completeness and accuracy.
- Recalculate the average number of employees employed during the year and agree this to the disclosure note in the financial statements.

Related parties

Audit objectives

13.57

- To identify any directors' current accounts and transactions with directors and other related parties.
- To confirm that all details of directors' advances, credits and guarantees have been appropriately disclosed in accordance with Section 1A of FRS 102.
- To confirm that all transactions with related parties which are outside the ordinary course of business have been adequately disclosed in accordance with Section 1A of FRS 102.

Audit tests

13.58

- Obtain a reconciliation of all directors' current accounts. Review the entries and consider their relevance in the context of anti-money laundering regulations.
- Review accounting records and remain alert for evidence of any undisclosed related party transactions.
- Review the bank confirmation letter and note any potential undisclosed related parties.
- Review debtors and creditors listings at the year-end for evidence of related party transactions and balances.
- Review the adequacy of the disclosures made in the financial statements and agree amounts to accounting records (note – small entities only have to make limited related party disclosures in accordance with Section 1A of FRS 102).
- Enquire of management as to the existence of any undisclosed related party transactions and consider reviewing the records held at Companies House (such as the directors' involvements with other entities) to identify any undisclosed related parties.
- Review the register of interests in shares to determine the names of the principal shareholders.
- Review the company's tax returns for evidence of additional related parties.
- Review correspondence and invoices from lawyers which may indicate the existence of related parties and transactions with those related parties.

Taxation

Audit objectives

13.59

- To confirm that the liability to corporation tax has been properly accounted for.
- To confirm that corporation tax returns have been submitted for all previous periods by the specified dates.
- To confirm all amounts in respect of taxation have been paid to HM Revenue and Customs by the due date.
- To ensure amounts in respect of deferred tax have been calculated appropriate (note Section 29 *Income Tax* of FRS 102 uses the timing difference plus approach).

Audit tests

13.60

- Obtain the corporation tax computation for the year under review and consider the need to have this reviewed by a tax specialist where necessary.
- Ensure that the tax charge/refund in the financial statements has been correctly allocated and the tax liability/asset is sufficiently disclosed.
- Ensure that provisions for penalties and interest have been correctly calculated and accounted for where appropriate (eg following a tax enquiry).
- Perform a reconciliation of the tax charge/credit per the profit and loss account.
- Agree the deferred tax balance and ensure correct accounting treatment (eg deferred tax in respect of non-monetary assets subject to revaluation have been taken to a revaluation reserve (eg owned property) or profit and loss (eg investment property) as appropriate).
- Ensure any deferred tax assets recognised are supported by sufficient and appropriate evidence to confirm that there will be sufficient future taxable profits in order to utilise such deferred tax balances.

Going concern

Audit objectives

13.61

- To confirm managements' assessment that the entity is a going concern is appropriate.
- To conclude whether a material uncertainty exists which may cast significant doubt on the entity's ability to continue as a going concern.
- To determine the implications for the auditor's report.

Audit tests

13.62

- Ensure that management have undertaken an assessment of the entity's ability to continue as a going concern for a period of at least 12 months from the date of approval of the financial statements (where this period is under 12 months and management have not made disclosure of that fact, the auditor should do so in the auditor's report).
- Consider whether management have included all relevant information found by the auditor during the audit when undertaking their going concern assessment.

- Review the adequacy of the disclosures in the financial statements where there are uncertainties relating to the entity's ability to continue as a going concern (note – going concern disclosures are an encouraged disclosure in Section 1A, Appendix D, paragraph 1AD.1(c) of FRS 102 and should be made where disclosing such uncertainties enables the financial statements to give a true and fair view).
- Consider managements' plans for future actions and whether such plans are feasible in the entity's individual circumstances for example if management plan to borrow money or undertake debt restructuring or increase capital expenditure.

Events after the reporting period

Audit objectives

13.63

- To obtain sufficient appropriate audit evidence to confirm that events occurring between the reporting date and the date of the auditor's report which require adjustment or disclosure have been appropriately reflected in the financial statements.
- To respond appropriately to facts that become known only after the date of the auditor's report and that, had the auditor known about those facts at that date, would have cause him/her to amend the report.

Audit tests

13.64

- Obtain an understanding of how management identify events after the reporting period.
- Inquire with management if they are aware of any events which may affect the financial statements.
- Review board minutes to identify any events which may require adjustment or disclosure in the financial statements.
- Review any management accounts or interim accounts prepared after the year-end to identify any events after the reporting period.
- Review correspondence from lawyers to identify any events which may require adjustment or disclosure in the financial statements (eg litigation).

Focus

- In addition to the audit evidence gathered during the fieldwork stage, the auditor should also obtain written representations (in accordance with ISA (UK and Ireland) 580 *Written representations*) for material areas of the financial statements. Such written representations should be dated on the same date as the auditor's report, or very close to that date, but not after.

AUDIT REPORTING

13.65 Audit reports are coming under increasing scrutiny by both regulatory bodies such as the Financial Reporting Council and the professional bodies. Over the years the audit report has been the subject of varying degrees of criticism from commentators and stakeholders who have questioned the usefulness of the audit report in terms of the jargon used and the information which it is conveying. Attempts have been made over the years to simplify the report and to make it more useful in terms of the language used. Indeed, this is evidenced by the International Auditing and Assurance Standards Board's new ISA 700 *(Revised) Forming and Opinion and Reporting on Financial Statements* which will be effective for audits of financial statements for periods ending on or after 15 December 2016. Such reports will include references to 'key audit matters' and, at the time of writing, the Financial Reporting Council are planning to consult on changing ISA (UK and Ireland) 700.

'Key audit matters' are those matters which, in the auditor's professional judgement, were of most significance in the audit of the financial statements of the current period. They can include issues relating to the valuation of financial instruments, goodwill, going concern, revenue recognition and issues which give rise to a significant risk (such as an accounting estimate(s)).

UK and Ireland audit reports

13.66 UK and Ireland audit reports are governed by the ISAs (UK and Ireland) in the 700 series, being:

- ISA (UK and Ireland) 700 *The independent auditor's report on financial statements.*
- ISA (UK and Ireland) 705 *Modifications to opinions in the independent auditor's report.*
- ISA (UK and Ireland) 706 *Emphasis of matter paragraphs and other matter paragraphs in the independent auditor's report.*
- ISA (UK and Ireland) 710 *Comparative information – corresponding figures and comparative financial statements.*
- ISA (UK and Ireland) 720A *The auditor's responsibilities relating to other information in documents containing audited financial statements.*
- ISA (UK and Ireland) 720B *The auditor's statutory reporting responsibility in relation to directors' reports.*

The auditor's report on the financial statements must contain a clear written expression of opinion on the financial statements taken as a whole. This opinion is based on the audit evidence obtained by the auditor during the course of the audit. Paragraph 8 of ISA (UK and Ireland) 700 says that the auditor must evaluate the conclusions drawn from the audit evidence obtained, including evaluating whether:

- sufficient appropriate audit evidence as to whether the financial statements as a whole are free from material misstatement, whether due to fraud or error has been obtained;
- uncorrected misstatements are material, individually or in aggregate. This evaluation shall include consideration of the qualitative aspects of the entity's accounting practices, including indicators of possible bias in management's judgments;
- in respect of a true and fair view framework, the financial statements, including the related notes, give a true and fair view; and
- in respect of all frameworks the financial statements have been prepared in all material respects in accordance with the framework, including the requirements of applicable law.

Paragraph 9 of ISA (UK and Ireland) 700 further expands on the above points and requires the auditor to evaluate whether:

- the financial statements adequately refer to or describe the relevant financial reporting framework;
- the financial statements adequately disclose the significant accounting policies selected and applied;
- the accounting policies selected and applied are consistent with the applicable financial reporting framework, and are appropriate in the circumstances;
- accounting estimates are reasonable;
- the information presented in the financial statements is relevant, reliable, comparable and understandable;
- the financial statements provide adequate disclosures to enable the intended users to understand the effect of material transactions and events on the information conveyed in the financial statements; and
- the terminology used in the financial statements, including the title of each financial statement, is appropriate.

Elements of the audit report

13.67 ISA (UK and Ireland) 700 outlines the form and content of the audit report and as such the report itself must contain certain elements, including:

Title

13.68 The auditor's report shall have an appropriate title (eg *Independent Auditor's Report to the Shareholders of ABC Ltd*).

Addressee

13.69 The auditor's report shall be appropriately addressed as required by the circumstances of the engagement (the addressee is usually the shareholders/members of the company).

Introductory paragraph

13.70 The introductory paragraph identifies the financial statements which have been audited, including the date of, and the period covered by, the financial statements.

Respective responsibilities of those charged with governance and auditors

13.71 The audit report must include a statement that those charged with governance are responsible for the preparation of the financial statements. It must also contain a statement that the auditor's responsibility is to audit and express an opinion on the financial statements in accordance with the applicable legal requirements and ISAs (UK and Ireland). In addition, the report must also state that those standards require the auditor to comply with the APBs Ethical Standards for Auditors (note the APB (Auditing Practices Board) no longer exists, but ISA (UK and Ireland) 700 still makes reference to the APB).

Scope of the audit

13.72 The auditor has three choices in outlining the scope of the audit in the auditor's report. The report must either:

- cross refer to the applicable version of a 'Statement of the Scope of an Audit' that is maintained on the FRC's website; or
- cross refer to a 'Statement of the Scope of an Audit' that is included elsewhere in the annual report; or
- include the following description (verbatim) of the scope of an audit:

> 'An audit involves obtaining evidence about the amounts and disclosures in the financial statements sufficient to give reasonable assurance that the financial statements are free from material misstatement, whether caused by fraud or error. This includes an assessment of: whether the accounting policies are appropriate to the [describe nature of entity] circumstances and have been con-

sistently applied and adequately disclosed; the reasonableness of significant accounting estimates made by [describe those charged with governance]; and the overall presentation of the financial statements. In addition, we read all the financial and non-financial information in the [describe annual report] to identify material inconsistencies with the audited financial statements and to identify any information that is apparently materially incorrect based on, or materially inconsistent with, the knowledge acquired by us in the course of performing the audit. If we become aware of any apparent material misstatements or inconsistencies we consider the implications for our report.'

Opinion on financial statements

13.73 The opinion paragraph must clearly state the auditor's opinion as required by the relevant financial reporting framework used to prepare the financial statements, including applicable law.

Where the auditor expresses an unqualified opinion on financial statements that are prepared in accordance with a true and fair framework, the opinion paragraph must clearly state that the financial statements give a true and fair view.

Opinion in respect of an additional financial reporting framework

13.74 Where the auditor is engaged to form an opinion on the compliance of the financial statements with an additional financial reporting framework, this second opinion must be clearly separated from the first opinion. The auditor will do this by using another appropriate heading.

Requirement specific to public sector entities where an opinion on regularity is given

13.75 The auditor shall address other reporting responsibilities in [a] separate section[s] of the auditor's report following the opinion[s] on the financial statements and, where there is one, the opinion on regularity. (This is usually found in a separate regularity report for clients such as an academy school – although a 'conclusion' rather than an 'opinion' is formed on an academy's regularity report due to the limited work required on the regularity report).

Opinion on other matters

13.76 When the auditor addresses other reporting responsibilities within the auditor's report, the opinion which arises from such other responsibilities are to be set out in a separate section of the auditor's report which follow the opinion(s) on the financial statements or, where there is one, the opinion on regularity.

> **Focus**
>
> - Auditors of companies which report under the Corporate Governance Code are required to include additional information to the above in their audit report. However, such companies are beyond the scope of this book and hence will not be considered further.

Types of audit opinion

13.77 The hope of many (if not all) auditors is that they can express an 'unqualified' opinion on the financial statements. However, situations can present themselves during the course of an audit which, if not resolved, can result in a qualified opinion being expressed (the term 'qualified' is also referred to as a 'modified' opinion in ISA (UK and Ireland) 705 *Modifications to opinions in the independent auditor's report*). It is important at the outset to point out that when the auditor uses an 'emphasis of matter' paragraph, they are not qualifying (or modifying) the audit opinion; rather they are modifying the audit report (an emphasis of matter paragraph alerts users to an issue relevant to the financial statements and cross-refers them to a disclosure in the financial statements – for example going concern disclosures).

13.78 An audit qualification can be one of three types:

- Qualified opinion.
- Adverse opinion.
- Disclaimer of opinion.

> **Focus**
>
> - It is important to ensure that the opinion expressed in the financial statements is not only correct, but also appropriate. In practice there are many situations which may present themselves where it might not be as clear cut as to what type of opinion should be expressed.

13.79 Closely interrelated to audit qualification is the term 'pervasive'. Paragraph 5 of ISA (UK and Ireland) 705 defines 'pervasive' as:

> 'A term used, in the context of misstatements, to describe the effects on the financial statements of misstatements or the possible effects on the financial statements of misstatements, if any, that are undetected due to an inability to obtain sufficient appropriate audit evidence. Pervasive effects on the financial statements are those that, in the auditor's judgment:
>
> (i) Are not confined to specific elements, accounts or items of the financial statements;
>
> (ii) If so confined, represent or could represent a substantial proportion of the financial statements; or

(iii) In relation to disclosures, are fundamental to users' understanding of the financial statements.'

The following table illustrates a distinction between the types of opinion:

Opinion	**Circumstances**
Qualified opinion 'except for'	The misstatement giving rise to the opinion, or the lack of evidence, is material but is not pervasive.
Adverse opinion	Misstatements, both individually and collectively, are both material and pervasive.
Disclaimer of opinion	The possible effect of the lack of evidence is both material and pervasive to the extent that the auditor cannot form an opinion.

Qualified 'except for'

13.80 This type of opinion is to be expressed when the auditor disagrees with a type of accounting treatment and the treatment applied is material to the financial statements. In addition, management may not have made adequate disclosure concerning an item which is material to the financial statements.

Example 13.2 – Qualified opinion 'except for'

The auditor of North Ltd is undertaking the completion phase of the audit for the year-ended 31 March 2017. The company is involved in research and development and during the year has capitalised significant amounts of research expenditure on the balance sheet. The audit senior has discussed the appropriate accounting treatment permitted under Section 18 *Intangible Assets other than Goodwill* stating that Section 18 does not allow research expenditure to be capitalised; instead it must be written off as incurred. The finance director has refused to make any adjustments to the financial statements. There are no other misstatements that have been found during the course of the audit.

As the company has failed to comply with the requirements of Section 18 and has not written off research expenditure to the profit and loss account, the auditor disagrees with the accounting treatment applied and hence expresses a qualified opinion. The 'Basis for Qualified Opinion' paragraph will explain the reasons for the qualification, including quantitative amounts, and the 'Opinion' paragraph will state that 'except for' the effects of the matter described in the Basis for Opinion paragraph:

(a) the financial statements give a true and fair view; and

(b) have been prepared, in all material respects, in accordance with the applicable financial reporting framework.

Adverse opinion

13.81 Such opinions are fairly uncommon, but do arise occasionally. An adverse opinion is expressed by the auditor when they conclude that the financial statements do not give a true and fair view due to material misstatement. A misstatement can be material both individually and when aggregated with other misstatements and the auditor will express an adverse opinion when the effects of the misstatement(s) are both material and pervasive.

Example 13.3 – Adverse opinion

During the audit of the financial statements of South Ltd for the year-ended 31 March 2017, it became apparent that the company had serious going concern problems. The bank have not renewed the borrowing facilities of the company for the forthcoming year to 30 June 2018 and various suppliers have withdrawn credit facilities and are suing the company for non-payment. The directors have not made any going concern disclosures within the financial statements on the grounds that they believe it may prejudice any potential lender's decision to refinance the company. In addition, the directors do not have any resources themselves to introduce into the company to help the company survive its financial difficulties and it is clear that the company will have to cease trading shortly.

The company has prepared the financial statements on the going concern basis and the auditors disagree that this basis is appropriate in light of the facts and evidence they have obtained during the audit.

As the auditor disagrees with an issue which is both material and pervasive (the going concern presumption), the auditor will express an adverse audit opinion. This also complies with the requirements of ISA (UK and Ireland) 570 *Going concern* at paragraph 21.

The 'Basis for Adverse Opinion' paragraph will outline the reasons why the auditor has expressed such an opinion and the 'Opinion' paragraph will explain that because of the significance of the matter described in the Basis for Adverse Opinion paragraph:

(a) the financial statements do not give a true and fair view; and

(b) have not been prepared, in all material respects, in accordance with the applicable financial reporting framework.

Disclaimer of opinion

13.82 Disclaimers of opinion are also rare, but have been known to have been issued in certain situations. The auditor will express a disclaimer of opinion when the inability to obtain sufficient appropriate audit evidence is so material and pervasive that they simply cannot form an opinion as to whether the financial statements give a true and fair view.

Example 13.4 – Disclaimer of opinion

East Ltd (East) has a year-end of 31 December 2016 and on 16 February 2016 appointed a new firm of auditors as relations with the old firm broke down. East manufactures household appliances for the retail industry and always has a material amount of stock and work in progress. No auditor attended the stock count which was held on 31 December 2016. In addition, during the year the company changed accounting systems and the old and the new system were not run in parallel. Unfortunately the new system contained significant errors and the opening balances had not been transferred correctly and whilst management have corrected many of the errors, there is still a major problem with the closing trade debtors which was still to be resolved at the date the audit report was to be signed.

The auditor has not been able to determine whether any adjustments may have been necessary to the recorded/unrecorded stocks and cannot quantify the levels of errors to trade debtors. As a consequence they will express a disclaimer of opinion because the issues are so material and pervasive to the financial statements as such balances will affect the profit and loss account and balance sheet.

The 'Basis of Disclaimer of Opinion' paragraph will explain that the auditor has not been able to obtain sufficient appropriate audit evidence on which to provide a basis for an audit opinion and the 'Opinion' paragraph will state that the auditor does not express an opinion on the financial statements.

Summary of opinions

13.83 ISA (UK and Ireland) 705 contains a useful table in the *Application and Other Explanatory Material* at paragraph A1 which outlines how the auditor's judgment about the nature of the matter giving rise to the modification, and the pervasiveness of its effects (or possible effects) on the financial statements:

Nature of matter giving rise to the modification	**Auditor's judgment about the pervasiveness of the effects or possible effects on the financial statements**	
	Material but not pervasive	**Material and pervasive**
Financial statements are materially misstated	Qualified opinion	Adverse opinion
Inability to obtain sufficient appropriate audit evidence	Qualified opinion	Disclaimer of opinion

Emphasis of matter paragraphs

13.84 Emphasis of matter paragraphs are dealt with in ISA (UK and Ireland) 706 *Emphasis of matter paragraphs and other matter paragraphs in the independent auditor's report.*

Over the years firms have been criticised for inappropriately using an emphasis of matter paragraph as a means of (incorrectly) qualifying the audit report or, conversely, not using an emphasis matter of paragraph at all when circumstances would indicate the need for one.

Focus

- An emphasis of matter paragraph is not a qualification to the audit opinion. The auditor uses an emphasis of matter paragraph when they consider it necessary to:
  - draw users' attention to a matter(s) presented or disclosed in the financial statements which are of such importance that they are fundamental to users' understanding of the financial statements; or
  - draw users' attention to any matter(s) other than those presented or disclosed in the financial statements that are relevant to users' understanding of the audit, the auditor's responsibilities or the auditor's report.

It follows, therefore, that an emphasis of matter paragraph is used to highlight something of importance that has been appropriately presented or disclosed in the financial statements and the paragraph itself should make it clear that it is not an audit qualification (eg by starting the paragraph with 'Without qualifying our opinion, we draw your attention to …').

Example 13.5 – Going concern

During the year to 31 December 2016, East Ltd had suffered from serious cash flow difficulties and reduced levels of sales and profits due to adverse publicity concerning one of its major products. In addition, a large customer went into liquidation and the company suffered a bad debt hit on its profit and loss account, the amount of which is material to the financial statements.

The directors have approached their bank with a request for a working capital loan in order to survive. The directors have produced detailed cash flow statements and forecasts which confirm that the company will return to profitability and stability if the loan is made as the company has just been awarded a large contract which is due to start in six months' time. At the date of approval of the financial statements the company had received confirmation from the bank that it would agree to the loan, provided the director-shareholders also introduce funds into the business and agree to provide personal guarantees, which they have.

Despite the bank agreeing to the loan, the directors still have a material uncertainty as to whether the company will survive for the foreseeable future because the contract which they have been awarded is initially 'cost-heavy' in the first couple of months and, in addition, it will also take some time to turn the business around. They have, therefore, made adequate disclosures in the notes to the financial statements about this material uncertainty as they recognise such disclosures are encouraged in Appendix D to Section 1A of FRS 102 and need to avoid any disagreement with the entity's auditors.

As the directors have made adequate disclosures relating to going concern, the auditor can still express an unqualified audit opinion (provided there are, of course, no other material misstatements which remain uncorrected). However, the auditor will include an emphasis of matter paragraph in the audit report which will cross-refer to the going concern disclosure note in the financial statements as a means of drawing users' attention to the issue relating the material uncertainty about the entity's ability to continue as a going concern.

The use of an emphasis of matter paragraph in the auditor's report

13.85 When the auditor considers it necessary to include an emphasis of matter paragraph in the audit report, the auditor shall:

- Include it immediately after the Opinion on Financial Statements paragraph in the auditor's report.
- Use the heading 'Emphasis of Matter' or other appropriate heading.
- Include in the paragraph a clear reference to the matter being emphasised and to where relevant disclosures that full describe the matter can be found in the financial statements.
- Indicate that the auditor's opinion is not modified in respect of the matter emphasised.

Other matter paragraphs

13.86 The auditor may consider it necessary to communicate a matter, other than those which are presented or disclosed in the financial statements, which the auditor considers is relevant to users' understanding of the audit, the auditor's responsibilities or the auditor's report. Where this is not prohibited by law or regulation, the auditor can do this through the use of an 'other matter' paragraph. This paragraph is included immediately after the Opinion paragraph and any emphasis of matter paragraph. Alternatively, the auditor can use an 'other matter' paragraph elsewhere in the auditor's report if the content of the other matter is relevant to the other reporting responsibilities section.

PITFALLS TO AVOID

- Failing to undertake an adequate programme of planning resulting in non-compliance with the UK and Ireland ISAs in the 300 series.
- Forgetting to discuss the susceptibility of material misstatement due to fraud with related parties or discussing the issue but not documenting it.
- Forgetting to calculate performance materiality.
- Ensuring that sample sizes are not bias in terms of focussing on the easier items to sample.
- Failing to attend the stock count where stock is material.
- Relying on inquiry as a form of sole audit evidence.
- Failing to document safeguards that have been applied to reduce ethical threats to independence and objectivity.

CHAPTER SUMMARY

- As well as UK and Ireland ISAs, auditors of small entities are also required to follow Ethical Standards which are primarily in place to maintain independence and objectivity.
- Audit planning is imperative and enables the audit strategy and audit plan to be developed.
- When the auditor devises audit procedures at the planning stage, they should do so having regard to the assessed levels of risk that the financial statements are materially misstated.
- Audit programmes are generally bought 'off the shelf' for modern day smaller audits; however, procedures must be tailored specifically to reduce audit risk and to obtain sufficient appropriate audit evidence.
- This chapter considers some of the key audit areas in the financial statements together with audit objectives and illustrative audit tests. The chapter does not consider every audit area because no two audits are the same and the illustrative audit tests are to be viewed as a guide rather than as comprehensive.
- Audit completion procedures should include a going concern review and a post-balance sheet events review (also referred to as a review of 'events after the reporting period'). Both should be done on the date of the auditor's report.
- Audit reporting is a crucial area and the UK and Ireland ISAs in the 700 series are particularly vital for such reports.
- There are generally three types of audit qualification (qualified 'except for', adverse and a disclaimer of audit opinion).

- An emphasis of matter paragraph is not a substitute for audit qualification, it is used to highlight a matter of importance within the financial statements to the users.
- An 'other matter paragraph' can be used when the auditor which to communicate a matter(s) which they consider relevant to the users' understanding of the audit which is not prohibited by law or regulation.

Chapter 14

The Transition to New UK GAAP

SIGNPOSTS

- The rules in FRS 102 *The Financial Reporting Standard applicable in the UK and Republic of Ireland* and FRS 105 *The Financial Reporting Standard applicable to the Micro-entities Regime* are retrospective and need to be applied as far back as the date of transition and hence a thorough programme of planning needs to be undertaken by small and micro-entities to ensure a smooth transition (see **14.1** and **14.2**).
- Section 35 of FRS 102 says that the 'date of transition' is the start date of the earliest period reported in the financial statements (see **14.3–14.5**).
- An opening FRS 102/105-compliant balance sheet will have to be prepared at the date of transition although this does not need to be disclosed in the financial statements (see **14.6**).
- There is a four-stage process that must be applied to achieve the transition and involves recognising and derecognising assets and liabilities where appropriate and reclassifying items where necessary (see **14.7–14.10**).
- As a means of simplification, there are four mandatory exemptions from retrospective application and 18 optional exemptions in FRS 102 and FRS 105 contains two mandatory exemptions and eight optional exemptions (see **14.11–14.36**).
- Practical issues range from choosing the relevant framework to report under (FRS 102 for small entities or FRS 105) to ensuring the financial statements of a small entity give a true and fair view (see **14.37–14.42**).
- Previously declared dividends will not become unlawful if reserves become negative following transitional adjustments provided the profits determined under the previous UK GAAP were declared out of profits that had been determined by reference to 'relevant accounts' (see **14.43**).
- As the rules are retrospective, it is likely that any transitional adjustments may have associated tax implications. Specialist tax advice should be sought in complicated or ambiguous circumstances to ensure the correct tax treatment (see **14.45–14.64**).
- Micro-entities are exempt from the requirement to make transitional disclosure information, but small companies are encouraged to make such disclosures to enable the financial statements to give a true and fair view (see **14.65**).

INTRODUCTION

14.1 Small companies adopting FRS 102 *The Financial Reporting Standard applicable in the UK and Republic of Ireland* for small entities and FRS 105 *The Financial Reporting Standard applicable to the Micro-entities Regime* as the financial reporting framework will have to apply the rules retrospectively. The effect of retrospective application means that the financial statements will reflect the provisions of the new regimes as if the new standards had always been in existence and therefore will serve to ensure that the financial statements are both comparable and consistent and hence the rules are applied as far back as the date of transition. This means that previously reported equity and profit (loss) will also be affected and this chapter considers some of the key issues relating to a transition.

14.2 The importance of a proper programme of planning for a transition cannot be over-emphasised because in many cases preparers may not have had exposure to undertaking a transition. Technical staff need to have a sound understanding of how both FRS 102 for small entities and FRS 105 work as the new standards bring about new accounting methodologies in key areas. **Chapter 2** examines the differences between 'new' UK GAAP and 'old' UK GAAP in more detail and **Chapter 12** examines the recognition and measurement aspects. **Chapter 11** examines the recognition and measurement aspects for micro-entities. In all cases, a sound understanding of what the differences are between 'old' and 'new' GAAP must be understood and this will also help to undertake an impact assessment of how small companies (and micro-entities) will be affected by the new regime.

Section 35 *Transition to this FRS* in FRS 102 and Section 28 of FRS 105 outlines the procedures which are required to be adopted when dealing with a transition from old UK GAAP to the new frameworks. For companies which are not small or micro-entities, the disclosure requirements in Section 35 are mandatory; for small companies the disclosure requirements are *encouraged* and for micro-entities the disclosure requirements relating to the transition are not required (although micro-entities could voluntarily choose to make the required transitional disclosures if they so wish).

Focus

- While the disclosure requirements relating to the transition to FRS 102 for small companies are encouraged (hence not mandatory), directors of small companies should carefully consider making the disclosures contained in paragraphs 35.12–35.15, particularly where there have been material impacts on previously reported equity and profits. Where such disclosures are needed to enable the financial statements to give a true and fair view, small company directors will have a legal obligation to make such disclosures as it is still a legal requirement for small company financial statements to give a true and fair view. The disclosure requirements are considered at the end of this chapter.

14.3 Section 35 and 28 are critical sections of FRS 102 and FRS 105 when using the new standards for the first time. These sections apply to all first-time adopters of FRS 102 and FRS 105 regardless of the previous financial reporting framework which was applied in the preparation and presentation of the entity's financial statements.

Focus

- On the face of it, the principles contained in Section 35 and Section 28 may appear very similar to the methodology applied when changing an accounting policy; ie retrospective application. Changes in accounting policy would be dealt with under the provisions in Section 10 *Accounting Policies, Estimates and Errors* in FRS 102 and Section 8 of FRS 105. Section 10 and Section 8 do not, however, contain the mandatory and optional exemptions from retrospective application which are contained in Section 35 and Section 28 and hence Section 35 and Section 28 must be applied on first-time adoption of FRS 102 or FRS 105.

IDENTIFYING THE DATE OF TRANSITION

14.4 In any transition, the first step is to identify the entity's transition date. The Glossary to FRS 102 defines the date of transition as:

> 'The beginning of the earliest period for which an entity presents full comparative information in a given standard in its first **financial statements** that comply with that standard.'

To sum up the definition, the date of transition is the start date of the earliest comparative period reported in the financial statements.

Example 14.1 – Date of transition

Westhead Enterprises Ltd (Westhead) has a year-end of 31 March 2017 and is reporting under FRS 102 with reduced disclosures for the first time. The financial controller is unsure as to what Westhead's date of transition is.

The date of transition is the start date of the earlier period reported in the financial statements. The current year is 31 March 2017, meaning the 31 March 2016 financial statements are the comparative year. The comparative year starts on 1 April 2015 and hence this is Westhead's date of transition.

Using quarter-end dates, the following table should also help to identify the entity's date of transition (assuming early adoption is not taken):

Year-end	Date of transition
31 December 2016	1 January 2015
31 March 2017	1 April 2015
30 June 2017	1 July 2015
30 September 2017	1 October 2015

14.5 It can be noted from the table above that in almost all cases, the date of transition will have been and gone and hence transitional information should have ideally been obtained in order to apply some of the transitional provisions in Section 35 and Section 28 (such as holiday pay accruals and any GAAP valuations at the date of transition).

Opening balance sheet at the date of transition

14.6 The fact that the rules are retrospective will mean that an opening FRS 102 or FRS 105 balance sheet (statement of financial position) will have to be prepared as at the date of transition. Assuming a small company has a 31 December 2016 year-end, the date of the opening FRS 102/FRS 105 balance sheet will be 1 January 2015 (in other words, amending the closing 2014 trial balance to arrive at the 2015 opening balances, which is essentially the opening balance sheet). The opening balance sheet at the date of transition must be compliant with the provisions in FRS 102 and FRS 105. This will mean, in most cases, either changing the entity's accounting policies to be FRS 102/ FRS 105-compliant and/or recognising and derecognising assets, liabilities, income, expenses and equity which FRS 102/FRS 105 requires or does not permit (which may have been the opposite way around under previous UK GAAP). In some cases the transitional adjustments required at the date of transition and in the comparative year will have tax consequences (discussed later in the chapter) which will also need careful consideration as tax may be payable by the entity or refundable from HM Revenue and Customs.

Undeniably, the use of reputable accounts production software will aid a transition process, although preparers must keep in mind that such software will need to be 'told' the information in order to enable the transition to be done accurately and hence is the pivotal reason why technical staff and partners involved in a transition must be thoroughly conversant with all aspects of Section 35 and Section 28 as well as the new standards in general. Many commentators are cited as saying 'there is no substitute for reading the standards' and this is true in all cases and while this books aims to cover all the practicalities of the new small companies' regime, it cannot cover every eventuality.

Focus

- Small companies reporting under the provisions in FRS 102 must apply the **full** recognition and measurement principles in FRS 102; it is only the disclosure requirements which are different and are contained in Section 1A *Small Entities* of FRS 102 in Appendix C *Disclosure requirements for small entities* and Appendix D *Additional disclosures encouraged for small entities*. This is the main reason why company accountants and practitioners need to understand how FRS 102 (and FRS 105) works so as to enable the financial statements to be properly prepared.

THE FOUR-STAGE PROCESS AND ACCOUNTING POLICY ALIGNMENTS

14.7 Once the date of transition has been established, the next step is to consider the client's accounting policies and to establish whether these are consistent with the principles in FRS 102/FRS 105. This is important because some accounting policies and treatments which were permitted under the Financial Reporting Standard for Smaller Entities (the FRSSE) are no longer permitted under FRS 102/105 (and vice versa). This is one of the primary reasons why preparers of financial statements for small companies must have a sound understanding of the differences between 'old' and 'new' UK GAAP.

Focus

- While FRS 105 is primarily based on FRS 102 principles, the standard itself removes all accounting policy choices, for example development costs are all written off to profit or loss; there is no option to capitalise such costs (the same point applies to borrowing costs). In addition, there are significantly fewer disclosure requirements in FRS 105 than under FRS 102 Section 1A or the previous FRSSE (effective January 2015). A table outlining the key differences between the accounting methodologies in the FRSSE and in FRS 105 are outlined at **2.11** in **Chapter 2**.

Example 14.2 – Accounting policy alignments

Molbert Ltd (Molbert) is a small company with a year-end of 31 December 2016 and does not fall to be classified as a micro-entity. The accountant is considering whether the company's accounting policies are compliant with FRS 102 principles so that the opening balance sheet can be prepared at the date of transition.

Molbert acquired shares in another company several years ago for £50,000 and the transaction did not give rise to the creation of a subsidiary, associate or joint venture. They were merely recorded at cost in Molbert's financial statements. A valuation of the shares obtained on 31 December 2014 showed that the shares were worth £100,000 and had increased to £150,000 on 31 December

2015. The value of the shares did not increase in the year to 31 December 2016. Molbert pays tax at a rate of 20%.

The financial controller has asked whether the company can carry forward the cost value of the shares, or whether they would have to be carried at fair value under FRS 102 principles.

Under FRS 102, the investment should be carried at fair value and hence the following adjustments should be carried out:

<u>At the date of transition – 1 January 2015</u>

DR investment	£50,000
CR profit and loss reserves	(£50,000)

Being increase in fair value of the investment at the date of transition

Deferred tax will also have to be taken into consideration as this is a non-monetary asset subject to the revaluation model and under Section 29 *Income Tax*, the entries will be:

DR profit and loss reserves	£10,000 (20% × £50,000)
CR deferred tax provision	(£10,000)

Being deferred tax on the increase in fair value of the investment

<u>Comparative year to 31 December 2015</u>

DR investment	£50,000
CR profit and loss*	(£50,000)

Being increase in fair value of the investment to 31 December 2015

A further charge to deferred tax will arise to conform with Section 29 principles as follows:

DR tax expense (profit and loss)	£10,000
CR deferred tax provision	(£10,000)

Being deferred tax on fair value increase to 31 December 2015

*The £50,000 increase in fair value can be taken to a line item called 'Fair value adjustments' in profit or loss and should be included within operating profit where applicable.

14.8 As can be seen from the example above, the alignment of accounting policies can give rise to transitional adjustments meaning that previously reported profit (loss) and equity balances will be changed.

> **Focus**
>
> - As the impact on profit or loss and equity is likely to change due to the transition from the FRSSE/previous UK GAAP to FRS 102 for small entities, it is advisable to inform clients/directors sooner rather than later so that any material impacts will not come as an unpleasant surprise.

Process of restatement

14.9 Section 35 principles require first-time adopters to apply a four-stage process when it comes to the transition (the same procedures apply in FRS 105 at Section 28):

- recognise all assets and liabilities where FRS 102 requires such assets and liabilities to be recognised;
- derecognise assets and liabilities which are not permitted under FRS 102 principles;
- reclassify items that were recognised under previous UK GAAP as one type of asset, liability or component of equity, but which are a different type of asset, liability or component of equity under FRS 102 principles; and
- apply the provisions in FRS 102 from the date of transition in measuring all recognised assets and liabilities.

Example 14.3 – Transitional adjustment

Westhead Enterprises Ltd has a year-end date of 31 December 2016 and falls under the scope of FRS 102 for small entities. The following opening trial balance as at the date of transition (1 January 2015) has been extracted from the accounts production software system:

	DR	CR
Plant and machinery – cost	100,000	
Plant and machinery – depreciation		30,000
Computer equipment – cost	30,000	
Computer equipment – depreciation		20,000
Investment property	140,000	
Stock	45,000	

	DR	CR
Trade and other debtors	85,000	
Cash at bank and in hand	60,000	
Trade and other creditors		50,000
Corporation tax		17,000
Ordinary share capital		10,000
Revaluation reserve (see Note 1)		25,000
Profit and loss account		308,000
	460,000	460,000

Note 1

The revaluation reserve relates to the investment property which was carried at open market value in accordance with the FRSSE (effective January 2015).

The investment property was accounted for under the FRSSE (effective January 2015) which required all fair value gains and losses to be taken directly to the revaluation reserve unless a deficit (or its reversal) on an individual investment property was expected to be permanent, in which case it was charged (or credited) to the profit and loss account of the period. Paragraph 16.7 of FRS 102 extinguishes the use of the revaluation reserve account for investment properties and fair value gains and losses are instead to taken to profit or loss and reported within operating profit. This treatment must be reflected in the opening trial balance at the date of transition and therefore the following transitional adjustments will be made as at 1 January 2015:

DR revaluation reserve	£25,000
CR profit and loss account reserves	(£25,000)

The next issue to consider is the deferred tax implications relating to this investment property. Under the FRSSE (effective January 2015), provision for deferred tax in respect of non-monetary assets subject to revaluation would only be made if there was a binding agreement to sell the asset at the balance sheet date and the entity has revalued the asset to its selling price and does not expect to obtain rollover relief. However, Section 29 *Income Tax* deals with the issue relating to investment property in paragraph 29.16 and requires deferred tax to be calculated in respect of investment property carried at fair value. Therefore, ignoring the effects of indexation, and assuming a corporation tax rate of 20%, the transitional adjustments will be:

DR profit and loss account	£5,000
CR deferred tax provision	(£5,000)

Once the opening FRS 102-compliant balance sheet has been prepared, the next step is to consider the effects of the accounting policy alignment on the previous year's comparative figures. For the purposes of this example, if it is assumed that as at 31 December 2015, the fair value of the investment property had risen to £160,000 (i.e. a £20,000 gain in the year), the entries under the FRSSE (effective January 2015) would have been:

DR investment property	£20,000
CR revaluation reserve	(£20,000)

As this accounting treatment is inconsistent with the requirements of FRS 102, an adjustment to the 2015 comparative financial statements will be made as follows:

DR revaluation reserve	£20,000
CR profit and loss (within operating profit)	(£20,000)

The additional deferred tax requirements will be:

DR income tax expense	£4,000 (20% × £20,000)
CR deferred tax provision	(£4,000)

14.10 Once the above four-stage process has been undertaken, the effect will be that the financial statements will reflect FRS 102 principles notwithstanding the fact that the small entity may have applied the FRSSE/previous UK GAAP for several years. Applying the principles in Section 35 will ensure that the financial statements are both consistent and comparable, traits which stakeholders value considerably to arrive at reasoned conclusions about the business.

Focus

- Regardless of the fact that prior year financial statements will more than likely change as a result of the transition, revised financial statements do not have to be submitted to HM Revenue and Customs or Companies House. However, it is advisable to carefully consider making transitional disclosures which explain the impact of the transition on previously reported equity values and profit or loss, particularly where there are associated tax consequences. The same applies to micro-entities.

MANDATORY AND OPTIONAL EXEMPTIONS FROM RETROSPECTIVE APPLICATION

14.11 As a means of attempting to make a transition as smooth as possible, Section 35 of FRS 102 allows certain exemptions from retrospective application of the standard. There are four **mandatory** exemptions from retrospective application (ie small companies have no choice but to apply the mandatory exemptions). In addition, there are also 18 **optional** exemptions from retrospective application of which small entities can choose to apply some, all or none of them.

Mandatory and optional exemptions under FRS 105

14.12 FRS 105 at Section 28 contains two mandatory exemptions from retrospective application which relate to:

- Derecognition of financial assets and financial liabilities.
- Accounting estimates.

FRS 105 also contains eight optional exemptions from retrospective application relating to:

- Business combinations and goodwill.
- Share-based payment transactions.
- Investment properties.
- Compound financial instruments.
- Arrangements containing a lease.
- Decommissioning liabilities included in the cost of property, plant and equipment or investment property.
- Dormant companies.
- Lease incentives.

Mandatory exemptions from retrospective application

Derecognition of financial assets and financial liabilities (also applicable to micro-entities)

14.13 Entities cannot recognise financial assets and financial liabilities which were derecognised under previous UK GAAP. For those instruments which would have been derecognised under FRS 102/FRS 105 and arose in a transaction which took place before the date of transition, but were not derecognised under old UK GAAP, there is a choice: either derecognise them on adopting FRS 102/FRS 105 or continue recognising them until they are disposed of or settled.

Accounting estimates (also applicable to micro-entities)

14.14 Entities cannot use hindsight to change the value of accounting estimates recognised at the date of transition. Should additional information have come to light about the estimate, this should be treated as a non-adjusting event and accounted for in the current (not previous) accounting period unless there is clear evidence that the accounting estimate is incorrect.

Discontinued operations

14.15 On transition to FRS 102, a reporting entity cannot change the accounting it followed under previous UK GAAP in respect of its discontinued operations and hence there will not be any reclassification or remeasurement for discontinued operations that have been previously accounted for.

Non-controlling interests

14.16 Entities cannot retrospectively change the accounting that was followed for measuring non-controlling interests.

14.17 The 18 optional exemptions (for small companies) are as follows, the eight optional exemptions noted in paragraph 14.12 above only apply to micro-entities:

Business combinations, including group reconstructions

14.18 A first-time adopter does not have to apply Section 19 of FRS 102 or Section 14 of FRS 105 *Business Combinations and Goodwill* to those business combinations which took place before the date of transition. However, where the entity restates any combination so as to comply with Section 19/14, it must restate all later combinations. Where the provisions in Section 19/14 are not applied retrospectively, all assets and liabilities acquired or assumed in a past business combination at the date of transition will be recognised and measured in accordance with paragraphs 35.7 to 35.9 (28.7 to 28.9 of FRS 105) (or if applicable, paragraphs 35.10(b) to (r) (28.10(b) to (h) in FRS 105). There are, however, two exceptions in respect of:

- intangible assets (not goodwill): intangible assets subsumed within goodwill should not be recognised separately; and
- goodwill: no adjustment is made to the carrying value of goodwill.

Share-based payment transactions

14.19 For equity instruments granted before the date of transition, a first-time adopter does not have to apply Section 26 *Share-based Payment* (Section 21 in FRS 105). This exemption also applies to liabilities arising from share-based payment transactions which were settled before the date of transition.

For micro-entities, a first-time adopter will not be required to apply Section 21 to liabilities which have been settled before the date of transition to FRS 105.

Where a first-time adopter has previously applied either FRS 20 *Share-based payment* or IFRS 2 *Share-based Payment* to equity instruments granted BEFORE the date of transition, the entity must then apply FRS 20/IFRS 2 (whichever applies) or Section 26 at the date of transition.

Fair value as deemed cost

14.20 For items of property, plant and equipment (Section 17 *Property, Plant and Equipment*), investment property (Section 16 *Investment Property*) or intangible assets excluding goodwill (Section 18 *Intangible Assets other than Goodwill*), the first-time adopter can use fair value as deemed cost on transition to FRS 102. The term 'deemed cost' is defined in the Glossary as:

> 'An amount used as a surrogate for cost or depreciated cost at a given date. Subsequent **depreciation** or **amortisation** assumes that the entity had initially recognised the **asset** or **liability** at the given date and that its cost was equal to the deemed cost.'

Note: micro-entities cannot use fair values in FRS 105.

Revaluation as deemed cost

14.21 Again, for items of property, plant and equipment, investment property or intangible assets (not goodwill), a first-time adopter can use a revaluation amount as deemed cost. This may be of particular benefit to an entity who wants to stop getting periodic revaluations and move back on to the depreciated historic cost model for its property, plant and equipment. Be careful, however, with this exemption. Valuations should be obtained at, or before, the date of transition but not after.

Note: micro-entities cannot use revaluations in FRS 105.

Individual and separate financial statements

14.22 Paragraphs 9.26, 14.4 and 15.9 of FRS 102 require an entity to account for investments in subsidiaries, associates and jointly controlled entities at either cost less impairment or at fair value in the individual or separate financial statements. Where cost is used, the first-time adopter must use one of the following amounts in the individual/separate opening balance sheet:

- cost per Section 9 *Consolidated and Separate Financial Statements*, Section 14 *Investments in Associates* or Section 15 *Investments in Joint Ventures*; or
- deemed cost – in this respect the deemed cost is the carrying amount at the date of transition which has been determined under previous UK GAAP.

Compound financial instruments

14.23 The use of 'split accounting' is used for compound financial instruments (where the debt and equity components of the instrument are accounted for separately). A first-time adopter does not have to use split accounting if the liability portion of the instrument has been settled at the date of transition. This exemption also applies to micro-entities reporting under FRS 105.

Service concession arrangements

14.24 A service concession arrangement is defined in the Glossary as:

> 'An arrangement whereby a public sector body or a **public benefit entity** (the grantor) contracts with a private sector entity (the operator) to construct (or upgrade), operate and maintain **infrastructure assets** for a specified period of time (the concession period).'

For such arrangements, a first-time adopter does not have to apply the provisions in paragraph 34.12I to 34.16A for service concession arrangements entered into before the date of transition as these arrangements will continue to be accounted for using the same accounting policies applied at the date of transition.

There are no provisions in Section 28 relating to micro-entities and service concession arrangements.

Extractive industries

14.25 Where a first-time adopter has previously accounted for exploration and development costs for oil and gas properties which are in the development/production phase in cost centres that included all properties in a large geographical area, it can choose to measure oil and gas assets at the date of transition on the following basis:

- Exploration and evaluation assets at the amount determined under previous UK GAAP.
- Assets in the development/production phase at the amount determined for the cost centre under previous UK GAAP (this amount will be allocated to the cost centre's underlying assets on a pro-rata basis using reserve volumes/values at the date of transition).

First-time adopters must test exploration and evaluation assets in the development and production phases for impairment at the date of transition in accordance with either Section 34 *Specialised Activities* or Section 27 *Impairment of Assets*.

There are no provisions in FRS 105 for micro-entities relating to extractive industries.

Arrangements containing a lease

14.26 First-time adopters can choose to determine whether an arrangement that exists at the date of transition contains a lease on the basis of facts and circumstances existing at the date of transition rather than when the lease was originally entered into. This exemption also applies to micro-entities reporting under FRS 105.

Decommissioning liabilities included in the cost of property, plant and equipment (PPE) (or investment property for FRS 105)

14.27 The cost of an item of PPE should include the initial estimate of the costs of dismantling and removing the item and restoring the site on which it is located. A first-time adopter can choose to measure this portion of the cost at the date of transition rather than on the date(s) when the obligation initially arose. This exemption also applies to micro-entities reporting under FRS 105.

Investment properties (FRS 105 only)

14.28 A first-time adopter of FRS 105 is not required to apply paragraph 12.15 retrospectively to determine the depreciated cost of each of the major components of an investment property at the date the micro-entities transitions to FRS 105. Where the micro-entity takes advantage of this exemption it will:

(1) Determine the total cost of the investment property, including all of its components. Where the micro-entity previously carried the investment property at open market value under the FRSSE (effective January 2015), the total cost can be calculated by reversing any revaluations gains or losses recorded in equity.

(2) Separate the cost of the land from the cost of the buildings (as land does not depreciate).

(3) Estimate the total depreciated cost of the investment property (excluding land) at the transition date. This is done by recognising accumulated depreciation since the date of initial acquisition which is calculated based on the useful life of the most significant component of the item property (usually the main structural element of the building).

(4) A portion of the estimated total depreciated cost calculated in (3) above is then allocated to each of the other major components so as to determine their depreciated cost. This allocation should be made on a reasonable and consistent basis (for example multiplying the current cost to replace the component by the ratio of its remaining useful life to the expected useful life of a replacement component).

(5) Any amount of the total depreciated cost which is not allocated under (4) above is then allocated to the most significant component of the investment property.

Dormant companies

14.29 A company which is dormant (as defined in the Companies Act) can retain its accounting policies for reported assets, liabilities and equity at the date of transition until such time that there is a change to those balances or the company enters into new transactions. This exemption also applies to micro-entities reporting under FRS 105.

Deferred development costs as deemed cost

14.30 The carrying amount of development costs capitalised under previous UK GAAP can be used as deemed cost on transition to FRS 102.

This provision does not exist for micro-entities as there is no option to capitalise development costs.

Borrowing costs

14.31 When a first-time adopter decides to capitalise borrowing costs as part of the cost of a qualifying asset, it can treat the date of transition as the date on which capitalisation of such costs commences.

This provision does not exist for micro-entities as there is no option to capitalise borrowing costs.

Lease incentives

14.32 A first-time adopter does not have to apply paragraphs 20.15A and 20.25A (paragraphs 15.15 and 15.25 in FRS 105) to lease incentives provided that the lease was entered into before the date of transition. The first-time adopter can continue to recognise any remaining lease incentive (or cost associated with lease incentives) on the same basis as that applied at the date of transition to FRS 102. This exemption also applies to micro-entities reporting under FRS 105.

Public benefit entity combinations

14.33 A first-time adopter does not have to apply paragraphs PBE34.75 to PBE34.86 to public benefit combinations which had taken place before the date of transition. However, if the first-time adopter restates any entity combination to comply with FRS 102, it must restate all later entity combinations.

Assets and liabilities of subsidiaries, associates and joint ventures

14.34 When a subsidiary becomes a first-time adopter later than its parent, the subsidiary measures its assets and liabilities at either:

(1) the carrying values that would be included in the parent's consolidated accounts. These values are based on the parent's date of transition to FRS 102 if no consolidation adjustments were made and for the effects of the business combination in which the parent acquired the subsidiary; or

(2) the carrying values required by the rest of FRS 102 which are based on the subsidiary's date of transition.

The carrying values in (2) could be different than (1) where the exemptions result in measurements which are dependent on the date of transition. In addition, differences could also arise where the accounting policies used by the subsidiary differ from those in the consolidated accounts.

Similar exemptions are available for an associate or joint venture which become a first-time adopter later than the entity which holds significant influence or joint control over it.

Conversely, where the parent or investor becomes a first-time adopter later than its subsidiary, associate or joint venture, the parent/investor will, in the consolidated accounts, measure the assets and liabilities of the subsidiary, associate or joint venture at the same carrying amount as in the subsidiary's, associate's or joint venture's financial statements. This will also take into consideration consolidation and equity accounting adjustments as well as the effects of the business combination in which the parent acquired the subsidiary or transaction in which the entity acquired the associate or joint venture.

Where the parent becomes a first-time adopter in respect of its separate financial statements earlier or later than for its consolidated accounts, the parent measures its assets and liabilities at the same value in both sets of accounts, except for consolidation adjustments.

Designation of previously recognised financial instruments

14.35 FRS 102 allows a financial instrument to be designated on initial recognition as a financial asset or financial liability at fair value through profit or loss, provided certain criteria are met. Section 35 allows an entity to designate any financial asset or financial liability at fair value through profit or loss provided the asset or liability meets the criteria in paragraph 11.14(b) at the date of transition.

Hedge accounting

14.36 There are exemptions available in respect of hedge accounting that may be applied in respect of:

- a hedging relationship existing at the date of transition;
- a hedging relationship which ceased to exist at the date of transition because the hedging instrument had expired, was sold, terminated or exercised before the date of transition;

- a hedging relationship which commenced subsequent to the date of transition; and
- entities that choose to take the accounting policy choice under paragraphs 11.2(b) or (c) or paragraphs 12.2(b) or (c) and apply IAS 39 *Financial Instruments: Recognition and Measurement* or IFRS 9 *Financial Instruments*.

Example 14.4 – Revaluation as deemed cost

Bart Baling Equipment Ltd (Bart) always reported its freeholding buildings using the revaluation model as permitted by the FRSSE and obtained updated valuations every five years, with valuations in the intervening years where the directors suspected there had been a material change in valuation.

The board of directors have decided that the use of the revaluation model is no longer appropriate for the business and have asked whether they can switch back to the depreciated historic cost model.

Under the previous UK GAAP, a change from depreciated historic cost to revaluation would have been a change in accounting policy (as it would be under the principles in FRS 102). An accounting policy is changed by an entity so that the financial statements give more relevant and reliable information (and hence present a truer and fairer view). It is also generally accepted that fair value is more reliable than historic cost. Because of this, it is inherently very difficult to switch back from the revaluation model to the depreciated historic cost model on the grounds of justifying why depreciated historic cost is more relevant and reliable than revaluation.

However, as FRS 102 is a whole new financial reporting framework, it would be possible to use a revaluation amount as deemed cost at the date of transition. Care, however, must be taken when using such revaluation amounts because the date of the valuation must be either AT or BEFORE the date of transition. GAAP valuations obtained AFTER the date of transition to FRS 102 would not be appropriate.

Example 14.5 – Lease incentives

On 1 January 2012, West Ltd entered into a ten-year lease to rent a building to house its administration and office facilities. The terms of the lease make provision for a break-clause to be exercised on 31 December 2016. On signing the lease, the landlord agrees to a one-year rent-free period and rent of £230,000 per annum is payable.

Under the FRSSE West would recognise the incentive up to the point at which the rentals increase to market rate (ie up to the break-clause point). On transition to FRS 102, it can continue to do this if it so chooses, or it can spread the incentive over the remainder of the lease term.

Under the FRSSE the charge to the P&L would be as follows:

Year-end	Paid	P&L charge	Balance sheet c/f
	£'000	£'000	£'000
31.12.2012	–	184	184
31.12.2013	230	184	138
31.12.2014	230	184	92
31.12.2015	230	184	46

The journal entries in 2012 are:

DR rent expense (P&L)	£184,000
CR balance sheet incentive	(£184,000)

In the years to 31/12/2013, 14 and 15:

DR balance sheet incentive	£46,000
CR rent expense (P&L)	(£46,000)

On transition to FRS 102, West Ltd will have a choice. It can either restate as if FRS 102 for small companies has always been the reporting framework; or it can continue with the previous UK GAAP treatment and spread the incentive up to the point at which the break-clause will be exercised.

Option 1: restate under FRS 102 for small entities

If West decides to restate as if FRS 102 for small entities has always been the financial reporting framework then a transitional adjustment at the date of transition will be made to the balance at the date of transition together with a prior year adjustment in the comparative year.

Year-end	Paid	P&L charge	Balance sheet c/f
	£'000	£'000	£'000
31.12.2012	–	207	207
31.12.2013	230	207	184
31.12.2014 (Date of transition)	230	207	161
31.12.2015	230	207	138

Year-end	**Paid**	**P&L charge**	**Balance sheet c/f**
	£'000	£'000	£'000
31.12.2016	230	207	115
31.12.2017	230	207	92
31.12.2018	230	207	69
31.12.2019	230	207	46
31.12.2020	230	207	23
31.12.2021	230	207	–

At the date of transition an adjustment will be needed as follows:

DR accumulated profit and loss £69,000

CR balance sheet incentive (£69,000)

Being the difference between £161k and £92k

In the comparative year an adjustment will be needed as follows:

DR profit and loss expense £23,000 (£207k less £184k)

CR balance sheet incentive (£23,000)

Being the difference in P&L charge under FRS 102 for small entities v FRSSE

There will also be consequential tax adjustments to factor into account.

Option 2: continue with existing UK GAAP

If West decides to continue with the FRSSE then the position will be as follows:

Year-end	**Paid**	**P&L charge**	**Balance sheet c/f**
	£'000	£'000	£'000
31.12.2012	–	184	184
31.12.2013	230	184	138
31.12.2014 (Date of transition)	230	184	92
31.12.2015	230	184	46
31.12.2016	230	184	–

As can be seen from the above comparisons, there are also tax implications to consider and in the above worked examples, it would be more advantageous from a tax perspective to use option 1 and restate as if FRS 102 had always been the reporting framework because the charge to profit and loss is higher (as the lease incentive is being written off over a longer period) and hence tax relief would be granted on the excess.

PRACTICAL ISSUES FACING FIRST-TIME ADOPTERS

14.37 The new small and micro-entities financial reporting regimes are going to bring about various challenges to first-time adopters and are being cited as the most 'radical' change in accounting for a generation. The time small companies' were given to gear up for the new framework was not long as the government was only given until July 2015 to transpose the EU Accounting Directive into companies' legislation. As a consequence, practitioners and company accountants had to get to grips with a new regime in a relatively short timescale; which was not ideal, but was an issue which, to a large extent, was beyond the control of the Financial Reporting Council given that the new requirements in company law take mandatory effect for accounting periods commencing on or after 1 January 2016.

Choosing the relevant framework

14.38 Directors of small companies must choose the relevant financial reporting framework carefully. In determining the most appropriate framework, directors should not simply opt for the one with the least disclosure requirements or the one which contains the least complex accounting methodologies.

Focus

- A company which falls to be classed as a micro-entity because it meets the eligibility criteria may not necessarily benefit from reporting under FRS 105; particularly if the micro-entity is expected to grow at a rapid pace or wishes to carry certain assets (for example investment property) at revaluation. In such cases the entity should report under a more comprehensive framework, (for example FRS 102 with reduced disclosures). Micro-entities which are expected to grow at a rapid pace would benefit from reporting under FRS 102 for small entities as there would be little in the way of change in accounting methodology as the entity continues to grow.

14.39 The Financial Reporting Council have suggested the following factors be taken into consideration when determining which reporting framework is most suitable for a small/micro-entity:

- Whether the entity is eligible to apply a particular regime. Eligibility criteria may include the type of financial statements (ie individual or group) being prepared, company size thresholds and entity type.
- Where a choice of regime exists, entities should consider which of the regimes is the most appropriate to the individual circumstances of an entity. Factors to consider will differ from company to company and may relate to certain characteristics or restrictions of a particular regime, the resources available and the information needs of users of the accounts, amongst many others.

Where the micro-entities' regime is concerned, there are some key points that should be taken on board when considering the appropriateness of FRS 105:

- The regime prohibits the use of the fair value accounting rules and use of revaluation amounts. For a company with an investment property on its balance sheet (or other assets stated at valuation) which chooses to use FRS 105, it will have to restate the value of the investment property to the amount that would be carried in the balance sheet under normal fixed asset rules (ie cost less depreciation and impairment). Restating such assets under historic cost models could have a detrimental impact on the company's balance sheet.
- FRS 105 only applies to incorporated companies which meet the eligibility criteria. It is not available to charities, financial institutions, limited liability partnerships, financial statements of a parent company which prepares consolidated financial statements or to the financial statements of non-parent companies whose financial statements are included in consolidated financial statements. The eligibility criteria is therefore very restrictive and should be carefully considered at the outset when considering the most appropriate framework to choose.
- Financial instruments and assets cannot be carried under the fair value rules or the alternative accounting rules.
- The disclosure requirements are very minimal (see **Chapter 2** for the disclosure requirements).
- Only a Format 2 profit and loss account can be prepared (although a choice of Format 1 or Format 2 exists for the balance sheet).
- Micro-entities are exempt from the requirements to account for some complex transactions, such as equity-settled share-based payment transactions and deferred tax.
- Defined benefit pension schemes are accounted for in the same way as a defined contribution pension scheme under FRS 105 principles.
- No accounting policies are required to be disclosed because there are no accounting policies contained in FRS 105.

Advising directors

14.40 Company directors need to be informed of the new financial reporting regime as early as possible in order that they can make decisions as to the best framework for them (although in a lot of cases it is likely that the company will seek the advice from the professional accountancy firm).

It is advisable to undertake an impact assessment which looks at how specific entities are going to be affected by the new reporting regimes and consider how the implementation of FRS 102 with reduced disclosures/FRS 105 is going to affect accounting and financial reporting systems. Accounting packages are going to need to be reconfigured in some instances to cope with the new accounting methodologies inherent in the standards, for example not taking fair value gains on investment property fair values to a revaluation reserve but to profit or loss instead.

Accountants will also need to undertake an impact assessment early on in the transition process to identify the effect that a transition will have on previously reported equity and profits (or losses). Each small business will have a varying number of transitional adjustments to ensure their accounting policies comply with the provisions in the new regimes. It is impossible to quantify an 'average' number of changes because each small business is different; some companies might only have one or two changes, whereas some may have significantly more. Additional factors that should be considered during an impact assessment for small (not micro) entities are:

Impact assessment for small (not micro) entities

14.41

- Does the entity have goodwill and intangible assets that have not been given a useful economic life or management are unable to arrive at a suitable economic life? If so these intangible assets must be amortised over a maximum ten-year period (note intangible assets cannot have an indefinite useful life under the new regime and any change of amortisation period should be carefully considered as this may be an error in management's original estimation rather than a transitional adjustment). Accelerated amortisation periods on transition should only occur in exceptional circumstances.
- Does the entity have investment properties? If so, fair value fluctuations are taken to profit or loss rather than a revaluation reserve.
- Does the entity have major spare parts/standby equipment? If so, these are to be capitalised as part of property, plant and equipment and the cost recognised through depreciation as opposed to inventory and cost of sales.
- Are leases appropriately recognised as finance/operating leases? FRS 102 does not contain a benchmark percentage of minimum lease payments that equate to fair value and therefore the eight criteria in Section 20 *Leases* must be carefully considered.
- Does the entity value stock using last-in first-out? If so, this will have to be changed to first-in first-out, average cost or another acceptable method of stock valuation.
- Does the entity have financial instruments that fall within fair value valuations (such as derivatives)? If so careful consideration will have to be given to the fair value assessment of these.
- Does the entity have intra-group loans at a below market rate of interest? If so the accounting for such loans is markedly different under FRS

102 than under previous GAAP (see **Chapter 12** for a more detailed examination of the new rules where intra-group loans are concerned).

- Have deferred tax issues been considered? FRS 102 uses a timing difference 'plus' approach which will give rise to additional situations where deferred tax can arise. Care must be taken with deferred tax assets in that they can only be recognised when there is evidence that the entity will make suitable taxable profit in succeeding years to offset the deferred tax asset.
- Have accruals been made for short-term employee benefits (such as holiday pay)?
- Have loan agreements/finance agreements been scrutinised for any embedded derivatives that may have been incorporated in the terms? If so, these will have to be recognised on the balance sheet at fair value with changes in fair value going through profit or loss?
- Is management satisfied that they have sufficient information and explanations in order to produce the opening balance sheet as at the date of transition to FRS 102?
- Has the opening balance sheet as at the date of transition been agreed to accounting policies and records? Are there any exceptions that need to be corrected? Note – many accounts production systems will throw up exception reports where there are issues with brought forward balances.
- Have errors been discovered in the prior year's financial statements when undertaking the conversion? If so, have these been distinguished separately from transitional adjustments?
- Has the profit reported under old UK GAAP in the comparative year been reconciled to the profit per FRS 102 in the comparative year?
- Have the financial statements in the comparative year been correctly adjusted in accordance with FRS 102?
- Have the directors considered the need to make a statement of compliance with FRS 102 as set out in paragraph 3.3 of FRS 102? (Note the Financial Reporting Council (FRC) encourages, but does not mandate, this disclosure).
- Have the directors considered the need to explain how the transition has affected the entity's financial performance and financial position as set out in paragraphs 35.12 and 35.13 of FRS 102? (Note the FRC encourages, but does not mandate, these disclosures).
- Have the tax implications of the transitional adjustments been considered?
- Have the financial statements been reviewed by an appropriate person to ensure they are complete and technical disclosures accurate?
- Do the financial statements give a true and fair view? If not, the client must make additional disclosures over and above the mandatory disclosures to enable the financial statements to give a true and fair view.

Focus

- The above list is not exhaustive but does consider some of the more common factors that need consideration when dealing with a transition to FRS 102 for small entity clients.

14.42 Crucially, the tax impact of any transitional adjustments will have to be considered because transitional adjustments may attract tax relief or require additional tax to be repaid to HM Revenue and Customs (see the section 'Tax implications' later in the chapter).

Impact of a transition on previously declared dividends

14.43 For many small companies, the transition across to a new financial reporting regime (FRS 102 with reduced disclosures or FRS 105) will be relatively straightforward and may only involve a few transitional adjustments due to accounting policy alignments. However, for other companies, life may not be as straightforward. The question arises as to how the transition may affect dividends that have been previously declared in the financial statements, which were lawful at the time they had been declared, but which may appear to be 'illegal' once the transition process is complete. Small companies and micro-entities which already had a low level of distributable reserves may find these reserves turn negative following a transition because of the recognition of additional liabilities (eg holiday pay accruals and deferred tax provisions on non-monetary assets subject to revaluation).

Tech 02/10 *Guidance on Realised and Distributable Profits under the Companies Act 2006* at paragraph 3.28 introduces circumstances which are due to changes in accounting policies on the adoption of IFRSs. While the guidance itself is IFRS-specific, the principles on adoption to FRS 102 with reduced disclosures will also apply.

Paragraph 3.29 then goes on to say that while the effect of a change to a new financial reporting framework may be to reduce, or even eliminate, a company's net realised profits, distributions which have already been made out of realised profits would not become unlawful on transition to a new financial reporting framework. The dividend must, however, have been declared out of realised profits that had been determined by reference to 'relevant accounts' and such accounts would have had to have complied with GAAP principles (subject to paragraphs 3.30 and 3.31 of *Tech 02/10*).

Focus

- The Companies Act 2006 defines realised profits and losses as a basis for determining the unlawfulness of a distribution as:

> 'Such profits and losses of the company as fall to be treated as realised in accordance with principles generally accepted at the time when the accounts are prepared, with respect to the determination for accounting purposes of realised profits or losses.'[1]

TAX IMPLICATIONS

14.44 The application of the rules in FRS 102 and FRS 105 as far back as the date of transition may result in several adjustments being made to the opening FRS 102/FRS 105 balance sheet and the comparative year's financial statements and these adjustments may well have associated tax implications.

The tax legislation (Corporation Tax Act 2009, section 46) require financial statements for tax purposes to be prepared under Generally Accepted Accounting Practice (GAAP). Section 1127 of the Corporation Tax Act 2010 (CTA 2010) says that GAAP for corporation tax purposes, as well as for individuals, entities that are not companies and non-UK companies is UK GAAP. For companies that prepare IAS accounts, however, GAAP means IAS accounts (section 1127(3) of the CTA 2010).

Focus

- Consolidated financial statements will have no influence on the entities' individual tax position.

The financial statements of a company reporting under new UK GAAP are going to be affected in two main areas where taxation is concerned:

- the way that corporation tax liabilities for the current year are calculated; and
- the way that deferred tax is calculated.

The first bullet being an impact on actual tax paid, the second bullet being an impact only on presentation within the financial statements.

Tax impact of accounting policy changes

14.45 An entity transitioning across to new UK GAAP is required to consider its accounting policies to assess whether they are compliant with FRS 102/ FRS 105. For micro-entities, FRS 105 contains no accounting policy choices, but such an entity will need to consider the practices it currently adopts for financial reporting purposes to ensure that they are compliant with FRS 105 principles.

1 Companies Act 2006, s 853(4).

The way that transitional adjustments are applied work in a similar manner to a change in accounting policy (in other words similar to a prior period adjustment) and may give rise to either a positive adjustment (one which increases profit or reduces a loss) or a negative adjustment. Positive adjustments are taxed as receipts, whereas negative adjustments are allowable as an expense. Chapter 14 Part 3 of CTA 2009 says that where there is a change from one valid basis to another valid basis, any adjustments are calculated to ensure that business receipts are taxed once and once only and deductions for tax purposes are given once and once only.

Deferred tax impacts

14.46 Chapter 12 examines the concept of deferred tax in more detail, but the accounting for such a concept becomes more onerous under the provisions of Section 29 *Income Tax*. It is to be noted, at the outset, that micro-entities are exempt from the requirement to account for deferred tax under the provisions of FRS 105.

FRS 102 with reduced disclosures uses the timing difference 'plus' approach in the calculation of deferred tax. The 'plus' part builds on old UK GAAP in the FRSSE (effective January 2015) by requiring deferred tax to be provided for in three additional situations:

- where non-monetary assets are subject to revaluation;
- for fair values in business combinations; and
- in relation to unremitted earnings in overseas subsidiaries and associates.

> **Focus**
>
> - Under the provisions of FRS 102, Section 29 prohibits deferred tax balances being discounted to present day values. In practice very few entities discounted deferred tax to present day values and hence this prohibition is largely going to go unnoticed. However, where a small business does discount deferred tax to present day values, it will need to be grossed back up at the date of transition and in the comparative year to comply with FRS 102 principles.

Current tax impacts

14.47

> **Focus**
>
> - This section covers some of the main issues relating to the tax impacts of a transition which are most pertinent to a small company. It does not, and is not intended to, cover a comprehensive range of

circumstances applicable to every company and preparers are advised to gain specialist advice to cover issues which are complicated or ambiguous to ensure the treatment for tax purposes is correct.

- HM Revenue and Customs (HMRC) have issued an *Overview Paper 'Tax implications on application of New UK GAAP, FRS 102'* which may be of assistance to preparers of financial statements. The HMRC paper can be downloaded from the GOV.uk website:
- www.gov.uk/government/publications/accounting-standards-the-uk-tax-implications-of-new-uk-gaap.

Tax legislation mandates a company to calculate profits (or losses) of a trade in accordance with GAAP, subject to any adjustment which is required by law in calculating profits for tax purposes. A typical adjustment in this respect would be adding back depreciation to accounting profit as depreciation is disallowable for the purposes of tax and then bringing into the tax computation any capital allowances which the small entity might be eligible to claim.

Adjustments to accounting policies as a result of the transition to new UK GAAP would be classed as arising due to the move from one valid basis to another and hence would be allowable (or taxable) under the provisions of CTA 2009, Pt 3, Ch 14, outlined in HMRC's Business Income Manual at BIM34070 and following.

The corporation tax treatment for companies relies heavily on the accounting treatment and therefore on transition there will be adjustments that have a direct tax consequence. The following outlines the view by HMRC as to whether certain transactions will, or will not, be allowable or taxable for the purposes of tax.

Errors

14.48 Under previous UK GAAP, an entity would correct an error by way of a prior period adjustment if that error was 'fundamental'. The term 'fundamental' was defined as essentially destroying the truth and fairness of the financial statements and the validity of those financial statements.

Under FRS 102 at Section 10 *Accounting Policies, Estimates and Errors*, an entity corrects an error by way of a prior period adjustment if that error is 'material' and hence it is more likely that more errors will be corrected through prior period adjustments under FRS 102/FRS 105 principles.

HMRC says that a material error would be a change from an invalid basis to a valid basis and therefore tax legislation requires the invalid basis to be corrected in the year that the error(s) first occurred and subsequent periods are then restated (see *'Tax implications on application of New UK GAAP, FRS 102'* at section 3). It would all depend on the time limits for making or amending self-assessments as to whether the consequential tax impact can be collected or repaid.

Financial instruments

14.49 Financial instruments are dealt with in Section 11 *Basic Financial Instruments* and Section 12 *Other Financial Instruments Issues*. Accounting for certain types of financial instruments (for example derivatives) is a complex area and the provisions in FRS 102 allow for three types of accounting policy choice as follows:

- FRS 102, Section 11 or Section 12;
- IAS 39 *Financial Instruments: Recognition and Measurement*; and
- IFRS 9 *Financial Instruments*.

For tax purposes, the general principle is that the tax treatment follows the accounting treatment because for most companies, most financial instruments will fall to be classed as loan relationships (under Part 5 CTA 2009), non-lending money debts (treated as loan relationships under Chapter 2 of Part 6 CTA 2009) or derivative contracts (under Part 7 CTA 2009). In addition, tax legislation also ensures that most items which are taken to reserves are brought into account (see CTA 2009, section 308(1) for loan relationship purposes).

A further rule exists within tax law which says that if a profit or loss from a loan relationship or derivative contract is recognised directly in equity then this is to be brought into account in the same way as if it were recognised in profit or loss through reserves (CTA 2009, sections 321, 605) (this would be the case for a financial instrument measured at fair value through other comprehensive income).

Derivative financial instruments

14.50 Under FRS 102, derivative financial instruments have to be recognised on the balance sheet with fair value fluctuations going through profit or loss. Subject to limited exceptions, gains and losses which have been recognised in profit or loss on derivatives (and foreign exchange transactions) will form part of taxable income.

Hedge accounting

14.51 FRS 102 contains special rules which allow an entity to use hedge accounting so as to reduce the volatility of derivatives valued at fair value passing through profit or loss. For tax purposes these adjustments will not apply due to the 'Disregard Regulations' (Loan Relationships and Derivative Contracts (Disregard and Bringing into Account of Profits and Losses Regulations 2004, SI 2004/3256), although there are special tax rules which may well be relevant in some circumstances. See *'Tax implications on application of New UK GAAP, FRS 102'* at section 4.

Investment property

14.52 The accounting for fair value changes in investment property is markedly different under the principles of FRS 102 than was the case under the previous UK GAAP. Fair value gains and losses are taken to profit or loss under FRS 102 principles (as opposed to a revaluation surplus). In addition, there is no exemption for property let to, and occupied by, group entities to be excluded from investment property classification.

HMRC's position is that the accounting treatment of investment properties does not determine, for tax purposes, whether the property is an investment property or whether a disposal of a property is a capital or a revenue disposal. Investment property income for tax purposes is brought into tax as it is recognised in the accounts (for example rental income). Movements on the fair value of investment property passing through profit or loss are not taxable. On disposal by a company, investment properties will be subject to corporation tax on capital gains.

There are also situations where a company holding investment property as a lessee under an operating lease may account for the property as an investment property. Where this happens, the investment property is recognised in the accounts at the lower of its fair value and the present value of the minimum lease payments with the associated creditor being recognised as a finance lease. In such cases the tax rules which apply to a finance lease will apply (see HMRC's Corporate Finance Manual at CFM21150).

Property, plant and equipment

14.53 There are relatively few changes brought about by FRS 102 where the accounting for property, plant and equipment (tangible fixed assets) are concerned and FRS 102 for small entities is broadly consistent with previous UK GAAP, except:

- FRS 102 requires that major spare parts are capitalised as part of property, plant and equipment;
- for assets acquired under terms beyond normal credit terms, 'cost' is measured by reference to the present value of all future payments;
- the concept of 'renewals accounting' is not permitted; and
- residual values are to be based on current, as opposed to historic, prices.

Under UK tax legislation, depreciation and revaluations in respect of capital assets are disallowed. HMRC grants capital allowances on some assets and hence the above accounting changes are not expected to have any significant tax impact.

There are some occasions when revenue expenditure is included in the cost of an asset and where this is the case, the tax treatment follows the accounting treatment by recognising amounts reflected in profit and loss by way of depreciation charges to the extent that they are a write-off of revenue expenditure. It follows, therefore, where depreciation charges under FRS 102 differ from that under the previous UK GAAP (for example due to revaluation of residual values), tax will follow the amount under Section 17 *Property, Plant and Equipment*.

As renewals accounting is not permitted in FRS 102, there may be an adjustment for tax purposes made under the change of basis legislation (see **14.47**).

Intangible assets (including goodwill)

14.54 The definition of 'intangible assets' under FRS 102 is wider and hence an entity may have to deal with more intangible assets than was previously the case under the previous UK GAAP.

Section 871–879 of Part 8 CTA 2009 provides a comprehensive set of rules for changes in accounting for intangible assets and especially for cases where what is included entirely as goodwill under the previous UK GAAP is disaggregated into different types of intangible assets, with different amortisation rates or impairment factors, under FRS 102.

FRS 102 also restricts the amortisation of intangible assets where a reliable estimate of the intangible asset's useful economic life cannot be made by management (this is now ten years under FRS 102 rather than five years in the previous version as the government increased the lifespan in transposing the EU Accounting Directive into company law). In addition, under FRS 102 a company cannot have intangible assets with indefinite useful economic lives – all intangible assets will therefore be amortised over their estimated useful economic lives under the new regime. Where the useful economic life cannot be determined, the asset is required to be amortised over a period not exceeding ten years.

Tax relief is generally granted on either the amortisation or impairment of goodwill and intangible assets recognised in the accounts, subject to certain possible exceptions such as under the transitional provisions relating to pre-Finance Act 2002 intangible fixed assets (ie assets created or acquired by the company before 1 April 2002, the commencement date for the intangibles tax regime), and also in relation to anti-avoidance rules regarding goodwill acquired from a related party (eg upon the incorporation of a business) (CTA 2009, Part 8, Ch 16; section 849B-849D with effect from 3 December 2014).

Sections 871 to 873 of CTA 2009 ensures that any write-up on transition to FRS 102 is a taxable credit for Part 8, and section 872 ensures that any such credit is limited to the net amount of relief already given. Any impairment from written-up cost will be deductible.

Furthermore, tax relief is unlikely to be affected if an entity has elected (under CTA 2009, section 730) for a fixed rate of 4%.

Software costs

14.55 The accounting treatment under FRS 102 means that software used in the business is to be treated as an intangible asset as opposed being treated as part of fixed assets. For tax purposes, tax relief is obtained through the amortisation charge in the financial statements rather than through capital allowances. Obviously, however, it is not possible to claim both.

Leases

14.56 Where a lessee receives a lease incentive, the treatment under FRS 102 is also different than what was the case under previous UK GAAP. The lease incentive is recognised over the entire period of the lease; whereas UITF 28 *Operating lease incentives* required that operating lease incentive in the lessee's books are spread over the period ending on the date from which it is expected that the prevailing market rent will be payable.

For lease incentives, the tax treatment will follow the accounting treatment provided that the incentives are not of a capital nature.

Focus

- There is an optional exemption from mandatory retrospective application where lease incentives are concerned and an entity could continue to apply the requirements in previous UK GAAP or they could restate the lease incentives at the date of transition and in the comparative year under the principles in Section 20 *Leases*.
- This issue should be carefully considered because there may well be a tax advantage where the small entity chooses the option to restate as if the accounting treatment in FRS 102 had always been in place because a higher rent charge will be taken to profit or loss as the lease incentive would be spread over a longer period. An example is provided above (see Example **14.5**) which illustrates this issue.

Revenue recognition

14.57 The wording in Section 23 *Revenue* is notably more relaxed than the wording in the FRSSE (effective January 2015) and previous mainstream UK GAAP and the wording in FRS 102 is not as specific.

It is to be expected that revenue will continue to be recognised in the same way under FRS 102 as it was under the previous UK GAAP and hence HMRC have taken the view that there will be no accounting or tax impact (see *Tax implications on application of New UK GAAP, FRS 102* at section 12).

It is also worth noting that the Financial Reporting Council have intimated that if there is any 'abuse' of the relaxed wording in Section 23, they will issue an Abstract to clarify the position (which would essentially confirm the same revenue recognition principles as the previous UK GAAP because there was never an intention to change revenue recognition principles). Small and micro-entities should ensure they continue to recognise revenue when a right to consideration arises.

Government grants

14.58 FRS 102 introduces a new 'performance model' whereby an entity recognises a grant in profit or loss when all the performance obligations have been fulfilled by the entity. **Chapter 12** examines the performance model in more detail.

For the purposes of tax, grants which meet revenue expenditure are normally trading receipts and this treatment will continue under FRS 102.

Share-based payment

14.59 Equity-settled share-based payment transactions will have to be recognised in the financial statements under FRS 102 for small entities rather than disclosed (which was the case under the FRSSE (effective January 2015)).

There is specific tax legislation pertaining to share-based payment treatments in Part 12 CTA 2009 (*'Other relief for employee share acquisitions'*).

Employee benefits

14.60 In respect of defined benefit pension schemes covered by Section 28 *Employee Benefits*, there are certain changes when compared to previous UK GAAP as follows:

- FRS 102 removes the multi-employer exemption on defined benefit pension schemes; and
- the calculation of net interest on defined benefit pension schemes comprises the expected interest income on plan assets, the interest cost on the scheme's liabilities and the interest on the effect of the asset ceiling (if applicable).

These changes are not expected to have any impact on the entity's tax position because tax legislation provides relief on a contributions paid basis (sections 196 and 246 of the Finance Act 2004; sections 1290–1296 of CTA 2009).

Section 28 also requires a reporting entity to make an accrual for unpaid holiday entitlement accrued by the employee but not paid by the reporting date. Many entities did not make such accruals under the FRSSE (effective January 2015) or previous mainstream GAAP and for the purposes of tax this accrual would be treated in line with the treatment of unpaid remuneration which is dealt with at sections 1288–1289 of CTA 2009 (*'Unpaid remuneration'*) in Part 20, Chapter 1 of CTA 2009.

Transitional adjustments

14.61 On transition to FRS 102 with reduced disclosures, a small company is required to apply the provisions in Section 35 *Transition to this FRS*. This requires that the entity:

- recognises all assets and liabilities whose recognition is required by FRS 102;
- does not recognise assets and liabilities if FRS 102 does not permit such recognition;
- reclassifies assets, liabilities and components of equity to ensure presentation is consistent with FRS 102; and
- measures all recognised assets and liabilities in accordance with FRS 102.

For trading profit, Chapter 14, Part 3 of CTA 2009 (*Adjustments on change of basis*) provides that where there is a change from one valid basis on which the trading profits have been calculated to another, an adjustment is calculated so as to ensure that business receipts are taxed once and once only and deductions are given once and once only.

Intangible assets transitional adjustments

14.62 It is possible that the carrying values of intangible assets are adjusted in the opening FRS 102-compliant balance sheet. A taxable credit or allowable debit is to be brought into account under Chapter 15 CTA 2009 at Part 8 (*Adjustments on change of accounting policy*), unless and to the extent that it is already brought into account by section 723 ('revaluations'), section 725 ('reversal of accounting loss') or section 732 ('reversal of accounting gain').

Where changes to the opening balances of intangible assets takes place and no section 730 election (ie for writing down at a fixed rate) has been made, sections 872 and 873 (ie dealing with adjustments in respect of a change of accounting policy) will treat an increase as a taxable credit and a decrease as an allowable debit, arising at the start of the later accounting period.

Financial instruments

14.63 EU-adopted IFRS has been in existence in the UK for several years (applied mainly by listed companies) and the tax consequences of the transition were addressed by regulations (Loan Relationships and Derivative Contracts (Change of Accounting Practice) Regulations 2004, SI 2004/3271). HMRC have confirmed that these regulations will be applicable on transition from old UK GAAP to FRS 101 *Reduced Disclosure Framework* and FRS 102.

Significant transitional adjustments arose in the accounting for financial instruments under EU-adopted IFRS and the effect of the regulations is to spread the transitional adjustment over ten years, starting with the first period in which the new accounting policy applies. The main exclusions are for transitional adjustments in respect of:

(1) A loan relationship which comes to a natural end in the accounting period that the transition takes place because it is repaid or redeemed on the date which is the latest on which, under its terms, it falls to be repaid or redeemed.

(2) An embedded derivative that is bifurcated out of a loan asset or liabilities described in (1) above.

(3) A derivative contract which hedges a loan asset or liability described in (1).

For further HMRC guidance on transitional adjustments, see *Tax implications on application of New UK GAAP, FRS 102* at Part B.

Borrowing costs

14.64 Section 25 in FRS 102 *Borrowing Costs* allows an entity to capitalise the interest incurred on specific borrowings for qualifying assets.

Section 320 of CTA 2009 ('Credits and debits treated as relating to capital expenditure') outlines specific rules which provides relief for capitalised borrowing costs, but only where they relate to a fixed capital asset or project. Tax relief is not available for entities where such borrowing costs are capitalised in the carrying value of an intangible fixed asset which falls within Part 8 CTA 2009 (see HMRC's Corporate Finance Manual at CFM33160).

DISCLOSURE REQUIREMENTS

14.65 A micro-entity reporting under the provisions of FRS 105 is exempt from the requirement to make transitional disclosures. A small company reporting under FRS 102 for small entities is encouraged to make the transitional disclosures in paragraphs 35.12–35.15. Such disclosures would be required where not making the disclosures would not enable the financial statements to give a true and fair view.

The disclosures are as follows:

- An overall explanation of how the transition to FRS 102 with reduced disclosures has affected the financial position and financial performance of the entity.
- A description of the nature of each change in accounting policy.

- Reconciliations of equity determined under previous UK GAAP to the equity determined under FRS 102 for small entities for the following two dates:
  - — the date of transition to FRS 102 with reduced disclosures; and
  - — the end of the latest period presented in the entity's most recent annual financial statements that was determined in accordance with previous UK GAAP.
- A reconciliation of the profit or loss determined in accordance with previous UK GAAP to the profit or loss determined under FRS 102 with reduced disclosures.
- Where errors have been noted, the reconciliations above must distinguish the correction of those errors from the transitional adjustments arising as a result of changing the entity's accounting policies to comply with FRS 102 with reduced disclosures.
- Where the entity did not present financial statements for previous periods, that fact should also be disclosed.

Example 14.6 – Disclosure of transitional information

	Note	At 1 January 2015	At 31 December 2015
		£	£
Capital reserves (as previously stated)		X	X
Recognition of derivative financial instrument	(i)	(X)	(X)
Short term employee benefits	(ii)	–	(X)
Capital and reserves (as restated)		X	X

Reconciliation of profit or loss for the year

	Note	31 December 2015
		£
Profit for the year (as previously stated)		X
Recognition of derivative financial instrument	(i)	(X)
Short-term compensated absences	(ii)	(X)
Profit for the year (as restated)		X

Notes to the reconciliations

(i) Financial instruments

Smallco Ltd was not previously required to recognise derivative financial instruments on the balance sheet as under the FRSSE (effective January 2015) the effects of such instruments were recognised in profit or loss on settlement. Derivative financial instruments are classified as 'other financial instruments' under Section 12 *Other Financial Instruments Issues* and are recognised as a financial asset or financial liability, at fair value, when the company becomes a party to the contractual provisions of the instrument. As a result, financial assets of £X and financial liabilities of £X have been recognised in the opening balance sheet as at 1 January 2015. Financial assets of £X and financial liabilities of £X have been recognised in the balance sheet as at 31 December 2015. Derivatives are measured at fair value with gains (losses) from changes in fair value going through profit or loss. The effect on profit for the year ended 31 December 2015 was £X.

(ii) Short-term compensated absences

Prior to applying FRS 102 for small entities, Smallco Ltd did not make provision for holiday entitlement earned but not taken prior to the year-end. Section 28 *Employee Benefits* requires the cost of short-term compensated absences to be recognised when employees render the service that increases their entitlement. As a consequence, an additional accrual of £X at 1 January 2015 has been made to reflect this. The additional provision as at 31 December 2015 is £X and the effect on profit for the year-ended 31 December 2015 is an additional expense of £X.

PITFALLS TO AVOID

- Forgetting that the rules in FRS 102 and FRS 105 are applied as far back as the date of transition, not just to the comparative year.
- Not running exception reports at each stage of the transition resulting in additional work to correct any errors made during the transition.
- Not considering the tax implications of any transitional and comparative year adjustments.
- Failing to advise directors well in advance about the potential changes to reported profit/loss and equity balances resulting in unpleasant surprises after the transition has taken place.
- Inappropriately adopting FRS 105 when a more comprehensive framework might be better for the company.
- Not disclosing the transitional information for a small company when the impact is material and hence the financial statements fail to give a true and fair view.

CHAPTER SUMMARY

- The 'date of transition' is the start date of the earliest period reported in the financial statements (ie the start date of the comparative year) and FRS 102 with reduced disclosures must be applied as far back as this date to enable the financial statements to be both comparable and consistent. FRS 105 must also be applied to micro-entities' financial statements as far back as the date of transition.
- Small entities must ensure their accounting policies comply with FRS 102 principles and change accounting policies where they are not compliant (eg where the small entity previously did not make any provision for short-term compensated absences accrued by the employee(s) at the year-end).
- There are four stages in the transitional process and preparers of financial statements under the new regime need to have a sound understanding of the detailed requirements in FRS 102 for small entities noting that while the presentation and disclosure requirements are reduced due to the EU Accounting Directive, the full recognition and measurement principles of FRS 102 still apply.
- Practical issues which must be considered are notifying the client as soon as possible (as transitional adjustments will affect previously reported amounts of equity and profit/losses) and amending bookkeeping programs to cater for the new methodologies contained in FRS 102 and FRS 105.
- Transitional adjustments and prior year adjustments as a result of the transition to FRS 102/FRS 105 are likely to trigger tax implications. HMRC have issued an *Overview Paper* which outlines their interpretation of how such a transition will affect an entity's tax position.
- Micro-entities applying FRS 105 will have significantly fewer disclosure requirements and no accounting policy choices. In addition, the disclosure requirements relating to first-time transition are not legally required (but a micro-entity could voluntarily choose to make the disclosures). Small companies are encouraged to make the disclosure requirements found in Section 35 of FRS 102 and these would be required if the financial statements would otherwise fail to give a true and fair view.

Appendix 1

Sample Micro-entity Financial Statements

The following sample of micro-entity financial statements are intended to be an illustration only. In all respects, accountants should consult the provisions of FRS 105 *The Financial Reporting Standard applicable to the Micro-entities Regime* where difficulties or ambiguities are present.

Microco Ltd
Profit and loss account
For the year-ended 31 December 2016

	2016	**2015**
	£	£
Turnover	X	X
Other income	X	X
Cost of raw materials and consumables	(X)	(X)
Staff costs	(X)	(X)
Depreciation and other amounts written off assets	(X)	(X)
Other charges	(X)	(X)
Tax	(X)	(X)
Profit	X	X

Microco Ltd
Balance Sheet
As at 31 December 2016

	2016		2015	
	£	£	£	£
Called up share capital not paid		X		X
Fixed assets		X		X
Current assets	X		X	
Prepayments and accrued income	X		X	
Creditors: amounts falling due within one year	(X)		(X)	
Net current assets (liabilities)		X		X
Total assets less current liabilities		X		X
Creditors: amounts falling due after more than one year		(X)		(X)
Provisions for liabilities		(X)		(X)
Accruals and deferred income		(X)		(X)
Net assets		X		X
Capital and reserves		X		X

NOTES TO THE FINANCIAL STATEMENTS

1. Directors' benefits: advances, credit and guarantees

During the year the company made an advance of £X to a director of the company in respect of a private loan. The balance was fully repaid at the year-end.

2. Guarantees and other financial commitments

The company is defending itself against a legal claim brought against it by one of its customers for breach of a contract. The lawyers have advised that the maximum potential liability amounts to £4,000. No provision has been made in the financial statements on the grounds that the solicitors consider the company has not breached the terms of the contract and the company will not be required to pay any amounts.

For the year-ended 31 December 2016 the company was entitled to exemption from audit under section 477 of the Companies Act 2006.

Directors' responsibilities:

- The members have not required the company to obtain an audit of its accounts for the year in question in accordance with section 476.
- The directors acknowledge their responsibilities for complying with the requirements of the Act with respect to accounting records and preparation of accounts.

These accounts have been prepared in accordance with FRS 105 *The Financial Reporting Standard applicable to the Micro-entities Regime*.

Approved by the board of directors and signed on behalf of the board:

....

J Smith
1 March 2017

Company registration number: 12345678

Appendix 2

Sample Small Company Financial Statements

The following sample of small company financial statements are intended to be an illustration only. In all respects, accountants should consult the provisions of FRS 102 *The Financial Reporting Standard applicable in the UK and Republic of Ireland* where difficulties or ambiguities are present.

These illustrative financial statements are not adapted, nor abridged. A Format 1 profit and loss account and balance sheet have been used in these illustrations. Companies Act terminology has also been used (eg profit and loss account rather than income statement and balance sheet rather than statement of financial position).

Smallco Ltd
Profit and loss account
For the year-ended 31 December 2016

	2016	**2015**
	£	£
Turnover	X	X
Cost of sales	(X)	(X)
Gross profit	X	X
Distribution costs	(X)	(X)
Administrative expenses	(X)	(X)
Bad debts	(X)	(X)
Operating profit *	X	X
Profit (loss) on disposal of fixed assets	(X)	(X)
Interest receivable and similar income	X	X
Interest payable and similar charges	(X)	(X)
Profit on ordinary activities before taxation	X	X
Tax on profit on ordinary activities	(X)	(X)
Profit for the financial year	X	X

Smallco Ltd
Statement of comprehensive income
For the year-ended 31 December 2016

	2016	2015
	£	£
Profit for the financial year	X	X
Unrealised surplus on revaluation of freehold properties	X	X
Taxation	(X)	(X)
Total recognised gains and losses relating to the year	X	X

*FRS 102 does not require operating profit to be disclosed, but where an entity chooses to disclose operating profit it must do so correctly.

Smallco Ltd
Balance Sheet
As at 31 December 2016

	2016		2015	
Company registration number: 12345678	£	£	£	£
Fixed assets				
Intangible assets		X		X
Property, plant and equipment		X		X
Investment property		X		X
Financial assets		X		X
		X		X
Current assets				
Stock and work in progress	X		X	
Trade debtors	X		X	
Cash at bank and in hand	X		X	
	X		X	
Creditors: amounts falling due within one year	(X)		(X)	
Net current assets		X		X
Total assets less current liabilities		X		X

	2016		2015	
Company registration number: 12345678	£	£	£	£
Creditors: amounts falling due after more than one year		(X)		(X)
Provisions for liabilities		(X)		(X)
Net assets		X		X
Capital and reserves				
Called up share capital		X		X
Share premium		X		X
Revaluation reserve		X		X
Profit and loss account		X		X
Shareholders' funds		X		X

These financial statements have been prepared in accordance with the provisions applicable to companies subject to the small companies' regime and in accordance with the provisions of FRS 102 *The Financial Reporting Standard applicable in the UK and Republic of Ireland* applicable to small entities.

These financial statements were approved and authorised on behalf of the board by:

……………………………………..

J Smith
1 March 2017

The notes on pages X to X form part of these financial statements.

Smallco Ltd
Statement of changes in equity
For the year-ended 31 December 2016

NOTE TO SETTER – WOULD THIS LOOK BETTER LANDSCAPE?

	Share capital	**Share premium**	**Revaluation reserve**	**Profit and loss account**	**Total**
	£	£	£	£	£
Balance at 1 January 2015 as previously stated	X	X	X	X	X
Prior period adjustment re change in accounting policy				(X)	(X)
Share issue in the year	X	X			X
Dividends				(X)	(X)
Balance at 31 December 2015	X	X	X	X	X
Prior period adjustment re change in accounting policy				(X)	(X)
Share issue in the year	X	X			X
Dividends				(X)	(X)
Balance at 31 December 2016	X	X	X	X	X

Smallco Ltd
Notes to the financial statements
For the year-ended 31 December 2016

1. Basis of preparation

These financial statements have been prepared in accordance with the provisions of FRS 102 *The Financial Reporting Standard applicable in the UK and Republic of Ireland* applicable to small entities.

2. Accounting policies

The principal accounting policies applied in the preparation of these financial statements are set out below.

These financial statements for the year-ended 31 December 2016 are the first financial statements that comply with FRS 102. The date of transition is 1 January 2015.

The transition to FRS 102 has resulted in some changes to accounting policies to those previously used by the entity. The nature of these changes and their impact on opening equity and profit for the comparative year are explained in notes X to X below.

The presentation currency is Sterling.

Goodwill and intangible assets

Goodwill is capitalised and is being amortised over its useful life of four years.

Tangible fixed assets and depreciation

Tangible fixed assets are measured using the depreciated historic cost model and are recognised at cost, less accumulated depreciation and less impairment losses. Depreciation is calculated so as to write off the cost of tangible fixed assets over their expected useful lives using the following rates:

Freehold land	–	no depreciation
Freehold property	–	2% on a straight-line basis
Plant and machinery	–	25% on a reducing balance basis
Fixtures and fittings	–	20% on a straight-line basis
Motor vehicles	–	25% on reducing balance basis

Leases

Property, plant and equipment acquired under finance leases or hire purchase contracts are capitalised and depreciated using the same basis as other tangible fixed assets. The associated obligations, net of future finance costs, are included in creditors.

Rentals payable under operating leases are charged to the profit and loss account on a straight-line basis over the period of the lease.

Investment property

Investment property is carried at fair value. Revaluation surpluses are recognised in profit or loss and deferred tax is provided on these gains at the rate expected to apply on the date the investment property is sold.

Inventories

Inventory is valued at the lower of cost and estimated selling price less costs to complete and sell. Cost comprises the cost of production and all directly attributable costs such as freight costs and direct labour costs. Estimated selling price less costs to complete and sell is the estimated selling price which would be achieved in a sale between knowledgeable and willing parties on an arm's length basis. Appropriate provision is made for obsolete or slow-moving items of inventory.

Turnover

Turnover is stated net of value added tax and trade discounts. The company recognises a sale on despatch of the goods, which is the point at which the risks and rewards of ownership pass to the customer. Revenue in respect of service agreements are recognised on a receivable basis when the company's obligation under the contract have been fulfilled.

Deferred tax

Deferred tax is provided under the timing difference plus approach which takes into account the timing differences between the treatment of certain items for accounts purposes and the treatment of certain items for tax purposes.

Pension costs

The company operates a defined contribution scheme for the benefit of its directors and employees. Contributions payable are recognised in profit or loss.

3. Fixed assets

	Intangible assets	**Tangible assets**	**Investments**	**Total**
	£	£	£	£
Cost:				
At 1 January 2016	X	X	X	X
Additions	X	X	X	X
Disposals	(X)	(X)	(X)	(X)
At 31 December 2016	X	X	X	X
Depreciation:				
At 1 January 2016	X	X	X	X
Eliminated on disposal	(X)	(X)	(X)	(X)
Charge for year	X	X	X	X
At 31 December 2016	X	X	X	X
Net book value:				
At 31 December 2016	X	X	X	X
At 31 December 2015	X	X	X	X

4. Financial assets

	Listed	Unlisted	Total
	£	£	£
Cost at 1 January 2016	X	X	X
Additions	X	X	X
Impairment		(X)	(X)
Disposals	(X)	(X)	(X)
Cost at 31 December 2016	X	X	X

5. Inventories

	2016	2015
	£	£
Raw materials and consumables	X	X
Finished goods	X	X
	X	X

6. Debtors

	2016	2015
	£	£
Trade debtors	X	X
Other debtors	X	X
Prepayment and accrued income	X	X
	X	X

7. Creditors: amounts falling due within one year

	2016	2015
	£	£
Bank loans and overdrafts	X	X
Trade creditors	X	X
Other creditors	X	X
Corporation tax	X	X
Social security and other taxes	X	X
Obligations under finance leases	X	X
Accruals and deferred income	X	X
	X	X

8. Creditors: amounts falling due after more than one year

	2016	2015
	£	£
Bank loans and overdrafts	X	X
Obligations under finance leases	X	X
	X	X

9. Bank loans and overdrafts

An analysis of creditors falling due after more than five years:

	2016	2015
	£	£
Aggregate of non-instalment debt falling due for repayment after five years:		
Bank loans	X	X
Finance leases	X	X
	X	X
Aggregate of instalments which fall due after five years:		
Bank loans	X	X
Finance leases	X	X
	X	X

10. Revaluation reserve

	2016	2015
	£	£
At 1 January	X	X
Revaluation during the year	X	X
Amortisation during the year	(X)	(X)
At 31 December	X	X

11. Profit and loss account

	2016	2015
	£	£
At 1 January	X	X
Profit for the year	X	X
Dividends	(X)	(X)
At 31 December	X	X

12. Controlling party

The directors consider that Mr J Smith is the controlling party by virtue of his controlling shareholding in the company.

13. Financial commitments

The company had total commitments under non-cancellable operating leases as follows:

	£
Operating leases which expire:	
Within one year	X
Within two to five years	X
After more than five years	X
	X

14. Average number of employees

During the year the average number of employees was X (2015: X)

15. Transition to FRS 102

Reconciliation of equity

		At January 2015	At 31 December 2015
		£	£
Capital and reserves (as previously stated)		X	X
Recognition of derivative financial instruments	(i)	(X)	X
Re-measurement of stock using spot rate	(ii)	–	(X)
Short-term compensated absences	(iii)	(X)	(X)
Capital and reserves (as restated)		X	X

Reconciliation of profit or loss

		Year ended 31 December 2015
		£
Profit for the year (as previously stated)		X
Recognition of derivative financial instruments	(i)	X
Re-measurement of stock using spot rate	(ii)	X
Short-term compensated absences	(iii)	(X)
Profit for the year (as restated)		X

Notes to the reconciliations

Financial instruments

(i) Smallco was not previously required to recognise derivative financial instruments on the balance sheet. Instead the effects of the derivative financial instruments were recognised in profit or loss when the instruments were settled. Derivative financial instruments are classified as 'other financial instruments' in FRS 102 and are recognised as a financial asset or a financial liability, at fair value, when an entity becomes party to the contractual provisions of the instrument. Consequently financial assets of £X and financial liabilities of £X have been recognised in the opening balance sheet at 1 January 2015. Financial assets of £X and financial liabilities of £X have been recognised in the balance sheet as at 31 December 2015. Derivatives are measured to fair value with gains (losses) from changes in fair value recognised in profit or loss. The effect on profit for the year-ended 31 December 2015 is an increase of £X.

(ii) The derivative financial instruments are foreign exchange forward contracts. In applying the FRSSE (effective January 2015), Smallco previously chose to translate purchases in foreign currencies at the rate of exchange specified in a matching forward contract. This is not permitted by FRS 102, which requires purchases to be translated using the spot rate exchange rate on the date of the transaction. FRS 102 does not provide an exemption from measuring stock bought in a foreign currency and paid for before the transition date in accordance with its required accounting policies, but the difference is not material and accordingly no adjustment has been made. Items purchased since the transition date have been re-measured based on spot exchange rate. Consequently stock at 31 December 2015 has been reduced and cost of sales for the year end has been increased by £X and costs of £X have been reclassified as administrative expenses rather than cost of sales.

Short-term compensated absences

(iii) Prior to applying FRS 102, Smallco did not make provision for holiday pay (ie holiday earned but not taken prior to the year-end). FRS 102 requires the cost of short-term compensated absences to be recognised when employees render the service that increases their entitlement. Consequently an additional accrual of £X at 1 January 2015 has been made to reflect this. The additional provision at 31 December 2015 is £X and the effect on profit for the year ended 31 December 2015 is an additional expense of £X.

Index

[*All references are to paragraph number and appendices*]